P9-DVG-267

Spy Watching

Spy Watching

Intelligence Accountability in the United States

LOCH K. JOHNSON

OXFORD
UNIVERSITY PRESS

OXFORD
UNIVERSITY PRESS

Oxford University Press is a department of the University of Oxford. It furthers
the University's objective of excellence in research, scholarship, and education
by publishing worldwide. Oxford is a registered trade mark of Oxford University
Press in the UK and certain other countries.

Published in the United States of America by Oxford University Press
198 Madison Avenue, New York, NY 10016, United States of America.

© Oxford University Press 2018

Library of Congress Cataloging-in-Publication Data
Names: Johnson, Loch K., 1942– author.
Title: Spy watching : intelligence accountability in the United States / Loch K. Johnson.
Description: New York, NY : Oxford University Press, 2018. |
Includes bibliographical references.
Identifiers: LCCN 2017015734 | ISBN 9780190682712 (hardback) |
ISBN 9780190682736 (epub)
Subjects: LCSH: Intelligence service—United States. |
Government accountability—United States. | Transparency in government—
United States. | Legislative oversight—United States. |
BISAC: POLITICAL SCIENCE / Political Freedom & Security / Intelligence. |
POLITICAL SCIENCE / Political Freedom & Security / International Security. |
HISTORY / Military / Strategy.
Classification: LCC JK468.I6 J665 2018 | DDC 327.1273—dc23
LC record available at https://lccn.loc.gov/2017015734

1 3 5 7 9 8 6 4 2
Printed by Sheridan Books, Inc., United States of America

To August Tiivas Swati and Loch Warren Swati,
may they live in an America that enjoys just the right mix of liberty and security,
and
to the memory of
Professor Harry Howe Ransom, Vanderbilt University

"I don't fear the ordeal of freedom. I fear the moment when we stop thinking of freedom as an ordeal."
—Azar Nafisi, "Surveillance States," *New York Times Sunday Magazine* (June 14, 2015), p. 25

"The truth is, there is no victory. There is only vigilance."
—Stephen Berry, "The Book or the Gun?" in J. Matthew Gallman and Gary W. Gallagher, eds., *Lens of War: Exploring Iconic Photographs of the Civil War* (Athens: University of Georgia Press, 2015), p. 231

CONTENTS

Contents

FIGURES AND TABLES

PREFACE

I have been studying, writing about, and, at times as a congressional and White House aide, engaging in intelligence oversight for more than forty years. During this time, I have written several articles and edited a number of books on the topic. Now with this volume I attempt to bring this scholarly and practical experience together, along with a number of research findings and interviews with intelligence officers and their supervisors that I have never published before. My intention is to present in one place an examination of the tensions that exist between secret intelligence agencies and open democratic societies, the history of how these tensions have played out in the United States during recent decades, and an analysis of the ongoing dilemmas of governance presented by the dusky world of espionage.

All democracies have had to wrestle with this challenge of tolerating secret services within otherwise relatively transparent governments. Democracies pride themselves on privacy and liberty; spies, however, enjoy heavily veiled budgets, and they are involved in the hidden collection of information around the world and the use of covert action against foreign regimes. Sometimes, as examined in this book, they have even turned their dark arts against the very people they were created to protect, as with the so-called COINTELPRO operations carried out by the Federal Bureau of Investigation (FBI) against civil rights and antiwar activists in the United States during the 1960s and early 1970s. In this sense, democracy and intelligence have been and remain a poor match. Yet Americans live in an uncertain and dangerous world, with an abundance of nuclear warheads, long-range missiles, chemical and biological weapons, aggressive foreign leaders (some of whom are thugs and dictators), failing states, and brutal terrorists. Without an intelligence apparatus scanning the globe to warn the United States about these threats, not to mention possible pandemics and environmental catastrophes, this planet would be an even more perilous place. Thus it is incumbent upon democracies to maintain strong, effective espionage capabilities; at the same time, though, to prevent the misuse of secret power, open societies must also take steps to ensure their intelligence services are closely watched by responsible overseers.

The massive leak of intelligence documents by government contractor Edward J. Snowden in 2013 has heightened interest in the question of intelligence accountability. Have the officials responsible for monitoring the secret agencies, such as the House and Senate Intelligence Committees, been so ineffectual that insiders like Snowden must resort to a breach of law to bring about public debate over controversial spy activities, such as the National Security Agency's massive "metadata" collection program aimed at American citizens? Must whistle-blowers provide the safeguards for liberty in the democracies, because more official organs of intelligence oversight have failed?

This book is an attempt to look at the results of intelligence accountability in the United States during the modern era. The Snowden affair, along with revelations about torture carried out by intelligence officers in the CIA and America's military intelligence units, call for a fresh examination of an age-old question: Who, if anyone, within a democratic society is able to protect citizens against the improper use of the dark powers that are concealed within the corridors of the government's spy agencies? Who will watch the spies?

Spy Watching

Introduction

Democracy and Intelligence

A Focus on Accountability

I have been studying the subject of intelligence ever since 1975, when I served as the special assistant or "designee" to the chairman of the Church Committee, Frank Church (D, Idaho). That year the U.S. Senate authorized that ad hoc panel to investigate allegations published by the *New York Times* during the autumn and winter of 1974. The newspaper charged the Central Intelligence Agency (CIA), known by insiders as "the Agency," with involvement in domestic spying—a violation of its statutory mandate laid out in the National Security Act of 1947 to engage in espionage strictly overseas and never inside the United States. George Orwell's *1984* seemed to have arrived a decade early, and the intrusions of Big Brother were even more unsettling in reality than they had been in the British author's chilling fictional account of a repressive future society.[1] Coming on the heels of the Watergate scandal of 1973 and public disillusionment over the war in Vietnam, this spy scandal added to widespread concern across the country about the trustworthiness of government, especially when the Church Committee discovered that the misuse of power by the nation's secret agencies had been far more extensive than suggested by the already eye-popping accounts in the *Times.*[2]

Ever since this season of inquiry in 1975, I have continued to find intelligence a fascinating and important topic, although one that is extraordinarily difficult to study because of the shrouds of secrecy that envelop America's espionage institutions and their operations. Based on the oversubscribed classroom enrollments in "strategic intelligence" courses offered at universities and colleges from California to Maine, students are clearly attracted to the subject. So is the general public, as measured by the popularity of James Bond and other spy films, the multiple television shows that feature secret agents, and the novels of such masters of espionage fiction as John le Carré and Charles McCarry.

1

In my classes, I have addressed the full range of intelligence activities, but with a concentration on three core missions: the collection and analysis of information about foreign and domestic threats to the United States; the use of covert action to shape events behind the scenes overseas, in a manner favorable to America's best interests; and a reliance on the shield of counterintelligence to defend this nation and its intelligence agencies against the machinations of hostile foreign espionage services and terrorist cells. Once my students and I have dug into these missions, the course capstone is to explore the topic of intelligence accountability, that is, the tangled problem of how, on the one hand, the U.S. government can promote effective spy services while, on the other hand, it attempts to safeguard its citizens against the abuse of hidden power of the kind revealed by the *Times* and the Church Committee.

My earlier books have been devoted mainly to an examination of the three core intelligence missions: collection and analysis, covert action, and counterintelligence. In this book, I narrow the aperture to the topic of intelligence accountability. My objective is to probe into the manner by which the United States has endeavored to keep its espionage activities within the boundaries of law and propriety. This responsibility is critical in an open society, where the presence of heavily barricaded secret government agencies stands as a contradiction to the expected democratic norms of openness and transparency.

The overmastering question posed by the subject of intelligence accountability is worth emphasizing: *Can the United States protect the privacy and liberty of its citizens while, at the same time, conduct effective intelligence operations that help to thwart threats from the enemies of democracy at home and abroad?* In the tropes of those skeptics who answer "no," the United States must instead have "a level playing field" in its sometimes dangerous global competition with adversaries; it must "fight fire with fire"; it must guard against the "micro-management" (read: emasculation) of America's security interests by ill-informed lawmakers and reformers—however well intentioned—and other would-be "outside" supervisors of intelligence operations. In rebuttal, those who seek to shine a light into the hidden recesses of government stress that insufficiently controlled spy agencies can be hazardous to open societies. In a nation based on liberty, these covert organizations require constant vigilance by citizens and their representatives in Washington—just like the other parts of government, only more so because intelligence officers surround their action with darkness. Journalist Richard Harris posed a fundamental question about America's democracy almost forty years ago. "If we have an inner, secret government whose acts cannot be controlled," he wrote, "has our political system been basically altered without our knowledge or approval?" For decades, le Carré and other spy novelists have pondered the threat to democratic principles posed by clandestine agencies with unrestrained powers.[3]

The Constitution of the United States is dedicated to two essential objectives: ensuring the liberties of citizens and, at the same time, providing for their safety against dangers that imperil the Republic.[4] The dilemma lies in how to keep a proper equilibrium between liberty and security—the twin sine qua nons for a true democracy. Former CIA attorney Fred F. Manget notes that "what is acceptable to Congress and the American public and what is lawful vary over time. Both," he continues, "are pendulums whose velocity and stopping points reflect the beliefs of factions in the country. Those beliefs vary according to the perceived imminence and seriousness of the threat."[5] Journalist Daniel Schorr, who covered the national security beat for CBS News during the 1970s, noted similarly that "there have always been in our country two great urges—one toward security, one toward liberty. The pendulum constantly swings between them."[6] Former secretary of state Dean Rusk said simply that: "Wiretapping ebbs and flows with the national mood."[7] The case of Ellen Knauff provides an illustration of how even well-regarded administrations like the Truman presidency can fall into the trap of overzealous devotion to security. In 1950, the Truman Administration sought to banish Knauff from the United States without sharing with her and her attorney, or the judiciary, the specific grounds for the expulsion. Dismayed by this action, Supreme Court Justice Robert Jackson observed in dissent that "security is like liberty in that many are the crimes committed in its name."[8]

A full tilt toward security would turn the United States into a North Korea, the supreme surveillance state; yet a full tilt toward liberty with little concern for security interests would make the United States highly vulnerable to attack, just as ancient Athens was to Sparta. "Privacy and security are a continuum," remarks a savvy retired CIA officer, Martin Petersen. "Where do you want to put the marker? The more we move it toward security, the greater the potential for abuse by law enforcement and the intelligence community (IC). The more we move it toward privacy, the more we limit the utility of law enforcement and the IC to collect the information needed to prevent an attack."[9]

In 2016, a debate in the United States over proper encryption policies vividly displayed the tension between security and privacy. Backed by President Barack Obama, the FBI sought access to encrypted information on an iPhone manufactured by the Apple Corporation and used by two terrorists—Syed Rizwan Farook and his wife—who carried out an attack in San Bernardino, California, in 2015, that killed sixteen people.[10] Apple balked at assisting the Bureau, out of concern that present and future customers would object to the corporation's cooperation with the government and the invasion of citizen privacy which that would represent. Perhaps, ran the fear, the telephones of any Apple customer might be next in line for inspection by federal agents. Behind the scenes, several other organizations in America's IC took a position that was at odds with the FBI. Siding with Silicon Valley companies, some U.S. spy agencies expressed concern within the inner circles of government that, if Apple's encryption were forced open by the Bureau, their own cybersecurity methods might be the next target for outsiders once these unlocking procedures had escaped the genie's bottle.[11]

At stake, too, in this controversy was the effort by America's intelligence agencies, under way for years, to improve their relations with technology companies as an ally to help combat digitally savvy terrorists—especially ISIS, a brutal army of terrorists in Syria, Iraq, and Libya, which had demonstrated a sophisticated use of social media to recruit young men and women to its cause. (ISIS, the Islamic State in Iraq and Syria, is also known just as the Islamic State; as ISIL, or the Islamic State of Iraq and the Levant; or, in Arabic, as *Dawlat* [The State] or as *Daesh*, another Arabic term viewed by ISIS members as insulting.) Adding to the controversy was a standoff between the government and Silicon Valley over another technology company: WhatsApp, owned by Facebook. A federal judge had approved a wiretap warrant for a criminal investigation (not a terrorist case), but law enforcement officers had been unable to break WhatsApp's encryption and had received no assistance from the company.

A *New York Times* reporter suggested the difference between the Apple and WhatsApp cases in these terms: "If the Apple dispute is akin to whether the F.B.I. can unlock your front door and search your house, the issue with WhatsApp is whether it can listen to your phone calls in the era of encryption."[12] Both were important issues—and both difficult to resolve, since the nation was torn between concern about the threat of terrorism but worried, too, about the government's intrusion into the private communications of Americans.

President Obama argued that most of the time user data belonging to communications companies in the private sector should be protected from government access; however, in a limited number of legitimate, high-profile terrorist investigations—backed by judicial warrants—security concerns for the safety of the nation would have to trump privacy safeguards. As two experienced counterterrorism officials in New York City put it, unlocking the San Bernardino iPhone could reveal "the identities of terrorists who influenced or directed the attack; such information, if pursued, could prevent future plots."[13] In response to this debate, Microsoft founder Bill Gates acknowledged that in a few specific instances "with the right safeguards, there are cases where the government, on our behalf—like stopping terrorism which could get worse in the future—that that is valuable."[14]

Under these conditions and safeguards (the government's requests in the iPhone and WhatsApp cases had focused on a single device and were based on a judicial warrant procedure), cooperation between the government and the private sector seemed to make sense; and surely such requests would be understood and accepted by most citizens who wished to prevent terrorist attacks in the United States. Yet Apple's CEO, Timothy D. Cook, worried about "setting a dangerous precedent that threatens everyone's civil liberties."[15] In a remarkable show of support, some forty Silicon Valley companies filed court briefs that backed Apple as Mr. Cook fought a judge's order to allow FBI access to the San Bernardino iPhone in question. There was an important business angle involved in the debate. As a *Times* analyst put it, Apple and other companies would "lose badly to competitors in other countries if it became clear the United States government has a way around their systems."[16] Moreover, other countries (China and Russia, for instance) might insist on the same access to terrorist communications that had been provided by Apple and other telecommunications companies to U.S. law enforcement and intelligence officials.[17]

Law enforcement officials in the United States did little to ease concerns when they spoke of hundreds of other cases where they might need the assistance of Silicon Valley—say, with drug-trafficking or child abuse investigations. Cook said that law enforcement agencies nationwide "have hundreds of iPhones they want Apple to unlock if the FBI wins this [San Bernardino] case."[18] Even the FBI director conceded that this case could be just the first of many similar requests in the future. At least, though, the Bureau and others were not asking for a blanket "back-door" option that would allow government officials access to all Apple cell phones at any time.

The director of the Open Technology Institute at the New America Foundation, Kevin Bankston, considered even the San Bernardino request unpersuasive. He called the president's alliance with the FBI against Apple "yet another disappointment in a string of disappointments when it comes to privacy." In counterpoint, Representative Adam B. Schiff (California, the ranking Democrat on the House Intelligence Committee and one of its more progressive members) pointed out that "if ever there was going to be a nod to the law enforcement view, this was the one to do it."[19] A House colleague, Jason Chaffetz (R, Utah), chairman of the House Oversight and Government Reform Committee, cautioned, however, that "the big question for our country is how much privacy are we going to give up in the name of security. And there's no easy answer to that."[20]

When it comes to gaining access into private encrypted telephone or computer data, no immutable formula exists. Each case would have to be examined separately by law enforcement officials and the private company involved, along with the courts and (in dangerous terrorist situations) the president—all working toward maintaining strict standards of privacy, but with a short-term government override in evidence-based conditions that indicated the nation was in clear and immediate danger. Vital in these instances would be a warrant procedure, as well as reports to congressional oversight committees on these (infrequent) security alliances between the government and Silicon Valley. The special code that observers thought Apple would have to write in order to enter the San Bernardino iPhone could be locked up subsequently in a secure Apple vault, thus assuring communications companies that their phone and computer access protocols would not be undermined. As for requests from places like China and Russia, if the evidence of an immediate terrorist attack upon them was compelling (again, an infrequent situation), the United States could work with the relevant communications company to help these nations avert calamity—just as would be expected from them if their companies could assist in shielding Americans from terrorist assaults.

"Will technology companies protect the privacy of their users or will they do work for the U.S. government? You can't do both," concluded Malkia Cyril, the executive director of an activist group called the Center for Media Justice.[21] In fact, though, the companies can and—in rare instances involving acutely pressing threats like a terrorist attack—must do both. As it turned out, in the San Bernardino case the FBI proved able (after some missteps and finally with help from an undisclosed outside company) to access the iPhone; therefore, the government dropped its lawsuit to force Apple's compliance. Without a doubt there will be similar cases in the future, though, so the debate over whether private U.S. companies have the right to place privacy above all other considerations—even the security of the American public—continued on. One could only wonder if Apple and other telephone companies really wanted to become, as a *Times* letter-to-the-editor put it, "the host and protector of all the world's criminal communications"?[22]

The intelligence oversight committees on Capitol Hill joined the encryption debate. The top leaders of the Senate panel, Chairman Richard M. Burr (R, N. Carolina) and ranking minority member Dianne Feinstein (D, California), combined forces to sponsor a bill that would require technical companies to provide access to encrypted data, if so ordered by a court warrant. "We need strong encryption to protect personal data," Senator Feinstein acknowledged, "but we also need to know when terrorists are plotting to kill Americans."[23] The most liberal member of the Senate Intelligence Committee, Senator Ron Wyden (D, Oregon), took the opposite position, defending the right of the tech companies and their customers to keep the privacy of their communications intact. Wyden threatened to filibuster the Burr-Feinstein initiative, if necessary.

Amusingly, some intelligence leaders, such as Michael V. Hayden, the former director of the National Security Agency (NSA) and later director of the CIA, who in those positions had been dedicated to the idea that private industry should help the spy agencies gain access to encrypted messages in instances involving terrorists, suddenly changed their tune when they retired from government and became consultants for Apple and other Silicon Valley corporations.

In sync with their new employers, inviolate telephone and computer encryption suddenly began to make perfect sense to them.

The *New York Times* reached this conclusion about the jockeying between the government and Silicon Valley: "the battle has essentially ended in a draw now that the F.B.I. has managed to get into the [San Bernardino] phone by paying an outside group to help hack it."[24] In the midst of all this fury, it was clear: government and private industry would eventually have to devise a protocol for surveillance that all parties could trust, accompanied by close review by the courts and the Congress—if, in fact, the government really even needed the help of Silicon Valley to access electronic technological devices. The debate between Silicon Valley and the government began to seem moot, if not farcical, when the anti-intelligence hacking organization known as WikiLeaks disclosed in March 2017—in the largest leak ever of CIA documents—that the Agency already enjoyed a capacity to bypass the encryption on Apple and Android smartphones.[25]

In times of crisis, the United States has naturally tended—for the sake of flexibility and efficiency in dealing with perilous situations—to shift the balance toward the security side of the ledger. A recent illustration is when extraordinary intelligence operations were adopted in the wake of the 9/11 attacks, from widening electronic surveillance activities to the use of covert action against the Taliban regime in Afghanistan (which had provided a safe haven for the Al Qaeda terrorist organization responsible for the attacks). In more normal times the equilibrium between security and liberty returns, or even leans toward an expansion of liberties. Regardless of the tilting one way or the other, depending on the state of perceived threats to the nation, a core of privacy values must be preserved within a democracy even during unsettling times—or else the claim to be a democratic society based on freedom is lost. Schorr's pendulum must have a constrained arc as it swings in both directions. In a democracy, one cannot "balance" core values; they must be preserved and protected.

"The challenge is to provide sufficient protections for both the security of the state and its inhabitants, and for civil liberties and privacy," writes Canadian intelligence scholar Wesley Wark about this security/liberty conundrum.[26] As the 2014 Nobel Laurate in Economics Jean Tirole once stressed, in matters of regulation—whether in government or in industry—controls must be light enough to allow for agility, morale, and innovation to thrive, yet strong enough to prevent abuses.[27] Unfortunately, though, officials in industry or in the executive branch of government often view regulations—including laws and guidelines from Congress—as merely roadblocks thwarting innovation. Bureaucracies may have little enthusiasm for troublesome laws, rules, and regulations; but, as President John F. Kennedy emphasized, in a democratic society "law is the strongest link between man and freedom."[28]

The balance between liberty and security is one of several challenges in trying to maintain a sensible equilibrium in the sphere of intelligence. For instance, intelligence officials must shield their sources (such as the names of its agents abroad) and their methods (such as the resolution capabilities of cameras mounted on surveillance satellites). Indeed, the National Security Act of 1947 that created the modern American intelligence apparatus places a special emphasis on the importance of shielding "sources and methods." Yet this mantra can become an excuse for intelligence managers to keep *all* information about their activities tucked away from overseers in Congress and the courts. A balance must be struck between the executive branch keeping certain intelligence data (such as the names of agents and the technical details of reconnaissance aircraft) off-limits to all but a few managers, while at the same time cooperating in the sharing of information about most intelligence activities with lawmakers and other authorized overseers in the government. Similarly with document classification, some information should be legitimately classified, such as agent names, the blueprints of surveillance machines, and plans for sensitive covert operations; nevertheless, virtually every study on the intelligence classification system in the United States has concluded that too many documents are stamped "classified," indeed upward of 85 percent more than needs to be—a stunning imbalance between proper security measures to protect sensitive information, on the one hand, and the public's right to know about government programs, on the other hand.[29]

Another balancing act often takes place when the media, whose reporting can provide a vital nongovernmental check against abuses of power, receives intelligence documents in the form of leaks. Occasionally some news organizations rashly publish secret or even top-secret documents without much thought about the consequences for national security. An example is when journalist Jack Anderson published a column about Operation Guppy, a CIA program in Moscow during the Cold War designed to eavesdrop on conversations inside Soviet VIP limousines by using concealed backseat listening devices.[30] The KGB eliminated these electronic bugs once informed by Anderson's newspaper column. Most of the time, however, responsible members of the media carefully weigh the pros and cons of transparency in their reporting versus the government's claim that national security interests should override publication.

Before a decision is made, media managers typically talk with government officials and deliberate among themselves, with a full understanding of the responsibility that rests on their shoulders. The memoirs of former *Washington Post* managing editor Ben Bradlee offer a sense of this dynamic. "Stories involving questions of national security are the toughest problems for an editor," he acknowledged in his chronicle of the give-and-take that goes on between the government and the media over whether a leak should be published. Media editors can face threats by intelligence agencies or the White House to prosecute them if they publish classified information, however innocuous the story may be.[31] Moreover, from time to time the government will simply lie to the media about the supposed monumental importance of keeping a story out of the newspapers. Bradlee recalls that only eighteen years later did the Solicitor General of the United States, Erwin N. Griswold, concede that publication of the Pentagon Papers, the first-ever attempt by the federal government to stop the media from publishing classified information, had never proposed "any trace of a threat to the national security." Yet Griswold had made precisely the opposite argument against the *Washington Post* and the *New York Times* before the Supreme Court in 1971, which the justices rebuffed by a vote of 6 to 3.[32] In an earlier event, Admiral Jim Stockdale admitted only twenty years after the fact that there had never been a Battle of Tonkin Gulf in 1964, the incident in which Navy officials and the White House claimed that U.S. destroyers had come under fire from North Vietnamese patrol boats.[33] This national security cover-up, kept from the media on grounds of national security, provided the pretext for America's entry into a prolonged and unsuccessful war against North Vietnam.

When the *Times* found out in 2004 that the Bush Administration had bypassed the Foreign Intelligence Surveillance Act (FISA) of 1978, which requires court warrants for national security wiretaps, its managers caved in to the White House's request—again based on a national security claim—for prior restraint on the story. The scoop remained bottled up for over a year, until finally the newspaper had second thoughts and printed the unsettling discovery that the administration had resorted to illegal wiretaps in response to the 9/11 attacks. The change of heart at the *Times* occurred chiefly because one of its lead journalists with an intelligence beat, James Risen, was about to publish a book—courageously, in the face of remonstrations by the White House and even his own bosses at the *Times*—that would reveal this brazen sidestepping of FISA, one of the most important safeguards against the government's misuse of secret electronic surveillance power. "Secrecy is often necessary to protect national security," observes Lincoln Caplan, "but it can just as easily be used as a convenient veil for the autocratic assertion of power and, as the courts may find about parts of the [NSA's] surveillance programs, for illegality."[34]

Of special concern are the balancing decisions struck by government and media leaders during crisis situations that democracies inevitably face from time to time. Under conditions of stress, the implications for democracy of the trade-offs between liberty and security are often poorly weighed, lost in the rush to shield against an attack directed at the nation, or to track down perpetrators after an attack. The fundamental constitutional rights that make life in America special and admired around the world can be suddenly brushed aside. Moreover, trying to revert back from entrenched emergency powers can be difficult once the emergency abates, especially in light of the ever more sophisticated and care-fully concealed snooping technologies available to a government's intelligence services. A great challenge to democracy in the United States, as in other open societies, is to remain devoted to both liberty and security, even when terrorists and other enemies are at the gates, when dangers tempt government leaders and citizens alike to abandon their basic values in an atmosphere of anxiety often fueled by an epidemic of fearmongering. "If we have another 9/11, it'll be hard to stop people from throwing out the Bill of Rights," comments a veteran coun-terterrorism specialist. "Therefore we need to put roadblocks in the way now, before there's another crisis, so we can at least slow down the loss of privacy. Once you give away rights, you can't get them back."[35]

The risk lies in overreaction in times of crisis, as happened in the United States during the hysteria of World War II when people of Japanese descent in this nation were falsely accused as spies for Japan, rounded up, and sent to incar-ceration camps. Only forty years later in 1983 did a Federal District Court judge, Marilyn Hall Patel, declare in a case brought by one of those sent to a camp in Utah that the imprisonments stand "as a caution that in times of distress the shield of military necessity and national security must not be used to protect governmental actions from close scrutiny and accountability."[36]

Sweeping—and lingering—emergency powers can quickly displace hard-won freedoms. This approach, a product of panic, must be rejected in favor of limited surveillance targeted against only those individuals and groups who, by all reasonable criteria and after careful judicial review, may represent a danger to the Republic. The values of liberty and security will clash from time to time. In those rare moments that may require a temporary abandonment of some liber-ties, democracies must steadfastly resist the siren calls of those who—driven by fear, hatred, xenophobia, or a sense of revenge against attackers—advocate mea-sures that cut the very bone of America's basic constitutional principles.

A Chapter Roadmap

The purpose of the chapters that follow is to join the ongoing debate about how best to control America's sprawling intelligence bureaucracy—an important part of the debate over how to ensure an acceptable balance between liberty and security. The question of the relationship between intelligence and democracy runs through this book like a golden thread. From time to time, concern about the quality of intelligence accountability has risen to the forefront of the nation's attention, stirred by such revelations as domestic spying by the CIA brought to light in 1974; the Iran-contra scandal in 1987; the mass surveillance of American citizens carried out by the NSA and exposed in 2013; and the Senate's still-classified "CIA Torture Report," whose detailed Executive Summary (at least) was released to the public in 2014. Inaccurate or incomplete reports prepared by the intelligence agencies have stirred controversy, too, and raised questions about how well the Congress has prodded the nation's spies to provide more reliable portraits of threats that confront the United States. The failure to pinpoint the time and place of the terror attacks in 2001 is a prime example. This tragic lack of warning from the CIA and its companion organizations was followed quickly in 2002 by a host of mistaken claims by the spy agencies about the likely presence of weapons of mass destruction (WMDs) in Iraq. These errors included misunderstandings about the purpose of aluminum tubes and mobile labs spotted in Iraq, plus a false report that Baghdad had purchased from Niger fifty tons of yellow-cake uranium to advance a nuclear-weapons program.[37]

This book seeks to evaluate the merits of arguments advanced by both intelligence reformers and anti-reformers. What have been the implications of the profound change in attitudes inside the United States regarding the proper degree of accountability over spy organizations, which shifted in the mid-1970s from a blind acceptance of a wide leeway for espionage activities toward advocacy of a regular spelunking by lawmakers and their staff into the hidden caves of the government's secret agencies? What reforms were adopted, as leaders in Washington searched for a way to maintain effective intelligence armor for the United States while simultaneously providing democratic restraints against the misuse of hidden powers? How well has this balancing act fared since the trail-blazing inquiries into intelligence scandals by government panels in 1975 through the disparagement of America's spy agencies by incoming President Donald J. Trump in 2017? Has this nation placed itself at a disadvantage in the struggle with global terrorists and autocratic regimes by imposing overly rigorous democratic safeguards on its intelligence activities? How do the views on accountability held by intelligence professionals contrast with the rest of the executive branch—especially the White House and the Department of Justice (DoJ)—as well as with members of Congress and the judiciary?

Chapter 1: Tracking an Elusive Behemoth

This story begins with a look at the meaning and significance of intelligence accountability (often referred to by political scientists as "oversight"). The major institutions that conduct reviews of America's espionage activities—within the legislative, the executive, and the judicial branches of government—are introduced and their differing approaches outlined. This opening chapter also lays out the startlingly wide range of agencies in the executive branch that engage in intelligence activities, as well as groups outside the government to whom espionage tasks are sometimes assigned—spy "outsourcing." The purposes of this opening commentary are to underscore the importance of intelligence accountability and to emphasize the daunting responsibility that overseers face in understanding and reviewing the nation's global, arcane, and nearly invisible intelligence operations.

Chapter 2: Intelligence Exceptionalism

This chapter looks at the exceptional status that intelligence agencies have enjoyed in the government throughout most of America's history. Until recently, the secret agencies operated free from any serious supervision by the Congress and the judiciary, or even from supervisors within the executive branch. This amassing of power into the hands of espionage services, without the counterbalance of clear constitutional limitations, was a sure prescription for the abuses eventually revealed by the *New York Times* in 1974. The philosophy advanced by James Madison at the nation's Constitutional Convention in 1787 warned against the concentration of power in the executive branch. The nation would pay a price for bypassing within the dark side of government this basic truth about the value of institutional checks and balances enshrined in the Constitution.

Further, this chapter introduces two primary schools of thought on intelligence agencies that are examined throughout the book. The first school argues that spies should be robustly supported and left unfettered by oversight restrictions, in the name of efficiency as the United States confronts a hostile world that abides by few—if any—rules of constitutional restraint. The second and quite different school maintains that the intelligence agencies should not be given exceptional privileges that trump America's traditional philosophy of checks and balances. Rather, in the name of civil liberties and privacy—and especially during a time of growing technological sophistication and rampant surveillance capabilities—spies should be monitored more rigorously than ever by supervisors who insist that they operate within the boundaries of U.S. law and cultural expectations.

Chapter 3: Democracy Comes to the Secret Agencies

The third chapter further explores the long-standing proclivity to give the secret agencies loose rein, and why, in 1974–1975, the nation broke from this unbridled approach to security. As a result of sweeping inquiries into domestic spy scandals by the Church Committee in the Senate (led by Frank Church, D, Idaho), the Pike Committee in the House (after its leader, Otis Pike, D, New York), and the Rockefeller Commission in the White House (after Vice President Nelson Rockefeller), a new era of accountability for spies began in the United States.[38] In place of intelligence exceptionalism emerged an uneasy partnership between the secret agencies and their overseers, as Congress, the White House, and the judiciary established tighter controls over America's espionage services. Following the recommendation of the Church Committee, members of the Senate voted across party lines in 1976 to establish a permanent standing oversight committee for intelligence; in the next year, the House followed suit with a counterpart committee of its own—respectively, the Senate Select Committee on Intelligence (SSCI, pronounced "sis-see") and the House Permanent Select Committee on Intelligence (HPSCI, "hip-see"). An experiment in serious and systematic intelligence accountability had begun—a first not only in the United States but also in the contemporary world and throughout all of history.

The relationship between the secret agencies and their new supervisors proved fraught. Lawmakers responsible for intelligence review often advanced conflicting proposals for the proper balancing of security and democracy. It was clear, on the one hand, that effective—and sometimes highly aggressive—intelligence agencies were necessary to guard the United States against threats at home and abroad; but, on the other hand, it was also understood that openness in government was the very anchor of democracy. Under the new set of rules for accountability established in 1975–1976, in the midst of the Cold War, would the United States still be able to compete with global Communism and the often harsh use of secret operations by the Soviet Union and China? Or would the new norms—legislative "micro-management," in the damning phrase of some U.S. intelligence officers disdainful of congressional "interference"—shackle the CIA and its companion agencies, sapping their initiative and endangering the United States? Soon after the new intelligence oversight procedures were put in place (such as regular reporting by the secret agencies to SSCI and HPSCI), Dr. Ray Cline, a senior CIA officer, raised doubts about the wisdom of abandoning the old way of doing things, namely, giving the IC carte blanche in its efforts to counter America's enemies. "Must the United States respond [to the Soviet threat] like a man in a barroom brawl who will fight only according to the Marquis of Queensberry rules?" he asked in exasperation.[39] On another occasion, Dr. Cline expressed anguish over how the New Intelligence Oversight meant that the CIA et al. had to put on the breaks, when instead "the intelligence agencies need *horsepower*!"[40]

Chapter 4: The Experiment in Rigorous Intelligence Accountability Begins

In the slipstream of the government investigations by the Church, Pike, and Rockefeller panels, the Congress enacted several measures to tighten legislative, executive, and judicial control over the spy agencies. Unhappy about Congress's rising role in foreign and security policy, a member of the President's Foreign

Intelligence Advisory Board (PFIAB, pronounced "piff-e-ab"), political scientist James Q. Wilson of Harvard University and UCLA, suggested in 1986 that the struggle between Congress and the executive branch had "become an alley fight—a cacophonous, decentralized, unmanaged public quarrel over every detail of every policy." He added that America's interests were not served by "detailed disclosures of intelligence-gathering operations." Although Professor Wilson failed to provide examples of what disclosures he had in mind, entirely clear was his preference for presidential dominance in all matters of foreign policy and intelligence.[41]

Whatever side of the accountability argument one embraced, whether leaning toward more security or more liberty, it was self-evident a decade after the inquiries of 1975 that the finely embroidered net of safeguards fashioned by intelligence reformers had failed to prevent the CIA and the staff of the NSC from engaging in the worst scandal in modern American history: the Iran-contra affair, which involved multiple violations of law. A national security adviser in the Reagan Administration, Admiral John M. Poindexter, testified on Capitol Hill a year after Professor Wilson's remarks and sounded very much like him—only now the administration faced an unfolding Iran-contra scandal that would send President Reagan's popularity in the public opinion polls spiraling precipitously downward by twenty-one percentage points. Poindexter's answer to Wilson's query about how best to handle the quarrel between the branches over security policy was straightforward: the admiral just hid his actions from the Congress. "I simply didn't want any outside interference," he explained in response to questions from congressional investigators as they probed into why the staff of the NSC (the highest-level White House advisory board for foreign and security policy) had secretly bypassed the legislative branch in pursuit of illegal objectives in Iran and Nicaragua.[42] The admiral seemed to think that Congress was a rank outsider rather than a constitutional partner in the shaping of American foreign policy. With his declaration of independence, Poindexter had carried Professor Wilson's dissatisfactions with accountability into the inner sanctums of the White House and the nation's security bureaucracy.

The overzealous Iran-contra operations included an attack on the Constitution itself when the Reagan Administration ignored the congressional appropriations process. Its national security officials sought private funding to conduct covert actions in Nicaragua that had been formally prohibited by the Congress (through the Boland Amendments, sponsored by Representative Edward P. Boland [D, Massachusetts], HPSCI chairman at the time). In the wake of this affair, lawmakers revisited their cratered attempts fashioned in the mid-1970s to restrain the abuse of secret power. Clearly the safeguards advanced by the Church, Pike, and Rockefeller inquiries would have to be retooled to strengthen intelligence accountability.

After the Cold War ended in 1991, the government of the United States soon conducted additional probes into the activities of its intelligence agencies. The first major investigation during this period was spurred by significant intelligence errors. The initial failure occurred in 1993 and involved a lack of warning about the strength of local militants in Somalia, who killed eighteen U.S. Special Forces in a gun battle fought in the unpaved alleyways of that nation's capital, Mogadishu. The second failure, a year later in 1994, sprang from the revelation that a senior CIA counterintelligence officer, Aldrich Hazen Ames, had been providing secrets to the Soviet Union and later to Russia for a decade. It was the worse instance of internal treason in the Agency's history. Responding to these twin concerns, Congress and the White House created a joint executive-legislative investigative panel to study the circumstances of these intelligence missteps.

The panel was known as the Aspin-Brown Commission after its two chairs, first former representative and secretary of defense Les Aspin (D, Wisconsin) and then, when Aspin died in the middle of the inquiry, former secretary of defense Harold Brown. (I served as special assistant to Aspin and remained on the Commission staff.) The Commission soon found itself laden with a much broader investigative mandate than the subjects of Somalia and Ames. Congress further charged the panel to determine how well the intelligence agencies were adapting to the post–Cold War world, which was no longer bipolar but had fragmented into a multitude of power centers around the globe (although the United States remained the world's preeminent military arsenal). The Aspin-Brown Commission, officially known as "the Commission on the Roles and Capabilities of the United States Intelligence Community," labored for a year on this complex agenda. Its main recommendation was that the United States needed to establish a true, not merely a titular, spymaster: a much stronger Director of Central Intelligence (DCI), armed with an enhanced budget and personnel powers to integrate and coordinate the entire IC, not just lead the CIA (the main job of the DCI in the past).

Chapter 5: Spy Watching in an Age of Terror

Five years after the Aspin-Brown Commission called—fecklessly—for the strengthening of U.S. intelligence capabilities, terror struck the United States from the skies on September 11, 2001, as hijacked commercial airlines flown by *jihadists* smashed into the Twin Towers of the World Trade Center in New York City and the Pentagon in Washington, D.C.—the most devastating direct assaults against the continental United States since the British torched the nation's capital in the War of 1812.

Once Americans overcame their initial shock and the government had organized a retaliatory strike against the terrorist group Al Qaeda, hiding in Afghanistan and responsible for the attacks, the questions began to pour out. How had the nation been taken by surprise in another Pearl Harbor–like disaster? How was it that the CIA and the other intelligence agencies had known so little about Al Qaeda? Would the nation be forewarned of, and defended against, future acts of terror—perhaps even the use of nuclear, biological, or chemical (NBC) weaponry against the United States? Lawmakers established a joint House-Senate panel of inquiry to augment the probes already underway by SSCI and HPSCI; but, public pressure—especially from the families of the 9/11 victims—forced the White House under President George W. Bush to establish a higher-profile presidential investigative commission.

This 9/11 Commission, chaired by former governor Thomas H. Kean (R, New Jersey) and former representative Lee H. Hamilton (D, Indiana), prepared a voluminous, well-written, and well-received report in 2004. One of its core findings was that intelligence accountability on Capitol Hill had become "dysfunctional."[43] Again the Congress would have to take a hard look in the mirror and determine how to improve its efforts at monitoring the nation's spy activities. A lingering question was whether the 9/11 attacks could have been prevented, had congressional overseers demanded better performance from the intelligence agencies before the attacks; and whether a stronger DCI, as recommended by the Aspin-Brown Commission, could have steered the nation's intelligence services toward a more effective gathering of information about terrorists—especially Al Qaeda. Then, on top of the 9/11 missteps, came the inability of America's intelligence agencies to determine accurately whether Iraq possessed WMDs. Most of these agencies said yes, but a U.S. invasion of Iraq proved that the answer was no.

Clearly the nation's spy apparatus needed some improvements. Instead of adopting the Kean Commission's recommendation for a strengthened DCI, however, Congress created an Office of the Director of National Intelligence (ODNI), which turned out to have many of the same weaknesses associated with the old DCI but with new ones added on—including a questionable physical separation of the DNI, the nation's new spymaster, from the nation's core strategic intelligence analysts who continued to be located at the CIA.

The necessity for closer intelligence accountability became all the more apparent when the news broke in 2005 that the NSA had bypassed the warrant process for national security wiretaps, as required by FISA in 1978. Rather than amend or repeal the law, the second Bush Administration had simply circumvented it. Subsequently, in 2013, came the unauthorized leaking of classified information by Edward J. Snowden, a computer specialist at the consulting firm Booz Allen Hamilton on assignment at the NSA. After stealing some 1.7 million classified documents, Snowden fled to Hong Kong, then on to Russia, to avoid arrest by U.S. law enforcement officers.

Among the documents that Snowden snatched and soon released to the media were papers that revealed the existence of a bulk "metadata" collection program being carried out by the NSA to track the communications patterns (though not the content) of American citizens: telephone records (the number of every call and its duration), as well as other contacts made through emails and other forms of social media. The metadata program had two targets: American citizens, in a program known as "215"; and foreigners, in a program known as PRISM. The 215 initiative, critics complained, was a national fishing expedition being carried out by the NSA in hopes of uncovering hidden terrorist connections within the United States. Critics insisted that a more acceptable method of counterterrorism in a democracy would be to target (with proper FISA warrants) specific individuals or groups based on a reliable suspicion that they might be engaged in terrorist activities, say, as a result of FBI informant reports from inside a New York City or Los Angeles mosque known to harbor radical sympathizers of foreign terrorist organizations. As during the Church Committee probe in 1975, the NSA was once more embroiled in a civil liberties scandal; and, again, it was clear that existing measures of accountability remained far short of reliable, regardless of how much they had improved since the "good old days" (as some intelligence officers like to remember the era before the sea change in attitudes toward oversight brought about by reformers in the 1970s).

In the midst of these controversies, anti-reformers pushed back against the idea of yet more layers of intelligence accountability. The CIA's former Deputy Director of Operations (DDO) was a chief architect of the torture program adopted by the Agency to interrogate suspected terrorists after the 9/11 attacks—an approach condoned by the CIA's leader at the time, Porter Goss (R, Florida), a former HPSCI chair. The DDO asked with rhetorical flourish, as if this observation settled the case in favor of torture, "Don't we want to stop terrorism?"[44] In light of recent terrorist attacks against civilian targets—in London; in Paris and Nice; Berlin, Brussels, and Bavaria; San Bernardino, Orlando, and Ft. Lauderdale; Lebanon, Istanbul, and Sousse (in Tunisia); Lahore, Baghdad, Mecca, and Bangladesh—this kind of rhetoric struck a responsive chord in some quarters. Channeling Professor Wilson and Admiral Poindexter, this CIA torture advocate (the DDO) viewed Congress with scorn—particularly the crafting of a critical "Torture Report" by SSCI's Democratic staff during five years of investigation into the Agency's interrogation methods. In the report's declassified Executive Summary, Democrats on SSCI presented to the American people details of the severe approach to questioning adopted by the CIA after

9/11, under authorization from the Bush White House and the Office of Legal Counsel (OLC) in the Justice Department.[45] In the aftermath of the Snowden revelations and the public misgivings about the CIA's harsh interrogation practices, the United States began in 2015 to move away from its obsession with security toward a restoration of respect for the traditional American values of liberty and privacy.

Chapter 6: A Shock Theory of Intelligence Accountability

The experiences of the United States with intelligence accountability suggest that, in a democracy, some degree of strain—even turbulence—is inevitable between intelligence officers and their overseers. James Madison reasoned that the exercise of checks and balances, what he referred to as "auxiliary precautions," would allow "ambition to counteract ambition" (to cite passages from his *Federalist Paper No. 51*), as the branches of government jostled over the proper sharing of authority and guarded against any one branch of government gathering too much power. For most of America's government, that is exactly what happened after the nation's founding; but not until "the Year of Intelligence" in 1975 did these wise restraints apply to the espionage services as well.

Since the creation of stricter intelligence regulations in the aftermath of the Church, Pike, and Rockefeller inquiries, a pattern has emerged in which lawmakers have been emboldened to establish "rules of the road" for the nation's secret agencies. At first, members of Congress keep a close eye on the spy organizations to ensure the new rules are honored. Before long, though, the interest and attention span of lawmakers begin to wane and the intelligence agencies are treated with a sense of benign neglect on Capitol Hill. Then, inevitably when left unwatched, the agencies—or, at any rate, some key individuals within these organizations—either misuse their powers in a manner that leads to scandal or they fail to perform effectively in their basic assignments to collect and accurately analyze information about world threats and opportunities.

The scandals and failures that follow the phase of benign neglect deliver a shock to the polity—a sudden punch in the gut to the distracted overseers, as occurred with the Iran-contra scandal in the mid-1980s and with the failure to warn the nation about the 9/11 attacks in 2001. Once a scandal or failure is revealed, members of Congress shake themselves out of their lassitude, rally to investigate what went wrong, and attempt to set the spy agencies back on a proper track with a fresh set of rules. In a repeat of the cycle, immediately after the scandal or failure, spy watching on Capitol Hill remains intense, but only for a while before dropping off again as interest in the hard job of intelligence supervision dissipates among lawmakers—only to result in yet another bout of scandal or failure, followed by a new rush to discover what went wrong. I first advanced this "shock theory" of intelligence accountability in an essay published in 2006.[46] As further explored in this chapter, the pattern that emerges from an examination of the ups and downs of intelligence oversight reveals a number of points in an accountability cycle that cry out for reform—at least by those who hope to prevent the dislocations of scandal and failure that emerge in the wake of the extended periods of benign neglect that dominate the cycle.

Chapter 7: The Media and Intelligence Accountability

My "shock theory" of intelligence accountability indicates that most lawmakers rarely engage in intensive intelligence oversight unless a major scandal or failure forces them to pay more attention to the hidden side of government. With respect to the media's coverage of intelligence and the response of congressional overseers to this coverage, a central point of interest can be stated with this key question: What degree of stunning news in the media regarding failures or scandals involving the intelligence agencies—a shock—is necessary to stir members of Congress into taking a closer look at the nation's secret operations? This chapter examines the ten significant intelligence shocks—the most prominent scandals and failures—since the creation of the CIA in 1947, exploring the extent of media coverage associated with each. These shocks include the unexpected outbreak of war on the Korean peninsula (1950); the Bay of Pigs fiasco (1961); the CIA and the National Student Association controversy (1967); a suspected involvement of the CIA in Watergate (1973); Operation CHAOS (the Agency's domestic spy program revealed in 1974); the Iran-contra scandal (1986); the Ames treason (uncovered in 1994); the 9/11 attacks (2001); the faulty intelligence regarding suspected Iraqi WMDs (2002); and, most recently, the NSA warrantless wiretap and metadata controversies (2005 and 2013, respectively, which may be viewed as a prolonged unfolding of a single NSA scandal involving overzealous metadata and warrantless collection operations—to critics, a slow-motion signals intelligence Bay of Pigs).

The findings suggest that the level of media coverage of a scandal or a failure often corresponds with the degree of congressional attention paid to intelligence oversight: a low level of accountability exists when the media coverage of a shock is at a low level; moderate if moderate; and high if high. For the most part, members of Congress are content to adopt a posture of benign neglect toward spy activities, even in the cases of scandals and failures—unless a steady drumbeat of media coverage draws substantial attention to these activities and the ensuing "public oversight" generated by newspaper, television, and social media stories compels lawmakers to respond with official inquiries.

Chapter 8: Ostriches, Cheerleaders, Lemon-Suckers, and Guardians

The record of intelligence accountability since the breakthrough inquiries of 1975 exhibits another pattern that sheds further light on the shock theory: a tendency for lawmakers on SSCI and HPSCI to play one of four major roles in their capacities as spy watchers, with periodic transitions from one role to another. Some members of Congress behave chiefly as "ostriches," displaying little interest in the concept of accountability, attending few committee and sub-committee hearings, and registering only desultory interest in the topics that come before SSCI and HPSCI. These lawmakers essentially have their heads in the sand when it comes to espionage activities, even though many continue to "serve" passively as members of the intelligence oversight committees and enjoy status in their home constituencies as the James Bonds of Capitol Hill.

Other lawmakers, indeed the most predominant category, take on the attri-butes of a "cheerleader," rallying to the defense of the intelligence services when-ever they are criticized in the media—without the members of Congress first (or sometimes ever) examining the facts, and almost regardless of what the allegations may claim against the intelligence establishment. Here is a return to a full, uncritical embrace of the spy agencies that prevailed in the pre–Church Committee days: the propensity to trust those in the espionage trade to conduct themselves as honorable individuals at home, while at the same time behaving ruthlessly abroad (if necessary) to protect the interests of the United States. The oversight lanterns carried by the cheerleaders flitter in the darkness of the intel-ligence agencies, rarely revealing anything beyond their foyers.

A third category of intelligence role-playing on Capitol Hill is the "lemon-sucker"—a favorite phrase of President Bill Clinton to describe economists, whom he chastised for always bringing him gloomy (sour) predictions. The lemon-suckers are, in the context of this chapter, lawmakers who have a sharply negative attitude toward secret government organizations and their activities. These members of Congress have virtually no confidence in most, if not all, intelligence operations. They view these opaque arts as anathema to democratic society, in light of their tendency to engage from time to time (as the Church Committee found) in lawbreaking at home—CIA spying against Vietnam War protesters, FBI harassment of civil rights activists, warrantless NSA eaves-dropping inside the United States—and their use of such extreme measures as assassination plots against foreign leaders and the toppling of regimes over-seas. Or, if not dismissing the intelligence services as immoral and lawbreaking, the lemon-sucker at least considers them incompetent to the point where they ought to be abolished, if only to prevent a waste of taxpayer money. A favor-ite example pointed to by some lemon-suckers is the CIA's supposed failure to predict the fall of the Soviet empire—although, in fact, the record shows that the Agency's analysts did a credible job of tracking this rapid and astonishing decline.[47]

Finally, and most desirable from the viewpoint of democratic theory, some lawmakers serve as intelligence "guardians." They are both partners and critics of the spy agencies. At times, like the cheerleaders, they publicly commend the performance of these organizations. With an understanding of how intelligence can serve as America's first line of defense against danger, guardians help justify to citizens the billions of dollars spent annually on clandestine operations around the world. Unlike the cheerleaders, however, they are not above disciplining the secret agencies when they err—much as a good parent relies on a mixture of encouragement and punishment as befitting the behavior of the child. An example is a former member of HPSCI and, later in his career, of SSCI: Democrat Wyche Fowler of Georgia. While serving on the oversight committees, he understood the importance of reliable threat assessments and warnings prepared by the intelligence agencies, and he defended them when appropriate; but he also championed accountability, arguing that "fresh air openness won't compromise our intelligence gathering."[48]

Rather than being frozen into one role or another, the cases examined in this chapter indicate that lawmakers may shift in their role-playing, as events and conditions modify their attitudes toward the IC. For instance, in HPSCI's early days, Chairman Eddie Boland largely deferred to the wishes of the spy agencies, doing his best to developing good working ties between the nation's lawmakers and the managers of the secret services. His goal was to smooth the tempestuous relations between the nation's spies and the House of Representatives that had erupted during the investigation into CIA activities by the belligerent Pike Committee in 1975. In fulfillment of this goal, he assumed the role of cheerleader. After the shock of the Iran-contra scandal, however, Boland grew angry and disillusioned with the CIA and switched dramatically to the role of lemonsucker. Once new reforms were put in place and the Iran-contra architects had been dismissed from government (at least until the second Bush Administration came to town, when several were rehired), Boland settled into a third posture: the role of guardian—no longer an arch-opponent of the CIA, but no longer a malleable cheerleader either.

Attempts to improve intelligence oversight on Capitol Hill must consider the individual role preferences of lawmakers, coming to some understanding of how they form and how they change throughout the cycle of accountability. Though at the time not stated in terms of this role-playing typology, the hopes of a bipartisan majority on the Church Committee was that future members of SSCI and HPSCI would act as vigilant but fair-minded guardians. That has not been the outcome and this chapter explores why.

Chapter 9: In the Trenches: Collection and Analysis, Covert Action

The modern IC has been molded since 1947 to serve the nation, above all, in the pursuit of a preeminent objective: the gathering and interpretation of worldwide information related to threats and opportunities for the United States. The collection-and-analysis mission is complex and subject to many points of potential failure. Chapter 9 looks at the challenges faced by members of Congress in trying to help the IC improve its performance in this domain, avoiding to the extent possible future catastrophes like the mistaken Iraqi WMD hypothesis in 2002. Most of America's intelligence services calculated that Iraq had a robust NBC weapons program that, by implication, would become increasingly threatening to the United States. What proved to be faulty analysis on this subject provided an impetus for war by the United States against Iraq. The Iraqi WMD case demonstrates the value of lawmakers helping the intelligence agencies improve their collection and analysis of information on worldwide events and conditions.

Covert action (CA) is another intelligence activity that demands attention from overseers. These operations are often the most controversial pursuits carried out by the CIA (and at times by the Pentagon), because they are designed to aggressively change events around the globe in a manner expected to advance the international interests of the United States. A CIA document from the 1960s (during the Johnson Administration) regarding Bolivia gives a flavor of the rationales used by national security strategists for embracing CA as an approach to American foreign policy during the Cold War:

> The basic covert action goals in Bolivia are to foster democratic solutions to critical and social, economic, and political problems; to check Communist and Cuban subversion; to encourage a stable government favorably inclined toward the United States; and to encourage Bolivian participation in the Alliance for Progress. The main direction and emphasis of CA operations is to force Communists, leftists, and pro-Castroites out of influential positions in government, and to try to break Communist and ultra-leftist control over certain trade union, student groups, and *campesino* organizations.[49]

The Agency's CA operations can include, often in combination, propaganda (or "perception enhancement" in the CIA's preferred euphemism), as well as political support to friendly nations, factions, and individuals abroad, including financial assistance—sometimes indistinguishable from bribery—for the campaigns of those parties and candidates in democratic regimes. Pro–U.S. Agency officers lugging plastic bags overseas filled with $250,000 or more was not unusual in efforts to persuade foreigners to see things the American way—the incentives of cash that MI6 officers in Britain refer to as "King George's cavalry." CA includes, as well, economic activities that, at the extreme, can involve such operations as mining foreign harbors and the sabotage of power plants; the release of viruses into foreign government computers; and the theft of financial assets belonging to terrorist organizations like Al Qaeda or ISIS. The most controversial CAs are paramilitary or warlike operations designed to kill adversaries by way of drone attacks and other lethal methods, or the overthrow of an unfriendly government through secret and often armed interventions. In 2013, for instance, under directives from the Obama White House (and urged by Secretary of State Hillary Clinton), the CIA began secretly arming embattled rebels in Syria.[50] All of these approaches are meant to be officially unattributed to the United States, although ironically they are often reported openly in the media through leaks or from dispatches by journalists overseas, creating an odd category of "overt-covert operations"—as with the CIA's well-known drone sorties against terrorists inside Pakistan and Yemen.

Given the high levels of secrecy that surround CAs, intelligence overseers on Capitol Hill find themselves especially tested while attempting to monitor the CIA (the chief practitioner) in this mode of activity. Moreover, the statutory guidelines that mandate timely reporting to Congress on CAs have been frequently ignored or they have been twisted from their original intention— namely, prompt reporting to lawmakers—by Democratic and Republican administrations alike. Intelligence officers and White House officials have also flatly lied to Congress about covert actions, most notably during the Iran-contra affair but in many other examples discussed in this book. Further, from time to time intelligence officers have conveniently forgotten—or outright refused—to inform lawmakers about important CA operations. In a further exercise in legerdemain, the intelligence agencies on occasion have used misleading language to deflect attention away from questionable operations—what Winston Churchill might well have referred to as "terminological inexactitudes," had he been a member of SSCI or HPSCI.[51] This chapter offers multiple illustrations of this evasiveness, and even the bold black letter of the law has sometimes been insufficient to corral spy activities in the murky domain of CA.

Moreover, debates are heated between Capitol Hill and the White House over when reports on CAs should come to lawmakers: before an operation (*ante facto* reporting) or after (*ex post facto* reporting). Advocates of rigorous intelligence accountability argue in favor of an *ante facto* standard, which provides members of Congress with an opportunity to object *before* an operation is launched and it becomes too late for the legislative branch to rein in a wrong-minded or even idiotic endeavor. To react after the horse has left the barn is to watch helplessly as it gallops off. The purpose of chapter 9 is to explore the successes and failures of Congress in supervising the core intelligence missions of collection and analysis, as well as CA. The latter responsibility is particularly critical, because today the use of missile-laden drones to achieve foreign-policy objectives has become the most deadly and controversial of all the intelligence activities conducted by the United States.

Chapter 10: In the Wilderness: Coping with Counterintelligence

If the collection-and-analysis mission lies at the heart of intelligence, and if CA is its most lethal and contentious form, counterintelligence (CI) is the least understood and the most slippery for overseers to handle. Within this mysterious mission fall efforts to thwart hostile espionage and terrorist operations directed against America's shores, as well as against U.S. personnel and facilities abroad. Counterterrorism is an important subset of CI.

Within the rubric of CI, spy catching is the name of the game, especially ferreting out "moles" recruited by foreign governments or terrorist organizations who have burrowed deeply into the boiler rooms of America's secret agencies. Spies are by nature stealthy, and uncovering their whereabouts can be a difficult task. Further, CI has unfortunately been responsible for many of the most egregious violations of democratic principles inside the United States, from Operation CHAOS (the CIA domestic spy program to find possible Soviet ties to antiwar and civil rights activists, which led to the Church, Pike, and Rockefeller inquiries) to the disquieting tactics embraced by the Agency during the torture of suspected terrorists after the 9/11 attacks.

The United States and every other democracy, notably in Europe, have suffered from the presence of moles inside their governments over the years—most grievously, Soviet "penetrations" during the Cold War. Conversely, the democracies have also had successes from time to time in their own infiltration of foreign government and terrorist cells. Given the fact that this topic is highly convoluted even for intelligence professionals, it is easy to understand why the CI mission is so difficult for lawmakers and other supervisors to monitor. As a way of illustrating the perplexities that accompany CI activities, this chapter recalls the problems the Church Committee faced while investigating the CIA's chief of counterintelligence, James Angleton.

Chapter 11: Intelligence Accountability and the Nation's Spy Chiefs

For several years, I have had conversations with several of the nation's highest intelligence officials: the DCIs—each one, from Richard Helms (1966–1973) to George J. Tenet (1997–2004). These individuals in many cases allowed me to tape-record our talks. This chapter examines the views of these spy chiefs on the new approaches to accountability initiated by the Church Committee, along with the more recent reforms advanced by SSCI, HPSCI, and various ad hoc committee and commissions on intelligence.

Most of the DCIs, as well as DNIs and other top intelligence officials, have supported the post–Church Committee approaches to accountability, as a means for sharing their difficult responsibilities with elected representatives. Others, though, long for the days before the Year of Intelligence (1975) came along—a happier era, as they see it, when the spy agencies were able to respond more effectively to foreign threats without the annoying restraints imposed by the new architecture of accountability. Any study of intelligence oversight must consider the view from the aeries occupied by America's top spy managers. The vantage point, expertise, experience, and wisdom of senior intelligence officers and managers are of obvious importance in the debate about accountability, not just the perspectives of lawmakers, judges, professors, think-tank analysts, and journalists.

Chapter 12: The Ongoing Quest for Security and Liberty

This final chapter provides an overall evaluation of America's experience with keeping the nation's spies accountability—a roller-coaster ride that has included troubling scandals and failures, major investigations, intense debates over spy modus operandi, and dramatic disagreements over how to proceed in this novel experiment of bringing democratic principles inside the once completely shuttered world of secret organizations. What has been the outcome of switching from the long-held tradition of American intelligence exceptionalism to a situation in which the espionage services are more scrutinized by overseers than any other intelligence organization in the world? Why has the United States suffered from so many ongoing intelligence scandals and failures, despite the great effort invested in developing a closer supervision of its secret agencies? Which reforms have been useful and which have proved feckless or unwise—perhaps even dangerous impediments to the functioning of an effective intelligence shield against the enemies of the United States and other democracies? In a word, have the laws and the new oversight committees—SSCI and HPSCI—made much of a difference in the accountability of America's secret agencies?

This chapter also explores the feasibility of an augmentation in the current approach to accountability on Capitol Hill, which relies chiefly on the good performance of SSCI and HPSCI, plus occasional special committees or commissions of inquiry. An important supplement to the current system would be the creation of a permanent Citizens Intelligence Advisory Board (CIAB). Equipped with subpoena powers and a knowledgeable staff, this organization could consist of a standing panel of national security experts based in Washington, with the White House, Congress, the Supreme Court, and a scholarly board each choosing members for a renewable five-year term.

The duty of CIAB members would be to assist with the responsibility for intelligence oversight. The Board would work closely with SSCI, HPSCI, and the FISA Court, as well as with the NSC staff, the Intelligence Oversight Board, and each of the inspectors general in the IC. It could devote more time to special projects (say, a review of U.S. intelligence capabilities for monitoring Iran's adherence to the 2015 nuclear-weapon prohibitions it agreed to); and, in the case of especially contentious charges against the intelligence agencies, the CIAB—as an outside entity—could provide a more politically neutral probe than is possible for members of Congress. Lawmakers labor under the weight of many additional committee assignments other than SSCI and HPSCI, as well as the political distractions they face as a result of reelection pressures (notably the time-consuming demands of campaign fund-raising)—not to mention the troubling condition of polarization that currently plagues the nation's capital.

Epilogue: Intelligence in the Early Trump Administration

As this book was about to go into production, the presidential election of 2016 brought the Trump Administration into the White House. This brief epilogue provides some observations about the initial handling of intelligence matters by President Trump and his team.

In the early stages of writing this book, a colleague asked me which approach I was going to take. Would it be a textbook, a theoretical study, a political science primer on congressional oversight, a narrative history of intelligence sprinkled with memoir-like insights from a former insider, a look at contemporary intelligence challenges? Granted, one book can't do everything and every author must make some hard choices; still, I think a book can be both theoretical and historical at the same time, while having a contemporary policy orientation and also weaving into the narrative some personal observations based on my years as an intelligence overseer in the Congress and the White House. I have attempted to blend a range of methodologies and disciplinary approaches. I have tried, further, to read everything of scholarly merit that I could find on the subject (see the bibliography).[52] Over the last forty years, I also interviewed everyone in the intelligence agencies who would talk with me, including several of the nation's intelligence directors since the 1960s, many officers at lower ranks, and several members of Congress and their staff aides. This adds up to hundreds of interviews since I began approaching knowledgeable insiders about this topic in

1975. Moreover, I present what I think are telling illustrations of accountability successes and failures that I have witnessed firsthand as a staff aide on Capitol Hill and in the Executive Office of the President.

"Whatever you do," suggested the helpful colleague, "you need to address a big question head on: Have the intelligence reforms instituted in the 1970s worked?" In these pages I try to follow his good advice.

PART I

THE MAGNITUDE OF THE CHALLENGE

Tracking an Elusive Behemoth

The Meaning and Significance of
Intelligence Accountability

Using the legislative branch as an illustration, the former chair of the House Permanent Select Committee on Intelligence (HPSCI), Lee H. Hamilton (D, Indiana), writing with political scientist Jordan Tama, spelled out the argument for government accountability—more commonly referred to as "oversight" on Capitol Hill. "Congress must do more than write the laws," they emphasized, "it must make sure that the administration is carrying out those laws the way Congress intended." Through oversight procedures, they continued, law-makers "can help protect the country from the imperial presidency and from bureaucratic arrogance . . . [and] help keep federal bureaucracies on their toes."[1] Senator Wyche Fowler (D, Georgia), a member of HPSCI when he served in the House and subsequently a member of its Senate counterpart, the Senate Select Committee on Intelligence (SSCI), has observed simply that "oversight keeps bureaucrats from doing something stupid."[2] A more formal definition would underscore that oversight is a government's ongoing attempt to monitor public policy proposals, budgets, and activities, with the objective of correcting missteps—whether mistakes or scandals—and improving the prospects for future initiatives. Is a program lawful? Is it effective? Here are the leading questions for those engaged in maintaining accountability over executive branch agencies.[3]

In addition to keeping members of Congress informed about policies and budgets, the intelligence bureaucracies have also been expected to report to the National Security Council (NSC), which lies within the organizational framework of the Executive Office of the Presidency (EOP, or the White House, for short); and, since 1978 in certain instances, to report to the Foreign Intelligence Surveillance Act (FISA) Court in the judicial branch.[4] At least one of the intelligence agencies, the CIA, has professed its allegiance to vigorous government oversight in the aftermath of major investigations carried out in 1975 into its activities. In 2016, for instance, the Agency's deputy director (DD/CIA) noted in a public speech that each month, as new CIA recruits are sworn in during a ceremony in the headquarters building at Langley, Virginia, a special effort is made to underscore the importance of oversight. He acknowledged that "there are no reporters, lobbyists or advocacy groups filling the seats at our closed congressional hearings." As a result, "robust oversight by the President and Congress—in environments where we can have open, yet still confidential discussions and debates about our mission and how we are executing that mission—is the entirely appropriate adjunct to, and substitute for, traditional oversight by the people and the press."[5]

This chapter introduces the main institutions in the United States devoted to intelligence accountability or oversight. It also outlines the challenges the government faces in its efforts to supervise the nation's secret agencies. I begin with a look at the legislative branch.

Intelligence Oversight by the Congress

Political scientist Joel Aberbach defines legislative accountability as the "review of the actions of federal departments, agencies, and commissions, and of the programs and policies they administer, including review that takes place during program and policy implementation as well as afterward." Aberbach sees oversight activities as "a significant facet of congressional efforts to control administration and policy."[6] His definition can be strengthened with an amendment: the best form of oversight includes not just *ex post facto* (after the fact) reviews of programs, but an examination of major policy proposals *before* they are implemented as well—*ante facto* reviews.

None of the most significant intelligence abuses that have come to light since the end of World War II were revealed to the public by the official institutions of accountability located inside the executive branch. Rather, they were disclosed by congressional investigators, the media, and whistle-blowers. Yet newspaper, magazine, and television correspondents, as well as bloggers, face high walls (literally and figuratively) in their efforts to track the activities of America's secret agencies; and whistle-blowers are often dissuaded from stepping forward by the limited protections they are afforded by the legal system.

One can debate the legitimacy of Edward J. Snowden as an idealistic whistle-blower when, in 2013, he stole more than a million documents from the National Security Agency and leaked them to U.S. and British newspapers. Was he a hero for bringing to light the NSA's domestic "metadata" program, which collected the communications patterns (though not message content) of millions of American citizens? Or was he just a disgruntled contract employee with a narcissistic personality, or perhaps even a traitor, since he eventually accepted refuge in Russia? If a legitimate whistle-blower and not a Russian agent, Snowden nonetheless felt the need to flee the United States with his purloined documents rather than take his case against the metadata program directly to the NSA's inspector general, to the Intelligence Oversight Board (IOB) in the White House, or to oversight committees (SSCI and HPSCI) on Capitol Hill.

After he fled from the United States, Snowden disclosed his highly classified information to the media, initially from a temporary base in a Hong Kong hotel and later from Moscow. Snowden never attempted to press upon members of SSCI or HPSCI his misgivings about the metadata program, the chief subject of his avowed moral concerns (although a program that represented only a small fraction of the massive theft of papers that he leaked, including detailed budget data for the entire IC). As for remaining within the United States and presenting one's case against suspected intelligence abuses to the media, a number of government leakers less controversial than Snowden have gone to prison for their disclosure of classified documents to newspaper and television reporters.[7] To encourage acting within the system, the IC established a National Intelligence Professional Awards program in 2016, which honors those who report wrongdoing in the spy agencies "through appropriate channels."[8] Whistle-blowers, nevertheless, fear government reprisals against them, even if they work within the system, and the historical record substantiates their concerns.

Lawmakers, with their subpoena powers, authority to hold hearings, and other constitutionally based investigative tools, are—in theory at least—in the best position to keep an eye on America's intelligence agencies. Furthermore, Congress has the significant added advantage that comes with control over the government's purse strings (Article I of the Constitution), a potent inducement for gaining the attention of officials in the executive branch. Given the sweeping powers of the legislative branch, this book focuses especially on its role as an institution for intelligence oversight. The evidence shows, however, that despite their many powers lawmakers *qua* overseers have performed far below their potential as guardians against inappropriate intelligence activities—even since the years from 1974 to 1980, when members of Congress and the White House put into place a new set of strong accountability laws and regulations.

As mentioned in the introduction to this book, following the major investigations into a litany of intelligence abuses revealed in 1974 and 1975, lawmakers established SSCI in 1976 and HPSCI in 1977. With memberships of around fifteen lawmakers and thirty or so staffers on each panel (the numbers have varied somewhat over the years), these two committees have had the primary responsibility in the legislative branch for monitoring the seventeen intelligence agencies, as well as the hundreds of operations, thousands of personnel, and billions of dollars that fuel the IC. Needless to say, given this ratio of congressional over-seers to intelligence operations and personnel, lawmakers must be highly selec-tive in what they choose to examine among the vast number of spy activities carried out by the United States.

An example of this necessary selectivity is SSCI's recent, and monumental, five-year study of the CIA interrogation program directed against suspected ter-rorists; this was a huge commitment of the panel's limited resources, but many have viewed the outcome as a worthy use of the committee's time and energy. In 2015, the CIA—"the Agency"—hounded its inspector general out of office for his efforts to provide a candid and critical appraisal of this counterterrorism (CT) program; only with the Senate's report did the public begin to understand the full dimensions of the interrogation activities. The government released a sanitized 499-page Executive Summary of the classified study to the public in December 2014, although copies of the full 6,500-page report remain locked up in government vaults. Rather than a report for the public to read and learn from, the longer document gathers dust in inaccessible archives, with copies secured in safes at the White House, the Justice Department, the CIA, and SSCI. This result stems from an unwillingness of the Agency, President Obama, and Republican members on SSCI to make it public, even though the names of foreign agents and tradecraft details ("sources and methods," in the favorite rationale of the IC for keeping documents hidden away from outside scrutiny) had been carefully deleted by SSCI investigators in consultation with CIA officials.

Jane Mayer concluded in the *New Yorker* that SSCI's chair, the energetic eighty-one-year-old Dianne Feinstein (D, California, the oldest member on the committee and the only woman to have chaired one of the Intelligence Committees), proved that "Congress can still perform its most basic Madisonian function of providing a check on executive-branch abuses, and that is reason for gratitude."[9] Not everyone agrees with the conclusion that the "Torture Report" was a valuable project for SSCI to take on. The CIA recoiled from the report, written by the Democratic staff on the committee (when GOP senators and their staff opted out), accusing SSCI of preparing a study that is filled with inac-curacies and biases. Former vice president Dick Cheney, a chief architect behind the use of torture as an interrogation technique (and earlier while in Congress in 1987 an apologist for the Iran-contra scandal as well), dismissed the SSCI find-ings on a television news show as "full of crap."[10]

The two congressional oversight committees for intelligence have had both advances and setbacks in their effort to supervise the nation's espionage activi-ties. Intelligence scholars Amy Zegart and Julie Quinn have attempted to mea-sure SSCI's accomplishments.[11] One of their indices is the amount of legislation introduced by the committee and passed by the Senate. They discovered a low volume. This measure strikes me as having little relevance though. One can have a robust review of intelligence activities without passing many (or even any) new laws—especially when the few key statutes that have already been adopted carry bold and far-reaching provisions (like the Intelligence Oversight Act of 1980, examined later in this book and reprinted in appendix C). Zegart and Quinn also argue that SSCI and HPSCI have become unattractive committee assignments; VIP members of Congress no longer sign up for duty on these panels. I don't find this measure particularly telling either; in fact, "movers and shakers" may be exactly the wrong people to count on for attentive oversight, because they are too busy in chamberwide leadership roles or off running for higher office. Further, intelligence reporting requirements in times of emergency rely on a "Gang of Eight" for top-secret briefings, which includes the top leadership in the Senate and House even though they are not active members of SSCI or HPSCI. Of greater concern is the Zegart and Quinn finding about the low number of hearings—even in executive session—held by SSCI, a record far beneath any other committee in the Senate. Of course, much of the material reviewed by the intelligence oversight committees is too sensitive for public hearings; but more closed sessions are certainly warranted, and even carefully planned public hearings are possible without jeopardizing sources and methods (past examples are presented later in this book). Public records on the attendance of lawmakers at hearings, open or closed, held by SSCI and HPSCI would be useful, too, so citizens could know who is representing them well in congressional oversight duties.

Even when SSCI and HPSCI have failed to perform as meaningfully as reformers hoped at the time these panels were created in the mid-1970s, the degree of spy watching from Capitol Hill is still far more thorough than before the existence of these committees; indeed, the differences in congressional supervision of spy operations prior to and after the "Year of Intelligence" in 1975 is like night is to day.[12] The fact remains, nonetheless, that lawmakers devote only a small amount of time to intelligence oversight activities. Their heavy workload on several committees, covering not just national security issues but a wide range of domestic and economic issues as well, has them running from hearing to hearing, and from markup to markup—that is, when they are not preoccupied with the raising of campaign funds and otherwise preparing themselves for the next election cycle. Keeping their jobs on Election Day is the concern that attracts most of the time and attention of incumbent lawmakers.

From a pool of usually self-nominated candidates, the leaders of the House and Senate select the membership of the Intelligence Committees, a process outside the usual framework of relying on party caucuses to make these personnel decisions. Since SSCI and HPSCI deal with such sensitive matters, the idea has been to rely on seasoned congressional leaders as a filter to keep inexperienced first-year—as well as rough-edged more senior lawmakers—off these sensitive committees. No "radicals" need apply: only moderates who enjoy the favor of the House and Senate leadership. When Ron Dellums (D, California) was elected and requested membership on HPSCI, he was denied by Speaker Tip O'Neill and the Democratic Party leadership, simply because his district included the University of California at Berkeley, viewed as a hotbed of radicalism. Dellums, an immensely talented lawmaker, eventually proved his worthiness to the House leadership and was named to the committee. He also rose to the chairmanship of the House Armed Services Committee.

The Senate Intelligence Committee presently has eight Republican and seven Democratic members, for a total of fifteen lawmakers; the House Intelligence Committee has thirteen Republicans and nine Democrats, for a total of twenty-two members. SSCI has never had an Oversight Subcommittee; in contrast, the House began with one in 1977 (on which I was the staff director). HPSCI has periodically eliminated this unit, however, although one existed in 2016. Even without a specific subcommittee on the topic, the two Intelligence Committees have been engaged in oversight through their other subcommittees and while sitting as full committees. I think the existence of a specific oversight subcommittee is a good idea, as a means for concentrating the attention of members on suspicions of wrongdoing or erroneous reporting by the IC. Over the years, the chairs of HPSCI have been equally divided ideologically, with half (six) from conservative states and half (six) from more moderate states; in contrast, SSCI has had ten of its chairs come from conservative states and only three from moderate states. Since its creation in 1976, SSCI has shown a slight dominance of members from the South, followed by the West, the Midwest, and the Northeast—a reflection perhaps of the South's strong interest in military and intelligence affairs. With respect to regional representation, HPSCI has recorded a tie between the South and the West, again followed by the Midwest and the Northeast.[13]

A Fire-Alarm Metaphor for Congressional Oversight

In the scholarly literature on Congress, a vivid metaphor suggests two models of oversight behavior on Capitol Hill: "police patrolling" and "firefighting"— what one might think of, respectively, as routine inspections by lawmakers in contrast to their engagement in intensive public investigations into failures or wrongdoing after they occur. The authors of this metaphor, political scientists Matthew D. McCubbins and Thomas Schwartz, offer an explanation of police patrolling: "At its own initiative, Congress examines a sample of executive agency activities, with the aim of detecting and remedying any violations of legislative goals and, by its surveillance, discouraging such violations."[14] As police patrollers, members of Congress take the initiative to review executive branch programs in advance, as well as while they are being implemented. In contrast, as firefighters, lawmakers assume a more reactive stance, responding to such stimuli ("fire alarms") as media revelations of wrongdoing or grievances presented by interest groups (such as the American Civil Liberties Union, or ACLU) and the occasional whistle-blower.

When on police patrol, a member of Congress searches routinely for program information and indications of inefficiencies or malfeasance—sniffing for "smoke" by, say, questioning bureaucrats in hearings (open or, more common, closed when the subject is sensitive intelligence operations) or through on-site inspections of the seventeen major intelligence agencies within the executive branch. The idea behind police patrolling is not to wait until there's a "train-wreck" (D.C. slang for a government failure or scandal) but, instead, to ensure through continual observation that America's laws and regulations are being honored by those officials in the executive branch charged with implementing them. Alternatively, as McCubbins and Schwartz put it, as firefighters, lawmakers may have to jump on their hook-and-ladder truck "in response to an alarm." Police patrolling is a sustained, day-to-day activity by members of Congress and their staff; firefighting is episodic and after-the-fact, driven by unanticipated and untoward events (significant failures and scandals).

McCubbins and Schwartz connect this metaphor with interest groups that alert lawmakers to bureaucratic errors. In this book, I find their metaphor helpful in the way it draws attention to routine (police patrolling) versus more energetic, investigative (firefighting) oversight. The interest-group connection in their theorizing is less relevant in the intelligence domain, however, simply because fewer outside groups have connections to the IC than is the case with more open government agencies. The media is the most important "interest group" for the monitoring of intelligence activities, a feature that does not play a central role in the McCubbins and Schwartz research framework. At the core of the analysis in this book is the question of when intelligence overseers actively monitor the secret agencies before a crisis (police patrolling), as well as what it takes to initiate a major reaction among overseers in response to mistakes or wrongdoing committed by the spy services (firefighting). Often the answer to this second question is intense and prolonged media attention. It is hardly revelatory to say that Congress tends to react after a failure or scandal; this book, though, goes a step beyond this well-established observation, asking the further questions of why and when, and with what results, does this reaction occur in the sphere of intelligence—and what might be done to encourage lawmakers to take steps toward preventing intelligence failures and scandals in the first place, before a "fire" breaks out.

McCubbins and Schwartz, as well as political scientists Morris Ogul and Bert Rockman, found the fire-alarm approach—responding in times of crisis—the most prominent means of oversight on Capitol Hill prior to the Watergate scandal in 1973, regardless of the policy domain.[15] Aberbach's research suggests, though, that in more recent years police patrolling has surpassed a reliance by lawmakers on fire alarms, at least within the domestic-policy fields that he investigated.[16] For him, the explanation for this change in congressional behavior stemmed from the transformation of public opinion that occurred during the 1970s and 1980s. Displaying a growing disenchantment with government performance—mainly because of the nation's experiences in the 1970s with the Watergate affair, the failure to win the war in Vietnam, and a CIA domestic spy scandal—the public has increasingly demanded that members of Congress pay less attention to the creation of new government programs and more on the close monitoring and improvement of programs that already exist.

This change in the political environment provided an incentive for some lawmakers to engage more energetically in oversight activities, with the best of them trying to be effective "police officers" by anticipating and preventing the outbreak of disastrous "fires." In this manner lawmakers are able to claim credit with the public (voters) for their vigilance as champions of accountability, rather than passively waiting for the shrill sound of fire alarms in the night. "As a consequence," writes Aberbach, "formal oversight proceedings (such as oversight hearings) became common activities in the 1970s, and it seems that aggressive information search[es] also became more common."[17] As we will see in this book, though, the dedication of lawmakers to persistent intelligence police patrolling has waxed and waned since the days of Watergate, Vietnam, and the CIA spy scandal.

Instruments and Sources of Leadership for Legislative Oversight

When members of Congress are inspired to engage in more active police patrolling of executive branch activities, what means do they use to carry out their program reviews? In order of frequency, the top methods uncovered by Aberbach when he looked at various domestic-policy domains were the following:

- staff communication with agency personnel, augmented by program evaluations carried out by congressional support agencies, such as the Government Accountability Office (GAO);[18]
- oversight hearings with participation by members of Congress;
- staff investigations and field studies;
- program reauthorization hearings with members of Congress; and
- program evaluations by committee staff.

Two features of oversight stand out in Aberbach's research findings. First, staff plays a major role; second, lawmakers personally become involved in their accountability duties mainly during hearings. Ogul has similarly noted that "hearings focus the members' attention." Here is where members of Congress seek out information.[19] Evocative of the police-patrolling and firefighting metaphor, political scientist Frank Smist has highlighted the presence of two kinds of oversight hearings on Capitol Hill: the routine and the scandal-driven—or, in his terminology, the "institutional" (or "supportive") hearing and the "investigative" hearing.[20]

As for oversight leadership within Congress, committee chairs prove to be first among equals. "Oversight is driven by the chairman," emphasized a senior SSCI staffer to me, in a common refrain.[21] Two-thirds of the senior staffers on the domestic-policy committees interviewed by Aberbach also said that the chairs of congressional panels exercised the most important influence on oversight decisions.[22] This was certainly what I witnessed firsthand in a yearlong observation of an executive-legislative investigative committee that looked into U.S. espionage activities in 1995: the Aspin-Brown Commission on Intelligence (discussed in chapter 4).[23]

Levels of Commitment to Oversight

Aberbach and some recent theorists are sanguine about the effectiveness of legislative oversight in the United States. Yet most studies on the subject have been less upbeat.[24] The general consensus among researchers is that lawmakers have been largely desultory in their exercise of accountability, across the policy board and down through the years, even if somewhat more energetic in this domain since the Watergate scandal in 1973. In the 1960s, for example, John Bibby referred to oversight as Congress's "neglected function."[25] In 1974, a congressional self-study reached the unanimous conclusion that the legislative branch was "just barely making a scratch on the oversight of the executive branch in any one year."[26] About the same time, Ogul found oversight more intermittent in its practice than comprehensive and systematic.[27]

Some lawmakers consider it an obligation in their capacity as overseers to serve as advocates for the executive agencies and programs within their legislative purview; others, adopting quite a different stance, view oversight as a personal responsibility to participate in a detailed examination and, if necessary, public criticism of an agency's shortcomings. Aberbach concluded that "most oversight takes place in a general advocacy contest"; that is to say, lawmakers tend to assume the posture of an agency's defender (referred to as "cheerleading" in chapter 8 of this book).[28] A study conducted in the 1990s discovered, however, a range of behavior in intelligence oversight hearings that went beyond that of cheerleader. Some lawmakers did act solely as an agency's defense counsel and advocate on Capitol Hill; others, though, cross-examined intelligence officials with a more critical—sometimes withering—assault of specific questions about program performance. In this sense, oversight hearings may be based on either a "softball" or a "hardball" approach to the questioning of executive branch officials, with Republican members of Congress tending to ask the more lenient questions of CIA witnesses.[29]

Rather than fully embracing one style or another, lawmakers are at their best, advises former HPSCI chair Lee Hamilton, when behaving as both "partners and critics."[30] In this vein, Joseph Wippl—a savvy former CIA senior officer and the director of graduate studies at Boston University's Pardee School of Global Studies—has spoken to the question of what lawmakers can bring to the table when it comes to accountability. "The advantage of real-time oversight," he told a reporter, "is that the Congress knows what the intelligence community is doing, and assisting it any way that it can to achieve the results; and also to say, 'Excuse me, guys. That's not going to work.'"[31]

On balance, even the optimistic Professor Aberbach is prepared to offer only "two cheers for Madison" when it comes to the conduct of accountability by lawmakers, conceding that "what the United States now has is far from perfect, not even pretty or neat." He adds, however, that "we could do far worse."[32] Similarly, looking broadly at foreign and defense policy, political scientist Christopher Deering found that legislative oversight "isn't nearly as bad as 'they' say it is; but it is not as good as it might be."[33] Deering's conclusion provides a fitting description of intelligence accountability as well, as the chapters that follow reveal. Most scholars of oversight have concluded that Congress has fallen short because of its lack of motivation to engage in accountability in a consistent, determined manner. This failure of motivation is, in turn, a product largely of constant fundraising demands on lawmakers for reelection purposes, along with the limited staff available to assist members with their oversight duties (despite a general misconception in the public mind that lawmakers have too many assistants).[34]

Intelligence Oversight by the Other Branches of Government

The Executive

Accountability for espionage operations requires attention not only to the organizations within the official IC (a set of secret agencies introduced later in this chapter), but also to the various smaller intelligence entities and outsourcing companies (D.C.'s "beltway bandits"). This is a staggering challenge. To assist with this supervision, the government has established five prominent oversight entities within the executive branch: the NSC staff; the President's Foreign Intelligence Advisory Board (PFIAB, whose name was changed after the 9/11 attacks to the President's Intelligence Advisory Board or PIAB, taking into account that the president needs counsel on both foreign and domestic intelligence matters); the Intelligence Oversight Board (IOB); a system of inspectors general (IGs) throughout the national security apparatus; and, last but not least, the Office of Legal Counsel (OLC) in the Department of Justice. "We learned the hard way," remembered the veteran foreign-policy official, Dean Rusk, the nation's second-longest serving secretary of state (after Cordell Hull of the Franklin D. Roosevelt Administration), "that senior officials of the executive branch must review the intelligence agencies; oversight should not be left to our substitutes or congressional committees."[35]

The NSC is the nation's highest-ranking forum for foreign-policy decisions, with four statutory members (the president, the vice president, the secretary of state, and the secretary of defense) and a staff of over one hundred (most of whom are on loan—"seconded"—from security-oriented agencies around the government).[36] At the top of the Council's staff is the national security adviser, and beneath him or her is an aide for intelligence. The chief duty of this intelligence aide is to serve as a liaison officer between the IC and the White House, but also to keep an eye out in the planning stages for any inappropriate espionage initiatives initiated by the spy agencies. During the Iran-contra scandal, the NSC staff unfortunately became not the guardian against, but rather the perpetrator of, improper intelligence activities, under the sway of national security advisers Robert C. McFarlane and John M. Poindexter, who served one after the other during the Reagan Administration.[37]

Even when it had more laudable staff leaders, the Council met to review covert action proposals (for instance) only once between 1972 and 1975.[38] In recent times, argues law professor Michael Glennon, "even the president now exercises little substantive control over the overall direction of U.S. national security policy."[39] The tendency, especially for presidents inexperienced in foreign affairs (usually the case, as recently with Bill Clinton, George W. Bush, Barack Obama, and most of all Donald J. Trump) is for the White House to follow the recommendations of the national security bureaucracy—especially the NSC, the Pentagon brass, and the intelligence chiefs. As a result, one could discern few differences in the defense and intelligence initiatives of the second Bush and the Obama Administrations—even though they were worlds apart on domestic policies.

Another organization within the executive branch meant to play a role in intelligence accountability is the PFIAB, or now PIAB. Since its creation in the 1950s, PFIAB had among its dozen or so members (the numbers varied from administration to administration, and the organization was temporarily closed down during the Carter years) several prominent experts on security, foreign policy, and science.[40] The latter gave the panel a special niche: the reviewing of science-based intelligence programs to assist the president in improving the technical side of espionage activities. Edward H. Land, the inventor of the Polaroid camera, is an illustration of a much-valued PFIAB member during the Eisenhower years; he significantly helped to advance the capabilities of America's spy cameras on satellites and reconnaissance aircraft. Some presidents, however, have used membership on the Advisory Board not so much as a means for monitoring and enhancing U.S. intelligence, but as a prestigious White House payoff to political allies who have contributed money to the president's election campaign and who relish having a business card with a White House address—a deplorable corruption of the original intent of the panel's existence.

The IOB, which initially after its creation in 1976 stood alone in the White House but has been folded into the PIAB as a subcommittee, is small with only three or four members and a budget of some $3 million (compared to the intelligence community's $70-plus billion in 2016). Occasionally it has conducted a serious inquiry into charges of intelligence impropriety (as in 1995–1996 when it examined a CIA foreign-agent scandal in Guatemala, and in 2016 when it looked into NSA collection activities); but it, too, has frequently been merely an honorific assignment, more decorative than effective as a protector against the abuse of secret power.

Further, the intelligence agencies and other organizations in America's security establishment have set up offices of inspector general, designed to investigate charges of wrongdoing inside the spy agencies, as well as offices of legal counsel on the lookout for questionable intelligence initiatives. Remarks a Hill staffer, "More people are doing executive oversight than ever before. The lawyers at the CIA are everywhere, not just in the IG Office, the Office of Legal Affairs, and the Directorate for Operations, but in every subdivision."[41]

In earlier years, IGs within the intelligence agencies were often given only limited responsibility for conducting inquiries into allegations of power abuse; typically, they spent their time looking into relatively minor bureaucratic grievances regarding hiring and firing, as well as other personnel disputes. In the aftermath of the intelligence investigations of 1975 and then the Iran-contra scandal in 1987, though, these offices have become steadily elevated in their authority to investigate charges of lawbreaking. In 1989, Congress substantially boosted the powers of the CIA's inspector general; by law, the holder of that office henceforth had to be confirmed by the Senate and, further, was expected to report to Congress on a regular basis—and immediately if inappropriate intelligence activities came to light inside the Agency. The office of the CIA/IG subsequently conducted probes into a number of allegations against the Agency, including the torture of captured terrorist suspects ("detainees"), with a seriousness of purpose unseen during earlier years when the authority assigned to that office was weak.

In another illustration, the Pentagon's IG undertook a major inquiry in 2015 into whether senior U.S. military officers in Iraqi had distorted analytic reports from the Defense Intelligence Agency (DIA) on the war against the terrorist organization known as ISIS. Intelligence analysts within the DIA complained that the brass in Iraq was trying to make the Pentagon's progress look more favorable to the White House than was actually the case. The Department of Justice also has an IG Office, but, as with the Pentagon, the staff devoted to accountability is dwarfed by the size of the institution—a serious imbalance in the "ecology of oversight," as a Hill staffer has put it.[42] In the Justice Department, for example, the IG office has 450 people to serve 10,000 employees.

In 2010, the intelligence community established an IG to handle all the secret agencies, in a reform that also installed an IC/IG hotline, which (according to a directive from the Office of the Director of National Intelligence or ODNI) "provides a confidential means for IC employees, contractors, and the public to report fraud, waste, and abuse." So far, though, few intelligence officers have availed themselves of this channel.[43] When grievances are expressed from anywhere in the IC, the IC/IG rapidly responds. In 2014, for instance, a civilian employee working in a military intelligence agency complained over the IC/IG hotline that an interagency data repository improperly contained the names of numerous U.S. citizens. The IC/IG found the lead credible enough to report the matter to the IOB in the White House. In 2014, Steven Aftergood of the Federation of American Scientists, which publishes a newsletter on government secrecy, spelled out the importance of the IG system. "In the concentric circles of U.S. intelligence oversight," he wrote, "Inspectors General are close to the center—receiving allegations, interviewing witnesses, formulating responses, and taking appropriate action." Yet, as he further noted, "the *Washington Examiner* reported allegations that some agency Inspectors General are improperly subservient to, and protective of, their agency leadership."[44]

Around Washington, plenty of organizations are supposedly involved in intelligence oversight. The question is: which ones take the job seriously, with objectivity and determination, and also have the necessary authorities and powers to carry out their mission? The OLC in the Justice Department is, as one of its former attorneys, John Goldsmith, has accurately described, "a frontline institution responsible for ensuring that an executive branch charged with executing the law is itself bound by law."[45] The OLC is often the final arbitrator when it comes to deciding on the legality of White House and other executive branch policy initiatives. Its view was decisive—and raised serious doubts about relying on this office to provide legal oversight for the intelligence agencies—when it reached the judgment soon after the 9/11 attacks that harsh interrogation techniques, such as waterboarding, were legal and could be used by the CIA against terrorist suspects (a position later reversed by a different set of OLC personnel, as discussed later in this book).

Attorneys in the OLC and within the intelligence agencies have been responsible, too, for the government's prosecution of leaks—with a record number of cases during the Obama Administration for unauthorized disclosures of classified information to the media. David Sanger and Mark Landler have reported on the mixed message the Obama Administration had sent on security matters. The president acknowledged that the IC overclassifies documents. "There's classified, and then there's classified," he said, in recognition that only a limited number of documents were truly worthy of a "secret" or "top secret" stamp. Yet by 2015 the administration had notched up nine leak prosecutions—three times the number of every other presidency in American history combined.[46] Further, President Obama's lawyers sought administrative penalties against leakers, including the termination of employment, loss of security clearances, and fines.[47]

Among the mix of institutions in the executive branch with intelligence oversight responsibilities is the Privacy and Civil Liberties Oversight Board (PCLOB), an independent agency established in 2004 on the recommendation of the 9/11 Kean Commission. The PCLOB enjoys a grand title and has produced some useful public reports, including an influential (and partially adopted) recommendation that the FISA Court (see below) establish a "pool of 'Special Advocates'" to represent the public interest in rulings related to intelligence collection operations.[48] The PCLOB's jurisdiction is limited, however, primarily to maintaining constitutional safeguards and providing advice within the realm of counterterrorism. The board's efforts to expand its jurisdiction for a wider look at signals intelligence (the programs of the NSA) have been rebuffed by a Republican majority on SSCI. Moreover, the PCLOB's attempt to examine covert actions was similarly shut down by SSCI Republicans. On the House side, HPSCI Republicans also blocked the board's aspirations for an expansion of its investigative authorities. The PCLOB chairman, who resigned in the summer of 2016, accused SSCI and HPSCI of trying to undercut oversight and "push the Intelligence Community back into the shadows."[49]

Despite these limitations, the PCLOB has played a significant role in reviewing the bulk metadata collection program carried out by the NSA and has been far more critical of these methods than has either SSCI or HPSCI—a subject on which the board and the congressional oversight committees have sparred from time to time. The board concluded that the metadata program should be shut down and, not long after, the Congress did place tighter restrictions on the metadata program through the USA Freedom Act in 2015 (examined in chapter 5). As a pro-PCLOB member of SSCI commented, "It has examined large, complex surveillance programs and evaluated them in detail, and it has produced public reports and recommendations that are quite comprehensive and useful."[50]

The PCLOB viewed the metadata collection activities as both unlawful and ineffective, while in contrast a majority of SSCI and HPSCI members initially gave a green light to the NSA programs. This kind of oversight pluralism in the government is healthy, potentially providing more venues for whistle-blowers to air their misgivings in a responsible manner. Yet, unfortunately, in the case of the metadata program, whistle-blowers were prohibited by law from going to the PCLOB, and the icy reception at SSCI and HPSCI toward previous whistle-blowers evidently persuaded Snowden to skip that option altogether. Had the law allowed, Snowden might have found a more receptive audience in the PCLOB, permitting him to make his case against the NSA without stealing documents and disappearing overseas. Even with SSCI, its members and staff say that they would have taken his criticisms seriously if only he had come to them. Efforts to change the law and open the PCLOB door to whistle-blowers failed in 2014, along with other efforts to bring more transparency to NSA activities. These results led two experts to lament the "staggering failure of oversight" on Capitol Hill.[51]

A much older organization, the Information Security Oversight Office (ISOO), created in 1981, is responsible for oversight with respect to national security classification and declassification activities throughout the government. Obviously, given the nearly unanimous belief that too many documents are classified, the ISOO has failed to strike a good balance between necessary secrecy and transparency—although in recent years the number of new secrets created has begun to drop dramatically.[52] Various interagency working groups are also dedicated to some aspect of intelligence oversight, including the Public Interest Declassification Board (PIDB), an advisory panel to Congress and the White House; the Security Classification Reform Committee (SCRC), led by the White House; and the Intelligence Community Transparency Council (ICTC), which reports to the Director of National Intelligence. According to one close observer, these organizations have "yet (with the possible exception of the PIDB) established a substantial record of achievement."[53]

The CIA also sponsors an in-house entity, called the Historical Review Program (HRP), which taps some well-known academicians to advise on document declassification possibilities. Serving on this advisory board requires a security clearance and the signing of a secrecy oath, however—requirements that cause some candidates to decline an invitation to participate, out of concern that all of their published research would have to go through the Agency's Publication Review Board, or PRB (which has been accused from time to time of heavy-handed, arbitrary, and intimidating behavior).[54] The Agency has established, as well, an External Advisory Board (EAB, in the alphabet soup that is

Washington) of outside citizens, although this panel has more the markings of a booster club than a hard-nosed evaluator of intelligence activities. Its two legislative members, for example, are former senator Saxby Chambliss (R, Georgia), the CIA's most loyal supporter when he served as SSCI's chairman and ranking minority member, as well as the Agency's lead defender of the torture program; and former senator Evan Bayh (D, Indiana), a member of the CIA-selected panel that exonerated the Agency for its attack (labeled a "misunderstanding" by these "investigators") against SSCI staff and computers during the time of the torture investigation (examined in chapter 5).

The Judiciary

The judicial branch of government can play a role in intelligence accountability, too, by (for instance) hearing lawsuits from Justice Department prosecutors in Washington that involve classified intelligence documents—most famously the Pentagon Papers (*New York Times Co. v. United States*, 1971).[55] In that case, the Supreme Court blocked the efforts of the Nixon Administration to squash reporting about a critical top-secret Pentagon study on the poor progress of U.S. military operations in Vietnam. The Supreme Court and lower tribunals have heard many other intelligence cases, from the violation of employee secrecy agreements and the constitutionality of various surveillance programs to the legality of holding detainee prisoners at America's Guantánamo base in Cuba for the purpose of ongoing intelligence interrogations.[56] Sometimes the White House or the intelligence agencies have lost these cases, but, most of the time, judges—who are rarely expert in the intricacies of national security and intelligence—have deferred to the White House, the Department of Justice, and the intelligence community on matters related to espionage.

The most conspicuous and controversial recent involvement of the judiciary in intelligence matters has been related to the work of the FISA Court and its appellate arm, the FISA Court of Appeals. Both courts were created by the Foreign Intelligence Surveillance Act of 1978—one of several reform proposals recommended and initially drafted by the Church Committee in the Senate. With FISA, judicial review became a routine part of intelligence oversight. One of the court's important features was its *ex ante* review, in contrast, say, to judicial review of intelligence surveillance in Germany, which is "always done *ex-post*."[57]

The FISA Court and its appeals court have overwhelmingly endorsed wiretap warrant requests from the executive branch (mainly the CIA and the FBI). This high acceptance rate—almost 100 percent—results, in part, because the requests brought to the FISA Court have been thoroughly vetted beforehand in informal interactions between intelligence managers and the court judges.[58]

Also, though, the judges are reluctant to second-guess intelligence officials about national security threats. Nor do these judges, overloaded with cases in their regular district courts (their main jobs), have much time to provide a safeguard against improper initiatives within the intelligence bureaucracy. Professor Glennon concludes that the FISA Court, instead of being a separate check in the third branch of government, "for all practical purposes might as well be within [the executive branch]."[59]

The FISA Court of Appeals leans toward deference to the executive branch as well. Again, it is not that its judges tend to be servile; on the contrary, they are usually talented individuals with keen intellects and a strong sense of independence on most matters. The real problem with this appeals court, as one of its long-time members told me, is that the "judges don't know much about foreign policy. In support of counterterrorism warrant requests, they tend to believe that it is better to be safe than sorry."[60] Even with this history of deference from the FISA Courts, in 2001 after the 9/11 attacks the second Bush Administration elected to bypass the judicial warrant procedure altogether, dispensing with this legal requirement for national security wiretapping. In 2005, this violation of the law came to light through investigative reporting published by the *New York Times.*[61]

Just as with the experience with the FISA Courts, American courts generally have yielded to the executive branch on matters of national security, usually refusing to allow plaintiffs standing in suits against the executive on grounds that sensitive classified information might be revealed in public court proceedings (a doctrine known as the state secrets privilege). "Under today's foreign intelligence surveillance system," concludes a report from the New York University School of Law, "the government's ability to collect information about ordinary Americans' lives has increased exponentially while judicial oversight has been reduced to near-nothingness."[62] Now and then, however, the judicial branch will surprise—as with the Pentagon Papers case. More recently, in 2015, a U.S. Court of Appeals in New York declared illegal the controversial NSA bulk collection operation related to U.S. telephone and social media communications (the metadata program revealed by Snowden), which had been in operation since soon after the 9/11 attacks.[63] This judicial judgment led to legislative reform of the NSA program, with Congress in 2015 setting stricter boundaries for metadata collection (as examined later in this book).

During recent administrations, lawsuits related to cases involving such matters as NSA surveillance and CIA extraordinary rendition have persistently run into the state secrets privilege. The end result has been for the executive branch to simply invoke this "privilege" to avoid judicial scrutiny of intelligence programs. In response, some members of Congress—working with outside groups like the ACLU—have efforts under way to develop procedures that would allow lawsuits to go forward while continuing to protect legitimate state secrets.[64]

Now and then, lawsuits have led to important changes in the practice of intelligence oversight. A case in New York City related to the local police department's surveillance of Muslims, for example, led to the restoration of outside accountability safeguards that had been eliminated in the name of "flexibility" after the 9/11 attacks. The city agreed to the placement of a civilian lawyer (appointed by the mayor) inside the police department to examine intelligence files and report improprieties to the police commissioner, the mayor, or a federal judge. "These safeguards will be a strong check against the discriminatory surveillance of Muslim communities that we challenged in our lawsuit," said the director of the ACLU's National Security Project, which represented the plaintiffs in one of the lawsuits. "We hope the settlement shows that effective policing isn't at odds with constitutional policing."[65]

Intelligence Oversight by the Media and Civic Groups

Reporting by journalists on the secret agencies provides another significant form of spy watching. In what British scholar Claudia Hillebrand refers to as "public oversight," the media has been able to keep the American people informed about some intelligence activities.[66] Further, journalists serve as a prod on the government toward a more serious engagement in accountability, as officials react to the public's concern about media reports on intelligence failures and scandals. (Chapter 7 explores these important relationships.)

Yet, even these formidable institutions combined—the government's various oversight panels in the three branches, plus the media—face a tough assignment in trying to keep track of the IC's multiple and heavily veiled components. Further, beyond the IC are scores of smaller spy agencies that are largely ignored (such as the Transportation Security Administration Office of Intelligence, part of the Department of Transportation). So are the dozens of beltway bandits (among them the giant Booz Allen Hamilton) engaged in "outsourced" espionage operations.

Before 1975, U.S. spy agencies were given wide latitude to fight the Cold War, with occasional directives emanating from the president and the NSC; since 1975, however, the IC has been forced by law to accept the kinds of constitutional checks and balances long endured by the rest of America's government. Yet the leviathan proportions and esoteric nature of the spy agencies present overseers in each branch of government, as well as media reporters, with a dauntingly complex problem.

The practice of intelligence oversight has benefited, at times, from the interests and actions of groups outside the government. Congressional and executive branch inquiries into intelligence activities, for example, can be helped by assistance from organizations in American society that wish to testify before panels of inquiry, or aid government committees with their investigative research behind the scenes. The ACLU, for example, has been consistently active in working with Congress, or on its own, to bring lawsuits against the intelligence agencies, as a means of protecting the privacy concerns of American citizens. On the individual level, some indefatigable academic researchers and journalists have gained access to documents held within the vaults of the intelligence agencies through the Freedom of Information Act (FOIA, enacted in 1967)—although often this process can take years and often fails altogether as one agency or another claims that the material is too sensitive for release.

During the Church Committee investigation in 1975, a host of pro-privacy organizations—most notably the Center for National Security Studies (CNSS, funded by the ACLU)—worked with the committee's staff to write the Foreign Intelligence Surveillance Act, as well as legislation that set up the two standing oversight committees on intelligence, beginning with SSCI.[67] Today, high-profile groups that provide valuable information to the public about declassified intelligence activities include the National Security Archive at George Washington University, as well as the Federation of American Scientists, whose newsletter (entitled *Secrecy News*) is a valuable source of information on declassification issues and other matters related to intelligence. These, along with other outside civic groups and individuals concerned about privacy issues, face the same dilemma as the media in their examinations of intelligence policy: a lack of access to reliable information about current espionage activities. Nevertheless, they have played a key role in keeping the public informed about activities that do come to their attention.

The intelligence agencies also have a constellation of interest groups who lobby the government and fend against rivals who, in their opinion, have slighted security interests in their advocacy of liberty and privacy. One especially active group is the Association of Former Intelligence Officers (AFIO), based in Virginia and featuring a large component of former CIA officers in its membership. The number of groups and individuals engaged in intelligence oversight, to one extent or another and on one side or another, is impressive. Yet they are dwarfed by the vast and largely hidden terrain occupied by the spy agencies (what Laura Poitras has called the "deep state"), making efforts by citizens to bring some light to these dark shores a sobering endeavor.[68]

The Intelligence Community:
An Espionage Behemoth

The phrase "intelligence community" is a misnomer used by security officials to describe a cluster of seventeen institutions that compose the nation's surveillance establishment. The word "community" suggests a far more harmonious relationship than the history of these agencies—each a "silo" or "stovepipe" unto itself—has displayed throughout the years.[69] As intelligence scholar Amy Zegart writes, the IC "was never a community at all, but a disjointed assortment of agencies created at different times for different purposes without strong unifying authorities or structures; common policies, personnel systems, or incentives; and cultures to ensure that they operated in a coordinated fashion."[70] In the tug-of-war over philosophies about the degree to which America's intelligence agencies should be subjected to the government's normal checks and balances, one thing is certain: during the Cold War (1946–1991), these hidden organizations mushroomed into an enormous and sprawling bureaucracy—the largest for the purposes of information gathering ever devised by any society in history.

Spending for Spies

In the aftermath of the 9/11 attacks (which killed 2,977 people), the budget for U.S. intelligence skyrocketed. For example, the funding for the NSA, America's premier electronic eavesdropping organization and the largest spy agency ever created, doubled between 2001 and 2006.[71] In the United States, the intelligence budget is divided into two core components: the National Intelligence Program (NIP), which supports the largest of the intelligence agencies and focuses on a strategic view of the world; and the Military Intelligence Program (MIP), devoted chiefly to service-level or tactical—above all, battlefield—intelligence collection (see Figure 1.1). The boundary between the NIP and the MIP fluctuates somewhat, however, from year to year. In 2006, for instance, the National Geospatial-Intelligence Agency (NGA)—another one of the large strategic organizations in the IC, with responsibilities for taking surveillance photographs from satellite "platforms" in space—received 70 percent of its funding from the NIP and 30 percent from the MIP. The next year, though, the respective figures were 90 percent and 10 percent; and, in 2010, 66 percent and 34 percent.

In 2014, the budget for the NIP stood at $52.6 billion and the MIP at $19.2 billion, or a total of $71.8 billion worth of spending on intelligence activities by the United States that year. In 2016, the budget projections displayed a slight increase for the NIP, at $53.5 billion, and a decrease for the MIP, at $16.8 billion, for a total of $70.3 billion. Though large, these figures are lower than the record-breaking $80.1 billion of 2010 (even though the Great Recession that began in 2008 continued to rock the nation at the time), but the 2016 funding was still an expenditure vastly greater than America's aggregate spy budget before the 9/11 attacks. These spending figures, as with the NSA figure presented earlier, amounted to roughly a doubling of the overall intelligence budget from pre-9/11

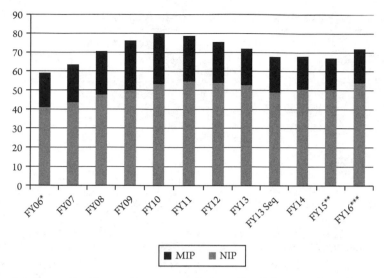

Figure 1.1 Recent Intelligence Community Budgets, Fiscal Years 2006–2016 (in $ Billions).

NIP = National Intelligence Budget Seq = sequestered budget

MIP = Military Intelligence Budget

* MIP budget estimated

** Budget requests (June 30, 2014)

*** Budget requests (February 2, 2015)

Note: "FY13 Seq" in the figure refers to the budget sequestration of 2013, when automatic spending cuts to the federal budget came into effect on January 1, 2013, as an austerity measure. Source: Mark McAlpine, Chair, Joint Forces Staff College, Defense Intelligence Agency, *The National Intelligence Community* (Washington, DC: Joint Forces Staff College, 2016), p. 29. (The data presented here are unclassified, based on ODNI and DoD press releases.) My thanks to Capt. Benjamin G. Williams of the United States Air Force, a former student of mine, for providing this figure.

levels.[72] (In stark contrast, the total British intelligence budget is reportedly about $3.6 billion a year.)[73] Given the Trump Administration's announced intention in early 2017 to raise the defense budget by 10 percent (a $54 billion or so increase), one would anticipate the intelligence budget to climb by a roughly equivalent amount, if history is any guide for this hard-to-predict administration. On the personnel side of the intelligence resource picture, the government revealed in 2009 that the IC employs some 200,000 people, a total that by all accounts has since increased.[74]

Drawing on leaks provided in 2013 by Snowden, the *Washington Post* placed into the public domain previously classified budget figures for America's key intelligence agencies. These data provide a sense of how spending on intelligence activities and personnel increased so dramatically from 2004 to 2013, driven chiefly by America's counterterrorism response to the 9/11 attacks

Table 1.1 **Major Intelligence Expenditures, by Agency, 2013 (in $ billions)**

Agency	Budget Figure	Percentage Increase since 2004
CIA	$14.7 billion	56
NSA	10.8 billion	53
NRO	10.3 billion	12
NGA	4.9 billion	108
Tactical Military Units	4.4 billion	3

Source: Barton Gellman and Greg Miller, "Black Budget" Summary Details U.S. Spy Network's Successes, Failures and Objectives," *Washington Post* (August 29, 2013), p. A1.

and a widespread anxiety about the need to shield the nation against further strikes.[75] See Table 1.1 for the *Post's* figures for the major intelligence expenditures, amounting to $45.1 billion of the roughly $53 billion aggregate spy budget in 2013.

These five programs accounted for fully 85 percent of the total budget, with remarkable funding surges recorded by the CIA, the NSA, and, in particular, the nation's chief geoint (geospatial-intelligence or imagery) agency, the NGA. (The NRO, or National Reconnaissance Office, is in charge of designing, building, launching, and managing surveillance satellites that serve the NSA and the NGA.) In 2015, as America and other antiterrorist coalition members struggled against the terrorist group ISIS in Syria and Iraq, as well as its rising terrorist presence in North Africa and the Arabian Peninsula, the synergy of several combined "ints"—human intelligence or humint (CIA), signals intelligence or sigint (NSA), and overhead surveillance or geoint (NGA)—helped significantly to direct allied bombing attacks against these enemies.[76]

The GOP, a party traditionally in favor of muscular national security budgets and broad discretionary powers for the secret agencies, has been a tireless advocate for these increases in the spy budget, both before and after the 9/11 attacks. Columnist David Brooks has noted that, above all else, "Republicans are against government."[77] Yet the expenditure of public funds on intelligence and military activities has long been a conspicuous departure from that steadfast antigovernment Golden Rule for the GOP. Security is that party's sacred cow, even for the nontraditional Republican president Donald Trump. For the most part, Democrats have been supportive of intelligence budgets, too, although this more liberal party has also displayed a greater concern than many Republicans for questions of civil liberties (although the GOP does have a libertarian wing resolutely devoted to privacy concerns). As a result, Democrats have been more inclined to oppose intelligence activities that might threaten the privacy rights of American citizens. In this concern for matters related to liberty, the Democratic

Party has been joined from time to time by GOP libertarians in efforts to keep government out of the lawful private activities of U.S. citizens—an unusual and unstable coalition of liberals and conservatives in defense of civil liberties.

America's Espionage Apparatus

The president and the National Security Council, known together as the National Command Authority (NCA), stand at the pinnacle of the behemoth intelligence complex. (See the diagram in appendix A.) Beneath these top institutions of command-and-control reside the nation's sixteen major spy agencies, where the shadows are numberless. From 1947 to 2004, these agencies were led by a Director of Central Intelligence (DCI) and, since 2005, by a newly created spymaster titled the Director of National Intelligence (DNI). The Office of the DNI—or ODNI, in Washington's unescapable forest of acronyms—is sometimes referred to as America's seventeenth intelligence organization. It is an "über-bureaucracy" in Jeff Stein's characterization,[78] responsible for coordinating, in theory at least, the mammoth spy bureaucracy. In reality, rather than a DNI in full command, the agencies that make up the IC have considerable independence. Within their stovepipes, each has its own director ("program manager") who runs the organization with considerable autonomy. "Gorillas in the stovepipes" is an unflattering, but telling, insider description of how powerful these agency directors are within the IC's fragmented management setting.

The spy agencies also have unique cultural norms that flow from their specialized approaches to intelligence gathering, such as humint, which relies on information gathered the old-fashioned way: by secret foreign agents—the CIA's chief means of intelligence collection. As a senior, retired Agency officer has put it: "Stealing secrets is the CIA's 'job one' overseas."[79] Several of the agencies rely on machines and technical devises for their intelligence gathering programs, a cluster of methods known as technological intelligence, or simply "techint." An example of a techint specialty is signals intelligence, or "sigint," which relies mainly on U.S. "listening posts" (large ground-based antennae) around the world, taps placed on underground and undersea fiber-optic cables, and eavesdropping satellites in space that sweep in telephone and social media intelligence ("socmint") from out of the ether.

The most common of these "ints" or "tradecrafts" (that is, intelligence collection disciplines) are humint; sigint; "geoint" or "imint" (imagery intelligence, with its new name, geospatial-intelligence or, in plain English, photography); "masint" (measurement and signatures intelligence, which uses scientific sensors to detect information about foreign weapons capabilities and industrial activities, say, the presence of nuclear materials at a supply depot in another country, or dangerous chemicals and biological substances in a warehouse); and "osint," open-source intelligence, which includes books, magazines, and news-papers that one can acquire at the local bookstore or newsstand. The purpose of the various combined ints is to discern, as well as mere mortals are able to, any unborn threat ripe in history's womb that may emerge to harm the United States. Some 90–95 percent of the content found in classified intelligence reports pre-pared for the president and other policy officials in the United States comes from osint, such as reports obtained through the purchase of Russian newspa-pers from kiosks in the streets of Moscow—easy today, riskier during the Cold War. Often, though, the most useful information must be stolen by a foreign humint agent (or "asset," in CIA lingo), say, by burglarizing a Beijing government safe at midnight or otherwise obtaining information through clandestine intel-ligence methods, whether facilitated by human spies, listening devices, chemi-cal sensors, reconnaissance aircraft (piloted or unpiloted), or costly surveillance satellites.

The Military Intelligence Agencies

Eight, or half, of the spy agencies in the IC (if one excludes the ODNI as an agency, because it is the IC's top managerial staff without operational responsi-bilities) are sheltered within the organizational framework of the Department of Defense (DoD), led by the mightiest "gorilla" of all in Washington: the secre-tary of defense. The SecDef is a bureaucratic King Kong who controls an annual budget of some $700 billion plus, as well as a massive war-fighting machine. (The intelligence budget is usually around 10 percent of what the United States spends on its overt military establishment.) The DoD is the largest and most aggressive consumer of intelligence—anything to help lift the fog of war in Iraq and Afghanistan, or wherever else U.S. fighting men and women face combat. Seven more intelligence agencies are located in civilian policy departments, such as the Department of State. Finally, one organization in the IC, the CIA, is a stand-alone, independent organization—or two organizations, if one wishes to count the ODNI as an intelligence agency, rather than a relatively small head-quarters and managerial staff created to bring a greater degree of integration to the overall community. These relationships are depicted in appendix A.

The military intelligence agencies include the giant of them all, the NSA (equivalent in floor space to the Pentagon), a codebreaking, encrypting, and sigint service engaged chiefly in telephone, email, and social media snooping; the NGA, dedicated to taking photographs of enemy troops, weapons, and facilities, using high-resolution cameras fastened to satellites in space, as well as on the wings of lower-altitude UAVs (unmanned aerial vehicles, popularly known as drones) and piloted reconnaissance aircraft; the NRO, the manager of the nation's surveillance satellites (both for sigint and geoint purposes); the Defense Intelligence Agency (DIA), which analyzes—that is, tries to make sense of—military-related developments around the world; and the intelligence units of the Army, Navy, Air Force, and Marines, each of which concentrates on the collection and analysis of tactical intelligence from war zones overseas and other places where U.S. personnel serve in uniform. Together, these military spy agencies account for some 85 percent of the total spent by the United States on intelligence each year, and they employ approximately 85 percent of the nation's intelligence personnel.[80]

The combat-oriented military intelligence agencies absorb such a high portion of the spy budget because of two main reasons: first, the protection and advancement of America's troops in battle is, understandably, a national priority of the highest order; and, second, the "platforms" (satellites and reconnaissance aircraft) used by the Pentagon for intelligence gathering are elaborate, big-ticket items. Each of the NGA's and NSA's surveillance satellites is often the size of a Greyhound bus and costs upward of a billion dollars just to launch into space, let alone the expense of the initial design, construction, and later management in orbits circling the planet. Expensive, too, are the global fleet of remote-controlled drones, operated chiefly by the Pentagon but also by the CIA in certain areas of the world (such as Pakistan, Somalia, and Yemen). These pilotless aircraft are equipped with sophisticated cameras and, frequently, with missiles to shoot down enemy targets that have been spotted through the camera lens.

Civilian Intelligence

Moving from one shadowy cluster of organizations to another, of the seven intelligence agencies embedded in civilian policy departments, four have been part of the IC for decades and three are newcomers. Among the older agencies, the FBI is located in the Department of Justice and is assigned both a counterintelligence (spy-catching) and a counterterrorism mission, along with its traditional law enforcement duties (the original reason why the Bureau was created in 1908). Another agency, the Office of Intelligence and Analysis, resides in the Department of Treasury and includes among its duties the tracking of hidden funds that support ISIS, Al Qaeda, and other terrorist organizations. The Bureau of Intelligence and Research (INR), the smallest of America's secret agencies, is part of the Department of State and is one of the most highly regarded members of the IC, because of its lucidly written and often prescient reports based in part on daily cable traffic from U.S. diplomats serving around the world. Further, the Department of Energy has an Office of Intelligence and Counterintelligence, which monitors the worldwide transit of nuclear materials, such as uranium, plutonium, heavy water, and nuclear-reactor parts. This office also has significant counterintelligence assignments: maintaining security at the nation's weapons laboratories, as well as protecting America's nuclear-weapons arsenal.

The triad of newcomers, which reside as well inside civilian policy departments, were all brought on board the IC after the 9/11 attacks. They include Coast Guard Intelligence; the Office of Intelligence and Analysis, an analytic unit within the Department of Homeland Security (DHS); and the Office of National Security Intelligence in the Drug Enforcement Administration (DEA), which, like the FBI, is part of the Justice Department. When admitted to the IC in 2001, Coast Guard Intelligence initially had its own direct line to the nation's intelligence director (the DCI at the time); however, when the second Bush Administration created the Department of Homeland Security in 2003, Coast Guard Intelligence was folded into this new department, because of their common mission to protect the U.S. homeland from the coastline inward. The DEA, America's lead agency in the (so far losing) effort to block the entry of illegal drugs into the United States, has been a part of the Justice Department for decades, but it became an official member of the IC in 2006.

The Office of the DNI and the CIA

ODNI

The two additional civilian intelligence organizations—the new, managerial-oriented ODNI and the long-toothed, legendary CIA—reside outside any of the policy (cabinet) departments. When the DNI replaced the position of DCI in early 2005, the new spy chief assembled within his organizational framework a set of deputies (DDNIs), a National Counterterrorism Center (NCTC, which also reports directly to the White House), and the former DCI's panel of top-flight analysts who collectively compose the National Intelligence Council (NIC). A primary purpose of each of these organizations is to help the DNI mitigate against the stovepipe behavior of the intelligence agencies, so that the surveillance community will work together more effectively toward the ultimate intelligence goal of providing policymakers with a reliable, timely, and holistic ("all-source") assessment of world affairs. Given that the law establishing the ODNI provided neither a clear-cut budget nor appointment powers for the new spymaster, the integration of the IC has been a daunting task. As elsewhere in government, inside the community: no peso, no say-so. The DNI has only limited control over the pesos spent on intelligence activities; thus, the job has led to frustrations in that office, resulting in a high turnover rate among the first three DNIs (see appendix B).

The fourth DNI, James R. Clapper, Jr., a retired three-star Air Force general, set a tenure record for this office, however, by persevering for six-and-a-half years. He was able to achieve a greater degree of cohesion among the intelligence agencies than ever before, despite the lack of strong formal managerial tools. "Intelligence community integration" was his favorite phrase and his primary day-to-day orientation.[81] A dramatic illustration of successful IC integration is the way in which the agencies worked together in the Bin Laden take-down in 2011. Clapper's modicum of success (the IC still remains quite fragmented, with its separate gorillas, stovepipes, and cultural norms related to the different ints) stemmed from the fact that he had served in the field of intelligence for five decades before becoming DNI and knew practically all the program managers and other top people in the community—several of whom he had mentored over the years. Relying on these personal ties, Clapper was able to persuade some of the gorillas, some of the time, to play nice with each other by coordinating their collection efforts more closely and sharing information obtained from their agencies' operations.

Lacking many sticks or carrots to coax all the spy agencies into harness, the DNI is at best a persuader—hardly a "spymaster" able to fire uncooperative gorillas or easily shift funds from one agency to another. Thus the United States is left with largely a cosmetic, not a true, intelligence leader, despite the impressive title "Director of National Intelligence" and the goal of reformers to create a stronger IC boss in the aftermath of the 9/11 attacks. In 2004, the Pentagon and its allies in Congress ambushed intelligence reform efforts when a bill that favored a meaningful DNI office—with budget and appointment powers over all intelligence agencies—wound its way through the parlous labyrinths of Capitol Hill. The Department of Defense, led by Secretary Donald H. Rumsfeld at the time, opposed the central idea in this initiative (the Intelligence Reform and Terrorism Prevention Act): namely, the establishment of a strong civilian DNI, who (Rumsfeld and the Pentagon brass feared) might divert funding from military intelligence operations toward a greater concentration on global diplomatic, political, economic, scientific, and cultural developments—in other words, in favor of civilian intelligence at the expense of protecting America's fighting men and women.[82] However unfounded this fear was (any DNI is likely to place the protection of U.S. troops foremost among intelligence priorities, or be fired quickly by the president), this argument won the day. One important reason for the Pentagon victory: Rumsfeld's iron will, extraordinary bureaucratic and lobbying skills, and long experience as a Washington insider (in his second stint as SecDef, the first one in the Gerald R. Ford Administration).

In the "wiring diagrams" of the federal government, the ODNI appears to be a neutral managerial agency—even having something of a civilian hue, residing as it does outside the Pentagon's organizational framework. After temporary quarters at the New Executive Office Building in downtown D.C. (near the White House), and then at the DIA's facility (located on Bolling Air Force Base, across the Potomac River from the Pentagon), the ODNI subsequently moved to quarters some twenty miles away from the Department of Defense, at a place called Liberty Crossing in North Arlington (a suburb of Washington in Virginia). This office is roughly six miles away from the CIA's Headquarters at Langley, the home of the erstwhile DCI and still the location where the NIC and most of the nation's top intelligence analysts prepare their reports. The ODNI occupies two upscale modern glass-and-granite buildings (home, too, of the National Counterterrorism Center, part of the ODNI structure). They are nestled among look-alike edifices in a part of northern Virginia that serve as headquarters for corporations and beltway bandits who thrive on government contracts. Yet this geographic distance from the uniformed military brass at the Pentagon notwith-standing, three out of the five DNIs have been former high-ranking Air Force or Navy officers, including the longest serving director, James Clapper. (The first DNI was a State Department diplomatic, and the fifth (and current) a former member of Congress—see appendix B.) There has often been, in short, a dis-tinctive military coloration to the ODNI, even if it does stand alone outside the Pentagon. Despite conjectures one way or another about the ODNI's civilian or military sympathies, in his final months in office, Clapper expressed an inter-est in honoring the notion of intelligence accountability and he authorized the establishment of an Intelligence Transparency Council (ITC), whose duties in part are to "ensure that the public has information that clearly presents the mis-sion, authorities, and oversight mechanism that direct and guide the IC."[83]

The CIA

Because the Agency—now in its seventieth year of existence—is outside the DoD's organizational framework, it is also considered civilian. It does boast a paramilitary unit, however, and engages periodically in warlike operations, most starkly in recent years with its use of drones to kill known and suspected terrorists overseas. During the Cold War, the CIA enjoyed a special cachet in Washington as the only espionage organization specifically named in the National Security Act of 1947, which constructed the scaffolding for America's modern national security apparatus. There was another, equally important reason for its high sta-tus and political clout in the nation's capital: the seventh floor of the CIA became the headquarters for the DCI, the leader of all the intelligence agencies in the IC from 1947–2004 (when the DCI office was replaced by the DNI office). This gave the DCI close access to the nation's top strategic analysts; the information and assessments of world affairs that they possessed turned into the power of knowledge for the DCI at high council meetings in the government. During the Eisenhower Administration, the DCI physically moved with the CIA from a cluster of antiquated Navy buildings in Washington near the Mall into new quarters located in Langley, Virginia, adjacent to the township of McLean.

As the names imply, the Central Intelligence Agency and the Director of Central Intelligence were originally meant to serve as hubs for America's entire spy apparatus, playing the role of coordinators for the IC's activities and collators of its all-source (all agency) reports, in an otherwise highly dispersed array of bureaucracies. R. James Woolsey, who held the position of DCI during the early years of the Clinton Administration, has described the DCI's role in this manner: "You're kind of chairman and CEO of the CIA, and you're kind of chairman of the board of the intelligence community."[84] He emphasized, though, that the DCI did not have the authority to give "rudder orders" to the heads of the various intelligence agencies. (Woolsey served for a time as undersecretary of the Navy.) Rather, he continued, "it's more subtle," a matter of personal relationships, private conversations, and gentle persuasion—the glue of trust and rapport rarely discussed in college textbooks on government but the essence of successful transactions in Washington (as DNI Clapper's relative success in integrating the intelligence community underscored).

While the DCI wore two hats as he (no women have held that office) led the IC while simultaneously guiding the CIA, today the DNI is free of responsibilities for day-to-day management of the Agency. The new spymaster is strictly in charge of coordinating the overall IC, while the CIA is now led by a director of the Central Intelligence Agency (DCIA or D/CIA). In a sense, though, the location of the DNI's offices miles away from the CIA Headquarters in Langley has been a liability. Both the earlier DCI and today's DNI have depended on knowledge as their source of authority in Washington—valuable information at their fingertips about what is going on around the globe. That is why they are invited to "the Oval" (the Oval Office in the White House) to meet with the president, as well as to sessions of the National Security Council. Since the ODNI is not on the seventh floor at Langley, the DNI's easy access to the nation's top analysts serving on the NIC and in the CIA's Directorate of Analysis (formerly the Directorate of Intelligence) is diminished compared to what the DCI once enjoyed. The DNI has benefited significantly, though, from not having to bear the pressures and anxieties that beset the DCI, as this earlier intelligence leader attempted to manage the Agency's daily transactions while trying—with minimal success—to integrate the broader community.

Not only do the sixteen intelligence agencies situated beneath the ODNI have cultures quite distinct from one another, based on which intelligence discipline ("int") they command, but—to make things even more complicated for their individual managers (the gorillas) and their outside overseers in Congress and elsewhere—there are also a variety of different cultures and subcultures that exist inside the units of each agency. The vastness of all these entities and their individual mores presents a daunting administrative challenge for the program managers (agency directors), as well as for intelligence overseers in the ODNI, in the White House, and on Capitol Hill. Admiral Stansfield Turner, who served as DCI during the Carter Administration (1977–1981), wrote about the tensions among (at the time) the four directorates within the Agency, not to mention the various covens within these directorates. During Turner's tenure, they were known as the Directorate of Operations (DO, which in 2005 became the National Clandestine Service, then reverted back in 2015 to the old DO name); the Directorate of Intelligence (DI, now the Directorate of Analysis or DA); the Directorate of Science and Technology (DS&T); and the Directorate of Administration (DA, now the Directorate of Support or DS). Each directorate was a "separate barony," as Turner recalls, emphasizing how the CIA has several identifiable cultures within its walls that are at times out of sync with one another and with the leadership cadre on the Agency's seventh floor.[85]

For example, those in the Directorate of Operations, whose paramilitary officers are sometimes referred to as "snake-eaters" (an image derived from the largely mythical image of them crawling on their bellies through Asian and African jungles on counterinsurgency missions during the Cold War), spend their time recruiting agents around the world and implementing covert actions. Those in Analysis, the "librarians," write reports for the president and other policymakers; those in S&T, the "geeks," construct gadgets useful for espionage, whether miniature cameras and microphones or mechanical "birds" (pigeons are a favorite) that can fly to the windowsills of foreign embassies where they sit, bob their heads, and listen; and those in Support, the "admin" (administrators), focused on the recruitment of new American recruits at home, as well as maintaining security at CIA facilities in the United States and abroad.

In 2015, the Agency created yet another directorate: the Directorate of Digital Innovation (DDI), responding to the importance of computers in today's world and the continuing concern about hackers and even the possibility of a major cyberattack against the United States—an electronic Pearl Harbor that would wreak havoc across our densely wired nation. In 2016, evidence emerged that some skilled hacker—perhaps even Russian intelligence—had engaged in a cybertheft of the NSA's top-secret computer code. If true, this security breach would overshadow even Snowden's considerable theft of NSA data in 2013.[86] Better documented in the public domain was hacking by Russian intelligence against the Democratic National Committee and other locations during the 2016 presidential elections, as well as the planting by the Russians of fake news stories in U.S. media and blogospheres, in an apparent effort to influence the outcome in favor of Donald Trump and against Moscow's nemesis, Hillary Clinton. (This possible Russian influence in the election remains a subject of ongoing investigation in Washington by the Justice Department, HPSCI, and SSCI.) At the cultural core of the DDI are computer "nerds" enthralled by monitoring foreign social media, as well as by the challenge of curbing hackers intent on finagling their way into Agency and other U.S. government computers. The intelligence officials in each of these CIA directorates all work for the same organization and the D/CIA, but they frequently have divergent interests, educations, methodologies, career paths, and personalities—all resulting in a complex and often elusive mosaic for overseers inside and outside the Agency's "campus" in Langley.

A key entity inside the Agency for dealing with external overseers is the Office of Congressional Affairs (OCA), which today boasts some forty professional staff members—compared to one individual assigned to "legislative liaison" duties during the first twenty years of the CIA's life (Walter L. Pforzheimer, a rotund, rich, and ribald graduate of Yale University, who was among the Agency's first hires); two in 1974; and about a dozen by 1991.[87] Approximately a third of these staffers come from the DO (sometimes a few more, given the high interest in covert action among lawmakers); a third from the DA; and a third from other Agency units, such as the Office of Security or (occasionally) the DS&T. Of the forty or so, only a handful are assigned lobbying responsibilities on the Hill. Quite often the more gregarious DO types are chosen for these duties, with their well-honed skills at endearing themselves to others (especially foreign government officials they hope to recruit). The rest of the OCA staff are specialists in deciphering the raft of oversight rules and reporting requirements promulgated by SSCI and HPSCI. The OCA works hand-in-glove with the Office of Legal Counsel at the CIA (OLC/CIA), the home of sixty attorneys (compared to two or three in the pre–Church Committee days). They count among their responsibilities the interpreting of intelligence-related laws and regulations crafted by Congress, as well as White House directives on intelligence.

The job of the OCA, located prestigiously on the seventh floor at Langley, is to keep the legislative branch happy by responding to questions from members and their staffs, along with fulfilling their document requests—even providing VIP parking at the Agency when they come to visit. (The ghost of James Madison must marvel at these elaborate oversight defenses that have evolved in the executive branch from his musings on the need for congressional accountability.) The Agency feels that its greatest obligations are to SSCI and HPSCI, plus the Appropriations Subcommittees in both chambers that deal with intelligence funding; however, intelligence officials prefer not to alienate any member of Congress and an attempt is made to be reasonably responsive toward all 535 of the nation's federal lawmakers (and scores of staffers).

This can stretch OCA resources and, from time to time, the office has had to refuse requests from outside its core oversight committees. In 2015, OCA officers participated in almost one thousand congressional engagements, from formal hearings to briefings for individual lawmakers.[88] Further, the Agency provides SSCI and HPSI with about two hundred written Congressional Notifications, or CNs, each year, ranging from one page to many pages and seek to provide the committees with insights into CIA activities. The CNs often stimulate requests for oral briefings or further documentation.[89] Then come the daily phone calls and emails from SSCI and HPSCI staff that request additional information. All of these queries intertwine into a rich network of communications between the congressional oversight committees and the OCA.

Even with this high level of attention paid to SSCI and HPSCI, dissatisfaction with accountability practices is often aired on the oversight committees and at Langley. Lawmakers and the more aggressive staff members complain that the Agency drags its feet on requests for information; and, at Langley (as well as the ODNI), the sense is that there are too many requests for information and documents, accompanied by unreasonable deadlines, prima donna behavior by some members and their staffs, and periodic attempts at micromanagement by Congress. High on the list of OCA grievances are "fences" set by lawmakers on Agency authorization and appropriations bills. Essentially this method amounts to a classified annex to bills that sets conditions the CIA must meet before the monies can become available to spend, even though these annexes are not voted on by the full House and Senate or sent to the president for White House approval or veto. The Agency grumbles about this use of what it views as "legislative vetoes" (declared unconstitutional in the Supreme Court case *U.S. Immigration and Naturalization v. Chadha*[90]); still, OCA tries to tolerate this technique rather than upset relations with the Hill.

The intelligence oversight committees have a different perspective on fences. "They are certainly established in custom as a proper legislative oversight tool," maintains a senior staffer on SSCI. He admits, though, that things can become "dodgy" in the interpretation of how a fence is satisfied. For example, say that SSCI fences a million dollars on a program, requiring the CIA to submit a report on some aspect of the program before the Agency can gain the release of the funding. But what if the report is submitted and the committee finds it unsatisfactory—perhaps because it is only a paragraph long when SSCI was expecting a more complete explanation? Especially combative is the situation when the report is in fact full-blown, but the committee still finds it inadequate because lawmakers simply do not like the underlying policy. "When you get into *Chada* problems, it is not with fences, per se," observes the SSCI staffer, "but in how the legislature deals with how the fences are satisfied. If there is a dispute, then you risk treading into 'legislating on appropriations' and other *Chadha* issues."[91]

The CIA's deputy director acknowledged in 2016 that "to be sure the CIA-congressional dynamic is not always one of complete harmony," adding "but this tension is to be expected, as it is more generally in the executive-legislative relationship."[92] He has a point: students of U.S. government have long commented on the tensions among the branches, as "ambition is made to counteract ambition." The highly regarded legal expert Professor Edward S. Corwin famously commented on the strains that arise from the Constitution's Article I (on the Congress) and Article II (on the presidency), characterizing the silences and ambiguities in these articles as an "invitation to struggle."[93] Still the overriding feature of the Constitution is the equality it created among the branches and, struggle though they may, this is no excuse for the executive branch to curb—as often happens—the flow of information to SSCI and HPSCI; the Intelligence Oversight Act of 1980 requires the executive branch to provide information to SSCI and HPSCI on all significant intelligence activities—and usually in advance of their implementation (a controversial expectation examined later in this book). Nor is there any excuse for the legislative branch to thumb its nose at *Chadha* and thrust upon the IC requests for an unreasonable number of reports.

Traveling congressional and staff delegations ("codels" and "staffdels") visiting U.S. embassies overseas—208 of these trips occurred in 2015—can be another source of oversight friction. These trips require considerable time from the Agency's chief of station (COS) in a foreign country and other personnel as they respond to, and try to woo, these Hill "inspectors." Yet there is a widely acknowledged positive side to these visitations. When lawmakers take a direct interest in the overseas activities of the spy agencies they can provide a boost to morale among intelligence officers in the field. Moreover, lawmakers and their staff usually come away with a better understanding of and appreciation for what case officers do in foreign capitals. Rarely are these trips "boondoggles," in which members are interested mainly in the night life or tourist attractions (although this does sometimes happen); usually serious interactions take place that educate lawmakers and their staffs, while keeping intelligence officers in the field on their toes. Typically, though, as one might guess, SSCI and HPSCI travelers are far more likely to visit London, Paris, Berlin, and Rome than Abuja, La Paz, Phnom Penh, or Port Moresby. A few lawmakers and staff, though, do pay visits to perilous places, such as Dakar, Khartoum, Mogadishu, and Nairobi—Boko Haram and Al Qaeda territory. These men and women put their lives on the line for the sake of intelligence accountability in the field, just as the intelligence officers they review have sacrificed their safety in order to gather information that could shield the American people from foreign dangers.

Intelligence Centers, Task Forces, and Mission Managers

To help overcome the fragmentation of America's intelligence establishment, both between agencies and within them, DCIs and now DNIs have resorted to the use of "centers," "task forces," and "mission managers"—staffed by personnel from across the broad IC—to deal with particularly heated international threats. The idea is to bring together all of the "ints" on a certain target, seeking (in intelligence lingo) "all-source fusion"—that is, a comprehensive dovetailing of findings from throughout the IC, woven together in reports and presented to decision makers in a timely fashion. For example, DCI John Deutch (1995–1996) established an Environmental Intelligence Center to examine how intelligence officers from across the community could cooperate with private-sector scientists on the security and ecological implications of global environmental degradation. Spies and scholars worked together using NGA satellite photography from more than fifty years to examine such matters as the depletion of rain forests in Brazil, with its economic, political, and ecological repercussions for Latin America; river water disputes in the Middle East; and the extent of iceberg melting in the Arctic Circle, with obvious ecological consequences but also of interest to Navy commanders who sometimes hide their submarines beneath these floes.[94]

During the First Persian Gulf War in 1990–1991, another DCI, William H. Webster (1987–1991), established a special Iraqi Task Force to coordinate "support to military operations" (practically everything inside the Pentagon is known by an acronym, in this case SMO). In the spirit of improved institutional integration and efficiency, the CIA similarly opted in 2015 to establish ten centers within its compound at Langley, each devoted to various topics (weapons nonproliferation, for instance) or geographical areas of the world. The prototype for this reorganization was the Agency's already established and effective Counterterrorism Center (CTC). These ten centers feature personnel—operatives and analysts—working together, cheek-by-jowl, in an ongoing management experiment initially emphasized by DCI Deutch in 1995 and known as "co-location": a combining of field knowledge with library knowledge. Each Agency center is guided by an assistant director, who is responsible for coordinating all the spying, analysis, covert action, counterintelligence, and liaison with foreign partners related to the center's topic or region. The end result has been a sometimes uneasy juxtaposition of snake-eaters and bookworms. The hope is to integrate the DO intelligence "ground truth" from the alleyways of foreign capitals and the DA epistemologically based research from libraries and the Internet; however, this effort at "jointness" has sometimes led to cultural tensions between the two types of intelligence officers. Nevertheless, despite initial cultural clashes, a former acting director of the CIA and himself an experienced analyst, John McLaughlin, maintains that "any time we've put analysts and operators together, the result has been a more powerful product."[95]

At the ODNI, Clapper created "mission managers" to coordinate community-wide intelligence on specific subjects and geographical regions. He also strengthened the emphasis on osint by establishing in 2015 an Open Source Center tied to his office (though physically located at the CIA—the same odd organizational arrangement as the panel of analysts that make up the National Intelligence Council). The idea of the osint center is to provide analysts with ready access to facts and figures about global affairs, drawn from libraries, bookstores, and the Internet; this open-source information is then combined with the "gold nuggets" of secret information acquired overseas through humint and techint methods, as with the sigint gathered by the NSA's giant listening antenna located in Alice Springs in northern Australia (aimed toward the Asia continent) and at other locations around the world.

A Nebulous Constellation of Smaller Intelligence Agencies

Added to this official array of major spy organizations—as if they were an insufficient undertaking for government overseers to properly supervise—are a plethora of smaller espionage units in Washington, D.C., and other locations, as well as a cornucopia of private institutions hired by agencies within the IC to help with their missions (the "outsourcing" of intelligence). The Department of Homeland Security, for example, has established in several state capitols around the United States a set of intelligence "fusion centers" for the purpose of sharing counterterrorism data (chiefly) with local intelligence and law enforcement units. In 2013, these centers employed 288 federal personnel, including representatives from the FBI and the CIA.[96] A *Washington Post* probe in 2010 uncovered the existence of 1,271 government entities involved in intelligence work of one type or another, along with an additional 1,931 private companies.[97] However troubling the question of what these various entities are doing and who is watching them, the significance of these smaller organizations pales in comparison to the IC's major organizations, where most of this nation's spy dollars are spent. These large secret agencies are the ones examined in this book, for they have demonstrated a proven capacity for controversy by drifting away (now and then) from the safeguards of accountability put in place by the Church Committee and other reformers in 1975–1977. They have also admirably served the nation on many other occasions.

On the side of controversy, it was the CIA during the Cold War that plotted assassination plots against foreign leaders and tried to overthrow governments around the world; today, it is the intelligence agency (along with the Pentagon) that flies disputatious drone attacks in the Middle East, Southwest Asia, and Africa—not to mention the Agency's use of extraordinary rendition, torture, and secret prisons overseas in the struggle against global terrorism; the NSA that violated FISA warrant requirements and implemented the dragnet "metadata" program; the FBI that spied on and harassed civil rights activists and anti–Vietnam War protesters; and the DIA that joined these agencies in signing onto an illegal master-spy proposal to place U.S. citizens under surveillance during the antiwar protests of the 1960s and early 1970s (the Huston Plan, discussed in a later chapter).

In contrast, widely admired is (among other examples) the CIA that disseminated vital information to President John F. Kennedy during the Cuban missile crisis; the NSA that intercepts the communications of terrorist organizations and often thwarts their attacks; the FBI that tracked Soviet spies within the United States during the Cold War and now has had some success in foiling terrorist plots inside the nation; and the DIA that now, as in the past, presents policymakers with useful analysis about foreign military threats.

Despite the sizable footprints left by the agencies that reside within the IC, some of the smaller espionage groups have contributed appreciably to America's security, too, and a recent commission report has called for the inclusion of some of them into the official framework of the community (including the Secret Service, as well as the Immigration and Customs Enforcement Office of Intelligence).[98] These less-noted agencies must be taken into account in any serious attempt to establish meaningful intelligence oversight, even if the current members of the IC demand the most attention based on their large budgets and, in some cases, their repetitive records of privacy abuse.

Outsourced organizations, in particular, can cause trouble on the intelligence accountability front. One of the most notorious examples in recent years was a firm called Blackwater (and later Xe Services, then Academi), based in North Carolina. This team of security experts and paramilitary officers (former CIA, NSA, and FBI personnel in many instances) won more than a $1 billion in government contracts after the 9/11 attacks, largely for the purpose of providing security to U.S. intelligence officers and diplomats overseas during the wars in Iraq and Afghanistan, as well as in other locations. The CIA even included Blackwater in its planning for executing terrorist leaders around the world—a covert action proposal that was scrubbed when the firm's employees developed a reputation for overzealous behavior in Iraq and Afghanistan. For instance, in 2007, Blackwater guards armed with machine guns and grenade launchers killed, in questionable circumstances, seventeen Iraqi civilians at Baghdad's Nisour Square. In 2015, despite this history, the new HPSCI chairman (Devin Nunes, R, California) named an Academi lobbyist as his staff director.

In another example of controversial outsourcing, as part of its counterterrorism program the CIA created a Rendition and Detention Group responsible for torture ("enhanced interrogation techniques" or EITs, in the Agency's euphemism), carried out in secret Agency prisons ("black sites") reportedly located in Afghanistan, Morocco, Lithuania, Poland, Rumania, and Thailand, among other locations abroad. Some 73 percent of the personnel in this program were outside contractors employed by Mitchell & Jensen Associations, a Seattle-based company led by two psychologists whom the CIA paid more than $80 million for their handiwork over four years (with the Agency officer who helped set up the firm retiring from government to run it as a well-paid CEO).[99] In yet another illustration of accountability problems in the world of outsourcing, recall that Edward Snowden—the most notorious leaker since Daniel Ellsberg and the Pentagon Papers—was an outside contractor, working for Booz Allen Hamilton.

Hand-in-hand with the well-known lobbying in Washington carried out by weapons manufacturers (which President Dwight D. Eisenhower derided in 1959, pointing as well to the Pentagon brass and the congressional Armed Services and Appropriations Committee, as an uncontrolled "military-industrial complex"), the arms industry now adds to its Capitol Hill shopping list potentially lucrative intelligence proposals that they hope lawmakers will fund. The list includes spy platforms, such as the expensive satellites used by NGA and NSA, as well as the mass production of drones for spying on and attacking terrorist cells overseas. Despite the controversies generated by outsourcing, companies like the former Blackwater organization continue to sell their services to help with security, counterintelligence, and covert action operations run by the CIA and the Pentagon.

As this chapter suggests, the scope of agencies carrying out intelligence operations on behalf of the United States is extensive. The purpose of this book is to evaluate the effects and implications of the novel experiment undertaken in Washington to extend the principles of democracy into the dark corridors of these agencies. How has America's experience in supervising the hidden side of government stacked up? The answer to this question requires, first, a look back over our shoulder at the place accorded intelligence accountability as the history of the nation unfolded.

2

Intelligence Exceptionalism

The Frustrations and the Glory of Democracy

Speaking in the House of Commons on November 11, 1947, Winston S. Churchill declared that "democracy is the worst form of government . . . except for all those other forms that have been tried from time to time."[1] While the great British prime minister emphasized the point with his signature wit, the imperfections of democracy had long been noted by philosophers, politicians, and citizens. Through the years, these imperfections have been tolerated, with sighs of resignation, for precisely the reason Churchill suggested: a more satisfactory means of governance has persistently eluded theorists, statesmen, and citizen reformers alike.

At the time of America's Constitutional Convention in 1787, the leaders of the newly formed Republic wrestled admirably with the shortcomings of democracy. In a sequence of arduous, spirited, and stunningly productive meetings in Philadelphia over a three-and-a-half-month period, they attempted to create a government in which the people would rule. This was a revolutionary idea in a world that, at the time, knew only monarchies and dictatorships.[2] The document they crafted—the United States Constitution—was hardly perfect. Slavery was allowed to continue, for instance, and women were banned from voting, let alone governing. As the decades passed, however, Americans further shaped their founding document with amendments and legal interpretations that allowed the nation to honor more completely its original commitment to full civic participation.

The evolution of democracy in the United States has been riven by periodic setbacks, delays, and even violent disagreements, including internecine warfare that almost tore the country permanently asunder during the Civil War. Even today, the nation faces much unfinished business as Americans continue to feel their way toward—as the Preamble to the Constitution promised—"a more perfect union." The reality is that life in the United States still lags behind the lofty rhetoric that extolled the virtues of liberty and equality at the time of the nation's birth. Moreover, concerns grow each year about the yawning economic chasm that separates the rich—the "1 percenters" —from everyone else in the nation. Despite these imperfections, however, it is fair to say that for the most part the Constitution drafted by the fifty-five founders 230 years ago has served the nation well. Further, this document has stood as a model for many people around the world who have established, or seek to establish, democracies of their own.

In 1787, the founders grappled with a wide array of thorny questions regarding the proper framework for governance. Having suffered under the heavy hand of monarchial suppression levied by King George III—with his edicts of taxation without representation, the quartering of British troops in the homes of Americans as Red Coat military commanders saw fit, and an arrogant disregard of grievances expressed by the colonists—rule by kingly might was a regime type quickly rejected by most of the founders. They were not interested in reliving "a history of repeated injuries and usurpations," as the Declaration of Independence put it. The singular George Washington, a victorious military hero exalted across the new American states, might well have been a worthy candidate for a coronation, but fortunately he, too, preferred a Republic.

A preference for republican rule and the successful construction of a Republic were two different matters, however. How should one fashion such a government at a time when the world's first democracy remained vulnerable to attacks from European powers; when America's industrializing Northeast seemed to have little in common with the rural South or the uncharted territories opening up in the West; when the frontiersmen displayed minimal allegiance to the nation's leaders on the eastern seaboard; when political wrangling over the proper scope of government was beginning to drive a wedge between the Federalists and the anti-Federalists; when some influential founders embraced the concept of limited government (James Madison, for one), while others advocated the benefits of an energetic national government (with Hamilton in the forefront)?

Controlling the Use of Power

The debates among the founders at the Constitutional Convention were often heated, and they relied on more than a modicum of goodwill, along with Washington's sure hand as chair of the proceedings, to achieve compromise and forward movement. The president would be strong (everyone assumed the first incumbent would be General Washington), but not too strong; authority would be shared among three "departments" of government: the executive, legislative, and judicial. One of the delegates in Philadelphia, Georgia's Abraham Baldwin, reflected the sentiments of his colleagues with these remarks: "It appears to be agreed that the government we should adopt ought to be energetic and formidable, yet I would guard against the danger of becoming too formidable."[3]

Elections would occur regularly as the primary check against the aggrandizement of power into the hands of one person, or a political cabal, at the national level of government. Other safeguards were put in place, such as the treaty power, which would be exercised jointly by executive and legislative officials with no major pacts entered into abroad without the approval of an extraordinary two-thirds majority of the Senate before final ratification by the president's signature. The founders lodged the authority for war-making—the most dangerous of the governmental powers—squarely in the hands of Congress, with a majority vote in both the Senate and House chambers required before war could be declared against another nation. (Not until 1973 did the Congress concede through passage of the War Powers Resolution that the president could initially use military force without legislative approval, but only for two days before lawmakers had to be informed and could then vote on whether to continue the armed aggression.[4]) The practical solutions reached by the founders in tackling these and a host of other government challenges gained them a reputation for thoughtfulness and creative genius that has endured.

Among those who gathered in Pennsylvania to write a Constitution, perhaps no one surpassed James Madison (whom historian Edward J. Larson has described as "the nerd" at the proceedings[5]) when it came to deep thinking about the future of the American polity. At the core of his philosophy was the conviction that (as he put it) "power, lodged as it must be in the hands of men, is ever liable to abuse."[6] Today, these words are etched in marble on a wall within the eponymous Madison Wing in the Library of Congress. Madison's anxiety about the dangers of concentrated power struck a responsive chord among his contemporaries. Although Thomas Jefferson was engaged in diplomatic representation for the United States in Paris at the time of the Constitutional Convention, his views on governance—as the chief author of the Declaration of Independence—were well known to the founders. Following his return home, a year after the thirteen states had ratified the Constitution, Jefferson reminded his fellow citizens that "confidence is everywhere the parent of despotism. Free government is founded in jealousy. . . . It is jealousy and not confidence which prescribes limited constitutions to bind down those we are obliged to trust with power." His prescription: "In questions of power, then, let no more be heard of confidence in man, but bind him down from mischief by the chains of the Constitution."[7] A hundred years after the drafting of the Constitution, in what would become one of the most famous aphorisms ever pronounced, Lord Acton succinctly captured the philosophy that seemed to be a part of the founders' DNA: "Power corrupts and absolute power corrupts absolutely."[8]

The brilliance of the Constitution comes from the safeguards it established to shield citizens from the potential corruption of governmental powers. The document's provisions were, in essence, a gift of freedom from the founders to their compatriots, passed down through the generations at home as well as to millions of immigrants who have arrived on these shores in search of liberty. In *Federalist Paper No. 51*, written soon after the Constitutional Convention, Madison explained the importance of the safeguards crafted in Philadelphia:

> If angels were to govern men, neither external nor internal controls on government would be necessary. In framing a government to be administered by men over men, the great difficulty lies in this: you must first enable the government to control the governed; and in the next place oblige it to control itself. A dependence on the people is, no doubt, the primary control on the government; but experience has taught mankind the necessity of auxiliary precautions.[9]

By "dependence on the people," Madison was referring to regular elections. The essence of democracy lies in the opportunity for the people to "throw the rascals out" if they wish, through the workings of the ballot box. But what about in between elections—that lengthy span of time wherein much mischief can occur before the judgment of the voter is pronounced? This is why Madison included a reference to "auxiliary precautions." He wisely foresaw the need for democratic safeguards beyond the ballot box, what today we often refer to as "checks and balances" —holding those with power accountable through a variety of methods, from congressional hearings and budget reviews to legislative investigations and, in the extreme, even impeachment proceedings. Important would be the doctrine of the separation of powers, that is, the idea (which Madison explored in *Federalist Paper No. 10*) of dispersing power across the government to avoid its concentration into the hands of any one branch or official, not even someone so universally admired as George Washington.

Looking back at the work of the founders more than a century later, Supreme Court Justice Louis Brandeis commented on Madison's approach to governance. "The doctrine of the separation of powers was adopted by the [Constitutional] Convention in 1787," Justice Brandeis wrote in *Myers v. United States* (1926), "not to promote efficiency but to preclude the exercise of arbitrary power. The purpose was not to avoid friction, but, by means of the inevitable friction incident to the distribution of the government powers among three departments, *to save the people from autocracy*."[10] In the roadmap for democracy laid out by the founders, liberty trumped efficiency, a republic—however messy—won out over tidy, but dangerous, hierarchical rule.

Thus, according to the prudent philosophy that suffuses the Constitution, a correctly functioning democracy had two essential ingredients: recurring elections and, in between, the vigorous use of "auxiliary precautions" to ensure that those with power were held accountable and made answerable to the public for their deeds. Safeguards to achieve this goal of accountability, such as the congressional gathering of information about executive branch activities through hearings, would be indispensable to prevent the gravitation of power into the hands of a few, which invariably—as history has shown repeatedly—corrodes and imperils the commonweal. In addition, a free press and an active citizenry would emerge as important components of constitutional democracy. Nothing remained so central to its success, though, as fair elections and a constant review of the government's activities—the very meaning of accountability or oversight.

For the most part, elections in the United States have been fair and open, despite well-documented pockets of corruption now and then. Further, the track record for accountability has been reasonably good when compared to other democracies, even though abuses of power have come to light from time to time—if sometimes only months or even years after the transgression (as in the Watergate scandal of 1973 and the Iran-contra scandal of 1986, respectively). At least most executive departments, agencies, and bureaus in the United States are relatively accessible to citizens, the media, and lobbyists, as well as to members of Congress and their staff. Plus, these government entities are required to engage in transparent budget reviews (with some exceptions when sensitive national security spending is involved); and, as a rule, they obey the rule of law. American society, further, has remained largely civil since the decidedly uncivil war of 1861–1865. As journalist David Brooks has written, "Despite all our polarization, we do accept the election results, even when the other party wins. People in New York do uncomplainingly send tax dollars to help people in New Mexico. We are able to assimilate waves of immigration."[11] On the whole, the Madison system of checks and balances has maintained the honor and intent of the Constitution's democratic principles, however belatedly and imperfectly at times, and even though much work remains to be done to fulfill the founding principles—especially a reduction in the influence of large corporations outside the government and the Department of Defense inside.[12]

Checks and balances in the American style have a potentially negative aspect: when the government is badly divided politically, say, with the Democrats in control of the White House and the Republicans in control of the Congress, the result can be a stymieing of policy initiatives, be they treaty proposals, sweeping reforms in health care, or some other major initiative. Regimes that are democratic, with parliamentary forms of government, where a prime minister's powers are outsized, have more flexibility in this respect. Yet, in the long-standing debate about the merits of a Madisonian versus a parliamentary form of government, the prudence of Madison's checks and balances against excessive executive power offers much to recommend.[13] True, Madisonian government—"a complex system of interlocking parts"[14]—requires for significant policy initiatives more of a national consensus and adroit leadership by a president and lawmakers, but that is just as it should be.

Intelligence—Beyond the Authority of the Constitution?

In the United States, as in countries around the world and throughout history, the norm has been to treat espionage agencies—the Realm of Night—as something special and apart from the rest of government. These agencies are clad in thick cloaks, have unique access to decision makers, and are given leeway to pursue their duties without the review of executive branch programs, personnel, and budgets normally carried out by lawmakers, the judiciary, and civic groups (in democracies at least). A nation's leaders avert their eyes as their secret services break laws overseas, a routine occurrence, and engage in unsavory activities—even assassinations and coups d'état—that would be deemed inappropriate for other government agencies. Jefferson may have advised "binding down" the government "with the chains of the Constitution," but America's intelligence operatives have long enjoyed the luxury of government laissez-faire. In 1787, the new Republic faced ongoing hostilities from European powers, as well as (quite legitimately and understandably) from Native Americans; as a consequence, the fledgling government was willing to surrender broad discretionary powers to its intelligence officers who, as the first line of defense against dangers at home and abroad, were expected to provide early warnings about perils to the Republic.

This hands-off approach to intelligence activities continued into the modern era. In the 1940s, for instance, the struggle against the Axis powers and then, immediately after, against the challenge of global Communism, encouraged special rules for America's secret services. As a top-secret study group, the Doolittle Commission reported to the Eisenhower Administration in 1954:

> We are now facing an implacable enemy whose avowed objective is world domination by whatever means and at whatever cost. There are no rules in such a game. Acceptable norms of human conduct do not apply. We must develop effective espionage and counterespionage services. We must learn to subvert, sabotage and we must destroy our enemies by more clear, more sophisticated and more effective methods than those used against us.[15]

This exceptionalism for spies was reinforced by a new threat that loomed on the horizon in the early 1950s: the possibility of a nuclear holocaust resulting from an all-out war between the United States and the Soviet Union. Indeed, just such a conflagration nearly ignited early in the Cold War during the Cuban missile crisis of 1962. Full-scale warfare between the U.S. and Soviet nuclear giants would have left Washington, D.C., New York City, Moscow, and thousands of other secondary targets smoldering in heaps of radioactive rubble. Shaken by this perilous slide toward the rim of Armageddon, leaders in Washington backed away from the dangerous game of brinksmanship. Given the global conditions of hostility and uncertainty, along with the disquieting and burgeoning arsenals of weaponry in the Soviet Union and the United States, the superpowers would rely more on their intelligence establishments to keep opponents at bay. In the United States, that meant that the CIA, established by the National Security Act of 1947, would have to fight the Communists "in the back alleys of the world" (as Secretary of State Dean Rusk in the Kennedy and Johnson Administrations described this hidden side of the Cold War[16]). America's secret agencies would need to be as tough as anything the Soviets could field, and they might well have to eschew the democratic restraints of checks and balances.

This is not to say that the CIA and its companion services were given carte blanche in the struggle against Communism. Most of what they did from 1947 onward was based on decisions approved by the NSC and periodically reported, in broad outline at least, to a few members of Congress and their aides. Yet the White House and congressional approvals for intelligence operations were frequently little more than open-ended grants of authority; and the reporting to lawmakers by the nation's spy managers proved to be irregular, perfunctory, sketchy, and usually of only passing interest to lawmakers—most of whom were content to let the "honorable men" of the intelligence agencies proceed as they must to vanquish the Communist foe. This approach to oversight (more accurately: overlook) also conveniently allowed members of Congress to escape culpability if things went wrong, as with the Bay of Pigs trainwreck in 1961.[17] Model democracy or not, the United States would mimic the traditional practice of other nations—open societies and dictatorships alike—in placing its intelligence agencies outside a rigorous framework of government supervision. The nation's spies would be allowed wide discretionary powers. If Americans were to be secure, a world bristling with nuclear weapons, well-armed Communist armies, and ubiquitous secret agents demanded no less.

Proponents of greater intelligence accountability during these early years of the Cold War argued that the time was long overdue for introducing more transparency into the activities of America's hidden agencies; the shielding of citizens against the chill of surveillance against them by their own Argus-eyed government depended on it. Yet, opponents of reform warned that shining a light into the hidden crevasses of government would result in exactly the opposite outcome. Subjecting the spy apparatus to the strictures of America's democracy would end up undermining the very security of its citizens; our espionage organizations would be hobbled in the struggle against the Soviets and other enemies who had no qualms about an unregulated, even brutal, use of secret operations against the United States. Intelligence had to remain an exceptional case, for the sake of America's survival in a hostile and uncertain world.

Efficiency versus Accountability

At its core, the ongoing debate about intelligence accountability has revolved around the values of security, efficiency, and effectiveness, on the one hand, and liberty, accountability, and privacy, on the other hand. In weighing the arguments on both sides, consider these intelligence vignettes from history, beginning with the security side of the equation.

Effective Intelligence

No one wants inefficient or ineffective intelligence agencies, especially when spending per annum anywhere from a high of $80 billion in 2010 to some $70 billion in more recent years on America's espionage activities—both figures a stupendous amount compared to the intelligence budgets of other nations, or even to this nation's own pre-9/11 spending on spies.[18] Often this has been money well spent, for security purposes large and small. Here are some illustrations, starting with a big—indeed existential—example.

The Prevention of World War III

Happily, World War III never erupted between the United States and the Soviet Union during the various superpower confrontations of the Cold War. The end result could well have been the destruction of both civilizations—possibly even a "nuclear winter" that could have frozen the planet, as soot and other debris from the nuclear bombings formed black clouds over the earth and blocked out the sun's rays for an indeterminate amount of time.[19] This fate, the end of humanity, was avoided for three main reasons.

First and foremost, the deterrence shield of both superpowers was sufficiently potent and credible to give an attacking opponent pause; starting a nuclear war would have been tantamount to committing national suicide, like two scorpions in a bottle stinging one another. The credibility of the deterrent shield depended in part on the ability of the U.S. intelligence community to know the location, number, and preparedness of Soviet military units: weaponry, troops, ships, and communications facilities. Further, meaningful deterrence required our intelligence agencies to have accurate maps and detailed coordinates on the whereabouts of high-value Soviet targets, for the potential delivery against them of tactical laser-guided "smart" bombs and missiles (precision-guided munitions, or PGMs) as well as transcontinental nuclear rockets. "The Cold War was a battle for information," recalls the imminent British scholar and former intelligence officer Michael Herman.[20]

Second, important as well was the memory of the carnage wrought by World War II, in which the Soviets alone lost over twenty million citizens. No one of sound mind wanted to unleash the awesome destructive potential of an all-out war in the Nuclear Age. As President Eisenhower put it, "The survivors would have envied the dead."[21] Intelligence analysts helped the United States understand the effects of nuclear weapons, which underscored the need to pursue arms control and nuclear-safety measures to prevent their use. Further, sophisticated intelligence collection systems gave the superpowers an ability to double-check that U.S.-Soviet arms control agreements were being honored by the Kremlin. "Trust but verify" became a popular slogan of the president and his defense officials during the Reagan Administration; and, stated in one form or another, this rule became the arms control mantra of subsequent administrations as well.

Third, the rising intelligence capabilities enjoyed by the superpowers diminished the danger of a military surprise attack, either nuclear or conventional, by one superpower against the other—a nuclear Pearl Harbor. Initially, policy officials in Washington had little dependable knowledge about conditions behind the Iron Curtain. This led to alarming rumors of a "bomber gap" and then a "missile gap," a fear—hyped by U.S. Air Force officials seeking more funding from Congress—that the United States was dangerously behind the Soviets in both of these categories of strategic strength. By the late 1950s, however, flights by U2 reconnaissance aircraft armed with high-resolution cameras began to piece together the reality of Soviet war-fighting capabilities in a manner more reliable than previously allowed by the lumbering U.S. reconnaissance spy planes of the prior decade that were occasionally able to slip into Soviet airspace (over twenty of which were shot down by the Soviets). The bomber and missile gaps proved to be myths; indeed, the United States was substantially ahead of the Soviet Union in both weapons categories. Moreover, the realization that the U.S.S.R. was actually behind the United States in weapons development in the early years of the Cold War allowed the Eisenhower Administration to cut back on defense spending and channel these funds toward education, infrastructure development (the famous construction of interstate highways during this era), and other domestic programs.

Then, in the 1960s, satellite surveillance became the mainstay for estimating ("bean counting") the number, type, and location of Soviet armaments, as well as the whereabouts of Red Army troops and tanks. As a satellite expert in the intelligence community has observed, the capacity of even the early satellites made it seem as though "an enormous floodlight had been turned on in a darkened warehouse."[22] On the other side of the Iron Curtain, leaders in the Kremlin also relied on their intelligence apparatus to provide improved knowledge about U.S. military capabilities. In Washington and Moscow, fingers on nuclear-response triggers could relax as the possibilities of a surprise attack by either superpower receded. Today, drones augment intelligence collection by satellite, another important addition to reconnaissance by piloted aircraft. Drones boast a nimbleness of movement, along with long-term hovering capabilities and a capacity for close-range observation. Their most attractive feature, though, is the safety of the drone "pilots," who guide their unmanned aircraft around the world by way of computers on well-guarded military bases in Nevada and other secure locations, far away from battlefields. (The negative features of drones are examined later in the book.)

The Missile Crisis in Cuba

The Cuban missile crisis of 1962 offers another illustration of how significant intelligence can be for the nation's security. The United States would have been unaware of the attempts by the Soviet Union to establish a nuclear missile base in Cuba, were it not for the reports of human assets (humint) and—much more reliable and compelling at the time—U2 aircraft photography (imagery intelligence or "imint," referred to by intelligence professionals today as geospatial-intelligence or "geoint"). The U2 photography provided irrefutable empirical evidence of the missile sites—a deeply unsettling discovery. Vital, too, was the realization from these images that the missiles would not be "operational" (that is, capable of being fired) for another two weeks, an interval in which President Kennedy could search for a more moderate response than the one initially advocated by the Pentagon and by CIA director John A. McCone: an immediate U.S. military invasion of Cuba.

Backing away from the invasion option, which would have led to the deaths of Soviet advisers on the ground in Cuba and the possible triggering of a thermonuclear war between the superpowers, President Kennedy settled on a more cautious series of diplomatic and military measures. As well documented in many studies, through diplomatic backchannels the president secretly traded off the dismantling of U.S. missiles in Turkey for the withdrawal of Soviet missiles in Cuba. Further, Kennedy established a naval "quarantine" (a gentler word than "blockade") around the Caribbean island, warning the Soviets to turn back their ships steaming toward Cuba. Fortunately, the Kremlin retreated. A relieved Secretary of State Rusk said at the time, "We are eyeball to eyeball and the other fellow just blinked."[23] The CIA had alerted President Kennedy to an alarming threat and provided information that gave him an invaluable breathing space in which to evaluate a range of responses other than a military invasion of Cuba and possible war with the Soviet Union.[24]

Less sweeping in scope and magnitude, but still important, are examples of the value effective intelligence can provide at lower levels of international affairs.

Thwarting a Range of Bad Actors

America's intelligence agencies have been able to halt the sale of fissionable materials, including uranium and plutonium, to irresponsible regimes; and they have been successful in intercepting shipments of illegal narcotics bound for the United States (although only about 20 percent of the total in recent years—up from just 10 percent, but still a long ways from victory over the drug lords). Further, intelligence officers have aided other nations in identifying and arresting human slave traffickers, as well as members of drug cartels. Among the notorious criminals and terrorists brought to justice through intelligence work have been the elusive terrorist Carlos the Jackal, tracked down in Sudan; the leader of the Shining Path terrorist group in Peru; Libyan terrorists involved in the Pan Am 103 bombing; and, most famously, the head of the Al Qaeda terrorist organization, Osama bin Laden, located through the labors of intelligence assets in the field, NSA sigint interceptors around the world, and CIA analysts at home. Based on these intelligence findings, U.S. Navy Seals were able to raid a guarded compound in Abbottabad, Pakistan, in 2011, and kill the terrorist leader when he resisted capture.

Humanitarian and Ecological Support

For nations experiencing natural disasters, environmental deterioration, and humanitarian crises, Western assistance has been forthcoming and often guided by the IC. America's spy organizations have provided critical support for humanitarian workers responding to political and health crises in Haiti, Rwanda, West Africa (during the 2014 Ebola crisis), Pakistan, and many other places around the globe; and they have assisted aid workers in rescue efforts after earthquakes, hurricanes, and tsunamis. Satellite surveillance has also helped Western officials pinpoint evidence of human rights abuses, as when NGA's geoint cameras spotted mass graves dug by Serbian soldiers to bury civilians murdered during the wars in Bosnia and Kosovo in the 1990s. War crimes tribunals in the Hague have often relied on U.S. and other intelligence sources for reliable criminal evidence in such cases. Further, information gained by the CIA and its companion agencies (especially NSA sigint) has prevented the carrying out of assassination plots overseas against allied leaders, leading to the capture and imprisonment of the conspirators.

On the environmental front, the CIA began in 1996 to share some of its satellite archives with prominent American scientists in a program called MEDEA. While photographing various Soviet and Russian military installations over the years, the Agency has also gathered (as an unintended by-product) a rich portrait of the planet's evolution: the status of forests, reefs, deserts, lakes, and seas, all awaiting scientific analysis by university and private laboratory ecologists. This greening of intelligence has been helpful to leading scientists.[25]

Backup for Diplomatic Initiatives

Time and again, America's spy agencies have provided indispensable information to assist the State and Defense Departments in successful efforts to intercede in rising hostilities involving nations abroad, including periodic flare-ups between Pakistan and India. Moreover, a staple of intelligence is to provide a heads-up to the United States and its allies when other countries have violated treaty provisions or bypassed agreed-upon trade sanctions. When allies have experienced financial crises, America's intelligence analysts have often anticipated these troubles, thus allowing the U.S. Treasury Department and global monetary institutions to help the faltering economies before they collapse (as in the case of Mexico in the 1990s). In addition, the IC routinely supports UN and NATO peacekeeping and related diplomatic operations.

Saving American Lives

Soon after the Cold War ended, an American ambassador and his family prepared to fly home after two years of service in an African republic.[26] Their domicile bustled with the packing of suitcases, accompanied by a joyful anticipation of rejoining friends and family stateside. At 9:15 in the evening prior to the day of their departure, a knock on the door at the ambassador's residence brought chilling news from a NSA intelligence officer assigned to the U.S. embassy. He reported to the ambassador on the contents of a sigint intercept obtained by the NSA in the country's capital. A brief telephone conversation between members of a known terrorist faction revealed that they intended to ambush the ambassador in the morning as he drove to the airport, killing the diplomat, his wife, and their two children, along with the embassy's security detail. Embassy personnel quickly arranged an alternate route to the airport, doubled the armed escort, and ensured that the ambassador and his family were safely homeward bound for the United States on a military aircraft. In this instance, the stakes were far less than warding off World War III or thwarting the installation of an enemy missile base in nearby Cuba, but the NSA did manage to save the lives of an American diplomatic family.

A former U.S. ambassador to Saudi Arabia (1996–2001), Wyche Fowler, recalls as well how NSA intercepts may have protected him on two occasions while he was traveling in the Middle East.[27] In another example, a CIA covert action team operating in northern Iraq in 1995 provided a timely warning to an American missionary living there that he had been targeted for death by Iranian Revolutionary Guards for his religious activities. He was able to flee before the assassins arrived at his home.[28]

A Successful Rescue Attempt

Another illustration of how intelligence can play a vital role even in small-scale situations, which are nonetheless important to the United States, took place in Iraq in 2003. The NSA participated in the successful rescue of Pfc. Jessica Lynch, who had been captured by terrorists and taken to a hospital in Nasiriya. To rescue Lynch, a U.S. military strike team relied heavily on blueprints of the facility's floorplan, which the NSA was able to obtain in the nick of time from a Japanese construction company that had built the hospital.[29]

Covert Action to the Rescue

The examples presented above were products of successful intelligence collection and analysis: mission No. 1 for the secret agencies. Sometimes covert action—the more aggressive use of intelligence agencies to manipulate events abroad—has also scored a bull's eye (although this approach has often failed, too, as chapter 9 relates). In the early days of the Cold War, for instance, secret funding and paramilitary guidance from the CIA (along with open assistance through the Truman Doctrine) helped turn the tide against Communist insurgents in Greece. The CIA's secret program to infiltrate literature into the Soviet Union—everything from editions of the Russian writer Aleksandr Solzhenitsyn's novel of the disgraceful Soviet system of forced labor camps (the *Gulag Archipelago*) to recent copies of *Time* and *Newsweek* magazines—seems to have contributed toward the goal of keeping dissent and hope alive behind the Iron Curtain in the courageous underground circles of resistance groups.[30]

In 1953, a coup in Iran brought to power a friend in the Middle East for the United States—the Shah of Iran, who allowed the West to purchase gasoline at a cheap rate and who stood as a bulwark against Soviet expansion in the region. The next year another regime change instigated by the CIA traded one repressive government for another in Guatemala, with the new tyrant offering at least the advantage of friendlier ties between that banana-rich nation and the U.S. corporate giant, the United Fruit Company. Moreover, and of comparable significance, this covert action ensured the establishment of another anti-Communist regime in Central America. Further, soon after the end of World War II until the mid-1960s, CIA covert propaganda and political assistance to the Christian Democratic Party in Italy staved off an Italian Communist Party election takeover of this NATO nation, barely escaping Moscow's access to military secrets in the West's top military alliance.

The CIA also successfully aided the Hmong tribesmen in Laos as they fought against Communists from 1962 to 1968, although when the Agency withdrew its support the Hmong resistance crumbled and these brave tribesmen were decimated by the Communists, who were well armed by the Soviets, the Chinese, and the North Vietnamese. Further, during the Reagan years, sophisticated CIA arms for the anti-Communist *mujahideen* in Afghanistan aided their victory over the Soviet Red Army; and, in the best example of all, later in Afghanistan a combination of CIA covert action, Pentagon special forces, U.S. Air Force bombing, and assistance from the local Northern Alliance in 2001–2002 managed to remove the Taliban regime (the old *mujahideen*, who had taken over the nation and provided Al Qaeda with a safe haven) from power after the 9/11 attacks.

Each of these covert actions had serious downsides, too, as examined below (and in chapter 9); but their positive results—at least over the short term— merit consideration.

Spying on Spies: Counterintelligence

The third intelligence mission, counterintelligence, has had its share of successes, too. High on the list has been the development of individual assets—and in some cases elaborate spy rings—around the world, which have yielded from time to time valuable humint for the United States on developments inside Communist nations and other places that might affect American interests (as in Indonesia, for example). The most well-known illustration is the counterintelligence asset Oleg Penkovski, a Russian military intelligence officer who provided high-value classified military documents to the CIA and to its British counterpart, MI6— including military-base designs that revealed how the Soviets constructed their nuclear missile sites in a Star of David configuration. These blueprints tipped off the Agency to the significance of the patterns on the ground disclosed in the photographs snapped by U2 pilots flying over Cuba during the superpower crisis of 1962.

Pointing to some of these examples, the Aspin-Brown Commission on Intelligence concluded in its 1996 report that "intelligence is an important element of national strength. The country should not lose sight of this amid the spy scandals and management failures of recent years. The performance of intelligence can be improved. It can be made more efficient. But it must be preserved."[31] In this same vein, a leading intelligence scholar, Richard A. Best, Jr., observes that "intelligence has been the glue that has often held together national security policymaking and military operations since the beginning of the Post–World War II era. The record of intelligence agencies is by no means flawless; it has in general, however, made a substantial contribution."[32] These observations point to a core truth about intelligence, often forgotten by its critics (including President Trump as he assumed office in 2017): the protection of the United States at home, as well as its military personnel and its diplomats abroad, often depends on the good work of the CIA and the other espionage organizations in the IC.

Accountability and Intelligence

Yet there is another, more somber dimension to intelligence that is also an important part of America's experience with spy agencies: they have been subject to failures and scandals that have harmed the United States. All human enterprises suffer shortcomings from time to time, and some even fall into the trap of serious moral lapses; however, the inherent secretiveness of intelligence organizations, and their use of violence in some operations, magnifies the consequences of their errors. In the black hole of an espionage agency, improper choices by intelligence officers can present a special danger to the principles of democratic government. Here are some illustrations.

Intelligence Failures

Within the three core missions of intelligence (collection and analysis, covert action, and counterintelligence), things can go wrong. This should hardly come as a surprise, since any institution staffed by mere mortals is going to have instances of incompetence or wrongdoing. Further, as former secretary of state Rusk liked to remind his aides, human beings lack a capacity to "pierce the fog of the future."[33] Nevertheless, many of the errors that befall intelligence officers and their organizations can be prevented, or at least reduced in their effects, and the best practices of accountability can help.

Collection and Analysis

The first major intelligence failure following the creation of the CIA in 1947 arose within the collection-and-analysis mission, namely, the conclusion reached by Agency analysts in 1950 (when they were still fairly new to the international spy trade) that war was unlikely on the Korean Peninsula. War did break out, though, as thousands of North Korean fighters swept southward toward Seoul in June, joined four months later by Chinese troops streaming from their homeland into North Korea from across the frozen Yalu River. Further, though on a smaller scale, a year earlier the CIA's analytic shop (the Directorate of Intelligence) and the other U.S. spy agencies, had misjudged by several years the date of the first Soviet A-bomb test, which took place in 1949, not in the early 1950s as anticipated.

After the war in Korea, which ended in a stalemate in 1953, the IC also failed to provide warnings of Soviet invasions into Hungary (1956), Czechoslovakia (1968), and Afghanistan (1979). Among more recent examples, this time closer to home and with devastating consequences for the United States, the spy agencies were taken by surprise when Al Qaeda struck New York City and Washington, D.C., in 2001. They were wrong as well when the regime of Saddam Hussein turned out to have no significant stockpiles of WMDs after all (beyond a few dated caches of chemical weaponry)—a discovery that ran counter to most intelligence predictions. The WMD hypothesis was disproven only after a costly U.S. invasion of Iraq in 2003 by the United States.

Covert Action

Covert action has suffered its share of missteps as well—more than its share, some would say. The most well-known instance is the Bay of Pigs episode in 1961, when a ragtag and delusional team of Cuban exiles sponsored by the CIA suffered a crushing defeat as they attempted to invade Cuba and overthrow the popular regime of Fidel Castro. Even earlier, the CIA (and British intelligence) had many of its agents captured, imprisoned, or murdered by Soviet and Eastern European intelligence services as they parachuted behind the Iron Curtain after World War II to conduct sabotage and related operations against the Communists. Several of the Western agents had been compromised by the Soviet mole Kim Philby, a high-ranking MI6 officer with access to key U.K. and U.S. operational plans, and who all along since his student days at Cambridge University had been working for his puppet masters in the KGB (Soviet foreign intelligence). Throughout the Cold War, covert action faltered periodically, and, with the Iran-contra scandal, it even precipitated a major scandal within America's government—a low point of U.S. intelligence looked at later in this book.

Counterintelligence

In the realm of counterintelligence, beyond the Philby calamity we now know that during the Cold War *every* CIA agent in Cuba and East Germany had been "turned" against the United States by the local intelligence apparatus, without the Agency realizing at the time that it had been double-crossed.[34] Further, counterintelligence officers in the CIA and the FBI spent much of the Cold War squabbling with one another over the bona fides of foreign intelligence officers who defected to the United States, with many cases never satisfactorily resolved. One contentious illustration was the Moscow defector Yuri Ivanovich Nosenko, who came to the United States in 1964 with a story that the KGB had nothing to do with the murder of President Kennedy. The CIA chief of counterintelligence, James Angleton, concluded Nosenko was lying and that the KGB may have been involved in the assassination. From his point of view, Nosenko had been sent to America by the Kremlin to sow confusion and convince U.S. counterintelligence officers to drop their suspicions of a KGB hand behind Kennedy's death. Yet, despite Angleton's lofty perch as CI chief at the Agency, the FBI and even others at Langley eventually accepted the Russian as a genuine defector—not a false "dangle" sent to spread disinformation and discord in the United States. Foreign defectors have often caused the U.S. spy agencies to spin their wheels in disagreement over their bona fides.

For the United States, the most painful failures in the murky world of counterintelligence were the acts of treason by Aldrich H. Ames and Robert Hanssen, both using their positions in counterintelligence high within the CIA and FBI (respectively) to sell top-secret information to their spy handlers in the Kremlin during and after the Cold War. Ames's treachery lasted from 1984 to 1994 and led to the execution by the KGB of nine Agency assets in Moscow, along with the rolling up of over two hundred of the CIA's collection operations under way against the Soviet Union. Hanssen's tenure as a traitor lasted even longer, from 1984 to 2001, during which time he confirmed much of Ames's reporting to Russia. He also provided additional information on the location of U.S. electronic eavesdropping devices inside the Russian Embassy in Washington, as well as information on the NSA's underwater listening capabilities in the Atlantic Ocean (potentially vital for tracking Russian submarines in time of war).[35]

In these instances of failure (a few well-known examples from a much longer list), the core question of accountability arises: Could closer supervision of the intelligence agencies by lawmakers and their staffs, as well as overseers within the executive and judicial branches, have led to fewer mistakes and greater effectiveness? In some cases, perhaps not; but, in others, quite possibly so. Consider the 9/11 tragedy. Inquiries into this surprise attack reveal that the CIA and the FBI had poor liaison ties with one another, leading to fateful delays and setbacks in their surveillance of the 9/11 terrorists after they had entered the United States over a year before the attacks. Prior to the attacks, congressional hearings on this rocky CIA/FBI relationship (well known in professional circles)—held in closed session to preserve secrecy—might have led to better communications between the two agencies and an arrest of the terrorists before they boarded commercial airliners on that horrible morning in September.

In the lead-up to the 9/11 attacks, an FBI special agent in Minneapolis became suspicious of a man, Zacarias Moussaoui, who once had links with terrorists in the Russian territory of Chechnya. The special agent sought permission from Bureau Headquarters in Washington for a FISA warrant that would allow her to search the suspected terrorist's apartment and computer. The FBI's leadership decided not to seek a warrant, despite the Chechnya connection and the special agent's discovery that Moussaoui had made the suspicious request of a local flight trainer to teach him how to fly a commercial airliner in midflight, but showed no interest in lessons related to take-off or landing skills. Prior to the attacks, what if SSCI or HPSCI had held executive session (closed) hearings on the relationship between the Bureau and the FISA Court, perhaps learning that the FBI's rules for moving forward with a warrant request were ambiguous and overly rigid? Had the Bureau's special agent been provided with a warrant to enter Moussaoui's apartment in Minneapolis, we now know that she would have discovered on his computer unequivocal ties between this "twentieth hijacker" and the nineteen terrorists who hijacked the airplanes involved in the 9/11 attacks. The information might have unraveled the plot before it proceeded.[36]

With respect to the Iraqi WMD failure, what if the congressional oversight committees on intelligence (SSCI and HPSCI) had held hearings on why the Department of State, the Department of Energy, and U.S. Air Force intelligence services had all expressed reservations about the hypothesis that favored the likelihood of NBC weapons (nuclear, biological, and chemical) hidden inside Saddam Hussein's regime? What if SSCI and HPSCI had demanded a National Intelligence Estimate (NIE) on this topic—not at the last minute as the Congress finally requested in 2002, but earlier when lawmakers would have had more time to study an NIE and debate the merits of the flimsy WMD evidence before voting in favor of a major ground invasion of Iraq? The war ended up being one of the longest ever fought by the United States, costing more American lives than the 9/11 attacks themselves, along with a more than $2 trillion (some say $3 trillion) surcharge on the U.S. federal treasury.[37]

One can imagine many instances when major intelligence reports based on collection and analysis could have been improved by a serious "reader over the shoulder" in the oversight offices of SSCI and HPSCI. The practice of elected representatives of the American people sitting down to evaluate the merits of key intelligence products, and suggesting how they might be improved, can be a valuable form of accountability. Indeed, these reviews are indispensable, given that the preparation of timely, accurate, unbiased intelligence reports is the paramount duty of the spy agencies.

Covert action and counterintelligence can also benefit from serious SSCI and HPSCI review: a check on the degree of care put into the planning of these intelligence operations, along with an assessment of their logic, cost, lawfulness, and ethics. What if executive session hearings had been held by Congress on the Bay of Pigs proposal in 1961, revealing that the CIA's staff in the Directorate of Operations (DO) had never spoken to intelligence analysts working on the Cuban portfolio in the Directorate of Intelligence (DI), who were highly skeptical that Castro could be ousted by a limited paramilitary operation? And further revealing that not a single person in the White House and NSC meetings had asked to be fully briefed on the invasion plans?[38] What if hearings on counterintelligence had yielded the fact that, at the time of the Ames debacle, the CIA rarely examined the banking records of its employees—even when they suddenly displayed signs of sudden wealth, whether in the form of a fancy sports car or a luxury home (both, in Ames's case)? Hearings on the Hill, carefully undertaken in the secure rooms of the oversight committees, provide an opportunity to critique and improve collection and analysis, covert action, and counterintelligence activities—sometimes amending or even rejecting dubious initiatives before they do harm to America's best interests and global reputation.

Intelligence Scandals

Intelligence mistakes are not the only source of damage to the national interest; scandals in the closeted world of America's spies have been catastrophic, too. The first spy scandal of major significance in the United States was Operation CHAOS, the codename for the CIA's domestic espionage operations directed against anti–Vietnam War protesters in the 1960s. The Church Committee investigation into this scandal revealed that in 1970 the Nixon Administration had approved domestic spying throughout the United States by way of the bone-chilling "Huston Plan," devised by a young White House aide, Tom Charles Huston. This master spy plan secretly ordered the CIA, FBI, NSA, and Defense Intelligence Agency (DIA) to conduct espionage operations against American citizens who were merely exercising their First Amendment rights to protest peacefully against the war in Vietnam. The Church Committee discovered, further, that spying inside the United States by the CIA and FBI had already gone on before the Huston Plan and resumed even after its recession by President Nixon.[39]

These surveillance excesses, and the FBI's harassment activities against anti-war protesters and civil rights activists through a program called COINTELPRO, led to the intelligence inquiries of 1975–1976, the creation of SSCI and HPSCI, and a cluster of statutes enacted to curb future espionage improprieties. An era of serious-minded intelligence supervision, by all three branches of government, had begun. Despite the creation of new oversight procedures, however, the Iran-contra scandal occurred in the mid-1980s—just a decade after the nation's remarkable turn toward the adoption of tighter reins over its spy agencies.[40] Then, in 2005, a third major scandal came to light in a series of revelations about the NSA and its bypassing of FISA procedures enacted in 1978 that required a warrant for national security wiretaps. In 2013, Edward Snowden's revelations about the NSA's metadata program added fuel to this fire. These scandals, along with revelations about the CIA's torture program, and the investigations they triggered, are explored in chapters to follow.

As with collection and analysis, so with covert action and counterintelligence: there are distinct downsides to intelligence, as well as gratifying successes. These two missions warrant separate handling later in this book; but, to touch here on covert action, one can consider the factions around the world that the CIA has supported over the short term, only to leave them to their own destiny—and powerful enemies—in the long term, as with the Hmong in Laos in 1968. Or consider the deaths of noncombatant civilians—women, children, the elderly— that have resulted inadvertently as "collateral damage" from drone strikes in the Middle East, Southwest Asia, and Africa.

From time to time, the esoteric field of counterintelligence has crossed bright lines, too, as with the Huston Plan in 1970, or with the use of torture techniques adopted by the second Bush Administration, despite a long American tradition of rejecting such methods. However hardworking and honorable most U.S. intelligence officers have been—putting in long hours, sometimes in dangerous situations (117 CIA officers have lost their lives on duty since 1947)—none of the triad of intelligence missions have been free of failure and scandal. All aspects of America's espionage practices could have benefited from a more concerted exercise of Madison's auxiliary precautions.

As these introductory remarks suggest, intelligence has been something of a domestic battleground where national security "hawks" and civil libertarian "doves" jostle with each other, and with everyone in between, in what has been an ongoing experiment to determine the proper balance between security and liberty in America's democracy. On the hawkish side of the debate, intelligence officers sometimes wonder why they must be limited by congressional rules and regulations in their efforts to defeat terrorists and other enemies of the United States. In response, a member of Congress has defended the dove position: "It is the irresistible impulse of government to assume more power. My role has been to say no."[41] Of special interest in this book is the extent to which lawmakers have been dedicated, in the spirit of James Madison, to a continuous inspection of intelligence activities as a means of reducing the odds of spy failures and scandals. Or have members of Congress, instead, undertaken oversight duties largely in the role of *ex post facto* investigators—objecting to failures and scandals only after these untoward events have come to light? Or perhaps displayed little or no interest at all in accountability, *ex post* or *ante*?

The Evolution of Intelligence Accountability

After close study of the period from 1947 when the CIA came into existence to 1970 in the middle of the Cold War, political scientist Harry Howe Ransom dismissed the devotion of lawmakers to intelligence oversight as "sporadic, spotty, and essentially uncritical."[42] Even with various reforms to improve the supervision of the IC during the following decade, a study published in 1980 found that among the members of the newly minted HPSCI only a few lawmakers spent much time on oversight activities.[43] A decade later, an intelligence scholar wryly concluded that "oversight" was "an aptly chosen figure of speech."[44] The historical record shows that attitudes toward intelligence accountability have fluctuated from time to time in both the executive and legislative branches, heavily dependent upon circumstances (police patrolling versus firefighting) and the personal philosophies of individual overseers.

The Eras of Intelligence Oversight in Modern Times

Since the end of World War II, intelligence oversight has gone through five major phases in Washington (see Table 2.1): first, an Era of Trust (1946–1974), which relied on blind faith that the spy agencies would do the right thing in the struggle against global Communism. This granting of extensive authority to the spy agencies had been the hallmark of the earlier years in the nation's history as well. Then, abruptly came the Year of Intelligence in 1975, as Congress, the courts, the executive branch, and the American people reacted with astonishment to the CIA domestic spying scandal (Operation CHAOS). This interval of upheaval and reform led to an Era of Uneasy Partnership (1976–1986), when the United States established full-fledged select committees in Congress dedicated to intelligence accountability and began to debate the proper approach to the closer supervision of the nation's spies. This decade-long attempt to craft a sensible intelligence partnership among the three branches of government came to a screeching halt when the Iran-contra scandal gravely set back the experiment to introduce democracy into the shrouded world of espionage. The Iran-contra affair ushered in an Interval of Distrust (1987–1991), as reformers pondered how the new intelligence safeguards had failed so abysmally and what might be done to prevent a repeat performance.

In the unfolding drama of "Democracy and America's Secret Agencies," next came an Era of Partisan Advocacy, as approaches to intelligence oversight—as

Table 2.1 **The Eras of Intelligence Accountability in the United States**

Era of Trust	Year of Intelligence	Era of Uneasy Partnership	Interlude of Distrust	Era of Partisan Advocacy	Era of Mass Surveillance	Era of Rebalancing
(1946–1974)	(1975)	(1976–1986)	(1987–1991)	(1992–2001)	(2002–2012)	(2013–)
Ch. 3	Ch. 3	Ch. 4	Ch. 4	Ch. 4	Ch. 5	Ch. 5

with other policy domains across the board in Washington, D.C.—began to fracture along partisan lines (1992–2001). This time of intense wrangling between Democrats and Republicans in the nation's capital gave way, in the wake of the 9/11 attacks, to an Era of Mass Surveillance (2002–2012). Both political parties, fearful of more terrorist attacks, tossed aside many of the most important efforts at intelligence accountability put in place since 1975. The second Bush Administration took off the gloves and secretly approved a fast-rising increase in spying—without legal warrants—against suspected terrorists, and it authorized detainee interrogation activities by America's intelligence services both at home and abroad.

Further, the administration opened the floodgates to poorly supervised sigint operations that included American citizens on the lists of collection targeting; indeed, millions upon millions of telephone and social media records about the communication patterns of Americans were swept into the NSA's vast data banks. These excesses finally led to a backlash in 2013, when Congress—their conscience pricked by the Snowden leaks about NSA's metadata operations— ushered in a new phase in intelligence oversight: a continuing Era of Rebalancing, in which the nation began to ask whether the equilibrium between security and liberty had shifted too far in the direction of eroded rights of privacy. Just a year later came the publication of the SSCI's Executive Summary of its Torture Report on the CIA's third-degree grilling of prisoners in its web of detainee prisons around the world, a practice that led to the deep bruising of America's reputation across the global latitudes. The time had come, as in 1975 after disclosure of Operation CHAOS and in 1987 after the Iran-contra affair, for a resumption of America's ongoing debate about the limits of intelligence, and how a more acceptable degree of spy accountability might be achieved.

A Search for the Proper Equilibrium

The on-again, off-again quest for an ideal equilibrium between the fundamental objectives of security and liberty goes onward, with privacy proponents— their voices temporarily discounted in the anxieties that followed the 9/11 attacks—again finding the ears of the American people and their represent-atives in Congress. The movement toward a rebalancing in favor of improved civil liberties gained momentum as the USA PATRIOT Act of 2001, which had provided broad and vaguely defined support for a widening use of intelligence collection methods after 9/11, was about to expire in June 2015.[45] In May, a fed-eral appeals court in New York found that the NSA's bulk-data collection (meta-data) operations were illegal, adding to the momentum moving the intelligence pendulum back toward the protection of civil liberties and privacy concerns. As lawmakers took steps through the USA FREEDOM Act (enacted in June 2015) to limit the NSA's dragnet surveillance program, the *New York Times* observed that the United States was moving away "from a singular focus on national secur-ity at the expense of civil liberties to a new balance in the post-Snowden era."[46]

This notion in the *Times* of a "singular focus" from 2002 to 2012 underes-timates the misgivings about the performance of the spy agencies felt by even some erstwhile supporters of the CIA and its companion agencies during the Era of Mass Surveillance. Key Republicans in Congress, for instance, questioned the effectiveness of America's intelligence agencies after the 9/11 and Iraqi WMD failures; and the libertarian wing of the GOP, joining privacy advocates in the Democratic Party, balked at the NSA's expanding surveillance programs. Nevertheless, the *Times* accurately captured the sense of a rising undertow in Washington that was carrying lawmakers in both parties on Capitol Hill, as well as others in American society, toward a fundamental readjustment of values at home as the nation continued its struggle against global terrorism. The time of freewheeling bulk-data collection by the NSA domestically and overseas, the torture of suspected terrorists by military intelligence units and the CIA, and an overreliance on drone attacks was coming to an end, accompanied by a greater devotion to safeguards against the abuse of power by the secret services. Or so reformers hoped. Should more terrorist attacks come against the United States, the pendulum's swing toward privacy would surely slow—and quite possibly reverse altogether.

Meanwhile, in France, the United Kingdom, Belgium, and some other European nations, the pendulum was moving in just the opposite direction from the United States, toward an increasing emphasis on security concerns and an expansion of intelligence activities. At a rapid rate, these countries were strip-ping away civil liberties and unleashing their spy agencies to combat the rising levels of Islamic extremism. As is often the case, the fear of danger overwhelmed concern for civil liberties, tipping the European balance toward security.

Occasional exceptions to this trend could be seen, as when the European Court of Justice (the European Union's highest court) ruled in 2015 against the storage of data about European users on American-based computer servers, out of a concern that U.S. companies like Google, Facebook, and others might be unable to protect the privacy of Europeans against NSA snooping into their files. More common, though, was the reaction in France. There the pro-security dynamic accelerated as a result of the murder in January 2015 of journalists who worked for the satirical weekly newspaper *Charlie Hebdo* in Paris, as Islamic *jihadists* in France reacted violently to the paper's cartoonish portrayals of the Prophet Muhammad. The *Charlie Hebdo* killings were accompanied by an additional attack against a kosher supermarket in Paris. Despite the threat of terrorism, the editor in chief of *Charlie Hebdo*, Gérard Biard, a target of the extremists, had steadfastly and bravely opposed the bend of the French government toward more intrusive and widespread surveillance operations. "I think that opportunistic laws are always bad laws," he said prior to his murder by *jihadists*.[47]

Soon an even bloodier massacre by terrorists erupted in Paris, when four simultaneous shootings and suicide bombings in November 2015 killed 129 innocent Parisians and wounded 352 more at popular cafés, a concert hall, and a soccer stadium. The prime minister of France, Manuel Valls, immediately called for extraordinary security measures. "The state of emergency, it's true, justifies certain temporary restrictions on liberty," he said, "but resorting to this, it's to give us every chance to fully restore these liberties."[48] The new French restrictions included some eight hundred police raids in Paris without warrants, aimed at apartments where suspected terrorists were thought to live. The police were allowed additional powers, among them the right—again without judicial warrants—to make house arrests and electronically tag those who were apprehended. Security forces were also permitted to dissolve radical groups running mosques; to block websites and other social media espousing terrorism; and to seize computer data related to suspected terrorist activities.

Some civil libertarians in France voiced concern that counterterrorism officials, operating in a climate of crisis, were engaging in executive overreach. Between November 2015 and March 2016, less than 1 percent of the 3,300 warrantless police raids in Paris resulted in new terrorism investigations.[49] Critics complained that the heavy price in freedom was not being offset by greater safety. Yet, across the English Channel, intelligence scholar Anthony Glees at the University of Buckingham chided the French for, unlike British intelligence, placing "a higher value on their privacy than their security, a dreamy premodern view."[50]

In Germany, the public reaction was sympathetic toward France after the attacks; however, memories of the Nazi experience, coupled with the threat posed by the Stasi secret police in Communist East Germany during the Cold War, had made Germans wary of emergency powers (exactly what Hitler had demanded early in his takeover) and aware of how important it is to keep a careful equilibrium between security and liberty—democracy's vital and sometimes vexing duality. As a result of these dark memories, the Germans were less willing than the French to give their intelligence agencies free rein in the name of counterterrorism. "German people are very sensitive, very hysterical [because of Germany's past]," remarked Thomas Wölfing, the German Deputy Consul General for the southern region of the United States.[51] Even a terrorist bombing plot against Germany, discovered soon after the attacks in Paris, failed to push Berlin down the pro-security pathway that France had chosen—although the right wing was on the rise in Germany in response to this plot and, even more important, there was a public backlash against so many immigrants (some of them unruly) entering the nation from Syria.

In the midst of the pendulum's swing back toward a concern for liberty in the United States following the Snowden revelations and the Torture Report, the terrorist attacks in Paris occurred, along with (a few days earlier) the downing of a Russian commercial flight departing from Cairo to St. Petersburg by a terrorist bomb smuggled into the airplane's cargo hatch. Renewed fears led some in Washington, D.C., and on the presidential campaign trail in 2016 to call for a ramping up of intelligence operations. The American public and their elected representatives seemed to oscillate between the values of liberty and security, like a donkey between two bales of hay. The menacing atmosphere in France wafted across the Atlantic, leading some members of the House of Representatives— Democrats and Republicans alike—to support legislation that made it more difficult for Syrian refugees to enter the United States. Republican presidential candidates, not just Donald Trump, expressed their anxiety that among the mainly old people and children coming from Syria might lurk agents dispatched by ISIS, the barbaric terrorist organization that claimed responsibility for downing the Russian airliner. Trump announced that he was prepared to permit Christian Syrian refugees into the United States, but certainly not those with a Muslim background—even though only a minuscule percentage of the billion-plus Muslims in the world support *jihadism*.[52] President Obama declared Trump's stance un-American and, in a rare moment, many other leading Republicans agreed with him.

To inflame matters further, in December 2015 terror struck the United States again, this time in the unlikely location of placid San Bernardino, California, a half-hour drive east of Los Angeles. A young man and his wife—he of Pakistani heritage but born in America, she an immigrant from Pakistan via Saudi Arabia—burst into a county health department building where the man was employed and gunned down fourteen coworkers while severely wounding several others. Both assassins were pursued by local police who, after a four-hour search, killed them in a highway shootout. Inspired by Internet ISIS calls for attacks on the West, this "lone wolf" assault added to the growing angst in the United States about the *jihadist* storm that seemed to be gathering against the coalition of nations fighting radical Islamic forces in Syria and Iraq. The San

Bernardino attack was followed by an even more shocking and deadly killing in Orlando, Florida, when in June 2016 another lone wolf, an American-born young man of Afghan descent, declared his allegiance to ISIS and then gunned down forty-nine late-night partiers at a gay nightclub—the worst mass shooting ever on American soil.

As a backdrop to this expanded sense of uneasiness in the United States was the specter of China as a rising Great Power, perhaps on a collision course with America over freedom of the seas in Asia. Added into the mix was the ongoing fighting throughout the Middle East with American troops directly involved in Iraq and Afghanistan, plus flying sorties (piloted and unpiloted) over Pakistan, Syria, Yemen, and elsewhere. Further, Russian leaders exhibited a military aggressiveness in Ukraine and Syria, accompanied by a truculent tone in their foreign-policy pronouncements and remarks about President Obama. These strains would deepen when U.S. intelligence agencies discovered evidence of Russian efforts to sway American public opinion in favor of Trump during the presidential election of 2016.

It was in this atmosphere of global unrest that Trump called for the zealous policy of blocking the transit of anyone of Muslim faith into the United States. Moreover, authorities in Texas attempted to prevent any Syrian refugees from being relocated in the Lone Star State, although a ruling from a federal judge squelched that initiative. In some places across the country, global humanitarian commitments were being pushed to the back burner and the heat turned up on the front burner of national security concerns. Fear in America about the threat of additional terrorist lone-wolf attacks—or worse—boiled over into a surging Islamophobia, as verbal and physical confrontations aimed at American Muslims tripled in number, according to news reports. With the right wing of the Republican Party notably full of passionate intensity about the dangers of terrorists lurking within the refugee movement streaming out of war-torn Syria, the level of anti-immigrant hysteria was on the rise from coast to coast in the United States. Loose talk among some politicians in D.C. and in European capitals went so far as to recommend the registration of all Muslims living in the West—another proposal Trump found attractive. This suggestion was painfully reminiscent of the Nazi Party's policy toward Jews during the early days of the Third Reich, a prelude to shipping those so enrolled off to concentration camps. In this time of stress, one began to feel in one's bones the fragility of democratic government.

At the CIA, Director John Brennan expressed a sense of scorn toward U.S. lawmakers and journalists who had been engaged in "hand-wringing" before the Paris attacks about the privacy risks associated with a strengthened authority for America's intelligence agencies, and toward those who fretted about the government's sharp criticism of leakers (above all, Snowden) who had spilled classified information about U.S. spy programs into the public domain. Without support for robust intelligence operations, Brennan insisted, it had become harder to track the "murderous sociopaths" who belonged to or identified with ISIS.[53]

At first, the San Bernardino terrorist event seemed to underscore Brennan's point when it was alleged that the woman involved in the attack had made several social media remarks about her embrace of militant jihadism long before she applied for admission as an immigrant to the United States. At the time the IC had been wary, on legal grounds, of accessing social media communications. After the attack, however, the FBI announced that contrary to reporting in the *New York Times* the San Bernardino terrorists had never expressed their pro-*jihadist* views via social media; rather they had used private online messages. The *Times* subsequently quoted intelligence officials to the effect that it "would be incredibly difficult, if not technically impossible," for America's spy agencies to search the social media posts of every visa applicant—the tens of millions of individuals who enter the United States each year to visit, work, and live.[54]

Given the importance of having good intelligence about potential Islamic extremists, how far would America be willing to go toward the goal of increased security at the expense of civil liberties and privacy? Although the event had occurred decades earlier, the memory remained green of President Franklin D. Roosevelt's internment of American citizens of Japanese descent into guarded military camps during World War II (Executive Order 9066, signed on February 19, 1942). "We've gone through moments in our history before when we acted out of fear, and we came to regret it," President Obama recalled in the aftermath of the Orlando shootings, cautioning against anti-Islamic sentiments. He went on: "We have seen our government mistreat our fellow citizens, and it has been a shameful part of our history."[55] Still in mind, too, from the 1960s was the record of CIA spying on anti–Vietnam War protesters; the NSA's interception of cable and telephone conversations by U.S. citizens; the FBI's efforts to spy on and disrupt the civil rights and antiwar movements during the 1960s—all uncovered by the Church Committee and the Rockefeller Commission in 1975. Moreover, the Snowden revelations about NSA's massive data-collection program against Americans had been revealed just two years prior to the Paris massacre. Would NSA's eavesdropping agenda expand again, perhaps going even beyond the bulk-data program disclosed in the Snowden leaks? Would citizens of Muslim heritage be registered, as presidential candidate Trump had advocated; or perhaps even sequestered in the manner of FDR's wartime policy against Japanese-Americans? Would the FBI infiltrate and harass nonviolent, lawful groups with ties to the Middle East and Southwest Asia? Could drones even be used inside the United States to hunt down and eliminate suspected terrorists, whether from abroad or citizens of this nation?

During the Reagan Administration, conspirators involved in the Iran-contra affair created "the Enterprise," a secret government organization privately funded to conduct covert actions in Nicaragua, even though this approach had been prohibited by Congress. With the creation of the Enterprise, the constitutional appropriations process was simply bypassed, as were laws that required reporting about covert actions to lawmakers on SSCI and HPSCI. In a PBS documentary about this scandal, journalist Bill Moyers offered an appraisal of the Enterprise. Given its invisibility, there would be "no watchman to check the door, no accountant to check the books, no judge to check the law." The invisible organization would operate outside the Constitution, following no laws or reporting requirements. Moyers raised the possibility that the Enterprise "might take on a life of its own, permanent and wholly unaccountable." And what if the Enterprise turned against the president? "Who would know?" he asked hauntingly. "Who would say no?"[56]

Could such things happen in the United States? Who would have believed during the Weimar Republic that the death of parliamentary democracy in Germany would have come about so quickly, as Adolph Hitler and his thuggish brownshirts came to power through open elections? Under the pretext of defending Germans against terrorists and other alleged rabble-rousers, in 1933 Chancellor Hitler promoted enactment in the Reichstag of an Enabling Act (*Gesetz zur Dehebung der Not von Volk und Reich*, or "Law for Removing the Distress of People and Reich"). This law gave him emergency powers over the control of budgets, treaties, and constitutional amendments for four years—a time limitation soon erased by the Nazis. Caught up in the hysteria of the times and the chancellor's spellbinding oratory, questions of accountability were thrown to the winds and Germany descended into a ring of hell unimagined even by Dante or Milton. The Social Democrats in the Reichstag tried to halt this slide away from democratic procedures, but, in a vote of 441 to 84, they were pushed aside by Hitler's security-obsessed coalition.[57]

In thirteenth-century England, one of the most important constitutional documents of all, the Magna Carta, struck a strong blow for individual freedom against the arbitrary authority of despotic kings. In the modern era, British historian Edward Gibbon restated the operative principle of democracy in his magisterial study of the Roman Empire: "constitutional assemblies form the only balance capable of preserving a free constitution against enterprises of an aspiring prince."[58] Leaders in the Weimar Republic threw this principle into the dust bin. In one balloting on one afternoon, German lawmakers—in a deification of executive power—chose to side with a despot, dispensing with the safeguards of accountability that accompany shared institutional authority. Some forty million people would pay for this decision with their lives during World War II.

Constitutional democracy is one thing on paper and quite another in practice. As the following chapters present, the five eras of intelligence accountability in the United States have displayed an ebb and flow both in the attitudes of lawmakers toward oversight as well as the proper equilibrium point between liberty and security. Chapter 3 explores the first era, which encompasses the timeline from 1947 to 1974 (a period of benign neglect toward the intelligence agencies), as well as the Year of Intelligence in 1975 when the tendrils of democracy began to insinuate their way into the hidden corners of government. Chapter 4 addresses the second and third eras, moving the story forward from the beginnings of this new approach to intelligence accountability in 1976 through its partial collapse with the onset of the Iran-contra scandal of 1986—a scandal that deeply jolted the democracy-and-intelligence experiment—and on to the fateful terrorist strikes against the United States in 2001. Chapter 5 looks at the fourth era: the state of intelligence accountability in the aftermath of 9/11 and during the early stages of America's struggle against global terrorism, when security concerns frequently swamped the practice of rigorous accountability. Chapter 5 explores, as well, the fifth and most recent era, beginning in 2013, whose hallmark is the effort to rebalance the tilt away from civil liberties that occurred in the climate of fear and revenge generated by the events of 9/11 and subsequent struggles against terrorists at home and abroad.

PART II

THE EVOLUTION
OF INTELLIGENCE
ACCOUNTABILITY

‖ 3 ‖

Democracy Comes to the Secret Agencies

The Era of Trust (1787–1974)

A Posture of Benign Neglect

Almost from the very beginning of the nation's history, there has been a conspicuous exception to America's bedrock governmental philosophy of checks and balances. At first, the Continental Congress ran America's espionage activities, with secret foreign agents on its payroll; but once Washington was elected president, lawmakers provided him (at his request) with a "Contingency Fund for the Conduct of Foreign Intercourse." When members of Congress attempted years later to establish accountability over the secret fund, President James K. Polk (1845–1849) quickly and successfully stiff-armed them, offering this admonishment: "The experience of every nation on earth has demonstrated that emergencies may arise in which it becomes absolutely necessary... to make expenditures, the very object of which would be defeated by publicity."[1] Congress backed off and thereafter Madison's auxiliary precautions—the safeguards built into the Constitution—were rarely applied to the nation's spy agencies.[2] Espionage would be supervised, to one degree or another, by the executive branch. A CIA publication concludes, "President Polk's defiant stance regarding congressional oversight effectively staved off significant oversight by the legislative branch for more than a century. It was not until after World War II and enactment of the National Security Act of 1947 that the Congress again tried to oversee US intelligence activities."[3]

Polk's belief in intelligence exceptionalism continued to guide the national security establishment during the Cold War that began following the end of World War II in 1945. The struggle against the Communist world required a strong intelligence response, free of congressional kibitzing—or so argued those who opposed supervision from Capitol Hill. In the nuclear age, a nation might not survive a surprise attack; America's secret agencies would have to be as hard-boiled and efficient as anything the Soviet Union and its intelligence agencies, the KGB (foreign) and the GRU (military), could muster. Even in this warlike climate, though, America's secret agencies had some limits placed on their discretionary powers. Most of their activities were approved by the White House and reported, in broad scope at least, to small intelligence oversight subcommittees in the House and Senate.[4] Political scientist David M. Barrett, the leading authority on intelligence oversight during this early period of the Cold War, finds that the devotion of lawmakers to intelligence police patrolling during the 1950s has been somewhat underestimated, and he presents good evidence to that effect, as does another expert on the subject, former SSCI counsel L. Britt Snider.[5] Yet Barrett quotes one of the key intelligence overseers in Congress during these early years of the Cold War, Senator Leverett Saltonstall (R, Massachusetts), as preferring not to "obtain information [from the CIA] which I personally would rather not have."[6] As various studies have shown, this was a typical response of intelligence overseers on Capitol Hill at this time.[7]

Snider underscores the limited detail and scope of the CIA's briefings to lawmakers, with the most sensitive discussions "reserved for one-to-one sessions between [the DCI] and individual committee chairmen."[8] Senator Saltonstall's son, William L. Saltonstall, who served as his legislative aide, remembers how his father would travel to DCI Allen Dulles's home in Georgetown during the 1950s for late afternoon socializing and face-to-face briefings about intelligence operations; or the senator would invite Dulles over to his home for chats.[9] The subcommittee in the Senate affiliated with the Armed Services Committee that supposedly kept an eye on the CIA met only once during 1951, once during 1956, never in 1957, and only periodically for short sessions in the intervening years.[10] On the House side, the counterpart oversight subcommittee convened with CIA briefers during the 1950s (as one participant recollects) "one time a year, for a period of two hours in which we accomplished virtually nothing."[11] As an Agency historian has written, during these years "congressional over*sight* was more akin to over*look*."[12]

The frequency of these meetings rose to five a year in the 1960s, a dramatic increase but still insufficiently often enough to count as vigorous accountability.[13] A DCI told Representative Les Aspin (D, Wisconsin) that, even in the 1960s, the intelligence oversight subcommittees for Armed Services and Appropriations in the House "preferred not to get involved"; and Frank Church (D, Idaho) recalls that when he came to the Senate in 1956 his senior colleagues on the intelligence oversight panels told him, in effect, "We don't watch the dog. We don't know what's going on and, furthermore, we don't want to know."[14]

Snider interviewed Walter L. Pforzheimer, the CIA's first legislative counsel and point man with Congress during the 1950s. "There were very loose reins on us at the time," Pforzheimer told him, "because the Congress believed in us and what we were doing. It wasn't that we were attempting to hide anything. Our main problem was, we couldn't get them to sit still and listen."[15] Inattention on Capitol Hill was only half of the problem; reticence in the executive branch comprised the other half. Spy chief Dulles said that he felt an obligation to tell only one person what the intelligence agencies were doing: the president of the United States—if he asked.[16] Other key officials in the executive and legislative branches were kept in the dark. An illustration is Secretary of State Dean Rusk, who remembered, "I never saw a budget of the CIA. . . . [It] apparently went to two or three specially cleared people in the Bureau of the Budget, then was run briefly by the President, turned over to Senator [Richard B.] Russell [D, Georgia], and that was the end of it. He would lose the CIA budget in the defense budget, and he wouldn't let anybody question it."[17]

On another occasion, Dulles said that he would "fudge the truth to the oversight committee, but I'll tell the chairman the truth—that is, if he wants to know."[18] The often phlegmatic chairmen normally did not wish to know. Congressional support for intelligence programs was deeply deferential, providing a long succession of DCIs with broad operational authority to fill in program details as they saw fit, all in the name of fighting global Communism. Encouraged by a roundelay of excuses from lawmakers for avoiding their oversight duties, the basic fact is that intelligence reporting to Congress during the first three decades of the Cold War was sketchy, perfunctory, and often unwanted on Capitol Hill.

The leading critic in Congress of this lackadaisical approach to intelligence supervision was a young, no-nonsense, and famously laconic lawmaker from Montana, Mike Mansfield (D), who would rise to the top of the Senate's hierarchy as majority leader later in his career. In 1955, he pilloried his colleagues for their "hodgepodge system" of CIA accountability, in which the Agency was given a pass from "regular, methodical review" by the legislative branch.[19] Mansfield formally introduced a proposal to establish a joint oversight committee for intelligence, with members of the House and Senate working together to ensure regular and thorough program reviews for all significant intelligence activities. The proposal drew a third of the Senate as cosponsors. It was one of the more than two hundred proposals introduced into Congress between 1947 and 1974 that attempted to improve intelligence accountability and, like all the rest, it failed.[20]

Mansfield's arch opponent was the formidable Senator Richard Bevard Russell, who hailed from the small town of Winder, Georgia, an eye-blink after an hour's drive east of Atlanta. He was widely considered the foremost authority in Congress on matters of national security, a function of his many years of service on the Armed Forces and Appropriations Committees in the Senate. During the debate on the Mansfield Resolution, Russell opined that "if there is one agency of the government in which we must take some matters on faith, without a constant examination of its methods and sources, it is the CIA."[21] Years later, in 1976, DCI William E. Colby would observe that "the old tradition was that you don't ask. It was a consensus that intelligence was apart from the rules . . . that was the reason we did step over the line in a few cases, largely because no one was watching. No one was there so say 'Don't do that.' "[22]

Senator Russell knew one thing even better than the subject of national security: how to line up votes in the Senate. He skillfully rallied support among the top hierarchy of senators against Mansfield's proposal (and others) for intelligence oversight reform. "It would be better to abolish [the CIA] out of hand," said one of Russell's close allies on the Senate floor, Wayne Morse (D, Washington), "than it would be to adopt a theory that such information should be available to every member of Congress and to the members of the staff of any committee." Never mind that the Mansfield proposal confined intelligence briefings just to a proposed joint committee, in closed and well-guarded sessions. The chairman of the Armed Services Committee, Carl Hayden (D, Arizona), agreed with Morse, adding, "How would it be possible to keep the American people fully informed and at the same time keep our Communist enemies in Moscow in the dark?"[23] Prior to the floor debate over the Mansfield proposal, the CIA's legislative counsel, the portly Pforzheimer, was delighted to provide "talking points" for the Agency's defenders in the Senate.[24] As the clerk went through the slow litany of a roll-call vote on the Senate floor, the headwinds proved too strong for the reformers. The tally was a lopsided 59–27 against the upstart Mansfield.

Stung by defeat, Mansfield left the field of intelligence reform (at least for a while) to an outspoken, reform-minded colleague, Eugene McCarthy (D, Wisconsin, who would run for the presidency in 1968). McCarthy was up in arms about the Bay of Pigs fiasco in 1961, when the CIA-sponsored paramilitary attempt to overthrow Fidel Castro of Cuba collapsed miserably.[25] With enthusiasm, he took up Mansfield's crusade for a joint intelligence oversight committee and introduced the proposal each year during the 1960s; and each year Russell and other Senate pooh-bahs, many from the South and in high positions in the legislative chamber, beat back the reformers. When the CIA refused to respond to his information requests, the handsome and charismatic Representative John Lindsay (R, New York) joined the intelligence reform efforts in the House favoring the creation of a joint oversight committee. McCarthy and Lindsay wrote impassioned essays in *Esquire* magazine appealing for improved intelligence accountability. They were labeled "sons of bitches" by the DCI at the time, John A. McCone, and the CIA renewed its behind-the-scenes lobbying to crush this latest reform boomlet on Capitol Hill.[26] Lindsay saw his joint committee initiative die in the back rooms of the House Rules Committee, a victim of a pro-CIA coalition led by another congressional panjandrum from Georgia, Carl Vinson (D), who served fifty consecutive years in Congress.

At least, though, the criticism from Mansfield, McCarthy, and Lindsay seemed to convince the CIA that it needed to meet with members of Congress more often in the formal setting of congressional hearing rooms. In 1965, for instance, the Agency convened with the Senate and House oversight subcommittees thirty-four times. How useful these meetings were is another matter. In the Senate, J. William Fulbright (D, Arkansas), a leading light on international affairs during the 1960s and chair of the prestigious Foreign Relations Committee, stopped attending Agency briefings because (as he put it) they "never reveal anything of significance."[27] Nor were lawmakers always at their best during intelligence briefings, with the sessions often poorly attended and, even when members were present, characterized by superficial questioning.

The reality of the passivity displayed by members of Congress toward intelligence oversight down through the years makes a *New York Times* report in 1966 quite misleading. After interviewing "more than 50" government officials, the newspaper reported that the Agency seemed "tightly controlled." Those interviewed offered their opinion that the establishment of more formal oversight institutions on the Hill "would probably provide little more real control than now exists and might both restrict the [CIA's] effectiveness and actually shield it from those who desire more knowledge about its operations."[28] This status quo orientation—everything's right, mate, leave us alone—would soon collapse under the weight of scandal and growing public concern about an imperial presidency in Washington.

A New Congress Rising

The Vietnam War experience, along with the Watergate scandal that drove President Nixon from office, began a shift in attitudes toward government reform, including a more favorable atmosphere for the improvement of intelligence accountability. Senator Stuart Symington (D, Missouri), for instance, became an ardent opponent of the CIA's paramilitary operations in Laos (1962–1968), and rumors in Washington about possible Agency complicity in the notorious break-in into the Watergate Hotel, home of the Democratic National Committee (DNC), fueled additional misgivings about the nation's premier spy agency. A major panel of inquiry formed in the Senate, the Ervin Committee, soon known as the Watergate Committee and chaired by the witty, folksy, and bushy eye-browed Sam Ervin, Jr. (D, North Carolina), began to probe a possible CIA-Watergate connection.[29] Given the widespread publicity that surrounded the Watergate scandal, the Agency—led by Richard Helms at the time—had little choice but to cooperate with Senate and House investigators. As Snider reports, "For the first time in its history, the Agency had allowed investigators from the Congress to review documents from its files and interview its employees."[30]

The Ervin Committee and other investigative panels failed to find any significant links between the Agency and Watergate.[31] Senator Ervin's panel did discover, though, that the CIA's Directorate for Science and Technology (DS&T) had provided—at the request of one of the Watergate burglars, E. Howard Hunt (a former DO officer)—a coppery colored wig and other disguise materials, but without knowing about Hunt's nefarious intentions to burgle the DNC. Lamely, the DS&T never inquired about his purpose.

Public distrust of government flourished in the United States in the mid-1960s and early 1970s, thanks especially to the twin disasters of Watergate and Vietnam.[32] Then, in the middle of these controversies came the blockbuster news in 1974 of CIA spying at home. The nation would now enter a new stage of intelligence supervision whose hallmark was a sweeping change in attitudes about how closely America's espionage agencies should be tracked by congressional monitors. Before this confluence of events, the United States—model democracy or not—followed the practice of regimes around the world (and throughout history) of placing secret agencies outside the normal framework of governmental supervision. If American citizens were to be secure, a hostile world demanded no less. So, at any rate, was the general consensus that stretched from Capitol Hill to 1600 Pennsylvania Avenue prior to Watergate, Vietnam, and the CIA domestic spying scandal known as CHAOS. When William Colby entitled his memoirs *Honorable Men*, the vast majority of the men and women who have served in the intelligence community deserved the "honorable" encomium—certainly the vast majority of the ones I had met over the years. Blind faith, though, is a careless form of democracy and accountability and, as CHAOS revealed, this approach proved harmful to the nation.

Joining Mansfield, McCarthy, and Lindsay, a few other lawmakers would engage in brief flurries of criticism of the CIA when things went wrong, as at the Bay of Pigs; however, intelligence reformers in Congress consistently failed to muster a majority in either chamber in support of strengthening intelligence safeguards through the creation of either two permanent standing committees in the Senate and House or a joint congressional committee on the subject. Other flaps, such as the shooting down of an American U2 spy plane over the Soviet Union in 1960, or a controversy surrounding CIA subsidies for U.S. student groups in 1968, set off fire alarms that stirred legislative debate and calls for reform. These alarms were insufficiently shrill and persistent, though, to trigger major inquiries and serious reform. Moreover, relatively little police patrolling went on between these flaps. Oversight remained largely a flat line of activity, whether measured by various potential forms of police patrolling (such as continual hearings) or firefighting (major investigations into intelligence mistakes or wrongdoing). Reformers would have to wait until October 1974, when a piercingly loud fire alarm sounded on the front page of the *New York Times*: CIA spying at home! This alarm and adjunct media coverage proved so shrill that even the most moss-backed of lawmakers felt a need to respond.

The Year of Intelligence (1975)

The notion of intelligence exceptionalism underwent a stunning reversal not because of any upheaval in world affairs, or the efforts of reformers like Mansfield to bring about change from within the Congress; rather, the stimulus came from a series of sensational news stories appearing in the *Times* in late 1974. Collectively, they were the equivalent of a five-alarm fire, accusing the CIA of multiple counts of power abuse. Reporter Seymour M. Hersh wrote the articles, based on a major leak—dubbed "the Family Jewels" at the Agency[33]—from a CIA insider. (This leaker was an early, but anonymous, Snowden type, although without his monumental disregard for the unauthorized disclosure of detailed budget and program information—legitimate secrets—from across the IC as he also dumped into newspaper hoppers data on the NSA initiative he avowedly opposed: the metadata collection operations against American citizens.) As Snider recalls, the *Times* reporting "was proof positive that the existing oversight arrangements did not work. The oversight subcommittees had known nothing of these activities."[34] Nor, as investigators would learn, had a series of the CIA's own inspectors general.

The reports astonished Americans, as the *Times* revealed that the CIA had engaged in the widespread opening of mail sent to and received by U.S. citizens, an operation known inside the Agency by the codename CHAOS. (At the time, I remembered from my English classes in college that "Chaos" in Milton's *Paradise Lost* was "a place of utter darkness.") The secret mail opening inside the United States was a blatant violation of the CIA's legislative charter spelled out in the National Security Act of 1947, which allowed the Agency authority to direct its operations strictly overseas—never at home. According to the *New York Times*, the CIA had tried as well to manipulate the free and democratic elections for the presidency in Chile during the 1960s and 1970s; then, when the White House's favored Chilean candidate lost in the 1970s, the Agency attempted (under secret presidential directives from Nixon) to undermine the regime of the election winner, Salvador Allende, who had been critical of the United States in the past. As newspapers across the country reprinted and commented on these disclosures—especially CHAOS—the CIA faced a major scandal in the making.

The Hughes-Ryan Act

In the midst of the early rumblings about the Agency's Operation CHAOS spy scandal, Senator James Abourezk (D, South Dakota, a gadfly in the upper chamber) attempted to prohibit all Agency covert actions—those secret activities aimed at influencing events in other lands. The senator hoped to limit the CIA only to intelligence collection, analysis, and counterintelligence. His bold proposal, known as the Abourezk Amendment, lost by a wide margin during a Senate roll-call vote. Once the CIA's Family Jewels—CHAOS and other missteps—became public knowledge, however, members of Congress faced spreading outrage among constituents across the country over the Orwellian spying allegations. The initial response of lawmakers was to enact, in response to the Allende revelations, the first-ever measure to place legal restrictions on the Agency's covert action operations: the Hughes-Ryan Act. This proposal was sponsored by Senator Harold E. Hughes (D), a former truck driver from Iowa who overcame alcoholism, became governor of Iowa, and was elected to the Senate, from which he retired after only one term; and by Representative Leo Ryan (D) from California, who was murdered in Guyana four years later while investigating the Jonestown religious cult (which had recruited the children of some of his constituents).

Incensed by the Agency's secret interventions against Chile's fairly elected president, Hughes and Ryan proposed that henceforth all important covert actions would have to be formally approved by the president and reported to Congress.[35] It was a major effort by lawmakers, in a time of shock over the *Times* revelations, to establish a clear trail of accountability—at least for covert actions—that would lead straight to the Oval Office. No more "plausible deniability," a doctrine that had allowed presidents to deny knowledge of (and therefore evade responsibility for) controversial intelligence operations that could include sabotage, coups d'état, and even the attempted murder of foreign leaders. Brief but powerful in its wording, the Hughes-Ryan Act required that

> [no] funds appropriated under the authority of this or any other Act may be expended by or on behalf of the [CIA] for operations in foreign countries, other than activities intended solely for obtaining necessary intelligence, unless and until the President finds that each such operation is important to the national security of the United States and reports, in a timely fashion, a description and scope of such operations to the appropriate committees of Congress.

From the verb "finds" in the text came the term "finding," that is, a document that states the scope of the operation and includes the president's formal approval for each covert action.[36] With its passage on December 30, 1974 (over the Agency's strenuous objections and fierce lobbying), the Hughes-Ryan Act initiated the movement toward serious—indeed, revolutionary—intelligence reform in the

United States and a tidal change in attitudes toward the prudence of allowing intelligence exceptionalism.[37] Day began to invade night.

Three weeks later in January 1975, lawmakers further reacted to public concern about the *Times* reports on CIA domestic spying by establishing investigative panels, one in the Senate and one in the House, to probe into the newspaper allegations.[38] Never before had America's secret agencies been subjected to major congressional inquiries into their activities. Not to be left behind and accused of laxity, the White House created its own presidential commission to examine the charges presented in the *Times*. These three inquiries continue to stand as extraordinary milestones in the evolution of intelligence accountability in the United States. For the first time since the founding of the Republic, lawmakers would carry the lamplight of Madison's philosophy of accountability into the most remote corridors of the nation's spy agencies.

The Church Committee: Intelligence Confronts Democracy

The Hersh articles rocked the nation and aimed the spotlight of public attention directly on the sunless fields of intelligence. "Huge C.I.A. Operation Reported in U.S. against Antiwar Forces, Other Dissidents in Nixon Years" bannered a *Times* headline on December 22, 1974, above photographs of a trio of CIA directors who stared grimly out at the reader.[39] The accompanying article claimed that the Agency had engaged in "massive" espionage against American citizens, snooping on the very people the CIA had been established to protect. Further, the articles provided details of the extreme measures adopted by the Agency (prodded by the Johnson and Nixon Administrations) to prevent the election of an Allende regime and, when he became president of Chile anyway in fair and open balloting, to destroy the new, socialist-leaning government.

Alone, the revelations about the CIA's covert attacks against Allende would probably not have enraged the American public, even if these bullying tactics had touched the raw nerves of Hughes, Ryan, and a majority of other lawmakers. Chile fell into the category of foreign policy, and public mentality during the Cold War continued to favor an aggressive intelligence response to perceived threats abroad—however tenuous at times, whether the Allende presidency or much later when the United States invaded Grenada in 1983 to quell an exaggerated Marxist presence on that sleepy Caribbean island. The surveillance of U.S. citizens—spying on voters—was, though, another matter entirely. This news had a seismic effect, carrying echoes of Nazi Gestapo tactics and rousing *1984* nightmares of possible government repression in America. Operation CHAOS, a revelation featured by hundreds of newspaper and other media outlets across the country, spurred an intense political outburst in Washington, D.C., and practically everywhere else in the United States.

The shock effect of CHAOS rippled across party lines, as both Democrats and Republicans rallied behind the launching of immediate investigations, exercising a vital tool available to lawmakers for the safeguarding of America's democracy. The "Year of Intelligence" was under way—or more somberly, "the Intelligence Wars," as many intelligence officers viewed this time of turbulence. For sixteen months, the Church Committee in the Senate, led by Frank Church (an expert on foreign policy and a former intelligence officer in World War II), looked into a broad spectrum of the nation's intelligence agencies and activities, not just the CIA and CHAOS.[40] For nine months, the Pike Committee in the House, led by Representative Otis Pike, conducted its own probe into the CIA; for five months, the presidential panel, the Rockefeller Commission, led by Vice President Nelson Rockefeller (R, New York), also focused on the Agency— though narrowly on its questionable mail opening and other forms of surveil- lance inside the United States. Combined, these investigations added up to the most intensive scrutiny of America's secret agencies in the nation's history, then or since.[41] For that matter, any one of these inquiries alone would have quali- fied for that distinction, given how isolated the intelligence agencies had become from the rest of the government over the years. Indeed, a former high-ranking CIA officer remembered sensing within the Agency "a potentially dangerous arrogance and a suffocating insularity in an organization whose work already inclined it toward both."[42]

The Church Committee, with its large staff and several nationally known sen- ators, was by far the most prominent and searching of the inquiries. It caught the wave of history and rode it to the far shores of genuine intelligence reform. In a scholarly study of the top hundred investigations carried out by the U.S. gov- ernment since 1945, Professor Paul C. Light concluded that "it is impossible to single out one investigation in this book as the best of the best, but I often return to the Church Committee's 1975 investigation of intelligence abuse as a model of the high-impact investigation."[43] The committee was guided by eleven sena- tors (six Democrats and five Republicans) and staffed by 135 people, including fifty-three investigators trained chiefly as lawyers and political scientists. I was among the latter group and served also as Senator Church's "designee" or special assistant.[44]

Leaving the topics of illegal operations at home (CHAOS) and dubious cov- ert actions abroad (Allende) to the Church Committee, Pike and his colleagues in the House honed in on the failure of the spy agencies (especially the CIA) to adequately collect and analyze information about foreign threats. The findings of the Pike panel revealed a litany of errors in the forecasting of world events by the Agency, a difficult task to be sure that—short of finding a magical crystal ball—will inevitably result in failures from time to time. Unfortunately for the Pike Committee's reputation, it had many shrill verbal battles in public with DCI William E. Colby and the White House; moreover, its top-secret draft report leaked anonymously to a New York City newspaper (the *Village Voice*). These set-backs came on top of the panel's already stained reputation resulting from accusations that it had been careless in the handling of classified documents (reminiscent of the recent charges leveled against Hillary Clinton for alleged misuse of classified email accounts while serving as secretary of state).[45]

Clearly the committee (like Secretary Clinton many years later) could have benefited from greater self-discipline, but the Pike Committee's negative reputation was not all of its own making. The CIA seemed out to smear the House investigation at every opportunity (as did the GOP against presidential candidate Hillary Clinton). The struggle between the Pike Committee and the Agency was, reported prominent journalist Mary McGrory, a "mismatch all the way." In contrast to the CIA's skills in the arts of propaganda and manipulation, refined over three decades against the Soviet Union and other recalcitrant foreign regimes, the House of Representatives was, she wrote, "a large, slow-witted, thin-skinned defensive composite that wants to stay out of trouble." If the Agency was drawn to cloaks and daggers, the House (McGrory continued) had "a penchant for earmuffs and blinders."[46] Fed up with the public antics of the Pike Committee, a majority of the House soon turned against its own controversial panel of inquiry and disbanded it.

At the White House, the Rockefeller Commission fared far better and displayed a greater willingness to work cooperatively with the CIA in an examination of the CHAOS improprieties. Despite these close relations, which critics feared might lead to a cover-up, the Commission produced a serious, highly critical dissection of the controversial domestic spy program—not at all the whitewash that many observers predicted would be the response of the Ford Administration.[47] The Church Committee, too, attempted to avoid a bitter clash with the intelligence agencies, working with them—forcefully, but without the public theatrics of the Pike Committee—to seek a fair but thorough inquiry. The style of the Rockefeller and Church Committees was one based on diplomacy and compromise, not confrontation, and as a result these two panels had much better success in convincing the CIA and the other spy agencies to turn over requested documents, to appear in public hearings, and otherwise to assist with the probes—although Rockefeller and Church did not always get their way by any means.

The Church Committee pushed back hard when the Ford Administration attempted to slow or undermine its progress, even going to court to gain access to selected intelligence documents. Further, the committee insisted—waving at the White House the threat of subpoenas—on the appearance of certain witnesses for hearings. In the case of CIA Chief of Counterintelligence James Angleton, a subpoena was prepared and approved by the committee; but, just before it was to be delivered, he decided to appear on his own volition. The committee also had to threaten Mafia witnesses with subpoenas to encourage their appearance; the mob eventually cooperated, but two of the witnesses were subsequently murdered in unsolved homicides soon after talking to the senators—a chilling sidebar in the Church Committee inquiry.

The Church Committee stopped short, however, of insisting on sensational public hearings about the FBI's harassment of Dr. Martin Luther King, Jr., or the CIA's assassination plots against foreign leaders. Such hearings may have been useful dramaturgy for attracting public support in favor of intelligence reform; but they would have likely dragged the panel into a political war with the White House and the secret agencies that would have undermined the committee's ultimate objective of finding a workable system of accountability, which is so dependent on institutional comity and cooperation between the executive and legislative branches. As Frederick "Fritz" A. O. Schwarz, Jr., the committee's chief counsel, recalls, "the key to our success [was] that we recognized the legitimacy of elements of secrecy. In contrast is the House Committee, which essentially didn't."[48]

Fortuna, as Machiavelli would put it, also played a part in the success of the Church Committee. A member of the panel, former senator Walter Mondale (D, Minnesota), recollected that

> we were lucky because J. Edgar Hoover was no longer around. The newspapers had already reported a lot of these abuses. And there were many people in the CIA, including its director [Colby], who felt the Agency was out of control and needed the oversight the Congress was providing. And Edward Levi, [President] Ford's Attorney General, wanted to help. His leadership over there [at the Department of Justice] was indispensable to our success.[49]

In addition, the Ford Administration was unlikely to have relished a major battle with the Church Committee over access to documents, given the recent Supreme Court decision against President Nixon in the Pentagon Papers case. Also, Fritz Schwarz remembers, "I think given how [President Ford] took over from Nixon, how he pardoned Nixon, I think he simply couldn't appear to be non-cooperative."[50]

The administration did find ways to counterattack the Church Committee, though, perhaps most conspicuously in December 1975 when a terrorist group killed an erudite officer by the name of Richard S. Welch, the Agency's chief of station in Greece. The administration falsely suggested that the Church

Committee had revealed his identity; in fact, it had not. Moreover, facts on the identity of the COS and where he lived were widely known in Athens. When Welch's body was flown back to Washington, D.C., the White House made a spectacle of the event in an effort to turn public opinion against the investigation—what the committee's chief counsel has referred to as "dancing on the grave of Richard Welch." The strategy seemed to work; public opinion polls supporting the Church Committee inquiry began to dip after this propaganda coup by the Ford Administration.[51]

A Debate on NSA Public Hearings

A good example of the Church Committee's approach to the successful conduct of a sensitive investigation is its internal debate over whether controversial NSA programs aimed at American citizens—Operations SHAMROCK and MINARET—and other aspects of this sigint agency's work could be the subject of a public hearing. After all, "accountability" risked descending into the category of an oxymoron, absent some degree of public transparency. SHAMROCK involved the interception of international cables sent to, and received by, American citizens ever since the Truman Administration; MINARET was a telephone-tapping program that listened to the conversations of U.S. citizens on a "watch list" of individuals suspected of being a danger to the nation. One faction on the committee, led by Chairman Church, argued in favor of open hearings; another, led by Vice Chairman John Tower (R, Texas), argued against.

The debate remains relevant today, because of the fresh controversies over NSA metadata (telephone and social media) collection programs involving Americans, as well as its violation of the FISA requirement for wiretap warrants, and because critics have scolded SSCI and HPSCI for avoiding public hearings into spy activities, on grounds that intelligence is too sensitive to be discussed openly. This Church Committee debate in 1975 also provides a portrait of the dynamics involved in the conduct of intelligence oversight, as lawmakers of different parties and persuasions review espionage programs. Overseers are typically forced to settle on a middle ground between the policy positions of the political left and right.

When Senator Church initially raised the possibility of public hearings on the NSA, which had never been tried before, Secretary of Defense James R. Schlesinger (who had moved to the Pentagon from his post as DCI at the CIA), and General Lew Allen, Jr., the director of the NSA (DIRNSA), appeared in closed session before the Church Committee on October 2, 1975, to oppose the idea of open NSA hearings, preferring to perpetuate the forbidding darkness that engulfs the sigint agency.[52] The NSA's methodology is far too delicate for a public hearing, argued Schlesinger, as he sat before the panel in a swirl of his pipe smoke in a low-ceilinged, bunker-like hearing room near the Capitol Dome. General Allen nodded in agreement. Any open hearing might accidentally disclose information that America's enemies could use to block the NSA's interception of foreign communications—the same argument heard more recently in opposition to public hearings on the NSA's metadata program. Schlesinger did concede that if the committee insisted on a public hearing, the proper approach would be to carefully choreograph the event, which would be based on a limited open review of a written report on NSA activities—carefully sanitized beforehand of classified "sources and methods" by the NSA's attorneys.

When Schlesinger and Allen departed, Church expressed his view that the committee would be able to exercise sufficient discipline in informing the American people about the NSA's activities (including SHAMROCK and MINARET), while at the same time "staying clear of topics that we know from these briefings are too sensitive for public disclosure." Senator Mondale supported Church, but both quickly ran into the buzz saw of John Tower, who expressed concern that the nation's fragile sigint capabilities might be torn asunder by open hearings. He expressed a willingness, though, to give the idea more thought; perhaps, he acknowledged, a limited, sharply focused hearing could work. No votes were taken and the issue remained unresolved. Church chose to interpret this relatively passive response of the committee members as tacit consent to move forward; so, after the meeting, he asked William G. Miller, the committee's staff director, to tentatively schedule an NSA hearing for the Russell Caucus Room in the next few days. The chairman was treading on thin ice.

The Ford Administration reacted fiercely against the idea of a public NSA hearing. Attorney General Levi carried the president's brief to the committee soon after the Schlesinger-Allen appearance. Because Levi was a noted legal scholar and former dean of the University of Chicago's School of Law, his views carried considerable weight. It soon became clear, however, when Church, Mondale, and Gary Hart (D, Colorado) questioned the AG, that this great legal mind had little knowledge of what the NSA actually does. Sidestepping detailed questions about sigint, Levi was content to deliver the administration's core message: public hearings would harm the national security interests of the United States. Period. He had nothing more to say and quickly departed the hearing room before more detailed questions could be asked.

As soon as the AG vanished, Senator Barry Goldwater (R, Arizona), who had missed the first Committee meeting on this subject, objected to any possibility of an open session on the NSA. "We're flirting with real trouble," he advised and called for a formal vote on the question. I was in the room seated behind the chairman and I could see a ripple of anger race through his shoulders, though for the time being he said nothing. Another well-known Republican, Howard Baker of Tennessee—famous for asking, while a member of the Watergate Committee, "What did the president know and when did he know it?"—stood up from his chair and announced that he had to attend another meeting. He left his proxy vote with Tower, saying as he left that he opposed holding a public NSA hearing the next day, as scheduled, but that he might be persuaded to allow one after further committee deliberation.

Speaking in favor of the general idea of public hearings, Senator Charles "Mac" Mathias (R, Maryland, home of the NSA at Ft. Meade) reminded his colleagues that "the committee has an educational responsibility."

Goldwater immediately repeated, "I call for a roll-call vote." The Arizonan seemed to seek felicity in the mission of blocking Democratic initiatives on the committee. A second to his motion came from Tower, who had decided to take a stronger stand against an open hearing. The two senior Republicans, both legends in the Senate, were now united in their opposition.

Mathias's face displayed puzzlement. "I'd like to offer an alternative," he said. "It looks like we've hit a sensitive nerve here. Let's find out what is going on. Let's sit down with the Secretary of Defense, the Attorney General, General Allen, whomever, and find out what the problems are."

Church turned in his chair toward Mathias, normally an ally, and said with exasperation, "We've already covered this ground several times."

A fellow Democrat, Robert Morgan (from North Carolina, and a former AG in that state) weighed in and added to Church's discomfort. "I don't agree with the chair that it is the responsibility of the committee to reveal all wrongdoings," he advised.

Without bothering to conceal his annoyance, the chairman replied, "Let's vote on the Goldwater motion to cancel any public hearings on the National Security Agency." When the votes were tallied by the staff director, the result was 5–4 against Goldwater's motion to bury any NSA open hearing, with Philip Hart and Baker absent. Two Democrats—Gary Hart and Morgan—had abandoned the chairman; two Republicans—Mathias and Richard S. Schweiker (Pennsylvania), both known for their progressive views—supported him. The lineup for pro-hearings (at least at some point) included Church, Mondale, Walter "Dee" Huddleston (D, Kentucky), Mathias, and Schweiker, with Tower, Goldwater, Morgan, and Hart voting for cancellation. Properly, Tower declined to use Baker's proxy, since the Goldwater motion opposed all NSA public hearings and the Tennessean had held out the possibility of a carefully conducted session later in the month. It was a pyrrhic victory for Church. The central fact was that his committee had fractured in half.

The chairman scrambled for a compromise solution: no public hearing on SHAMROCK or MINARET, the most disputatious of the NSA's activities, in part because they involved a complicated and questionable tie in with the private

U.S. communications sector that could embarrass the corporations. Instead, a public hearing could look strictly into the NSA's "watch list"—the kinds of people it had targeted for surveillance. Again, Mathias brought him up short. The Maryland senator had been unwilling to endorse a blanket "no" against NSA public hearings, but he opposed moving forward the very next day with even the constricted agenda of the watch list.

"Let me repeat," Mathias said. "I believe we ought to defer *any* hearings on the NSA until we've had further meetings. I believe I have a motion to this effect."

"What have we been doing but meeting day after day!" Church exploded, his voice trembling with barely muted anger. Then he quickly regained his composure. "I offer a substitute to your motion," the chairman continued, glancing at Mathias, a personal friend of his, "that we defer SHAMROCK [and, by implication, MINARET] and hold hearings on the watch list."

When the roll was called, Mondale, Huddleston, and Schweiker stayed in the Church camp, while Tower, Goldwater, Baker (Tower exercised his proxy for Baker this time), Morgan, and Hart joined Mathias in opposition. The chairman had lost his committee and was visibly shaken. The defection of fellow Democrats Gary Hart and Morgan was an especially hurtful and unexpected blow. Church left the room with his head down. Adding insult to injury, President Ford telephoned him later in the day to emphasize the inadvisability of open hearings on the sigint agency.

Only momentarily in doubt, in a couple of days the chairman shook off these concerns and, like a beleaguered Odysseus struggling to make his way home, he tried once again to sell his colleagues on the idea of at least some kind of NSA public hearing. He reminded the committee members that both Mathias and Baker had requested further deliberation on the possibilities of a hearing. As a next step, Church asked Mathias and Huddleston to consult with the White House on the matter, then report back. They did the next day, but the White House merely repeated to the senators what the president had already said to Church: an NSA hearing was a no-go. During this back-and-forth debate within the committee, newspapers published op-eds about spying on American citizens by the CIA and possibly other intelligence agencies, and about a House subcommittee led by Bella Abzug—a fearless Democratic congresswoman from New York—which had been delving into Operation SHAMROCK, in public hearings no less. Also, Church Committee staffers had completed their painstaking research into SHAMROCK, MINARET, and the NSA watch list; they were now in anguish, as time ticked by and their pleas for a public hearing on their hard-gained findings fell into limbo.

In a last-ditch effort, the chairman decided to raise the question of a hearing one last time, even though no indication of compromise had emerged from the White House or the NSA. "I don't see why we can't have an open session tomorrow morning," Church pleaded on October 28. Mondale, who had become a reliable ally of Church (at least on this topic), forcefully presented the staff's argument that a public hearing would be feasible, as long as senators stayed away from delicate sigint tradecraft. He diplomatically avoided pointing out that the technology of the NSA's operations was clearly beyond the knowledge of law-makers anyway. Although Tower and Goldwater were absent, a majority of the senators (with a "no" proxy from Goldwater) continued to oppose a hearing on SHAMROCK or MINARET. Each of these programs was deemed too sensitive, the senators maintained, adopting the NSA's line—despite expert views of their own staff to the contrary. The naysayers were finally willing, though, to allow a session on the watch list. Frustrated but prepared to accept half a loaf rather than no loaf at all, Church retreated from SHAMROCK and MINARET. He directed the staff to go forward with a watch-list hearing.

The hearing, held in a packed Russell Caucus Room (today renamed the Edward Kennedy Caucus Room, after the late, long-serving senator from Massachusetts and brother of President Kennedy), went well—however lim-ited. It demonstrated, without jeopardizing sensitive sigint modus operandi, that open hearings could indeed be held to explain to the American people why the NSA is important; how its watch list had strayed from the agency's obligation to honor the privacy of law-abiding citizens; and what might be done to ensure that its good work continued without further violations. As Tower and Goldwater sat scowling at the hearing table, Church began by explaining how "the com-mittee had worked diligently with the agency to draw legitimate boundaries for the public discussion that will preserve the technical secrets of NSA and also allow a thorough airing of agency practices affecting citizens." He told the audi-ence about how the NSA had developed a watch list containing more than 1,500 American names, and it had distributed sigint information extracted from its wiretaps to the CIA, the FBI, and other intelligence agencies. Some of the tar-geted individuals might have qualified as legitimate national security concerns, he said, but their constitutional rights were inadequately taken into account.[53] Tower spoke next, declaring that he had opposed any kind of public hearing on the NSA, because its technology included "the most fragile weapons in our arse-nal." Staring out at the news reporters gathered in the front row, the vice chair-man maintained that "there comes a point when the people's right to know must of necessity be subordinated to the people's right to be secure"—a fundamental dichotomy that resides at the center of intelligence accountability and the bal-ancing act between liberty and security.

Directly opposite Church and Tower sat the NSA witnesses for the hear-ing: General Lew Allen and his deputy, Bensen Buffham, the agency's top leaders. Reading from a prepared statement, Allen testified that between 1966 and 1973 the NSA had intercepted the telephone messages of 1,680 citizens and groups (on the MINARET watch list), all without warrants or the explicit approval of the president or the AG. He stressed that the agency had avoided surveillances against strictly domestic communications; at least one "terminal" had to be on foreign soil. The NSA had carried out this sigint collection on behalf of the CIA, the FBI, the Secret Service, the DIA, Army Intelligence, and the old Bureau of Narcotics and Dangerous Drugs (now the DEA). In one instance, a sigint intercept had helped the FBI halt a major terrorist plot in an American city, the director noted, carefully avoiding specifics but underscoring the value of the watch list. The interceptions had provided the necessary information, General Allen added, to seize many illegal drug shipments into the United States.

During the Q and A, Mondale examined the less shiny side of the coin. He observed that one of the NSA intercepts was simply an invitation from a "peaceful" antiwar activist to a foreign singer, requesting a financial contribution to the anti–Vietnam War movement. The effect of that kind of spying, the senator said, was to "discourage political dissent in this country." When the questioning had come to an end, Church tossed a lightning bolt. Once again, only this time in a public forum, the chairman raised the matter of holding a similar public hearing on another key NSA "program" that the committee had been reviewing in closed session. (The chairman never used the term SHAMROCK, which remained classified at the time.) He explained how such a hearing would not violate vulnerable technology, because the program no longer existed and new technologies had been developed. As to whether the private U.S. companies that had cooperated in the program might be embarrassed by an outing of their involvement, Church said the companies should have been hesitant in the first place to comply with government requests until it was clear they were lawful and ethical.

Tower was having none of it. "President Truman decided that this matter should be kept secret," he said, revealing how far back in time the NSA had been conducting SHAMROCK and MINARET surveillance. Tower added, "President Ford has personally and specifically requested of the committee that it be kept secret." Morgan agreed with the vice chairman, expressing how he was "awfully reluctant to go against the word of the president of the United States." Mondale countered that "we are no longer a coequal branch of government" if the Senate permitted the White House to dictate what it could do and not do. As in earlier closed sessions, the committee had reached a stalemate, bogged down over parliamentary questions about the right of Senate committees to conduct sensitive public hearings. Like the stone of Sisyphus, SHAMROCK rolled back down the hill or, in this case, the Hill.

This episode offers a portrait of how difficult intelligence oversight can be when lawmakers from different parties and contending philosophies clash over Madison's separation-of-powers doctrine. Such is the nature of democracy, which is especially complex in a nation as large as the United States (with more than 300 million citizens from places as different as Vermont is to Arizona). At least, though, the Church Committee engaged in a debate about the subject of NSA hearings in public; while the chairman and other strong advocates of intelligence accountability had to make compromises and even abandon some objectives, controversial spying operations were at least addressed—in closed session most of the time, but even occasionally in open hearings (as with the NSA watch list). This had rarely been the case before 1975. The debate over NSA public hearings demonstrates, further, that with careful preparation so as not to reveal classified information, oversight committees can conduct open sessions in their efforts to inform the American people—in broad outline at least—about how their secret agencies perform. This can be a boon to the agencies, since their staggeringly high budgets could stand some public justification.

The Church Committee Findings

Each of the three investigations in 1975 produced impressively detailed and thoughtful reports, including that of the Pike Committee—regardless of all its histrionics. The inquiries confirmed that the *Times* had been correct about widespread CIA surveillance within the United States, as well as the Agency's pursuit of questionable covert action in Chile. The investigators soon realized, however, that the media accounts had only scratched the surface of wrongdoing by the intelligence community. After 126 full committee meetings, 40 subcommittee hearings, 800 witness interviews, and the scouring of 110,000 documents, the Church Committee discovered that the CIA had

- opened the mail to and from selected American citizens, which generated 1.5 million names stored in the Agency's computer banks (CHAOS), including such "subversives" as John Steinbeck, Leonard Bernstein, Arthur Burns, and even Richard Nixon and Frank Church;
- engaged in drug experiments against unsuspecting subjects, two of whom died from side effects;
- manipulated elections around the world and even in democratic regimes like Chile, as the *Times* had reported (although without examining the worldwide extent of such operations, as the Church Committee did);
- infiltrated religious, media, and academic organizations inside the United States; and,
- plotted assassination attempts against foreign leaders, but without succeeding in killing anyone on the target list.[54]

Further, Church Committee investigators found that several other intelligence agencies had joined with the CIA, or acted independently, in a secret assault on America's traditions and laws related to privacy and civil liberties. Army intelligence units had compiled dossiers on 100,000 U.S. citizens during the Vietnam War; the vast computer facilities of the NSA had pursued Operations SHAMROCK and MINARET, intercepting the communications of American citizens; and the IRS had allowed tax information to be misused by intelligence agencies for political purposes.

Among the most chilling of the Church Committee discoveries was found in the secret vaults of the FBI. The Bureau had created files on more than one million Americans and carried out more than 500,000 investigations of "subversives" from 1960 to 1974, without a single court conviction.[55] Among its dubious operations was a campaign to incite violence among African-Americans, as a way of setting back the civil rights movement in the 1960s. As the Church Committee learned, a Bureau office in California boasted in a memorandum back to FBI Headquarters about "shootings, beatings, and a high degree of unrest continu[ing] to prevail in the ghetto area of southeast San Diego. Although no specific [FBI] counterintelligence action can be credited with contributing to this overall situation, it is felt that a substantial amount of the unrest is directly attributable to this program."[56]

The efforts to drive African-Americans to one another's throats was just one of many operations that fell into a broad category known inside Bureau headquarters as the Counterintelligence Program, or COINTELPRO, a set of operations targeting American citizens involved in civil rights or antiwar activities and carried out in the 1960s and early 1970s. As Senator Mondale recalls, "No meeting was too small, no group too insignificant" to escape the FBI's attention.[57] Motivated by racism when it came to civil rights activists and a misplaced sense of patriotism in the case of the antiwar protesters, Bureau Director J. Edgar Hoover had undertaken unilateral action in these cases—without authority from the White House, Congress, or the Department of Justice, although clearly President Nixon set a tone for targeting antiwar students by referring to them publicly as "bums."[58]

In his disruptive COINTELPRO operations, Hoover also went after the Ku Klux Klan—any group that failed to fit into his image of how Americans should be: conformists confined to a narrow, moderate spectrum of political views. The United States had to appear like a Norman Rockwell *Saturday Evening Post* cover—or else. The FBI director and several of his special agents had become a law unto themselves, with minimal accountability to anyone outside Hoover's spacious office. In discussions about government surveillance, my students often say to me, "I don't care about that; I don't have anything to hide." As COINTELPRO should remind everyone, an individual's political orientations and other beliefs might one day be used against them by opponents with secret government power. The chilling effect alone of a Big Brother watching our every move can be profound in itself; when the government comes after dissident citizens, who are only exercising their lawful First Amendment rights to speak out, the results can be catastrophic for the targeted individuals and for democracy.

From 1956 to 1971, the Bureau carried out smear campaigns against thousands of groups and individuals, simply because they had expressed opposition to the war in Indochina or joined the civil rights movement.[59] One of the victims whom I met with personally during the investigation was Professor Anatol Rapoport, a brilliant social scientist and a concert pianist at an early age. He was the author of an influential book on game theory, entitled *Fights, Games and Debates*.[60] His "crime" while at the University of Michigan had been to speak out against the war in Vietnam. This made him a Communist, in the eyes of J. Edgar Hoover, especially in light of the fact that Rapoport had been born in Russia—although he left with his parents while still a baby, when his Jewish family fled to the United States to escape religious persecution. A flood of anonymous letters to the university's president, the governor of Michigan, and other officials complained about Rapoport's alleged ties to the Soviet Union. The harassment finally drove him to leave Ann Arbor for the University of Toronto, where he was warmly welcomed as he continued his illustrious academic career. All of the anti-Rapoport letters, the Church Committee learned, had been written anonymously by FBI agents under Hoover's orders. In 1975, Church Committee staffers traveled across the country to meet with some of the COINTELPRO victims. We showed them their FBI files, which the Bureau had declassified at the committee's request. By now an elderly man with snowy white hair, Rapoport wept as I went through his file in the living room of his modest apartment in Toronto. He had never dreamed the government of the United States had been behind the smear campaign that forced him to leave the University of Michigan.

Ecumenical in its distrust of anyone who failed to fit tidily into Hoover's vision of a patriotic American citizen, the Bureau also went after groups on the extreme right.[61] Target number one for Hoover, though, was any and all civil rights activists. Hundreds of anonymous letters went out to members, black and white, involved in the movement, attempting to sow dissension among their families and friends. Hoover had one major goal in particular: to ruin the reputation and the life of Martin Luther King, Jr., the famed civil rights leader. King became the victim of a multitude of FBI secret operations, including a blackmail attempt in 1964 that sought to push him toward suicide on the eve of his acceptance of a Nobel Peace Prize.[62]

One of the most distinguished members of the Church Committee was Phillip A. Hart (D, Michigan), a soft-spoken, bearded (uncommon for senators), and unassuming man, said to be "the gentlest and kindest" member of the upper chamber of Congress and widely thought of as its "conscience."[63] (The newest of the three Senate office buildings, completed in 1982, is named after him.)

Hart was terminally ill with cancer during the committee's hearings, but he managed to come to a public session on the FBI's COINTELPRO activities. As he spoke barely above a whisper, the cavernous Russell Caucus Room—filled with reporters, congressional staffers, tourists, and more spies than the Duc Hotel in Saigon during the Vietnam War—fell silent. He related a story about how his family of political activists had complained at the dinner table, during the time of antiwar marches in Michigan, that the FBI was attempting to discredit the protesters. He had waved aside their arguments, attributing them to the frustrations that accompany dissent. Then, in a broken and emotional voice, he said that his family had been correct all along and he had been wrong in defending the Bureau.

"I've been told for years by, among others, members of my own family that this is what the Bureau has been doing all this time," Hart recalled during the hearing. "As a result of my superior wisdom in high office, I assured them that they were on pot; it just wasn't true. [The FBI] just wouldn't do it." Only a remote burial ground at midnight could have matched the stillness of the Caucus Room as the senator summarized the staff's findings about COINTELPRO. "What you have described is a series of illegal actions intended to deny certain citizens their First Amendment rights—just like my children said," Hart concluded. It was the most poignant moment in the life of the Church Committee. Many in the audience, including some hardened staffers on the committee, were reaching for handkerchiefs to dry their eyes.

The testimony of witnesses in hearings, open and closed, held by the committee revealed an IC that had drifted far away from its original mandate to protect the American people against foreign and domestic threats. Here is one exchange between Senator Mondale and chief counsel Schwarz in a public hearing about the FBI's attacks against Dr. King:

MONDALE: [No one] showed up a single suggestion that Martin Luther King had committed or was about to commit a crime. Is that correct?
SCHWARZ: That is correct. . . .
MONDALE: Was he ever charged with fomenting violence? Did he ever participate in violence? Was it ever alleged that he was about to be violent?
SCHWARZ: That was the very opposite of his philosophy, Senator.[64]

As Schwarz has noted in a commentary on the experiences of the Church Committee, a suspected violation of the law is "the only legitimate ground to investigate Americans."[65] The intelligence agencies had slipped far below that standard. One of the witnesses before the committee was Tom Charles Huston, the youthful architect of a master spy plan drafted in 1970 and bearing his name. The Huston Plan was endorsed by the leaders of the CIA (Helms), the

FBI (Hoover), the NSA (Admiral Noel Gayler), and the DIA (Army General Donald Bennett). Among the foremost targets of the plan were campus protesters who opposed the war in Vietnam. In public hearings, a repentant Huston conceded that this approach, which he had devised at President Nixon's request, had brought with it the potential for the intelligence agencies to "move from the kid with a bomb to the kid with a picket sign, and from the kid with the picket sign to the kid with the bumper sticker of the opposing candidate. And you just keep going down the line."[66]

In another exchange with a witness during the Church Committee's sole public hearing on the NSA, this time with Buffham, the agency's deputy director, Senator Mondale again probed the legal aspects of the sigint agency's involvement in domestic spying:

MONDALE: Were you concerned about its legality?
BUFFHAM: Legality?
MONDALE: Whether it was legal?
BUFFHAM: In what sense? Whether that would have been a legal thing to do?
MONDALE: Yes.
BUFFHAM: That particular aspect didn't enter into the discussion.
MONDALE: I was asking you if you were concerned about whether that would be legal and proper.
BUFFHAM: We didn't consider it at the time, no.[67]

Nor did the FBI give much thought to the law. William Sullivan, the Bureau's deputy director during the COINTELPRO operations, told the Church Committee, "No holds were barred. We have used [similar] techniques against Soviet agents. [The same methods were] brought home against any organization against which we were targeted. We did not differentiate. This is a rough, tough business."[68] Sullivan testified further that he had never heard a discussion about the legality or constitutionality of any aspect of COINTELPRO, or any of the other FBI internal security programs. "We were just naturally pragmatic," he explained. He offered an excuse for his conduct that was reminiscent of Hannah Arendt's remarks on the banality of evil.[69] "I was so inured and accustomed to any damn thing I was told to do," Sullivan said. "I just carried it out and kept my resentment to myself. I was married and trying to buy a house with a big mortgage and raise a family."[70]

In a critique of the Church Committee, a prominent legal scholar Peter M. Shane concluded that "its investigation created a historical record that Americans could rely on as a basis for democratic debate about national security and intelligence gathering."[71] Looking at this record, Henry Steele Commager astutely observed further that "perhaps the most threatening of all the evidence that [emerged] from the findings of the Church Committee" was the indifference of the intelligence agencies to constitutional restraint.[72] As a result of the *Times* reporting and the Church, Pike, and Rockefeller investigations, Congress set out to change this attitude by adopting restrictive laws and regulations, and, above all, a new philosophy of more meaningful involvement by lawmakers in the supervision of the secret agencies, in place of the earlier attitude of benign neglect.

"If there is one lesson that our Committee felt above all must be learned from our study of the abuses which have been reported," said Senator Mondale as the Church panel wrapped up its inquiry, "it has been the crucial necessity of establishing a system of congressional oversight."[73] The committee had many recommendations that were subsequently adopted, including a ten-year term limit on the tenure of the FBI director (no more Hoover-like dynasties) and the creation of a warrant procedure for national security wiretaps (the Foreign Intelligence Surveillance Act, enacted in 1978). Its most important reform proposal, though, was the creation of SSCI and HPSCI—permanent committees on Capitol Hill devoted to intelligence accountability.

The Church Committee's findings pointed to an obvious conclusion: Madison, Jefferson, Lord Acton, Brandeis, and all the other sage observers over the years who had warned about the corrosive effects of unchecked power were correct—perhaps doubly so when it came to the risks associated with secret power. A new experiment in the evolution of American democracy was about to begin, one that had never been attempted in the history of the United States or any other society, namely, the dissemination of democratic principles into the stygian blackness of the nation's spy agencies. "We were able to redefine what was right and what was wrong in the light of contemporary circumstances," recalls the committee's staff director, Bill Miller, adding, "I think we preserved [the] balances of the branches set forth in the Constitution."

Congress Adopts New Intelligence Safeguards

A central finding reached by the Church Committee was that the law works. Each of the security objectives sought by the intelligence agencies during the Cold War could have been achieved without descending into the hellish pit of COINTELPRO and the other overzealous operations uncovered by the committee. The United States could fight a totalitarian state, the Soviet Union, without becoming one itself. Liberty and security had to be kept in balance, if America were to stay true to its core values and traditions.

Forty years later, in 2015, as Congress pondered (via the USA FREEDOM Act) a cutback in the NSA metadata program that Edward Snowden had revealed, a modern-day overseer on the House Judiciary Committee, Representative Jason Chaffetz (R, Utah), posed the same seminal question faced by the Church Committee: "How much liberty are we going to give up for security?"[74] In 1975, and again in 2015 with the FREEDOM Act, lawmakers decided the nation had gone too far in the security direction and they began to reset the compass in the direction of protecting the liberties of American citizens. The NSA could continue to have considerable leeway for its sigint operations in the struggle against global terrorism; the agency, though, would have to operate under new rules. The role of the FISA Court in providing warrants before surveillance could take place would have to be honored. In almost every instance, so would the privacy of individuals at home and abroad who were customers of the U.S. telecommunications companies; and if an exception were sought in dire terrorist circumstances, a warrant would still be required, along with reporting to SSCI and HPSCI.

When Iran took U.S. diplomats hostage in Tehran during the Carter Administration, former secretary of state Dean Rusk thought it was fortunate the United States did not, in return, seize Iranian diplomats in Washington. "We are not that kind of country or that kind of people," he reflected.[75] A similar point of view guided a majority on the Church Committee in the midst of the Cold War: a conviction that the United States was different from the Soviet Union. Our nation is also different, today, from ISIS and Al Qaeda. The nation was, and remains (despite global grumblings about the Trump Administration), the world's premier democracy, and that standing has helped win international support for America.[76] Most members of the Church Committee felt that when this nation ignored its fundamental democratic principles, it risked losing that support—and its identity. Similarly, Senator J. William Fulbright of Arkansas, a leader of a congressional resurgence in foreign policy during the mid-1960s, believed deeply that America's democracy is "more likely to be destroyed by the perversion or the abandonment of its true moral principles than by armed attack from Russia."[77]

The inquiries in 1975 stressed the importance of applying traditional Madisonian checks to the hidden side of government, not just to the more open agencies and departments. The CIA obviously has a different mission than the Department of Agriculture and it operates in a nasty global setting; but, in their adherence to basic constitutional principles, both government organizations should be subject to meaningful and ongoing reviews of their programs, not just by executive branch supervisors but by Congress and the courts as well. The venerable maxim of checks and balances that undergirds the spending, subpoena, and investigative powers of the Congress found in Article I of the Constitution provides America's "parliament" with a uniquely strong claim to oversight authority, even within the hidden recesses of the intelligence agencies.[78] The question in the air as the Church Committee wound down its investigation in 1976 was whether its reforms would end in a cloud of dashed hopes or lead to better checks and balances, even within the opaque world of spies.

Today, as a result chiefly of the Church Committee's push for permanent intelligence oversight committees, the nation's espionage institutions must now take into account the likely reactions to their programs by members of SSCI and HPSCI, the bartizans for intelligence accountability on the Hill.[79] A key question haunting the effort to bring some semblance of democracy into the nebulous province of spying was whether the lawmakers and staffs of these committees would be able to keep the nation's secrets as they carried out their oversight responsibilities. From their beginnings, SSCI and HPSCI have worked closely with CIA and FBI security and counterintelligence personnel to ensure the sanctity of classified documents held in the vaults of the oversight committees, and that the closed hearings of these panels were protected against eavesdropping by foreign intelligence services. As the years passed, it became clear, both committees could be counted on to preserve the nation's secrets—although with the right, as well, to debate the merits of these secrets and pursue their declassification (if appropriate) through proper channels. (The question of under what circumstances SSCI or HPSCI are able to declassify executive branch documents is a tangled but important topic, addressed later in this book.)

The vote was 72–22 in favor of creating SSCI and, a year later (a gap during which the House continued to reel from the Pike Committee dust-up), the vote was 227–171 in favor of HPSCI. On the Senate side, SSCI had jurisdiction over the National Intelligence Program, or NIP (see chapter 1); but it relinquished to the Armed Services Committee authority for "tactical foreign military intelligence activities"—today's Military Intelligence Program, or MIP. In contrast, HPSCI assumed authority over both strategic (NIP) and tactical (MIP) intelligence programs for purposes of oversight and budget authorization. (Such odd differences between the Senate and the House in their structuring of intelligence oversight unnecessarily complicates life for IC officers trying to work with the Congress). Further, both committees arranged to have some "cross-over" (joint) memberships with the Armed Services, Appropriations, Foreign Relations, and Judiciary Committees, as a means for encouraging a degree of intelligence coordination and shared understanding among the premier national security panels in Congress. Thus, for example, SSCI would have two senators who also sat on the Armed Services Committee, two on Appropriations, and the like—in all, eight SSCI members would serve on related standing committees.

Further, SSCI members would serve a maximum of eight years and HPSCI members for six years (the two chambers make their own rules, which are sometimes different from one another). Such term limits were unique for congressional committees and designed to prevent SSCI and HPSCI members from becoming too cozy with the intelligence agencies and "co-opted"—a political science term to describe when lawmakers sell out to the executive branch by assuming a posture of unalloyed deference. In 2004, SSCI decided to abandon the term-limit provision, in favor of allowing members to accrue greater intelligence experience by remaining longer on the committee, as well as to motivate greater commitment to oversight among members who could now aspire to stay on the committee and perhaps become its chair.[80] The House kept its ceiling in place, but it waived this rule for HPSCI chairs and ranking members.

Jurisdictionally disputes would come to trouble SSCI and its House counterpart. Indeed, every major commentary of intelligence reform in recent years usually begins by calling for a clarification of the lines of oversight authority for intelligence among the committees of Intelligence, Appropriations, Armed Services, Foreign Relations (Foreign Affairs, in the House), Homeland Security, and Judiciary—a morass of reporting obligations faced by the spy agencies. SSCI and HPSCI have sole formal authority only over the CIA and the ODNI, but the Intelligence Committees must jockey with the other congressional panels when it comes to accountability for the rest of the IC. Sometimes important topics slip through the jurisdictional cracks, as in the late 1990s when the FBI's counterterrorism program escaped attention from SSCI and HPSCI, which thought the Judiciary Committees were handling this review—and vice versa![81] As argued later (chapter 12), few reforms related to accountability are as pressing as the need to clarify and simplify these zones of oversight authority, especially when it comes to the relationships among the Intelligence, Armed Services, and Appropriations Committees.

During the debate on the creation of SSCI, reformers were forced to adopt a compromise that designated the proposed intelligence oversight committee as "B" panels, secondary in importance to the well-established "A"-level standing committees (like Armed Services). As a result, future SSCI members could be expected to devote most of their time to "A" committee assignments, where members were not required to rotate off and, therefore, had an opportunity to rise to the panel's chairmanship. This "inferior" status for intelligence oversight, if one chose to see it that way, was the Senate's *quid* for the *pro quo* of approving the unusual procedure of membership rotation off SSCI. When the committee removed this tenure ceiling in 2004, it also discarded the "B" designation, thereby elevating the committee's status in the Senate. HPSCI has yet to embrace these useful reforms.

The purpose of SSCI and HPSCI was to prevent a further erosion of American liberties at the hands of the secret agencies, as spelled out in the CIA's Family Jewels and the Church Committee findings. "We can't slide back into the days of J. Edgar Hoover" was the Church Committee's neon-light message, stressed by a senior staff expert on the panel, with its COINTELPRO findings printed indelibly in his mind.[82]

The CIA as Rogue Elephant

Despite Professor Light's conclusion that the Church Committee serves as a model of firefighting accountability, some observers have viewed its work quite negatively.[83] A few have gone so far as to suggest that the committee undermined America's intelligence capabilities, leaving the nation vulnerable to the attacks that occurred on 9/11.[84] William Colby, DCI during the Year of Intelligence, helped to set the record straight. In his words, the committee provided a "comprehensive and serious review of the history and present status of American intelligence."[85] Further, an internal Agency summary of the committee's effects on intelligence noted that the Church Committee had found that "the CIA and other intelligence agencies had made important contributions to the nation's security and had generally performed their missions with dedication and distinction."[86] Senator Church himself, in his most important speech given on the floor of the Senate during the investigation, praised the work of the CIA and its companion services.[87] What the senator and a bipartisan majority of his committee objected to were the activities of the spy agencies that strayed outside the boundaries of the law, as with CHAOS, SHAMROCK, MINARET, COINTELPRO, and other programs. That had to end.

In postmortem evaluations of the Church Committee, the CIA (in internal documents and in public comments by its leaders) pointed out that Senator Church's colleagues rejected his observation that the Agency had been out of control before 1975. Early in the committee's life, Church had speculated on a national television news show that the CIA may have become "a rogue elephant." It was a line that had come to him from McGeorge Bundy, the former Harvard University dean and national security adviser during the Kennedy Administration. Over breakfast the morning before the television show, the two men discussed in general terms the course of the Senate investigation. Church complained to Bundy about the Huston spy plan and how the CIA had continued to engage in domestic espionage, even after President Nixon rescinded the plan a few months after his initial approval.[88] Church was dismayed, too, by his committee's early discovery of shellfish toxins and other highly poisonous substances still stored at the Agency and in military facilities in Maryland, even though these substances had been banned by an international treaty and supposedly destroyed during the Nixon years. Over breakfast, Bundy expressed his view that the CIA had come to resemble "a rogue elephant on a rampage." When Senator Church went on television, he repeated this characterization, perhaps having in mind as well that the committee had just learned about the Agency's MK-ULTRA program, in which the CIA had used the mind-bending drug LSD against one of its own scientists as an experiment without his knowledge. The scientist committed suicide soon afterward by leaping out the window of a hotel room in New York City.[89]

In coming up with the "rogue elephant" phrase, Bundy also had some historical evidence to draw upon from his service in the White House during the Kennedy years. For example, the CIA on its own volition asked for help from U.S. mobsters in its efforts to murder Fidel Castro. When Attorney General Robert Kennedy, the president's brother, found out about the Mafia connection (thanks to J. Edgar Hoover, who had a low regard for the CIA), he demanded that these ties be severed. The Agency officer in charge, William Harvey of the DO, was supposed to have terminated the relationship with the mob, but in fact the underworld continued to carry out the Agency's bidding—just under a different CIA officer in charge.

Moreover, Harvey remained active in Operation MONGOOSE, Robert Kennedy's CIA-led initiative to eliminate Castro, although this time without mob involvement. Harvey sent several Agency teams onto the island for sabotage and other secret efforts meant to disrupt the Castro regime—all without the knowledge of the White House point man for these endeavors, Edward Lansdale. These secret teams remained at work in Cuba even during the middle of the missile crisis in October 1962, when Robert Kennedy had explicitly ordered the CIA to stand down from further MONGOOSE operations during this tense period. One objective of these teams was to blow up Russian ships in Cuban ports. Harvey knew these sabotage activities were under way during the crisis, but he did nothing to stop the teams. Further, some evidence indicates that Harvey had an assassination team in Cuba intent on eliminating Castro at the same time the United States was involved in anxious negotiations with the Soviets over removal of their missiles from the island.[90]

As well, looking at the CIA's operations against Lumumba in the Congo, one of the Agency's assets—appropriately codenamed WI/ROGUE—was described by internal documents found by the Church Committee as "without pangs of conscience." This asset could "rationalize all actions" and was "rather an unguided missile . . . the kind of man that could get you in trouble before you knew you were in trouble."[91] No wonder Bundy had doubts about how well the CIA was supervised. One of the top staff attorneys on the Church Committee has underscored a central concern of investigators in 1975: "to what extent should the CIA or other agencies be permitted to make their own interpolations of what they should be doing in the interest of the president, based on some vague statements?"[92]

Despite these fragments of evidence about "roguish" Agency behavior, Church clearly had spoken prematurely in public on the news show in 1975, before his committee had a chance to dig deeply into its research on intelligence operations. The chairman's colleagues reprimanded him at the next committee meeting, and he would be hounded by the statement thereafter. He never again spoke of the CIA as a rogue elephant, but he did stick to his view that the Agency had lacked proper supervision at times. Many years later, in 2014, columnist David Ignatius wrote that the SSCI's Torture Report "revives the notion of the CIA as a 'rogue elephant' that was propounded by Frank Church's committee in the 1970s but has been rebutted by many historians."[93] In this column, Ignatius unfairly shifted an off-the-cuff, Sunday morning news show remark by Senator Church onto the shoulders of the entire Church Committee and its final report. Closer to the mark is the conclusion Ignatius presents later in his op-ed, which embraced a position well documented by the Church Committee's reports. "The real story of intelligence abuses in the 1950s and '60s," Ignatius continued, "is that they were ordered by presidents or their henchmen, who didn't want to know the dirty details." Despite the truth of this observation, one should not dismiss the fact (as the CIA likes to do) that significant instances of "roguishness" have occurred within the Agency and other organizations in the IC—most obviously during the Iran-contra scandal of the 1980s and in the post 9/11 period, as examined in the next two chapters.[94]

My study of the Church Committee published in 1986 ended with an expression of concern that intelligence accountability "may well be too demanding, as well as devoid of an outside constituency, to stir [lawmakers] into a struggle against the strong forces in the executive—and within Congress itself—that resist change."[95] The Iran-contra affair confirmed the fragility of the system of accountability put in place by Congress during the Year of Intelligence. As with all statutes (as against homicide, for instance), the legal framework for oversight remained vulnerable to individuals and institutions who elect to flout the rule of law.

When SSCI and HPSCI came into existence, the nation's experiment with intelligence accountability began—trying to bring the rule of law into the Deep State. The experiment would suffer significant setbacks that underscored the difficulty of the task and the ongoing resistance from brawny opponents; nevertheless, a significant change had taken place. "Steadily, during and after 1975, CIA would move from its exclusive relationship with the President," writes former DCI Robert M. Gates, "to a position roughly equi-distant between the Congress and the President—responsible and accountable to both, unwilling to act at presidential request without clearance from Congress."[96] The next chapter chronicles the rough patches of resistance that SSCI and HPSCI would soon encounter in their pursuit of this objective.

The Experiment in Rigorous Intelligence Accountability Begins

The Era of Uneasy Partnership, 1976–1986

The Church Committee and the other investigations of 1975 produced a sea change in perspectives within the United States about the need for closer supervision of the nation's intelligence agencies. Before, accountability had been thin; members of Congress were content to let the secret side of government go its own way for the most part during the Cold War, guided by broad directives from the White House and the NSC, with only occasional spurts of interest by Congress. Lawmakers decided to let the "honorable men" of the CIA and the other spy agencies determine what operations to conduct and when.[1] Intelligence would be an exception to the normal rules of American government and the canons of accountability; clandestine operations were simply too delicate and dependent on secrecy for government as usual. Espionage operations simply would not fit, without endangering the nation, into the procrustean bed of Madisonian safeguards. In the domain of national security activities, such "auxiliary precautions" were an indulgence prohibited by the perils of the Cold War.

Further, lawmakers were too busy with other activities—not least, fundraising for their next election campaign—to worry much about covert actions and other stealthy activities aimed at the Soviet Union and other Communist regimes. Besides, the less members of Congress knew about spy operations, the easier it would be for them to dodge culpability if things went wrong, as with the Bay of Pigs invasion in 1961. Not just presidential, but congressional plausible deniability could be a handy thing.

Operations CHAOS and COINTELPRO, however, brought an end to this philosophy of blind trust. Now the American public and their representatives began to understand that constitutional protections were required even within— perhaps especially within—the rabbit hole of the secret agencies. Yet a change in attitudes among lawmakers, though important, was not enough. Genuine accountability required new guidelines to serve as buoys for the secret services, marking more clearly for intelligence managers the precise lines of probity. Even in the small interstice of time between the *New York Times* reporting on CHAOS in 1974 and the creation of the Church Committee in 1975, these new rules had begun to take shape with passage of the Hughes-Ryan Act. They would continue to expand over the next forty years, with debate on their merits still a lively topic today—thanks to the controversy generated by the NSA metadata controversy, along with the notoriety of the CIA "enhanced interrogation" practices, its use of extraordinary renditions, and other controversial spy programs.

How well the new oversight laws and less formal guidelines have been enforced by members of Congress since 1975 provides an index of the commitment on Capitol Hill to intelligence accountability. The results have been mixed, stretching from a passivity that harkens back to the days of benign neglect before the Church Committee, to occasional subsequent bursts of formal oversight investigations (firefighting) rarely seen in the days preceding the Year of Intelligence. Before these patterns can be understood and evaluated, however, one must first know something about the new rules and the demands they have placed on both the intelligence agencies and their overseers.

New Oversight Rules for Intelligence

The Era of Trust that ended in 1974 rested on a foundation of good faith by overseers toward the intelligence community, a "don't ask, don't tell" mentality shattered by the exposure of the "Family Jewels" and the follow-on findings of the Church, Pike, and Rockefeller inquiries. Beginning with passage of the Hughes-Ryan Act in December 1974 and carrying on through the Iran-contra exposé in 1987 and the 9/11 terrorist attacks in 2001, members of Congress, presidents, and leaders of the IC have attempted to fashion a workable relationship between effective espionage and democratic openness—between security and liberty. With the establishment of the standing intelligence oversight committees, SSCI and HPSCI, lawmakers now had the authority and the tools to carry out all the police patrolling they desired. The result, beginning in the wake of the Church Committee's report issued in 1976, was increased attention inside the legislative branch to intelligence activities. The difference in the level of accountability for spies before and after the Church Committee was dramatic.

Each step of the way toward the establishment of the new forms of intelligence oversight was riven by debate, intense negotiations, and sometimes bitter wrangles in Washington, D.C. The efforts to create SSCI and HPSCI, the most important institutional changes to emerge from the Church Committee investigation, had to overcome formidable opposition from the IC, as well as resistance from the congressional Armed Services Committees, which objected to their loss of jurisdiction over authorizations for intelligence programs and spy machines related to military matters. Not to mention powerful individual lawmakers allied with the spy agencies—the inheritors of the Richard B. Russell mantle of CIA advocacy on the Hill.

HPSCI Grapples with the New Oversight

Once up and running, members of SSCI and HPSCI found they often had to struggle in their attempts to acquire from the spy agencies timely and full reporting on intelligence activities, even with respect to covert actions (as expressly required by the Hughes-Ryan statute). Sometimes the most intense tug-of-wars occurred not between the committees and the CIA, but within the committees themselves—as had frequently been the case with the Church and Pike Committees. An example came early, during a meeting of HPSCI in 1978 when members gathered for their first briefing on a covert action finding.[2]

Chairman Edward P. Boland (D, Massachusetts), at the time a sixty-five-year-old bachelor who would soon marry and sire four children, welcomed DCI Stansfield Turner of the Carter Administration to his first Hughes-Ryan briefing before HPSCI. A former Rhodes scholar and lineman on the Naval Academy football team (as well as a classmate of President Carter), the admiral smiled confidently at the semicircle of lawmakers arrayed around a mahogany bench in the committee's isolated hearing room near the Capitol dome. He seated himself before the lawmakers and read aloud from the short "finding" statement— the document presenting the president's approval of the covert action. Then he leaned back in his chair with a bemused look, awaiting any response.

Of the committee's thirteen members, only seven (six Democrats and a Republican) had showed up for what was likely to be one of the more interesting and certainly historic briefings provided to HPSCI by the intelligence director. After almost a full minute of silence, disturbed only by the hum of neon lights in the bunker-like room, Representative Roman Mazzoli, a feisty Democrat from Kentucky, cleared his throat and with palpable relish launched into a critique of the skimpy document Turner had just read. How much would the covert action cost? Mazzoli wanted to know, grinding forward like a tractor in low gear. What risks were involved? How long would it last? The DCI clenched the teeth in his square jaw before offering a spirited defense of the operation.

Mazzoli was unimpressed by the DCI's rationales for the covert action and, much to the admiral's surprise and annoyance, the congressman set forth a series of objections. Soon Chairman Boland held up his hand to end the exchange. "I'd like to have a serious debate," the chairman said, "but this is not the place."[3] I was in the room as a senior staffer and I remember thinking to myself, if this was not the place to have a serious debate about a covert action proposal with legislative overseers—in a closed meeting, guarded by Capitol Hill policemen, within the inner sanctum of HPSCI's suites of windowless offices—then where was a good place? "I don't want any adversary proceedings between this committee and the intelligence agencies," Boland concluded flatly, with a stern glance at the junior member from Kentucky.

Mazzoli sank back into his chair, an expression of dismay tinctured with irritation registering on his face. A few other Democrats turned toward the chairman in wonderment, but said nothing. Mazzoli was on his own if he wished to cross swords with Eddie Boland, who was also the second-ranking member on the mighty Appropriations Committee, as well as a close friend of House Speaker Thomas "Tip" O'Neill (a fellow Democrat from Massachusetts). The chairman pronounced the meeting over. Admiral Turner and his aides departed from the room draped in smiles, no doubt pleased to have someone of Boland's stature as an ally on the Hill. Maybe Eddie Boland could become the next Senator Russell—or, since this was the House, that other reliable Georgian, Carl Vinson—for the intelligence community.

When he silenced Mazzoli, Chairman Boland likely had the memory of the Pike Committee on his mind. That panel's controversial skirmishes with the CIA and the NSA had left a sour taste in the mouths of House members and delayed the establishment of HPSCI for more than a year after the Senate created SSCI. As HPSCI's first leader, Boland was determined to avoid the confrontational approach to oversight adopted by Otis Pike; he preferred a more cooperative relationship. No more fireworks. Debates, if needed, would be conducted in the inner sanctum of the chairman's office, with Boland—not the full committee— confronting the DCI. Boland had assumed the posture of peacemaker; comity, not conflict, would be HPSCI's guiding principle.

The HPSCI chairman's stance was understandable, given the memory of the Pike panel within the House of Representatives. What good could come from a strained relationship with the intelligence community right at the beginning of this experiment of filtering strands of democracy into the sequestered world of espionage? To a large degree, the tradition of separate institutions sharing power in America's form of government depended on goodwill among the branches. Besides, the House simply would not tolerate another Pike Committee; Speaker O'Neill himself had cautioned Boland against confrontations with the spy agencies. Yet this warm-and-fuzzy approach had a downside: a chummy relationship with the DCI was unlikely to place the IC on notice that, from then on, they faced serious review on Capitol Hill. The danger was that lawmakers might slip back into the good old days of benign neglect.

Director Turner returned in a few weeks with another covert action finding authorized by President Carter, who seemed to have embraced this option as a way of secretly dealing with foreign-policy problems. Small in stature but with a spine of steel, Mazzoli listened intently to the DCI's briefing, then brushed aside Boland's earlier warning and fired a volley of pointed questions at the admiral regarding this latest initiative to send the CIA on a covert mission designed to manipulate another country's politics. This time Representative Les Aspin (D, Wisconsin), who had missed the first covert action briefing and Boland's tirade, joined with Mazzoli in a withering barrage of questions about the finding, as both displayed high sparks of commitment to the practice of accountability. Aspin held a Ph.D. in economics from MIT and had a mind like a searchlight; moreover, he was a battle-scarred alumnus of the Pike Committee, accustomed to verbal fisticuffs with senior intelligence officials. As well, by nature he relished a good debate; he was a classic policy wonk, once described by *Times* journalist Johnny Apple as someone who attempted to "look at all five sides of a triangle."[4]

At this second meeting on a finding, the committee's staff director had requested the presence of a transcriber in the room, a congressional stenographer (or "reporter" in the lingo of Capitol Hill) cleared to record top-secret intelligence briefings. The stenographer's job was to take down a verbatim account of what was said in key briefings and hearings, along with the responses of committee members. This would provide HPSCI with a record of the proceedings, should its members need one at some point. Less than two minutes into his presentation, Admiral Turner suddenly stopped as he belatedly took notice of the stenographer. The DCI advised Chairman Boland that having a "stranger" in the room would be a breach of Agency security. The room fell silent. Finally, Boland said "okay" and dismissed the stenographer. As the perplexed man gathered his recording equipment, a HPSCI staff aide slipped a note to Aspin that read: "We *must* have a record of these briefings! How else are we going to have any memory of what the DCI said, and whether the president and the CIA are living up to their assurances? It'll be the DCI's recollection against ours." Aspin tucked the note in his coat pocket and, venturing out on a limb, spoke up against the chairman's banishment of the stenographer. Just as quickly, Mazzoli backed Aspin. The air grew taut in the HPSCI bunker.

Boland took on the severe look of a headmaster before disobedient schoolboys as he waved aside the objections offered by Aspin and Mazzoli. The DCI weighed in with the chairman, further explaining the security risks presented by the existence of a stenographic record. Besides, Turner said, the committee will have a copy of the finding in its files. Not easily dissuaded, Aspin responded forcefully that a short finding—one sentence in this case—was not enough; the dialogue between HPSCI members and the director would capture in greater detail the goals and methods of the operation. Glowering at Aspin, the chairman repeated that he saw no need for a transcript and again ordered the dazed stenographer off the premises. Unbowed, Aspin thrust his head and shoulders across the green baize benchtop around which the members sat. He stared along its curvature toward Boland. "I call for a vote on this, Mr. Chairman," he said, without emotion. "Second," chimed in Mazzoli. His careworn face shading from crimson to an even angrier darkening hue, Boland pushed his chair back from the bench in disgust and ordered the committee's clerk to call the roll.

It was gut-check time on the Boland Committee—a still point in a turning world. The chairman was unlikely to forget who challenged his authority at the beginning of his tenure as HPSCI's boss. The clerk slowly called out the names of those present, eleven of the thirteen this time. When the tally came to an end, the outcome was 6–5. Les Aspin had won by a single vote. While comparisons between such disparate individuals as Frank Church of Boise and Eddie Boland of Boston are fraught, like Church in 1975 over SHAMROCK hearings, so had Boland momentarily lost his committee. Senator Church had pushed too hard for vigorous accountability and Representative Boland not hard enough, as both of their committees oscillated in an uncertain arc above the volatile and ill-defined Golden Mean where security and liberty might theoretically meet in perfect balance. From now on, HPSCI would keep a word-for-word record of DCI briefings on covert actions, along with the Q and A that followed. Once the SSCI staff heard about this vote, their senators also demanded a verbatim record of all Hughes-Ryan briefings before their committee.

The skeletal reporting requirements set by Hughes-Ryan had thus evolved into serious forums on Capitol Hill, one in SSCI and another in HPSCI, for the discussion and evaluation of covert actions. Some of the debates in the coming years would be deeply thoughtful, and a few saw heated sparks flying between the committees and whichever DCI or DNI was in office at the time. Hughes-Ryan and subsequent laws have never called upon the oversight committees to actually vote their approval before a covert action could proceed. That step seemed to erode too much the separation-of-powers doctrine and the command-in-chief clause of the Constitution and was unlikely to gain majority support in Congress. (Further, in 1983, the Supreme Court case *INS v. Chadha* seemed to rule out that kind of "legislative veto" over executive actions.) Nevertheless, if members of the committees raised strong objections to a covert action, this would be duly noted by intelligence chiefs delivering the Hughes-Ryan briefing and reported back to the White House. The result could be a de facto veto of the proposal, because presidents are reluctant to start fights with key congressional panels—and so are DCIs, D/CIAs, and DNIs, since their annual funding relies on good relations with SSCI and HPSCI (along with the Appropriations Committees).

Much depends on which lawmakers object during a session on a covert action approval briefing, as well as how many object.[5] If the dissent comes from just a junior member on HPSCI, say, the White House can weather that kind of storm; if the dissent includes the committee's leaders or even just the chairman, however, that is a different matter. Most of the time since lawmakers adopted the Hughes-Ryan Act in 1974, the executive branch has worked in a spirit of comity with the dissenters—at least if they were important committee members, or if a panel majority was up in arms—to modify a covert action, making it more palatable to the lawmakers. On rare occasions, members of SSCI or HSPCI (or both) have taken a formal vote on a covert action proposal, even if Hughes-Ryan is silent on this possibility. The results were not legally binding on the CIA; nevertheless, a formal negative tally sends a powerful message to the executive branch: Rethink this covert action! On occasion, a president has canceled a proposed covert action operation, based on this kind of explicit signaling from an oversight committee or committees.

These dynamics underscore the political aspects of Hughes-Ryan briefings: beyond the explicit black letter of the statute lie opportunities for lawmakers to modify, or even curtail, executive branch activities by signals of objection, such as through fences, letters, or visits to the White House by disgruntled lawmakers, or even committee formal votes on HPSCI and SSCI; and sometimes an agitated committee can decide to retaliate against a recalcitrant administration by shutting off spending for the operation in question, or through the cancellation of funding for other programs dear to the administration. In the most extreme case related to intelligence, an exasperated Eddie Boland—growing more and more wary of the nation's spy activities as he chaired HPSCI—took his proposal to halt paramilitary operations in Nicaragua before a highly unusual joint secret session of Congress in the mid-1980s, where he won majority support for his initiative.

A series of additional Boland Amendments led the Reagan Administration to descend into underground passages where it could conduct its Iran-contra operations out of sight, without answering to Congress or its legal prohibitions. The administration would not be denied; it would seek its objectives to overthrow the Nicaraguan regime through its own novel form of off-the-books covert action, guided by the super-secret organization known as the Enterprise. As a former CIA officer has suggested, adoption of a covert action is "something the President can do when he's frustrated. It's what you do when you want to feel tough."[6] Intelligence accountability went from the soaring hopes of the Church Committee to a wretched setback during the Reagan years as the NSC and the DCI turned their backs on Congress and its Hughes-Ryan rules of accountability.

Early in the history of HPSCI and SSCI, Boland and his Senate counterpart, Daniel K. Inouye (D, Hawaii), had been pushed by the impassioned vigilance of two junior HPSCI members, Aspin and Mazzoli, toward a more serious form of accountability. Now lawmakers could monitor the ongoing performance of the intelligence agencies in light of assurances made by the IC's top leader, as recorded in previous briefings. Turner would test the limits of tolerance on

Capitol Hill in other ways, too. Soon after the confrontation over the steno-graphic record, the DCI informed Boland that some subjects in the IC were just too sensitive for him to bring to HPSCI; he would be able to only brief the chair-man alone. This went too far for Boland and he replied that the committee would expect to have access to everything. Feeling increasingly wary of being manipu-lated by the intelligence agencies, the chairman insisted that the full committee had to be informed on all significant intelligence activities.

Throughout the start-up days of the Boland Committee, the give-and-take continued between the chairman and outspoken junior members—boats against the current—especially (along with Aspin and Mazzoli) Wyche Fowler (D, Georgia), Morgan Murphy (D, Illinois), and Kenneth Robinson (R, Virginia). Representative Robinson's approach was less to pose thoughtful questions in hearings than to pore over intelligence budgets, line by line, late into the evening in HPSCI's suite of offices. Sometimes Boland had a major-ity on his side and sometimes a majority joined the Young Turks, as the House Committee felt its way forward in this new terrain of intelligence accountability. Then the Reagan Administration arrived in Washington in 1981, with a DCI by the name of William J. Casey who had no temperament for congressional over-sight. Intelligence, from his vantage point, was a presidential prerogative. Even Eddie Boland, still trying to avoid major confrontations with the intelligence community, found the new director's uncooperative attitude more than he could tolerate. The once neurasthenic HPSCI chairman began to move away from his "make-nice" philosophy of oversight and toward a rising skepticism about Casey and the CIA that would eventually ally him with his erstwhile nemeses, Aspin and Mazzoli (a transition explored in chapter 8).

Building a Framework for Intelligence Accountability

As the Canadian intelligence scholar Wesley Wark has noted, "Primary legisla-tion should set down limits on what the intelligence machine can be used for, to remove fears that the power of modern intelligence methods will become ubiquitous and thus seriously erode individual liberty."[7] The rule of law is para-mount. History has shown that if an important guideline for executive agencies is not placed into the form of a statute, it can become a plaything for presidents and bureaucrats. Constitutional democracy is a decision to place the rule of law above capricious reliance on power.

The FISA Initiative

Following the establishment of SSCI and HPSCI, Congress enacted a bold over-sight law in 1978: the Foreign Intelligence Surveillance Act (FISA), initially drafted three years earlier by the staff of the Church Committee. The staff found that wiretap surveillance powers had been misused over the years for political purposes by both Democratic and Republican administrations, a discovery sobering enough to produce a 95–1 vote in favor of the bill in the Senate and a wide margin in the House as well. The law required a "prior judicial warrant [involving] all electronic surveillance for foreign intelligence or counterintelligence purposes in the United States in which communications of U.S. persons might be intercepted."[8] It also established a FISA Court to evaluate the merits of a warrant application, as well as a FISA Appeals Court. In line with the recommendation of the Church Committee, the statute provided a constitutional safeguard against arbitrary wiretaps against U.S. citizens and aliens with permanent residency status. Two exceptions were granted to the "prior" warrant requirement: first, in emergencies, the executive branch could carry out electronic surveillance for twenty-four hours (later changed to seventy-two hours) before obtaining a warrant; and, second, if Congress declared war, electronic surveillance could be pursued without a warrant for fifteen days (maximum) against suspected enemies of the United States.

Forbidden by the law was any claim of unfettered executive power to engage in electronic surveillance. Many years later, in 2005, FISA would attract extensive public commentary when the *New York Times* revealed that after the 9/11 attacks the second Bush Administration—with Dick Cheney a champion of unchecked executive powers as its vice president—ordered the NSA to bypass the warrant requirement and conduct wiretaps as considered necessary against terrorist suspects (a rash White House decision examined in chapter 5).

An Intelligence Charter

As members of Congress continued the search for a proper balance between security and liberty, a majority in the Senate rejected an attempt by reformers to pass an omnibus intelligence "charter." This proposal was meant to cover almost every aspect of intelligence, from collection and analysis, counterintelligence, and covert action to the relationships of the secret agencies with practically every group in American society, including students and professors, missionaries, aid workers, and journalists.

When SSCI came into existence, Senator Dee Huddleston (formerly on the Church Committee) was named a member and he spearheaded its effort to codify his old panel's key recommendations into a comprehensive "omnibus charter," an initiative given the designation S.2525 and introduced on the Senate floor for debate in February 1978. Among its provisions were prohibitions against extreme covert actions and counterintelligence activities, such as (respectively) the creation of food or water shortages in a target nation, or the use of torture during interrogations. The charter effort collapsed under its own weight, however; the proposal was too long and detailed (over 250 pages), drawing attacks from many quarters.[9] It became the target of skillful lobbying by the spy agencies, which relied on allies among members of Congress to gut most of its content. Further, several of its provisions (although not the prohibitions against extreme covert actions and torture) had already been adopted in an executive order signed by President Jimmy Carter in 1976. This made the charter proposal superfluous in the minds of some critics.[10]

The Intelligence Oversight Act of 1980

In place of the lengthy charter proposal, Congress enacted in 1980 a dramatically pared-down—indeed skimpy—two-and-a-half-page encapsulation of the charter's core principles. Though short, the version of the charter that survived—known as the Intelligence Oversight Act of 1980 (or, more formally, the Accountability for Intelligence Activities Act[11])—was of pivotal importance in the evolution of intelligence accountability. Adopting language from the resolutions that had created SSCI and HPSCI, this dwarf-like Oversight Act stressed that the intelligence agencies were expected to keep the committees "fully and currently informed" of their activities, to include any "significant anticipated activities." This wording, though, had been nonbinding in the earlier resolutions; now with the 1980 Oversight Act, the spy agencies were required by the mandatory language of the law to inform SSCI and HPSCI about *all* significant intelligence activities *in advance* of implementation (see appendix C for a copy of the law). This wording, the Holy Grail of *ante facto* reporting, would provide lawmakers with an opportunity to shut off the funding for an intelligence activity that they had found ill-advised *before it was implemented*.

The 1980 Oversight Act allowed an exception in times of emergency, which made it more palatable than the unconditional "prior" reporting envisioned in the language of the omnibus Intelligence Charter proposal. In extreme circumstances, the executive branch would be required to report in advance only to eight members of Congress, who became known informally as "the Gang of Eight." This octet included the top two overall leaders in the House and in the Senate for both parties, plus the top two Democrats and Republicans on SSCI and HPSCI. Even in an emergency situation, however, the full SSCI and HPSCI memberships expected to be briefed on the operation within a couple of days after the Gang of Eight had already been given advanced notification.[12] Even with the emergency exception, this reporting requirement went far beyond those laid out in the trail-blazing Hughes-Ryan legislation; the 1980 law rejected its *ex post facto* formula of reporting "in a timely fashion"—informing SSCI and HPSCI only *after* an operation was already under way. The reporting requirement in the 1980 law also surpassed the legal expectations of other major statutes of the time. The Case-Zablocki Act of 1971, for example, gave the executive branch a ninety-day leeway for reporting to Congress about the signing of U.S. executive agreements with other nations; and the War Powers Resolution of 1973 established a risky two-day *ex post facto* reporting clock.[13]

Mandated reporting requirements provide vital assistance for congressional police-patrolling responsibilities, because they force executive agencies to keep lawmakers informed about their activities. The language of "in advance" and "prior" in the Intelligence Oversight Act of 1980 was truly a striking step forward in the establishment of meaningful intelligence accountability—assuming the executive branch would honor the statute's wording and penumbra of intent. As it has turned out, the reporting to SSCI and HPSCI under this law has proven inconsistent—and sometimes nonexistent (as related later in this book). In fact, the overall record of IC compliance with SSCI and HPSCI reporting mandates has been nothing less than discouraging. For instance, according to a congressional staff analysis, between December 2001 and April 2002—a five-month period—SSCI expected eighty-four reports from the IC. Of these, eighteen were late, eight were incomplete, and a whooping fifty-one never arrived at all! Only seven reports met the deadline, which adds up to an 8 percent compliance rate.[14] When SSCI complained about this poor response, the intelligence agencies improved for a short period of time, then returned to their more cavalier ways—a similar pattern to the experiences Congress had with reporting on executive agreements under the Case-Zablocki Act.[15]

James Clapper, the DNI, complained to me from time to time that there are too many reports sought by the Intelligence Committees, and some staffers on the Hill have admitted to me that he is right. One recent example had to do with reporting on every slight shift of a space-based surveillance satellite antenna. "SSCI and HPSCI don't know the difference between oversight and micromanagement," a senior intelligence official vented to me in the summer of 2016. Other staffers, though, reject the notion that there are too many mandated reporting stipulations. In 2016, SSCI included in its FY Intelligence Authorization Act (S.3017, Sec. 809) additional reporting requests, including the submission of copies of all memoranda of understanding (MOU) among or between the intelligence agencies, as well as notification of all classified and unclassified presidential directives to these agencies. As one authority noted, "the bill would reset the terms of the congressional intelligence oversight relationship, seemingly dispensing with comity and imposing mandatory disclosure to Congress of various categories of records." In an understatement, he concluded: "Executive branch resistance may be anticipated."[16] These proposed requirements strike me as sensible; the Intelligence Committees, however, should cut back on its overly long list of reporting mandates of lesser significance. On its side, the intelligence community needs to be far more responsive than it has been in honoring SSCI and HPSCI information requests.

Despite setbacks in efforts to improve intelligence accountability (such as the rejection of comprehensive charter legislation), members of Congress have managed to put in place serious, ongoing reviews of spy programs and budgets within the hearing rooms of SSCI and HPSCI, as well as in the quarters of the Appropriations Subcommittees that deal with intelligence budget approvals. (The House and Senate Judiciary Committees demand continuing jurisdiction over the FBI and its intelligence activities; and the Armed Services Committees in the House insist on keeping an oar in when it comes to tactical military intelligence.) In place of a philosophy of benign neglect, an opportunity had arrived in the wake of the Church Committee for a dedicated police patrolling of America's secret agencies. Staff experts and at least some devoted lawmakers on SSCI and HPSCI began to scrutinize intelligence budgets line by line; read closely all the reports that had been requested from the spy agencies; hold regular hearings (mostly in closed session), where often thoughtful, probing questions are posed to the spy agency representatives; and engage with intelligence officers in an ongoing review of their programs at their agency headquarters and overseas. As intelligence scholar Gregory F. Treverton has observed, America's secret services had been forced to join the rest of the government and now faced the normal array of Madisonian checks and balances.[17]

Legislating on Behalf of the Intelligence Community

In the wrestling match between pro-security and pro-liberty proponents inside the government, members of Congress have sometimes leaned toward liberty, as with the reporting requirements for covert action advanced by Hughes-Ryan and the even more stringent demands of the 1980 Intelligence Oversight Act for prior reporting; and sometimes they have leaned toward security, as with the rejection of an omnibus Intelligence Charter, which opponents found too intrusive into the activities of the IC. A further illustration of the security tilt—part of an effort by SSCI and HPSCI to build up rapport with the intelligence community in the new oversight relationship—is another law passed in 1980: the Classified Information Procedures Act (CIPA).[18] This measure allowed the government (read CIA, in most cases) to redact or rephrase classified information to protect sources and methods in espionage-related lawsuits, so long as the defendants' rights were properly protected. This removed the "graymail" problem faced by the IC, when now and then the government had to drop a court action out of concern that secrets might have to be revealed in a fully open court proceeding.[19]

Again, in 1982—still early in the accountability experiment, which was viewed as highly dubious by the new Reagan Administration—the Congress weighed in further to help the intelligence agencies, through the enactment of an Intelligence Identities Protection Act.[20] This law established a red light against the exposure of undercover intelligence officials through the publication of their names. Henceforth, such revelations would be a criminal act. During the time of the Church Committee, some far-left groups in the United States and abroad had sought via their underground publications to destroy the CIA by exposing the names of its officers. One former Agency officer, Philip Agee, wrote a book, published in the Year of Intelligence (1975), that revealed—with many inaccuracies—the names of 2,500 U.S. intelligence officers and their assets (agents who were foreign nationals).[21] Further, in 1976, leftists in the United States published *Covert Action* and *The Covert Action Information Bulletin* that opposed the use of covert action and attempted as well to identify Agency officers and assets by name—again, with many inaccuracies, but with damaging repercussions overseas. Branded a traitor by the CIA and with his U.S. passport revoked by the Department of State, Agee became a pariah in the United States and lived abroad for the rest of his life (although banned from France, the Netherlands, and West Germany). With passage of this law, members of Congress demonstrated how they could be helpful to America's secret agencies, not just corral them with regulations.

A third measure to assist the IC, enacted during the early days of the Reagan Administration, was the CIA Information Act of 1984. This measure exempted specific kinds of information in the Agency's operational files from Freedom of Information Act (FOIA) requests, such as documents related to covert action proposals and counterintelligence cases.[22] A deputy director of the CIA at the time claimed to lawmakers that Agency officers often spent more time on FOIA requests—as much as 5 percent of their day—than any other matter dealt with by the organization.[23]

The Casey-Goldwater Clash

When the Reagan Administration came to power in 1981, the new president chose William J. Casey, his national campaign manager, to serve as DCI. Throughout his tenure (1981–1987), Casey struck a combative stance toward efforts by lawmakers to maintain accountability over "his" agencies. In a stunning display of *comédie humaine*, Casey even managed to alienate Senator Barry Goldwater (R, Arizona), the chair of SSCI from 1981 to 1985—an ironic turn of events, given that Goldwater had been an arch-opponent of intelligence accountability and a champion of all things related to the executive branch in the conduct of foreign policy. While on the Church Committee, Goldwater voted against the very creation of SSCI in 1976. "I don't even like to have an intelligence oversight committee," he remarked before becoming SSCI's leader.[24] Goldwater was an arch-critic of oversight, that is, until Casey was less than forthright with him and other SSCI members. During a briefing to the committee in 1984, the DCI slipped quickly and inaudibly—he was notorious for mumbling his words—over the fact that the CIA was mining the harbor in the port city of Corinto, Nicaragua, in an attempt by the Agency to discourage commercial shipping and ratchet up pressure on the regime in Managua in hopes of engineering its collapse. Casey mentioned this extreme economic covert action in a single muffled sentence during a hearing that lasted more than two hours. Goldwater and other senators missed the remark.

Soon after this briefing, the CIA assured SSCI that the Operations Directorate had not mined the harbor, as post-hearing rumors had claimed. Upon further questioning by committee members, however, it became clear that the CIA was playing a semantic game with SSCI members. The Agency had not mined the Corinto *harbor*; it had mined *piers* in the harbor. Goldwater was incensed over the legerdemain practiced by Casey and the CIA. He wrote a letter to the DCI, mailing a copy to the *Washington Post*. A passage in the letter read "It gets down to one, little, simple phrase: I am pissed off."[25] The ranking Democrat on the committee, Daniel Patrick Moynihan (New York), who had been a sponsor of the 1980 Oversight Act, said that Casey's briefing was neither "full," "current," nor "prior," as required by the law.[26] Members of HPSCI often felt overlooked, too. "We are like mushrooms," said Representative Norman Mineta (D, California), an inaugural member of the House committee. "They [Casey and the CIA] keep us in the dark and feed us a lot of manure."[27]

Following this loss of trust in Casey, Goldwater transformed into a different kind of arch-critic; his ire was now aimed at the DCI, not at the concept of intelligence accountability. This run-in between the DCI and the SSCI chair (a breach taken up in more detail in chapter 8) was the first significant setback in congressional relations for the CIA since the beginning of the new intelligence accountability in 1976. A retired DCI, Stansfield Turner, offered an appraisal of the collision. Casey had perhaps honored the letter of the law, the admiral observed, but "hardly the intent." Turner added: "The CIA did go through the motions of informing, but it wasn't speaking very loudly."[28] The admiral's critique was generous; in fact, the DCI and the CIA had made a mockery of intelligence oversight with their "piers" charade.

Casey's hopes of returning intelligence oversight to the Era of Benign Neglect backfired. He attempted to make amends with Goldwater through what became known as "the Casey Accords"—a written promise from the DCI to SSCI members that he would be more cooperative and more transparent in future briefings before the committee. Even after this conciliatory outreach, however, both SSCI and HPSCI continued to complain (according to SSCI's chief counsel) that "it was taking too long for them to receive findings, and notifications, that they were not getting the actual texts of findings, and that the Agency was overusing the option of giving notice to the 'gang of eight' rather than the full committees."[29]

The Gang of Eight technique proved irresistible to this and subsequent administrations, who conveniently seemed to forget that this was meant to be an emergency—not a normal—reporting provision. Worse still, the executive branch soon invented the concept of a Gang of Four in the case of intelligence activities other than covert actions—an excuse just to brief the top four leaders of SSCI and HPSCI, rather than the full committees, on important collection and counterintelligence activities. Unfortunately, the oversight panels all too often allowed the spy agencies to get away with these truncated briefing presentations.[30] In 2009, Leon Panetta would concede during his confirmation hearings as CIA director that the Gang of Four approach had been "overused by the previous [Clinton] White House, and, therefore, abused."[31] He vowed to cut back on the practice, and did; but, following his departure, the second Bush Administration turned back to Gang of Four reporting.

Even the early altercations between DCI Casey and the Congress over briefing methods were relatively placid, though, compared to the heavy seas that Casey and the Agency were about to sail into as they descended into a stunning intelligence scandal that would forever stain the history of the CIA.

The Iran-Contra Scandal

Intelligence accountability seemed to work reasonably well from 1976 through the first term of the Reagan Administration (Casey's mumbling notwithstanding), with SSCI and HPSCI serving as alert watchdogs for the most part. President Reagan liked to say, "It's morning in America," signaling a new beginning for the United States (an earlier variety of President Trump's "Make America Great Again"); it was also morning in the intelligence oversight experiment. Then, all of a sudden, two major pillars of established law in this domain—Hughes-Ryan and the Intelligence Oversight Act of 1980—seemed as though they were merely sandcastles washed away by the morning tide. The staff of the NSC and their CIA co-conspirators would proceed with Reagan Administration foreign-policy objectives in Latin America as if these statutes, and a new law prohibiting covert action in Nicaragua, had never existed.[32]

Unlike the circumstances at the time of Operations CHAOS and COINTELPRO, the Iran-contra affair erupted in 1986 when elaborate procedures for intelligence accountability were in place and operating well—or so it seemed. Strong oversight committees—SSCI and HPSCI—now existed, along with clear oversight statutes such as Hughes-Ryan, FISA, and the Intelligence Oversight Act of 1980. As it turned out, though, fading like a photograph was the will of lawmakers to use these instruments with rigor for the review of intelligence activities. Missing, too, with even greater consequences, was the willingness of the executive branch to honor the new rules. It was not that lawmakers at the time lacked industriousness; they just weren't industrious as intelligence overseers. Members of SSCI and HPSCI busied themselves raising campaign funds to buy television ads for their next election cycle, met with influential constituents (notably business executives with deep pockets), and engaged with selected policy issues that promised a larger payoff in their home states and districts—highway projects, for example—than the often arcane and largely invisible duties of intelligence review unlikely to make headlines back home. Matters of intelligence accountability became merely a penumbra outside their central obsession of raising funds to run successful reelection campaigns.

The new rules that required executive branch reporting on all important covert actions (the Hughes-Ryan Act) were ignored during the Iran-contra affair, as the NSC staff and the top echelons of the CIA—including DCI Casey himself—set out to oust the Sandinista government in Nicaragua through covert actions and replace it with more pliable, pro-American contra insurgents. Secretly discounted, too, were a fresh set of specific intelligence restrictions: the Boland Amendments, named after their sponsor, the HPSCI chair, who had become less sympathetic toward the IC in light of its irascible new director, William J. Casey. The Boland Amendments were a series of seven laws beginning in 1982, each becoming progressively more severe in shutting down CIA covert actions in Nicaragua. The version adopted by Congress in 1984 banned the further use of paramilitary operations to overthrow the Sandinista government in that Central American nation.[33]

The Iran-contra affair began in the Middle East, as the Reagan Administration sought to free U.S. hostages in Lebanon through an arms-for-influence deal with the Iranians. Tehran's religious leaders had ties with terrorists in Lebanon and were in a position to serve as intermediaries in secret negotiations for the release of American hostages held there, including the CIA's chief of station in Lebanon, William Buckley, a personal friend of Casey's. The DCI feared—rightly so—that Buckley was being tortured to death by his captors. After some assistance from Israel (which continued to have backchannel contacts in Tehran despite the tensions between the two nations), along with months of bargaining accompanied by foot-dragging and multiple duplicities on the Iranian side, a few hostages were finally released to the United States in exchange for a discounted sale of missiles to Iran—a form of ransom. Unfortunately, Buckley died at the hands of his torturers before the deal was completed, a death for which not only the terrorists but also the leaders of Iran bore responsibility.

As the Republican White House focused on the plight of Buckley and his fellow hostages, the Democrats (who enjoyed a wide majority in the House throughout the 1980s) focused on curbing covert actions against the government of Nicaragua, which had been recognized as a legitimate regime by the Carter Administration. Once at least some of the hostages were freed by Lebanon, the Reagan NSC turned its full attention to Central America. In response to the Boland Amendments, staffers on the Council secretly concocted extraordinary measures to achieve the president's regime-change objectives in Nicaragua, even as they continued to jockey for the release of additional hostages in Lebanon. The NSC staff created what they referred to in their circles as "the Enterprise," a heavily veiled, privately funded organization situated outside the official framework of government, beyond the reach of the congressional appropriations process or the scrutiny of SSCI and HPSCI overseers.

The Enterprise, referred to by deputy national security adviser Col. Oliver "Ollie" L. North (who said he was quoting DCI Casey) as an "off the shelf, self-sustaining, stand-alone" entity, would carry out the covert actions in Nicaragua desired by the administration, despite the Boland laws. No more annoying budget hearings; no more green-eyeshade sessions with SSCI and HPSCI staff experts; no more Q and A during Hughes-Ryan briefings; no more probing by the likes of Aspin, Mazzoli, and (increasingly) Eddie Boland. These vital forms of congressional accountability would be dismissed, as caterpillars within the National Security Council staff swarmed the wholesome herbs of constitutional government. So what if President Reagan had signed the Boland Amendments into law; what else could he have done in the face of a Congress dominated by Democrats? If the Democrats in Congress were too ignorant to understand the threat posed by the Marxist Sandinistas, the Reagan NSC would come to the rescue without the help of these misguided lawmakers, like the cavalry in Hollywood Westerns. White House Communications Director Patrick Buchanan warned that Soviet allies were "just two days driving time from Harlingen, Texas" and the map of Central America might soon be "covered in a sea of red, eventually lapping at our own borders."[34] Col. North's secretary, Fawn Hall, provided biblical justification for the NSC taking extreme measures to defeat the godless Communists. "We were responding to a higher law," she later told investigators.[35] This Manichaean philosophy would lead the administration into a series of darkening consequences.

Reacting to rumors circulating in Washington about a scheme hatched by the NSC staff to circumvent the Boland Amendments, prominent members of SSCI—Chair David Durenberger (R, Minnesota) and Vice Chair Patrick Leahy (D, Vermont)—went to the White House in 1985 for a meeting with the Council staff leaders, National Security Adviser Robert C. McFarlane and his deputy, Lt. Col. Oliver L. North. The lawmakers questioned them about executive branch adherence to the Boland restrictions. Sitting face-to-face with these senior legislative overseers, the senior NSC staffers denied knowledge of the Enterprise. Representative Lee H. Hamilton, the HPSCI chair, joined by some of his colleagues, had the same experience with McFarlane and North. When the scandal finally broke in 1986, McFarlane acknowledged that he had engaged in "tortured language" in his talks with the members of Congress who were looking into the rumors.[36] Earlier in 1986, McFarlane's successor, Vice Admiral John M. Poindexter, who had graduated first in his class at the U.S. Naval Academy, continued the deception when queried by SSCI and HPSCI overseers. Unfortunately, this questioning of McFarlane and then Poindexter was never under oath. The oversight committees never took the next steps of holding hearings with sworn witnesses, or subpoenaing documents related to the reactions of the Reagan Administration to the Boland Amendments. The value of these steps would have to be learned the hard way.

In the midst of this charade, North convinced McFarlane and Poindexter to help finance the Enterprise with profits from the missile sales to Iran. Next the busy and innovative colonel, as conspiratorial as a Venetian prince in medieval times, decided that additional funds for the Enterprise could be raised from foreign potentates friendly to the United States—even though the president's chief of staff, James Baker (an attorney), warned at the time that obtaining money from other countries "is an impeachable offense."[37] Undeterred, North—snappy looking in his Marine Corps uniform—marched forward. The Sultan of Brunei alone provided an immediate lump sum of $7 million, making the King of Arabia with his slow-roll $1 million a month initially look like a piker—although he made up for this with an eventual total of $32 million for the contra cause. North tapped, as well, into the coffers of homegrown Reagan conservatives, such as Joseph Coors, the Colorado brewer, who was good for several thousand. Who needed congressional oversight, budget hearings, and the whole maddening appropriations process? Government by secret fiat was much easier.

Legal scholar Laurence H. Tribe has spelled out the implications of allowing something like the Enterprise. A fundamental concept in the Constitution— that all government spending must be approved by Congress (Article I, Section 9)—"would be rendered utterly meaningless," he has written, "if the President, seeing himself not as an agent of the Government but as an outsider, could preside freely over the creation of a shadow treasury designed to aid his shadow intelligence network in pursuit of his private schemes."[38] The battlements of congressional accountability were substantially weakened by this fateful decision of the Reagan Administration to bypass SSCI, HPSCI, and the Appropriations Committees altogether.

In 1986, the Iran-contra scheme came to a sudden halt, though, when the Lebanese magazine *Al-Shiraa* revealed the basic facts about the arms sales in

Iran and the diversion of funds to the contras in Nicaragua. Now the legal violations were public knowledge. Members of SSCI and HPSCI joined together to conduct a major inquiry into the startling operations: the Inouye-Hamilton Committee (named after the two committee chairmen, respectively). When the panel held extensive public hearings in 1987, the truth came tumbling out. The extent to which the Reagan Administration dismissed the new procedures of intelligence accountability was profoundly troubling. Members of SSCI and HPSCI had been persistently lied to, and the nation's appropriations system tossed into the dustbin. The abuse of power ran deep, far surpassing President Bill Clinton's improper sexual behavior with a White House intern that led to his impeachment in the House, or even President Nixon's Watergate cover-up, a felony crime but at least less of a devastating assault directly upon the Constitution itself.

Deceiving Congress was a central part of the Reagan Administration's strategy in the conduct of the Iran-contra operations, an approach supported by Casey and a few other officials at the CIA. For example, the operations chief for Latin America, Duane "Dewey" Clarridge, prepared for covert actions against the Sandinistas and against Cuba without a finding; an Agency officer, on loan to the NSC staff, ran a program that attempted "to manipulate the media, the Congress and public opinion to support the Reagan Administration's policies" against Nicaragua; and McFarlane denied that the Boland Amendments applied to the NSC staff, even though the reporting requirements of the Intelligence Oversight Act of 1980 stress that its provisions extended to all "entities" in the government. Further, Agency officers Clair George and Alan Fiers flatly denied Agency involvement in the affair, as they (in George's words) tried to "protect the Central Intelligence Agency." Here were perfect candidates, one and all, for the Four Pinocchios Award. Moreover, an even more effective method than mendacity was adopted by the administration: to tell Congress nothing at all. "I don't think the intelligence community has ever lied to us," SSCI Chair David Durenberger (R, Minnesota) said about the Reagan years. "The problem is what they don't tell us."[39]

President Reagan's secretary of state, George Schultz, viewed the Iran-contra affair as "Watergate all over."[40] Yet a GOP addendum to the Inouye-Hamilton Committee report (with Representative Dick Cheney, R, Wyoming, among the signatories) dismissed the entire affair as merely the legitimate use of presidential power. Cheney and his Republican colleagues concluded that "the mistakes of the Iran-Contra Affair were just that—mistakes in judgment, and nothing more. There was no constitutional crisis, no systematic disrespect for 'the rule of law,' no grand conspiracy, and no Administration-wide dishonesty or cover-up."[41]

The public found the majority report more persuasive. Caught in the undertow of the affair, President Reagan's popularity plunged in the opinion polls. The other perpetrators of the scandal suffered lasting humiliation, and they would have gone to jail had not George H. W. Bush, the vice president during the scandal, won the presidency in 1988 and eventually pardoned each of the conspirators with a get-out-of-jail-free pass, thereby avoiding a criminal trial that may have drawn Bush himself more explicitly into the circle of culpability. ("Where was George?" was a popular lapel pin in D.C. during the Iran-contra congressional inquiry.) The special prosecutor who investigated the scandal called the president's pardon "the last card in the cover-up."[42]

When the Iran-contra scandal first broke, Casey claimed—and President Reagan agreed—that it was unnecessary to report to Congress in situations like those posed by the hostages in Lebanon and the threat to the United States arising in Nicaragua, because informing the oversight committees might undermine the president's constitutional authority.[43] Here was a variation of the "unitary theory" of the presidency that Vice President Dick Cheney would espouse subsequently during the second Bush Administration, in the context of unleashing the NSA's sigint powers against American citizens. Contrary to the nation's founding principles, the notion was that the president knows best when it comes to national security and foreign policy—a refrain often heard from Trump and his aides during the start-up period for his administration. Indeed, in Cheney's *Weltanschauung*, the president enjoyed *inherent* powers within the security and foreign-policy domains that Congress and the judiciary may not limit or try to control. "Trust the executive" was a philosophy of governance that held little attraction to the delegates at the Constitutional Convention of 1787, who had just ended by force of arms the executive tyranny practiced by George III against the American colonies.[44]

With the Iran-contra affair, the experiment in intelligence accountability had gone into a tailspin. It was a time when, according to the chief counsel of the Inouye-Hamilton Committee, a "mentality" descended on the Reagan Administration "that made it patriotic to lie to Congress, to circumvent checks and balances through covert actions, and to create the Enterprise to do what the CIA was not permitted to do."[45] It was a time, as well, when people in the White House would do "anything to protect the president"—reminiscent of what had happened with John Dean, White House counsel during the Nixon Administration, and other aides entangled in the Watergate cover-up a decade earlier, their career ambitions varnished with zeal.[46] The tone an administration sets is vital. It is hard to imagine the excesses revealed during the Iran-contra investigations ever happening under Dwight D. Eisenhower or Jimmy Carter. Their high standards for abiding by the law and acting in a moral manner were clear to those who worked for them. Moreover, unlike President Reagan, their management styles were sufficiently hands-on and focused that mischief of this magnitude would never have gone unnoticed and uncorrected by the chief executive. As the ancient Greek philosophers understood, the quality of individuals selected for high office is of utmost importance in the pursuit of "good government" and for the success of accountability safeguards.

An Interval of Distrust, 1987–1991

The Iran-contra affair dealt a staggering blow to the principles of intelligence oversight. In the years preceding the scandal, the leaders of SSCI and HPSCI—Boland, Durenberger, Hamilton, Inouye, and (at times) even Goldwater—had tried to develop a civil working relationship among Congress, the secret agencies, and the White House. With the onset of a major scandal, however, accountability had fallen into the acrimonious pit of a major congressional inquiry in 1987, followed by an interval of distrust that yielded additional legislation to tighten the rules governing the spy agencies. The scandal brought with it a disheartening message for lawmakers: even the elevated levels of police patrolling that had become a regular feature of executive-legislative relations in the realm of intelligence activities—far more hearings, staff interaction with intelligence professionals, and budget reviews than before 1975—had failed to prevent the lawless transgressions that took place in Iran and Nicaragua.

Within the CIA, the end result was the firing of two senior officers for their involvement in improper operations with the contras. A handful of additional officers received slaps on the wrist for intentionally withholding information from Congress about the affair. Within the legislature, the outcome was a mixture of discouragement and a determination nonetheless to hit the "reset" button in the intelligence oversight experiment, with additional safeguards in place. Casey, McFarlane, and Poindexter had been the top-ranked officials leading the Iran-contra affair. The DCI died from brain cancer in March 1987, so he missed the opportunity to defend his actions in public. The reputations of the two national security advisers were deeply tarnished, which did not deter the second Bush Administration from hiring Poindexter (and other Iran-contra conspirators) to work on foreign policy and intelligence matters.

Much of the success of police patrolling depends on the personalities of the key officials in the IC and on the Hill, as Casey—an oversight disaster—illustrates. Before him, in sharp contrast, Admiral Turner of the Carter Administration enjoyed reasonably cordial relations with SSCI and HPSCI, once he got over losing the "stenographer argument" to Aspin and Mazzoli on the House panel. Beyond Casey's difficult personality, which would have created problems on Capitol Hill one way or another, the major irritants to a solid working relationship between lawmakers and spies during the 1980s was the deep-seated partisan disagreement over both the threat posed by the Sandinista regime in

Nicaragua, and the question of whether highly intrusive covert actions ought to be used as a means for ousting this quasi-Marxist government.

Prior to the emergence of this prickly issue of Nicaragua, virtually all significant intelligence decisions made by SSCI and HPSCI had enjoyed a bipartisan consensus. The Democrats on SSCI and HPSCI from 1975 to 1991 had been tougher in their questioning of CIA witnesses at hearings during the Carter Administration than during the Reagan years.[47] In a foreshadowing of what would become common behavior in Washington, however, Nicaragua split the oversight committees sharply along party lines, with Republicans in favor of regime change in Managua and Democrats willing to work with the Sandinistas. Party wrangling would soon become commonplace on practically every topic coming before SSCI and HPSCI, as was the case with the rest of Congress.

In the aftermath of the Iran-contra scandal, lawmakers strengthened the internal investigative powers of the CIA's inspector general through passage of the CIA Inspector General Act of 1989, despite Langley's best efforts to torpedo the proposal.[48] Henceforth, the Agency's IG would be subject to confirmation hearings in the Senate, and the IG was required to report to SSCI and HPSCI twice a year—or immediately when wrongdoing was discovered in the Agency. As Snider has noted, this law gave the congressional Intelligence Committees "a window into the Agency's operations that they had not had before," as well as "a place they could go within the Agency to ask for oversight inquiries that exceeded the committees' own capabilities."[49]

As the Cold War wound down, Congress also attempted in 1990 to enact a new Intelligence Oversight Act that featured significant language related to accountability.[50] This law provided the first detailed definition of covert action; required all findings to be written (no more oral findings, as President Reagan had resorted to during Iran-contra); banned retroactive findings (again, a Reagan innovation); and clarified the *ante facto* reporting requirements that had been set forth in the revolutionary Intelligence Oversight Act of 1980. This last measure proved contentious. With respect to covert actions, the Congress wanted strictly a one-day delay in reporting to the full SSCI and HPSCI memberships whenever the president triggered the Gang of Eight emergency reporting provision. In contrast, the White House sought more flexibility and preferred the Hughes-Ryan standard of "in a timely fashion."

When Congress proved stubborn, the first President Bush exercised his pocket veto authority—the first and, so far, only one of two instances of any form of presidential veto aimed at an intelligence measure (see chapter 8 for a veto exercise by the second President Bush). In a second try in 1991, lawmakers grudgingly adopted Bush's preferred "timely fashion" wording, but they maintained their insistence in dialogues with the White House that the full memberships of SSCI and HPSCI had to be notified within "a few days," which was

interpreted in the legislative colloquy accompanying the bill to mean just a couple of days—forty-eight hours. Again the White House balked at signing the
bill; however, the following year—while still less than delighted about the two-
day interpretation but willing to show good faith—the president exchanged letters with SSCI and HPSCI in which he promised to cooperation and to keep the
committees well informed. He then accepted the revised law, known formally as
the Intelligence Authorization Act of 1991, and less formally as the Intelligence
Oversight Act of 1991, now trimmed down and finally signed by the president
in August 1991. The first major Oversight Act passed in 1980 had borne teeth;
now, angered by the Iran-contra transgressions, lawmakers had sharpened their
points by way of this new statute.[51]

   In the years that followed the Iran-contra scandal and as the Cold War came to
an astonishing conclusion in 1991, DCIs William H. Webster (1987–1991) and
Robert M. Gates (1991–1992) attempted to heal the ruptured relations between
Congress and the IC wrought by Casey, MacFarlane, Poindexter, North, and the
other Iran-contra schemers. Unlike Casey, Webster and Gates understood and
sympathized with the concept of intelligence accountability; they were willing
to nurture a national security partnership with Congress, in part to have lawmakers share the blame when intelligence operations ran awry. Webster "set a new
standard in comity between the branches of government," concluded political
scientist Marvin C. Ott. "Intelligence oversight had reached its full flowering."[52]
Similarly, Gates developed a close working relationship with SSCI chair David
L. Boren (D, Oklahoma). The duo became a simulacrum of comradeship as
they braided their professional lives together for the sake of improved IC-Hill
relations. The bleakest chapter in the annals of intelligence accountability, Iran-
contra was impossible to banish from memory; nevertheless, the congressional
Intelligence Committees returned to their police-patrolling duties—now with
a redoubled commitment and, at least for a while, better cooperation from the
White House and the IC.

   Beginning in 1992, though, the nation was about to enter into yet another
phase of intelligence accountability: a time of intense partisan warfare in
Washington, in which the concept of reaching across the aisle in friendship and
comity came apart like a frayed rope. Prominent lawmakers, most notably Newt
Gingrich (R, Georgia), introduced a high level of discord into cross-party relations in the nation's capital, as a means of relentlessly discrediting the Democrats
and finally achieving a Republican majority in Congress. By 1995, the GOP had
achieved this goal in the House; attack-dog politics—however unseemly—had
worked wondrously. Republicans lifted their leading firebrand, former West
Georgia College history professor Gingrich, into the speakership, and they
soon controlled the Senate as well. "What is distinctive in the period after the
Republican takeover in 1995," Aberbach observes, "is the level of oversight

hostile not only to the intent and behavior of political appointees, but to the missions of many federal programs and agencies."[53]

Oversight became a cudgel used by the GOP for a comprehensive attack on the Democratic Party and "Big Government" (the Department of Defense always excepted in the GOP's primer on the evils of Washington). "Gotcha oversight" had arrived full throttle in Washington; and, since this partisan approach to "accountability" can be a two-way street, the Democrats soon joined the game of one-upmanship, trying to score points themselves against the GOP in the name of accountability. "We're just going to stick it to you," became the mentality in D.C., recalls a Republican former member of Congress from Virginia. "We focus on what's not going well because our political system rewards that sort of thing."[54]

The Era of Partisan Advocacy, 1992–2001

The rising *Sturm und Drang* of Washington politics was about to invade the Intelligence Committees. In 1992 members of SSCI and HPSCI, who once viewed intelligence as above politics, joined in the partisan fray. Arrant lawmakers bivouacked in separate party encampments, casting votes and often verbal stones against the opposition. Stephen Knott attributes this polarization in part to a Republican wariness of President Bill Clinton's foreign-policy initiatives, as well as to a "simple partisan payback for years of perceived Democratic hectoring of Republican presidents."[55]

One arena where party disputes played out was the intelligence confirmation process. This procedure, during which a president's nominees for DCI and a few other high IC positions are evaluated by the Senate, provides an important opportunity for direct, hands-on accountability, as lawmakers have a chance to examine the qualifications of individuals picked by the executive branch to lead the nation's espionage activities. The United States is the only nation in the world, or ever, to have lawmakers play a central role in selecting intelligence chiefs. Unfortunately, though, during this period politics sometimes vitiated the review; a procedure that had been quite ordinary most of the time suddenly became fraught.

The heated nomination of Robert M. Gates for DCI in 1991 (his second try) was a turning point leading to a new and regrettable era in intelligence accountability tainted by partisan polarization on SSCI and HPSCI, as the GOP rallied behind President George H. W. Bush's choice of former CIA analyst Gates "as a matter of political loyalty and obligation."[56] In an attempt to rise above the partisan divide, Senator Boren, the Democratic chair of SSCI, joined the Republican members in a strong endorsement of Gates and the nominee eventually succeeded, but the hearings and the final vote took place in a swirling storm of party-driven acrimony.

Boren's laudable attempts to hold back the forces of partisanship soon failed. Another DCI confirmation hearing in 1997, this time to consider President Clinton's candidate, national security adviser Anthony Lake, led to an even more tense struggle between the political parties—indeed, a ruction. These vitriolic hearings were punctuated by the most barbed public exchanges across party lines in SSCI's history, fueled in part by the unsubstantiated suspicions of Chairman Richard Shelby (R, Alabama) that Lake had misled SSCI by failing to clarify the CIA's role in arms trafficking to Bosnia. Moreover, Lake's formal application had failed, in Shelby's view, to be sufficiently forthcoming about his personal stock holdings.[57] Shelby was a far more partisan and ideological committee leader than Boren had been and this contrast burned brightly throughout these hearings. Lake finally withdrew his name from consideration, condemning the confirmation process—in theory at least, an important form of intelligence accountability in the Senate—as little more than a political circus.

A further dimension of intelligence oversight began to emerge during this period. With an occasional exception, most members of SSCI and HPSCI became more outright advocates of the CIA and the other secret agencies, instead of performing as gimlet-eyed, hard-nosed reviewers of their programs. The next SSCI chairman, Bob Graham (D, Florida, who was more in the increasingly rare Boren mold when it came to a bipartisan spirit), admitted in 2002, for example, that "we probably didn't shake the [intelligence] agencies hard enough after the end of the Berlin Wall to say: 'Hey, look, the world is changing and you need to change the ways in which you operate . . . new strategies, new personnel, new culture.' We should have been more demanding of these intelligence agencies."[58] Caught up in the euphoria of the Cold War's end and the vanishing of the Soviet threat, on Capitol Hill the interest in intelligence—and intelligence oversight—began to wane. The growing threat of global terrorism and the proliferation of failed states in the world would eventually shatter this lack of concern.

The Alpirez Controversy

In 1995, an intelligence flap occurred in Washington that underscored ongoing deficiencies of accountability. The matter involved two killings in Guatemala. The first victim was an American innkeeper, Michael Devine, with a CIA asset by the name of Col. Julio Roberto Alpirez implicated in the death; the second was Efrain Bamaca Velasquez, a guerrilla fighter whose wife was a vocal and angry U.S. attorney with a Harvard law degree and great skill at shining the light of publicity on her husband's murder. Again Alpirez was implicated. Language in the landmark Intelligence Oversight Act of 1980 required the DCI to report any intelligence failure or suspected impropriety to SSCI and HPSCI. The fact that a suspected killer—Alpirez—was on the Agency's payroll qualified as a reportable event. Yet, for three years, the Agency had failed to inform Congress. Senator William S. Cohen (R, Maine), a member of SSCI who had also been a leading Iran-contra investigator on the Inouye-Hamilton Committee in 1987, told Acting DCI William O. Studeman sternly that "the oversight committees have been misled and . . . may have been lied to."[59]

When he arrived at the CIA to relieve Studeman from his duties as Acting DCI in 1995, John Deutch promulgated a rule—known as the "Deutch rule"—that barred the CIA from recruiting heinous individuals like Alpirez and other blatant violators of human rights. The exception: any potentially useful asset who could help the United States infiltrate terrorist organizations. As a result, outside of the counterterrorism domain (where all possible assets are taken seriously and groomed for humint duties), the Agency broke off its relations with a hundred or so foreign assets "because they committed murder, torture, and other crimes."[60]

The Alpirez incident surfaced an unsettling question, as well, about whether congressional overseers could be trusted to keep secrets. Representative Robert G. Torricelli (D, New Jersey), a member of HPSCI, had taken it upon himself to identify—in a one-man press conference—Colonel Alpirez by name, even though at the time his identity was classified. Torricelli claimed to have spoken out in moral outrage over the colonel's alleged criminal activities, although some claimed that the congressman was essentially a publicity hound intent on advancing his prospects for a Senate seat in New Jersey (which in fact he won the following year, although his political career as a U.S. senator eventually cratered in a corruption scandal that sent him to prison). The *New York Times* concluded that Torricelli sometimes came across as a "bumptious grandstander."[61]

Regardless of motivation, Torricelli had no right to reveal Alpirez's name or the identity of any other CIA asset. Instead, he could have expressed his concerns privately in any number of places: to the CIA's inspector general, the Justice Department, SSCI or HPSCI, the Intelligence Oversight Board, or the NSC and the president. Instead, he went to the media—a breach of trust that momentarily cast a shadow over the reliability of Congress to keep the nation's secrets. Anyone familiar with the history of the Intelligence Committees understood, however, that Torricelli was the single significant exception to the rule that SSCI and HPSCI had kept secrets well since the panels were established in the mid-1970s. Yet, thanks to Torricelli, a cloud settled over the committees for a while and their critics were given misleading ammunition to impugn the entire notion of legislative accountability over the spy agencies.

In SSCI hearings on the Alpirez controversy, Admiral Studeman admitted that the Agency had failed to inform the oversight committees about the suspected criminal actions of its asset in Guatemala. The Acting DCI explained the error as a result of a bureaucratic slip-up, noting that "someone in the CIA was thinking about it, but it never connected.... It slipped under the carpet." Studeman's eye-rolling explanation led SSCI member (and later chairman) Richard Shelby to remark: "That's a big carpet over there at Langley, isn't it? To hold all the things that have slipped under it. It'd have to be a large carpet."

"[SSCI and HPSCI] should have been informed," the admiral repeated, probably wishing he were on an aircraft carrier somewhere in the middle of the Pacific Ocean. "And we do have lists that describe the kinds of information and categories of data that we are to convey to this and the other committee [HSPCI]."

"I guess whoever is carrying out that list didn't come to work that day," Shelby, a master of performance art, concluded dryly. Studeman vowed to improve the Agency's notification procedures in instances of suspected Agency improprieties or intelligence failures.

The curtain came down on this exchange with a statement of concern from Senator Cohen, who earlier had been one of the leading Iran-contra investigators. "In the past, we used to have a mentality that if you asked the wrong question of the Agency you never got the right answer," he said. "If you asked the right question, you got only half the right answer."[62] That had been my experience, too, on occasions when I had taken depositions from leading intelligence officials while on the Church Committee's team of investigators. For instance, I had a difficult time trying to pry information out of former DCI Richard Helms about why, in 1970, he had signed a presidentially initiated—and clearly improper—master spy plan (the Huston Plan that ordered the CIA, the FBI, the NSA, and the DIA to engage in domestic spying).[63] "I can't recall" was Helms's refrain as I attempted to awaken details sleeping in his memory. It seemed unlikely to me that a DCI would forget his endorsement of an illegal domestic espionage scheme of this magnitude.[64] An attorney on the Church Committee staff had a similar experience with another canny witness, Richard Bissell, Jr., the CIA's deputy director for plans at the time of the Bay of Pigs. "In retrospect," the attorney recalls, "maybe he was only revealing layer two and layer three of the onion and there might have been fourteen layers."[65]

Forgetfulness seemed to be a chronic malady for Helms, appearing like an eruption of measles whenever he had to testify before an investigative panel. In front of the Rockefeller Commission in 1975, he again offered the testimony "I don't recall" when asked by investigators about whether (in 1963) he had considered the possibility of a connection between the assassination of John F. Kennedy and the CIA's several murder plots against Fidel Castro. Nor could he recall during his time as the head of the Operations Directorate whether he had ever briefed the new DCI John McCone about the assassination plots. Further, when asked if CIA poison pills were smuggled into Cuba to kill the Cuban leader, his answer was, once more, "I don't recall." During follow-up questions before the Church Committee on this subject, he resorted to a series of "I don't recalls." Senator Robert Morgan (D, North Carolina) of the Church Committee asked Helms if he had been forthcoming with the Warren Commission during its investigation of President Kennedy's murder:

MORGAN: "You were asked for [information] and you didn't give it?"
HELMS: "That's right, sir."[66]

Former DCI William E. Colby once maintained that "Congress is informed [about intelligence] to the degree that Congress wants to be informed."[67] There is great validity in this observation; if lawmakers are lazy or lack an interest in accountability, they are unlikely to acquire the information they need to understand the nation's spy operations. Even when members of SSCI or HPSCI have been persistent and pushed hard for the facts, though, there has been no guarantee they will be informed by the executive branch about key intelligence activities. The tide of truth in congressional testimony has sometimes sunk to a dangerous low. During the Iran-contra scandal, for example, CIA officers frequently misled lawmakers about the Agency's involvement in rogue covert actions against Nicaragua. When subsequently called on the carpet, one high-ranking Agency official argued that his sworn testimony to SSCI had been "technically correct, [if] specifically evasive."[68] That kind of gobbledygook makes oversight nearly impossible. Just as night darkens the streets, so was his vague testimony meant to obscure the CIA's involvement in the scandal. At the time of the hearing on the Alpirez case, Senator Cohen expressed his worry that the old mentality of evasion remained alive and well at Langley.

President Clinton directed the Intelligence Oversight Board in the White House to look into the Alpirez case. The IOB found fault with the Agency's handling of its ties with the Guatemalan colonel, especially its failure to inform SSCI and HPSCI about his likely involvement in the homicide; the board concluded, though, that the error was inadvertent (as Studeman had emphasized) rather than an attempt to evade lawmakers. In response to the congressional and IOB criticism, Studeman reprimanded a dozen Agency officers for their incompetence in dealing with the matter, two of whom were forced to retire.

The Aspin-Brown Commission

As well in 1995, the government undertook another major investigation into the intelligence community—an inquiry into U.S. spy activities second only to the Church Committee in its depth and scope. Carried out by a panel of lawmakers and executive branch appointees, and chaired in succession by former secretaries of defense Les Aspin (once an upstart HPSCI member) and Harold Brown (a former president of Cal Tech University), the investigation attempted to determine how America's spy agencies might best confront the challenging new world that had emerged at the end of the Cold War. The experience of the Aspin-Brown Commission sheds further light on the "firefighting" investigative form of intelligence accountability, an approach that is extreme, reactive, and often controversial.[69]

The Creation of the Commission

The initial incident that led to the establishment of the Aspin-Brown Commission was a U.S. military encounter in Somalia in October 1993, in which a ragtag force led by a Somali warlord killed eighteen Special Forces soldiers. Televised images of the dead American warriors, stripped naked and dragged through the city's alleyways, stunned viewers in the United States. The tragedy pointed to a disturbing intelligence failure regarding the strength of the opposition forces on the Horn of Africa, coming on top of an unnerving (if ineffectual) terrorist detonation of explosives in a rental truck at the base of the World Trade Center in February of the same year (a precursor to the 9/11 attacks eight years later).

Vice President Al Gore and Secretary of Defense Aspin sought an explanation for the wrenching debacle in Somalia. So did members of Congress, especially Republicans, quick to blame the Clinton Administration for the defeat. As criticism mounted on Capitol Hill and in the media, President Bill Clinton fired Aspin in December 1993, less than a year into his job, forcing him to take the hit for the administration. To soften Aspin's fall, Clinton appointed him chairman of the President's Foreign Intelligence Advisory Board (PFIAB). In this capacity, Aspin gained permission from the White House to investigate the intelligence deficiencies that had contributed to the Somali calamity.

Conservative members of Congress, though, had a different agenda. They were even more worried about the hemorrhaging of American secrets to the Russians. In 1994, CIA counterintelligence officers had discovered that for over a decade one of their own, Aldridge Hazen Ames, had spied against the Agency on behalf of the Soviet Union and then Russia. He had provided the Kremlin with specifics on hundreds of operations and the names of at least nine U.S. agents in Moscow, all quickly dispatched by the KGB. If the CIA were to be a subject of an investigation, congressional conservatives reasoned, this counterintelligence failure should be the focus.

Moreover, other lawmakers questioned whether the Agency had adequately considered its post–Cold War mission. The DCI at the time, R. James Woolsey, had been unable to communicate a vision of the role intelligence should play in this new era—at least, not to the satisfaction of SSCI members. A leading senator, John Warner (R, Virginia, and SSCI's vice chairman), soon entered the debate and recommended the Senate create its own commission of inquiry into the broad question of the IC's proper orientation now that the Cold War had ceased. "Warner's commission proposal is the only way to get [the CIA] back on track, because Woolsey hasn't put it there," declared SSCI Chairman Dennis DeConcini (D, Arizona), who seemed to view Woolsey as another rebarbative DCI in the style of William J. Casey.[70] Woolsey's cocksure personality, interpreted by some as arrogance, had managed to alienate key lawmakers, notably DeConcini, who accused him of "total obstructionism" with respect to the Congress.[71] As well, the DCI had been widely admonished on the Hill for merely reprimanding eleven CIA officers in their failed supervisory roles over Ames, instead of dispensing harsher penalties.

In frustration, when Warner refused to leave the investigative field to PFIAB, Aspin finally proposed a combined executive-congressional commission. It was a take-it-or-leave-it proposal: either this hybrid or two separate inquiries. Satisfied that he would have enough clout on the proposed commission (including his own membership) to rein in the liberal Aspin faction, Warner agreed to the deal. Congress approved the creation of the bipartisan Commission on the Roles and Capabilities of the United States Intelligence Community and the president signed the bill in October 1994, setting a March 1, 1996, deadline for the panel's final report.

Starting Up the Commission

The *New York Times* warned in January 1995 that unless the panel got moving it would soon be "roadkill," run over by HPSCI, which was gearing up under the leadership of its chairman, Larry Combes (R, Texas), to conduct a House probe of its own into the state of intelligence in the wake of the Cold War.[72] The House Committee planned a series of hearings labeled "IC21," an abbreviation for the "Intelligence Community in the 21st Century."

Among the commissioners, Aspin and Senator Wyche Fowler had served on HPSCI earlier in their careers. In addition, two others commissioners were incumbent HPSCI members: Norman D. Dicks (D, Washington) and Porter J. Goss (R, Florida). Later elected to the Senate, Fowler had also gone on to serve as a member of SSCI. Warren B. Rudman (R, New Hampshire), the Commission's vice chair, had served on SSCI, too, as well as the Inouye-Hamilton Committee on the Iran-contra affair; and J. James Exon and John Warner were SSCI incumbents. So the Commission had the benefit of seven members with hands-on experience as congressional overseers for intelligence.

The IC was well represented among the commissioners, as well, with high-ranking former NSA officials General Lew Allen, Jr. (who had opposed the Church Committee public hearing about his agency in 1975), Ann Z. Caracristi, and Robert J. Hermann. For some, their presence amounted to letting the fox into the hen house; but, at the same time, their technical knowledge and experience in signals intelligence were considered a valuable asset to the Commission, because much of America's intelligence collection overseas relied on sophisticated sigint machines—from miniature listening devices to giant satellites in space.

Aspin's main concern in these start-up weeks was to think through how to organize the Commission's work. In a list of the Commission's first- and second-order priorities came a catchall "cats and dogs" category that included counterintelligence, covert action, and, last of all, accountability. A week later, accountability was dropped from the list altogether. During a session early into the inquiry, the Commission's staff director and former SSCI chief counsel, L. Britt Snider, echoed the chief objective for the Commission espoused by Warner (who had urged Aspin to select Snider for the job of staff director). "Our goal is to *sell* intelligence," Snider declared. "We have to establish a political consensus in the country favoring intelligence."

In March 1995, President Clinton persuaded John Deutch, an MIT chemistry professor on leave as a high-level Pentagon official, to accept the DCI position when Woolsey resigned. If Deutch, the Commission, or the public needed any reminding of the importance of intelligence, they got it—miserably—on April 19, when a truck filled with explosives demolished the Alfred P. Murrah Federal Building in Oklahoma City, killing 168 people in the worst terrorist attack in the United States since a bomb had exploded on Wall Street in 1920. "I think we are going to see more of this," warned Acting DCI Studeman.

At the time, I was Aspin's aide on the Commission and he asked me to prepare a study on U.S. counterterrorism capabilities. '"Aerial terrorism' seems likely at some point," a CIA counterterrorism specialist told me when I sought out his assistance, "filling an airplane with explosives and dive-bombing a target." America was still six years away from comprehending the full implications of this warning and of how a passenger plane—loaded with highly volatile aviation fuel—would serve well enough as a devastating bomb without landing first for added explosives.

A Commission Retreat

To attempt some bonding of the diverse set of commissioners, Aspin decided to have the panel escape the hectic pace of Washington for a couple of days of meetings in the Virginia countryside. The retreat took place in early May at a wooded

CIA facility ("the Farm") used chiefly as a training site. The featured speaker was former DCI Gates. He displayed some passion as he turned to the subject of intelligence oversight. When SSCI and HPSCI were created, lawmakers placed term limits on membership, he reminded the commissioners: eight years for the Senate panel and six for the House. Gates thought this was a mistake, forcing members to rotate off the committees just as they were beginning to really understand the details of the intelligence business. "Experience matters," he said.[73]

Gates also opposed the nostrum, gaining some currency at the time, of having only one oversight committee: a joint intelligence panel to replace SSCI and HPSCI. Those who embraced this notion argued that a single committee would save the DCI precious time in the presentation of briefings (an appearance on the Hill once instead of twice for any given briefing), plus supposedly the leak potential would be less. With astonishing candor and a gleeful grin, Gates said that he preferred two committees because then "the DCI can manipulate one against the other." If SSCI didn't like a proposed intelligence operation, perhaps HPSCI would, or vice versa. The DCI could use these disagreements to his own advantage.

Above all, Gates recommended more informal meetings between the DCI and the oversight committees. I doubted that an increase in the number of afternoon kaffeeklatsches on the Hill, or evening cocktails in the DCI's suite of offices on the seventh floor at Langley, would have done much for the Woolsey-DeConcini relationship or mellowed out Bill Casey. Still, Gates had a valid point: good relations between the branches rested on the development of rapport and trust among individuals on the Hill and in the executive agencies, and that meant getting together for informal chats now and then.

During the Q and A with Gates, the first question was (to my delight) about oversight. This gave the former DCI an opening to chastise what he viewed as a tendency among SSCI and HPSCI lawmakers to "micromanage." This was a favorite word among spy professionals used to ridicule the participation of Congress in the intelligence community's sensitive activities. The core thesis was that lawmakers often become too involved in the details of delicate spy operations, without the requisite training and experience to understand them. Their clumsy meddling could harm espionage tradecraft and endanger lives. I had heard this critique from intelligence officers time and again, during and after the Church Committee investigation. For some people in the community, "micromanagement" was coded language that meant "stay the hell of out of our business, you morons. Just let us do what we think is right for the security of the United States." The phrase was a Trojan horse in their efforts to weaken legitimate safeguards.

Most people who advanced the micromanagement viewpoint had no examples to back up their claims, but to his credit Gates offered some illustrations. He said that lawmakers had recently forced the CIA to buy computers, while "leasing would have been smarter." If this had been the best example the former DCI could provide of micromanagement, his criticism would have been rather weak. His second example, though, was more damning. "I remember Senator Malcolm Wallop [R, Wyoming]," Gates continued, "trying to tell me exactly how many analysts to assign to each country." This was clearly over the line. The Wallop example, though, struck me as a rare illustration of overstepping by a member of Congress.

During the Q and A period, Senator Warner again underscored his philosophy about the Commission's charge. "A few of us were desperately concerned that someone was going to go in and cut up the intelligence budget," he said. "This Commission was meant to stop that—and it has succeeded. Our mission is to explain to the American people that intelligence is important." The senior SSCI member *qua* commissioner was proving to be an adroit cheerleader for the Agency. Richard Russell would have been proud.

The Loss of a Chairman

Soon after the Commission's retreat at the Farm, Aspin suffered a major stroke and died at the Georgetown University Hospital. President Clinton asked Harold Brown to take his place as the Commission chair. When former national security adviser Lt. Gen. Brent Scowcroft subsequently appeared before the panel, one of the commissioners asked him how it was that some oversight commissions succeeded and some failed. "It depends on the subject and the circumstances," Scowcroft replied. "President Reagan and the Congress were at loggerheads over the Commission on Strategic Forces in 1983. It went nowhere. There was another commission on defense management during the Reagan years that attracted little public interest, because the subject didn't seem that urgent. Your commission suffers from that same lack of interest." Still, Scowcroft viewed the Aspin-Brown inquiry as an "unusual opportunity" to sit down with the DCI, as well as other community leaders, and focus on their problems.

Former DCI Helms also appeared before the Commission and addressed the question of oversight. He expressed reservations about the new rules promulgated since the Church Committee and the ability of lawmakers to comprehend the intelligence trade; but he did concede that "there had been no leaks from Congress."

"That's because you didn't tell them anything, Dick!" interjected Vice Chairman Rudman in a jocular moment.

Commissioner Porter Goss, who had served in the CIA's Operations Directorate as a young man, circled back to the subject of oversight. "What's the best way to do this?" he asked Helms.

"Keep it small. Use a joint committee. Rely on trust and confidence," was his staccato response. The idea of a join committee was a favorite approach embraced by those who "favored less oversight rather than more," in the experience of a long-serving SSCI staffer.[74]

In between closed hearings held in a conference room at the New Executive Office Building near the White House, commissioners and staff met with other witnesses in their offices around Washington. Seldom did the subject of intelligence oversight come up, although former DCI Webster stressed that "Agency officials must learn that they will be held accountable for their transgressions." Occasionally, a witness argued against any form of intelligence supervision from the Hill. "Congress has no business in the area of intelligence," declared William G. Hyland, a former CIA analyst who had also directed the State Department's intelligence unit (INR). His primary example was all the occasions when the DCI had to trek up to Capitol Hill—"more than the secretary of state!" Rather than dilly-dallying with SSCI and HPSCI, Hyland believed that intelligence officers could more profitably spend their time running spies, managing satellites, and working to bring about greater integration to the IC.

A Second Retreat

In September, the Commission convened for its second retreat, this time at a conference center in Leesburg, Virginia. No votes were taken; rather, the plan was to identify worthy recommendations through further discussion. The commissioners went in a dozen different directions. Covert action—from CIA propaganda to paramilitary operations—caused the most fireworks, with little consensus for or against. "It's a dirty diaper pail," a commissioner concluded. Disputatious, too, was an idea floated to consolidate all technical intelligence under one command. "Wait, imint is different from sigint!" objected a commissioner who had served in the NSA and balked at lumping together photographic intelligence with telephone intercepts. One thing was certain: with three commissioners and two senior staffers from the NSA on the panel and present in the room, that agency was unlikely to lose its control over signals intelligence. Discussion of the intelligence budget also generated sparks, with different factions in favor of either downsizing, increasing, or holding spending exactly where it was. Harold Brown grew fidgety during these clashes, his right fist doubled and pumping up and down on the arm of his chair.

As the Commission began to wind down the first day of these meetings, one of the more progressive members warned, "We are in danger of becoming a status quo Commission."

"We will have some changes." Brown replied, with an edge to his voice.

"According to whom?" the commissioner responded. "The DCI? The SecDef?" The chairman's jaw hardened. "Let's put this discussion off to later."

On the last day of the retreat, Brown reviewed the topics that he thought the Commission had decided were most important. The list included economic intelligence; the relationship between law enforcement and national security; covert action; whether the office of DCI should be strengthened; whether to consolidate the military intelligence agencies; personnel issues; improving the management of space surveillance (DCI Deutch's pet project); whether to declassify the aggregate annual intelligence budget figure; whether to trim the budget; whether policy departments and agencies that wanted intelligence should be charged a fee by the DCI; oversight (revived as a Commission subject, thanks to Goss and Fowler); counterintelligence (the Ames problem); and the state of humint. Aspin's earlier interest in the Somalia intelligence failure had been shunted off to the Pentagon to figure out and correct.

Brown was leery of trying to pass a new law to increase the DCI's authority, at the expense of the eight-hundred-pound gorilla in the Department of Defense: the SecDef. "It is really telling the secretary of defense how to run his shop; so as a member of the club, I'm of two minds about that. . . . I would not want to write this into legislation, but," he added weakly, "rather urge the secretary of defense to make those changes."

Preparing the Final Report

Rumors of financial irregularities at the National Reconnaissance Office grew into a media spectacle in September 1995, as the Commission was drafting its final report. The NRO had secretly accumulated over $1.5 billion in public monies without keeping Congress informed of the unspent funds. The agency then asked the Congress to appropriate more money for satellites, again without acknowledging that it already had enough funds stowed away from past appropriations to cover the costs of the new surveillance machines. Deutch said publicly that the NRO had "ignored a directive from Congress" issued several years ago to reduce the amounts it was carrying over from year to year.[75] On top of this charge, news surfaced in January 1996 that the NRO had managed to misplace more than $2 billion in classified funds the previous year, a result of its chaotic accounting systems and poor management.[76] The lost appropriations were finally located when Deutch ordered an outside audit. HPSCI Chairman Combest remarked that "the NRO has a credibility problem here," adding: "One of the real complaints I have [is that] they have had a history of evading questions. They do not answer a question fully."[77]

On October 13, the staff huddled with commissioners in an attempt to hammer out exactly what language and recommendations the members desired. Goss's ongoing concern about oversight received added attention, given the revelations that the NRO had played shell games with its funding. He tried once more to advocate a joint oversight committee to replace SSCI and HPSCI.

"That's not even worth talking about," Rudman responded, pointing out that most lawmakers did not want to have only one committee on intelligence; the Senate and the House preferred to have their own separate panels. As usual, opposition from Brown or Rudman was tantamount to sticking a pin into a balloon. Abandoning the joint committee idea, Goss pursued another proposal: a ten-year term limit for SSCI and HPSCI members to replace their shorter tenures and, thus, provide better experience on the committees. No one voiced opposition to that notion.

Later in October 1995, Brown and Rudman visited Congress to update key lawmakers on the Commission's work and to solicit their opinions. During a meeting with Combest, Harold Brown noted that matters of oversight had been raised at a Commission retreat, including the possibility of establishing a joint intelligence committee to replace SSCI and HPSCI. Combest replied immediately: "That's a bad idea. Hell, we can't even get those senators to a conference committee meeting!" The HPSCI chair did believe, however, that the Commission should look at some issues related to accountability, such as removing the term limits for HPSCI and SSCI membership. Worth examining, too, he observed, were jurisdictional controversies on the Hill. As things stood in 1995—and still today—the Judiciary Committees, Armed Services Committees, and Appropriations Committee shared intelligence jurisdiction with SSCI and HPSCI, which led to a confusing tangle of oversight responsibilities. Cautiously, Brown mentioned that the Commission might look at these issues, "but leave the solutions to Congress." Combest nodded his head in approval.

At a subsequent Commission session, the troublesome issue of the intelligence budget—a core oversight responsibility—came up. Dicks and Goss opposed a 15 percent spending reduction on espionage activities over ten years, as recommended by General Allen (a rare position for an IC leader to take). "We ought to stabilize intelligence, not cut it," argued Dicks, who represented a district in the state of Washington where spy satellites were constructed. He continued: "That kind of cut wouldn't muster 100 votes on the Hill." Fowler countered that the Commission should do what is right, not what might be politically palatable; cuts were the right thing to do, since (in his words) "appetites [for more money] are insatiable. . . . The public expects savings." The extended debate made it clear that the Dicks-Goss faction had the votes on the Commission if it came to a formal division, including the most important ballot: Chairman

Brown's. General Allen eventually threw in the towel, saying, "If I can't convince you to save money, then, okay, I'll go along."

On January 18, 1996, the commissioners convened to go through the staff's draft report again. "Remember the underlying reason for the Commission," Warner emphasized: "to restore confidence in intelligence." Goss agreed: "We shouldn't paint such a black picture. I'm not trying to whitewash, but let's tone this down." The wide range of views on the Commission and the hope for consensus had the effect of blurring important issues, a common outcome for investigative panels. "This will be viewed as an extraordinary apologia for the intelligence community," Fowler said, drawing foul looks from Brown, Goss, and Warner.

"We've got to move along," Brown insisted.

"I plead for self-restraint," Rudman seconded. "We'd all write this differently."

Nerves fraying, the commissioners took a break. When they returned, the budget received the most attention. "We better try to cut 5 percent if we are going to have any credibility—except with the defense contractors," Rudman suggested.

Goss was not convinced. "It's more difficult to track a bunch of snakes [emerging world threats] than one dragon [the Soviet Union during the Cold War]," he said, paraphrasing a metaphor made popular by former DCI Woolsey. "Therefore, we need more money for intelligence, not less." Once again, forces pulling in opposite directions left the Commission stuck in the middle with the status quo. One of the few budget matters most commissioners could agree on was the release of the aggregate annual budget figure for the intelligence community.

"Nothing will give us more credibility than releasing the top figure," said Rudman.

"We'll look silly if we don't," Brown agreed.

By the time the commissioners had worked their way through the full draft, they looked exhausted. "My head is exploding," Fowler commented to me on the way out of the conference room. "These people [the commissioners] don't understand that the press and the public are going to be interested mainly in accountability, covert action, and counterintelligence, not dry, sterile treatises on bureaucratic changes—moving boxes from here to there." His face was a portrait of dismay.

The Commission Reports

Though some were unhappy about the compromises that had been made, each commissioner signed the report. Later that day, the staff released the two-hundred-page document to the public.[78] At a press conference, Brown summed up the main recommendations. When it came to spending on spies, the Commission had taken the easy way out, suggesting that Congress and the executive branch should think of ways to trim overlap and waste—as if that responsibility had not been part of the Commission's charge in the first place. The Commission leaders gave a slight nod to oversight by suggesting that the term limits on SSCI and HPSCI be raised a few years to enhance the level of experience on the panels—a sensible reform that both committees finally adopted in 2004 (eight years later). The report concluded: "By most accounts, [SSCI and HPSCI] provide rigorous and intensive oversight"—a stretch, to say the least, although no doubt politically prudent, as the Commission was about to ask those very committees to advance its recommendations on Capitol Hill.

The intelligence community was largely unaffected by the Aspin-Brown inquiry—or, for that matter, the similar reform proposals offered in HPSCI's "IC21." The spy budget remained intact; counterintelligence received little attention; the limits of covert action were never defined; the weaknesses in accountability went largely unaddressed; the DCI's powers remained stunted; and the threat of "aerial terrorism" garnered little attention. Nonetheless, the existence and the nudging of a blue-ribbon panel did encourage the DCI and the IC's agency directors at the time to concentrate intently on current problems and find redress for them—or risk attracting unwanted public criticism from commissioners in their report. In this sense, the Commission had a significant influence on the IC. The Pentagon studied the Somalia errors closely; the CIA and the FBI carefully examined what counterintelligence lessons could be derived from the Ames case; pension systems were reviewed; collection-and-analysis shortcomings were given a scrub. None of this attracted headlines or impressed the editorial boards and reporters of leading newspapers, and the flaws in the system of intelligence accountability failed to gain much traction during the Commission's probe. Nonetheless, the panel's investigations were in themselves a healthy exercise in oversight, coaxing the IC toward internal—if undramatic—reforms that few media and academic observers understood and appreciated at the time.

A Darkening Sky

Two years after the Aspin-Brown inquiry, President Clinton formed another national commission, at the urging of Speaker Gingrich, this one placed under the auspices of the Defense Department and entitled the U.S. Commission on National Security in the 21st Century. Its cochairs were former senators Gary Hart (who had served on the Church Committee) and Warren Rudman (the former Aspin-Brown vice chair). The Hart-Rudman Commission issued three thoughtful reports about America's security, which focused for the most part on the vulnerability of the United States ("the homeland") to attack by terrorists. Adversaries would resort to "forms of violence shocking to our sensibilities," the Commission concluded.[79]

The Hart-Rudman Commission labored for two and a half years on its reports, yet, as Hart recalls, "no one listened."[80] This is a great pity because few, if any, government reports have been so prescient. Less than six months after the Commission released its findings, terrorists struck the United States in the 9/11 attacks, bringing great tragedy to the nation and ushering in a new era in intelligence accountability. The world had changed, and along with it the balance between liberty and security within the United States. A few years later, a former Church Committee staffer would write that "the process of congressional oversight of intelligence, including covert action, so carefully crafted in the 1970s, is now regarded as something of a joke in Washington. Terrorism is frightening enough to the body politics to justify almost any action in response."[81] The next chapter examines these responses.

|| 5 ||

Spy Watching in an Age of Terror

The Era of Mass Surveillance, 2001–2012

In all of American history, the most piercing alarm signifying a failure of national security rang out on September 11, 2001, when the terrorist group Al Qaeda hit the United States. The traumatizing effects of this disaster continue to unfurl in debates over the proper balance between liberty and security. The attacks claimed the lives of nearly three thousand Americans as commercial airliners hijacked by terrorists slammed into the World Trade Center and the Pentagon. Passengers in revolt against hijackers brought down another airline in a rural field in Pennsylvania, with everyone onboard perishing. As partisan squabbling continued to roil SSCI and HPSCI, its members now confronted a much more troubling situation than finger-wagging between Democrats and Republicans: the spy agencies and the White House had proved unable to defend the homeland and, by implication, so had those responsible for intelligence supervision on Capitol Hill.[1]

Anger and fear spread across the nation after the terrorist attacks. How could they have happened on this scale inside our own country? Were more attacks coming? In the executive branch, counterterrorism budgets raced upward; the CIA, for example, saw a quick 35 percent increase in its funding.[2] On Capitol Hill, SSCI and HPSCI members merged into an ad hoc Joint Committee to investigate the tragic national security failure.

The Joint Committee and the Kean Commission

The Joint Committee, led by SSCI Chairman Bob Graham (D, Florida) and HPSCI Chairman Porter Goss (R, Florida), held extensive hearings throughout 2002, but the panel was often on the defensive. It fired its first staff director; then, in a second dust-up, the Bush Administration accused the panel of leaking classified information. The Joint Committee allowed the FBI, one of the agencies it was supposed to be investigating, to launch a probe into the leaks, thereby compromising the independence of the congressional investigation. Weathering these early setbacks, the committee managed to rebound and complete a serious examination of mistakes made by the intelligence agencies prior to the 9/11 attacks, especially the inability or unwillingness of the CIA and the FBI to share information with one another regarding the whereabouts of some of the 9/11 terrorists inside the United States during the months leading up to that awful day.

The Joint Committee's slow start caused it to run out of time, so its exasperated members proposed the creation of a special commission to continue and widen the inquiry. President Bush initially opposed the idea of yet another probe, but the skillful lobbying in Washington by family members of the attack victims generated a groundswell of support in favor of an expanded inquiry into why America was taken by surprise. The president begrudgingly relented and, in 2002, Congress and the White House named five members each to a bipartisan "9/11 Commission," known formally as the National Commission on Terrorist Attacks Upon the United States, or, after its chair, the Kean Commission, led by the Republican former governor of New Jersey, Thomas H. Kean. The Commission's vice chair was the experienced and much-heralded practitioner of intelligence accountability, Lee H. Hamilton, the former HPSCI leader at the time of the Iran-contra affair and the co-chair (with SSCI's Senator Inouye) of the investigation in 1987 into that scandal.

The life of the 9/11 Commission was turbulent, beginning with the president's initial opposition to its efforts at gaining access to key documents held by the spy agencies, especially the *President's Daily Brief*. The *PDB* is a highly classified report on day-to-day intelligence findings that the CIA is loath to allow anyone to see, other than top officials in the executive branch—even versions that are decades old.[3] Moreover, even the first step of finding someone to lead the Commission proved difficult. Former secretary of state Henry Kissinger, and then former Senate Majority Leader George Mitchell (D, Maine), turned down the opportunity, probably because (according to speculation at the time) they were reluctant to open up their personal finances for public scrutiny—a prerequisite for taking the job, to ensure no conflicts of interest (such as Kissinger's rumored consulting ties with Saudi Arabia, home for fifteen of the nineteen 9/11 hijackers). Reliable police patrollers on SSCI and HPSCI were hard enough to come by; now potential firefighters for the 9/11 Commission were scattering like quail.

In Thomas Kean, the president at last found an able and willing candidate to guide the inquiry. At the time, Kean was president of Drew University in New Jersey. Avuncular and known for his ability to work across party lines, he brought a high degree of earnestness and a sense of fairness to the helm. Hamilton, too, was low key, also in his senior years, and well regarded as trustworthy and willing to set partisanship aside. The Commission's membership was made up of retired politicians, plus a combination of D.C. lawyers and former bureaucrats. Given the specter of political polarization that had become an enduring feature of life in Washington, the Commission's membership was purposefully divided evenly along party lines. Within months, Senator Max Cleland (D, Georgia) would resign in disgust over what he claimed was the panel's excessive obeisance to the White House. Senator Bob Kerrey (D, Nebraska), an SSCI member, replaced him.

The Commission sifted through more than 2,500,000 pages of documents, interviewed 1,200 people, and held a dozen open hearings. The hearings garnered high TV ratings as a result in part of such celebrity witnesses as former secretaries of state Madeleine K. Albright and Colin L. Powell, Secretary of Defense Donald H. Rumsfeld, DCI George J. Tenet, former national security advisers Samuel R. Berger and Condoleezza Rice, former counterterrorism guru Richard A. Clarke, and FBI leaders Louis J. Freeh and Robert S. Mueller III. Further, the sometimes acerbic exchanges between commissioners and witnesses made for captivating drama. The Commission also privately interviewed the president, who tried to evade having to testify only to bow again to effective lobbying by the 9/11 families.

In the summer of 2004, after more than a year's worth of research, the Commission reported.[4] The narrative began in this way: "Tuesday, September 11, 2001, dawned temperate and nearly cloudless in the eastern United States. Millions of men and women readied themselves for work. Some made their way to the Twin Towers . . . or for those heading to an airport, weather conditions could not have been better for a safe and pleasant journey. Among the travelers were [terrorists] Mohamed Atta and Abdul Aziz al Omari, who arrived at the airport in Portland, Maine."

From this calm opening, the story builds to the gripping climax of the attacks. Here was a report that would have been hard to write without inducing a sense of drama. Who could fail to remember where they were at 8:46 on the morning of September 11 when the first airplane struck the North Tower of the Trade Center in New York, and then the telling next plane crash into the South Tower at 9:03? Who did not want to know more about how this horror had unfolded?

Yet it is one thing to relate the events of 9/11 and quite another to prescribe how to prevent terrorist attacks from recurring, or to offer guidance on how to improve intelligence accountability that might strengthen the spy agencies against future failures. Here is where the Commission stumbled, presenting a raft of recommendations that were often poorly thought out and ambiguous, such as the idea of turning CIA covert paramilitary operations over to the Pentagon. Belittling this notion, a former secretary of defense, James R. Schlesinger, had said to me at the time of the Church Committee in 1975 that "the Pentagon can't do anything small or quiet."[5]

Even the description of the events left much to be desired from such a high-powered, lengthy, and expensive inquiry. For example, the Commission never explained why it took Rice, the national security adviser during the first term of the Bush Administration, eight months—from January 25 to September 4, 2001—to place Al Qaeda on the NSC's agenda, even though she had been repeatedly cautioned by counterterrorism expert Richard A. Clarke of the departing Clinton Administration that no danger at the time was greater to the United States.[6] Nor was it adequately explained to the public why the FBI had rejected warnings from its field offices in Phoenix and Minneapolis about Arab visitors engaged in suspicious flight training in their states; or why warrants to search the homes of these individuals were never sought by FBI from the FISA Court. An anxious Bureau agent in Minneapolis even warned superiors in Washington that this was an important matter of "trying to keep someone from taking a plane and crashing into the World Trade Center" (an alarm that Headquarters found fanciful).[7] Cloudy, too, were the reasons why in early 2001 the CIA and the FBI had been unable to cooperate in tracking down two suspected terrorists entering California who became participants in the attacks.

Further, the Kean Commission failed to note the important fact that the CIA had warned of "aerial terrorism" as early as 1995.[8] Despite this red flag, neither the Clinton Administration nor lawmakers on SSCI or HPSCI did anything to alert airport security personnel, airline pilots, or the Department of Transportation about this startling threat assessment. Moreover, during this period, why weren't SSCI and HPSCI able to push the spy agencies and policymakers toward greater counterterrorism cooperation? Answers are not to be found in the Commission's report.

Critics who bemoan the lack of warning about the 9/11 attacks point to the CIA and cry: "Intelligence failure!" True, in the sense that the Agency never provided specific ("actionable") intelligence about how and when the United States might be struck from the skies by terrorists. The intelligence community did provide alerts, however, of a severe danger of terrorist attacks against the U.S. mainland in its aerial terrorism report from the CIA's Counterterrorism Center (CTC) in 1995; and, on August 6, 2001, a month before 9/11, a PDB underscored the high likelihood of an Al Qaeda strike against the nation, including a reference to a rumor that in 1998 the Al Qaeda leader (Bin Laden) had "wanted to hijack a US aircraft" to gain the release of one of its operatives held by the United States.[9] The lack of response by the nation's leaders to these red flags—what the PDB referred to as a "blinking red light" in August 2001—leads to the equally valid proposition that 9/11 was, as well, a profound policy failure. Neither Presidents Bill Clinton nor George W. Bush properly responded to the intelligence warnings. Further, the tragedy was a failure of intelligence account-ability, with lawmakers equally passive toward the warnings coming from the IC. These realities are never properly underscored in the report.

Especially disturbing was the inability of the Commission to assign any blame among intelligence managers, policymakers, or lawmakers for errors related to the tragedy. Anyone who knows anything about intelligence under-stands that mistakes are inevitable. Still, much could have been done to lessen the odds of failure in the events leading up to 9/11, such as taking more ener-getic steps to develop spy rings in the Middle East and Southwest Asia. Or, at home, FBI and CIA computers could have been integrated so that these two vital agencies could share intelligence more readily about suspected terrorists operating against the United States—especially those already inside the country. The public learned through media reporting, not from the Kean Commission, that the FBI's computer systems at the time were archaic. These are all matters that rigorous accountability on the Hill and inside the executive branch should have addressed.

Less satisfactory still were the Commission's recommendations. The central one was a proposal to establish a Director of National Intelligence (DNI). This was hardly a novel idea. Strengthening the authority of the DCI had been high on the agenda of intelligence reformers from early commissions in the 1950s to the Aspin-Brown Commission in 1995. The Intelligence Authorization Act of 1991 (known widely as the Intelligence Oversight Act of 1991) initially proposed the establishment of a DNI, but that part of the initiative never mus-tered sufficient support and was dropped from the original bill. When the Kean Commission again embraced the notion of a strong national spy chief in 2004, it erred in failing to adequately explain what authorities that office would need to have, or even where the new spymaster would be located. This ambiguity set the stage for a brawl on Capitol Hill among the intelligence agencies, DoD officials, lawmakers, the 9/11 families, and members of the Kean Commission over legis-lation to establish an Office of the DNI.

In December 2004—in the face of strong opposition from the CIA and DoD—Congress belatedly passed a reform measure entitled the Intelligence Reform and Terrorism Prevention Act (IRTPA), which embodied the DNI pro-posal and some other Kean Commission recommendations.[10] While pinballing its way through the legislative process, however, the IRTPA proposal became more and more ambiguous about the nature of the DNI office. This left many complex matters for the first DNI, former ambassador John D. Negroponte, to sort out. He faced the enormous task of trying to break down the stovepipes that separate each of the spy agencies from sharing information effectively—a chal-lenge of both information technology and, even more difficult, rival bureaucratic cultures. Negroponte and his successors, further, had to establish the right of the DNI to influence funding and personnel decisions throughout the sprawling intelligence community—all without a clear legislative mandate.

An obvious solution would have been simply, at long last, to give the DCI the powers that President Truman had envisioned in the first place, before he retreated from the DoD's cavalry charge to protect its grip on the military intelligence agencies.[11] These powers would include full budget and appointment authority for each one of the sixteen intelligence agencies, not just the CIA. The Kean Commission shied away, however, from rewarding the Agency—everyone's favorite scapegoat for the 9/11 failure—by increasing the DCI's authority in his seventh-floor aerie at Langley. Instead, the Commission embraced the model of a stand-alone DNI, removed from the other intelligence agencies and given little authority.

This anti-Agency stance suited many (perhaps all) of the other intelligence agencies, who over the years had built up resentment against the CIA's posture as the premier secret service in the government, and whose officers at Langley had sometimes worn that mantle with arrogance. Others no doubt thought that in light of recent CIA mistakes (such as its erroneous prediction in 2002 that Iraq possessed unconventional weaponry), it would have been fatuous for the Commission to increase the Agency's status by reestablishing and building up the DCI's powers. By enacting IRTPA, lawmakers went so far as to expressly prohibit in the language of the law any possibility that the new DNI would have his or her office at Langley.

The end result of these "reforms" has been to create a DNI who is placed at a distance from the substantial intelligence collection, analysis, production, and dissemination capabilities that had evolved for more than fifty years inside the CIA. Ambassador Negroponte located his headquarters at the New Executive Office Building in downtown D.C., then at the DIA's new, glassy headquarters building across the Potomac River from National Airport. The next two DNIs served only a short time (see appendix B), until President Obama appointed General Clapper to the position in 2010.

The first DNI to last beyond two years, Clapper went on to serve in that capacity for the remainder of the Obama Administration, ensconced in plush new quarters at Liberty Crossing, near Arlington, Virginia, with his offices in a sleek suburban building a half-dozen miles away from the CIA, where most of the government's senior strategic analysts work. As highlighted in chapter 1, his powers to hire, fire, and spend continued to be vague; nevertheless, his fifty years of services as an intelligence officer provided him with a deep understanding of the spy business and a vast network of contacts throughout the IC. As a result, Clapper proved far more successful than his three predecessors. Moreover, he had mentored a number of the agency directors, which helped dismantle some stovepipes—despite the DNI's lack of formal authority to shape budgets and take uncooperative agency heads to the woodshed or fire them outright.

The ambiguities of the Kean Commission's report, coupled with the success of the DoD and its congressional allies in diluting the powers of the new DNI, have led to an odd and unfortunate situation: an even weaker national intelligence chief than before the 9/11 attacks! The United States now has a spymaster, but one without an institutional base (as the DCI enjoyed at the CIA) or legal authority over community-wide budgets and appointments.

The Kean Commission presented some thoughtful reform proposals, at times prosaic but still useful, such as the need to streamline and centralize the nation's security clearance procedures; however, in light of its failure to define clearly even its most important recommendation (the need for a DNI), it should come as no surprise that many of the Commission's other proposals were also blurry. Its conclusions about intelligence accountability were almost nonexistent, as the panel booted this topic into the long grass. The commissioners noted accurately that intelligence oversight on Capitol Hill had become "dysfunctional," yet they failed to hold even a single hearing on the subject. Nor did they marshal evidence about how oversight had faltered since the high hopes of 1975, or what might be done to bolster intelligence accountability. In one of its few observations about supervising America's spies, the Commission urged the Appropriations Committees quixotically to give up their long-standing powers over intelligence spending and leave that to the authorizing committees, SSCI and HPSCI—an unlikely event running counter to over two centuries of congressional practice using a sequence of authorization and appropriation in the legislative process.

Feeling little heat from the 9/11 Commission or from the public, Congress did virtually nothing to put its own house in order. Far too many committees—Judiciary, Armed Services, Foreign Relations, and Appropriations in both chambers, in addition to SSCI and HPSCI—continued to engage in intelligence reviews of one kind or another, with jurisdiction lines between them twisted into a Gordian knot. A sensible solution would be to assign only the Intelligence and the Appropriations Committees, respectively, with the tasks of intelligence authorization and appropriations, along with allowing participation by the Judiciary Committees on surveillance warrants and other matters related to the FISA Court. The Judiciary, Armed Services, and Foreign Relations Committees have plenty on their plates already; besides, each of them, recall, has a few lawmakers who simultaneously sit as members of SSCI or HPSCI.

The pathos that enveloped the Commission came from the fact that it had held the nation's riveted attention, only to stumble in its attempts to craft reforms that would truly make a difference—especially in the domain of intelligence oversight. With IRTPA as its chief legacy, the Commission came to resemble (as H. G. Wells is reputed to have said of Henry James) a hippopotamus rolling a pea.

Rallying behind Security in a Time of Crisis

The cornucopia of minor intelligence reform proposals that spilled out of the Kean Commission notwithstanding, oversight on SSCI and HPSCI during this era came to mean for the most part rallying behind the president, the IC, and the Pentagon in their efforts to combat global terrorism and to fight a war in Iraq. This tilt toward an emphasis on security would come to mean an embrace by the Bush Administration of new, more aggressive forms of spying—even if they crossed legal bright lines—and less attention to the government safeguards against abuse put in place since 1975. The great worry of policymakers and their overseers was the specter of another 9/11—perhaps even an attack that included the use of NBC weapons. That could not be allowed to happen. Accountability would have to take a back seat to action in support of greater security.[12] Dana Priest of the *Washington Post* discovered in the fall of 2002 that no more than six senators, and just a handful of House members, had bothered to read the National Intelligence Estimate (NIE) on Iraq's nonexistent WMDs; moreover, few lawmakers had taken the time to examine the congressional Joint Committee's report on 9/11 issued in 2003.[13] Intelligence oversight on the Hill still went on at a much deeper level and greater purpose than before the Year of Intelligence in 1975, including detailed budget reviews; for the most part, though, lawmakers crooked their knees to the White House in a time of national crisis.

Even before 9/11, a decline in intelligence police patrolling had become evident. Before the attack, SSCI held only two hearings on the subject of Al Qaeda, despite the IC's warnings about global terrorism. On the House side, Representative Goss (once a champion of accountability while on the Aspin-Brown Commission) presided over HPSCI as its number of hearings steadily declined, with only two sessions on terrorism from 1998 to 2001—the fewest of any panel on Capitol Hill during the period leading up to the attacks on New York City and D.C.[14] According to a reporter with an intelligence beat, the relationship between the oversight committees and the IC had "degenerated into a mutual admiration society for secret agencies."[15] Given all the intelligence mistakes associated with 9/11 and suspected Iraqi WMDs, some lawmakers remained ambivalent about the value of the spy agencies. For most who worked on Capitol Hill, though, security concerns largely trumped questions of accountability and most of the time the intelligence community faced a stop light with just one signal: green.

The initial domestic response to the 9/11 attacks on Capitol Hill was enactment of the USA PATRIOT Act, a vaguely worded proposal rushed through Congress by the Bush Administration that gave the executive branch carte blanche to create extensive surveillance programs. Professor Karen J. Greenberg of Fordham University School of Law has skillfully chronicled how the administration exalted intelligence collection over constitutional protections.[16] The White House claimed that Section 215 of the PATRIOT Act permitted NSA access to metadata on U.S. communications patterns: the telephone numbers called by Americans, the time of day when a call was made, and the duration of the call. Further, as Professor Laura K. Donohue of the Georgetown University School of Law has noted, the government no longer had to show that the target was a foreign power: "It need only state that the records are sought as part of an investigation to protect against terrorism or clandestine intelligence."[17] With section 215, adds Professor Greenberg, the NSA could "collect and retain vast quantities of information about US citizens, including those who were not suspected of crimes, and thanks to the weakened FISA courts and the compliant federal courts, it had been free to carry out its intention without any real check from the judiciary. This was executive-ordered dragnet surveillance plain and simple."[18]

The administration's alacritous response to the terrorist attacks on 9/11 was understandable; the nation needed to build up its defenses immediately and hunt down the individuals responsible for the cowardly acts. Unfortunately, though, Congress passed the PATRIOT law with only minimal study of its provisions. The 350 pages and 161 separate sections of the act, including the passages that enhanced electronic surveillance powers for the NSA and eroded the FISA Court warrant procedures, were more than could be properly absorbed by lawmakers in the dash toward approval. Moreover, as members of Congress, the media, and the public attempted to understand the implications of the new law, the Bush Administration quietly disseminated a spate of supporting executive orders—secret presidential directives—that further expanded the authorities of the NSA, the FBI, the CIA, and other intelligence agencies.

In a few clauses of this statute, lawmakers displayed their concern for privacy and the PATRIOT Act nodded in the direction of accountability. For example, it required law enforcement officers to obtain a warrant before wiretapping the telephone of a suspected terrorist—a reemphasis on the FISA requirement established in 1978. Moreover, the PATRIOT Act included a sunset provision, that is, a mandatory review at the end of four years (a requirement that continued each time the law was renewed). The law never mentioned the NSA, however, let alone the idea of bulk "metadata" collection of telephone and social media records (the logs of communications without the actual conversation content). The White House secretly turned loose the sigint agency to carry out warrantless electronic surveillances against Americans and others, without evidence to suggest they were involved in terrorist or other legal violations.

NSA on the Loose—Again

Both the Bush and Obama Administrations chose to ignore the PATRIOT Act's limits on surveillance and they took advantage of loopholes; plus, the legal standard of probable cause of criminal activity was set aside. At the time, members of Congress anticipated neither the NSA's warrantless wiretaps nor its metadata collection. The PATRIOT Act and FISA were further modified to permit the NSA to tap the telephones of terrorists who communicated to one another overseas, but whose conversations were routed through international communication nodes located in the United States. This was a sensible idea, but one that should have been adopted as an amendment to FISA through the normal legislative process, not stuffed down the throats of lawmakers by executive branch insistence.

The upshot of this maneuvering by two consecutive White Houses (Bush and Obama), under the flimsy cover of the PATRIOT Act, eventually became clear: the three branches of government had approved sweeping surveillance programs that were out of step with a democratic public's right to privacy, even in an era of global terrorism.[19] At first, the Bush Administration informed the top four members of SSCI and HPSCI (the Gang of Four) about the sigint programs, plus the top House and Senate leadership in both parties (four more lawmakers, summing to the Gang of Eight). But as had become usual, the briefings were skimpy and devoid of an opportunity for staff study.[20]

In tandem with the PATRIOT Act, the Bush Administration also pushed through Congress practically overnight a law known as the Authorization for the Use of Military Force (AUMF). This ambiguous statute gave the military and the intelligence agencies vast new powers for fighting terrorism overseas, including—officials in both the Bush and Obama administrations maintained—authority to conduct drone strikes, seemingly wherever terrorists might be. The Bush White House argued, as well, in private meetings with select lawmakers that the AUMF allowed the commander-in-chief—President Bush—to engage in NSA wiretaps and data collection without warrants. At first the FISA Court was told nothing about this policy; then the Bush Administration informed the presiding judge about the new sigint programs in 2002, followed by the rest of the FISA judges four years later.[21] As usual, the court deferred to the executive branch, although only after agonizing about the issues involved. A former judge on the FISA Appeals Court has commented to me on the likely reason why his colleagues bent toward support of the White House's sigint requests. "Can we afford to take the chance of not having a metadata program?" he said that they had probably wondered.[22]

This new Era of Mass Surveillance yielded three major challenges to liberty, or what one could call phones, moans, and drones: namely, the NSA's expanded sigint programs, the CIA's phantasmagoria of harsh interrogation techniques, and the DoD's and CIA's attacks against suspected terrorists overseas using missile-bearing drones. (The subject of drones is addressed in chapter 9.)

Skirting the Law

The NSA may not be much of a conversationalist (according to an old complaint among legislative overseers, "NSA" means "never say anything"), but it is well known as a good listener. Too good perhaps, depending on where one's marker is on the security/liberty continuum. On October 4, 2001, the Bush Administration hatched what it referred to as the President's Surveillance Program, which bore the NSA codename STELLARWIND and remained in operation until 2005, when its existence was reported by the media. Under the auspices of this initiative, the White House ordered the NSA to cast aside the FISA warrant procedures and pursue a Terrorist Surveillance Program (TSP) designed to eavesdrop on the content of international telephone calls and Internet messaging (social media) patched through U.S. communications switchboards. This traveling through switchboards inside the United States is a fact of life for most international communications, since America has served as a telephone and email hub for decades as a result of its early role in the development of global communications networks.

Aligned with the TSP objectives was another NSA collection scheme codenamed PRISM. This operation was subject to FISA Court approvals and reporting—although not by way of individualized warrants as envisioned in the original FISA of 1978, but rather through a broad blanket approval under Section 702 of the FISA provisions. PRISM was constrained, however, by an important accountability safeguard: the content of any telecommunications linkage listened to by NSA's big ears had to include an overseas participant (a foreigner) known, or suspected, to be an associate of the Al Qaeda terrorist organization responsible for the 9/11 attacks.

Another offshoot of STELLARWIND, the NSA's 215 Program (based on Section 215 of the PATRIOT Act), took the sigint agency into even more controversial territory: the gathering of bulk data on U.S. telephone communications patterns—the metadata program. Yet another program, known as "pen register trap and trace," authorized the gathering of Internet metadata on email communications and other social media. These operations added up to dragnet surveillance inside the United States—an intelligence fishing expedition of the kind one might expect in North Korea, not the world's oldest and most famous democracy. In eerie echoes of SHAMROCK and MINARET, the NSA was spying on Americans again—only this time on an even wider scale. By way of these authorities (STELLARWIND, TSP, PRISM, 215, trap-and-trace, and related eavesdropping activities), the NSA's wily director, Lt. Gen. Michael V. Hayden—typically with a suppliant knee toward the Bush White House— had dispatched the nation's sigint spies deep into unlawful territory. With little hesitation, the NSA director and his lawyers were content to have Article II of the Constitution (the commander-in-chief clause) bury Article I (the powers of Congress). In the ensuing years, the NSA would gather through these collection operations "billions of phone records."[23]

This decision to unleash the NSA was finally disclosed by the *New York Times* in December 2005, after the newspaper had uncovered the story but sat on it for more than a year in deference to the Bush Administration's argument that reporting on the breach of FISA law would harm U.S. national security. STELLARWIND had already been in operation for four years before the *Times* decision to publish. The news story, with its revelations of domestic surveillance far greater than previously reported—the 215 metadata program and the fact that the communications content of some Americans were being captured in the TSP and PRISM intercepts—"shocked the world," remembers Jane Mayer of the *New Yorker*, a seasoned journalist reporting on the state of civil liberties in the United States (and one of several reporters that Gen. Hayden accused of lusting for "espionage porn").[24] James Risen of the *New York Times*, one of the reporters who broke the STELLARWIND story, wrote that "the Bush administration has swept aside nearly thirty years of rules and regulations."[25] In response to these disclosures, Hayden had the chutzpah to proclaim that the NSA was "the most aggressive agency in the intelligence community when it comes to protecting U.S. privacy."[26] In truth, the NSA had become the most aggressive violator of U.S. privacy, leading to a crisis in executive-legislative relations.

Despite this posture of arrogance in the White House and General Hayden's spreading of disinformation about the effectiveness of these operations, a coz-ened Congress was content nevertheless to pass amendments to the PATRIOT Act and FISA during the period from 2006 to 2008 that were, according to a scholarly analysis, "intended precisely to make lawful much of what had been of dubious legality, at best, under the Bush Administration."[27] An illustration is the FISA Amendments Act (FAA) of 2008.[28] This law revised the original FISA of 1978 by permitting the government to intercept the content of communications by U.S. citizens without a warrant, under the authority of Section 702—a provision originally designed by Congress for use against *foreign* terrorist suspects, not Americans. Now the intelligence agencies had even more discretionary authority for its warrantless collection programs, aimed at message content. The law also provided immunity to telecommunications companies that had cooper-ated with the earlier NSA warrantless wiretap programs under STELLARWIND and TSP. As a frustrated SSCI member, Ron Wyden (D, Oregon), underscored in 2014, "if intelligence officials are deliberately searching for and reading the communications of specific Americans, the Constitution requires a warrant."[29]

Moreover, the FISA Court soon backed the 215 Program, further formalizing what the Bush Administration was already doing: carrying out bulk metadata collection without the knowledge or approval of the court. The predictable end result of these measures was a state of intelligence overreach. "These statutory changes represented a return to pre–Church Committee processes," concluded a study in 2016, "and tipped the scale once again toward 'security' at the expense of 'liberty.' "[30]

In support of the expanded and warrantless sigint operations, Vice President Cheney—Polonius ever hovering near the Oval—remained convinced that in foreign and security affairs, presidents reigned supreme and had the right to proceed as they wished, laws or no laws: this was the "unitary theory" of the presidency, popularized by the administration's Justice Department attorney John C. Yoo and acted upon by Cheney at every opportunity.[31] The PATRIOT Act, and even the AUMF (originally designed to guide U.S. overt warfare in Iraq, not responses to terrorism worldwide), were handy window-dressing that—at least for Article II groupies—added to the legitimacy of inherent presidential powers. As the vice president told the NSA's Hayden at the crucial White House meeting to green-light a bypass of the FISA rules, "Mike, I understand your concerns, but here are some things we're going to have to do. And I think I have the authority to authorize you to do things that you've outlined."[32] Visions of Article II danced in the vice president's head. When Hayden returned to Ft. Meade, he told his legal aide, "The President is going to do this on his own hook. Raw Article 2, commander-in-chief stuff. No new legislation."[33]

The vice president's attorney, David Addington, wrote up the order and had it signed by the president. He then personally carried it to the CIA, the AG at the Department of Justice, DoD, and then NSA Headquarters at Ft. Meade for further sign-offs. When Hayden consulted with the NSA's deputy general counsel, the lawyer concluded that "there was no doubt in our mind that it was a legitimate use of the president's Article 2 authority."[34] In 2004, however, the Justice Department's Office of Legal Counsel (OLC) and the AG began to balk at further support of NSA collection programs that targeted the metadata, and sometimes the communications content, of American citizens. So the archly complacent Hayden, who seemed to believe he could sweet-talk a polar bear into a move to Florida, went to the more malleable FISA Court. In this forum, he gained authority from the presiding judge, Colleen Kollar-Kotelly, to skip the nuisance of individual warrants for sigint targets (as required by FISA). The president continued to say publicly, and falsely, that his administration was consistently operating within the framework of the PATRIOT Act and obtaining specific FISA warrants for each sigint operation against a suspected terrorist.[35]

Rather than suggest to the president and vice president that they seek to amend or repeal FISA before proceeding with the administration's proposed warrantless wiretaps or a metadata-collection program, the NSA director quickly agreed to the operations. He left the agency in 2005 to assume the office of Deputy Director of National Intelligence, at which time he was awarded a fourth star; he would subsequently become the CIA director, where he again displayed a willingness to interpret intelligence safeguards loosely, advising Agency offices that they should have "chalk on the cleats."[36]

The administration claimed to have informed SSCI and HPSCI members about these NSA surveillance programs. A closer look reveals, however, just how limited this "informing" was. Representative Jane Harman (D, California) fumed in a letter to President Bush that even the Gang of Eight, of which she was a part as the ranking minority member on HPSCI, "cannot take notes, seek the advice of their counsel, or even discuss issues raised with their committee colleagues."[37] Further, the 1980 and 1991–1992 intelligence oversight laws say nothing about a Gang of Four, a still even more attractive forum for presidents and their aides. This is a term invented by White House attorneys to avoid even having to report to a Gang of Eight. Moreover, the intelligence oversight laws anticipate reporting to *all* the members of SSCI and HPSCI after—at the most—a two-day delay in extraordinary circumstances.[38]

If an administration could freely and easily wave aside the FISA statute of 1978, along with established reporting requirements in Hughes-Ryan and the oversight acts of 1980 and 1991–1992 (together, the backbone of modern intelligence accountability), why not dismiss other oversight laws as well? These drastic measures taken by the second Bush Administration were a product of a siege mentality similar to the ones exhibited by the Nixon Administration in 1970 and the Iran-contra conspirators of the Reagan Administration. Regrettably, the Gang of Four on SSCI and HPSCI often passively accepted this limited reporting—or even allowed briefings to just a Gang of Two: the chairs of the committees.

This laxity put a large dent in the reporting expectations laid out in the nation's key intelligence oversight laws. Only after the *Times* disclosure of the warrantless wiretaps did the Bush White House start to brief the full memberships of SSCI and HPSCI about the NSA's operations; even then, a majority on the oversight committees lethargically accepted the necessity of gathering sigint through extraordinary means. Most of the lawmakers agreed that the agency's efforts might help against terrorism. The oversight committees would eventually regret their failure to take a closer look at the NSA's activities related to warrantless wiretaps when Snowden revealed them to the world, including several SSCI and HPSCI members who had never been briefed. Had they paid better attention, they would have learned that, as an extension of the TSP program, the Bush

Administration had authorized extensive sigint operations against the telephone and social media records of U.S. citizens.

The Era of Rebalancing, 2013–

Metadata and the Snowden Leaks

The controversial metadata-surveillance program was disclosed through the most significant breach of classified information in American history: over a million documents reportedly stolen, and many leaked to the media, by Edward J. Snowden in 2013. The fear and anger generated by the September 2001 terrorist attacks had caused the United States to turn rapidly toward an emphasis on security over liberty; the pendulum would begin to swing back toward liberty, however, as a result of public reaction to the Snowden revelations about the NSA's intelligence dragnet operations.

As related earlier in this book, before releasing the first of his stolen documents, Snowden fled the United States in search of a safe haven that would protect him from prosecution by U.S. authorities. His first stop was Hong Kong; then, when other options in Latin America and Scandinavia fell through, on to Russia. His leaks represented a stunning disclosure of classified operations rivaled in their effect only by the anonymous "Family Jewels" sent to the *New York Times* in 1974, which uncovered Operation CHAOS; and the Pentagon Papers in 1971, which revealed the copious misjudgments by the Johnson and Nixon Administrations related to the war in Vietnam.[39]

Even when the public reacted negatively toward metadata collection, only two SSCI members voted against its continuation: Ron Wyden and Mark Udall (D, Colorado). They failed in their combined attempt to declassify the program. "What happens when you get on [SSCI]," Wyden has noted, "right away the Intelligence Community sweeps in and basically starts the process of trying to kind of say, 'Well, these are tough issues.' And, in effect, only one point of view gets conveyed." He continued: "It's our job to do vigorous oversight and not just get caught up in the culture that makes you, in effect, something more like an ambassador [for the IC] than a vigorous overseer."[40] For another leading senator, John McCain (R, Arizona), what happened in the metadata case was simple: "Clearly, [the members of SSCI] have been co-opted. There's no doubt about that."[41]

A Brookings Institute report found that "while maintaining the secrecy of the metadata program, Congress failed to assess the security value of mass records seizures, to weigh the resulting harm to privacy interests, or to impose standards or requirements to minimize that harm." (The same could be said about the response of SSCI and HPSCI members when they first learned about the

CIA's torture program; see below.) The Brookings study went on: "the Snowden revelations exposed a profound failure by Congress to understand and deliberate about the government's massive collection of phone and email records. It dealt with the need for secrecy by leaving the decisions entirely to the president or the intelligence agencies themselves, while pretending to maintain statutory standards."[42]

Pushing back on criticisms leveled at the oversight committees for supposedly being patsies, top staffers on these panels explained to me the reasons for their support of the sigint programs. In HPSCI, for example, a senior aide said, "I favor bulk collection, because you never know where the terrorist trail is going to lead. Therefore, you should be looking at *all* the telephone numbers, not just those from a suspected terrorist to one or two links or 'hops' [degrees of association] out in his network of calls. The fewer the links you allow, the greater the risk."[43] Another HPSCI staffer, though, has said publicly that the program was "unethical, illegal, and unconstitutional."[44] A senior SSCI staffer told me that he was wary of unlimited linkage (looking at one telephone or social media contact after another), but he emphasized that the current program "is not a dragnet. The NSA uses only relevant numbers and just two links."[45]

Among the lawmakers supporting the metadata approach was SSCI chairwoman Dianne Feinstein (D, California), who even managed to hold an open hearing on the topic. (Frank Church would have been impressed by that feat, if not her pro-metadata stance.) Snowden claims that Feinstein's apparent coziness with the NSA during this session inspired him to leak the documents about the program, rather than try to work with SSCI and HPSCI toward modifying or eliminating it—although (as I have mentioned earlier in this book) staff members on both committees emphasized to me that they would have been happy to meet with Snowden to fairly assess his grievances. On the Senate Judiciary Committee, the top Republican—Chuck Grassley (R, Iowa)—supported the metadata program, but he acknowledged that it was handled poorly from the point of view of public accountability. "There's a lot more we could have made public," he said. "If there had been more information out there, there would have been less suspicion and not all of these questions being raised."[46]

Grassley's Democratic counterpart on Judiciary, Chairman Patrick Leahy (D, Vermont), had quite a different view. He said that Feinstein had been too easy on the NSA, and he directed his committee to hold five open hearings related to the metadata debate. Leahy was particularly skeptical of the sigint agency's claim that the program had prevented more than fifty terrorist attacks. He was right to be skeptical: under the pressure of open scrutiny, the agency reduced that figure to three or four—and even then the evidence proved shaky.[47]

Like Feinstein, HPSCI chair Mike Rogers (R, Michigan; a former FBI agent), gave the metadata activities a pass, noting that there was "nothing illegal, nothing untoward, no rogue agency" at work. "Not liking it is different than not overseeing it," Rogers said, adding: "Huge difference. And I take exception to those that say there was not proper oversight." Echoing John Tower and Barry Goldwater on the Church Committee, Rogers believed that holding open hearings on the NSA was a mistake, since they could give away too much to America's enemies. Transparency for him was the requirement that NSA officials explain their programs to HPSCI and SSCI in closed sessions. "The transparency part," he underscored, "is they can't do these activities without coming to elected representatives in the U.S. Congress and having these debates for approval and policy review and funding. That all happened."[48] The Senate Majority Leader, Mitch McConnell (R, Kentucky) put the case more simply still, with reference to ISIS (the rising new terrorist organization in Syria): "This is the worst possible time to be tying our hands behind our back."[49]

An HPSCI staffer, though, told me that the NSA had been less than forthcoming with the House committee, especially regarding the degree of internal debate in the agency about the merits of the metadata approach. The staffer recalled that Director Hayden had denied "anything except enthusiasm" among the NSA workforce for the metadata program, even though several employees had raised informal and formal objections to senior managers at Ft. Meade.[50] "Even when we have classified briefings," further admonished Representative Justin Amash (R, Michigan), "it's like a game of twenty questions and we can't get to the bottom of anything."[51]

The leaders of SSCI and HPSCI, and eventually the full memberships of both committees, had heard the secret metadata briefings and—with only a few dissenters—supported the program both in its early years and, more formally, through the FISA Amendments Act of 2008. Nonetheless, the appropriateness of the bulk-data method of intelligence collection would soon become a subject of heated discussion among citizens in the United States and Europe, thanks to the Snowden leaks.

Further, the number of SSCI and HPSCI members in support of the NSA programs began to shrink as more knowledge about the details of these programs came to light—especially when an Obama-appointed study panel (the President's Review Group, established on August 27, 2013), led by Professor Geoffrey Stone of the University of Chicago Law School, issued a highly critical report in December 2013.[52] Stone told the media that he thought Feinstein and Rogers had been hoodwinked by the NSA. "Just given human nature, it's not surprising that they've circled their wagons," he told *Politico*. "I don't think they asked all the right questions."[53] (Feinstein had already acknowledged that the "no staff" rule—whereby the NSA insisted that SSCI members not discuss the metadata briefings with staff experts—needed to be changed.[54]) Another prominent law professor, Jack Goldsmith at Harvard University, said that "the program was an example of the Administration going it alone, in secret, based on inadequate legal reasoning and flawed legal opinions."[55] With such criticism mounting, President Obama started to have second thoughts about his unquestioning adoption of the Bush Administration's electronic surveillance programs.

For many, the demand from the Bush and Obama Administrations for actionable intelligence about terrorism had overruled the venerable American values of privacy and liberty. Shock, fear, uncertainty, and revenge had commingled to erase the established legal standards for surveillance. The Bush Administration, along with Hayden and his immediate successor at NSA, preferred a vacuum-cleaner approach to electronic surveillance, rather than (as advocated by civil libertarians) a more pinpointed targeting of individuals based on a standard of reasonable suspicion that they might be involved in terrorist activities. Hubris seemed to have played a role, too, in the pursuit of metadata—a belief at the NSA that "since we have the latest spy technology, let's use it." As a top CIA official intimately familiar with the NSA's warrantless surveillance activities concluded, "The NSA had largely been collecting information because it could, not necessarily in all cases because it should."[56] Accompanying this mentality—indeed, driving it—was the steady rise of a dizzying array of new sigint surveillance capabilities.

Part of the debate over sigint during this period dealt with the appropriateness of Snowden's behavior. Central to the debate over the legality, ethics, and wisdom of the Snowden leaks stood the question of whether he was a patriot for revealing to the public a questionable intelligence program, or a traitor for his unauthorized disclosure of classified information (much of it going beyond the metadata program that he claimed morally justified his actions—including detailed intelligence budget figures for FY 2013). Director Hayden's successor, General Keith B. Alexander (at the helm of the NSA when Snowden was cleared to work there), called the leak "the greatest damage to our combined nations' intelligence systems that we have ever suffered."[57] Alexander conceded that the NSA collection of social media records had produced little of value, but he insisted the telephone taps had been crucial to America's counterterrorism activities.[58] His replacement in 2014, Admiral Michael S. Rogers, deplored Snowden's leaks; however, he downplayed their damage, saying he could see no indication "the sky is falling."[59] The Times had noted earlier that none of the U.S. spy agencies had presented "the slightest proof that [Snowden's] disclosures really hurt the nation's security."[60]

In 2016, a movement began among civil rights groups (including ACLU, Human Rights Watch, and Amnesty International) for the pardon of Snowden by President Obama during the waning months of his presidency. Members of HPSCI unanimously—Republicans and Democrats alike—signed a letter to the president (dated September 11, 2016) in opposition to a pardon. The letter advised that "Mr. Snowden is not a patriot. He is not a whistleblower. He is a criminal." In an accompanying classified report, the committee concluded in an unclassified Executive Summary that "Snowden caused tremendous damage to national security, and the vast majority of the documents he stole have nothing to do with programs impacting individual privacy interests—they instead pertain to military, defense, and intelligence programs of great interest to America's adversaries."[61] One of the reporters given documents by Snowden—Barton Gellman of the *Post*—dismissed the HPSCI letter as "contemptuous of fact."[62]

The Worm Turns

As the public debate continued to roil over the NSA's bulk-data program, as well as the merits of Snowden's behavior, Congress passed the USA FREEDOM Act, proposed by Senator Leahy of the Judiciary Committee. The bill, designed to overhaul the PATRIOT Act of 2001 (about to expire), passed by a vote of 338–88 in May 2015. The new law trimmed back the reach of the PATRIOT Act and the NSA's metadata activities, by modifying FISA's Section 215 (the source of authorization in the PATRIOT Act for the "bulk collection" of metadata). The FREEDOM Act also allowed, but did not require, the FISA Court judges to appoint "amici"—special advocates representing the public interest before the court. The FREEDOM Act was clearly a step in the right direction toward a better balancing of security and liberty, but its text was suffused with ambiguous language. Clearly worded laws are vital to ensure executive branch adherence to rules set by Congress and, in this sense, the FREEDOM Act left much to be desired. It was in this same month that the U.S. Court of Appeals for the Second Circuit in New York declared metadata collection illegal, a judicial decision that bolstered the efforts of Leahy and his privacy-oriented colleagues on Capitol Hill to rebalance the equilibrium between security and liberty.

President Barack Obama, who had largely adopted George W. Bush's approach to counterterrorism (with the significant exception of the CIA's program of harsh interrogation methods), continued to endorse the NSA metadata program, but at least he instituted improved safeguards. Since the USA FREEDOM Act adopted his proposed added privacy protections, Obama signed the bill— much to the chagrin of Hayden and former Bush Administration AG Michael B. Mukasey. In their view, the statute was "exquisitely crafted to hobble the gathering of electronic intelligence."[63] Senator Mark Rubio (R, Florida), an SSCI member and soon to be an unsuccessful GOP candidate for the presidency in 2016, agreed. In his opinion, a "gutted" sigint program might lead to "a horrifying result."[64]

The key provisions of the new law included an emphasis on limiting metadata collection to only two communications linkages out from an initial terrorist suspect, along with the storage of this more constricted data in the files of the telephone companies—not within the NSA's massive computer storage banks in Utah. Further, the data could be kept for no more than five years. Only with a proper FISA warrant could the NSA access these files to examine the intelligence as it related to terrorist suspects. These provisions met the primary concerns of SSCI's Ron Wyden, who consistently argued that the NSA should be required to seek probable-cause warrants, just as FISA had required.[65] Some critics, though, including another soon-to-be-unsuccessful GOP presidential candidate, libertarian Senator Rand Paul of Kentucky, buoyed by the New York Appeals Court decision, continued to attack the NSA metadata approach as overreaching even under the new rules of the USA FREEDOM Act.

The decision of the New York court and the enactment of the USA FREEDOM Act strongly signaled a change in attitudes about the proper balance between national security and individual privacy, both vital for any viable democracy. "I'm not going to vote for an extension of a law [the PATRIOT Act] that has recently been declared illegal by a federal circuit court," declared Senator Chris Coons (D, Delaware). And Senator Paul asked his colleagues on the Senate floor, "Are you really willing to give up your liberty for security?"[66] Now opinion was swinging against national security hawks and back toward civil liberty doves. The coalition in favor of an intelligence rebalancing was made up of Democrats and libertarian Republicans who brought, the *Times* reported, "a changing tide in post–Sept. 11 America, where privacy concerns have become as important as national security interests for many people."[67]

Further complicating this ongoing debate between proponents of security and defenders of civil liberties was a ruling by the FISA Court, in the summer of 2015, that the NSA did indeed have a right to continue its metadata program— regardless of the New York Second Circuit opinion—at least until the Congress made clearer exactly what the boundaries were going to be for the agency's surveillance practices. "Second Court rulings are not binding" on this panel, declared Michael W. Mosman, a FISA Court judge.[68] The judge had become persuaded that a metadata program, had one existed in 2001, might have stopped the 9/11 attacks; however, other reports pointed to the fact that the CIA had lots of information about a couple of the eventual terrorists hiding out in San Diego fully two years before the attack but had never shared this information with the FBI, which is responsible for domestic counterintelligence. "There was no need for a metadata-collection program," concluded a thoughtful commentator. "What was needed was [CIA] cooperation with other federal agencies."[69]

Still badly divided by partisan squabbling, Congress would have to continue its debate—set aside until after the 2016 presidential election—over the long-term fate of the metadata and related NSA surveillance operations. Had these programs unequivocally led to successes in curbing terrorist attacks, the argument in favor of their continuation would have been more persuasive; in fact, though, the NSA and the White House were unable to offer instances compelling enough to quell the defenders of civil liberties—just as was true with the CIA's use of torture against suspected terrorists.

The Senate Torture Report

Soon after the 9/11 attacks, President Bush gave the CIA authority to capture, detain, and kill Al Qaeda operatives around the world; then, in the next year, he waived Common Article 3 of the Geneva Conventions that prohibited "cruel treatment and torture." (The United States had also ratified the Convention against Torture in 1988, signed by President Ronald Reagan.) Further, in 2002, the head of Justice's OLC provided the CIA with additional after-the-fact authority to engage in harsh interrogation.[70] Just how many of the now 100-plus attorneys in the CIA's Office of General Counsel (OGC) objected to the program, if any, remains unknown.[71] As Jane Mayer writes, "unthinkable cruelty" was becoming official U.S. policy.[72]

The CIA Reacts to 9/11

In September 2002, the CIA at long last briefed a few members of HPSCI and SSCI about its interrogation activities. The chair of the Senate committee, Bob Graham, requested additional information, but the Agency slow-rolled and stonewalled him, knowing that he was about to retire from the Senate in a few months. One outside observer concluded that the Agency's approach to SSCI and HPSCI during this time was one of "disdain and evasiveness."[73]

Early in 2003, the CIA's top lawyer informed SSCI and HPSCI leaders that the Agency was videotaping the prisoner interrogations, at which point the lawmakers presciently advised against destroying the tapes and issued a "preservation order." (The potential for oversight review of interrogation videotapes is one of the best checks against excesses in the questioning of terrorist suspects.) At the end of the year, Secretary of State Colin Powell and Secretary of Defense Rumsfeld were belatedly informed about the specifics of the interrogation practices. In May 2004, the CIA's own inspector general concluded in an internal report that some of the interrogation methods were likely illegal, causing DCI George Tenet to temporarily suspend the program; in June, the new OLC head, Jack Goldsmith, revoked the earlier permissive torture authority granted by the Justice Department.[74] In 2005, however, yet another OLC head, Steven G. Bradbury, reauthorized the use of the interrogation methods. The authority for torture had become a dog's breakfast.

In 2005 things began to fully unravel in the torture program. During November, Dana Priest of the *Washington Post* reported on the existence of CIA prisons aboard. Soon afterward, the Deputy Director of Operations (DDO, the top covert action officer at the Agency) destroyed videotapes of the torture sessions, despite the earlier admonitions from SSCI and HPSCI.[75] (This unauthorized action was reminiscent of the time when the Iran-contra scandal began to surface, leading the CIA to demolish and bury implicating Agency aircraft in Costa Rico being used by the Enterprise.[76])

Two years afterward, the *New York Times* learned about and reported on the destruction of the videotapes. "There is only one reason why [the tapes] were destroyed, because certain people wanted that information never to be available," concluded SSCI Chair Feinstein, who may have accepted the NSA's sigint operations as a counterterrorism tool but decidedly did not approve of torture and thought the disposal of the tapes had all the earmarks of a blatant cover-up.[77] "Some lawmakers, and even some CIA lawyers, may not have understood how appalling and gory the torture sessions really were," an SSCI staffer said to me, in an argument in favor of still having the videotapes to prove the brutality to any doubting Thomas.[78]

Only in April 2006 did President Bush receive a briefing on the harsh interrogation techniques. According to CIA records of the meeting, Bush displayed discomfort with the "image of a detainee, chained to the ceiling, clothed in a diaper and forced to go to the bathroom on himself." In the summer, the Supreme Court weighed in on the subject, ruling that Common Article 3 applied to U.S. detainees. During the fall, the CIA finally briefed the full SSCI membership on the interrogation program for the first time—five years after its initiation. Hayden, now the CIA's director, gave the briefing in his typically self-assured and pugnacious manner. He vouched for the effectiveness of the interrogation methods and, in one of his more egregious moments of peddling fiction, claimed that they were actually quite benign: merely "tummy slapping," as Senator Feinstein recalls him saying.[79] Feinstein later remembered that Hayden had presented "the entire set of techniques as minimally harmful and applied in a highly clinical and professional manner. They were not."[80] The Senate Torture Report states, further, that the CIA eliminated references to one of the harsher techniques—waterboarding—in many of its subsequent briefings.[81]

In contrast, Porter Goss (the DCI when the torture program was under way) said that "there was congressional oversight of the RDI [rendition, detention, and interrogation] program." He elaborated: "the specific enhanced interrogation techniques were briefed and discussed with the top committee leaders. I recall no objections being made."[82]

When the *Times* reported on the destruction of the interrogation videotapes in 2007, Hayden—whose role model seemed to have been Candy Cummings, the inventor of the curveball—rushed to assure SSCI that, no, the tapes had not been destroyed. Oops, wrong again. The SSCI staff would record thirty misstatements just in one session of Hayden's testimony presented to them during their probe into the CIA's interrogation activities. Regardless of this growing criticism, President Bush in October 2006 had once again authorized the Agency's continuation of its interrogation activities. A year later, as criticism swelled further, the CIA at last terminated this approach to counterterrorism.

The Senate Inquiry into the Practice of Torture

While these events were evolving, SSCI decided in March 2009—too belatedly, critics would complain—to initiate a staff investigation into the Agency's interrogation practices. Prodded by public calls for a "truth commission" to examine "torture" and other rumors of brutal acts levied against detainees, as well as upset by the unauthorized destruction of the interrogation tapes, the SSCI voted 14 to 1 in favor of a formal inquiry. The lone holdout was Senator Saxby Chambliss (R, Georgia), the vice chairman of the committee, who went even beyond Senator Russell in his almost blind devotion to the CIA (but, unfortunately for the Agency, without Russell's clout in the Senate).[83] After Chambliss retired from the Senate, the new SSCI vice chairman, Kit Bond (R, Missouri), withdrew Republican support on the committee for the inquiry, using the excuse that the Department of Justice had just launched a criminal investigation into possible CIA counterintelligence abuses. This DoJ probe, he argued, made it impossible for the SSCI staff to interview Agency personnel, since its director Leon Panetta had excused his officers from having to testify twice and possibly place themselves in legal jeopardy. "The GOP pulled out early when the threat of prosecutions of participants in the program went live," recalls a senior Republican staffer on SSCI.[84] The DoJ inquiry eventually concluded that the Agency had committed no prosecutable offenses.

Yet in its files SSCI already had troves of interviews and oral histories with key Agency personnel knowledgeable about the interrogation methods, including a session with DCI George Tenet on the subject. Moreover, the SSCI and CIA staffs had engaged in continuous back-and-forth discussions about the report as it was being prepared, which in themselves amounted to a large number of "interviews." It is not as if the Agency's views on the matter were unknown. Feinstein attempted to convince the Republicans to stick with the committee's investigation, but to no avail. As an SSCI Democratic staffer recalled to me, "We asked the Republicans to join in the investigation and at first they said yes. Then it became so political."[85] The truth of the matter was that the GOP did not want to be viewed as hobbling the CIA in an age of terrorist threats and, thus, Republicans on the committee opted out. The Democratic staff members—who also have respect for what the CIA does day in and day out, but were concerned about interrogation excesses—soldiered on, poring over 6.3 million pages of Agency documents. In December 2012, the committee approved the Democratic staff report (at 6,700 pages with 38,000 footnotes, probably the most thorough accountability study ever produced by a congressional panel on a single intelligence activity) by a vote of 9 to 6: eight Democrats and one lonely member of the GOP, independent-minded Olympia Snowe (Maine), against a half-dozen Republicans.

A Declassification Battle

The report was then sent to the CIA and the White House for a declassification review, which took months to complete. The committee studied and debated the revisions and redactions proposed by the executive branch, whose censors had taken scissors to about 7 percent of the study. During the course of the inquiry, the CIA had adroitly erected one barrier after another against the investigators, taking (for example) more than three years to provide SSCI with the documents it requested; now, in the end game, the Agency became fiercely resistant to the idea of releasing the full report, even in a heavily redacted form. Finally, in April 2014, a fatigued committee voted by a margin of 11 to 3, with one abstention (Chambliss), to give up on publication of the full report and settle for the release of just a sanitized Executive Summary—if even that could be achieved. Three senators, all Republicans, did not want to see even the declassification of an Executive Summary: they were James Risch (Idaho); Dan Coats (Indiana, who would become President Trump's DNI in 2017); and the would-be presidential candidate Rubio.

After eight more months of additional wrangling over declassification decisions—the CIA, the Bush Administration, and the Obama Administration together broke all records in slow-rolling the Congress—SSCI at last gained permission from the Obama White House near the end of 2014 to publish the Executive Summary. (At no point during or after this long review did President Obama ever say a word to Senator Feinstein about her committee's findings.) Even in its truncated form, at 499 pages and with 2,725 footnotes, the report was a lengthy and searing document.

Reaction to the Torture Report

The committee—or at least a portion of its membership—had displayed a rare and laudatory tenacity in its study of the Agency's use of interrogation practices against 119 detainees. Some of the victims had been snatched off the streets in European capitals by CIA operatives and flown to secret interrogation sites on the Continent or at other "black sites" abroad, an intelligence operation known as "extraordinary rendition" and involving at least one mistaken identity. Then the extreme forms of counterintelligence tradecraft, known as enhanced interrogation techniques, or EITs in Agency vernacular (and, in an earlier iteration of cosmetic labeling, called "intelligence educement"), were used against the terrorist suspects.[86]

Six members on the SSCI staff—all from the Democratic side of the aisle, when GOP leaders called their staff off the investigation—spent over five years trying to determine the authorization for the Agency's use of torture. They also examined the nature of the around-the-clock interrogation techniques, which ran from waterboarding three detainees (in the instance of Khalid Sheikh Mohammed, 183 times) and rectal feeding, to mock executions and sleep deprivation lasting for days (seven and a half days in one case, with the subject moved from cell to cell to eliminate any chance to sleep—what guards called the "frequent-flier program"), along with confinement in cramped coffin-like boxes. According to the Executive Summary of the SSCI report, one of the waterboarded detainees, Abu Zubaydah, "became completely unresponsive, with bubbles rising through his open, full mouth."[87] The report said that one ploy used by the CIA was the "hard takedown," whereby five Agency people would jump a detainee, hood him, cut away his clothing, punch him, and drag him down a hallway.

The Obama Administration's last director of the CIA, John O. Brennan, has said that the report is full of exaggerations and errors—an incomplete and selective picture of what occurred, in his view. Republicans on SSCI echoed this judgment in a minority report. Yet, in 2016, the chief military prosecutor at Guantánamo, General Mark Martins, read the document and commented publicly that the facts were accurate, based on his knowledge of the interrogation program.[88]

The SSCI investigators studied, as well, whether these methods had elicited useful information that shielded the United States from further terrorist attacks. Brennan eventually acknowledged: "We have not concluded that it was the EITs within that program that allowed us to obtain useful information from the detainees subjected to them." Ultimately, though, in his opinion, the question of whether torture had been useful was "unknowable."[89] In contrast, the conclusions reached by SSCI investigators were that the methods used by the CIA were far more barbaric than the Agency had claimed (one partially naked detainee, who had been apprehended in a case of mistaken identity, died of hypothermia in 2002), and that the effectiveness of the methods had been grossly exaggerated by Hayden and others at the CIA, the White House, and the Justice Department.[90] Brennan eventually ended up speaking out against the future use of waterboarding, declaring that "as long as I'm director of CIA, irrespective of what the president says, I'm not going to be the director of CIA that gives that order. They'll have to find another director."[91] President Trump's CIA director, Mike Pompeo (R, Kansas, and a former HPSCI member), has similarly vowed to resign rather than adopt torture techniques.

Effective? Ineffective? The more important point was the damage the use of torture has done to America's global reputation for fair play and dedication to human rights. As President Obama said about the SSCI report, it "reinforces my long-held view that these harsh methods were not only inconsistent with our values as a nation, they did not serve our broader counterterrorism efforts or our national security interests . . . upholding the values we profess doesn't make us weaker, it makes us stronger."[92]

The long-known principle that anyone being tortured will fabricate information in order to prevent further pain could be seen at work again in these protracted interrogation sessions at the Agency's secret prisons overseas, inside such cooperative nations as Afghanistan, Poland, and Thailand, as well as at the U.S. Guantánamo base in Cuba.[93] It was a reality that James Angleton, the chief of CIA counterintelligence for twenty years, emphasized to me during the days of the Church Committee when I had asked him about the Agency's lengthy detention of the Soviet defector Yuri Ivanovich Nosenko during the 1960s at the Farm.[94] Angleton had been close to Israeli intelligence, which had tried many of these techniques against enemies and confided to him that they were of little use. In contrast to this "abuse interrogation," the winning over of a detainee through a more civilized approach to questioning (known as "rapport" or "soft" interrogation) has demonstrated a higher chance of success in the experience of seasoned FBI (and Israeli) counterterrorism experts.[95]

Even if torture does work in some isolated instances—and might have to be resorted to in an extreme (and unlikely) "ticking bomb" scenario—the question of its legitimacy remains in question and President Trump has said that he supports its use (see this book's epilogue). At the time of the Abu Ghraib torture sessions carried out by Army intelligence personnel against suspected terrorists in a Baghdad prison by that name in 2003, photographs making their way around the Internet vividly captured the horror, with victims—naked and in dank prison cells—being hosed down with powerful sprays of cold water; subjected to the snarling lunges of German shepherd dogs; and humiliated by their nudity in front of taunting U.S. female intelligence interrogators. Some senior Republican leaders in the Bush Administration blanched at these excesses. "Unhelpful," commented Donald Rumsfeld when asked about the torture practices at Abu Ghraib, while GOP strategist Karl Rove estimated that it would take a "generation" for America to recover its good image in the world.[96]

At the time of the Abu Ghraib revelations, a scholarly conference on intelligence studies was under way in Oslo. During breaks between conference presentations, participants from all over Europe would spill into the hallways, expressing astonishment over the methods used by the United States in the Baghdad prison, as captured by the Internet photographs. In anguish, a respected senior scholar from Sweden came up to me (as the only American at the conference) and asked, "How could you do this?"[97]

Two years later, the top student in my undergraduate seminar on national security at Yale University (where I was teaching as a visiting professor) asked if he could talk with me privately.[98] The student told me he had applied to the CIA for employment and things were moving along well toward his acceptance, but that he had experienced a change of heart based on early reports about the Agency's involvement in the torturing of "detainees" (the CIA's euphemism for "prisoners"). He seemed shattered that his earlier zeal for intelligence work and the clear career pathway that lay ahead of him were now in ruins. The student sought out counseling from me about other possible avenues to serve his country in the national security field. I reminded him that only a small component of the CIA had been involved in torture; that intelligence analysis, for example, remained an important Agency endeavor, with its Intelligence Directorate (now Analysis Directorate) providing timely reports to the president and others that improved the quality of foreign-policy decisions made in Washington. Yet, disheartened that torture evidently had the imprimatur of the Agency's top leadership, the student had reached a point where he was dead-set against an intelligence career. As I do with all my students, I talked with him about the many other opportunities for public service in Washington, from Capitol Hill to Foggy Bottom.

How many other idealistic and talented young Americans across the country have been turned off to intelligence work by the CIA and the military's excesses is anyone's guess. Suffice it to say that the moral goodness of one's actions matter—not only to Swedish professors and Yale undergraduates but to people around the world. Soft power is real, even if discounted by some cynics who see the world largely in terms of military and economic power.

On an International Relations list-serv in the academic world, a recent exchange regarding the effects of torture drew this comment from a prominent pillar of wisdom in the field: "Soft power is not worth a plug nickel."[99] I thought Supreme Court Justice William O. Douglas had been closer to the mark when he observed that people around the world—like the disappointed Swede at the Oslo conference—admired the United States not "so much for our B-52 bombers and for our atomic stockpile, but for the First Amendment and the freedom of people to speak and believe and to write, [and to have] have fair trials." Here was the "great magnet" that attracted friends for the United States, said Justice Douglas.[100] He would have been appalled by America's resort to methods more likely to occur in the basements of the Lubyanka in Moscow, or cellars in

Pyongyang, than within the facilities of a U.S. government agency or its secret prisons abroad. Equally appalled would have been another admirable voice lost in the march of time: the former chairman of the Senate Foreign Relations Committee, J. William Fulbright (D, Arkansas). "If America has a service to perform in the world—and I believe it has," he said, "it is in large part the service of its own example."[101] Torture is not the example Fulbright would have chosen.

The Senate Committee's torture investigation, while not matching the Church Committee in scope, stands as a significant example of serious intelligence accountability, with the staff having to struggle against both a spy organization expert at sheathing itself in bureaucratic armor and wily opponents within SSCI itself. The investigation may not have answered every question—such as why members of SSCI (and HPSCI) had failed to halt the torture program in the first place, when some of them found out about it a few years after its initiation; nevertheless, in the fullness of time the report did place the topic of torture before the public, allowing another national intelligence debate (accompanying the NSA metadata program) on the value of this approach to intelligence gathering. The SSCI staff paid a price, though, in terms of cohesion, with Democratic and Republican appointees at one another's throats during the research and writing of the report—and since. "There was blood on the floor after that report," observed one of the senior GOP staffers on the committee.[102]

The Senate Torture Report raised vital questions about whether secret agencies had gone too far in the direction of security by adopting counterterrorism measures alien to America's fundamental ethical principles, entering (to borrow a phrase from Dante) "a dark wood in which the straight way was lost." When the Japanese military used the technique of waterboarding against U.S. soldiers in World War II, American officials at the Tokyo trials called it torture and pursued convictions against the Japanese for war crimes; now, under the second Bush Administration, waterboarding was being used against suspected terrorists, with some key lawyers in the White House, the Justice Department, and CIA attorneys arguing that this method no longer qualified as torture. Vice President Cheney recalled that at the time of the 9/11 attacks "we gave our intelligence officers the tools and lawful authority they needed to gain information . . . through tough interrogation, if need be."[103] The vice president's devotion to an imperial presidency became the ladder upon which General Hayden and others ascended into forbidden land.

The senior lawyer at the CIA, John Rizzo, wrote in his memoirs that he could not bring himself to cancel the Agency's interrogation program, because he feared that another attack against the United States might occur and he did not want to be responsible for removing a program that might have prevented the disaster.[104] In a public forum another recently retired CIA attorney made the further argument that waterboarding is not torture "if done carefully."[105] Many

Americans were skeptical, though, that waterboarding and the other harsh interrogation methods employed by the CIA could be considered lawful operations.
So were the SSCI staff investigators who wrote the Torture Report. "There is
no careful way to waterboard," one of them—who had seen minute-by-minute
written transcripts about these episodes—told me when I mentioned the former CIA attorney's comment. His conclusion: "It's essentially drowning someone."[106] As we spoke in a remote corner of the Hart Building cafeteria, the staffer
seemed overwhelmed by a sense of sadness as he related to me details from the
packet of medieval tricks adopted by the Agency.

The Torture Report produced by the SSCI Democratic staff was roundly
criticized by leaders in the Bush Administration, as well as by the CIA's senior
management team and their retired counterparts from the Bush years—and,
indeed, by most of the Republicans on the Senate committee itself. They maintained that the facts in the report were often wrong and partisan. A retired Dick
Cheney called the SSCI study "a bunch of hooey."[107] He had also panned the
majority report on the Iran-contra scandal in 1987 and, as a member of Congress
from Wyoming, he had joined in a minority report from the Inouye-Hamilton
Committee that attempted to exonerate those involved in the scandal. Jose
A. Rodriguez, the Agency officer who ordered the destruction of video evidence
related to the torture program, insisted that the CIA's approach to interrogation
was "legal and effective."[108] Hayden dismissed Congress with the observation
that it had "lacked the courage or the consensus to stop [the interrogation pro-
gram], endorse it or amend it."[109]

SSCI Chair Feinstein, the most senior member of the Senate but full of life
and driven by dismay about the Agency's use of waterboarding and other unsavory methods, countered with arguments that the committee's study on torture
had been painstakingly researched by professional staff, drawing on the CIA's
own documents. She said that it was "the most significant and comprehensive
oversight report" in SSCI's history and that the Agency's actions had been
"improper."[110] Before taking on this burden, Feinstein had a reputation for being
"one of the CIA's most faithful supporters."[111] No longer.

The debate over the substantive merits of the report aside, the SSCI study
was a noteworthy oversight accomplishment, if for no other reason than the way
it had succeeded in drawing the nation's attention to the torture program and
how it stimulated widespread discussion about the wisdom of this approach
to counterterrorism—exactly what should happen in a democracy. Senator
Feinstein and her colleagues who supported the investigation deserve, along
with their staff aides, the nation's appreciation for their tenacity in standing
up to the intelligence bureaucracy, some senators on SSCI itself, and the two
administrations that tried to block their work. Yet this case points to intelligence
oversight failures, too. Why haven't Congress and the White House shown the

courage to release the complete Torture Report (with appropriate edits to protect sources and methods)? And why weren't they engaged in a more robust dialogue about proper counterterrorism techniques long before the disastrous interrogation program was ever adopted?

Officials in the CIA have claimed that, from the outset, SSCI and HPSCI lawmakers were adequately briefed on the scope of the harsh interrogation program. "We briefed the Congress 65 times between 2002 and 2008," recalls an Agency spokesman.[112] Yet, it is worth emphasizing again, the briefings often included only a few members of SSCI and HPSCI (sometimes not the Gang of Eight or even the Gang of Four); moreover, each among the anointed who were briefed was given just a partial accounting. Looking back, one cannot help but remember the vague responses of several CIA witnesses before the Church Committee, too, as well as DCI Casey's attempts to fool SSCI about mining harbors in Nicaragua, and, more recently, how Agency officials whispered into the ears of selected lawmakers about the NSA metadata program, warning them not to discuss it with colleagues or staff (who could have provided an evaluation of the technical explanations about sigint activities). These approaches amount to gaming the oversight system, rather than trying to treat SSCI and HPSCI as responsible partners.

The CIA Attacks the SSCI Staff

Also in 2014, in the context of the torture investigation, the Agency further contributed to a growing sense in the United States that the time had come to rebalance the security-liberty equation. In a move that set a new standard of brazenness and disdain toward congressional overseers, CIA officers hacked into computers—four times—that the SSCI staff had used during the torture inquiry. The Agency's cyberwarriors removed 870 documents during one hit, and 50 on another occasion.[113] The CIA director, John Brennan, claimed—falsely, it turned out, although perhaps he thought his statement was correct at the time—that SSCI staffers had first hacked into the Agency's computers. In fact, the Agency had accidentally sent to the SSCI staff's computers its internal examination of Agency interrogation practices—the so-called Panetta Report, named after then CIA director Leon Panetta, who had ordered an internal inquiry into the uses of torture. Amazed and pleased to stumble across this unknown study, which the Agency should have shared with SSCI in the first place, the committee staff was gratified to learn that the in-house study closely paralleled their own findings.

Unhappy that the Senate investigators now had inadvertently been provided with the Panetta Report, some people in the Agency—including the director— tried to turn the tables on their Hill tormentors by claiming that the SSCI staff had stolen the document by way of illegal hacking. The tradecraft of the CIA against foreign countries often includes the use of deception and manipulation; these dark arts were now turned against "Sissystan," as Agency officers had nicknamed SSCI—as if it were a Russian satellite nation. The Senate committee was, essentially, now just another hostile target for covert action. Even Senator Chambliss blanched at these accusations from the D/CIA. "John [Brennan] didn't handle that right," he managed to say in rebuke.[114] An SSCI member observed at the time: "It's WWIII between the CIA and Senate."[115]

Feinstein wrote to Brennan, reprimanding the Agency for its search into SSCI's computers, which she said might well have violated the separation-of-powers doctrine that lay at the heart of the Constitution (not to mention the CIA's founding law in 1947, which clearly prohibits Agency operations inside the United States). The director took weeks to respond. A Senate colleague of Feinstein's told the SSCI chairwoman that Brennan's intentions on behalf of the CIA were "to intimidate, deflect, and thwart legitimate oversight."[116] Subsequently, Brennan would concede in testimony before the full committee that a "trust deficit" had opened up between SSCI and the Agency, and he apologized to Feinstein and Chambliss for the hacking transgression.

At this same time, though, Brennan turned loose former CIA officers to proselytize the company line, including Hayden, Rizzo, and a former deputy director, John McLaughlin (who is also an amateur magician). In a major PR campaign reminiscent of the one aimed at the Church Committee by the Ford White House, the Agency trashed the committee and its Torture Report on every major television talk show in the country, as well as through a blizzard of newspaper op-eds, a "ciasavelives.com" website, and even Twitter messaging.[117] The CIA was able, further, to insinuate itself as an adviser to Hollywood in the making of the film *Zero Dark Thirty*, which portrayed torture as helpful in tracking down the Al Qaeda leader Bin Laden—a contention rejected in the Senate report.

McLaughlin, whose sleight-of-hand skills clearly went beyond hat-and-bunny tricks, stressed on one show that the CIA's interrogation approach was "a valuable program when it existed, in the time that it existed, and the circumstances it existed." He also testified to SSCI that the interrogations were nothing like what occurred at Abu Ghraib; in truth, though, several of the methods were exactly like those used in the Iraqi prison.[118] In an attempt to hoist defenders of the torture study on their own petards, he posed this question (part of the standard script echoed by several Agency advocates of the interrogation program in their media appearances): "Wouldn't it be equally immoral if we failed to get this information and thousands of Americans died? If there was another 9/11? How immoral would that be?"[119] This rhetoric comes from the common-law defense of "necessity." McLaughlin and his Agency colleagues hoped to find shelter in the argument that even though one may have engaged in a questionable deed, it was only for the purpose of averting a greater evil.[120]

Such "what if" questions, however, allow an unacceptable elasticity of moral vision, permitting a government to do practically *anything*, on the pretext of trying to protect the nation. To save democracy, nothing would be impermissible, including surveillance operations against every citizen or engaging in unsavory methods like torture that soil the honor of the United States. America transformed into North Korea. The McLaughlin position does remind us, though, that definitions of what constitutes legitimate intelligence oversight can vary widely. Even someone who billed herself as an aggressive HPSCI overseer, Representative Jane Harman (D, California), bought into a wide range of questionable interrogations techniques just below the threshold of waterboarding. "I'm O.K. with it not being pretty," she told a journalist.[121] President Obama had a different perspective. As he said in his Nobel Peace Prize acceptance speech, "We lose ourselves when we compromise the very ideals that we fight to defend."[122] That is the view the CIA and the rest of the IC should have had mapped into their value system.

The CIA used many of the same approaches against SSCI that the Ford Administration had embraced against the Church Committee. For example, the CIA—and others in the Bush and Obama Administrations—argued that the release of details about the interrogation program would endanger Americans around the world (just as supposedly publication of the Church Committee report on assassination plots would have done, but didn't). The Obama Administration went so far as to recruit the well-liked Secretary of State John Kerry to trot out this tired argument. Moreover, McLaughlin attempted to defend even the outsourcing of the interrogation program, saying that the external psychologists hired by the Agency "came to the effort with knowledge and experience that very few people in the CIA had."[123] In fact, according to Senator Feinstein, these contractors "had no experience in interrogation, no experience with counterterrorism, no experience with Al Qaeda, no understanding of the language."[124]

The CIA engaged in other forms of harassment against the committee's investigators, too. The Agency's acting chief counsel went after the SSCI staff with a vengeance, perhaps distressed by the fact that his name had come up more than 1,600 times in the Torture Report (each of which he managed to have deleted during the White House declassification wars). He referred to the Justice Department for investigation the names of the SSCI staffers who wrote the Torture Report. The CIA knows how to intimidate its critics. In the light of these anti-oversight activities, the Agency's understanding of, and allegiance to, the existing laws on accountability became a subject of profound concern on Capitol Hill and in the media. Senate Majority Leader Harry Reid (D, Nevada) warned Feinstein: "Look, you can't stand by anymore! The CIA is leaking stuff. They're making your staff out to be the bad guys!"[125] The Agency's efforts to spy on SSCI staffers were an unprecedented violation of the oversight relationship—an operation carried out with impunity, despite the strong, even angry complaint delivered by Feinstein in a press conference.

Brennan appointed a panel to look into the charges. Three of the five members of this group were CIA officers, and the other two were outside individuals known to be friendly toward the Agency. After a brief "investigation," the CIA absolved itself of any blame and announced, with its practiced skills of agitprop, that the whole episode had just been a "misunderstanding."[126] In sharp contrast, the CIA's own inspector general had reported earlier that the Agency's hacking into SSCI computers was improper, as was the effort by the acting general counsel to file a crimes report with the Department of Justice against committee staffers. The IG, David Buckley, soon found himself discredited and ostracized inside the CIA; he resigned as the Brotherhood closed ranks against him.

In 2015, the findings of the Torture Report significantly influenced the Senate vote of 78 to 21 in favor of banning America's use of any interrogation techniques in the future, unless they were specifically authorized in the list of less draconian methods found in the Army Field Manual. In an odd ending to the debate in Washington, the new chairman of SSCI, Richard Burr (R, North Carolina), asked President Obama in January 2016 to return all copies of the still-classified full Torture Report to his committee. Burr seemed determined to make sure it was never released to the public, beginning with this move apparently designed to block FOIA requests for the document (since FOIA does not apply to congressional records). Senator Feinstein strongly objected, fearing that Burr's ultimate goal was to destroy every copy of the final report.

The White House appeared happy to ignore Burr's request, as well as SSCI's newest internal confrontations. In 2016, in a unanimous ruling, the U.S. Court of Appeals for the D.C. Circuit in Washington ruled that records that Congress shares with federal agencies cannot be disclosed if there is a "clear intent" by lawmakers "to control the files."[127] It appeared as though in these circumstances the full Torture Report would remain forever bottled up, short of a Supreme Court judgment otherwise—or the election of more enlightened lawmakers. In 2017, agencies in the government—the CIA, the FBI, the DNI, among others—began returning their copies of the report to Senator Burr. Three copies, though, remained outside the chairman's clutches: one in the Obama presidential papers (frozen for twelve years); one at the Pentagon; and one in the vaults of the D.C. District Court (so ordered by the judge hearing cases from former CIA detainees).

A Mixed Record

A former SSCI chair, Jay Rockefeller, summed up the CIA's response to the interrogation inquiry as an "active subversion of meaningful congressional oversight."[128] To some degree, however, SSCI and HPSCI bear blame for allowing the CIA torture and the NSA metadata programs to move forward for so long before they took a closer look at them. Accepting at face value Hayden's "tummy slapping" remarks (or Robert McFarlane's earlier assurances about the nonexistence of the Enterprise during the Iran-contra episode) proved to be painful mistakes. Overseers must learn to be more skeptical and tenacious—using hearings with witnesses sworn under oath, as well as subpoena powers—until they are reasonably sure all the facts are known.

Further, as several CIA directors have noted, once they were finally informed by the executive branch about the interrogation activities, SSCI and HPSCI members "missed a chance to help shape the program—they couldn't reach a consensus. The executive branch was left to proceed alone, merely keeping the committees informed."[129] Journalist David Ignatius concurs. He accepted the SSCI Torture Report as "immensely valuable," but tagged the committee for not addressing "Congress's own failure to oversee these activities more effectively." He wondered: "Did the members of Congress push back hard, as we now realize they should have? Did they demand more information and set stricter limits? Did they question details about the interrogation techniques that were being used?" His correct response: "they did not."[130] Legal scholar Mike Glennon asks, too, "Where was SSCI while all this was going on?"[131] He might have added: "And where was HPSCI?" Neither committee visited any of the CIA's black sites overseas, for example.

At the same time, SSCI earns high marks in persevering with its inquiry into the interrogation program, despite great adversity and pitiful cooperation from the executive branch (for example, the executive branch—at the CIA's instigation— blocked 9,000 pages of documents from going to SSCI during its investigation, evoking the doctrine of executive privilege so thoroughly discredited during the Watergate inquiries). The Torture Report is no doubt flawed. It would have been especially good to have bipartisan participation in the effort, at the staff and member levels. The Republicans could have made this happen, but they abandoned their Democratic colleagues as a means of trying to slow and discredit the investigation. They would have had plenty of opportunities along the way to insert their dissenting views into the report and set the record straight when they thought the Democrats were off-mark. In this sense, the Republican strategy did the CIA a disservice. Only courageous Olympia Snowe on the GOP side displayed a bipartisan spirit and a willingness to search for the truth with colleagues across the aisle.

Critics have charged the Democratic staffers working on the report with allowing their ethical objections toward torture to override a dispassionate weighing of the program's effectiveness. The staffers deny this, arguing that their purpose was to lay out the facts.[132] At any rate, the facts did indicate that torture was not very effective (just as the value of the NSA's controversial sigint programs were routinely exaggerated by intelligence officials—and even by Senator

Feinstein).[133] As outside expert, Professor James P. Pfiffner of George Mason University, concludes: "It is possible that some useful intelligence was gained as a result of EITs, but the inability of the CIA to cite convincing evidence of any major breakthroughs produced by these methods is telling."[134]

One could hardly blame the SSCI staff investigators for experiencing some emotion during their inquiry, given the unsavory—even brutal—activities they had uncovered. These staffers have told me that the document made public, the Executive Summary, is mild compared to the gut-wrenching, nitty-gritty facts laid out in the full report about the agony experienced by the torture victims. The torture videotapes were destroyed; but the staff did gain access to transcripts of these sessions. In the full report that remains classified, these transcripts apparently describe the torturing in hair-raising detail. The picture that emerges, Senator Feinstein and her staff say, is stunningly different from the mild descriptions that Hayden tried to pass off to SSCI in his 2006 briefing.

Senator Feinstein, the accountability hero throughout this doleful torture episode, well captured the report's normative sentiments. "We're not Nazi Germany," she said. "We don't torture people. We don't waterboard them 183 times until they nearly stop breathing. We don't put them in coffins and attach them to walls for, like, 100 hours."[135] Hayden dismissed her views as "emotional," but she was not alone in her outrage. Senator McCain for one, himself a victim of torture at the hands of cold-blooded North Vietnamese interrogators during the war in Vietnam, said that "this question isn't about our enemies; it's about us."[136] In the same vein, Professor Pfiffner expressed a feeling that was widespread in the academic world: "Even if one concedes that the CIA did obtain useful intelligence as a result of EITS, the question remains whether the bits of intelligence gained were worth the cost of using torture—in terms of moral compromises, our international reputation, and precedents set." He continued: "The primary objection to torture is not that it doesn't work, but that it is wrong—by virtually universal religious proscriptions as well as the principles of the United States Constitution, international law, and American values."[137] The torture debates underscore another important dimension of accountability. Reviewing executive branch adherence to laws and reporting requirements is not enough; overseers must also make some important ethical judgments.

On December 30, 2005, torture became illegal for the United States when Congress enacted a law sponsored by Senator John McCain, entitled the Detainee Treatment Act.[138]

What patterns emerge when the historical experiences with intelligence accountability—the ups-and-downs discussed in part II of this book—are examined more analytically? The next chapter searches for explanatory patterns.

PART III

THE PATTERNS OF INTELLIGENCE ACCOUNTABILITY

|| 6 ||

A Shock Theory
of Intelligence Accountability

Patterns of Intelligence Accountability
on Capitol Hill

In the aftermath of the *Times* revelations about the CIA domestic spy scandal known as Operation CHAOS, members of Congress tried from late 1974 through 1980 to institute major improvements in the supervision of America's intelligence agencies. As we have seen in earlier chapters, their most notable achievements were the creation of SSCI (1976) and HPSCI (1977), along with the enactment of the Foreign Intelligence Surveillance Act (or FISA, 1978) and the Intelligence Oversight Act (1980). (Recall that, even before the Church Committee's findings, lawmakers had passed the Hughes-Ryan Act of 1974, based on Seymour Hersh's reporting in the *Times* on the covert actions against Allende.) Despite these dramatic reforms, the jaw-dropping Iran-contra affair erupted in the 1980s. This scandal, unmatched in constitutional implications by any other involving the nation's espionage agencies, led to the adoption of additional legislation and executive rules fashioned to hem in inappropriate spy activities (most notably, the Intelligence Oversight Act of 1991, as redrafted and passed with the more formal title of the Intelligence Reorganization Act of 1992). Nevertheless, two decades later in 2004, yet another panel of inquiry, the Kean 9/11 Commission, reached the disheartening conclusion that congressional accountability for intelligence—and obviously for counterterrorism—was simply not working.[1]

Nor have various American citizens been able to protect themselves in court against questionable U.S. intelligence operations, thanks to the "state secrets privilege." This doctrine rests on the notion, embraced by the executive branch, that federal courts cannot judge certain lawsuits without jeopardizing national security. As Louis Fisher explains, such cases might contain "state secrets" and thus, for the sake of national security, had to be "closed down before damage to the nation occurs." Judges have accepted this reasoning and, therefore, Fisher continues in criticism of this approach, they have surrendered "judicial independence and become an arm, willing or not, of the executive branch." To automatically accept executive claims that a state secret might be jeopardized "degrades the judiciary, undermines the rights of private litigants to bring a case charging the government with illegalities, and sends a green light to the executive branch that it may violate statutes, treaties, and the Constitution without any accountability."[2]

On Capitol Hill, prominent members of Congress have acknowledged the inadequacies in their attempts to track the activities of America's hidden government. "We really don't have, still don't have, meaningful congressional oversight," concluded Senator John McCain in 2004.[3] Frustrated by yet another intelligence controversy that took Congress by surprise—the warrantless wiretaps carried out by the NSA in violation of FISA, disclosed by the *New York Times* in December 2005[4]—the leading Democrat in the House of Representatives, Nancy Pelosi, proposed that her colleagues create a bipartisan, bicameral working group to recommend improvements for the intelligence oversight process.[5] Nothing of significance emerged from this initiative. Then, breaking ranks with her chairman, Representative Peter Hoekstra (R, Michigan), HPSCI member Heather A. Wilson (R, New Mexico) urged a "painstaking" review of the controversial NSA eavesdropping program. Again, little happened as the House Intelligence Committee (like its Senate counterpart) closed ranks, with few exceptions, behind the NSA's sigint programs. Most of these lawmakers embraced even the highly controversial metadata operations, with little consideration of the privacy implications. This chapter explores patterns of behavior among SSCI and HPSCI members that might help explain their uneven commitment to monitoring the elusive components of the intelligence community.

Shock as a Stimulus for Intelligence Accountability, 1974–2016

As touched on in chapter 1, political scientists Matthew McCubbins and Thomas Schwartz have offered a useful metaphor contrasting the "police-patrolling" and "firefighting" activities pursued by members of Congress.[6] As patrollers, lawmakers *qua* overseers regularly review executive branch programs, just as a police officer might walk the streets, check the locks on doors, and shine a flashlight into dark corners—all to maintain vigilance against potential acts of crime. In contrast, firefighters classically respond to alarms only after flames have ignited. In a similar fashion, lawmakers may carry out routine but careful reviews ("patrols") of executive branch programs; or they can wait until disaster strikes, then rush to the scene after an alarm sounds to indicate a program has run afoul of the law or other societal expectations.

The research on intelligence accountability on Capitol Hill presented in earlier chapters supports the observation of Professor Harry Howe Ransom, among the first to study this topic, that over the years patrolling of the spy agencies by lawmakers has been spotty and rarely critical.[7] The chief cause of this inattentiveness (again, with some exceptions among members of Congress, as seen in earlier chapters) derives from the nature of the legislative branch of government. Above all else, in most cases lawmakers seek reelection; they have political careers and they want to keep them moving forward and, if possible, trade in a lower office for a higher one. Thus, they usually come to the conclusion that passing bills with their names on them—visibility—and raising campaign funds are much better uses of their time than the often tedious and seldom-reported review of executive programs. This is especially true when it comes to the monitoring of intelligence operations, which must take place for the most part in closed committee sanctuaries far from public view. Absent constituents' awareness of this hard labor, a lawmaker's opportunities for credit-claiming back home—so vital to reelection prospects—become difficult.[8]

Counterterrorism guru Richard A. Clarke has observed that "America, alas, seems only to respond well to disasters. . . . Our country seems unable to do all that must be done until there has been some awful calamity that validates the importance of the threat."[9] An analysis of intelligence accountability in the United States since 1974 indicates a pattern in which a major intelligence scandal or failure—a profound shock to the body politic—rapidly converts normal, perfunctory patrolling by lawmakers (or often no patrolling at all) into a burst of intense firefighting. This after-the-fact, five-alarm, hook-and-ladder response to oversight obligations is followed by a limited phase of dedicated patrolling that often yields remedial legislation or other reforms designed to curb a repeat of failed or improper intelligence activities in the future.

Less significant mistakes or instances of wrongdoing can generate fire alarms, too, but they are below the five-alarm threshold that is of main interest in this book. These lesser shocks to the system can present opportunities for improving accountability as well, but they fall short of stimulating a full SSCI, HPSCI, or special commission response in the form of high-profile inquiries and noteworthy remedial legislation. Examples of lower-threshold alarms related to analysis would include the intelligence failures to anticipate widespread rioting in Colombia (1948); the Suez Canal crisis (1956); the Soviet invasions of Hungary (1956) and Czechoslovakia (1966); the Indian underground nuclear test that surprised U.S. intelligence analysts (1998); and the attack against the U.S.S. *Cole* in the Gulf of Aden (2000). And related mini-scandals are (for example) the CIA assassination manual discovered during the Reagan Administration (even though President Gerald R. Ford had banned such practices by executive order); and the Alpirez controversy in 1995 (discussed in chapter 4).

Sometimes the high-intensity patrolling in the aftermath of a major alarm can last for months and—if the original shock has been particularly strong and accompanied by a media tsunami, as occurred with the Operation CHAOS revelations—even years. Once the firestorm has subsided and reforms are in place, though, lawmakers return (either quickly or sometimes slowly) to a state of relative inattentiveness to intelligence concerns.[10] Just as Constant Hijzen has noticed in his study of parliamentary oversight in the Netherlands, "it is possible for Parliament to switch from a fundamental passive to a now and then active role vis-à-vis the world of intelligence."[11] This sequence, in which vigorous accountability comes and goes like the Cheshire Cat, is depicted schematically in Figure 6.1.

To reach an alarm or shock level, an allegation of intelligence wrongdoing—a scandal such as Iran-contra or a major mission failure, say, a significant analytic error in the understanding of world events (such as the faulty prediction that Iraq possessed WMDs in 2002), or a disastrous collapse of a covert action operation or counterintelligence shield—appears to require

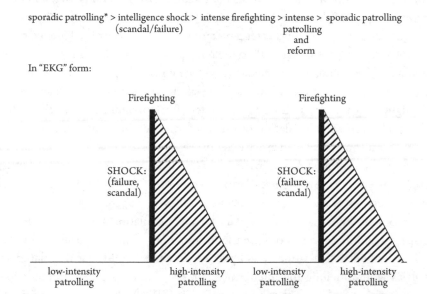

The pattern:

sporadic patrolling* > intelligence shock > intense firefighting > intense > sporadic patrolling
                        (scandal/failure)   patrolling
                                                                     and
                                                                     reform

In "EKG" form:

              Firefighting   Firefighting

SHOCK: SHOCK:
(failure,   (failure,
scandal)   scandal)

  low-intensity   high-intensity   low-intensity   high-intensity
   patrolling   patrolling   patrolling   patrolling

Figure 6.1 The Dominant Pattern of Intelligence Accountability on Capitol Hill, 1975–2016.
* A result of insufficient opportunities for credit-claiming and the enhancement of re-election prospects, which in turn produce an inattentiveness to oversight duties and a concomitant ripening of conditions for scandal or failure.

sustained media coverage. This attention in leading newspapers must last over several weeks running, with at least a few front-page stories. In 1974, for instance, the *New York Times* had an unusually high number of stories about the CIA published between June and December: over fifty articles, including nine stories on the Agency that made the front page in December. Here was a steady drumbeat of mainly negative reportage about operations arising from Langley, leading to a strong public reaction—along with a concomitant rise in congressional and presidential attentiveness—to the most explosive of the news items: the CIA's alleged involvement in spying on American citizens from coast to coast (Operation CHAOS). Similarly, on the eve of the next major intelligence scandal, the Iran-contra affair, the *New York Times* carried—in both October and November 1986—eleven front-page stories about possible abuses related to improper covert actions in Iran and Nicaragua. The coverage leaped to eighteen front-page, above-the-fold stories in December. This set the stage for a major congressional investigation into the scandal in 1987.[12]

This relationship between media coverage and the onset of major investigations into intelligence scandals or failures is explored more fully in the next chapter. Suffice it to say here that, at the time of the Church Committee, Professor Ransom had reason to observe that when it came to intelligence activities "the press, with all of its problems, remains the chief accountability enforcer." This assessment stands in stark contrast to President Trump's dismissal of the media early in his presidency as an "enemy of the people."[13] Obviously, Congress has more authority than the media to investigate intelligence operations, including (rare among parliaments around the world when it comes to intelligence accountability) the power of the subpoena.[14] Another significant source of congressional leverage is the powerful grip on the nation's purse strings enjoyed by lawmakers. Frequently, though, the media has stronger incentives—attracting an audience of readers or viewers, selling newspapers and products, perhaps winning distinguished prizes for reporting—and, thus, a greater will to engage in the serious day-to-day probing of government activities. Although a favorite piñata for American politicians, the media in the United States has served for the most part as a vital protector of liberty. This is rather a different role than (for instance) the one assigned to the Chinese media by President Xi Jinping, who said publicly in 2016 that journalists in his country have a singular raison d'être: to serve as propaganda tools for the Communist Party, pledging their fealty to Mr. Xi.[15]

Even saturation media coverage may not be enough in itself, however, to sound a penetrating fire alarm and bring overseers out of their lassitude. Such considerations as the personalities of SSCI and HPSCI leaders (especially the committee chairs), or the presence or absence of divided government, play a role as well in determining to what degree lawmakers will undertake a major investigation into an intelligence scandal or failure.[16] In early 2006, the media coverage of possible presidential abuse of the FISA warrant procedures for wire-taps was extensive, even if less than for the spy domestic scandal of 1974 or the Iran-contra scandal of 1987. The Republicans, however, controlled the White House (the second Bush Administration), as well as both chambers of Congress, and they resisted Democratic calls for a major probe into the allegations of these NSA espionage crimes.[17] Moreover, angst from the 9/11 attacks remained fixed in the nation's *gestalt*; lawmakers continued to have security far more on their minds than concerns about privacy.

Major Shocks and Alarms

Forty-three years have passed since Congress began to take intelligence account-ability seriously in December 1974, following the newspaper charges about CHAOS.[18] Since then, lawmakers have devoted approximately six years of close attention to full-scale investigations (firefighting) into intelligence controversies. The remaining thirty-seven years, or 86 percent of the total, consisted of police patrolling at a much lower level of intensity. The "checking-up" duties associated with patrolling displayed varying degrees of energetic commitment among over-seers on Capitol Hill—some of it vigorous in the immediate aftermath of a "fire," but mostly of a quotidian nature.

The time span examined in this chapter, from 1974 to 2016, began with CHAOS, the first intelligence five-alarm scandal since 1945 in the United States of sufficient intensity to bring about a major congressional response. Four more major alarms would ring out during the coming decades. These prominent events in the annals of modern intelligence accountability are outlined below.

Alarm No. 1 (1974): A Domestic Spy Scandal

Recall, the Senate and House investigative committees (the Church and Pike panels), established by Congress in the wake of the *Times* exposés in 1974, dis-covered extensive spying at home not only by the CIA, but also by the NSA, the FBI, and various military intelligence units. As we saw in chapter 3, the findings of these panels (along with the Rockefeller Commission) not only confirmed but also went far beyond the allegations leveled by the *Times*. The Church Committee issued a voluminous set of reports critical of a wide range of domes-tic intelligence operations, as well as the CIA's involvement in assassination plots against foreign leaders and other questionable covert actions.[19] At the center of its reform proposals issued in 1976, the panel recommended the creation of a permanent oversight committee in the Senate: the SSCI, created that year.

On the House side, the Pike Committee blasted the poor quality of intelligence assessments ("analysis") of worldwide threats over the years, but soon fell into a struggle with the CIA over access to documents and witnesses. The committee eventually collapsed during this confrontation with the Agency, amid innuendoes suggesting that its lawmakers and staff had dealt with classified materials in an unprofessional manner. Despite these hurricanes of charge and countercharge, when the winds finally settled, representatives in the lower chamber went on to establish a companion to SSCI: the HPSCI, which set up shop in 1977.

The Congress had reacted vigorously—too vigorously, critics would maintain—to the domestic spy scandal, working hard for a couple of years to ensure that the CIA and its companion agencies would never spy on Americans again, unless authorized to do so with proper FISA warrants and reports to lawmakers. With SSCI, HPSCI, and the new arrangements for improved intelligence accountability in place, lawmakers shed their firefighting posture and moved to police-patrolling duties (embraced with varying degrees of enthusiasm and diligence by individual lawmakers). Not until the next fire alarm would members of Congress—at least most of them—exhibit another high level of collective devotion to accountability.

Alarm No. 2 (1986): The Iran-Contra Scandal

In its determination to free American hostages held by terrorists in the Middle East and to rid Central America of a perceived Marxist influence in Nicaragua, the Reagan Administration pushed aside the nascent intelligence oversight rules and conducted unreported covert actions by way of a small cabal within its own NSC staff and a few top personnel at Langley (see chapter 4). When this end run was discovered in 1986, Congress established a combined Senate-House investigating panel (the Inouye-Hamilton Committee: HPSCI and SSCI blended into a Joint Committee) that confirmed the unlawfulness of the intelligence activities. Neither the administration's arms sales to Iran or aggressive paramilitary operations aimed at Nicaragua had been reported to Congress, as required by the Hughes-Ryan and 1980 Oversight laws. The Nicaraguan side of the scheme also violated the specific prohibitions of the Boland Amendments against paramilitary covert actions in Nicaragua. The new intelligence oversight was under secret assault, spearheaded by the "Enterprise"—a clandestine organization invented by DCI William Casey and the NSC staff that amounted to an off-the-books mini-CIA within the White House. After extensive research and dramatic public hearings, the Inouye-Hamilton Committee issued a detailed report on improprieties committed by the NSC and the Agency (with some side assistance from the NSA) during the period in which the scandal unfolded (from 1981 to 1986).[20]

Alarm No. 3 (1994): Intelligence Failures in Somalia and with CIA
Counterintelligence

Less than a decade after Iran-contra, Congress joined with the executive branch (the Aspin-Brown Commission) in another probe of intelligence problems that had cropped up. The White House was spurred into a firefighting stance by the intelligence failure associated with the killing of U.S. Special Forces soldiers on the Horn of Africa in 1993. On Capitol Hill, lawmakers focused, as well, on the counterintelligence failure involving the Soviet recruitment in 1984 of an American agent (Aldrich Ames) within the upper echelons of CIA Headquarters. Ames remained undiscovered by Agency or FBI counterintelligence officials until 1994, by which time he had sold important secrets to the U.S.S.R. about CIA operations directed against the Communist empire.

The Aspin-Brown Commission published a report calling not only for improvements in counterintelligence and improved tactical intelligence support for Special Forces operations, but also for across-the-board reforms of intelligence activities (chapter 4). After the Church Committee, it was the second most intensive examination of U.S. intelligence by lawmakers.[21] Upon issuing their findings in 1996—largely to an uninterested America enjoying the peaceful interlude of the immediate post–Cold War years—the commissioners returned to their normal duties, which, for the lawmakers involved in the inquiry, meant mostly desultory police patrolling (if any at all). Five years later, the nation would awaken abruptly from its slumber.

Alarm No. 4 (2001): The 9/11 Attacks

The failure of the intelligence agencies to provide specific warning to the nation about the catastrophic terrorist attacks against the American homeland in September 2001 (beyond the important but insufficiently detailed 1995 CIA/CTC "aerial warning" report and the August 6, 2001, *PDB*'s "blinking red light," discussed earlier in this book) led Congress to roll out the hook-and-ladder truck again, with great fanfare. Lawmakers formed another joint panel of inquiry—the Graham-Goss Committee, guided by the chairs of SSCI and HPSCI, respectively, at the time—and, subsequently, urged the creation of a presidential investigative panel (what became the Kean Commission) to further examine the events that led to the national tragedy.[22] Under Representative Goss's leadership, HPSCI also conducted a separate probe into CIA human intelligence, especially in the Middle East and Southwest Asia (prime breeding grounds for terrorism), producing a critical internal report on worldwide Agency humint inadequacies that had contributed to the 9/11 intelligence and policy failures.[23] On the military front, the United States attacked Afghanistan, where the Taliban regime had provided safe haven to the Al Qaeda terrorists responsible for the attacks. America's longest war—now in its sixteenth year—had begun.

Alarm No. 5 (2003): Weapons of Mass Destruction in Iraq

Following the major reports presented to the public by the Joint Committee and the Kean Commission, overseers again fell back into patrolling mode— although not for long. The ramp-up to war against Iraq in 2003, along with the discovery that (despite White House and IC claims) Baghdad had no WMDs after all, set off an alarm that brought lawmakers hastening back into the role of firefighters. The engines on the hook-and-ladder trucks had barely cooled from the 9/11 inquiry before they were revving up again in just two years, the nation's shortest interlude between major intelligence "fires." The first four fire alarms have been looked at in earlier chapters; the fifth—the surprise lack of WMD in Iraq—warrants further attention here.

The mistakes of intelligence analysis, policymaking, and accountability that led to this crisis were numerous, each disquieting. An October 2002 NIE concluded (as did most of America's intelligence agencies and outside scholarly analysts at the time) that WMDs were probably present in Iraq. This assessment—rapidly prepared, read by few on Capitol Hill, and its dissents buried in the document with no references to them in the "Key Judgments" cover section (the Executive Summary, which is all that many busy people bother to read)—appears to have been based on three primary sources of inaccurate information.[24]

First, IC analysts had extrapolated from what they knew about Iraq when Americans (and their intelligence officers) had boots on the ground in Iraq during the First Persian Gulf War of 1990–1991. At that time, the Agency discovered that its estimates regarding the presence of WMDs in that country had been dramatically off the mark; Saddam Hussein's nonconventional weapons program had advanced fully five years beyond what U.S. analysts had calculated. Without reliable ground-based sources after 1991 when U.S. troops withdrew from Iraq (soon followed by U.N. weapons inspectors, thrown out of the nation by Saddam because of the presence of CIA officers in their ranks), America's intelligence analysts compensated in the 2002 NIE for their earlier underestimates by this time *overestimating* the probability of WMDs.

Second, reliance on what appeared to be valuable humint sources proved to be an error. Testimony from a German asset who escaped from Iraq, a Baghdad scientist known (prophetically, as it turned out) by the intelligence codename "Curve Ball," factored into the CIA's assessments. German intelligence officials vowed that he was a reliable asset, and the Bundesnachtrichtendienst rejected Agency requests to let its own analysts interview the man. Only after the Second Persian Gulf War began in 2003 did the Germans concede that Curve Ball had turned out to be a pathological liar (among other character flaws). In another case, the DIA interrogated an Al Qaeda member by the name of Ibn al-Shaykh al-Libi, who had been captured by the U.S. Army in Afghanistan after the 9/11 attacks. His testimony also failed to hold up. Soon after the U.S. invasion of Iraq, Al-Libi finally admitted that he had invented the stories about WMDs in Iraq just to end the torture inflicted on him by Egyptian intelligence officers in Cairo, to whom the CIA had rendered him for further "cross-examination."

Third, a pressure group in the United States—the exiled Iraqi National Congress (INC), led by Ahmed Chalabi—managed to convince the Bush Administration that it knew all about Saddam's activities inside Iraq. A charming, well-spoken physician from Baghdad, Chalabi encouraged the White House and the intelligence community to accept the probability that Iraq was seeking to acquire WMDs—including nuclear warheads—that could be used against invading U.S. armies or even against the American homeland. The INC rapidly lost credibility, though, after the U.S. military flooded into Iraq in 2003 and found no such weaponry. Again only after the invasion did the Bush Administration come to realize that Chalabi had a different agenda than ridding the world of Iraqi WMDs: his own rise to power in Baghdad.

On top of all this dubious "intelligence" on Iraq, U.S. analysts had been persuaded by MI6 (the British counterpart of the CIA) and other foreign spy services in the Western democracies that Saddam was in fact busy manufacturing large-scale weaponry. Yet subsequent inquiries in the United Kingdom after the invasion revealed that, in truth, the worries of MI6 analysts had been more about Saddam using *tactical* chemical-biological weapons against any U.S. or U.K. invasion force, rather than *strategic* WMDs to strike more distant targets like Washington and London (as originally claimed by the Bush White House and No. 10 Downing Street, in a campaign of fear-mongering designed to gain public support for the invasion). Saddam's own foolhardy public harangues buttressed the WMD hypothesis, because he often boasted of Iraq's nuclear, biological, and chemical weapons capabilities—probably in a desperate hope of deterring an invasion of his land by a hostile neighbor, Iran.

Before the U.S. invasion, Secretary of State Colin L. Powell visited Langley several times to study the current intelligence on Iraqi WMDs, especially on the eve of his appearance before the United Nations (February 3, 2003) to argue in favor of an attack against Saddam's regime.[25] During these visits, the secretary picked up on some disagreements among Agency analysts about the WMD hypothesis; moreover, even within the Bureau of Intelligence and Research (INR) in his own State Department, dissent on some aspects of the WMD hypothesis was palpable. So, too, did dissent simmer inside U.S. Air Force Intelligence and the Department of Energy intelligence unit—the latter an organization notably expert when it comes to global nuclear issues, which it tracks daily.

These agencies offered insights that departed in significant ways from the IC's majority viewpoint in support of the Iraqi weapons hypothesis. For instance, one point of dispute centered on the 60,000 high-strength aluminum tubes purchased by Iraq that might have been meant for a uranium centrifuge in a nuclear-weapons program. Important, too, especially for Powell's U.N. presentation in support of an invasion of Iraq, were the testimony of Curve Ball as well as some imint products that seemed to reveal the presence of mobile chemical-weapons labs in Iraq. Yet INR analysts in Powell's own building at Foggy Bottom, as well as other analysts in the Department of Energy's intelligence unit, maintained that the aluminum tubes were most likely combustion chambers for conventional rockets, not components of a uranium centrifuge; in addition, the mobile labs could just as well have been—and indeed turned out to be—just fire trucks, not chemical decontamination vehicles that accompany chemical weapons. Further, analysts in Air Force Intelligence questioned the prevailing view in the IC that Iraq's UAVs had a long-range capability.

This questioning trio of small, though well-regarded, spy agencies should have induced some skepticism in the Bush White House about Iraq's alleged quest for strategic weaponry. Yet the giants among the intelligence agencies—CIA, NSA, DIA—brushed them aside, as well as their own internal dissenters, and persisted with the argument that an advanced WMD program pursued by Baghdad made sense and was probably already well under way. Compelling, too, was the fact that DCI George Tenet, head of the IC and a favorite at the White House because of his jovial countenance, supported the majority WMD opinion.

Even in the face of these various caveats from INR, Air Force, and the Energy Department, Powell deferred to the IC's powerful majority coalition. All of these debates occurred chiefly among professional intelligence analysts, outside the purview of the American public and with no meaningful SSCI or HPSCI participation. The three small intelligence agencies found themselves overruled by the judgments of their much larger companions—and by the DCI himself. In the end, despite some lingering doubts, Powell, who was given only four days to prepare his high-profile speech, did his best to defend the conventional wisdom—the WMD hypothesis—before the United Nations.

President Bush at least took the time to question DCI Tenet directly about his confidence in the conclusions of the 2002 NIE that supported the notion of Iraqi WMD (though he never met with, or even perhaps knew about, the dissenters within the IC). Was the DCI absolutely sure there were such weapons in Iraq? Tenet's response, reported by Bob Woodward of the *Washington Post*, is now well known: "It's a slam dunk, Mr. President."[26] The few outsiders who have read the NIE say, though, that the analysts who wrote it were by no means claiming any such sweeping conclusion.[27] While they did state that the odds were in favor of finding WMD in Iraq, the Estimate presented—although buried in the middle of the document—a number of caveats about the assessment's softness, including the reservations expressed by INR, the Air Force, and the Energy Department.

This sense of uncertainty about many key points, like the true nature of the suspected mobile weapons labs, is precisely what Tenet should have underscored for the president, emphasizing that the NIE was hardly a definitive report and that more on-the-ground fact-finding was badly needed to fill in the gaps; that the CIA was uneasy about the humint from Curve Ball and Al-Libi, and about the motives of Chalabi. A DCI briefing along these lines to the president—or in response to tough questioning of Tenet by SSCI and HPSCI lawmakers—would have highlighted the need for a delay in the invasion plans until U.N. weapons inspectors had been able to reenter Iraq and clear up the intelligence ambiguities (the course of action favored by two of America's most important allies, Germany and France). Instead, the White House seems to have been all too ready to embrace the WMD argument, which conveniently happened to run parallel to the policy desires of neoconservatives in the administration to knock out the Saddam regime—in part as a favor to Israel, as well as to create a democratic beachhead in that part of the Middle East. As he mentions in his memoirs, the president also had his own personal interest in an invasion: avenging Saddam's failed plot to assassinate his mother and father when they had visited Kuwait after the First Persian Gulf War.

Prior to his slam-dunk remark, Tenet had failed to set the record straight during another significant moment in the WMD debate. Inserted into the president's State of the Union address in January 2003 was an assertion that Saddam Hussein had sought to purchase fifty tons of yellow-cake uranium from Niger, suggesting that, yes, the Iraqi dictator was in hot pursuit of a nuclear weapons program. The CIA had looked into this allegation, dispatching a former U.S. ambassador to make direct inquiries on the ground in the African nation. The ambassador found no evidence to support the allegations and reported this finding to Langley, which in turn passed on the information to deputy national security adviser Stephen Hadley—all well in advance of the State of the Union address. Yet the speech included the false yellow-cake claim anyway, even though Tenet had personally telephoned Hadley and advised removal of the passage.[28] The notion that Saddam had tried to buy large quantities of yellow cake was now cloaked in the legitimacy of the president's own words in an important nationally televised event. Neither Tenet nor the National Security Council corrected the public record after the speech; Tenet claimed further, with limited credibility, that he had never had a chance to read the State of the Union address in advance.

In light of the mistaken NIE published in 2002 that had predicted the presence of WMDs in Iraq, President Bush authorized an executive order to create still another presidential investigative panel (the Robb-Silberman Commission) to investigate the analytic failure.[29] Further, SSCI undertook an inquiry of its own into the faulty estimate, which was considered so sound and significant that the committee eschewed its more usual partisan divisions and voted 15–0 in support of the final report.[30]

Once the flap over the erroneous Estimate had settled down, the wars in Iraq and Afghanistan ground on and intelligence overseers settled back into patrolling activities, which they had largely abandoned during the NIE "debate" (such as it was). The NSA metadata program and the CIA's involvement in torture would soon jolt lawmakers into a more intensive pursuit of police patrolling; but these intelligence controversies (see chapter 5) never managed to trigger major firefighting inquiries, as lawmakers continued to be gripped above all by concerns about security—no more 9/11s—even at the expense of an erosion of liberties that had taken place in the face of the ongoing global terrorist threat.

As the commitment of lawmakers to patrolling ebbed and flowed in the Congress over these years, the staffs of SSCI and HPSCI continued to conduct research, examine budgets, critique analytic reports, and weigh the merits of covert action and counterintelligence activities. They also regularly visited IC facilities inside the United States and abroad, organized routine but useful hearings (mainly in executive session), and wrote briefing books and position papers for members of the committees. Here was an ongoing degree of intelligence oversight unknown before the advent of the reforms inspired by the Church Committee in 1975—even if seldom at the level of the intensive police patrolling hoped for by intelligence reformers.

The Policy Results of Intelligence Accountability

As displayed in Table 6.1, Congress adopted several key legislative proposals related to intelligence during the time span from 1974 to 2016. Of the eighteen significant oversight initiatives presented in this table, only seven occurred during a phase of police patrolling, outside the context of a major fire-alarm response.

Police-Patrolling Oversight Initiatives

Lawmakers enacted the first three laws related to intelligence police patrolling during the early 1980s (the Reagan Administration). This trio grew out of what might be called "empathetic police patrolling" by lawmakers, that is, they were the result of instances when Congress responded favorably to the requests of

Table 6.1   **Types of Stimuli and Oversight Responses by Lawmakers, 1974–2016**

Year	Stimulus	Oversight Response	Purpose of Response
1974	FA (#1)	Hughes-Ryan Act	Controls over covert action
1976–1977	FA (#1)	Est. SSCI, HPSCI; critical repts.[1]	More robust accountability
1978	FA (#1)	FISA	Warrants for electronic surveillance
1980	FA (#1)	Intel. Oversight Act	Tightening oversight rules
1980	P	Intel. Information Procedures Act	Eased legal action against leaks
1982	P	Intel. Identities Act	Protect intel. officers/agents
1984	P	CIA Information Act	Limits on FOIA requests
1987	FA (#2)	Critical report[2]	Improve intelligence oversight
1989	FA (#2)	CIA Inspector General Act	Improve internal CIA oversight
1991	FA (#2)	Intelligence Oversight Act	Further tightening of oversight rules
1996	FA (#3)	Est. DCI assistants; critical repts. [see above for 1976–1977][3]	IC management improvements; strengthening CI
1997	P	Intel. Authorization Act provision	Controls on CIA use of journalists
1998	P	Whistle-blowers Protection Act	Improving procedures for whistle-blowing
2001	FA (#4)	USA PATRIOT Act; authorization of war against Al Qaeda and Taliban regime, AUMF; increases in counterterrorism funding	Increase surveillance of suspected terrorists; paramilitary counterattacks against Al Qaeda and Taliban
2004	FA (#4)	Critical repts.[4]	Improving humint and analysis

Table 6.1 **Continued**

Year	Stimulus	Oversight Response	Purpose of Response
2004	FA (#4, #5)	Intel. Reform & Terrorism Prevention Act (IRTPA)	Strengthening CT, IC coordination, est. Director of National Intelligence
2008	P	FISA Amendments Act	Supporting NSA metadata program
2015	P	USA FREEDOM Act	Improved safeguards for NSA operations

Abbreviations:

FA = fire alarm (#1 = domestic spying; #2 = Iran-contra; #3 = Ames; #4 = 9/11; #5 = WMDs in Iraq)

P = patrolling

[1] The Church Committee Report (Select Committee to Study Governmental Operations with Respect to Intelligence Activities, *Final Report*, 94th Cong., 2nd Sess., Sen. Rept. No. 94-755, 6 vols. [Washington, DC: U.S. Government Printing Office, 1976]); Rockefeller Commission Report (Commission on CIA Activities within the United States, *Report to the President* [Washington, DC: U.S. Government Printing Office, June 1975]); and Pike Committee Report ("The Report the President Doesn't Want You to Read: The Pike Papers," *Village Voice*, February 16 and 23, 1976).

[2] The Inouye-Hamilton Report (*Report of the Congressional Committees Investigating the Iran-Contra Affair*, Sen. Rept. No. 100-216 and H. Rept. No. 100-433, 100th Cong., 1st Sess., U.S. Senate Select Committee on Secret Military Assistance to Iran and the Nicaraguan Opposition and U.S. House of Representatives Select Committee to Investigate Covert Arms Transactions with Iran [Washington, DC: U.S. Government Printing Office, November 1987]).

[3] Aspin-Brown Commission Report (*Preparing for the 21st Century: An Appraisal of US Intelligence*, Report of the Commission on the Roles and Capabilities of the United States Intelligence Community [Washington, DC: U.S. Government Printing Office, March 1, 1996]); and Staff Study, *IC21: Intelligence Community in the 21st Century*, Permanent Select Committee on Intelligence, House of Representatives, 104th Cong., 2nd Sess. [Washington, DC: U.S. Government Printing Office, March 1996]).

[4] The Graham-Goss Committees Report (*Joint Inquiry into Intelligence Community Activities before and after the Terrorist Attacks of September 11, 2001*, House Permanent Select Committee on Intelligence and Senate Select Committee on Intelligence, Sen. Rept. 107-351, 107th Cong., 2nd Sess. [2002]); the Goss Committee Report (*Intelligence Authorization Act for Fiscal Year 2005*, House Permanent Select Committee on Intelligence, H. Rept. 108th Cong., 2nd Sess. [2004]); and the Roberts Committee Report (*US Intelligence Community's Prewar Intelligence Assessments on Iraq*, Senate Select Committee on Intelligence, Sen. Rept. 108-301, 108th Cong., 2nd Sess. [2004]).

spy managers for legislation designed to help them run the IC more effectively. William Casey had served as national campaign manager to the successful GOP candidate, Ronald Reagan; and so, as DCI, he had close ties to the Oval, as well as solid relationships with most Republicans and even some Democrats in Congress. With Iran-contra still brewing underground and not yet a controversy, lawmakers *qua* police patrollers were willing to work with the new intelligence director.

Foremost among this group of statutes is the Intelligence Identities Act of 1982. This law was the result of a willingness by lawmakers, at the urging of President Reagan and DCI Casey, to enact a measure that set stiff penalties against anyone who revealed without proper authorization the name of any U.S. intelligence officer or asset. The other two initiatives included one, the Intelligence Identities Act, to address so-called graymail, making it easier for the Agency to sue individuals in court without having to reveal classified information; and a second, the CIA Information Act, that placed limits on filing FOIA requests, which (according to the administration at least) had become a time burden to the Agency. During the 1990s, the next two police-patrolling initiatives required the DCI to report any exception to established rules prohibiting the Agency's reliance on U.S. journalists for spying activities (a provision in the Intelligence Authorization Act of 1997), and to improve whistle-blower protections (the Whistleblowers Protection Act of 1998). The final laws during this period that stemmed from police patrolling were the controversial FISA Amendments Act in support of the NSA metadata program (2008) and the USA FREEDOM Act that, in contrast, placed new restrictions on metadata collection.

The media-related law passed in 1997 was a reaction to a *Washington Post* allegation that the CIA had recruited journalists for intelligence-related matters, even though Agency regulations from the Church Committee era prohibited its operational contact with reporters accredited to U.S. media organizations.[31] John Deutch, DCI at the time of the *Post's* revelation, said that the CIA had in fact honored these restrictions; but, he added, the intelligence director had the right to waive this rule (established by executive order, not by an act of Congress) in times of emergency—say, using a journalist to gain access to a terrorist who intended to detonate a nuclear device in an American city.[32] The apparent (and previously unknown) malleability of this rule raised shackles on Capitol Hill. Members of Congress were further aggravated when former DCI Stansfield Turner subsequently admitted that he had invoked this privilege three times during the Carter Administration without informing the congressional oversight committees.[33] To prevent misuse of these media contacts by Deutch or future DCIs, lawmakers placed a provision in the Intelligence Authorization Act of 1997 (signed into law by President Clinton) that allowed a waiver in times of urgency, but only with formal presidential authorization and timely reporting to SSCI and HPSCI.[34] Here was a Hughes-Ryan safeguard for emergency contact between the CIA and journalists.

Two years later, lawmakers were persuaded that whistle-blowers in the government needed more protection in order to encourage their assistance with intelligence accountability. The result was the Whistleblowers Protection Act of 1998. This law evolved within SSCI and HPSCI over a long period of time, pushed forward by a sense that an intelligence officer with a serious complaint against a spy agency should be shielded by Congress against retaliation by the executive branch.[35]

The penultimate oversight initiative springing from police patrolling rather than firefighting was the FISA Amendments Act a decade later, in which Congress decided—with little serious debate—to endorse most of the controversial NSA sigint programs started by President George W. Bush and Vice President Dick Cheney. When President Obama came into office, he reversed his earlier concern about runaway eavesdropping by the NSA and threw his weight behind the Amendments. In 2015, though, Obama reversed fields to some extent and signed the USA FREEDOM Act, which introduced some protections against the overzealous use of sigint programs targeting American citizens (chapter 5)—the last of the police-patrolling measures adopted during this time.

High-Threshold Firefighting Oversight Initiatives

The eleven other oversight measures presented in Table 6.1 carried weightier implications for the IC. Each came about as a result of a major intelligence shock and resultant alarm, followed by full-bore investigation into the spy agencies and (initially at least) more aggressive forms of patrolling by members of Congress and their staffs. Most of these proposals took a fair amount of time for the lawmakers to craft and then attract majority support for their enactment.

Major Fire Alarm No. 1

An illustration is the Intelligence Accountability Act of 1980, which, as with the creation of SSCI, HPSCI, and the passage of FISA, was a proposal that emerged from the Senate inquiry associated with fire alarm no. 1—Operation CHAOS. After germinating in the reform petri dish of the Church Committee for a year, it took supporters yet another four years to gain sufficient backing in both chambers to pass the Oversight Act. This watershed law had several vital provisions for the future of genuine intelligence accountability. It required, recall from chapter 4, the DCI to report to the Congress *in advance* on *all* important intelligence activities. The president could delay contacting lawmakers only in "extraordinary circumstances." Even then, the White House was expected to report immediately to the Gang of Eight and later to the full memberships of SSCI and HPSCI "in a timely manner" (understood to mean within one day or, at the most, two days).[36]

Another illustration is the earlier enactment in 1978 of FIAS, which set up a warrant procedure for national security surveillances—a marked departure from earlier practice. Reformers more rapidly won passage of this initiative; it became law within just two years after its preliminary drafting by Church Committee staff. This relatively speedy success was aided by the fact that Walter Mondale, a former Church Committee member and a chief sponsor of FIAS, had become vice president in the Carter Administration. From that perch, he was able to assemble a powerful legislative affairs team that lobbied Congress relentlessly on behalf of the bill's enactment.

Major Fire Alarm No. 2

The response of Hill overseers to the Iran-contra scandal yielded a congressional report (prepared by the Inouye-Hamilton Committee) that was highly critical of the Reagan Administration's infringements of law and the Constitution. Another report, issued on February 26, 1987, was written by a presidentially appointed review panel (the Tower Commission, led by John Tower, a former Republican senator from Texas and another erstwhile member of the Church Committee). It faulted President Reagan for an overly permissive management style, with reins so loose that the NSC staff was allowed to run afoul of the Boland Amendments and other intelligence oversight laws. This was the general conclusion, too, of yet a third report on Iran-contra, presented on August 4, 1993, by Independent Counsel Lawrence E. Walsh, whose pen flowed with acid rather than ink. In the wake of these inquiries, Congress passed the 1989 CIA Inspector General Act and the Intelligence Authorization Act of 1991 (commonly known as the Intelligence Oversight Act of 1991). The latter reinforced its 1980 forerunner by defining covert action more fully (delineating it from less controversial secret diplomatic negotiations), as well as by underscoring the necessity for signed findings and timely (two-day) reporting to SSCI and HPSCI on all significant intelligence activities (not just covert actions).

Major Fire Alarm No. 3

The third major fire alarm, set up by intelligence failures on the Horn of Africa and by the Ames treachery, led to the creation of the Aspin-Brown Commission, with its modest reform proposals favoring some strengthening of the DCI office.

Major Fire Alarm No. 4

Then came 9/11 and a fourth truly screeching alarm. The terrorist attack resulted in a turn away from intelligence accountability as America responded to the global terrorist threat. A congressional Joint Committee and the Kean Commission did call, though, for a major overhaul of the IC, especially improvements in the sharing of information among the spy agencies—the top recommendation of the Kean Commission.

Major Fire Alarm No. 5

Driven by the embarrassing and consequential analytic errors regarding the presence of WMDs in Iraq—what former secretary of state Colin Powell has referred to as "one of the worst intelligence failures in U.S. history"[37]—the fifth fire alarm produced the Robb-Silverman Commission as well as an SSCI report, both critical of CIA intelligence reporting on the Middle East. Further, Congress passed the Intelligence Reform and Terrorism Prevention Act (IRTPA) and thereby established a DNI Office and National Counterterrorism Center, in hopes of further advancing the goal of improved institutional integration in the fragmented intelligence community. The DNI position was another Kean Commission proposal, although its members envisioned a stronger version of a national spymaster.

The Frequency of Intense Intelligence Accountability

The War of 1812 aside, the most important intelligence "wake-up call" for congressional overseers in the period before the formal creation of the CIA and America's modern intelligence community in 1947 had been the Japanese surprise attack against Pearl Harbor on December 7, 1941. The sections of the National Security Act of 1947 that established the CIA were a delayed response, in part, to that terrible intelligence failure. Important, too, in the creation of the Agency was President Truman's desire for a more streamlined and coordinated flow of intelligence into the Oval Office instead of the separate stacks of reports from various spy agencies that were piling up on his desk. Most of all, though, the creation of the CIA sprang from a growing concern in Washington about a new peril to the United States: the Soviet Union, an emerging and heavily armed global rival guided by a Marxist philosophy anathema to America's espousal of market-based liberal democracy.[38] America needed better information about this existential threat.

Several low-threshold fire alarms sounded during the early years of the Cold War—significant events involving intelligence mistakes or scandals, but not earthshaking enough to produce major government inquiries. Among the most notable stemmed from the Agency's failure to predict the outbreak of war on the Korean Peninsula (1950), followed by the Bay of Pigs disaster (1961), the controversy over CIA ties to the National Student Association and other domestic groups (1966), and an alleged Langley connection to the Watergate burglars (1973).[39] I refer to them as low-threshold alarms here because none of them came close to being as shattering as the subsequent high-threshold shocks delivered by CHAOS, the Iran-contra affair, the Ames and Somalia cases, the 9/11 attacks, or the mistaken WMD report that helped fuel—or at least provide cover for—an American war in Iraq in 2003. With the possible exception of the Ames and Somalia cases, these blaring alarms captured the attention of vast numbers of Americans across the nation, which in turn (or, in some cases, simultaneously) led lawmakers to take more seriously the events that caused the alarms to sound. Whether or not the Ames and Somalia cases attracted broad citizen interest, the act of high treason at the CIA and the tragic death of U.S. Special Forces on the Horn of Africa were worrisome enough to trigger in 1994 a double-sourced major fire alarm heard by national security officials and lawmakers in the nation's capital.

The CHAOS alarm was a no-brainer; spying on American citizens was beyond the pale and caused a ruckus across the land. As for the Iran-contra scandal, members of Congress might have reacted sharply even if the public had shown little concern, since it amounted to a provocative disregard for the congressional appropriations process, covert action reporting requirements, and the Boland Amendments. Moreover, the likes of the phantom Enterprise were too chilling to ignore. Lawmakers reacted strongly as well to the Ames counterintelligence case, since a Soviet penetration at the highest levels of the Agency was difficult to dismiss, striking as it did at the heart of the CIA's mandate in the 1947 National Security Act to protect "sources and methods." At the time, the Ames treachery was instantly acknowledged as the worst counterintelligence failure in American history. Further, when sizable numbers of American troops are brutally ambushed and murdered in a nontraditional battle zone, as happened in Somalia in 1993, officials in the federal government are not going to sit on their hands; they want to know how it happened. The closeness in time of these two headline events—Ames and Somalia—led to a combined fire alarm responding to both, followed by the establishment of the Aspin-Brown Commission. The 9/11 and the WMD failures were also too momentous for overseers to ignore.

The low-threshold alarms, Korea in 1950 and the Bay of Pigs in 1961—while obviously disconcerting, to say the least—dealt with situations outside the United States and, prior to the war in Vietnam, Congress and the public had given the executive branch wide latitude in such cases. "Politics stops at the water's edge," was the venerable saying. The CIA's relationships with students, however, and with the Watergate episode both took place at home. Yet the former came across as a fairly narrow issue, chiefly involving improper Agency support for U.S. students attending international conferences; and the latter proved to have little substance beyond a rust-colored wig and a small camera supplied by DS&T for E. Howard Hunt (a former CIA officer) and thick glasses for G. Gordon Liddy (a former FBI agent). These two erstwhile intelligence officers turned Watergate conspirators were known in the White House as "the Plumbers Group" (assigned to stop further leaks like the Pentagon Papers, a DoD history provided to the media by Daniel Ellsberg, which revealed serious missteps taken by Presidents Johnson and Nixon in the conduct of the Vietnam War). More formally, the conspirators were referred to by White House insiders as the secretive Special Investigations Unit, or SIU. Preceding the Watergate Hotel "black-bag" operation, this dubious duo orchestrated another break-in, this time into the office of Ellsberg's psychiatrist in hopes of finding material to smear the man who leaked the Pentagon Papers. Both "second-story" jobs were felony crimes.

In the wake of the Watergate scandal, several investigations found that the CIA's DS&T had failed to inquire—lamely—into the purpose of the Hunt and Liddy disguises, and it had no prior knowledge of Hunt's Watergate and Ellsberg-related antics. As for the burglary into the psychiatrist's office (abetted by three Cubans whom Hunt had met during his service in the Agency), the Hunt-Liddy team discovered nothing they could use against Ellsberg. This caper, though, according to a White House aide who helped direct both burglaries, was "the first irreversible step by which a presidency ran out of control."[40] Other than these few foolish support activities—undertaken by naïve or incompetent lower-level bureaucrats at Langley without understanding the intentions of Hunt and his colleagues, and on the margins of the break-in operations—the CIA strenuously steered clear of Watergate, especially the attempts by the Nixon Administration to draw DCI Richard Helms and his crew at Langley into the conspiracy cover-up. Their resistance to White House blandishments and threats stands as a high-water mark in the Agency's history—although the disguises, the camera (containing pictures taken in Ellsberg's office and later developed for Hunt by DS&T), the Cuban assets, and the ties to Hunt remain disturbing examples of poor accountability in the bowels of the CIA.

An examination of the frequency of notable alarms, both low- and high-threshold (see Table 6.2), highlights the periodicity of intelligence scandals and failures in the modern era.[41] Eliminating the CIA-Watergate "scandal," since it consisted of negligible intelligence participation (however important the burglary and cover-up was as a political and historical event in the United States), a significant, five-bell intelligence alarm has sounded roughly every seven and a half years, on average. The second longest gap—at thirteen years or almost twice the average—occurred between the domestic spying scandal exposed in 1974 and the Iran-contra affair that came to light in 1986.

The most recent major fire alarm leading to an investigation was the 2003 Iraqi WMD controversy. The gap of no major fire alarms since then sets a new record of fourteen years and growing between intelligence-related major firefighting alarms. The Snowden leaks on the NSA metadata program in 2013 generated considerable publicity, but this event never led to a major government inquiry.

Table 6.2 **The Frequency of Low- and High-Threshold Intelligence Alarms, 1941–2013 (with high-threshold years in bold and underscored)**

Year	**1941**	1950	1961	1966	1973	**1974**	**1987**	**1994**	**2001**	**2003**	2013 …
Alarm	F	F	F	S	S	S	S	F	F	F	S
	^	^	^	^	^	^	^	^	^	^	
Internal (Yrs.)	9	11	5	7	1	13	7	7	2	14+	

Average Interval: 7.6 years*

The Events		Thresholds
1941	Pearl Harbor attack**	High
1950	Outbreak of war on the Korean Peninsula	Low***
1961	Bay of Pigs	Low
1966	CIA–National Student Association scandal	Low
1973	CIA–Watergate "scandal"	Low
1974	Domestic spying scandal (CHAOS)	High
1987	Iran–contra scandal	High
1994	Somalia attacks and the Ames failure	High
2001	9/11 attacks	High
2003	Faulty WMD analysis (Iraq)	High
2013	Snowden leaks	Low

* Excluding the CIA-Watergate case (see text).

** Not examined in this book, which concentrates on the period since the establishment of the CIA.

*** "Low" and "High" in this table simply indicate intelligence mistakes or scandals that never triggered a major government inquiry ("Low") and those that did ("High").

Abbreviations:

F = failure of collection and/or analysis

S = scandal or impropriety

The muffling of this fire alarm was a result, most likely, of the various global terrorist events that occurred during this time, especially in England, France, and Spain, plus a few in the United States (most notably, the killing sprees in San Bernardino in 2015 and Orlando in 2016). Washington officials were loath to be seen as interfering with robust intelligence collection against Al Qaeda, ISIS, and their collaborators in the midst of this ongoing terrorist activity. Further, it was not exactly astounding for the public to suspect already that the U.S. government might be eavesdropping on telephones and social media—even those belonging to Americans—in search of terrorists. As a political scientist has noted, "this information [about NSA spying] turned out to be *already known* by the public to some degree, even if not officially."[42]

The domestic spying scandal known as CHAOS and the ensuing investigations (Church, Pike, Rockefeller) were profoundly traumatic to the intelligence agencies, whose officers remember 1975 as an *annus horribilis*. The investigations established a new standard of ethics and accountability for the IC that may have significantly contributed to the reduced incidence of improper behavior by intelligence officers over the next thirteen years. This encouraging early record came to an end, however, when the obsession of the Reagan Administration with bartering for U.S. hostages held in the Middle East and with cleansing Nicaragua of Sandinista rule led NSC staffers and the CIA to misuse the government's intelligence capabilities—and even develop their own secret organization (the Enterprise) to conduct covert actions against the regime in Managua.

The briefest interlude between major alarms occurred from 2001 to 2003, with the revelation about the IC's faulty Iraqi WMD projections coming rapidly on the heels of the 9/11 failure—a double blow to the reputation of the Agency and a primary reason for its dramatic decline in 2004–2005 as the heartland of America's intelligence activities. After these twin failures, the CIA became just one of seventeen entities in the IC and no longer its exclusive "central" hub (regardless of the enduring word "central" in its name). In 2004, Congress moved this premier leadership role to the new DNI office, as a result of the Intelligence Reform and Terrorism Prevention Act (IRTPA) passed in 2004. The next year, the White House informed the director of the Central Intelligence Agency (D/CIA) that he would no longer be a regular attendee at NSC meetings or the lead person to conduct the daily intelligence briefings for the president. The DNI, though, would soon revert to a reliance on close assistance from the D/CIA and the Agency's analysts for these time-consuming and high-pressure White House briefing responsibilities.[43] The CIA was on the rise again.

Steady Patrolling at the Staff Level

The portrait presented here that depicts a periodic inattentiveness of lawmakers in the guise of patrollers should not overshadow the fact that intelligence oversight since 1975 has been vastly more robust than "in the good old days," as some mossback intelligence professionals recall the years before 1974 when Congress left the secret agencies largely to their own devices.[44] Intelligence overseers since 1976–1977 have benefited greatly from the existence of the two standing intelligence oversight committees, SSCI and HPSCI, each armed with budget and subpoena powers and staffed by intelligence experts. The authority of these panels over intelligence extends far beyond that enjoyed by any other spy oversight panels in any legislative chamber in the world, today or in the past.

Moreover, while some lawmakers have been less than fully engaged in patrolling, in the extraordinary circumstances when major scandals or intelligence failures erupt most members of Congress selected for investigative duties have become dedicated—even zealous—firefighters. Here is vigorous oversight, practiced at no time more actively than when television cameras are in the hearing room. With the klieg lights in place and the cameras rolling, the possibilities for credit-claiming become attractive—along with a chance perhaps to launch a campaign for a Senate seat (if in the House) or for the presidency (if in the Senate).

At a lower level on SSCI and HPSCI, even during the more routine years of patrolling since 1976, the staffs of these committees—some fifty to seventy individuals combined, who are for the most part well educated and experienced—have regularly queried intelligence professionals about their activities, studied annual budget requests, inspected intelligence installations at home and abroad, and prepared thick briefing books for the use of committee members during hearings. It is worth emphasizing again that very little of this kind of persistent staff work was carried out before 1975, a fact that underscores the deep structural changes wrought by the domestic espionage scandal of 1974 and the intensive Church, Pike, and Rockefeller investigations.

Intelligence Failures and Scandals

An important feature of the findings presented here is the contrast between what I have referred to as intelligence failures and scandals. Intelligence failures—errors of collection and analysis—are frequently inadvertent, perhaps resulting from the lack of a well-placed agent overseas, a well-timed surveillance satellite in a relevant orbit, the rapid translation of an intercepted terrorist telephone conversation in Farsi, or a wise and experienced analyst. Of course, less excusably, an intelligence officer might also be just lazy; an agent might have been doubled; or an analyst might be poorly trained. Whatever the case, often as not failures are a result of human fallibility and, in that sense, they are inevitable.[45] This condition can be mitigated to some degree through improvements in a nation's capacity to gather reliable information from around the globe, say, by building more sophisticated spy satellites or reconnaissance airplanes, or by establishing a larger number of capable spy rings in "hot spots" overseas. Nevertheless, the probability of failure can never be eliminated; the future is an unknown place, shrouded in mist.

Through the expenditure of as much as $80 billion plus on intelligence (an astronomical amount compared to every other nation, just as with America's overt military spending), the United States attempts to cut through the mist to the extent possible. Full global transparency, though, remains the stuff of dreams. The planet is too large, and adversaries are cunning at hiding their activities—whether planning attacks against the United States from remote caves in Afghanistan or constructing atomic bombs in deep underground caverns in North Korea. Further, some things are simply unknowable in advance. Here are the "mysteries" of the intelligence world, as opposed to the "secrets" that might be stolen from a Beijing safe at midnight or otherwise gathered by agents and technical means. An example of a mystery is the question of who will follow Vladimir Putin as the next Russian president, or the probable leadership succession in China. No one can know the answers to these questions with any degree of certainty, until it happens—just as Donald Trump's presidential victory in 2016 was a surprise to most election observers and the general public. When intelligence-based forecasting failures do occur, as with the outbreak of war in Korea in 1950 or the absence of WMDs in Iraq in 2003, the United States takes steps to improve its collection and analysis. Nevertheless, new and unexpected threats continue to emerge around the world (intelligence analysts refer to them as "pop ups"), such as the appearance of a new disease like Zika, which suddenly surfaced and surprised medical researchers.

In contrast to failures, scandals and improprieties are intentional. Someone violates a law, a regulation, or a standard operating procedure in order to achieve a goal. The perpetrator hopes to avoid discovery, and he or she may be convinced that the importance of an objective surpasses all other considerations—including the rule of law. Recall how, when called upon to explain why they had violated intelligence statutes during the Iran-contra affair, some NSC staffers from the Reagan Administration testified that they were responding to God's "higher law," which required them to fight Communism in Central America through extraordinary means. It wasn't their fault that Congress had been foolish enough to pass the Boland Amendments.

In theory at least, intelligence scandals could be eliminated by recruiting only virtuous people for high office: men and women who would never succumb to illegal spying against U.S. citizens, or flaunt laws like the Boland Amendments, let alone infiltrate and subsidize student groups and other organizations in American society; provide disguises to former intelligence officers without checking on the purpose; or lie to congressional overseers. Yet virtue is often in limited supply among mere mortals; thus, intelligence scandals have proven to be as inevitable as failures of collection and analysis. Indeed, the entire rationale for accountability prescribed by Madison in *Federalist Paper No. 51* rests on the supposition, persistently confirmed, that human beings should not be confused with angels (grandchildren excepted). So, with respect to failures and scandals in the intelligence agencies—or any other organizations, public or private—one can anticipate more of both.

At the same time, a nation can take steps to decrease the odds of mistakes and wrongdoing by improving its intelligence collection-and-analysis capabilities, carefully recruiting men and women of high integrity into the secret agencies, and steadfastly patrolling the IC in search of incipient gaps in performance and signs of corruption in the human character (such as Aldrich Ames's abuse of alcohol and his luxury spending on personal goods that went far beyond a CIA officer's government salary). That is why oversight patrolling is so important: ideally, one would like to find and correct conditions that might lead to an intelligence "fire" before the conflagration ignites. Implicit in the notion of accountability is the hope that a few more eyes of elected officials available to examine policy initiatives—from the vantage point of Capitol Hill, the judiciary, and other oversight forums, not just from the White House—might help discover questionable practices before they turn into government catastrophes.

Taking the Shock Out of the Shock Theory

After the 9/11 terrorist attacks, some members of Congress lamented their inattention to intelligence oversight duties. "We didn't understand . . . the need for human intelligence," reflected SSCI overseer Mike DeWine (R, Ohio), for example. "We simply did not provide the resources."[46] Recall, too, that Bob Graham, the SSCI's leader who cochaired the Joint Committee investigation into the 9/11 intelligence failure, said, "We should have been more demanding of these intelligence agencies"; and that the HPSCI chair at the time, Porter J. Goss, who served as the other cochair of the Joint Committee inquiry, issued a separate report in 2004 prepared by his committee that was scathing in its criticism of CIA human intelligence (yet the Agency still has fewer case officers overseas recruiting agents than the FBI has personnel in New York City).[47]

What if these lawmakers and their colleagues had been sufficiently exercised about such intelligence deficiencies in the years preceding September 11, 2001? The planned attacks might have been uncovered in advance with better humint, faster translation of communications intercepts from Al Qaeda plotters, and more focused analysis on global terrorism. Would it have been possible to avoid, or at least lessen the effects of, the five major intelligence shocks if lawmakers had been more dedicated to their patrolling duties in the lead-up to the failures or scandals? It is worthwhile examining each of the alarms from this vantage point, although one should do so with the humble understanding that Monday morning quarterbacks always play better at home than their weekend counterparts in the NFL. Nonetheless, an examination of past outcomes can sometimes yield useful insights for the future.

The 1974 Domestic Spy Scandal

From the perspective of intelligence accountability, one would like to know why lawmakers had to rely on the astonishing leak of the "Family Jewels" to realize that many things were awry at the Agency—and not just Operation CHAOS. Thorough, day-to-day oversight might well have uncovered at least some of these "Jewels." Yet the small intelligence oversight subcommittees that existed on Capitol Hill before 1975 were operating in an era when Congress had, for the most part, a "hands-off" attitude toward intelligence activities. Further, with small staffs on the subcommittees (at times just one person), lawmakers were poorly equipped for serious and continuous intelligence-program review, even though these staff personnel were well regarded at the time and did engage in some serious budget and program dissection. Tracing through budget figures, though important, is unlikely to lead to information about a program like Operation CHAOS, however, which was buried and disguised in the funding for the Office of Security at the CIA. That kind of discovery would have taken a larger staff and intensive probing beyond financial spreadsheets.

Even with a larger staff, the philosophy of benign neglect that dominated the thinking at the time among lawmakers with intelligence oversight duties would have proscribed meaningful day-to-day patrolling. For the Congress rather than DCI Schlesinger to have uncovered the Family Jewels, lawmakers needed to have been fully engaged in continual hearings and the posing of thoughtful questions about ongoing intelligence activities—ideally with the witnesses under oath on sensitive topics. Further, members of Congress and their staffs would have had to pay visits to the secret agencies; converse with intelligence officers at various levels of government; and carry out all the other approaches used by overseers with earnest intent.[48] Little of this kind of concentrated, ongoing review occurred prior to 1975.

The 1987 Iran-Contra Scandal

This scandal occurred well after Congress had set up its new intelligence oversight procedures in 1976–1980, yet these safeguards failed to prevent or even reveal the affair. (Recall that a Middle East newspaper broke the scandal in 1986.) Rumors to the effect that the Reagan Administration had continued to pursue covert actions in Nicaragua, despite the Boland Amendments, circulated throughout D.C. in 1984–1986. Finally, SSCI and HPSCI lawmakers sat across the table from top NSC officials at the White House and asked them point-blank whether the Council's staff had secretly raised funds to seek covert action in Nicaragua in violation of the Boland statutes. The staff lied to the overseers, denying any NSC involvement. The lawmakers took their disclaimers at face value and dropped the topic. The accountability lesson: when the allegations are particularly grave, overseers must question suspects under oath on Capitol Hill. The witnesses may still prevaricate, but the odds are reduced; penalties rise sharply when one has committed perjury, perhaps enough to make would-be dissimulators think twice before giving the finger to Congress.

The 1993 Somalia and 1994 Ames Failures

The United States failed to realize in 1993 that Somalian warlords and their undisciplined soldiers could mount a potent resistance even to America's highly trained Special Forces units. Urban guerrilla warfare in the dirt streets of Mogadishu taught this lesson in blood, with eighteen U.S. soldiers killed by Somali clans who stripped off the clothing of the Black Hawk crew members and dragged their naked bodies though the city's streets. Seventy-five other American troops were wounded in the battle.[49]

At CIA Headquarters, lessons of a different kind were to be learned from the Ames treachery. Usually counterintelligence is a neglected stepchild on the congressional oversight agenda—and, for that matter, within the IC—although the Snowden leaks, as well as Russian and Chinese hacking against U.S. government computers (periodically in recent years) and the Democratic National Committee (in 2016), have refocused attention on protecting the secret agencies and their documents from cyberattacks carried out by disgruntled intelligence officers—the "insider threat"—as well as hostile intelligence organizations. Counterintelligence is an arcane art, requiring the type of patience that George Smiley exhibited in John le Carré's early novels. James Angleton, the CIA counterintelligence chief, did not refer to this discipline as a "wilderness of mirrors" for nothing. Tracking down defectors, false defectors, dangles, and double agents requires an intense devotion to archival research and a persistent cross-checking of bona fides that is unlikely to appeal to many members of Congress or even their staffs. Yet SSCI and HPSCI have an important obligation to maintain a close watch over how well the intelligence agencies are shielding their own facilities, plans, operations, personnel, names of foreign assets, and classified documents from foes—the essence of counterintelligence.

Had they shown more interest in the state of U.S. intelligence in the world's backwaters where American troops have often been sent since the end of the Cold War, lawmakers on SSCI and HPSCI might have prodded the CIA's analysts toward a better understanding of North African warlords and their tribes, including how well armed they were. Had they held more closed hearings on counterintelligence, lawmakers might also have prodded Agency security and counterintelligence officials toward a keener attention to the question of whether hostile intelligence services might have managed to penetrate the Headquarters Building at Langley and successfully recruited someone like Ames. If SSCI and HPSCI had constantly asked pointed questions about the state of analysis and counterintelligence, perhaps the CIA (as well as DIA) could have warned Special Forces about the dangers present on the Horn of Africa and could have stimulated the CIA's counterintelligence and security corps to look more closely at the blue-chip lifestyle of Ames. The same could be said about the FBI, whose counterintelligence personnel failed to perceive the erratic behavior of the Bureau's worst traitor, Robert Hanssen—another Soviet recruit during the 1980s who inflicted much damage on U.S. intelligence operations in Russia before being apprehended in 2001.

When William Colby fired Angleton in 1974, counterintelligence plunged as a priority at Langley as the DCI shifted responsibility for this mission to decentralized elements through the Agency.[50] While Angleton had his own deep flaws as CI chief (see chapter 10), this management decision left no one at a high level to skillfully guide the CIA's counterintelligence defenses, or the recruitment of foreign "moles" of its own within hostile intelligence services—the best of all counterintelligence defenses. As a result, the Agency became more vulnerable to successful penetrations by America's adversaries. Not long after Angleton's demise, the nation experienced its worst ever counterintelligence setbacks: not only Ames and Hanssen, but also several other traitors during the "Year of the Spy" in 1985 (examined in chapter 10).

The 2001 Terrorist Attacks

Recall how, in 1995, a top-secret memo (now partially declassified) came from the CIA's Counterterrorism Center (CTC) to the Aspin-Brown Commission, warning that "aerial terrorism seems likely at some point—filling an airplane with explosives and dive-bombing a target." This startling prediction appeared in the *President's Daily Brief*, delivered by the CIA to President Bill Clinton and his top national security advisers. Moreover, the Agency briefed members of SSCI and HPSCI about this sobering possibility. Yet, six years before the forecast became a reality, and following another *PDB* warning about terrorist hijacking of airplanes (dated August 6, 2001), no policymakers—either in the Clinton or the second Bush Administrations—took steps to alert U.S. commercial pilots to the danger; seal cockpit doors in aircraft; increase the number of sky marshals in the air; urge the FBI to watch flight training schools more closely; or tighten airport security. Nor did SSCI or HPSCI.

When George W. Bush replaced Clinton as president, both the White House counterterrorism expert Richard A. Clarke and the CTC provided fresh alerts to new national security adviser Condoleezza Rice (as well as, again, to members of SSCI and HPSCI) that Al Qaeda might resort to aerial terrorism and other methods of attacking the United States. The Bush Administration ignored these warnings from January until early September 2001, without a single NSC meeting held on Al Qaeda; the congressional oversight committees also did little to improve America's defenses against airplane attacks by terrorists and held precious few hearings on the subject of global terrorism.[51] The 9/11 tragedy was an intelligence failure, certainly, but it was a policy failure, too, during both Democratic and Republican administrations. Further, it was a failure of accountability on Capitol Hill, again implicating both parties. What if SSCI and HPSCI had held extensive, executive session hearings on the CTC's alert about aerial terrorism, then followed through to see whether commercial pilots, the FBI, and airport security understood the danger and were taking steps to protect the public?

Moreover, government inquiries have discovered that the intelligence agencies failed to coordinate and act on the few shards of specific information they did possess regarding the September 11 terrorists.[52] For instance, the agencies proved unable to track two of the nineteen terrorists inside the United States, despite warnings—though slow to be delivered—from the CIA to the FBI about their arrival in San Diego. The Bureau also failed to respond to red flags raised by its own agents in Phoenix and Minneapolis about suspicious flight training undertaken by foreigners in those cities; and the Department of Defense appears to have smothered questions raised by an "Able Danger" group of military intelligence officers, whose research had apparently come across the presence of sixty suspected foreign terrorists inside the United States—almost two years before the 9/11 attacks.[53] On the Able Danger list were four of the September 11 hijackers, including their Egyptian-born leader, Mohammed Atta. While it would have been difficult—but certainly not impossible—for SSCI and HPSCI to have known about the specific CIA-FBI liaison snafus in 2001, or the internal Bureau memos from field agents in Phoenix and Minneapolis, the committees in fact did know about the Able Danger allegations. What if they had taken them more seriously? And to what extent were lawmakers and their staffs keeping up with the always important—and always troubled—question of CIA-FBI liaison relationships, especially with respect to the sharing of intelligence on terrorist threats to the United States after the bombing of U.S. embassies in Kenya and Tanzania in 1998 and the attack against the U.S.S. *Cole* in 2000?

At a deeper level, September 11 was an intelligence failure because the CIA had no assets within Al Qaeda. Further, the NSA had fallen far behind on translating relevant sigint intercepts involving suspected terrorists (yet the Bush

Administration would soon have it collecting even more data that would go untranslated and unread—a few potentially valuable "signals" destined to drown in a sea of "noise"). All of America's intelligence agencies lacked sufficient language skills and understanding about nations in the Middle East and South Asia, or even about the objectives and likely motivations of Iraq's Saddam Hussein or the Al Qaeda leader Osama bin Laden. To what extent were SSCI and HPSCI probing these questions and encouraging (for example) better humint recruitment and training? These deficiencies have not gone away.

The 2003 WMD Failure

The intelligence failures regarding Iraqi WMDs were, in some ways, even more unsettling than those that led up to the 9/11 attacks. The NIE of October 2002 concluded, as did most intelligence agencies and outside analysts, that unconventional weapons were likely to be present in Iraq. This assessment was based on several inaccurate sources of information. Recall how the IC had no significant human assets in Iraq during the years between America's two military interventions in Iraq (1991–2003); therefore, the CIA's analysts extrapolated from what they knew when the Pentagon last had "boots on the ground" there as part of the U.S. war effort in 1991 and with UN inspectors in the early 1990s. In the run-up to the Second Persian Gulf War against Iraq, Agency analysts decided to compensate for their earlier underestimates by this time overestimating the probability of WMDs in the Middle East nation.

Also factored into the IC's miscalculations, remember, were reports from the German asset "Curve Ball," an Iraqi exile whose reliability was vouched for by that nation's equivalent of the CIA—the BND (or, in the German jawbreaker, Bundesnachtrichtendienst). Only much later, after the American invasion of Iraq, did the Germans admit that their Iraqi asset was a thoroughly unsavory and untrustworthy individual who had fabricated his reports on Iraqi WMDs. Added to these sources of incorrect information were the lobbying of Ahmed Chalabi and the Iraqi National Congress, along with the false confessions of Ibn al-Shaykh al-Libi. Moreover, consider the skepticism of analysts in the INR arm of the State Department and in the Department of Energy about the aluminum tubes purchased by the Iraqi regime; INR's questions about the Iraqi mobile biological weapons labs; and the reservations of Air Force Intelligence about the alleged long-range capability of Iraqi drones.

Had SSCI and HPSCI taken testimony from these dissenters, the committees would have understood that the 2002 NIE was anything but a definitive report on Iraqi WMDs—regardless of Tenet's description to the president that the existence of unconventional weaponry in Iraq was a "slam dunk." In reality, the Estimate provided to Congress on the eve of war was a rush job prepared in days, rather than the usual time of several months for an NIE. The result, according to a *New York Times* analysis published a year and a half after the invasion, was "one of the most flawed documents in the history of American intelligence."[54] Lawmakers on SSCI and HPSCI who were conscientiously involved in intelligence oversight could have learned—before the astronomical costs of going to war against Iraq—that additional on-the-ground fact-finding was sorely needed; and that many intelligence analysts felt uneasy about the humint reporting provided by Curve Ball, Al-Libi, and Chalabi.

Armed with this information, the Congress could then have contributed in a major way to the debate on whether war against Iraq was justified in March 2003 or should await further intelligence on the WMD hypothesis. Instead, lawmakers (as well as the *New York Times* reporter covering the topic in the White House, Judith Miller) swallowed whole the WMD arguments of the Bush Administration in favor of war. What members of Congress lacked was countervailing evidence, which was available if they had only taken the time to listen to the dissenting voices expressed in the NIE. Did SSCI and HPSCI know about the dissent to the WMD hypothesis inside INR, the Energy Department, and U.S. Air Force Intelligence? If so, why weren't these objections made a more visible aspect of the war "debate" (such as it was), both inside the Congress and for the public?

Two Sides of the Oversight Coin

Success in improving intelligence oversight on Capitol Hill will require, above all, stronger motivation among the members of SSCI and HPSCI—one side of the oversight coin. Since the creation of these committees, their members have already outperformed their marginally engaged predecessors from 1947 to 1974; and their staffs are considerably larger and better prepared. Even so, the efforts of the two panels have fallen short of full engagement at the member level; and even the best of staffs cannot compensate for lawmakers who treat their oversight responsibilities as a secondary concern, although a few lawmakers over the years have been deeply committed to their oversight responsibilities.[55] Worse still, the all-consuming partisan bickering on the intelligence oversight committees since the early 1990s have often plagued cooperative efforts on accountability and overturned the earlier tradition on Capitol Hill of keeping sensitive intelligence issues apart from party rivalries.[56]

Neither SSCI nor HPSCI managed to sniff out the Iran-contra operation; the weakened counterintelligence posture that allowed the acts of treason by Ames, Hanssen, and others; the poor humint prior to the 9/11 attacks; or the erroneous WMD analysis that provided a rationale for the war against Saddam

Hussein. The venerable saying "Eternal vigilance is the price of liberty" is wise counsel not always well followed by the intelligence oversight committees.[57] If overseers are unwilling to pay this price, they should be replaced either by the congressional leadership or by voters in their own constituencies.

Lawmakers must really want to be effective overseers, or else the constitutional protections extolled by the founders, as well as the accountability laws passed from 1974 forward, are doomed to failure. The nurturing of this motivation depends upon building into the congressional culture better incentives to encourage attention to oversight duties. These incentives could include prestigious awards presented by the congressional leadership and civic groups to dedicated and accomplished overseers; Capitol Hill perks dispensed by the leadership to the most outstanding members of SSCI and HPSCI (providing them with offices that have a coveted view of the Capitol Dome, for instance, and underground parking closer to their offices); publicity in national and hometown newspapers underscoring admirable achievements in accountability by individual members of Congress; and more discussion of accountability in schools and colleges. Voters must also become more aware of the importance of congressional oversight, honoring those lawmakers on Election Day who work industriously to make existing laws work better and to improve the performance of the federal bureaucracy. Journalists and educators can contribute a great deal to this task of raising civic awareness.

Congressional motivation is, however, only half of the challenge. The other side of the accountability coin depends on the willingness of the executive branch to cooperate with lawmakers in the quest for improved intelligence supervision. Former president George H. W. Bush, who served as DCI after William Colby near the end of the investigations carried out by the Church and Pike Committees, has referred publicly to the members and staff of those panels as "untutored little jerks."[58] In 2006, the chairman of the Republican National Committee pointed to the reforms of the Church and Pike Committees as a primary source of America's intelligence weaknesses on the eve of the 9/11 attacks.[59] These critics evidently wish to turn the clock back to the pre-1975 era, when oversight was weak and the intelligence agencies slipped into domestic spying, excessive covert actions aimed at regime change even in democratic societies (Chile, for example), assassination plots against foreign leaders, and other questionable activities. The actual reasons for the intelligence weaknesses prior to the 9/11 attacks and throughout the slide toward war in Iraq in 2003 are far more complex, mainly revolving around America's shallow understanding of the Middle East, Southwest Asia, global terrorism, and Islamic radicalism. They have nothing to do with the investigations of 1975, which were designed to weed out wrongdoing by the intelligence agencies and focus their energies on more effective collection and analysis.

If the executive branch insists on viewing lawmakers as "an outside interference," as Admiral Poindexter thought of the Congress during the planning of the Iran-contra operations, and as the second Bush Administration treated lawmakers in the controversy over NSA's sigint programs, then overseers will be cut off from the information they need to properly evaluate intelligence programs.[60] The end result will be an intelligence community more and more isolated from any semblance of checks and balances, and increasingly likely to present the nation with its next major intelligence failure or scandal. When Congress attempted to investigate the 9/11 failure, the White House, the DCI, and various intelligence officers delayed and obstructed the work of the Joint Committee. They also opposed the creation of the Kean Commission, and they adopted the same approach of outright resistance—and, when that failed, the fallback methods of stonewalling and slow-rolling. The same methods were taken up again during the congressional probes into the NSA's controversial STELLARWIND programs and the CIA's embrace of harsh interrogation methods—including even spying on and carrying out harassment attacks against SSCI in the latter case. The use of dilatory practices by the executive branch is a prime enemy of accountability, which makes it an enemy as well of the constitutional form of government advocated by the nation's founders. The goal should be to have executive officials and lawmakers working in harness to prohibit inept and improper intelligence operations, not to be at constant loggerheads.

The Persistent Reporting Problem

Accountability setbacks are often a result of the executive branch refusing to provide information on its activities to oversight committees. Less explosive than Iran-contra, but still profoundly unsettling, are several instances of the spy agencies failing to keep the Congress well informed of its activities, as required initially by the Hughes-Ryan Act of 1974 for covert action, and strengthened by the requirement of "prior notice" in the Intelligence Oversight Acts of 1980 and 1991 for covert action and every other intelligence activity of importance. "It is my business to know what other people don't know," Sherlock Holmes told Dr. Watson.[61] It is the business of overseers, as well, to know what the general public does not know about the secret agencies, to ensure that these invisible organizations are operating efficiently, lawfully, and ethically on the public's behalf.

Yet, as we have seen, too often instead of briefing SSCI and HPSCI in their full complement, intelligence managers have elected to whisper into the ears of only a few members, say, the chairman and vice chairman of the oversight committees, cautioning them not to discuss the "briefing" with anyone else.

Some lawmakers are prone to obey these edicts, since the requests for confidence descend from the cloudy summits of executive authority. Author Patrick Radden Keefe has commented on this approach:

> You have the individual senator or member of Congress who's brought in and read into a program. They're not allowed to bring any staff with them. They're not necessarily allowed to communicate any of what they've heard to their staff. In some instances, they're not lawyers, so they may not understand all of the legal fine points. In most instances, they're not technologists, so they may not be able to grasp what it is precisely that they're being briefed on, or the implications of it.[62]

A former CIA attorney has noted the difficulties that these ground rules present to lawmakers (as the Agency well knows). "It is virtually impossible for individual members of Congress . . . to take any effective action if they have concern about what they have heard," she acknowledges, adding: "It is not realistic to expect them, working alone, to sort through complex legal issues [or] conduct the kind of factual investigation required for true oversight."[63]

In 2001, then Speaker of the House Nancy Pelosi (D, California) wrote to Gen. Hayden, complaining about the lack of clear answers from the NSA about its post-9/11 surveillance programs; and SSCI's Jay Rockefeller expressed his frustration to Vice President Cheney in 2003 about the artificial fog that had blocked Congress's ability to see the IC clearly. Neither Pelosi nor Rockefeller received helpful responses.[64] Pelosi would charge the CIA in 2009 with failing to brief her fully on the detainee interrogation program, which the Agency has said is untrue. According to my conversations with staffers in the Agency's Office of Congressional Affairs in 2016, "Pelosi was conveniently forgetful"—a charge she continues to deny.[65]

Sometimes the information in the briefings will change from one session to another, since these one-on-one sessions take place over time and situations can alter. This adds to the confusion of lawmakers who think they are receiving the same briefing on a subject as a few other anointed colleagues, but in fact the substance may be different. No wonder even a dedicated overseer like HPSCI's Representative Jan Schakowsky (D, Illinois) has said, "In terms of the oversight function, I feel inadequate most of the time."[66] On top of these constraints is the ever-present chilling effect that comes from a concern that "sources and methods" might be revealed inadvertently by a lawmaker during hearings or on the floor. At the time of the Iran-contra scandal, SSCI counsel Dan Finn expressed the sense of the "political vulnerability" felt by members and staff alike: "a concern that if you went too far, you could be accused of leaking secrets."[67] This concern is a major leverage that the IC uses over its congressional overseers.

Political scientist Carl Friedrich of Harvard University often spoke of "the law of anticipated reactions." The potential for a negative response from committees on Capitol Hill is known to have a sobering effect on bureaucrats who must obtain annual funding from lawmakers. When the intelligence agencies can finesse having to explain their activities to the full complement of SSCI and HPSCI, this important check is significantly diminished. Further, to challenge an intelligence activity often takes majority support on the oversight committees; individuals, or even small groups usually have insufficient clout to make an impression at the White House, the NSC, the ODNI, or Langley (the Aspin/ Mazzoli coalition discussed in chapter 4 was an exception to the rule). Here is another strong incentive for the IC to keep its briefings limited. "Because you can't go public, it takes a majority of this committee to get any action going," Judiciary Committee member Sheldon Whitehouse (D, Rhode Island) has remarked, "and I don't think the Intelligence Community is unaware of that fact."[68]

Sometimes there have been no briefings at all from the IC or the White House, not even sepulcher whispers; instead, lawmakers have learned about controversial intelligence operations in their morning newspapers or from television news shows. During the Iran-contra affair, President Reagan made it explicit to his national security aides when approving the finding for the Iranian arms sale: Do not tell Congress. As Gregory F. Treverton has observed, "Excluding the designated congressional overseers, also excluded one more 'political scrub,' one more source of advice about what the American people would find acceptable"[69]—the essence of why accountability is vital. More recently, after the Boston Marathon bombing in 2013, an HPSCI member voiced his dismay that the FBI had not provided the committee with information about possible flaws in the Bureau's counterterrorism operations—especially its failure to prevent that terrorist attack. "What I am looking to do is identify our security shortcomings and change them," Representative William Keating (D, Massachusetts) wrote in a letter to incoming FBI Director James B. Comey. "Without forthright information from the F.B.I. we are prevented from taking the critical steps needed to protect the American public." On the Senate side (and on a different subject), lawmakers on SSCI sought access to Department of Justice legal opinions justifying drone operations, but the AG refused to provide full access to these documents.[70]

Moreover, even when briefings and hearings have taken place in a timely manner, intelligence officers have sometimes elided the most important facts. A former intelligence officer told an interviewer that his briefings to select SSCI and HPSCI members, about an attempt during the Clinton Administration to kill Osama bin Laden, lasted "about two minutes" over a secure telephone. He admitted that this interaction was "meaningless . . . there was no oversight of any kind."[71] Worse yet, as we have seen in earlier chapters, intelligence briefers have simply lied to overseers. This was blatantly the case in the lead-up to the Iran-contra investigation;[72] and SSCI staffers maintain, too, that the CIA "lied to the White House and the Congress periodically during the torture investigation."[73] In recent years, the NSA has been one of the leading culprits when it comes to poor reporting to Congress, and lawmakers have been reluctant to demand better communications between the two institutions. Some members of Congress have been either too busy or too lethargic, and some are also wary of weakening U.S. counterterrorism capabilities through legislative tinkering. Moreover, members have little interest in sharing blame with the spy agencies, should intelligence operations fail or become controversial. Yet, as historian Dexter Perkins has wisely stressed: "Blind acceptance of the views of the executive would not be consistent with the principles of democracy."[74]

Accountability and Public Education

If the Church Committee investigation can be viewed as intelligence accountability at high tide, the Iran-contra scandal was low tide. For those seeking meaningful oversight for America's secret agencies, sometimes their hopes have been shattered, as with the arrogant dismissal of the new accountability rules by the executive branch during Iran-contra; sometimes they have been realized, as with SSCI's confirmation hearings for DCIs and DNIs, which have been thorough reviews into the fitness of candidates for those important jobs (although this process has been marred occasionally by excessive partisan wrangling, as with the Lake nomination by President Clinton, discussed in chapter 4). In the world of intelligence accountability, like everywhere else, life has a penchant for doling out an array of successes and setbacks.

It bears repeating that, even though intelligence accountability since 1975 has been infinitely more serious than before that watershed year, it is nowhere near as effective as it can and should be, if this nation hopes to reduce the odds of another major intelligence failure or scandal in the future. In place of sporadic patrolling and ad hoc responses to fire alarms, lawmakers and their staffs will need to redouble their commitment to a continuous, day-in, day-out scrutiny of spy activities, praising meritorious operations, suggesting ways to improve new or faltering programs, and rooting out improper initiatives and miscreant officials before they produce full-blown disasters that harm the nation's security and good reputation. For this to work, the public will need to acquire a better understanding and appreciation of accountability. Scholars, journalists, and public officials must engage in more effective "public diplomacy" at home to educate

Americans about the value of intelligence oversight, as carried out by members of Congress along with institutions of accountability in the executive and judicial branches. None of this will be easy. Yet, as America's founders understood, the virtue of democracy lies not in its ease, but in its promise to protect the people from the dangers of concentrated power—especially secret power.

In chapter 7, this exploration of the shock theory of intelligence accountability turns more specifically to the role of the U.S. media as a source of vigorous oversight. Newspapers and television have often played a major role in prodding lawmakers toward important intelligence investigations, and new forms of journalism (blogs, podcasts, and the like) show promise in this regard, too.

7

The Media and Intelligence Accountability

Media Coverage of Spy Missteps

"Democracy begins with a free discussion of our sins," observed W. H. Auden, yet free discussion about intelligence activities rarely occurs on Capitol Hill until a major scandal or failure—an intelligence shock—forces lawmakers to shine a light into the far recesses of the spy agencies. This chapter zeros in on ten major intelligence shocks since the creation of the CIA. The purpose is to explore whether widespread and deep media coverage of an intelligence shock (or "sin") has been associated with an increase in congressional accountability related to the shock. Or perhaps, alternatively, lawmakers have either engaged in or entirely disregarded intensified oversight after a shock quite apart from the degree of media attention given to the failure or scandal. High media coverage and no increase in oversight, or low media coverage and an increase in oversight, are results that would suggest the absence of a meaningful relationship between media attention to a shock and intelligence accountability. In contrast, high media coverage and a clear increase in oversight, or low media coverage accompanied by minimal oversight, would suggest an association between the two phenomena. The question of how lawmakers have monitored this nation's secret agencies—perhaps the most challenging form of government account-ability—in times of low or high media coverage of shock events may provide insights into when and why members of Congress engage in the serious supervi-sion of the espionage agenices.[1]

As earlier chapters have recounted, the performance of Congress in review-ing the nation's intelligence activities has fluctuated widely during the Cold War years and since. Even after the introduction of a more dedicated form of intelligence accountability in the wake of the Church Committee investigation, scholarly studies have discerned a waning of legislative attention to this responsi-bility as Operations CHAOS, COINTELPRO, MINARET, and SHAMROCK receded into history and the fear of terrorism rose. In addition to intelligence accountability, research on legislative oversight across the policy board has revealed a decline in oversight activities on Capitol Hill during the early 1980s, along with—at best—merely an episodic practice of these duties since then.[2]

As we have noted along the way in this book, the chief cause of inattentiveness derives from the nature of Congress itself. Its members seek reelection as a primary objective; yet inquiries into spy operations must take place mostly in closed committee sanctuaries with only limited or, usually, no media coverage. The Senate Select Committee on Intelligence (SSCI), for instance, held only a single public hearing in 2012. Nonetheless, just as oversight activity often ebbs on Capitol Hill, so does it occasionally flow. The previous chapter illustrated that a close look at intelligence accountability in the United States since the Year of Intelligence in 1975 reveals a cyclical pattern of attention to oversight duties. A major intelligence scandal or failure transforms the perfunctory performance of oversight into a burst of intense program scrutiny. This deep-dive involvement in the review of spy activities is followed by a continuing, but temporary, high level of engagement in police patrolling that often yields remedial legislation or other reforms designed to curb inappropriate intelligence operations in the future. Then this "shock cycle" returns to a state of middling legislative involvement in matters of spy watching.

I have described this up-and-down pattern in this book as a sequence of police patrolling and firefighting, to highlight differences in commitment by lawmakers to oversight responsibilities, a theoretical framework introduced in chapter 1.[3] A prominent member of Congress has also used the policing analogy. "There has been no cop on the beat," lamented Representative Henry A. Waxman (D, California), when he served as chair of the House Oversight and Government Reform Committee, who accused Republicans in 2007 of abandoning their accountability responsibilities. "And when there is no cop on the beat," Waxman continued, "criminals are more willing to engage in crimes."[4] As depicted in the previous chapter, in contrast to police patrolling, firefighting involves an emergency reaction to a calamity inside the government. At the blare of the fire alarm, members of Congress qua firefighters jump on the hook-and-ladder truck and race to put out the "fire" of gross government mistakes or abuse of power.

As described in the previous chapter, sometimes the high-intensity period of police patrolling that typically follows firefighting can last for months and, in those cases when the original shock has been strong enough to yield profound concern among lawmakers, even years. Once the firestorm has subsided and reforms are in place, however, most lawmakers soon return to a state of relative laxity toward the nation's espionage activities. They assume their "normal" posture of low-intensity reviews of intelligence programs—or perhaps bow out of even limited police patrolling, at least until they are rattled into action by the next shock. I depicted this on-again, off-again approach to oversight—the "shock" cycle—in Figure 6.1 of the previous chapter.

To reach the level of a shock that sets off a major "fire alarm," stimulating a strong oversight reaction on Capitol Hill or in the White House, an allegation of intelligence scandal or failure may have to attract sustained media coverage, with at least a few front-page stories in well-regarded media outlets. Members of Congress, as well as executive branch officials, are busy and distracted; it may require the persistent drumbeat of media coverage before they give a "shock" due consideration. The facts and interpretations presented by the media may well be the most vital aspect of the coverage; but just the sheer fact of sustained reporting on a shock event can be important, too, as a means of emphasizing its merits as a policy controversy worthy of closer consideration by overseers. In 1974, for example, in the lead-up to the Church Committee inquiry into allegations of domestic spying, the *New York Times* published a long run of stories on the CIA from July through December: fifty-two articles in all. In December alone, nine articles on the Agency made the front page—unprecedented at the time for that intelligence organization. The *Times* headline on December 22, for instance, had a provocative lead-in that charged the CIA with "massive illegal domestic intelligence operations."

Intense media coverage may be insufficient in itself, though, to bring out the firefighters on Capitol Hill, or to stir meaningful reform initiatives within the executive branch. For example, the warrantless wiretaps of the second Bush Administration garnered considerable media attention in December 2005, and again after the Snowden leaks in 2013, but yielded no major congressional inquiry; an executive inquiry was unlikely, since the questionable wiretaps had been authorized by the White House and, further, the nation remained fearful of more terrorist attacks. Such considerations as the personalities of congressional overseers and top executive branch officials—especially the attitudes of the SSCI and HPSCI chairs on Capitol Hill, and those of the president and vice president in the White House—can play a meaningful role in determining the vigor of intelligence accountability. The philosophies and motivations of leaders in Congress and the executive branch matter, and they sometimes trump extensive media coverage of a shock event in the determination of whether a major congressional or executive inquiry will take place. Nonetheless, at times, the extent of media coverage may well be important in grabbing the attention of busy and distracted policy officials—that, at any rate, is the supposition probed in this chapter.

The Intelligence Shocks

Forty-three years have passed since Congress began to take intelligence accountability seriously at the end of 1974. As noted in the preceding chapter,

Table 7.1 **Stimulus Source and the Key Intelligence Accountability Responses, 1945–2016**

Year	Stimulus	Oversight Response	Outcome of Response
1950	Korean War surprise	Closed cong. briefings	Minimal cong. probing of CIA analytic methods
1961	Bay of Pigs fiasco	Taylor Comm. Rept.	Modest wrist-slapping; some improvements in covert action planning
1967	Nat'l Student Assn. scandal	Katzenbach Comm. Rept.	Modest clarification of CIA ties to U.S. groups
1973	CIA-Watergate "scandal"	Cong. hearings	Modest efforts to probe CIA involvement in Watergate
1974*	Operation CHAOS	Major inquiries in both branches	Est. standing oversight panels (SSCI, HPSCI); new oversight laws (Hughes-Ryan; FISA**); 1980 Oversight Act); critical repts.
1986*	Iran-contra scandal	Major inquiries in both branches	CIA/IG statute enacted; 1991 Intel Oversight Act; critical reports
1994*	Ames failure	Major exec.-leg. panel of inquiry (Aspin-Brown Commission)	Management improvements; counterintelligence strengthened; critical rept.
2001*	9/11 attacks	Major exec. and leg. investigations	PATRIOT Act; war against Al Qaeda and Taliban; increases in CT funding; IRTPA ('04)
2002*	Iraqi WMD failure	Major exec.-leg. panel of inquiry	Critical repts.
2005, 2013– 2015	NSA warrantless wiretaps; metadata collection	Closed cong. briefings and hearings on wiretaps; hearings on metadata	Tightening of wiretap and metadata supervision

* The asterisk here and in the text below indicates that major inquiries were undertaken (firefighting).

** Foreign Intelligence Surveillance Act of 1978.

throughout this period lawmakers have devoted about six years of their time to intensive investigation (firefighting) in the intelligence domain, after being sufficiently prodded by five major spy-related controversies or shocks (alarms) to take up rigorous oversight. (See Table 7.1.) This pentad of prominent shocks included the following:

- the CIA domestic spy scandal (Operation CHAOS) of 1974;
- the Iran-contra affair of 1987;
- the Ames spy scandal of 1994, when the FBI (working with CIA counterintelligence) belatedly unmasked Aldrich H. Ames as a Russian spy;
- the intelligence failure related to the 9/11 terrorist attacks of 2001; and,
- the intelligence failure associated with a faulty U.S. intelligence estimate about the likely presence of WMDs in Iraq in 2002.

During the other thirty-seven years, members of SSCI and HPSCI spent most of their time engaged in intelligence police patrolling—sometimes vigorously in the immediate aftermath of a shock, but for the most part in a more desultory manner. Similarly, the White House remained relatively passive most of the time when it came to intelligence accountability. Occasionally, though, presidents reacted in a fashion similar to lawmakers, by creating special investigative commissions at the same time Congress chose to respond seriously to the fire alarms through the establishment of committee inquiries on Capitol Hill. Often members of Congress embarrassed a quiescent White House into taking action before an administration finally reacted (as with the Rockefeller Commission in 1975 and the Kean Commission in 2002).

Five other significant intelligence shocks that took place during the period from 1947 to 2016 had a different outcome: they failed to result in major legislative or presidential investigations. Four took place prior to the watershed year of 1975:

- an intelligence failure related to the outbreak of the Korean War in 1950;
- the Bay of Pigs fiasco in 1961;
- the CIA-Watergate "scandal" in 1973 (although this event involved more the perception of scandal than the reality when it came to Agency involvement);
- and the National Student Association affair in 1967, also involving the CIA.

The fifth and most recent shock that failed to reach a high-enough threshold for a major inquiry occurred in 2005, stimulated by media allegations that the Bush White House had misused the NSA to carry out warrantless wiretapping against American citizens (prohibited by FISA).

This latest shock was soon reinforced in 2013 by an additional media revelation, based on the Snowden leaks, that the NSA was also engaged in gathering records—"metadata"—about the telephone and social media communications of U.S. citizens and had circumvented the FISA Court warrant procedure for some content-oriented telephone wiretaps. In this slow-motion unfolding of news stories about questionable intelligence activities, next came coverage in

2014 related to the release of SSCI's Executive Summary of the CIA's torture practices after the 9/11 attacks (this media coverage is not examined in this book). Further, in and around these stories was ongoing media reportage on the CIA's use of drone attacks overseas, including the targeting of a few Americans thought to be dangerous terrorists living in the Middle East and Southwest Asia. Yet, even though near to one another in time and each one rather startling, the cumulative effects of these media reports never pushed the government to a "firefighting" threshold of concern sufficient enough to spur major formal investigations.

As shown in Table 7.1 (an offshoot and elaboration of Figure 6.1), Washington officials have embraced several key initiatives related to intelligence accountability during the time span from 1974 to 2016, though relatively few prior to 1974. Recall from Table 6.1, only seven of the eighteen noteworthy intelligence oversight initiatives have arisen outside the context of firefighting: the Intelligence Information Procedures Act (1980); the Intelligence Identities Act (1982); the CIA Information Act (1984); the Intelligence Authorization Act, with its provision against the Agency's recruitment of U.S. accredited journalists (1997); the Whistleblowers Protection Act (1998); the FISA Amendments Act (2008); and the USA FREEDOM Act (2015). The other eleven congressional oversight initiatives were the result of specific shocks and the sounding of five-bell alarms, followed by inquiries of some magnitude and then a period of aggressive police patrolling.

Of primary interest in this chapter is the question of why some high-threshold shocks have produced a strong legislative and executive reaction—in the direction of increased accountability through the establishment of major investigations into spy activities—while other low-threshold shocks have failed to reach a sufficient level of societal concern to produce major inquiries and the concomitant adoption of significant remedial measures. In this sample of ten significant shocks since 1947 (which combine the 2005–2015 NSA and CIA counterterrorism torture controversies into a single, drawn-out series of low-threshold related alarms), there turns out to be five instances of high-threshold alarms and five instances of low-threshold alarms, as depicted in the findings presented here.[5]

Evidence-Based Intelligence Studies

In the field of health care, evidence-based medicine (EBM) has gained prominence as a research tool.[6] This approach incorporates methods from science, engineering, and statistics, with the goal of replacing *ex cathedra* pronouncements by "experts" with empirical "best evidence" results to guide those engaged in the practice of medicine. The animating philosophy is one of scientific validation.

Unlike many subfields in the social sciences, often missing in the relatively new field of intelligence studies are empirical data and analysis.[7] The reason why has to do mainly with the classified nature of most espionage activities. The outside researcher simply does not have systematic access to the number of cases necessary to make reliable statistical inferences about the hidden side of government, in the manner that one has (say) in electoral studies or for the correlates of war. Nevertheless, empirical research can be carried out even in this veiled domain and scholarly, evidence-based intelligence studies (EBIS) is to be encouraged whenever feasible. This study pursues a modest quantitative examination of media coverage related to intelligence "shocks." Although its small "*n*" (only ten cases, albeit important ones) prevents formal hypothesis-testing or attempts to report statistical levels of significance, it does provide a preliminary sense of the relationship between media reporting on major intelligence missteps and the oversight reaction in the executive and legislative branches of government.

The puzzle placed under the microscope here can be stated simply: Has a high volume of media coverage been associated with the creation of formal panels of inquiry—the most intensive form of accountability—to probe controversial activities of America's secret agencies? Directionality is almost always a dilemma when studying the media. Does media coverage trigger interest among government officials to investigate wrongdoing, or do the publicly expressed concerns of officials about wrongdoing lead to greater media coverage? One can readily imagine both directions occurring simultaneously in a complex interaction, perhaps in a fashion that is so interwoven that the vectors become impossible to gauge. It would be noteworthy, though, if inquiries occurred despite minimal media coverage, or if they failed to occur even in the face of widespread reporting by journalists. These are the kinds of broad, and admittedly modest, outcomes this chapter explores.

In my experience as a staff aide in the House, the Senate, and the White House, extensive media coverage of intelligence does in fact stir interest in a topic among government officials. In remarks to a group of journalists, a former DNI has commented on this relationship. "What is it I look at first [in the morning] . . . it's the same thing everybody in this town [Washington, D.C.] looks at first, particularly if you are more senior, and that is what is in the press. . . . I'm looking for what you all found out and what you have said because that is going to *frame the debate*."[8]

The *New York Times* is usually read—or at least scanned—each day by top officials in Washington, along with the *Washington Post*, the *Wall Street Journal*, and back-home newspapers. For the purposes of this analysis, the *Times* is used as the source of media coverage on intelligence. Relying on the hard-copy indexes of story topics addressed in the pages of the *Times*, my research assistant and I counted the number of articles printed that dealt with the major intelligence shock events (scandals or failures) for the relevant period of time that preceded the government's decision about how to react to the allegations. This reaction, taken jointly or separately by the executive and legislative branches, might have entailed downplaying or even ignoring the shock; reacting to it with a moderate expression of concern; or undertaking a major inquiry into the charges (high-threshold shocks). The key time period for the analysis stretches from when the shock first became a matter of public discourse to when the government for-mally responded—or perhaps failed to respond at all (with hopes that the story would soon disappear on its own accord).

Although beyond the scope of the analysis presented here, valuable, too, would be an examination of reporting on intelligence in the *Post* and the *Journal*. Stories about intelligence scandals and failures published by the leading newspa-pers in each of the fifty states could be insightful as well, since lawmakers (espe-cially) take seriously these local media sources as well—even closer to heart in those states where the *Times*, the *Post*, and the *Journal* are rarely read by constitu-ents. This wider research task would present a huge data-collection challenge for the individual researcher, though, and would best be undertaken by a team. Useful, too, would be an examination of television reporting on the intelligence shocks, especially as presented on the major network evening news. For this chapter, I found it daunting enough just to wade into the *New York Times* cover-age of intelligence shocks.

The Ten Major Intelligence Shocks since the End of World War II

The findings for the ten major shock events from 1945 to 2016 are displayed in Table 7.1. Five of the events triggered a major inquiry, as designated by an aster-isk next to the year in which the events below occurred. The first of these major inquiries is the CIA domestic spy scandal of 1974. Another five shocks never led to a major investigation (and, therefore, have no asterisk in the table); in this category is, first, the surprise outbreak of war on the Korean Peninsula in 1950.

1. Korean War Failure (1950)

On June 25, 1950, war erupted on the Korean Peninsula when mainland Chinese- and Soviet-supported Communist forces in the northern region of Korea invaded the pro-Western southern region. Analysts at the CIA failed to predict the invasion, although they did duly report that the North Korean Army was massing on the border between the north and south regions, and that the Communist regime had evacuated women and children along the border. A National Intelligence Estimate dated June 20, 1950, described in detail the concentration of North Korean troops and armaments arrayed along the border. Whether the North Korean military maneuvers—hardly the first time they had taken place—was bluff and bravado, or a genuine preparation for invasion, was harder to say. The question of *intentions* has always been far more difficult for intelligence analysts to fathom than an adversary's military *capabilities*, such as the "bean-counting" of weapon systems photographed by reconnaissance aircraft. The capabilities were clear: North Korea had fielded an imposing army. The intentions, however, remained a mystery.

Two days before the invasion, DCI Rear Admiral Roscoe H. Hillenkoetter (1947–1950) appeared before a secret session of the House Foreign Affairs Committee and said nothing about a likely outbreak of hostilities in Korea. It was the most significant intelligence failure in the CIA's young life. Under the umbrella of a United Nations Coalition, the United States entered the war against the Communists in June 1950 and, after the loss of more than 35,000 American troops, the war ended in a stalemate three years later. Tensions between the two Koreas, divided along the 38th parallel, have remained taut ever since—with North Korea now armed with atomic bombs and long-range missiles, and South Korea defended by U.S. troops and their nuclear armaments.

At the time of the invasion in 1950, the *New York Times* reported on the intelligence failure, concluding that Republicans in Congress appeared "likely to follow up and make a national issue." Indeed, lawmakers were clearly upset by the absence of warning about the attack. For example, Senator Styles Bridges (R, New Hampshire), chairman of the all-mighty Appropriations Committee, vowed to examine the CIA's methods of analysis "in some detail." He asked, "Why wasn't the Central Intelligence Agency on the job?" During the early weeks of June 1950, the *Times* also published several articles that criticized the lack of warning.

Nonetheless, little happened by way of a formal inquiry into the intelligence failure—beyond a few closed committee hearings on Capitol Hill, punctuated by occasional public criticism from one member of Congress or another. A majority in both chambers showed few signs of desiring a full-scale investigation into the matter. Most representatives and senators, especially on the Republican side, were content to focus their unhappiness on President Harry S. Truman and his controversial secretary of state, Dean Acheson—the chief architects of government bloat and softness on Communism, according to their GOP detractors. "In that inflamed political environment," writes political scientist David M. Barrett, "the CIA was less of a target." Was the Agency blameworthy? "No consensus answer would emerge in 1950," Barrett concludes.[9]

In this case, the media coverage and the degree of government intelligence accountability were both low (see Table 7.2). The *Times* printed only seventeen articles related to the CIA and the Korean intelligence failure, and they were diffused over a lengthy time period that extended (off and on) all the way throughout most of 1952. This distinction between diffuse coverage that lasts from several months to more than a year with only occasional articles, on the one hand, and concentrated coverage that is dense and focused within a few contiguous months, on the other hand, is important. Concentrated coverage is more apt to be dramatic and to have a reinforcing effect that makes the subject difficult for government officials to dismiss. Just as the media coverage related to the outbreak of war in Korea was modest, so was the government's response to the intelligence failure. At the end of 1952, General Walter Bedell Smith, a popular DCI whose managerial competence in the wake of a less organized Hillenkoetter had done much to reassure lawmakers that the Agency had improved its analysis, stepped down from office. During Smith's tenure (1950–1953), no movement took hold—in either the executive or legislative branches of government—in favor of a major investigation into why the analytic capabilities at Langley had been flawed on the eve of the Korean conflict.

2. The Bay of Pigs Failure (1961)

On April 6, 1961, eleven days before the Bay of Pigs paramilitary operation began, the *New York Times* accused the CIA under the Kennedy Administration of planning an undeclared covert war against Cuba.[10] Over the next several weeks, newspapers "had a field day socking the CIA," complained Senator Stuart Symington (D, Missouri) in an enthusiastic defense of the Agency at the time.[11] Five days after the failed invasion, with the *Times* continuing to cover the event closely and often on page one, President John F. Kennedy appointed General Maxwell Taylor to head up a committee that would delve into what had gone wrong. Attorney General Robert Kennedy (the president's brother), DCI Allen Dulles (1953–1961), and Admiral Arleigh Burke served as the other members of what became known as the Taylor Committee. On Capitol Hill, twenty-two days after the initial *Times* report and eleven days after the invasion, Dulles responded to Senate concerns by providing a briefing to the Foreign Relations Committee in closed session.

The Taylor Committee convened periodically throughout the rest of 1961, then at year's end issued an anodyne accounting of the disastrous invasion. A few individual members of Congress called for a more significant probe, and for immediate intelligence reform (most notably Senators Wayne Morse, D, Washington, and Allen Ellender, D, Louisiana). The vast majority of lawmakers, however, were content to let the CIA review its own mistakes and make

Table 7.2 **The Media as Pressure for Intelligence Accountability in the United States, 1945–2016**

Significant Intelligence Shock	Media Coverage* (# of Story Cites Preceding Government Decision)	Threshold Levels**	Degree of Government Response	Close Media/ Oversight Association
1. Korean War (1950)	17 (diffused)	Low	Low	Yes: low/low
2. Bay of Pigs (1961)	37 (concentrated)	Moderate	Moderate	Yes: mod./ mod.
3. NSA scandal[1] (1967)	54 (concentrated)	High	Moderate	No: high/mod.
4. CIA-Watergate (1973)	66 (diffused)	Moderate	Moderate	Yes: mod./ mod.
5. Domestic spying scandal (1974)	52 (concentrated)	High	High***	Yes: high/high
6. Iran-contra scandal (1987)	618 (concentrated)	High	High	Yes: high/high
7. Somalia/Ames (1994)	93 (concentrated)	High	High	Yes: high/high
8. 9/11 failures (2001)	472 (concentrated)	High	High	Yes: high/high
9. Iraqi WMDs (2003)	220 (concentrated)	High	High	Yes: high/high
10. NSA warrantless wiretaps[2] (2005)	89 (concentrated)	High	Low	No: high/low
Metadata (2013–2015)	204 (concentrated)	High	Moderate	No: high/mod.

[1] NSA = National Student Association

[2] NSA = National Security Agency; the warrantless wiretap and metadata operations are treated here as a single, ongoing, and still unfolding sigint controversy.

* Based on reported coverage in the *New York Times Index: The Book of Record* and the *New York Times Index Online,* as measured by the number of article citations during the time period leading up to a government decision about whether to begin an inquiry—modest or major—into the intelligence failure or scandal. The core time periods examined are as follows:

(*continued*)

Table 7.2 **Continued**

1. Korea: June 23, 1950 (war begins in Korea), to November 11, 1952 (*Times* confirms DCI General Walter Bedell Smith's intentions to leave office). The annual volumes used, along with the page numbers, are 1950: p. 1169; 1951: p. 1098; 1952: p. 1178.

2. Bay of Pigs: April 17, 1961 (invasion date), to September 29, 1961 (the president fires DCI Allen Dulles). 1961: p. 1044.

3. National Student Association: February 14, 1967 (*Ramparts* reveals scandal), to December 20, 1967 (the CIA accepts the Katzenbach guidelines). 1967: pp. 1269–1273.

4. CIA-Watergate: June 17, 1972 (Watergate break-in revealed), to July 13, 1974 (the Senate Watergate Committee disbands). 1972: p. 2297; 1973: pp. 2473–2474; 1974: pp. 2539–2541, 2681–2725.

5. Domestic spy scandal: July 16, 1974 (CIA articles begin), to January 21, 1975 (Church Committee formed). 1974: pp. 2540–2541; 1975: pp. 2583–2585.

6. Iran-contra affair: November 3, 1986 (scandal revealed in Middle East newspaper), to January 6, 1987 (Senate investigative committee formed, soon joined by House participation in a Joint Committee inquiry). 1986: pp. 667–678; 1987: p. 632.

7. Ames: February 21, 1994 (Ames is arrested), to October 14, 1994 (creation of Aspin Commission). 1994: pp. 1170–1172.

8. 9/11: September 11, 2001 (Al Qaeda attacks), to June 4, 2002 (congressional investigative committee formed). 2001: p. 1625; 2002: pp. 1840–1902.

9. Iraqi WMDs: January 7, 2002 (articles on WMDs begin), to June 1, 2003 (SSCI inquiry; presidential commission formed). 2002: pp. 963–991; 2003: pp. 882–957.

10. Warrantless wiretaps: December 16, 2005 (*Times* reveals warrantless wiretaps), to February 17, 2006 (Senate rejects wiretapping inquiry, and HPSCI opts for a minimal probe). 2005: pp. 1871–1876; 2006: pp. 1668–1682.

NSA metadata: June 5, 2013 (Snowden's first leak to the *Washington Post*), to August 12, 2013 (when President Barack Obama appointed a Review Board on Communications Technologies, which reported four months later and concluded that privacy must be better protected in the United States [*Liberty and Security in a Changing World* (Washington, DC: U.S. Government Printing Office, December 12, 2013)]. Given the small size of the board (five members) and its short duration (four months), its work—though widely recognized as first-rate—cannot be viewed as a major firefighting inquiry in the same league as the early examples in this table. Reporting on the Snowden affair continued in the coming years, but still without a major presidential commission or congressional investigation ever taking place. Passage of the USA FREEDOM Act on June 2, 2015, however, included key provisions from among those recommended by the Presidential Review Board, and the new law, strengthening privacy (see chapter 5), was probably influenced by the board, along with ongoing news articles and television coverage of Snowden's activities, plus strong lobbying by privacy groups. 2013: statistics from the *New York Times Index Online*, accessed in 2016.

The hard copy *New York Times Index: The Book of Record* for each year is unsystematically organized and often even absent clear references to the "Central Intelligence Agency." In some cases, one must search through various categories, such as "U.S. Government—Intelligence," or sometimes "Intelligence agencies," "Espionage," or "Counterintelligence." With respect to the Watergate case, the researcher has to pore through separate sections on "Watergate," searching for the occasional intelligence reference. For the 9/11 case and for the warrantless wiretaps case, one must turn to a special section on "Terrorism." (The *New York Times Indexes* contain thousands of citations to the 9/11 attacks; this study, though, focused only on those that had some reference to intelligence.) For the WMD case, one must search under "Iraq." For the NSA controversies: "National Security Agency," "Snowden," "FISA," "wiretaps," and "metadata." Given this lack of uniform indexing, the numbers in this table must be treated as approximations, although one can be reasonably certain

Table 7.2 **Continued**

they reflect the general degree of attention devoted to each case by the *Times*. Further, the numbers are comparable to those listed in the online Lexus-Nexus reference base for the *Times*. This reference is easier to follow than the *Times Index*, but Lexus-Nexus lacks its nuances and that is why the *Times Index* was used, despite the more difficult research demands. The hard-copy *Index* was no longer available for years after 2007, so I turned to the *New York Times Index Online* to examine the Snowden-related entries in 2013.

  ** The benchmarks are based on the number of articles about the scandal or failure. A visual inspection of the distribution of the ten data points led to this classification: 17 articles in the *Times* about the event were designated as "low"; 37 as "moderate"; 52 to 93 as "high"; and above 200 "very high." With respect to the Watergate scandal of 1973, the 66 rating was downgraded to "moderate," because the number of *Times* articles in this instance was so widely diffused over a long period of time, and most had nothing to do with the CIA or other intelligence agencies. The threshold presented here—low, medium, high—refer to the newspaper coverage associated with an intelligence mistake or scandal, whereas in chapter 6 the terms "low-threshold" and "high-threshold" were employed in a different and more general manner that simply indicated that some "shock" events had drawn little attention and some considerable attention on Capitol Hill.

  *** In each of the "High Government Response" cases, the decision by officeholders was to establish both a presidential commission and one or more legislative inquiries. Each occurred in the post-1975 climate of a new, more rigorous approach to intelligence accountability.

appropriate internal reforms as its managers saw fit. Some senators recommended the CIA change its now tarnished name, but Dulles let even this rose-water proposal quietly expire.

As for the White House, President Kennedy was enraged at first when the operation failed. He reportedly declared to staff aides his intention "to splinter the CIA into a thousand pieces and scatter it to the winds."[12] Instead, he settled for firing DCI Dulles. The president soon turned back to the Agency for help with fresh efforts to destabilize the Castro regime in Cuba (Operation Mongoose) and to pursue a wide variety of other covert operations against Communism around the world. His predecessor, Dwight David Eisenhower, who had initially authorized the Bay of Pigs planning, cautioned publicly against a full-scale inquiry into the controversial operation; even Senate Majority Leader Mike Mansfield (D, Montana), a champion of intelligence reform a decade earlier, concluded that "this is no time for a congressional investigation." The Taylor Report and Dulles's Foreign Relations Committee briefing were, at best, a moderate reaction to such a colossal Agency calamity.

Despite the lack of a major inquiry, the CIA did take the Bay of Pigs outcome seriously. It could hardly do otherwise, given the embarrassment caused by the operation. Agency managers launched an internal inquiry and issued a scathing postmortem for Langley's own use, written by its inspector general Lyman Kirkpatrick. In the grand scheme of things, however, the Bay of Pigs had a limited effect on the CIA and how it conducted its future business—other than to temper some of the hubris displayed during the 1950s inside Agency

Headquarters and at the White House that America's foreign-policy woes could be easily resolved by a magic waving of the covert action wand.

In the Bay of Pigs case, an association between media coverage and government reaction was again present. The *Times* gave moderate coverage to the intelligence failure, including twenty-two stories in April and May (some on the front page). "By year's end, the *Times* had published a record amount about the CIA—fifty-seven articles, columns, editorials and letters," Barrett reports.[13] (My count in Table 7.2 is thirty-seven, a difference attributable to the fact that, unlike Barrett's tabulation, this chapter does not include letters to the *Times* in its tabulation.) In contrast to the reporting on the Korean War failure, the news articles in this case were also less scattered over time. They accumulated into a dramatic punch during April and May 1961. Moreover, on its editorial pages, the newspaper had pressed hard for a full-blown inquiry. While designated "moderate" in this study (in comparison to the much greater media coverage of the CIA in later years), at the time the coverage on the Bay of Pigs by the newspaper was quite extensive.

Similar to the *Times*, the White House and the Congress responded to the failure in a relatively moderate manner (again, compared to later years), namely, the Taylor Committee probe and secret DCI briefings for lawmakers. Both branches encouraged the Agency's managers to improve their covert action operations but left it at that. Calls for intelligence reform from Senator Eugene McCarthy (D, Minnesota), not yet a national figure, fell largely on deaf ears on the Hill and throughout Washington. The moderate media attention proved an insufficient stimulus to sound a loud-enough fire alarm to set in motion inquiries of any consequence. Still, the government was more critical of the CIA than it ever had been before and, thus, in Table 7.2 the event qualifies as a "moderate" (rather than a "low") degree of government response. Enmity toward Fidel Castro among Washington officialdom, along with some sympathy for President Kennedy in dealing with the bearded Communist irritant, superseded the notion of putting the Agency's Operations Directorate through a formal investigation.

3. The National Student Association Scandal (1967)

Recall that by virtue of its founding statute (the National Security Act of 1947), the CIA is expected to operate overseas, not within the United States. Yet, over the years, the Agency developed ties at home with a wide variety of groups and organizations deemed helpful for its foreign missions of espionage, covert action, and counterintelligence. Some observers tolerated these relationships for the sake of advancing U.S. security interests; others found them beyond the pale of what should be allowed within a democratic society. When news came that the CIA had been secretly using American students in the National Student

Association (a different NSA than the mammoth sigint agency discussed elsewhere in this book) for purposes of spreading anti-Communist propaganda at international student conferences, the media revelations—beginning with a report in a left-wing periodical, *Ramparts*, and then taken up by the *New York Times*—led to a domestic intelligence scandal or, at any rate, a mini-scandal.

From the day the *Times* first reported on the story, February 14, 1967, until the day when Congress decided on a response, February 25, 1967, the newspaper carried fifty-four stories about the NSA controversy—a large amount that surpassed even the Bay of Pigs coverage and included ten front-page stories in as many days. Regardless, lawmakers decided against a formal inquiry. At the other end of Pennsylvania Avenue, President Lyndon B. Johnson merely assigned a senior official, Under Secretary of State Nicholas Katzenbach, as chair of a committee to write a report on the matter, rejecting the creation of a higher-profile presidential commission. The other members of the committee were DCI Richard Helms, along with Health, Education, and Welfare Secretary John Gardner. The Katzenbach Report recommended later in the year that "no federal agency shall provide any covert financial assistance or support, direct or indirect, to any of the nation's education or private voluntary organizations." The Agency was little affected by the scandal.

A close association between media coverage and intelligence accountability is absent in this instance. Regardless of the extensive coverage given the scandal by America's newspaper of record, Washington officials reacted only modestly to calls for meaningful intelligence reform. Lawmakers held a few executive-session hearings, and the White House settled for ordering up the Katzenbach Report, which was shaped chiefly by the CIA's own boss, Helms. At least, though, managers at Langley had learned to steer clear of U.S. student groups for purposes of its international propaganda operations—although it continued to have widespread and intricate relationships with other U.S. organizations, from the media to academe.[14]

4. The CIA-Watergate "Scandal" (1973)

The most notorious political scandal in modern American history is known by the tag line "Watergate." The name comes from the Watergate Hotel in Washington, D.C., the site of a burglary aimed at the Democratic National Party Headquarters in 1972 and directed by aides in the Nixon White House. Subsequently, after an alert hotel security guard apprehended the burglars in the act, President Nixon joined his staff in a cover-up attempt. This criminal offense became the linchpin of the impeachment proceedings against the president, leading to his resignation on the eve of what was likely to be a conviction in the Senate.[15]

Responding to the security guard's telephone call, D.C. police arrested the burglars on June 17, 1972, and the president resigned from office on August 9,

1974. This was an epic event in American politics that preoccupied the media throughout more than two years. The research presented here is concerned with only a small slice of the episode: whether the CIA aided and abetted the burglary and the attempted cover-up, as rumored in the capital at the time. According to Samuel Dash, the chief counsel of the Senate Watergate Committee (led by Senator Sam Ervin, Jr. [D, North Carolina]), committee member Senator Howard Baker (R, Tennessee)—a Nixon loyalist—tried to pin the Watergate caper on the Agency, but could find no evidence to support his theory. Neither could the Ervin Committee as a whole nor, two years later, the Church Committee.[16] The CIA-Watergate relationship proved not to be a scandal after all.

The record shows that when the Nixon Administration had attempted to suborn the Agency into a cover-up role, the CIA's leaders refused to be drawn in. It is true, recall from the previous chapter, that the Agency's DS&T provided a wig of reddish hue and other disguise materials to the Watergate conspirators; true, as well, some of the other Watergate burglars had once worked for the Agency. Nonetheless, many a lawmaker who has looked into this matter concluded that the relationship never brought the Agency into either the burglary or the cover-up.[17] Members of Congress scolded DS&T's managers for its carelessness, but neither the legislative nor the executive branches pursued a more extensive, stand-alone inquiry into the CIA's connections to the notorious scandal.

The association between the media and intelligence accountability holds in this case. The *Times* offered several articles that explored the CIA's relationship with Watergate (sixty-six in number), a coverage that—on the surface—might seem to allow a "high" designation" in Table 7.2; nevertheless, this coverage is placed instead in the "moderate" category, because the articles were diffused over a three-year period. Similarly, the branches of government turned away from establishing a full-fledged investigation into the Agency's role in the scandal; but they did spend enough time with various probes into the charges to qualify collectively as a "moderate" government response. The Subcommittee on Intelligence, a unit of the House Armed Services Committee, looked into the question, as did the Ervin Committee—albeit as a minor aspect of its larger inquiry into the White House cover-up; and so did the Church Committee to a modest extent. (Senator Baker served on both the Ervin and Church panels.) By all indications, however, like Gertrude Stein's Oakland, there was no there there.

5. The Domestic Spying Scandal (1974)*

The *Times* reporting on Operation CHAOS began in the summer of 1974 and by the end of December—fifty-two articles later, in a concentrated period of time (six months), including several front-page stories in December—the Congress had enacted the first ever law in America's history spelling out provisions for intelligence accountability. Appalled by the CIA's operations against Allende's democratically elected regime, lawmakers approved the Hughes-Ryan Act to provide closer executive and legislative supervision over covert actions. Then, following up this action quickly in January 1975, the Senate set up the Church Committee; the House, the Pike Committee; and the White House, the Rockefeller Commission—all created to investigate the *Times* allegations. As related in chapter 3, these inquiries resulted in the creation of SSCI and HPSCI; enactment of FISA; and passage of the Intelligence Oversight Act of 1980, with its requirement for prior notice (*ante facto* reporting) to SSCI and HPSCI of all important intelligence operations—a dramatic departure from the tradition of *ex post facto* intelligence reporting (if any reporting at all) in earlier days.

The CHAOS case displays a close fit between media coverage and attempts at closer government accountability over the secret agencies. The *Times* series ran throughout the summer, autumn, and winter of 1974, painting a disturbing portrait of the Agency's involvement in prohibited domestic operations. On Capitol Hill, CHAOS—spying against American citizens—was hard to ignore and brought about a "high" government response (the first in the annals of U.S. intelligence). The Year of Intelligence was under way, with what would stand as the most extensive investigations ever aimed at America's (or any other nation's) spy services. The outcome was a new set of expectations in the nation's capital. Henceforth, the espionage agencies would be deemed a more normal part of American government, subject to checks and balances like all the other parts—including intensive police patrolling and, when necessary, firefighting. (The asterisk above indicates a major inquiry.)

6. The Iran-Contra Scandal (1987)*

Even though the investigations of 1975 ushered in a more serious approach to intelligence accountability, the United States would learn a decade later that its secret agencies could still succumb to questionable behavior. In Congress, the Inouye-Hamilton Committee examined the Iran-contra allegations in 1987 and discovered, as related in chapter 4, that the NSC staff and a few CIA officers had entered into unlawful intelligence operations by (among other offenses) violating the Boland Amendments that prohibited covert action in Nicaragua. In the executive branch, the Tower Presidential Commission similarly found wrongdoing and criticized President Ronald Reagan for failing to supervise his own staff and its questionable activities in Central America. On Capitol Hill, these investigative findings led to the enactment of the CIA Inspector General Act of 1989 and the Intelligence Oversight Act of 1991 (redrafted and passed as the Intelligence Reorganization Act of 1992), which clarified the definition of covert action and strengthened the approval and reporting procedures for that intelligence mission.

The *New York Times* offered extensive—indeed, record-setting—coverage of the scandal, with a rising crescendo of articles in the weeks of November and December 1986 and January 1987. The coverage dwarfed even its earlier attention to Operation CHAOS and the covert actions against Allende. The efforts by elements in the Reagan Administration to seek secret financing from American conservatives and foreign potentates for covert action against the Nicaraguan regime especially grated on many lawmakers who did not appreciate the administration's efforts to bypass the appropriations process, Hughes-Ryan and the 1980 Oversight Act, and the Boland Amendments. Nor did they appreciate having been lied to by NSC staff officials, including national security advisers Robert C. McFarlane and John M. Poindexter when SSCI and HPSCI leaders asked them about the rumors around Washington hinting at the possibility of covert action improprieties in Nicaragua. With their institutional pride injured, and with a backdrop of persistent clamors from the *Times* and other media for a major investigation, the Congress created the Inouye-Hamilton Committee. President Reagan responded with the Tower Commission, which (as it turned out) did not treat him as gently as he might have hoped and expected with a fellow conservative Republican, John Tower, at the helm.

An association between extensive media coverage and a rise in intelligence oversight is evident in this case. The *Times* reporting of the Iran-contra affair was expansive—618 articles, mostly in November and December 1986—and the government launched major inquiries. A caveat must be added, however: media coverage was not the only influence that bore upon the establishment of the congressional investigation. The leadership of Lee H. Hamilton, the HPSCI chair, who had been misled by McFarlane and others, contributed significantly to the movement on Capitol Hill toward an inquiry. So did the personal outrage of several other members of Congress. Still, the story's domination in the *Times* added to the sense in Washington and around the nation that the scandal warranted a solemn probe.

7. The Somalian Analysis and Ames Counterintelligence Failures*

In 1993, the killing of U.S. Special Forces troops in Somalia by a tattered band of local warriors in Mogadishu, spurred an interest in Washington—especially in the White House—toward examining the flaws of intelligence analysis that had failed to warn America's soldiers about the military threat posed by warlords on the Horn of Africa. Also, in 1994, as we have seen in earlier chapters, an FBI inquiry brought to light the fact that the Soviet Union had successfully recruited a mole at the center of the CIA: Aldrich Ames, a high-ranking counterintelligence officer who had been working on behalf of his Moscow spy-handlers for more than a decade—the most spectacular counterintelligence failure in the Agency's history. The unmasking of Ames, a high-profile story that surpassed even the coverage of the Somalian debacle, stimulated extensive media coverage during the period from the first *Times* story on February 21, 1994, when the FBI arrested Ames, until the establishment on October 14, 1994, of a presidential-congressional investigative panel, known as the Aspin-Brown Commission. The Commission published a report in 1996 calling for reforms related to intelligence analysis and counterintelligence, plus (as the Commission took up topics beyond Somalia and Ames) the lack of managerial integration in the intelligence community.

The Aspin-Brown Commission left it to the Pentagon and military intelligence to improve collection and analysis against the Somalian warlords and related targets, while it concentrated on the Ames flap as well as a wide range of other intelligence issues concerning the difficulties in redirecting the IC away from a Cold War global environment and toward the new world of failing states and proliferating terrorist cells. The relationship between media articles on Somalia, Ames, and the transition of the intelligence agencies toward a post-Communist environment indicates a correspondence between extensive journalist reporting on these subjects and an uptick in intelligence oversight. The media coverage included ninety-three articles about the Somalian tragedy and about Ames (including four front-page stories); in harmony with this coverage, the Aspin-Brown Commission was a significant government response, notably to the Ames counterintelligence failure and the Commission's concern about the need for a new global orientation beyond the IC's previous concentration on the Soviet Bloc. Again, though, media coverage was only part of the picture. Aspin energetically sought the creation of a commission that could look into both the Ames affair and the intelligence failures in Somalia in 1993—a military fiasco that had cost him his job as secretary of defense. Further, many lawmakers— including the influential SSCI vice chairman, John W. Warner—pressed for a commission as a vehicle to restore the sullied reputation, and protect the funding, of the CIA (an organization in his Virginia constituency) after the discovery of Ames's treachery.

8. 9/11 Intelligence Failure*

The inability of the intelligence agencies to adequately warn the nation about the terrorist attacks against the American homeland in September 2001 led Congress to form a Joint Committee of inquiry (the Graham-Goss Committee) and, subsequently, to urge the creation of a presidential investigative panel to probe further into intelligence and related weaknesses in the U.S. defense posture. Energetically lobbied by families representing some of the people who died during the 9/11 attacks, the Bush White House finally consented to create a presidential panel (the Kean Commission) to further study the catastrophe. Moreover, inspired in part by the poor human intelligence—the lack of effective spy rings in the Middle East—leading up to the 9/11 attacks, HPSCI undertook a critical evaluation of the Agency's espionage recruitment programs around the world, stressing the lack of good agents in key locations.

At first, SSCI elected not to examine questions about the poor use of warning intelligence by policy officials in the Clinton and second Bush Administrations. Here was a hot potato. Over a year later, though, the panel finally turned to the policy side of the equation and found, as had already been widely reported in the media and in scholarly articles, that the executive branch under both Clinton and Bush had been culpable in the 9/11 intelligence failures. Both administrations had failed to take action on the counterterrorism warnings they had received, of which the most vivid and prescient was the CTC's 1995 report on aerial terrorism (see chapter 4).

As one would expect, the *Times* covered the 9/11 attacks closely, including the intelligence failures (472 articles were related to this aspect of the tragedy), and the newspaper called for major investigations. Once again high media coverage and major government inquiries went hand in hand. Once again, though, a caveat must be added: major investigations would probably have occurred anyway, given the horrendous nature of the attacks, along with the pressures brought on the government by the families of the victims who lobbied fervently and effectively in favor of a meaningful inquiry.

9. Iraqi WMD Intelligence Failure*

Throughout 2002 and early 2003, the United States and its allies, plus various members of the United Nations, engaged in heated debates about whether Iraq possessed WMDs and posed a grave danger to international peace. Recall that a controversial October 2002 NIE indicated a likelihood that the Middle East regime did have such weaponry. When the United States led an invasion into Iraq in March 2003, however, the anticipated armaments were nowhere to be found. In light of these developments, Congress supported the creation of a presidential commission on intelligence in June 2003 (the Robb-Silberman Commission) to investigate this conspicuous and consequential intelligence failure. Moreover, SSCI undertook a parallel probe of its own (the Roberts Committee) into the faulty WMD estimate, focusing on the CIA's errors.

Preceding the establishment of these panels of inquiry, the *New York Times* provided extensive coverage about the intelligence disputes related to possible Iraqi WMDs, including 220 articles from January 2002 through May 2003 and with a particularly high saturation in the early months of 2003. This case suggests an association between strong media reporting on Iraqi WMDs and a significant government reaction to the intelligence mistakes that were made about this supposed weaponry. Yet, given the high stakes involved—war in the Middle East—high-profile inquiries may well have been undertaken anyway. As in several of the shocks examined here, one can only say in this instance that the direction of media coverage, which stood lopsidedly in favor of pursuing serious inquiries, paralleled the consensus in Congress that—by way of formal inquiries—answers had to be found to explain the disastrously wrong WMD rationale for a war in Iraq.

10. The Warrantless Wiretap and Metadata Scandals (2005, 2013)

In 2005, *Times* correspondents James Risen and Eric Lichtblau reported that, in the wake of the 9/11 attacks, the second Bush Administration secretly over-turned thirty years of law related to wiretapping for national security purposes (FISA). At the request of the White House, based on alleged national security considerations, the *Times* sat on the story for more than a year.[18] When the newspaper finally published the piece, Risen and Lichtblau won a Pulitzer Prize for exposing the administration's improper approach to wiretap activities. Eight years later in 2013, when Edward Snowden leaked the documents that revealed the NSA's further controversial use of sigint against American citizens—including, this time, the metadata program—the initial uncase about the FISA violations ballooned into heightened anxieties among proponents of liberty and privacy that the NSA had truly gone too far. It was this overreach by the sigint agency that stirred a movement in 2014–2015 back toward a better balance between security and liberty—even without a major investigation into the sigint abuses.

Congress had enacted FISA in 1978 to prohibit the misuse of electronic spying against American citizens by the national security apparatus; henceforth, wire-taps and other forms of surveillance by the NSA and other spy agencies would have to acquire a warrant from a special FISA Court. Yet Risen and Lichtblau discovered that President George W. Bush had given the NSA authority to con-duct surveillance on communications inside the United States—including the targeting of this nation's citizens—without FISA Court rulings. The disclosures in the *Times* were a sobering confirmation of rumors that privacy in America was being trammeled in the rush to hunt for terrorists.[19] Legal authorities around the country chastised the Bush Administration's surveillance programs for their vio-lation of the Fourth Amendment of the Constitution (which bars unreasonable searches), as well as for bypassing FISA.

The *Times* pursued the warrantless wiretaps story relentlessly in December 2005 and into January and February 2006: sixty-one articles in a compressed period of time. The newspaper reporting noted that only a few SSCI and HPSCI members had been informed about the wiretap operations. Some of these lawmakers had balked, with Jay Rockefeller the most vigorous in the questions he raised privately with the Bush Administration—all to no avail. As Risen has commented, "By giving the lawmakers secret briefings with no staff present and then demanding that they never discuss the matter with anyone, the congressional leaders were paralyzed."[20] The close attention paid to this topic by the *Times*, including several op-eds by the editors of the newspaper calling for a major congressional investigation into the NSA program, failed to result in a decision by members of Congress to establish a special panel of inquiry. Some outside groups argued for a major investigation, as well, but without success.[21]

Members of SSCI and HPSCI did hold closed-session hearings on the subject of warrantless wiretaps and, eventually, the Bush Administration made some minor adjustments in the surveillance program (adopted via the FISA Amendments Act of 2008); but the validity of the administration's legal memoranda in support of ignoring the FISA law, and the question of why the NSA agreed to go along with this lawless use of secret power—even after being publicly embarrassed in 1975 by the Church Committee for comparable transgressions—were never explored through a significant probe carried out by Congress or the executive branch. Assurances from Bush Administration officials that they would provide more complete briefings on its wiretap programs to SSCI and HPSCI leaders had led, concluded the *Washington Post*, to "a dramatic and possibly permanent drop in momentum for a congressional inquiry, which seemed likely two months ago."[22]

The response of the Bush Administration was to claim, as one of its legal briefs put it, that "the government may be justified in taking measures which in less troubled conditions could be seen as infringements of individual liberties."[23] It was an eerie and chilling echo of an argument made to the Church Committee by former president Nixon, whose philosophy of governance was an early manifestation of the "unitary theory" of the presidency later advocated by Vice President Cheney and John Yoo, a high-ranking attorney in the Department of Justice. As Yoo has written, the policies of the executive branch must reign supreme on matters of security.[24] The same rationale for the overreach from 2001 to 2005 would be advanced again by the Bush Administration for its post-9/11 metadata excesses (chapter 5).

This case of unfettered NSA surveillance represents the most salient illustration of disharmony between extensive media coverage and aggressive oversight action by the government. The *New York Times* persistently featured the questionable NSA programs in 2005–2006, and again in 2013–2014 (see Table 7.2); but neither Congress nor (no surprise here) the perpetrators of the NSA program—the Bush White House and NSA Director Michael V. Hayden, followed by NSA Director Keith Alexander—saw fit to support a major investigation. As when they had stampeded to pass the USA PATRIOT Act in 2001, which also lifted restrictions on intelligence activities, lawmakers had again rushed in their support of expanded NSA sigint operations to project an image of themselves as resolutely antiterrorist.[25] Existing laws and civil liberties in the United States were thrown, for the time being, into the back seat.

The Obama Administration eventually responded to public and media pressure to examine the NSA's programs. The president appointed a small review group on August 27, 2013, led by Professor Geoffrey Stone of the University of Chicago Law School (see chapter 5). The panel's research was outstanding and its final report, issued later in the year, provided a thoughtful and articulate criticism of the NSA's overreach; but these findings received only limited attention from the media and the public. The review group contributed to the national debate over the NSA's excesses and probably influenced, at least moderately, passage of the USA FREEDOM Act in 2015; however, it was too small and short-lived to be considered a major inquiry.

The Influence of Media Reporting on Intelligence Accountability

A summary of the newspaper coverage for these ten shock events, and how the coverage either supports or erodes the notion of an association between media attention and intelligence accountability, is presented in Table 7.2. The degree to which news articles were concentrated or diffuse is a consideration. In the cases of the Korean War and the Watergate episode, for instance, the number of articles was spread out (diffuse coverage) over a long period of time and probably had less of an effect than in the many other cases where the *Times* displayed a persistent downpour of attention to a topic over a short period of time (concentrated coverage). In eight out of ten cases, a close relationship between media coverage and accountability was present, although certainly not in any conclusive statistical sense with such a low "*n*." Despite the limited number of cases (however important they were), the results do suggest, however, at least a tentative general conclusion: high media coverage of intelligence shock events is likely to be associated with the establishment of special panels of inquiry—the most intensive form of accountability. This relationship was evident in five cases: CHAOS; Iran-contra; the Somalia and Ames cases; 9/11; and Iraqi WMDs—with these last four occurring in the era of more rigorous intelligence accountability that began in 1975. In two other cases, the Bay of Pigs and the Watergate episode, moderate media coverage corresponded with a moderate government response. Finally, in the first case presented in this chapter—the

Korean War intelligence failure—low media coverage was accompanied by a low government reaction.

In the remaining two cases examined here, extensive media coverage occurred but without an accompanying high-profile special inquiry: the National Student Association scandal and the NSA sigint controversies of 2005–2006 and 2013–2015. (The NSA sigint disputes were reinforced as possible subjects for a major government inquiry by the SSCI Torture Report, as well as widespread concern over the use of drones for killing terrorist suspects. Both of these intelligence activities generated extensive media coverage [not tabulated here], but they never stimulated a major probe that might have looked into the efforts, for example, of the CIA to stifle the SSCI Democratic staff researching into torture practices, or to the use of drone attacks against American citizens living abroad.) The CIA-student scandal happened before the Church Committee investigation in 1975, which was the main impetus for the creation of SSCI and HPSCI. These committees, in turn, had the effect of bringing intelligence activities more into the mainstream of government checks and balances, accompanied by regular reporting to lawmakers on the budgets and operations of America's secret agencies. As Glees and Davies have put it, this new oversight moved intelligence "into the sphere of overt, public discourse and debate."[26] Reporting by the *New York Times* on, and government inquiries into, intelligence failures and scandals became more the norm than had been the case before 1975. Moreover, the student scandal seemed to many observers at the time as something the Johnson White House could easily resolve, without major inquiry (which it did). This NSA flap paled in interest compared to the day-to-day heartbreaking stories coming out of the stagnating war in Vietnam.

The second case—questionable National Security Agency and CIA activities—displayed the widest gap between media coverage and an intensive oversight reaction. The warrantless wiretapping and metadata controversies occurred after the establishment of the new accountability standards and institutions recommended by the Church Committee, as did the Agency's use of torture and assassination drones. All of these activities received extensive and lasting media coverage, and the research of the Senate Democratic staff brought significant attention to the torture program. Still, both the NSA and the CIA managed to escape an intensive special probe—a full-blown Church- or Kean-like inquiry into their disputatious counterterrorism programs. As I have speculated in earlier chapters, this outcome is probably a result of wariness among lawmakers about conducting a major intelligence investigation at a time when the United States was engaged in two wars (Iraq and Afghanistan), as well as a struggle against the terrorist group behind the 9/11 attacks—Al Qaeda—still at bay (in the 2005 case) and ISIS on the march in Syria, Iraq, and Libya more recently.

The CIA and the other intelligence agencies have garnered significantly more year-by-year attention in the *Times* since the domestic spy scandal of 1974. According to Lexus-Nexus entries, for example, coverage on "the CIA" went from 94 articles in 1969 to 1,068 in 1975, then to 1,328 in 2004 (the high-water mark), before declining to around 400 per annum in recent years (still far above the average recorded before the Year of Intelligence). Media considerations, though, rarely explain on their own why officials in Washington opt to carry out major investigations into intelligence activities. Media attention probably helped move the government in that direction with the Church, Pike, and Rockefeller inquiries in 1975, the Iran-contra investigations in 1987, and the Somalia and Ames failures in 1995; but with the 9/11 and Iraqi WMD shocks, the instant destruction and tragedy accompanying the former, along with the widespread sense of a profoundly mistaken rationale for war associated with the latter, would have led most likely to significant inquiries even if the media coverage of these intelligence errors had not set record marks. Still, in the absence of significant media coverage, major government investigations seem less likely in most circumstances.

This chapter suggests the possible existence of a media threshold for the triggering of a major inquiry into intelligence shocks: a data point of a necessary minimum of fifty articles, all relatively concentrated in time. This is not to argue that high coverage by the *New York Times* of a scandal or failure *causes* Congress to take up more serious forms of accountability; the evidence is not clear enough to make that argument. Rather, the notion is that a serious spy inquiry rarely occurs without a backdrop of extensive and concentrated reporting on a shock event.

Related as well to the question of a media threshold is the timing of a shock. Did it come before or after the watershed year of 1975, when the United States adopted more rigorous legal standards, along with clearer measures of effectiveness and propriety for its secret agencies? Unlike "the good old days," the shock of the CIA's domestic spying in 1974 made the intelligence agencies fair game for investigative reporting and intensive government probes. Important as well is the question of leadership. For example, long-time intelligence reformer Senate Majority Leader Mansfield was determined to have a major investigation into the domestic spy charges of 1974; and Les Aspin and John Warner, key Washington figures at the time, pushed strongly (respectively) for the Somalia and Ames combined inquiry in 1994. Absent well-placed and aggressive leadership sympathetic to the need for a major investigation, media drumbeats—however persistent—may be without serious consequence.

The nature of the shock event is pertinent as well. In 1994, Aspin was primarily concerned about the 1993 intelligence failure in Somalia that took place when he was secretary of defense. Yet he could not convince enough key officials in Washington to conduct a major inquiry into that matter alone; the topic was viewed as too narrow and was already being addressed by the Pentagon anyway. So Aspin was forced to combine the Somalia intelligence failure with the Ames counterintelligence failure of 1994 that had attracted more attention on Capitol Hill. By joining forces with Senator Warner, who supported the Ames inquiry, Aspin succeeded in his goal of launching an intensive intelligence investigation that would also include (through the back door) the Somalia debacle, along with a range of other intelligence issues related to the shift of America's spy agencies from a bipolar Cold War setting to a new unipolar world dominated by the United States following the collapse of the Soviet empire in 1991. Earlier, in the case of the domestic spying allegations of 1974, Senator Church had no trouble garnering support for a full-blown investigation, given how Operation CHAOS had raised Orwellian anxieties across the country that the CIA had become a Gestapo—although support from Mansfield was pivotal as well.

Tipping the Scales toward Firefighting

Many ingredients enter into why government officials decide to become investigative firefighters, rather than only police patrollers. One of the most important influences can be the extent of media coverage associated with an intelligence shock. In most cases, more coverage is associated with a greater probability that Congress or the White House will create a high-profile panel of inquiry. If an event is startling enough in its own right (like CHAOS), tragic enough (as with 9/11), or has led to the launching of a major war based on false premises (Iraq in 2003), the extent of media coverage may still be important; in these instances, however, lawmakers are apt to conduct probes anyway, because of the manifest significance of the events and a prevailing sense that the government must do something to correct the IC's mistakes or wrongdoing. Further, if a shock event has taken place after the Year of Intelligence—when Congress and the executive branch began to place higher standards of propriety and performance on the secret agencies—the climate has been more favorable for a strong government reaction in the form of a special inquiry into improper or ineffectual espionage operations.

Significant, as well, is the kind of scandal or failure that occurs. If it deals with domestic spying on American citizens, concern will be extensive. If instead, the topic is, say, poor intelligence in Somalia during the lead-up to America's failed humanitarian intervention there in 1993, interest may be more narrowly confined to those (like SecDef Aspin) directly involved in the original decision to intervene. Finally, in times of rising global threats (say, when ISIS expanded rapidly into Iraq from its base in Syria, or when "lone wolves" carry out terrorist attacks inside the United States), government officials may be reluctant to engage in an investigation that might divert attention from the immediate and pressing challenges to U.S. security. The pursuit of a major investigation might lead to political accusations that the advocates of a high-profile inquiry are interfering with the nation's safety in parlous times. Here are the apparent reasons why no major government inquiries were established to probe into the NSA and CIA excesses from 2002 through 2015, despite the high media coverage in both 2005 and from 2013 to 2015. Of course, the 9/11 and Iraqi WMD inquiries did take place in a time of terrorism; however, both of these major probes fairly screamed out for a significant investigation—in the first instance, a direct attack against the United States, and, in the second, an unfortunate and avoidable slide into a war in the Middle East that has proved costly in blood and treasure.

The media can be important in American society as a stimulant for more energetic government accountability. Even if the reporting does not lead to a major inquiry, it may nudge desultory police patrollers into a more active review of intelligence programs. An illustration, presented earlier in this book, is the *Washington Post* disclosure that DCI Deutch claimed to have authority to waive prohibitions against CIA-media alliances. This news story never warranted a level of coverage that might have initiated a formal inquiry, but it did stimulate passage of stricter decision rules and reporting guidelines for the use of any such waivers (required by the Intelligence Authorization Act of 1997). As a central conclusion of this chapter suggests, though, media reporting—however influential at times—is not the sole consideration when the government ponders whether to launch major investigations into intelligence scandals and failures.

Moreover, even though my files of *New York Times* newspaper clippings on intelligence since 1975 indicate an ongoing strong attention to this subject, it is widely known that U.S. media coverage of foreign and national security affairs has tapered off dramatically in recent years. According to a 2012 study, only six newspapers and chains now have dedicated reporters in Washington, D.C., to cover the foreign affairs beat, down from thirteen in 2003; and the number of foreign correspondents employed by the ten largest American newspapers fell 24 percent, from 307 in 2003 to 234 in 2011.[27] In light of this shrinkage, it becomes increasingly tenuous for overseers and the public to rely on journalists for alarms about intelligence failures and scandals. Further, during the 2016 presidential election, television reporter Matt Lauer's mishandling of an interview with GOP candidate Donald Trump reminded us that some reporters are insufficiently well versed in complex issues of foreign policy to even pose thoughtful questions and follow-ups. Lauer had come across as poorly informed and unable to probe into Trump's misstatements, such as the nominee's widely discredited claim that he had been opposed to the 2002 invasion of Iraq.[28]

Considerable research remains to be done on the range of media, societal, and Washington leadership influences that might explain when lawmakers and presidents feel compelled to engage in firefighting activities, or at least stepped-up police patrolling, as a means for reviewing intelligence activities. The next chapter takes a look at how individual members of Congress have reacted to the challenge of more rigorous intelligence accountability. Their behavior suggests a continuum of oversight dedication among lawmakers, stretching from genuine enthusiasm to nearly total disregard.

8

Ostriches, Cheerleaders, Lemon-Suckers, and Guardians

Intelligence Oversight and Individual Members of Congress

Despite the sizable amount of spending on the seventeen organizations in the intelligence community, the American people know relatively little about their nation's spy activities. Only those in charge of the "purse strings"—the elected representatives on Capitol Hill—and top officials in the executive branch are able to monitor systematically how these secret agencies are used and the success of the outcomes. As elected officials located outside of the executive branch and potentially free of pro–White House or pro–intelligence agency biases, lawmakers have a unique obligation to supervise the nation's espionage operations and, when possible without jeopardizing sensitive sources and methods, to keep the public informed of their endeavors.

Even though these accountability duties are of great importance, as underscored by the startling revelations in 1974 and 1975 of Operation CHAOS and COINTELPRO—not to mention the extraconstitutional maneuvering involved in the Iran-contra scandal—the practice of intelligence oversight on Capitol Hill has often been sluggish, even since the reforms of the mid-1970s and early 1980s. The number of oversight hearings—both open and closed—on the CIA and the other spy agencies has declined in recent years, for example, and attendance of lawmakers at executive-session hearings has been spotty (according to my interviews with SSCI and HPSCI staff). Members of Congress have been drawn instead to fund-raising events and legislative activities on the Hill that give them much more public visibility, such as the sponsoring of bills and high-profile public hearings on such matters as airport security delays or the dangers of opioid addiction. Only during times of perturbation—domestic spy scandals, catastrophic world events, questionable covert actions, drones accidentally bombing wedding processions or health clinics in Southwest Asia—have lawmakers been jolted into a closer look at intelligence operations.

Reform-minded members of the Church Committee had hoped in 1975 for a much higher level of intelligence accountability on Capitol Hill than has turned out to be the case. They anticipated that, through extensive hearings (mostly closed-door), budget reviews, and agency visitations, the Congress could help the spy agencies avoid mistakes and scandals before they happened, rather than having to investigate them breathlessly as firefighters after the fact.

Ninety-seven lawmakers have served on SSCI and 133 on HPSCI since their creation in 1976 and 1977, respectively, for a total of 230 overseers.[1] Among these individuals, the committee chairs—fourteen on SSCI and a dozen on HPSCI (see appendix B)—have been particularly influential in determining the vigor of committee oversight. Throughout Congress, committee chairs are well known to be first among equals. Recall from chapter 1 that two-thirds of the senior staffers interviewed by Joel Aberbach in his study of congressional accountability practices related to domestic-policy programs found that the chairs of congressional panels exercised the major influence in oversight decisions.[2]

On both of the Intelligence Committees, the average "liberal" voting score (tabulated by the interest group Americans for Democratic Action, or ADA, whereby a tally of 100 is the most liberal record one can achieve and 0 the most conservative) was 48 for SSCI chairs and 42 for HPSCI chairs—both in the moderate range.[3] This apparent middle-of-the-road profile conceals, however, some extreme ideological swings along the way as the committees have evolved. For instance, SSCI Chair Dianne Feinstein (D, California) recently had a 93 ADA score, compared to 10 for her successor and current chair, Richard Burr (R, N. Carolina); HPSCI Chair Silvestre Reyes (D, Texas) recorded a score of 81, followed by Mike Rogers (R, Michigan) with a score of 1, then for Devin Nunes (R, California, the current chair) with a score of 0. (See Table 8.1.) In the second half of its existence, HPSCI in particular has displayed in its leadership a steady slide toward one side of the political spectrum: conservative. The only exception has been Silvestre Reyes (D, Texas).

Despite the importance of the chairmanship, from time to time the ranking minority member on one of the oversight committees, or even a junior member (whether Democrat or Republican), has displayed strong leadership abilities and interests, contributing notably to the committee's responsibilities for oversight. During the early days of HPSCI, for instance, minority member J. Kenneth Robinson (R, Virginia) spent more time than any of his colleagues, in either party, dissecting intelligence budget proposals. As a result, he excelled in closed hearings on intelligence funding decisions. A paragon among dedicated

Table 8.1 **Regional and Ideological Profiles for SSCI and HPSCI Members, 1976–2017**

Name	Years as Chairman	Party	Region/State	Ave. ADA Score/Term
SSCI				
Daniel Inouye	1975–1979	D	West/Hawaii	51
Birch Bayh	1979–1981	D	Midwest/Indiana	62
Barry Goldwater	1981–1985	R	West/Arizona	7
David Durenberger	1985–1987	R	Midwest/Minnesota	42
David Boren	1987–1993	D	South/Oklahoma	44
Dennis DeConcini	1993–1995	D	West/Arizona	78
Arlen Specter	1995–1997	R	NE/Pennsylvania	58
Richard Shelby	1997–2001	R	South/Alabama	5
Bob Graham	2001–2003	D	South/Florida	83
Pat Roberts	2003–2007	R	Midwest/Kansas	10
Jay Rockefeller	2007–2009	D	South/West Virginia	85
Dianne Feinstein	2009–2015	D	West/California	93
Richard Burr	2015–present	R	South/North Carolina	10
			Average:	48
HPSCI				
Edward Boland	1977–1985	D	NE/Massachusetts	71
Lee H. Hamilton	1985–1987	D	Midwest/Indiana	57
Louis Stokes	1987–1989	D	Midwest/Ohio	83
Anthony Beilenson	1989–1991	D	West/California	83
David McCurdy	1991–1993	D	South/Oklahoma	50
Dan Glickman	1993–1995	D	Midwest/Kansas	65
Larry Combest	1995–1997	R	South/Texas	3
Porter Goss	1997–2004	R	South/Florida	4
Peter Hoekstra	2004–2007	R	Midwest/Michigan	5
Silvestre Reyes	2007–2011	D	South/Texas	81
Mike Rogers	2011–2015	R	Midwest/Michigan	1
Devin Nunes	2015–present	R	West/California	0
			Average:	42

Note: My thanks to my undergraduate research assistant at the University of Georgia, Zachery Hawkins, for gathering these data in 2016 from tabulations prepared by the Americans for Democratic Action (ADA) in Washington, D.C. A 100 score is for perfect liberals, from the ADA's reckoning; a 0 score is for perfect conservatives. See Americans for Democratic Action, *Voting Records* (1976–2016), http://www.adaaction.org/.

overseers, Robinson would point to obscure sections in authorization bills that had weak justifications and wield a nimble pen-as-scalpel during committee markups.[4]

Recall, too, from chapter 4, how two HPSCI junior members, Les Aspin and Roman Mazzoli, though mindful of the importance of the intelligence agencies and willing to praise witnesses and programs when warranted, became the House committee's most vocal critics of inadequately planned covert action proposals. They were also unyielding in their cross-examination of DCIs and other officials who appeared before the committee in executive-session hearings. Some members would ask one or two questions of witnesses; Aspin and Mazzoli grilled them at length. Often their questions went into the details of operations in great depth, with the goal not of micromanagement but rather to ensure the proposals had been carefully thought out. Vigilant but fair, they achieved a balance between criticism and support. As the chair of HPSCI's Subcommittee on Oversight, Aspin also managed to choreograph several open hearings on intelligence, without jeopardizing sources and methods—a publicity boon for him in his Wisconsin congressional district but, more important, also a way of informing the American public about at least some aspects of how their taxpayer dollars were being spent on intelligence activities. For example, his public hearings on ties between the media and the CIA, held in the House Rayburn Building in December 1979, filled the room, garnered widespread media attention, and helped further define guidelines for this ambiguous relationship.[5]

Personality and the Practice of Oversight on Capitol Hill

Personality matters. Consider this tale from the 1950s about an Agency briefing to lawmakers on covert action—still remembered with glee at Langley.[6] One afternoon, in a police-guarded Senate hearing room, two young CIA officers stood on either side of an easel that supported charts they had brought with them from Agency Headquarters. One of the officers braced the charts, while the other occasionally moved a pointer up and down the slope of red-and-blue trend lines. Seated near them was a thick-haired man, who was a senior Agency briefer in his fifties. He read from a typed statement, speaking precisely, and seldom looking up from the classified documents before him, his words falling onto the witness table in a dry monotone. All three men wore starched white shirts with buttoned-down collars and striped ties. They might well have been marketing consultants tracing annual sales for the edification of corporate board members.

This "board," though, showed remarkably little interest in whatever profits or losses the charts revealed. Nor was the room anything one might expect to find in a corporate headquarters. It was elegant, even stately. Doric pillars, carved from wood, embellished the rich walnut paneling on the walls; a grand chandelier sparkled at the center of the ceiling. Beyond the spacious windows, draped in purple velvet curtains, was a courtyard where a fountain spewed a column of water high into the frigid morning air. Pigeons pranced along the edge of the fountain. This was no suburban industrial park, but rather the venerable Old Senate Office Building of the United States Senate (which would be named in the 1970s after Richard B. Russell, Georgia's pro-CIA stalwart).

A U-shaped bench dominated the hearing room, its prongs facing the three CIA men as if they were trapped in a magnetic field. Within the concave space of the bench sat a stenographer, his fingers dancing lightly on the keys of a recording machine. A pair of elderly lawmakers sat at the head of the bench, each a United States senator and a member of the secretive Subcommittee on Intelligence Oversight—the only ones to show up for this covert action briefing. They listened as the briefer at the table droned through his prepared statement on the CIA's paramilitary activities around the world. As the deputy director for Operations (DDO), he was expected to present a report—however elliptical—now and then to the Congress.

One of the senators rested his head in his arms and soon fell into the arms of Morpheus. His colleague, the panel's chairman, stared blankly at the CIA briefer, nodded once in a while, and discreetly stole glances at his wristwatch and at the front page of the *Washington Post* folded in front of him on the bench. This was not the first time the DDO had experienced a distant look in the eyes of a lawmaker, or even the first time he had seen one nod off. His job was to provide an update on the DO's activities; how the report was received on the Hill was not his problem.[7] He raised his voice for a moment, more to relieve his own boredom than to stir his small audience. "*Paramilitary activities,*" he emphasized, "have been an important part of our program since the early days of the Cold War."

The new inflection in the briefer's voice woke the slumbering senator with a jolt. "*Parliamentary activities?*" he bellowed. "You fellas can't go messin' round with parliaments. I won't have it!"

A silence fell over the room. The stenographer's fingers stopped their dance. The DDO pursed his lips and looked at the subcommittee chairman.

"Senator, this briefing is on paramilitary, not parliament, activity," the chairman softly told his colleague.

"Oh, well, uhruumph," the sleepy-eyed senator replied, clearing his throat. He paused and tugged at his ear. "Well, all right, but y'all stay away from parliaments, ya hear?" With that warning, he rose from his chair and shuffled out of the room. At a nod from the chairman, the DDO resumed his statement to an audience that had now dwindled to one.[8]

This oft-related portrait of congressional oversight is unfair to members of Congress, several of whom—and not just Mansfield, McCarthy, and Lindsay in the 1960s (see chapter 3)—have valiantly attempted to monitor America's secret foreign policy. Too few, though, have pushed hard for details, or asked well-considered follow-up questions during briefings or more formal hearings. Whether the story of the snoozing octogenarian is factual or imagined remains in question; but it is true that Agency appearances before Congress during these years often lacked a seriousness of purpose—on both sides—that genuine accountability requires. The story also underscores the importance of what kinds of people serve on SSCI and HPSCI to carry out oversight duties: their ideologies; degrees of partisanship; energy levels (which may or may not be correlated with age); views on the separation-of-powers doctrine; their margin of victory in the last election; the degree of stability in their personal lives; their sheer interest in the subject of intelligence and knowledge of world affairs; and other factors that make up the dizzying complexities of human behavior. Some members simply don't seem up to the task of engaging in accountability activities. One HPSCI chairman, for instance, couldn't respond to a reporter in 2006 as to whether Al Qaeda was Sunni or Shia in its religious orientation. The answer is Sunni, as those with even the slightest acquaintance with global terrorism know.[9]

One's basic interest in intelligence is a particularly important attribute. Robinson was fascinated by spy budgets; Aspin was dogged in his attendance at HPSCI meetings, because he loved the back-and-forth banter with intelligence officers about their secret operations.[10] Aspin deeply enjoyed the intellectual discussions that sometimes ensued in hearings about the propriety, logistics, costs, and likely success of foreign operations. Some lawmakers relish the James Bond status of being on one of the congressional Intelligence Committees; but they really don't have the burning desire, or fortitude, to plunge headfirst into the hard work of becoming an intelligence expert.[11]

How well intelligence accountability is pursued on Capitol Hill and elsewhere will depend in part, then, on the quality and motivations of the individuals engaged in this task. Institutional constraints are also important in the life of Congress, such as whether one is in the majority or minority,[12] but Washington is far more than the boxes depicted in the wiring diagrams of organizational charts. As famed political scientist Harold Lasswell once put it, "Political science without biography is a form of taxidermy." A pioneer in the study of personality and government, he realized that knowledge of political institutions was vital to an understanding of public policy but, he stressed, so was the behavior of men and women in high office—what another prominent political scientist, J. David Singer, has referred to as the "psycho-political process" in foreign and security affairs.[13]

An analysis of this human dimension in governance can take several approaches. Lasswell dwelled on the Freudian antecedents of individual political behavior. He described "political man" (*homo politicus*) as a power seeker driven primarily by a desire to overcome feelings of low self-esteem, as engendered by early life experiences—perhaps growing up with a domineering father or suffering from a pronounced physical handicap. In a less speculative manner, other scholars have cast government activities more in terms of "statecraft," defined by Stanley Hoffman as "the way in which the leader conceives of and carries out his role as statesman, his relations with and impact on his followers or opponent."[14]

Lasswell might see the failure of the League of Nations in terms of Woodrow Wilson's ongoing struggle with his powerful father, as manifested in the president's adult life during his confrontations with the domineering, father-like threat of the strong-willed, anti–League of Nations chairman of the Senate Foreign Relations Committee, Henry Cabot Lodge (R, New Hampshire). Wilson reacted out of proportion to Lodge's criticisms of the League proposal. Instead of trying to negotiate and compromise with the senator, Wilson vented an emotional response that Lasswell traces to an earlier latent anger toward his father, who was a prominent and stern Virginia clergyman when Wilson was a boy. Commenting on this line of research, Lasswell wrote, "[It calls] attention to the significance of Wilson's relationship to his father, noting the inner necessity for over-reacting against any subsequent authority figure who reawakened incompletely resolved unconscious conflicts."[15]

In contrast, Hoffman would explain the failure of the League in the simpler terms of inept lobbying of Congress by the president and his aides, coupled with an isolationist political tide in the nation that ran against the devotion of an internationalist White House to the League concept for many reasons—none of them having to do with father–son relationships during Wilson's adolescence. From Hoffman's statecraft perspective, not psychological demons but rather external realities guide foreign and security policy.

Regardless of the methodology one embraces to examine the influence of personality in government, the subject of intelligence oversight cannot be fully addressed without a look into the mental pictures that individual lawmakers carry around in their heads about the spy trade, as well as the degree of energy and interest that overseers bring with them to their review of intelligence programs. The approach adopted here, more in line with Hoffman than Lasswell, simply attempts to sketch out four general approaches or roles used by lawmakers as they face their supervisory duties as members of SSCI and HPSCI.

These different roles can be viewed as dynamic "centers of gravity" in the styles that lawmakers bring to their accountability duties, with periodic movement between the centers rather than a sharply delineated and enduring persona adopted by a lawmaker throughout his or her tenure on SSCI or HPSCI. That is to say, the roles (presented in Table 8.2) are not set in stone. The typology of approaches includes the ostrich, the cheerleader, the lemon-sucker, and the guardian. Unfortunately, researchers have very little access to reliable systematic data on Hill personality types overseeing intelligence—even their attendance records at SSCI and HPSCI hearings; so the typology examined here must be considered fragmentary, more heuristic than definitive. It is a pity that even basic attendance records at hearings are kept from the public; they would provide some insight into how engaged committee members really are.[16]

The Ostrich

Some intelligence overseers come across as "ostriches." Here is the lawmaker who embraces a philosophy of old-fashioned benign neglect toward the intelligence agencies, a member of Congress content to keep his or her head in the ground, largely oblivious of intelligence operations and budgets, willing to trust the honorable men and women of the IC to get the job done in a world that can be nasty, even brutish. A classic example of the ostrich throughout much of his service on SSCI is Senator Barry Goldwater. He had previously served, recall, as a member of the Church Committee that investigated the spy scandals in 1975, a time during which that panel's chief counsel recollects: "I don't remember anything constructive that Goldwater did."[17] Senator Goldwater joined SSCI when it was established in 1976 and, ironically—given the fact that he had voted against the very creation of the committee—he rose to its chairmanship in 1981. It was one of those bizarre card tricks that history loves to play. While a member of the

Table 8.2 **A Typology of Roles Assumed by Intelligence Overseers in the U.S. Congress**

		Responsibility for Intelligence Support	
		Low	High
Responsibility for Intelligence Evaluation	Low	1 The Ostrich	2 The Cheerleader
	High	3 The Lemon-Sucker	4 The Guardian

Church Committee, he also opposed most of the other reforms recommended by his colleagues, including closer judicial scrutiny of wiretapping operations inside the United States (the FISA safeguard).

Goldwater was content with the system of oversight that existed before 1975: an occasional, usually perfunctory review of secret activities by subcommittees housed within the Armed Services and the Appropriations Committees.[18] Those entities had been largely passive; they never knew about the domestic spying revealed in 1974 (Operation CHAOS), for example, or the plots carried out by the CIA to assassinate selected foreign heads of state, the FBI's attacks against antiwar protesters and civil rights activities (COINTELPRO), or the many other controversial operations uncovered by the Church Committee. Representative (and later President) Gerald R. Ford (R, Michigan) served on the House intelligence oversight subcommittee in the days prior to HPSCI and later recalled that he had never heard a word about CHAOS or the Agency's assassination plots.[19]

A former SSCI counsel has commented on how this head-in-the-sand approach to accountability is ultimately harmful to the intelligence agencies themselves. Looking back on the feckless system of subcommittees prior to the establishment of SSCI and HPSCI, he notes that

> had they taken a more active role, problems might have been prevented. . . . However appealing cursory congressional oversight might seem, in the end it undermines congressional, as well as public, support for the Agency. Better to have overseers who understand and are able to defend the Agency's interests than to have overseers who are largely ignorant of them.[20]

The Cheerleader

A second role type among intelligence overseers is the "cheerleader." In this approach, a member of Congress has removed his or her head from the sand, but only for the purpose of cheering more loudly on behalf of the spy agencies. The life of this kind of lawmaker is mottled by excessive deference to the executive branch and the intelligence community. The cheerleader is interested primarily in advocacy on behalf of intelligence officers and their operations, the uncritical support of espionage budgets (along with the unquestioning grant of spending supplements when requested), and the zealous advancement of clandestine operations at home and abroad against suspected U.S. enemies—or, for that matter, even friends if they get in the way of America's global interests. Senator Dianne Feinstein, the SSCI chair during the committee's writing of its Torture Report, once described this method of accountability: "Some people around here look at oversight as being the best buddy, and always support them, no matter what."[21] A classic illustration in my experience was House Speaker Newt Gingrich (R, Georgia), perhaps the highest placed uber-advocate in Congress that the CIA has ever enjoyed. He routinely arranged to add extra funding to the Agency's budget, whether it requested the money or not. Once when I was in the DCI's office at Langley for an interview, the director related to me the essence of a telephone call with Gingrich that had interrupted our visit—an offer of an extra $1 billion for a CIA program favored by the Speaker.

Cheerleading was the preferred posture of almost all members of Congress before CHAOS exploded into the public conscience in 1974; and, according to an experienced SSCI staffer, Republicans on that committee today "tend to be cheerleaders, while Democrats even criticize their own administrations."[22] A journalist who has written thoughtfully on intelligence issues, James Bamford sees the Hill overpopulated with cheerleaders across the board—Republicans and Democrats alike. "Today," he says, "the Intelligence Committees are more dedicated to protecting the agencies from budget cuts than safeguarding the public from their transgressions."[23]

One compelling reason why politicians find the roles of ostrich and cheer-leader most comforting is that they fear being blamed for the next Bay of Pigs fiasco, or for failing to support intelligence activities that might have halted in their tracks terrorists bound for America on a mission of destruction. The flip-side of this argument, though, is this: What lawmaker wishes to be responsible for intelligence failures and scandals—Iran-contra, poor CIA-FBI liaison, the Iraqi WMD blunder—that might have been stopped if only more vigorous over-sight had been in place? In trying to motivate the Bush Administration to take Al Qaeda and terror attacks against the United States more seriously, the counter-terrorism specialist Richard A. Clarke wrote a prescient insider warning to the NSC in the days before the 9/11 attacks. *"Decision makers should imagine them-selves on a future day when the CSG [the government's Counterterrorism Security Group] has not succeeded in stopping al Qida attacks and hundreds of Americans lay dead in several countries, including the US,"* he said in a memo to national security adviser Condoleezza Rice. He continued: "What would those decision makers wish that they had done earlier? That future day could happen at any time."[24] Rice finally got around to calling an NSC meeting on Al Qaeda just a few days before the 9/11 attack.

During hearings, the cheerleader specializes in "softball" pitches—easy questions designed for hitting over the center-field fence by witnesses from the intelligence agencies.[25] In press conferences, the cheerleader acts as a defense attorney for America's spies, hinting at their behind-the-scenes, "if you only knew" successes; lauding the heroism of intelligence officers and agents;

castigating journalists for printing classified leaks that supposedly imperil the nation (remember the James Risen case in 2004–2005); and warning of threats at home and abroad that could lead to another 9/11 if the intelligence agencies are hamstrung. Such statements by cheerleaders are often true (intelligence officers have behaved heroically as times, for example, as during the covert actions against Al Qaeda in Afghanistan after the 9/11 attacks), yet they can be one-sided, too—completely devoid of a critical eye.

An example of a cheerleader is Representative Edward P. Boland when he became the inaugural chairman of HPSCI in 1977. He had witnessed firsthand how, two years earlier, the Pike Committee had prepared a shrill final report, widely discredited for its partisan tone and anti-CIA biases, and eventually leaked (whether by the committee or by the CIA to discredit Pike remains in dispute). Recall how, appalled by the manner in which the Pike panel had behaved and its ultimate collapse, a majority of House members refused to create a permanent intelligence oversight committee of their own at the time when the Senate established SSCI in 1976. It took another year of debate, and a cooling of anger over how the Pike Committee had embarrassed the House, before representatives voted to establish HPSCI in 1977. To overcome the negative impression left by the Pike Committee, Eddie Boland made a concerted effort in the early days of his HPSCI leadership (from 1977 to 1982) to tamp down partisanship on the panel and to cooperate with intelligence officials. He often swallowed personal skepticism about some covert operations and expressed his support for the secret agencies, determined to show that his committee could be a responsible partner in the world of intelligence (see chapter 4). If he had anything to do with it, the Boland Committee would not be Son of Pike.

Chairman Boland was fortunate that the Constitution gave confirmation powers to the Senate, not the House, and this helped him avoid the partisan warfare that struck SSCI as members reviewed the credentials of individuals nominated by the White House for the DCI position. Moreover, the next six HPSCI leaders were (like Boland) mild-mannered; and, during a period of high turnover during the committee's early years, none of its chairmen served more than two years—an insufficient period of time to gain the requisite experience and knowledge that would allow deep-tissue critiques of IC proposals.

The Lemon-Sucker

A third role type examined in this chapter is the "lemon-sucker," a phrase drawn from President Bill Clinton's characterization of economists. During his tenure, they would come to the White House, all too often bearing sour news. This role—like the cheerleader—is also one-sided, but at the opposite extreme from the cheerleader. For the lemon-sucker, a dedicated skeptic, nothing the intelligence agencies undertake is likely to be worthwhile. Spying is inherently immoral: reading other people's mail, eavesdropping on telephone conversations and social media, stealing documents, perhaps even killing people with exploding cigars, dart guns, daggers, or drones. Ethics aside, the lemon-sucker may also charge the IC with incompetence, say, by pointing to the CIA's inability to dispatch any foreign leader on its assassination hit list during the 1960s, despite many attempts. The failure to anticipate the precise day when the world would witness the fall of the Soviet Union, or aerial terrorist attacks against the United States, provided additional fodder for oversight lemon-suckers.[26]

For the most pure of the lemon-suckers, there is but one solution to their laments: shut down the CIA and its companion agencies. In 1996, for instance, SSCI Senator Daniel Patrick Moynihan (a former Harvard University professor) was dismayed by the Agency's inability to predict the collapse of the Soviet empire. He called for the outright abolition of the CIA.[27] Representative Robert Torricelli (D, New Jersey) became such a zealous lemon-sucker in 1995 that he resorted to an inexcusable tactic for a member of HPSCI or SSCI: he disclosed to the public classified information regarding the Agency's recruitment of a disreputable—indeed, by all accounts, murderous—Army colonel in Guatemala (the Alpirez case, discussed in chapter 4).[28]

Few thoughtful observers of intelligence embrace the role of lemon-sucker. Most lawmakers (as well as intelligence experts in academia) believe that the American spy services—whatever their flaws—are necessary to provide timely information and insight on world affairs to the president and other key decision makers in Washington and throughout the U.S. military commands and diplomatic posts abroad.

The Guardian

The fourth type of intelligence overseer is the guardian. This role conforms best with the aspirations of reformers in 1975. Senator Frank Church, among others, favored a legislative branch that would conduct an ongoing and meaningful review of the nation's intelligence activities. Rather than simply responding to intelligence failures and scandals, Church hoped to prevent these blunders before they occurred. A voracious reader of books on the fall of ancient Rome while an undergraduate and law student at Stanford University, Church would have come across this passage from Gibbon: "Unless public liberty is protected by intrepid and vigilant guardians, the authority of so formidable a magistrate [a monarchy with full powers over government] will soon degenerate into despotism."[29] This perspective became his mantra as a young man when he was elected to the Senate at age thirty-two.

Representative Lee Hamilton, the HPSCI chair from 1985 to 1987 and a blue-chip overseer who consistently displayed seraphic equanimity even in the face of the most exasperating lack of cooperation from the executive branch, has argued that the ideal intelligence supervisors on the Hill are both "partners and critics" of the spy agencies—the very definition of a guardian.[30] Another HPSCI member, Norm Dicks (D, Washington), told an interviewer that "overseeing the intelligence community is like being a good parent: you have to encourage and discipline."[31]

As "partners" with the IC, lawmakers must educate the American people on the virtues of maintaining a robust intelligence capability. Moreover, the secret agencies sometimes legitimately need a friend in court. The members of SSCI and HPSCI are in a position to defend the agencies against unreasonable charges, such as their failure to anticipate fast-moving calamities (as with the rapid disintegration of the Soviet Union that no one could have reasonably foreseen) and the allegation—for which there is no evidence whatsoever—that the CIA has financed its operations through the sale of illegal narcotics over the years, or from earnings generated by the establishment of Agency fronts (false businesses, known as "proprieties" and used as covers for espionage activities).[32]

Without defenders—the cheerleading side of the guardian role—on Capitol Hill, the IC is at a distinct disadvantage in gaining public support for its hidden activities and large budgets. Lawmakers on SSCI and HPSCI can provide citizens with some assurance that the money for their espionage operations are being used properly in the pursuit of valid security objectives. When mistakes are made and scandals occur, citizens then expect their elected representatives to take steps—the critic side of the guardian role—that will prevent them from happening again. Or, better yet, to reduce the number of mistakes and scandals in advance through purposeful *ante facto* hearings, field investigations, and budget reviews (police patrolling).

As effective overseers, lawmakers must also be critics when necessary: searching for, acknowledging, and correcting program flaws. This role requires a capacity, above all, to be objective and to speak out against questionable activities (in closed hearings when operations are too sensitive for public review). Widely considered an avatar of accountability, Lee Hamilton has come as close to this ideal as any member of SSCI or HPSCI. As head of HPSCI, he regularly convened committee meetings, paid close attention to memos and reports from his staff and the intelligence agencies, followed up on media allegations of intelligence wrongdoing or mistakes, and spent oceans of time (like Representative Robinson) reviewing spy budgets in HPSCI's guarded quarters and talking to intelligence professionals there or on their own turf. He was also willing to reach out to other lawmakers involved in intelligence accountability in one way or another, say, building a closer relationship with the chair and members of the House Defense Subcommittee on Appropriations. In this way, Hamilton was able to develop a vital link between the twin congressional procedures of authorization and appropriations. This link would dissolve in later years when lawmakers paid less attention to the establishment of personal ties among colleagues for the good of intelligence accountability and more toward scoring partisan debating points. Hamilton recalls: "I tried to persuade them [members of the Defense Subcommittee] of the value of [HPSCI's] recommendations."[33]

Yet, as seen earlier in this book, Representative Hamilton's tenure as a guardian was blotched by a serious misstep during the Iran-contra scandal of the mid-1980s. When NSC staffers assured him that they were not involved in illegal operations (the Enterprise), Hamilton—along with other SSCI and HPSCI leaders—took these assurances at face value. When *Al-Siraa*, a Lebanese weekly, subsequently revealed the scandal, it was clear that national security advisers McFarlane and Poindexter, along with their deputy, Lt. Col. Oliver L. North, and other officials in the Reagan Administration, had failed to tell the truth to Hamilton and his congressional colleagues about the involvement of the National Security Council in the affair.[34]

The Dynamic Nature of Intelligence Accountability

"All the world's a stage, and all the men and women merely players," wrote Shakespeare in *As You Like It*. "They have their exits and their entrances; and one man in his time plays many parts."[35] During their tenures, some members of SSCI and HPSCI have also played many parts, exhibiting more than one approach to intelligence supervision during their tenures. In addition, even lawmakers who fall into—and remain in—just one of the four "cells" in Table 8.2 can often be some distance apart from one another within that particular "center of gravity." For example, some cheerleaders and lemon-suckers may be mild in their advocacy or criticism (respectively), while others may be rabid. In the case of the ostrich, some lawmakers may poke their heads out of the sand at least once in a while, if only to shout out a cheer or two for the CIA, while others may prefer to stay constantly in the dark. As for guardians, some may be better than others at maintaining an even keel between offering praise and finding fault.

A look at two prominent intelligence overseers at the time of the 9/11 attacks, Senator Pat Roberts (R, Kansas) and Representative Porter Goss (R, Florida), provides a sense of just how dynamic the approaches to intelligence account-ability can be, with changes in viewpoint from time to time even by the same individual.

The Roberts Committee

As the Kean Commission went forward with its work in 2002–2003, SSCI and HPSCI displayed a changed attitude toward intelligence oversight: a for-mer sense of unequivocal support for the IC among most members switched to a new sense of ambivalence. Some members of a Joint Committee that had formed to investigate the 9/11 failures, a panel led by Senator Bob Graham and Representative Goss, publicly scolded the intelligence agencies at the time for their mistakes. Even as a prominent Republican on SSCI (who became its chair in 2003), the once arch-defender of the CIA, Senator Pat Roberts, rued in 2004 that not a single official in the IC had "been disciplined, let alone fired" for the errors related to the terrorist attacks and the subsequent war in Iraq (based in part on the false WMD hypothesis). In dismay, Roberts concluded that the "community is in denial over the full extent of the shortcomings of its work."[36] For well over a year, though, the Roberts Committee stopped short of carrying forward the Senate's 9/11 inquiries by looking into the policy mistakes made by the Clinton and Bush Administrations, let alone any look at how SSCI and HPSCI themselves had never engaged in meaningful oversight activities related to counterterrorism prior to the 9/11 attacks.

With his disappointment in the IC mounting, Roberts metamorphosed into a paladin of spy reform. In July 2004, he released an SSCI report remarkable for its bipartisan consensus and the severity of its critique of the spy agencies, although the chairman continued to waffle on the inattention to intelligence displayed by policymakers (including members of Congress) in the months prior to the inva-sion of Iraq.[37] The Roberts Report excoriated the CIA's forecast in 2002 that Iraq possessed WMDs and might well use them against American homeland targets. This latter argument became central to the Bush Administration's public justi-fication for the invasion of Iraq in 2003, although privately its officials seemed determined to invade Iraq regardless—for a host of reasons, including the desire of the neoconservatives with White House and DoD ties to protect Israel against Saddam Hussein, the Iraqi dictator.[38]

By August 2004, Senator Roberts was ready to propose sweeping changes for the IC, including the dismantling and dispersal of the CIA's component parts into several new agencies led by a National Intelligence Director, or NID.[39] Roberts's embrace of a bipartisan reform effort proved short-lived, however; he soon issued a laundry list of proposals for change endorsed by all but one of the SSCI Republican members, but the chairman never solicited the views of Democrats about these reform initiatives. Moreover, the persistent partisan infighting within both SSCI and HPSCI prohibited the committees from even passing intelligence authorization bills from 2005 to 2009, let alone sweeping reforms. The bills disintegrated under the weight of several contentious provisions, such as a clause in the FY2008 authorization bill proposed by Democrats that tried to force the CIA into using only the softer interrogation techniques spelled out in the Army Field Manual rather than waterboarding and other extreme methods. This proposal caused President Bush to pull out his veto pen. The HPSCI chair at the time, Pete Hoekstra (R, Michigan), bemoaned the inability to enact intelligence authorization bills: "The executive branch can disregard us. . . . So we are irrelevant in that dialogue, and we can't have an impact."[40]

Fortunately, though, SSCI and HPSCI were able to pass six authorization bills in a row after that standoff. The difference? "Authorization bills get passed when lawmakers exercise the restraint required to keep controversial matters—which lead to the bills failing, an administration threat of a veto, or an actual veto—off of those bills," explains a senior SSCI staffer. "Legislating—and governing—requires restraint, not controversy."[41]

During the periods of authorization failures, the House and Senate Appropriations Committees had the budgeting field largely to themselves, setting intelligence spending levels with little concern about what SSCI and HPSCI might prefer to authorize. Newly elected Speaker of the House Nancy Pelosi attempted to reform this imbalance by establishing a Select Intelligence Oversight Panel (SIOP) on the House Appropriations Committee to advise the panel's Defense Subcommittee about annual intelligence funding. While somewhat helpful, SIOP was viewed by most lawmakers as a second-class citizen in the budget process; it had nowhere near the clout that a standing subcommittee on intelligence would have enjoyed on the Appropriations Committee. In 2004, a special resolution passed in the Senate (No. 445) adopted the idea of a formal Subcommittee on Intelligence for its Appropriations Committee; but even though the measure was adopted by senators, the Appropriations Subcommittee on Defense has never let this panel become a reality.

Predictably, the intelligence agencies began to spend more time nurturing their relationships with the Senate Appropriations Subcommittee on Defense, responsible for the spy budget, than with their official overseers on SSCI. The former had become a handy way to obtain extra funding that SSCI and HPSCI opposed—all in all, a devastating blow to the reputation and power of the intelligence authorizing committees. "The Intelligence Community knows [this] and exploits it," observed former HPSCI chair Hamilton.[42] Like the ongoing confusions over military intelligence supervision—presently divided in the House between the Intelligence and the Armed Services Committees—sensible accountability over espionage spending cries out for jurisdictional clarifications between the Intelligence and Appropriations Committees, accompanied by stronger authorization authority for SSCI and HPSCI, as well as the establishment of an Appropriations Subcommittee on Intelligence in both chambers of Congress. Roberts, though, understood the difficulties of change on Capitol Hill. "The No. 1 issue for any chairman of any committee is that you don't give up your turf under any circumstances," he said, "not a spadesful."[43] It is a perverted rule of governance followed by the agencies in the intelligence community as well, exacerbating the DNI's job to improve integration and coordination among the secret agencies.

The Roberts intelligence reform proposals astonished many Capitol Hill observers. The 9/11 attacks and the poor intelligence on WMDs in Iraq had jarred the SSCI chairman and many of his colleagues out of their ostrich and cheerleader postures and into taking a fresh look at the imperfections of the spy agencies. As well, Roberts may have been miffed at the Senate leadership for brazenly assigning intelligence reform to the Government Affairs Committee (perceived by Senate leaders as less partisan) in 2004, rather than to SSCI, during the time in which the Intelligence Report and Terrorism Prevention Act (IRTPA) was being considered. A former SSCI general counsel and CIA IG viewed this humiliation as "the low point" in SSCI's history.[44]

Despite his momentary zeal for reform, Roberts had another and eventually more dominant side to his approach to intelligence: he continued to support virtually every counterterrorism measure proposed by the administration. Moreover, he could be counted on by intelligence professionals to grant their every funding request. The SSCI chair, in brief, displayed a kaleidoscope of role types during the years immediately following the 9/11 attacks.

The Goss Committee

In the House, the dominant Republican leader responsible for intelligence oversight at the time of the 9/11 attacks was Representative Goss, a former operations officer in the CIA as a young man, a member of the Aspin-Brown Commission, and (before he became the last of the DCIs) chair of HPSCI from 1997 to 2004. As HPSCI's leader, Goss was widely considered a diehard supporter of the intelligence agencies.[45] Taken in by General Michael V. Hayden's self-confident briefing style, Goss once recalled: "You really wanted to believe what Mike had to say and absorb it and digest it, rather than question it."[46] Goss's standard response to questions about waterboarding was: "It's a professional interrogation technique."[47]

Goss largely eschewed theatrical displays of partisanship during the earlier years of his HPSCI chairmanship. An exception to this rule was the potshot he took at Bill Clinton on the eve of his retirement from the presidency. Goss claimed on a television talk show: "'We don't care about national security,' said the Clinton people."[48] As a member of the Aspin-Brown Commission, Goss had witnessed firsthand the president's indifference to intelligence matters. It was not until 2003, however, that Goss really laid into the departed Clinton Administration for its neglect of intelligence. The incumbent DCI George Tenet had announced his retirement, effective in 2004, and the sense in Washington at the time was that Goss—still HPSCI's chairman—was angling with the second Bush Administration for this top intelligence job by underscoring at every opportunity his GOP bona fides and deep dislike for Bill Clinton, the favorite Republican bogeyman at the time. Like Roberts did with SSCI, Goss kept HPSCI out of any serious inquiry into the Iraqi WMD errors made during the Bush presidency.

The strategy worked. In 2004, President Bush selected this fellow Yalie for the DCI position vacated by Tenet, who had been thoroughly discredited by mistakes associated with 9/11 and by the faulty predictions about Iraqi WMDs. Goss proved inept as DCI, with widespread managerial snafus that a journalist labeled "fumbling" and "near-comical"—a perspective shared by many observers.[49]

When Goss served as HPSCI chair, the committee's reports on the IC could be graded mostly with "As" for their thoroughness. Further, Goss was the only leader of that committee to keep an office in its suite near the Capitol Dome, and he spent more time on the premises than any previous chair—even beating Hamilton's impressive record of personal engagement in the committee's work. He had also been one of the more energetic members of the Aspin-Brown Commission, pushing steadily for greater attention to oversight issues (although Chairman Brown pushed back harder and, moreover, some of Goss's reform proposals were dubious—such as his desire for a single joint committee for intelligence).[50] The degree of time spent by a lawmaker on oversight activities is, however, no indicator necessarily of the role he or she may play.

As the HPSCI chair, Goss was far more supportive of almost all intelligence programs than were the panel's Democrats; and he consistently advocated increases in the annual intelligence budget (as he had on the Aspin-Brown Commission). Nor during Goss's reign did HPSCI carry out any major intelligence reforms. In an exception to this attitude of unalloyed support for intelligence, HPSCI under Goss did issue (as mentioned in an earlier chapter) in 2004 a blistering critique of CIA human intelligence in key parts of the world, such as the Middle East. So the record that emerges with respect to the Goss Committee is one of fairly energetic reviews of intelligence activities, with a special interest in humint (Goss had served in the DO); however, usually the chairman wore rose-tinted glasses as he reviewed IC activities.

As the final person to serve as DCI (confirmed by the Senate in September 2004 before the DNI position kicked in during early 2005), Goss continued to press sensibly for stronger centralized authority in the IC under the DCI office, as a vital step toward improvements in the interagency sharing of intelligence. As director, though, he was also inclined to go along with the budgetary and program requests of the various agency managers, without much of an in-depth program review. During his DCI confirmation hearings, he vowed to approach the job of intelligence director in a strictly nonpartisan manner; but, once in office, he became a highly partisan, even shrill critic of the Democratic Party and its leaders, especially Bill Clinton's record—although the paramount responsibility of a DCI (or a DNI) is to provide timely, objective information to policymakers, free of partisan coloration. This responsibility relies on a degree of rapport and cordial interaction with the White House, as James Clapper managed with President Obama, despite the DNI's conservative political leanings—although without crossing over into the realm of politicizing intelligence reports to suit the political needs of an administration.

A Wider Set of Role Types

These brief portraits of the SSCI and HPSCI leaders Roberts and Goss indicate how difficult it is to confidently place overseers firmly in one of the four "boxes" of role types. Nevertheless, on balance, both Roberts and Goss qualified most of the time as cheerleaders; other lawmakers, too, display distinct centers of gravity in their approaches to accountability—usually in the cheerleader category. Of course, beyond the four types presented here, one might imagine other roles that overseers could assume. During the Aspin-Brown inquiry, for example, a member of that panel, Senator James Exon (D, Nebraska), rarely bothered to come to Commission meetings, let alone read draft reports, interview witnesses, travel to examine U.S. intelligence programs overseas, or engage in any other tasks carried out by his colleagues on the Commission.[51] Exon showed up for the first meeting; once again midway through the inquiry when a celebrity witness came before the Commission in secret session (former secretary of state Henry Kissinger); and, finally, when the panel's report was finished and the commissioners were invited to brief President Clinton and Vice President Gore on their findings in the Oval Office. In terms of role types, one could invent the "prairie dog" just to fit Exon, for he poked his head out of his underground hole every now and then to see what was going on, only to disappear quickly if it looked like work was on the horizon.

Another role might be the "sleeping watchdog," based on the CIA tale of the slumbering congressional response to a paramilitary briefing in the 1950s; or perhaps a "junkyard dog," reminiscent of when Representatives Aspin and Mazzoli clamped their teeth around the ankle of DCI Turner and refused to let go.[52] A former seasoned CIA officer, who once served as an Agency liaison officer to SSCI and HPSCI, suggested to me some additional role types (as he vented against Congress). "How about 'grandstander,' for the politician who bashes intelligence for political gain?" he asked, only partially tongue-in-cheek. He continued: "Or 'weasel'—a member of Congress who evades responsibility by being ostensibly shocked by matters on which they were fully briefed?"

This same intelligence officer, a former Agency chief-of-station in Europe with decades of overseas experience as well as liaison service on the Hill, pointed to Frank Church as a prototypical grandstander. "Church had presidential ambitions," he argued, "and used a public investigation of intelligence as a grandstand for his ambitions. Those ambitions colored his approach to oversight." For "weasel," his favorite candidate was HPSCI member Jane Harman (D, California), someone "always in sending mode, never in receiving." The weasel, in his lexicon, was another form of lemon-sucking: complaining about an intelligence agency without bothering to learn more about its perspective—listening rather than just criticizing. He is right on that point: good oversight practice requires both. This intelligence officer's favorite target of ridicule was those overseers on the Hill who (he believed) had been fully briefed on both the CIA interrogation program and the NSA metadata operations, but who later found it convenient— when these activities became public and controversial—to maintain they had never had any useful briefings at all. Former House Speaker Nancy Pelosi was his favorite illustration.

The experiences of this good CIA officer in dealing with SSCI and HPSCI had soured him on Congress. He thought the roles lawmakers played were often phony. "Members of Congress are fallible human beings, capable of their own brand of deception and distortion," he wrote to me. "As a result, intelligence officers have a reasonable point-of-view in distrusting Congress and the oversight process."[53] My sense was quite different: that Church had worked hard on the investigation in 1975 and only got seriously involved in presidential politics after this work was essentially completed in December of that year;[54] and that Speaker Pelosi had been briefed, but in such a Delphic manner (no details, and no opportunity to speak with colleagues or staff) that one could understand how she might have later felt misled.

Role Playing in a State of Flux

The two-by-two depiction in Table 8.2 that generates the four role types of ostrich, cheerleader, lemon-sucker, and guardian may well be too confining. "Thus play I in one person many people," declared Shakespeare's Richard II.[55] Still, I think the roles presented here do capture basic oversight proclivities among members of SSCI and HPSCI. I would underscore the caveat, though, that lawmakers may shift from one role to another—and sometimes back again—during their careers. Further, it is worth noting that in a manner most all of the lawmakers on SSCI and HPSCI have been ostriches, in the following sense. Using a different metaphor, a former senior SSCI staffer has observed that "the members never get down into the boiler room, let alone the hold. They're always on the pilot's deck—and driven by stories in the *Washington Post*." He continued: "Their eyes glaze over as soon as one speaks of 'analytic layers' or other complicated intelligence topics. They are interested only in what's in the newspapers."[56]

In Table 8.3, I attempt to illustrate this state of flux among some members of Congress by highlighting the migration of selected lawmakers between over-sight roles. A further caveat: the labeling of lawmakers according to these roles has a certain element of subjectivity to it and is shaped, in part, by how impor-tant the observer believes guardianship is (as, say, opposed to cheerleading). A good balance between support and criticism of the secret agencies—being a guardian—is, in this book, the essence of admirable accountability. Yet, admit-tedly, what may appear as vigorous guardianship to one observer may come across as grandstanding to another.

Senator Ron Wyden (D, Oregon), for instance, strikes many scholars who track intelligence oversight as a smart, hard-driving, conscientious, indefatigable questioner about the state of IC surveillance in the United States and abroad. A level-headed Democratic staffer on SSCI said to me, however, that he viewed Wyden as "a show horse, misleading people into thinking that things are worse than they really are." Nor did he think much of the other chief SSCI dissenter against NSA's programs at the time (2014), Senator Mark Udall (D, Colorado), whom he accused of "milking the metadata program to win votes with libertar-ians in Colorado" as he faced a tight race for reelection (which he lost).[57] My own interpretation is that these senators were sincerely upset by the NSA's activ-ities and the CIA's use of harsh interrogation methods, and that they had the intestinal fortitude to speak out. I mention these examples just to underscore the fact that judgments about role playing can be tricky to substantiate in the murky world of intelligence. Empirical measures are elusive; starting with the attendance records for SSCI and HPSCI meetings (which, recall, are kept locked up in committee files). Thus, one is stuck, as I am here, with insider interviews, media reports, personal observations, and what the overseers themselves say in public.

The Boland Migration

During his HPSCI chairmanship, Representative Boland (as an example) felt it necessary to be a strong partner of the intelligence agencies in the years from 1977 to 1982, as a way to offset the terrible impression left in the minds of his

House colleagues and the public about the Pike Committee's strident attacks against the CIA (chapter 4). As the 1980s progressed, however, Boland— guided by the radar of accumulating experience—began to move away from the posture of cheerleading to assume a more balanced stance as guardian. By 1982, however, he had become exasperated about the intentions of William J. Casey, especially the DCI's use of covert action to advance the agenda of the contras against the Sandinista regime in Nicaragua. Boland, along with a majority in the Democrat-controlled Congress, concluded that the mining of Nicaraguan harbors and the blowing up of power lines (along with other extreme paramil- itary operations pursued by the Agency) were excessive responses to the min- imal threat posed by the quasi-Marxist government in Managua. Here was a galvanizing moment in Boland's movement away from waving pom-poms and toward taking a harder look at intelligence programs. His mutiny against ongo- ing deference to a discourteous Casey was under way. Remember how, between 1982 and 1985, Boland introduced and guided to passage seven successive amendments bearing his name, each further restraining the use of covert action in Nicaragua. Finally, the Agency was prohibited altogether from conduct- ing paramilitary and economic sabotage against the Sandinistas, although the CIA officers were allowed to continue more benign propaganda operations in Nicaragua.

Near the time that his tenure at HPSCI's helm came to an end in 1985, Boland's relations with Casey had dramatically deteriorated. The normally phlegmatic chairman had metamorphosed from cheerleader to guardian to full- fledged lemon-sucker (see Table 8.3). In terms of Tables 8.2 and 8.3, he began in cell two (cheerleader), traveled to cell four for a brief period (guardian), and then settled in cell three (lemon-sucker). Casey had managed to alienate an important figure on Capitol Hill and an erstwhile ally of the IC.

In Boland's case, the stimuli for these changes were twofold: first, what he perceived as the Reagan Administration's overwrought response to events in Central America; and second, a new and aggressive, even arrogant, DCI who did nothing to hide his disdain toward the whole concept of congressional intel- ligence oversight. Policy (paramilitary operations in Nicaragua) and personality (Casey's irascibility) had transformed Chairman Boland's approach to intelli- gence accountability from cheerleader to sourpuss.

Goldwater's Odyssey

Senator Goldwater went on a similar, though still more convoluted, odyssey while at SSCI's helm. With his head in the sand most of the time during the first few years of his SSCI chairmanship (beginning in 1981), Goldwater ini- tially played the role of ostrich, deferring to DCI Casey and the intelligence

Table 8.3 **Illustrations of Role Migration and Stability among Intelligence Overseers in Congress**

Ostrich	Cheerleader
Goldwater (1981–1983)	Boland (1977–1980)
Shelby (1997–1998)	Goldwater (1985)
	DeConcini (1993)
	Graham (2001)

Lemon-Sucker	Guardian
Goldwater (1984)	Boland (1981)
Boland (1982–1985)	Aspin (1977–1982)
Shelby (1999–2004)	Mazzoli (1977–1982)
DeConcini (1994–1995)	Robinson (1977–1982)
Graham (2002–2004)	Hamilton (1985–1987)

agencies. He reasoned that the intelligence bureaucrats should be trusted to do a good job under the trying circumstances of the Cold War. In his mind, the relationship between the CIA and world politics was simple: the Agency versus the Hammer-and-Sickle. During the debate on the War Powers Resolution and efforts by Congress to restore its war powers in 1973, Goldwater had opposed the resolution, arguing that the president knew best when it came to matters of war-making.[58] When Boland began introducing his restrictive amendments against covert action in Nicaragua, Goldwater (his Senate counterpart) declared that the laws proposed by the HPSCI chair were "unconstitutional."[59] He added: "It's another example of Congress trying to take away the constitutional power of the President to be Commander-in-Chief and to formulate foreign policy."[60] As was the case with Vice President Dick Cheney in the second Bush Administration, Goldwater was a leading proponent of the theory of presidential dominance in foreign and security affairs.

An exception to Goldwater's ostrich posture arose during the early period of his SSCI chairmanship, when the Reagan Administration launched an effort to draft a new executive order (eo) on intelligence without meaningful consultation with SSCI and HPSCI.[61] At the time, Admiral Bobby Inman served as Casey's deputy, forced upon the DCI by Goldwater, Birch Bayh (D, Indiana), and several other SSCI members who admired Inman. The admiral had a reputation for being thoughtful and, when he had served earlier in the capacity of NSA director, as someone who had firmly backed FISA and the Intelligence Charter proposal. With Inman, SSCI knew it had a friend highly placed at Langley. He didn't remain

Casey's deputy for long, but the admiral was on the CIA's seventh floor for enough time to warn SSCI that it was being steamrolled by the DCI during the drafting of the new eo. This led Goldwater, upset that his committee was being ignored by Casey, and prodded by Senator Bayh (whose designee was John T. Elliff, the experienced leader of the FBI Task Force on the Church Committee), to bypass Casey and work directly with the Reagan White House. The lobbying by Bayh, plus Goldwater's sense of institutional pride in the Senate—pricked by Casey's cavalier attitude toward the legislative branch of government—led the SSCI chair to slough off his lizard-like dormancy and insist that his oversight committee had to be consulted throughout the entire eo drafting process.

One of Casey's objectives during the drafting of the executive order was to exempt the CIA from Freedom of Information Act (FOIA) requests related to covert action. Goldwater, again urged on by Bayh as well as fellow SSCI member Patrick Leahy (D, Vermont), demanded that the lawyers in the Agency and the White House work out a compromise with the American Civil Liberties Union (ACLU, a champion of expanding FOIA access) that would give something to each side. The result was an "operational files" exception for the CIA, but one that did not cover all covert action records.

The FBI director during this eo squabble was Judge William Webster, a calm and moderate person. He helped SSCI dilute Casey's intentions to roll back the intelligence oversight reforms enacted since 1975. As Elliff recalls, Goldwater also deserves "tremendous credit for all of this" effort to block a rollback to the "good old days."[62] It is a reminder that even ostriches may come up for air now and then—if sufficiently poked by colleagues, staff, and institutional pride. For the most part, though, intelligence accountability remained a subject situated low on the chairman's radar screen. After the clash over the executive order on intelligence, Goldwater put his head back in the sand—at least for a while, until Casey jerked it out again.

In 1984, DCI Casey managed to do the seemingly impossible: he singlehand-edly turned the intelligence community's most reliable ostrich on Capitol Hill—Barry Goldwater—into one of its most vocal skeptics. It was a most remarkable *volte-face*. The catalyst in this transformation (as examined in chapter 4) was Casey's misleading testimony during an appearance before Goldwater's committee. When asked by an SSCI member whether the CIA was mining harbors in Nicaragua, the DCI said no—in his inimitable mumbling fashion. Only later did it become clear that Casey had relied on a misleading technical point: the Agency was not mining *harbors*, it was mining *piers* within the harbors. The DCI seemed mired in binary thinking: the United States versus the Soviet Union; good versus evil; the executive branch (or, more accurately, it turned out, the underground "Enterprise") versus the legislative branch.

Casey's attempt to toy with the SSCI angered its leader, leaving him with a deep bruise of humiliation. Largely a Casey doppelgänger, Goldwater's institutional instincts as a U.S. senator now flared and, temporarily at least, overwhelmed his core blind allegiance to the president and the CIA on anything to do with security. Recall from chapter 4 that he fired off a letter to Casey, with a copy to one of the best venting venues in the nation's capital: the *Washington Post*. The letter castigated Casey for his attempts at wool-pulling on Capitol Hill. "I am pissed off!" declared the SSCI chairman, revealing the stress fractures that can occur when the executive and legislative branches collide.[63]

During this time when Goldwater took the job of top SSCI overseer seriously, the committee attempted to expand the FISA Court warrant procedure to cover FBI physical searches ("black-bag jobs"), augmenting the law's authority for electronic surveillance (also requiring a warrant). The Reagan Administration managed to stymie this effort, though, relying on a Cheney-like doctrine of inherent executive authority—a central tenet of conservative constitutional ideology—to authorize warrantless physical searches by the Bureau. "The ideologues had to live with FISA," Elliff recalls, "but could not bring themselves to expand it."[64] The Reagan Administration won this fight, but without any assistance from Goldwater (normally a reliable ally). Only after the shock of the Ames counterintelligence failure, disclosed in 1994, was the warrant requirement extended to FBI physical searches.

Goldwater's ire over Casey soon receded, however. The SSCI chairman drifted back into a cheerleading role and remained in that mode for the remainder of his tenure through 1985; he and the secret agencies were once again copacetic. This pom-pom approach to oversight better suited his long-standing deference to the executive branch than did the role of lemon-sucker. Never again while captain of SSCI, though, did Barry Goldwater find it prudent to assume the posture of an ostrich; and, as a cheerleader, he kept up with current intelligence initiatives just enough to leave open the possibility that (as before) he just might discover some operations worthy of serious questioning. Herein lies the slim advantage of having a cheerleader, rather than an ostrich, as overseer.

DeConcini Demurs

In another example, DCI R. James Woolsey (1993–1995), whose rebarbative personality could shift mercurially from charming to flatulent to churlish, managed a similar feat with another SSCI chair, Dennis DeConcini (1993–1995), much to the detriment of the intelligence agencies.[65] The two men were as different as chalk and cheese. Woolsey wanted more satellites, while DeConcini wanted him to concentrate on improvements in humint. Moreover, Woolsey had punished only lightly those responsible for failing to catch Aldrich Ames much earlier in his treachery, while DeConcini wanted to see harsher penalties meted out.

Worst of all, when Woolsey proved unable to get his way on satellites, he tried an end run around SSCI by going to the Armed Services Committee (where he had once been a staffer) for help with his request. He may as well have poked a stick into a hornet's nest. Usually a mild-mannered individual, this affront infuriated DeConcini. Woolsey's sometimes imperious manner, buoyed by a Yale law degree and a Rhodes Scholarship, further alienated the SSCI chairman. As Bill Clinton might put it, one would be more likely to see a blue dog driving a school bus than DeConcini and Woolsey having a cordial conversation. Again, a DCI's style, coupled with basic disagreements over intelligence programs and the intelligence reporting procedures expected by DeConcini, turned an oversight committee chair from supporter to staunch critic.

Shelby Sulks

Two additional illustrations about the dynamic nature of intelligence oversight roles come from the period just before and right after the 9/11 attacks against the United States. Richard C. Shelby (R, Alabama) initially came to Congress as a Democrat in 1987 and eight years later joined most of his southern colleagues in a switch to the GOP as a Republican brand of conservatism spread across Dixie. Shelby led SSCI from 1997 to 2001, initially oscillating between the roles of ostrich and cheerleader, apparently seeing few imperfections in the work of the IC during his first year in the committee's wheelhouse. This sanguine outlook would soon begin to fade. In 1998, after India tested a nuclear bomb—an event the CIA had predicted would not happen—Shelby queried DCI George Tenet over the telephone about the intelligence failure. "Senator, we were clueless," replied the DCI, a troubling response that triggered doubts in Shelby's mind about the competence of the nation's spymaster.[66]

Subsequently, on April 26, 1999, Tenet failed to invite the SSCI chairman to the christening of the new George H. W. Bush Center for Intelligence (so named by Congress after the only DCI to become president). The Shelby-Tenet relationship circled the drain in the aftermath of this perceived slight. Finally, after the 9/11 attacks, Shelby came to the conclusion that Tenet had failed to warn the nation sufficiently about the Al Qaeda terrorist peril. The DCI needed to go.[67] Thereafter, the SSCI chair waxed ever more critical of Tenet and the intelligence agencies during the rest of his time on SSCI (where he remained for an additional three years as the ranking minority member when his chairmanship came to an end as the Democrats took over the Senate in 2001). In the case of

Richard Shelby, the 9/11 and Indian A-bomb test failures, coupled with a sense of personal insult over being excluded from the Bush Center ceremonies, transformed a cheerleader into a lemon-sucker. Shelby's periodic histrionics about being slighted by the DCI and the IC became a form of performance art on Capitol Hill. The episode was reminiscent of the time when a plume-plucked Speaker of the House, Newt Gingrich, led an effort in 1995 to shut down the government after the Clinton Administration injured his pride by providing him only secondary seating on an Air Force One trip. At that time, the Speaker said he felt "snubbed," "appalled," and "insulted."[68]

Graham Crackles

The next SSCI chairman (2001–2002), Bob Graham, likewise moved from cheerleader on the Senate Committee (in 2001) to a lemon-sucker (from 2002 to 2004, with Senator Roberts assuming the chairmanship in 2002), as a result of yet another confrontation between an SSCI chair and a DCI—George Tenet again. In this instance, Graham's pique stemmed from procedural slaps in the face, some of which the chairman (á la Shelby) took as a personal affront.[69] Recall that after the 9/11 attacks, Graham became cochair (along with HPSCI's Porter Goss) of a special Joint Committee that temporarily combined SSCI and HPSCI to investigate the 9/11 intelligence failures. Once hearings began, Graham and Tenet soon clashed over the committee's authority and procedures. When Graham asked Tenet to be succinct in his introductory remarks to the panel during hearings, the DCI instead carried on at length—and, according to a newspaper report, in a "somewhat defiant tone."[70] With a preternatural obstinacy, Tenet also refused to declassify some intelligence documents that Graham believed were important for the public record. Furthermore, the DCI frequently caused havoc in the committee's proceedings by denying access to basic intelligence documents related to the 9/11 attacks. He also refused at the last minute to allow scheduled intelligence officers to testify before the committee, even canceling his own appearance scheduled for a closed hearing. Tenet's approach to the Graham-Goss inquiry seemed to have been guided by the final words of King Lear: "never, never, never, never, never."

This is not the way senators—particularly committee chairs—like to be treated. As the Joint Committee wandered through shades of night while the DCI continued to stonewall and slow-roll the investigation, Graham began his transition from cheerleader to lemon-sucker. After Tenet's continued disruptions and disrespect, Graham finally exploded and accused the intelligence chief of "obstructionism" and "unacceptable" behavior.[71] The SSCI chairman had become an eighteen-wheeler with the high beams on. His anger increased further when the executive branch refused to declassify a section of the Joint

Committee report (twenty-eight pages) that, according to Senator Graham, spelled out troubling ties between the 9/11 terrorists and Saudi Arabia.[72]

Feinstein's Metamorphosis

In more recent years, SSCI Chair Dianne Feinstein underwent a startling transformation from cheerleader to lemon-sucker and on to guardian. In the early days of her tenure as the committee's leader (2009–2014), Feinstein supported virtually any intelligence program that came along, including the NSA's adventures in skipping over the FISA warrant requirements, as well as its freewheeling metadata exploration of the telephone and social media contacts of American citizens. Then Democratic staff aides on SSCI presented Feinstein with its finished report on the CIA's use of harsh interrogation techniques. She found the Agency's resort to the brutal questioning of detainees—especially the adoption of waterboarding—beyond the pale of acceptability for the United States. Her revulsion to these methods alone may have pushed her into the posture of lemon-sucker, but push turned to shove when she and her staff began to be attacked by Agency Director John Brennan and his Office of Legal Counsel. When confronted by an aggressive CIA, a once pliable overseer was on the road to becoming unseduced, unawed, unmoved, and unafraid.

The final straw was when the Agency hacked into SSCI staff computers four times (see chapter 5)—a truly egregious violation of the committee's right to conduct an investigation into the CIA's practices without the chilling clandestine arts of that organization being turned against the Senate, as if it were a foreign country that needed to be penetrated and intimidated by spooks. From being a reliable friend in court, Senator Feinstein plunged toward the posture of an angry juror. She had grown as disenchanted with D/CIA John Brennan during her service as an oversight chair as Boland and Goldwater had been with DCI Casey in earlier times. Wearing the armor of institutional and personal pride, Feinstein morphed into a combatant at war, in public, with the maladroit managers at Langley. Remembers a former Agency officer: "[Feinstein] was a serious overseer, knowledgeable, interested in the work.... She was such an important asset, for the CIA. I thought, for the Agency to lose that is horrifying."[73]

Another attribute of Feinstein's that made her an outstanding SSCI chair and eventually a guardian was her willingness to reach across the aisle to Senator Saxby Chambliss (R, Georgia), the panel's vice chairman. Often as not, they disagreed with one another on policy and certainly on politics, but they did so with admirable courtesy.[74] Chambliss lived up to the courtly charm expected of a southern gentleman, even as he voted consistently in the manner of a cheerleader at the same time Feinstein was donning the mantles of lemon-sucker and then guardian.

Feinstein's support for, or opposition to, the IC had been up-and-down during her SSCI tenure. She had been supportive of the NSA's expansive sigint activities, but ardently opposed to the CIA's use of torture. She was again supportive— although this time more thoughtfully, in the manner of a guardian—of the IC's request of Silicon Valley companies to help the FBI gain access to terrorist cell phones, in cases where individuals were suspected of plotting an attack against the United States (an intelligence debate examined in the introduction to this book). She and SSCI Chairman Burr, polar opposites in most respects, surprised observers by cosponsoring a bill that would require (with court warrants) the cooperation of Silicon Valley in such extreme cases—another instance of intelligence bipartisanship on the Hill that had been rare since the early 1990s.

Cheerleaders Rule

Over in the House, HPSCI Chairman Mike Rogers had a different vantage point than Feinstein on the proper responsibilities of an overseer. He was an undeviating defender of the NSA's sigint bulk-collection program, and he often noted that "*we* in the intelligence community" could not afford to miss a clue that might disrupt a terrorist event against the United States—as if HPSCI were a part of the spy bureaucracy, rather than its supervisor.[75] Rogers had once been a FBI agent and seemed to consider himself still part of the IC. When the Obama Administration sent a letter to Congress in 2011 that explained the NSA's metadata program (a decade after its commencement!), Senator Feinstein shared it with her entire committee, as the president requested, while Rogers withheld the letter from several HPSCI members. While chairman of the House committee, he appeared on Sunday television talk shows sixty-two times[76]—far more than any member of SSCI or HPSCI ever, and his message was almost always that of a cheerleader. On one of the shows, he insinuated that Edward J. Snowden was a Russian agent, though he had no evidence to offer in support of this assertion (which no one in the U.S. counterintelligence cadre had ever claimed, let alone substantiated).

Richard Burr, Senator Feinstein's successor as SSCI chair when the Republicans took over the Senate in 2014, displayed all the earmarks of an unquestioning defender of the IC. Like Goss, though, he worked long hours, coming in to the Hart Building (where SSCI is housed) sometimes at 3:30 in the morning to examine new documents sent to the committee from the spy agencies. Even though several of his colleagues had expressed their discontent about inadequate briefings from intelligence officials, Burr said, on National Public Radio, "I don't know that in recent history we've had any problems with the information that's been shared with the committees. Typically, the problem is when information that is meant to stay secret becomes public."[77]

Recall, too, that Chairman Burr attempted to deep-six the SSCI Torture Report by asking that all copies be returned to his committee's quarters, where they would be shielded from FOIA requests and never released to the public. Senator Feinstein persuaded the White House to back away from this request and President Obama did—although the full report still has never been released and Burr has resumed his efforts to ensure the final report never sees the light of day. Burr also wanted to return back to Langley the committee's sole copy of the Panetta Report on CIA torture practices (an in-house review ordered by DCI Leon Panetta), but Senator Feinstein rallied her colleagues against that move, too. Further, Burr opposed the firing—or even the reprimanding—of CIA officers involved in the torture program, including the DDO who unilaterally destroyed the torture videotapes after being told not to by the Congress.

During his first year as the SSCI's leader, Senator Burr cancelled one of the few traditionally open hearings held by the committee: an annual threat analysis presented by the D/CIA or the DNI. By his second year, though, SSCI members were able to persuade Burr to reinstate the practice, as one of the limited opportunities to let the American people gain a glimpse into the global perils the IC is trying to protect the nation against, including military threats, terrorism, pandemics, and other dangers from afar. As for the Agency's internal study that exonerated its spying tactics against SSCI computers, Burr dismissed the criticism from Feinstein and others with the casual observation that "it was a thorough review."[78] Here is Burr's own assessment of his prowess as an overseer: "I believe we do an incredibly effective oversight job on all of the CIA's programs."[79]

In contrast, a savvy observer in Burr's own state of North Carolina, William E. Jackson, Jr., a former Senate staffer, has concluded that the SSCI chairman "is a cog in the machinery of the national security state and an apologist for the multiple intelligence agencies, spurning a substantive discussion of his oversight responsibilities—including when appearing frequently on TV talk shows."[80] A manifestation of this apologetic approach to oversight was Burr's efforts to carry out the wishes of the Trump Administration to squash media stories about Russian attempts to influence the 2016 presidential election, before SSCI had gotten far into organizing its bipartisan probe into the allegations in 2017—a premature stance reminiscent of Frank Church's "rogue elephant" remarks on television in the preliminary stages of his committee's inquiry. "If Chairman Burr is discussing classified matters with the press and pre-judging the Committee's investigation, all at the behest of the White House, it's hard to imagine how he could convince me or the public of his impartiality," SSCI member Ron Wyden said. "If that is the case, I intend to co-sponsor legislation creating an independent commission to investigate Russia's interference in our democracy."[81]

The contrast between Burr and two of the most vocal watchdogs on SSCI, Senators Wyden and Udall, could not have been more stark. Udall, who had shifted from a guardian into a lemon-sucker when he became incensed by NSA and CIA excesses after the 9/11 attacks, said on the Senate floor that "it's not just that Democrats on the Senate Intelligence Committee reached a damning conclusion about CIA torture—the CIA itself reached the same conclusion [in the Panetta Report], but won't admit it. . . . Director Brennan and the CIA today are continuing to willfully provide inaccurate information and misrepresent the efficacy of torture." Udall concluded: "In other words, CIA is lying."[82] As the *New Yorker* reported in the summer of 2015, "Brennan's relations with Democrats on the Intelligence Committee remain hostile."[83]

Wyden was also upset about what he saw as misleading comments from intelligence managers. "Again and again the leadership of the Intelligence Community has said one thing in public and done quite another in private," he complained. "You cannot have good oversight by the Congress if the Congress can't get straight answers from the intelligence leadership."[84] He was especially upset that DNI James Clapper may have misled him about the NSA's metadata activities—a widely reported quarrel between the two men that I have recounted elsewhere, one that ended in some people questioning Clapper's honesty with Congress. I and many others (including Senator Feinstein) have interpreted this run-in as an unfortunate, and unintentional, misinterpretation by the DNI about Wyden's line of questioning in a public hearing, with Clapper thinking that the senator was talking about warrantless wiretapping procedures when in fact the lawmaker was probing into the metadata program. Over the years, Clapper had testified scores of times on the Hill without incident and I think he simply misunderstood the query—an error he soon rectified publicly, providing Wyden with an answer to his original metadata question.[85]

Burr the Protector; Wyden and Udall—the most recent versions of Aspin and Mazzoli—the Questioners. Conservatives versus Liberals; Spy Huggers versus Tree Huggers. Members of Congress come in many stripes, with multiple beliefs about the ideal virtues and best practices of intelligence accountability.

On the HPSCI side of the Hill, Burr's counterpart—also new to the job—was Chairman Devin Nunes (R, California). He got off to a promising start by announcing that his goal was "to make sure we are getting our members out to every corner of the world." He added: "You cannot conduct serious oversight work without getting on the ground and actually talking to the folks that are doing the work."[86] Nunes, though, had opposed publication of SSCI's Executive Summary of the Torture Report. He also accepted the NSA's expansive surveillance practices whole hog; and when HPSCI's ranking Democrat, Adam Schiff (also from California), proposed an amendment to require an annual report on U.S. drone-strike casualties, Nunes led the opposition to defeat the measure in committee (winning by a vote of 15 to 5). Pom-poms in both hands, he was well on his way to leading a series of HPSCI pep rallies on behalf of the IC. In the manner of his SSCI counterpart, Nunes—prematurely and at the request of the Trump White House—rejected the possibility of any inappropriate communications between Trump aides and Russia, even though his committee was still in its planning stage for a formal probe into the subject.[87] Both Burr and Nunes (a member of President-elect Trump's transition team) publicly acknowledged they were assisting the Trump Administration push back against media coverage about contacts between Russian intelligence officers and Trump aides during the presidential campaign.[88] Suspected of being too close to the White House to lead fairly the HPSCI inquiry into possible collusion between Trump aides and the Russians in the election (in early 2017, he had even gone to the White House by himself to confer with top officials about the subject), Nunes had to withdraw himself from chairing the House investigation. He was turning out to be the kind of congressional overseer that DCI William J. Casey would have loved.

Casey was not the only high-ranking intelligence manager who had smoke coming out of his ears when I have raised the topic of congressional accountability in interviews. Another senior intelligence officer I interviewed in Washington, D.C., in the summer of 2016, suddenly erupted into volcanic scatology at the mention of intelligence oversight on Capitol Hill. Outdoing even Casey in his frequency of f-bomb dictional punctuations, this individual (who wished to remain anonymous) excoriated the SSCI and HPSCI staff as mediocre, and he viewed the lawmakers on these Committees as inattentive to their duties. Besides, it was he—not they—who had been in the intelligence business for decades, including during two major wars when he was in the field. Even SSCI's Richard Burr, widely known as a reliable intelligence cheerleader, came in for a tongue-lashing as a good supporter on TV but poor at delivering funds for spy programs.

I agreed that the level of inattentiveness of some SSCI and HPSCI members was unfortunate; but, in my experience, the SSCI and HPSCI staffs were first-rate—across the aisle. Many of those who had left these Committees mid-career had gone on to illustrious achievements elsewhere; and most who stayed were smart and dedicated overseers, working longer than normal hours to improve U.S. intelligence capabilities and to maintain a proper balance between security and liberty.

A target of ire, as well, during the interview was the amount of time IC leaders were expected to spend talking with a proliferation of intelligence oversight panels within the executive branch, on top of the endless requests for appearances on Capitol Hill—"a bottomless time sump," he said. I reminded him of why accountability was important, pointing to CHAOS, COINTELPRO, and Iran-contra, plus the most recent excesses of the CIA (renditions, torture) and the NSA (FISA violations, metadata collection). He would have none of it. "Who's watching the Congress is what I want to know!" he burst out. I was tempted to answer "the voters," those citizens across the land who had no opportunity to cast ballots on the behavior of bureaucrats, but who could signal their displeasures to their own representatives in Congress. Then I could have gone into Madison's warnings about the corrupting influence of power. I had a recent example in mind: just that week, Vice Admiral Ted "Twig" Branch, the director of Naval Intelligence, and Rear Admiral Bruce Loveless, another Naval intelligence officer, became the focus of a criminal investigation for corruption.[89]

As he continued to express his frustration with Congress, he shifted his focus to Burr's House counterpart—Devin Nunes—who drew the most vitriol, for punishing the IC with budget cuts when it failed to respond to the representative's requests for help back in his home district. The Nunes family is of Portuguese descent, having immigrated to California from the Azores. Some of his constituents boast this heritage, too, and continue to have financial holdings in the Azores. When the Pentagon threatened to sharply reduce the profile of the U.S. base there, Lajes Airfield, Nunes went into action to protect these assets. Lajes is the second largest employer in the Azores and the lawmaker wanted to shield and stimulate the economy in the islands, not stand by and witness its decline. Nunes introduced a bill called the Africa Counterterrorism Initiative Act which, he argued, would strengthen Lajes as a major forward base for fighting against terrorism on the African continent. The Pentagon resisted Nunes's initiative, however, preferring to save some $35 million by downsizing the airfield. As HPSCI chairman, Nunes threatened to cut family benefits for DIA personnel, unless his wishes were fulfilled by making Lajes one of America's major staging spots for counterterrorism operations in Africa. In the view of the senior intelligence officer, Nunes had crossed the line—blatantly—that separates oversight from micromanagement, and misused his authority for narrow constituency interests over the national interest.

SSCI dissenters Udall and Wyden did have at least one kindred soul in HPSCI's ranks: Representative Rush Holt (D, New Jersey). He often expressed a regret that most of his colleagues on the committee saw their roles "as enabling the intelligence agencies to operate unencumbered, even to the extent of allowing the Intelligence Community to make the American public a target in order to protect the public"—an allusion to the NSA metadata program. Pointing to his committee's report on the annual intelligence authorization bill introduced in 2014, Holt noted:

> Nowhere in the Committee report is there any acknowledgement of the public's concern over mass surveillance. Nowhere is there a hint that the NSA has acted improperly in subverting encryption standards used in software installed on personal computers, nationwide. Nowhere

does the Committee note the NSA's practice of breaking into shipping boxes that contain American electronic products, inserting covert surveillance technology, resealing the boxes, and sending them on to the purchasers, to the detriment of U.S. industry.

Lamenting the "staggering failure of oversight," Holt, who appreciated the value of good intelligence work and was more of a guardian than a lemon-sucker, posed the question: "Who watches the watchmen? For now," he said, "the truthful answer is 'nobody.' We can do better."[90]

Wanted: More Guardians

The government of the United States is built on the concept of sharing power among the three branches. In addition to making laws, a primary duty of the legislative branch is to keep watch over the sprawling bureaucracy that lies at the feet of the president. Before 1975, members of Congress largely overlooked their responsibility to supervise spy activities, because the job was considered too time-consuming as well as daunting in the expertise it required. Intelligence oversight also cut into time reserved for campaign fund-raising, and it provided little opportunity for credit-claiming back home vital for reelection purposes, since most intelligence operations are too sensitive for public discussion. Better to spend the working hours raising campaign funds and pursuing legislative goals that are more closely covered in the newspapers and on television. Finally, and not least of the lawmakers' concerns, to know about an intelligence operation was to share culpability if, like the Bay of Pigs, it blows up—not an inviting scenario for a politician.

Ever since the advent of the post-1975 era of intelligence accountability, lawmakers have continued to feel these tugs that shift their attention away from monitoring the nation's spy activities. Yet what if there are future intelligence failures that lead to even more devastating attacks against the United States than 9/11? What if lawmakers could have prevented these failures by way of a more thorough review of intelligence activities, as well as by probing into the state of information sharing in the IC and into the quality of intelligence collection and analysis? What member of Congress will want to explain to constituents why he or she was too busy fund-raising to ensure—through hearings, budget analyses, and program reviews—the readiness of intelligence agencies to protect the United States?

Being a dedicated intelligence overseer is a job that does carry some risk, particularly having to share the blame if things go wrong. During the Cold War, most members of Congress thought it best to let America's spies go their own way in the back alleys of the world, fighting a hidden war against global Communism. The 1975 revelation of domestic spying against American citizens—the same citizens the CIA and its fellow agencies had been created to protect—thoroughly discredited that philosophy of legislative trust and benign neglect. Operation CHAOS stirred a realization among many elected representatives, as well as overseers in the executive and judicial branches, that it was vital for them to become more involved in matters of intelligence accountability.

In the years since 1975, however, these overseers have exhibited varying degrees of commitment to the task of supervising the hidden side of government. Among the oversight roles of ostrich, cheerleader, lemon-sucker, and guardian, the first two types have proven to be predominant in the Congress—especially cheerleading. Sometimes lawmakers on the intelligence oversight committees in the House and Senate have migrated from one role to another. This movement can occur because lawmakers have been personally affronted or irritated by their relationships with DCIs, DNIs, and other IC leaders; or because they have been shocked into a different posture than normal by a serious intelligence failure or scandal. One of the chief catalysts for motility has been a sense of injured institutional pride, when SSCI and HPSCI members perceive that intelligence officials have treated Congress with a lack of proper institutional respect.

Scholars and journalists need to conduct further investigations into the motivation behind the oversight roles selected by members of Congress, as well as how these roles may change over time. Especially important will be efforts to fathom why most SSCI and HPSCI members have failed to act as guardians. This model was widely accepted by reformers in 1975 as the ideal, because it balanced support for intelligence with a determination—through persistent program review—to avoid future intelligence failures and scandals. How can members of Congress be encouraged to spend more time on serious program evaluation, gladly tasting the fruits of their oversight responsibilities? What incentives can be introduced into the culture of Capitol Hill to make accountability more of a valued pursuit?

One might think that enough incentives already exist. After all, it is plain to see that robust intelligence accountability in the United States will help defend the American people against additional spy scandals. Another powerful motivation should be the desire to temper the nation's intelligence shield, warding off future terrorist attacks; or to avoid additional faulty conclusions about events and conditions abroad that may draw the nation into unwarranted foreign military adventures, as occurred when the false assumption of unconventional weaponry in Iraq led the United States into an expensive, unpopular, and enduring war.

Regardless of all the good reasons for being a dedicated spy overseer, most observers agree that members of Congress are performing far below their potential when it comes to supervising the secret agencies. Oversight remains a neglected stepchild on Capitol Hill—a distant concern. Correcting this condition is a worthy challenge for educators, journalists, civic groups, the congressional leadership, and indeed all public-minded citizens. And, as always, the vote is available as a powerful tool to rid the Congress of members who fail to understand the importance of their duty to provide a check on secret power.

PART IV

THE PRACTICE OF INTELLIGENCE ACCOUNTABILITY

9

In the Trenches

Collection and Analysis, Covert Action

Hands-On Accountability

As outlined at the beginning of this book, America's intelligence community has three primary missions: the collection and analysis of information from around the world, especially regarding threats and opportunities that face the United States; the use of covert action to advance the nation's global interests with a hidden hand; and counterintelligence, of which counterterrorism is a vital subset, defined briefly as those activities designed to protect the nation against hostile intelligence services and terrorists. The organizations devoted to intelligence accountability for this triad face towering obstacles, given that each of the missions is enveloped in secrecy. This chapter explores the question of oversight for collection and analysis and for covert action, focusing especially on the latter for two reasons. First, the literature on collection and analysis (the least opaque of the missions) is vast and the requirements for improved accountability are reasonably well understood.[1] Second, covert action—a fraught topic with a nimbus of perilous glamour—is concealed by so many curtains of secrecy that it remains widely misunderstood, subject to controversy, and held to insufficient levels of accountability. Oversight for counterintelligence is addressed in chapter 10.

As we have seen in earlier chapters, five significant intelligence shocks—failures and scandals—have occurred since 1975 when the United States adopted rigorous standards for maintaining genuine legislative supervision over the secret services. Each of these shocks—Operation CHAOS; Iran-contra; Somalia/Ames (a combined stimulus, as explained in chapter 4); the 9/11 attacks; and the Iraqi WMD analysis—led to prominent investigations. Three other significant spy-related controversies occurred after the 9/11 attacks; however, they did not reach a high-enough level of public and official concern to trigger major inquiries, although they did provoke considerable dispute. They included the NSA's sigint operations aimed at Americans; the CIA's harsh

313

interrogation techniques used against suspected terrorists; and the firing of missiles from Agency-controlled drones at suspected individual terrorists and their encampments, attacks accompanied by the "collateral" casualties—the death of innocent civilians—that inevitably occur when bombs are dropped on cities and villages. (The subject of drone covert actions is examined later in this chapter.) Where each of these benchmark events fits within the triad of intelligence missions is displayed in Table 9.1.

The collection-and-analysis category has one-and-a-half of the most significant firefighting shocks: the failures in Somalia and the suspected WMDs in Iraq. (The former accounts for half of the reason why a fire alarm sounded in 1994 that led to the establishment of the high-profile Aspin-Brown Commission, the other half being the Ames case.) The counterintelligence/counterterrorism

Table 9.1 **Major and Near Major (Firefighting) Failures and Scandals, by Intelligence Mission, 1975–2016**

	Intelligence Mission		
	Collection and Analysis	*Covert Action*	*CI/CT**
Year			
1975			Operation CHAOS
1987		Iran-contra	
1995	Somali military <————————————> threat**		Aldrich Ames**
2001			9/11 attacks
2003	Iraqi WMDs		
2005–2013			[FISA Court bypass and metadata controversy***]
2014			[Torture***]
2008–2016		[Drone attacks***]	

* Counterintelligence and counterterrorism.

** These two events combined to reach the threshold for a major intelligence investigation (the Aspin-Brown Commission).

*** These counterterrorism activities never reached a high-enough threshold of concern to trigger major national inquiries and are thus bracketed in this table; but they were subjects of wide debate in the media and the government nonetheless and are therefore discussed in this chapter. As noted in the text, since drone assassinations are both a PM and a CT tool, Table 9.1 has the entry labeled "Drone attacks***" straddling both the "Covert Action" and the "CI/CT" columns.

(CI/CT) category has two-and-half of the major shocks, including CHAOS and Ames, plus 9/11. This CI/CT is also the "mission home" of the three events that proved contentious across the nation from 2005 to 2015 (and continuing), but have yet to reach a firefighting threshold: the NSA's FISA Court bypass and metadata controversies, the CIA's resort to torture, and the use of drones in counterterrorism operations. Drone assassinations have another "mission home" as well: they are paramilitary operations, which fall into the "Covert Action" category (in addition to the CI/CT category). This shared "mission home" is illustrated by having "Drone Attacks" straddle these two categories in Table 9.1 The NSA excesses, the CIA torture program, and drone assassination attack—each on the verge of triggering major national inquiries (and each worthy of this level of attention)—never made the "hook-and-ladder truck" list, probably because they occurred in the anxiety-ridden post-9/11 environment of global terrorism. After the events of 9/11, many intelligence overseers were concerned about being labeled as leaning too far toward liberty and privacy at the expense of counterterrorism and security.

Public dissent against the NSA's programs, once finally revealed—partially by the *Times* in 2005 and more by Snowden in 2013—did cause President Obama to appoint a small commission to examine sigint operations directed against Americans, known as the President's Review Group on Intelligence and Communications Technologies (see chapter 5). This panel issued a report that was highly critical of NSA's overreaching, but the group's work never attained the level of public attention to qualify as one of the major firefighting episodes. The same is true of the SSCI Torture Report. Though an impressive Democratic staff inquiry (whatever one thinks about its widely discussed flaws), it also was never a major, bipartisan national inquiry led by high-profile investigators—including members of Congress or presidential appointees (sometimes both) actually engaged in the investigative work, as with the other hook-and-ladder events. The public discussion of drone paramilitary warfare has also garnered broad and sustained attention, but so far it has not led to an investigative probe in the manner and magnitude of the Church or the Inouye-Hamilton Committees.

Finally, the covert action category in the triad has just one example as a high-profile inquiry: the Iran-contra affair—although remember that drone assassinations (still below the firefighting threshold) fall into the covert action category as well as the CI/CT category. Arguably, though, the covert action side of the scandal that focused on Nicaragua threatened constitutional government in the United States more than any of the other intelligence-related events, as a result of the Reagan Administration's creation of a secret "government" known as the Enterprise, along with its disregard of the Boland Amendments, the Hughes-Ryan Act, the 1980 Intelligence Oversight Act, and Article I of the Constitution (the congressional appropriations authority).

While some of these abuses of power within the triad have been more devastating than others, the bottom line is that failure and scandal can arise within all three intelligence missions and, therefore, attention to vigorous accountability is vital across the triad.

Accountability and the Collection-and-Analysis Mission

Prevention against further assaults against the homeland, or to U.S. interests abroad and the safety of American citizens living or traveling overseas, requires reliable information about world affairs. Further, since threats may arise at home as well (consider the bombing of the Murrah Federal Building in Oklahoma City by white supremacists in 1995, and the terrorist killings in San Bernardino, California, in 2014), the United States must also keep an eye out for internal threats—be they harmful leaks from within the government or violence perpetrated by deeply alienated individuals or foreign agents operating within America's borders. The obligation of the IC to warn the nation against this broad range of perils is, as a DCI once emphasized, "the absolute essence of the intelligence profession."[2] In this portion of the book, I look at intelligence collection against targets that are neither terrorist organizations nor hostile foreign intelligence services; that subject is addressed in the next chapter on counterintelligence. Here I am interested chiefly in military, political, and economic threats, as well as opportunities abroad, that the IC is expected to uncover and track. At the center of this mission stands a process known as the "intelligence cycle."

The Intelligence Cycle

Planning and Collection

To simplify a complex set of relationships and activities for purposes of clarity, the concept of "collection and analysis" may be thought of as a shorthand expression for the gathering and interpretation of information that features several phases, accompanied by multiple, ongoing interactions and periodic interruptions. The opening phase in this "cycle" consists of planning sessions conducted each year in the White House, with ongoing updates, to decide exactly what kinds of information should be collected from a long list of possibilities (see Figure 9.1).[3] This formal "threat assessment" attempts to rank potential targets into a hierarchy of priorities, which may change from time to time. For example, at the top of the threat assessment list may be the terrorist groups ISIS, Al Qaeda, the Nusra Front (an Al Qaeda offshoot), and Boko Haram at the top, along with concern about cyberattacks against the United States, followed by WMD proliferation, North Korean belligerence, and Russian threats toward Eastern Europe, all the way down to an interest in oil sales in Venezuela or, at the bottom, perhaps the plight of polar bears in an age of melting ice floes. (Polar bears and snowy owls only make the list if the White House has someone high up who is concerned about the implications of climate change in all of its manifestations, as was the case during the Clinton Administration in the person of its vice president and noted environmentalist, Al Gore.[4])

On the cyber front, intelligence specialists in this domain worry especially about the defensive side of the picture. The United States is already proficient at cyberattacks against adversaries, when necessary. More difficult is defending against such attacks aimed at North America. These attacks have included Russian hacking of computers in the Democratic National Committee and state election databases in Arizona and Illinois in 2016, in a worrisome set of clandestine operations evidently designed to tamper with the U.S. presidential election. Cyberattacks now absorb considerable attention from cyber units throughout the IC, in cooperation with intelligence counterparts in the Canadian government.[5]

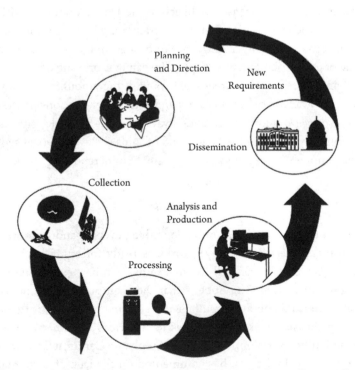

Figure 9.1. The Intelligence Cycle. Source: Adapted from *Factbook on Intelligence*, Office of Public Affairs, Central Intelligence Agency, October 1993, p. 14.

Collection

The next phase is the assignment of assets for the actual gathering of the desired information set forth in the threat assessment: human agents (humint), as well as machines (techint) such as reconnaissance aircraft (piloted and unpiloted), satellites, blimps, and ground-based listening devices as small as a fly or antennae as large as several adjoining football fields.[6] Machine "platforms" crisscross the skies over enemy targets at various altitudes, from deep in space to drones hovering close over a mountain village. Humint "case" or "operational" officers attempt to recruit foreign assets in every important venue, say, the prime minister's speechwriter, the trade minister's lover (or the trade minister herself), or the general's chauffeur. Data on current wheat yields in China, a photocopy of an Asian president's appointment calendar, the sources of weaponry purchased by ISIS on the black market, the state of Boko Haram's penetrations throughout northern Africa, and thousands of other small rivulets of information then accumulate into a flood tide of data pouring back from around the world to the CIA, NSA, NGA, and their companion agencies.

Processing

Once the information is transmitted back to the United States, it must be processed into a readable format. That means translating key sigint intercepts from Arabic (or some other foreign language) into English; interpreting the meaning and value of geoint photographs snapped by cameras orbiting on satellites or on drones flying quietly over a target—always with the amount of incoming data outracing the availability of translators and interpreters to convert these "raw" findings into useful information; and always with the valuable "signals" in the information only specks in the huge cloud of "noise" that composes sigint interceptions, geoint photography, masint data, and humint reporting (see chapter 1).[7]

Analysis

At this point the information, combined with an ever expanding array of opensource (osint) materials in today's world, is ready for study by Ph.D.-toting area or subject experts, as well as thousands of other specialists inside the IC—in a word, analysis. The hope is that they can provide an understanding of global events and conditions sufficiently edifying to yield reports helpful to Washington decision makers, as well as to America's diplomats, development officers, and military personnel overseas.[8] Stephanie Carvin, a Canadian professor of international relations, has commented on the lack of accountability in her country when it comes to the intelligence cycle. "There is no guidance as to how this role should be done," she writes, ruing the lack of adequate oversight "as to the delivery of intelligence products, how those products are produced, or whether those products are delivered in a timely manner."[9] Her concerns apply to the United States as well.

Here is the crux of the intelligence cycle: to give meaning to the buzz and confusion of world affairs, and to the possible machinations of subversives inside the United States (the counterintelligence side of collection). The core function of intelligence, as Michael Goodman has put it, is "to keep readers as informed as possible, to reduce ignorance, and to provide context for decision making to take place."[10] Etched on a wall in the office of the DNI is a motto that speaks of intelligence as a search for "decision advantage." Who is scheming in what manner and against whom, and when, with what likely consequences for the United States?

Given the size of the planet, along with methods adopted by America's adversaries for concealing their activities (North Korea's construction of atomic bombs in deep underground caverns, for instance), along with the sheer limits that human beings labor under in their inability to anticipate future events (no crystal balls in real life), this assignment of bringing insight to the unevaluated information is a staggeringly difficult task, replete with multiple opportunities for misjudgments and omissions. Even an annual expenditure of $80 billion—or double that amount—will not tear away all of the veils that hide anti-American intrigues hatching in unfriendly foreign capitals or evasive terrorist cells; yet, as a matter of national survival, the United States (like every other nation that can afford it) tries to strengthen its intelligence capacities—often referred to as the "first line of defense" against danger. Generous spending can help, but necessary, too, are well-trained information processors (linguists, photo interpreters, information technology whizzes) who must prepare and gather information for study and interpretation, which is performed by experienced and talented analysts in the "Analysis" phase of the cycle.

Dissemination

Indispensable as well, and the final step in this sequence, one must have receptive policy officials willing to take the time to absorb intelligence reports, smart enough to understand them, and courageous enough to make decisions based on reliable data rather than just whims or domestic political calculations.[11] In this dissemination phase of the cycle, two potentially fatal traps lie in wait— even after all the other difficult terrain has been traversed, from wise planning, to successful collection, thorough processing, and deep-thought analysis. The first trap is the challenge of attracting the attention of beleaguered policy officials, no mean feat that requires the cultivation of rapport between intelligence officers and decision makers—or else the information will simply languish on the desks of analysts at Langley or other IC agencies, with intelligence reports becoming just so many "self-licking ice cream cones" (the disparaging phrase in Washington for ignored spy reporting). National Intelligence Estimates, or for that matter the exclusive *President's Daily Brief*, often face a distracted readership, as frenetic policymakers race from one meeting to another with little time for pondering intelligence reports. Or, in some cases, policymakers are just plain lazy or incompetent; they have no interest in wading into a serious analysis of world affairs. Even such popular presidents as Ronald Reagan and Bill Clinton had little interest in studying—or even reading—intelligence reports, a stance that got Reagan into profound trouble with the Iran-contra scandal, and Clinton into the tragedy of the Somali attacks against U.S. Special Forces and, soon after, the Rwanda massacre. More recently, no president has publicly expressed more disdain for intelligence than Donald J. Trump as he entered the White House in 2017.

The second trap, and worse still, intelligence reports can be politicized at the stage of dissemination, that is, twisted by intelligence leaders to please superiors in the White House. One thinks of DCI George Tenet and his offering of intelligence-to-please during the Iraqi WMD disaster. In these circumstances, the necessary degree of rapport between intelligence and policy officials turns into sycophancy. More common, though, is for policymakers themselves to pluck out from intelligence reports only those items that support their biases, dismissing the rest—a phenomenon known as "cherry-picking." Even more damaging, policymakers have been known to alter intelligence reports to suit their own political needs, or they have dismissed reports altogether. These forms of "politicization" are the cardinal sins of the collection-and-analysis mission.

One example was the refusal of the Bush Administration to accept reliable reports from the CIA that indicated Iraq's Saddam Hussein had never purchased tons of yellow-cake uranium from Niger, as rumors embraced by the White House alleged in 2002.[12] Another recent illustration emerges from a House report prepared by GOP representatives in 2016, concluding that senior officials in Centcom (United States Central Command) doctored assessments of American efforts to defeat ISIS. Supposedly these officials sought to make it appear that the U.S. troops were doing better in countering the terrorist group in Iraq than was actually the case. The officials, so the argument goes, wanted to support the optimism projected to the public by the White House about its counterterrorism activities. A DoD spokesman cautioned, though, that before assuming the worst one should remember that "experts sometimes disagree on the interpretation of complex data."[13] Republican chairs for a coalition of House national security committees in Congress (HPSCI among them) established a task force created to examine the controversy—a laudable police-patrolling exercise. The task force found that Centcom analysis had good reason to believe that their superiors were doctoring the bleak assessments regarding U.S. efforts to defeat ISIS.[14] Democrats on these panels wrote their own report, which largely agreed with the GOP findings. As inquiries continued, the Obama Administration denied exerting pressure on the senior military Centcom officials accused of altering the analysts' conclusions.

The Ingredients for Good Analysis

Along the way, as information moves from the field to the Oval and other key decision arenas, the evolving product—the intelligence report, be it a high-status document like the *PDB* or merely a short profile (a "baseball card") on the personality of a foreign trade negotiator—will ideally meet several criteria of excellence. Whether these standards are achieved may well determine the security of the United States or, at least, its success in achieving policy goals, large and small. When they review the quality of intelligence reporting, overseers must take into account this list of desired attributes for reporting from the secret agencies—the end result of the billions of dollars spent on collection and analysis:[15]

- **Accuracy**: While no analyst will be clairvoyant, he or she must strive for reliable reporting. The NIE on Iraqi WMDs was a case of abject failure. From this fateful episode, the IC learned—among other hard lessons—not to accept liaison sources at face value (such as Germany's "Curve Ball"), and to eschew blind extrapolation of earlier data (as from Iraq in 1991). The accidental bombing of the Chinese Embassy in Belgrade in 1999, based on an out-of-date NGA map that indicated the building was still an arms depot, is an example of an inaccurate report that had unfortunate consequences. Many Chinese continue to believe the bombing was intentional.

    Another major controversy over the question of accuracy arose just the previous year. In 1998, CIA masint devices seemed to have sensed a chemical weapons precursor called Empta, required for the production of the lethal nerve agent VX, in a pharmaceutical factory near Khartoum. In light of the fact that Osama bin Laden had once had ties with this factory when he lived in Sudan, Agency analysts put two and two together and concluded that it was in fact producing chemical weapons. President Clinton approved a cruise missile attack on the factory. Afterward the president of Sudan, his factory in ruins, angrily claimed that the facility was merely producing aspirin and other common medicines. Several journalists covering the story also thought the Agency had reached a premature conclusion. The top WMD proliferation specialist at Langley conceded that assessments of this kind were difficult to make, because "the turning of a few valves can mean the difference between a pharmaceutical company and a chemical or biological plant." Nevertheless, he and staff remained resolute that the CIA had gotten this one right, protests to the contrary notwithstanding.[16]

- **Timeliness**: No one likes to read yesterday's newspaper. The acronym OBE ("overtaken by events") is not what an analyst wants to see scrawled in ink by a policymaker at the top of a rejected report.

- **Relevance**: The best way to end up with a self-licking ice cream cone is for an analyst to write on something devoid of any connection to the problems that have silted up a decision maker's inbox. Al Qaeda, ISIS, WMDs, North Korean missiles, Iranian adherence to its nuclear arms agreement with the United States, the state of sectarian fighting in Libya and Syria—these reports will be read, not ones that focus on "Vodka Consumption among Males in Siberia" or "Fishing Practices in the South Pacific" (a subject of significance to New Zealand intelligence services concerned about the threat of Japanese fishermen intruding into Kiwi waters, but not to the White House and the NSC). An important way to enhance relevance is for the intelligence agencies, or the DNI, to place intelligence liaison officers within the various policy departments and agencies. By hanging out around the water cooler, going to lunches, and attending staff meetings, the liaison officer can return to his or her home intelligence agency at the end of the day with advice about what the policymakers are working on. In this manner, agency analysts can steer back to policymakers data and insights that correspond with the problems currently in their inboxes.[17]

The risk always exists that something seemingly unimportant now may become significant later. The spy agencies didn't bother much with Rwanda in the 1990s—until it turned into a bloodbath of tribal warfare. The possibility of such "pop-up" events in world affairs requires some attention in the IC, even in cases of seemingly remote possibilities. Moreover, since New Zealand is an ally, assistance with its concerns about Japanese fishing excesses may be a worthwhile (if secondary) subject for some sharing of U.S. satellite surveillance with Wellington on the location of Tokyo's marauding fishing boats.

- **Readability**: A recent examination of PDBs from the 1960s—a rare public release of this closely kept, highly classified document—suggests a surprisingly poor level of writing quality. "A sticky situation could be brewing in Buenos Aires," suggested an analyst, without much substance to back up this florid assessment.[18] Reports must be cleanly written in basic English prose, á la Strunk and White. Purple prose, or analysis that is mathematically or conceptually dense beyond comprehension for policymakers—as if torn from the pages of the *American Political Science Review* or an econometrics journal—will find few readers in the lofty perches of the executive branch. (The Les Aspins and Harold Browns of the world—secdefs, with Ph.D.s and avid appetites for reading esoteric reports—are uncommon.) Four-color graphs, smooth sentence structure, short paragraphs, eye-catching photographs: here is the prescription for readability. It is not enough for an analyst to be bright; he or she must also learn to *market* intelligence findings. Toward that objective, a reputation for lucid exposition is of enormous value.

- **Brevity**: Shakespeare understood that "brevity is the soul of wit, and tediousness the limbs and outward flourishes."[19] So did General George C. Marshall, who cautioned his aides during World War II (including Dean Rusk, who told me about this admonition) to "avoid trivia." Keep it short. When dealing with busy policymakers, getting to the point is the point. In an oral briefing, one successful analyst simply held up a one-page diagram of Chinese aid to Africa spiraling downward. The secretary of state at the time got the message and moved to increase the number of U.S. development projects in this oft-ignored continent.

- **All-Source Fusion**: The 9/11 Commission Report criticized the IC for its failure to share information that had been collected and analyzed by the separate spy agencies about the activities of Al Qaeda prior to the attacks against the United States. The best intelligence reports are usually based on a blending of intelligence findings from each of the agencies, a synergism of the "ints," which is known in the IC as "all-source fusion" (or "jointness" in the Pentagon). This elusive goal of intelligence integration has existed since the founding of the CIA in 1947 and remains imperfectly met today. The most troubling example in recent years is the failure of the CIA and the FBI to coordinate their intelligence about the 9/11 hijackers as these terrorists infiltrated the United States. The foremost goal of the longest-serving DNI, James Clapper, was to further knit together the sixteen major espionage agencies, in hopes of a more frequent achievement of all-source fusion in intelligence reporting.

- **Objectivity**: As mentioned earlier, politicization is the most dreaded of all intelligence shortcomings. Above all, reporting from the IC has the foremost obligation of being unbiased—and accepted as such by policymakers (unless they have good evidence to conclude otherwise).

As straight as the CIA could call the unhappy news of impending military defeat in Vietnam, however, neither President Lyndon Johnson nor President Richard Nixon could accept its analysis. Nixon attempted to fire officers at Langley who questioned his policies in Indochina—indeed, fully 50 percent of the Agency's senior staff. The president recoiled from, as he put it, the "primarily Ivy League and the Georgetown set" at the CIA. (In the Agency's early days, it had been chastised by some outsiders for being too pale, male, and Yale; but by Nixon's time, the CIA had diversified, with, for instance, Notre Dame University and Brigham Young University becoming popular recruitment sites.) In 1972, President Nixon ordered White House hatchet men Bob Haldeman and Fred Malek to act aggressively on his objective to rid Langley of nay-saying analysts and managers, noting, "Of course, the reduction in force should be accomplished solely on the ground of its being necessary for budget reasons, but you will both know the real reason." The president further advised that his aides should ensure that the government stopped recruiting "from any of the Ivy League schools." He preferred combing schools in the Midwest, the South, and "even possibly some in the far West (not, of course, including Stanford or Cal) where we would have a better chance to come up with people who would be on our side."[20]

In a more recent illustration of undermining intelligence objectivity, it was improper of DCI Tenet to play down the dissent within the IC regarding the likely presence of WMDs in Iraq (which, recall, Air Force Intelligence, INR, and Energy Department Intelligence all questioned, but were largely shunted aside). Speaking truth to power is notoriously difficult, for it may place one's career at risk. Sometimes it requires courage and tenacity—and perhaps even a resignation from office in protest, if the matter is of great importance to the nation. In a good example of useful oversight, lawmakers on the Hill recently directed the CIA to develop a plan that would foster analytic objectivity inside the Agency. This exercise seems to have had some effect in reinforcing what everyone in the IC knows is an analyst's solemn duty: remaining true to the facts. As an official at Langley has noted, objectivity has long been a top priority at the CIA, but congressional focus on this topic "certainly helped to bring greater attention to this issue."[21]

- **Actionable**. Decision makers long for specificity. When, exactly, is a threat expected to occur? With respect to the 9/11 hijackers who would seek to board U.S. domestic airliners that would carry them to New York City and Washington, D.C., from what airports would they fly, at what time of day, and carrying what weaponry? This degree of precision can be extremely difficult to acquire, but specificity remains the gold standard of intelligence reporting. Armed with such information in 2001, policymakers could have ensured that 9/11 never happened; and, as we now know, details that could have unraveled the plot were indeed available beforehand, yet the information was discounted—such as the terrorist background of Zacharias Moussaoui in Minnesota; the entry of two of the hijackers into San Diego, California; and the odd flight training requests of some hijackers in Minneapolis, Phoenix, and elsewhere, as reported by their American instructors ("I just want to learn how to fly an airliner, not how to take off or land").

The Implications for Intelligence Accountability

This brief introduction to collection and analysis suggests a number of ways in which SSCI, HPSCI, and other oversight entities might engage in meaningful, helpful reviews of the IC within this foremost intelligence mission. Imagine the following queries, for example, as entry points for executive-session hearings by oversight panels on how well the secret agencies understand and cope with the dangers and opportunities presented by world affairs.

Planning

How sensible is the threat assessment document put together by each incoming administration? How often, and how well, is it updated? Does the assessment have room for "pop-up" contingencies, with funding sheltered for collectors and analysts working on obscure but potentially important topics—such as the effects of a rapidly declining population in Japan on that nation's political stability? Are such nontraditional topics as pandemics and global climate change given adequate consideration in the drafting of threat assessments? Is cybersecurity afforded the attention it merits, especially when it comes to blocking cyberattacks against the United States; and are the fragmented government efforts at cybersecurity being integrated effectively? (The answer to that last question is, presently, a resounding no.)

Collection

In the assignment of collection instruments is there a sensible balance between humint and techint? Have humint managers paid enough attention to deep cover: the nonofficial-cover (NOC) option, whereby intelligence officers operate in civil society overseas, say, as language instructors, tourist guides, archaeologists, or bartenders (rather than being sequestered in an American embassy), then when night darkens the streets assume their second job of spying? The NOC approach is used well by the Russians and the Chinese, but far less by the United States. At the same time, are the secret agencies respectful of existing prohibitions against the inappropriate use of U.S. journalistic credentials as a cover, as well as other organizations that are off limits, including the Peace Corps and the Fulbright Scholarship program? If exceptions must be made in the CIA's ties to American journalists in times of emergency, are these instances reported to SSCI and HPSCI in a timely manner? Within techint, has the fascination of lawmakers with shiny satellites—coupled with the effects of lobbying by the corporations that earn multimillion-dollar contracts for building these "platforms"—unduly swayed budget decisions toward this form of techint spending, at the expense of investments in humint? Or at the expense of low-tech machines, such as less costly but effective basketball-sized satellites rather than gigantic platforms in space that carry every conceivable bell and whistle on board?

Further on the collection side, what have the NSA and CIA learned from the metadata and torture controversies—practically and ethically? What is being done to ensure that these agencies resist a drift back into questionable practices, unless clearly authorized by an administration, with support from SSCI and HPSCI after full and timely briefings, as well as the acquisition of proper warrants from the FISA Court?

Processing

How well is the IC recruiting foreign-language translators? Photo interpreters? Data sifters? To what extent has the community worked closely with Silicon Valley to improve its skills in information technology (IT), especially the ability to cull signals from noise—searching for the proverbial needle in the haystack?

Analysis

How well is the IC attracting some of the nation's top minds to help the president and the Congress understand threats and opportunities confronting the United States? How honed are the skills of these individuals, as rated by the list of attributes for effective intelligence reporting presented earlier in this chapter? Especially, how professionally attuned are they to the dangers of politicization?

Dissemination

What improvements can be made so that whistle-blowers and other dissenters can step forward to IG offices, as well as the IOB, SSCI, HPSCI, and other inside review forums, to express concerns about possible cherry-picking and other forms of politicization, as well as suspected illegal activities? What can be done to encourage policymakers in the executive and legislative branches to read intelligence reports, and to interact with analysts about the findings in these reports? To attend committee hearings and to visit the spy agencies at work, both at home and abroad, as well as to discuss intelligence findings and operations firsthand with lower-ranking officers?

These sample questions are simply meant to suggest the richness of the agenda for those with responsibilities for intelligence accountability, just with respect to the mission of collection and analysis. More demanding still is the responsibility of coming to grips with covert action—the mission that has often blackened the eye of the United States in world affairs, but which at the same time has been useful now and then for protecting the nation and advancing its interests. Few subjects are more tightly shuttered within the CIA, which is the usual practitioner of covert action. As a result, several myths have evolved that must be addressed and dispelled by overseers if they are to be effective in monitoring this most aggressive of all the nation's intelligence activities.

Covert Action: The Quiet Option

The fact that covert action (CA) is among the most tightly held operational secrets in the government of the United States presents a mighty challenge to overseers, not to mention to the theoretical notion of an informed public in a democratic society.[22] As a starting point, members of SSCI and HPSCI, along with other American citizens, must come to grips with the mythology that surrounds covert action before they can attempt to evaluate the merits of any single proposal. The misunderstandings begin with basic definitions.

The Myths of Covert Action

Myth No. 1: The Meaning of Covert Action Is Clearly Delineated

The first myth has to do with the false notion that the border of covert action and its intersection with overt foreign policies has been carefully mapped. With the Intelligence Oversight Act of 1991–1992, the government did—at last—craft a formal statutory definition of covert action as "an activity or activities of the United States government to influence political, economic, or military conditions abroad, where it is intended that the role of the United States Government will not be apparent or acknowledged publicly."[23] In plain language, covert actions consist of secret government attempts to influence events and conditions overseas through the use of propaganda (the most frequently used instrument in this toolbox[24]), political and economic operations, and paramilitary or warlike activities. The god-like aspiration is to manipulate history so that it flows in a direction more favorable to the United States, as when the NSA and its "Tailored Access Operations" unit (TAO, operating in a joint effort with Israeli intelligence) reportedly inserted the Stuxnet virus into key Iranian computers as a means for sabotaging its nuclear-weapons program. The operation was said to have wiped out about a thousand nuclear centrifuges (20 percent of Iran's capacity at the Natanz uranium enrichment plant) and is considered "a turning point in the use of digital attacks" by one nation against another—indeed, Stuxnet was the world's first cyberweapon, with all the chilling prospects of future cyberwarfare that it presaged.[25]

The idea of secret influence is a spongy concept, though. A range of diplomatic and military objectives have seeped into the definition, often blurring the distinction between hidden activities run by the CIA, on the one hand, and by diplomats and soldiers, on the other hand. Defenders of the Iran-contra affair in the 1980s argued, for example, that the Reagan Administration's hidden support for "freedom fighters" in Nicaragua (by way of privately raised funds outside the Constitution's budgetary provisions) was really a matter of "secret diplomacy," not covert action. They reasoned that since the leaders of Nicaragua were aware of the CIA's involvement in the affair, the operation could not be truly considered a covert action. Yet the fact that they were kept in the dark about this scandal until it leaked led lawmakers to conclude that the operation's secrecy, along with its reliance on the CIA and the goal of influencing events in Iran and Central America, unequivocally made it a covert action.[26]

In 2004, under the orders of Secretary of Defense Donald R. Rumsfeld during the second Bush Administration, the Pentagon began to creep into the covert action domain by disguising its "special operations"—which sometimes closely resemble CIA covert actions—as traditional military activities. One illustration is the military training of foreign armies or rebels carried out by U.S. Special Operations Forces, which on occasion deploy soldiers out of uniform and on an unacknowledged basis—precisely the kind of activity engaged in by the Agency under the rubric of paramilitary (PM) covert action. By calling such activities "traditional military operations" (including even Pentagon-guided assassination operations using drones against terrorists outside of an authorized battlefield setting, as in Yemen in recent years), the DoD has been able to sidestep the formal legal procedures for covert action laid out in the Hughes-Ryan Act of 1974.[27] As discussed in chapter 3, these procedures require presidential approval for all important covert actions, by way of a signed "finding" ("The president finds that . . ."); and the law mandates, as well, reporting on the scope of the finding to SSCI and HPSCI.[28] In contrast, all the military brass has to claim is that its soldiers are engaged in a "war against terrorism" and the finding-and-reporting requirements of Hughes-Ryan—important accountability checks—melt away.

These definitional obfuscations have allowed generals to evade the Hughes-Ryan safeguards, which are much more rigorous than the rules followed by the Pentagon for their versions of covert action. After Rumsfeld decided (fueled by a strong dislike of the CIA) to enter the military into the covert action business in 2004, New York Times reporter Mark Mazzetti observed that "it became harder to see real differences between the mission of the military and the mission of the CIA."[29] The Pentagon, often the "hammer" among the implements of American foreign policy, would now compete with the CIA (more of a "scalpel") in the execution of paramilitary covert actions. Billowing clouds of ambiguity surrounded how these separate organizations would coordinate their similar tasks. Mazzetti reports that with respect to drone strikes in Yemen the "CIA maintained one target list, and JSOC kept another."[30] Overseers on HPSCI and SSCI would do well to insist that the CIA be responsible for covert actions, with any exceptions—such as the military's effective role in working with the Agency to dispatch Osama bin Laden—subject to Hughes-Ryan procedures.

Myth No. 2: Covert Action Offers a Quiet Approach to America's Foreign Relations

An appealing aspect of covert action is the promise that the United States may be able to address vexing problems abroad in a low-key manner, perhaps even without the target nation or group overseas even realizing that Washington was the silent hand behind the ill fate that has fallen upon them. Indeed, one of the euphemisms for covert action inside the U.S. government is "the quiet option."

Some forms of covert action fulfill this expectation. Throughout the Cold War, for instance, the CIA planted propaganda around the globe in foreign newspapers and magazines, as well as in radio and TV programs—upward of eighty covert media insertions a day at the height of the Cold War.[31] In the early period of the superpower confrontation, the Agency supported anti-Soviet guerrillas in the Greek countryside; parachuted agents into Poland, Albania, and elsewhere behind the Iron Curtain; and backed anti-Communist coups in Latin America and the Middle East. "The palette of covert activities was broad," notes Louis Menand.[32] Most of these operations went smoothly, with the U.S. government's sponsorship undetected. Nonetheless, even within the relatively benign realm of secret propaganda, the wheels can sometimes fall off the wagon. In the early 1970s, for example, the CIA's backing of Radio Free Europe and Radio Liberty leaked to the world, undermining their claim of independence. So did the CIA's ties to selected American publishing houses that printed anti-Soviet works on behalf of the government. These revelations called into doubt the objectivity of U.S. media outlets, tarnishing America's reputation for having a "free press." They raised questions, too, about the independence of some authors and their publishers.[33]

Much noisier still were various economic and paramilitary CAs, which may have been quiet at home—few knew about them inside the United States, including overseers on Capitol Hill—but not overseas where they were taking place. Well-known examples include the disastrous Bay of Pigs invasion in 1961 and, a little over two decades later, the use of mines to blow up cargo ships in Nicaraguan harbors. There was nothing silent about these activities or the CIA's paramilitary ventures in a host of other countries aimed at (among others) Vietnam during the 1960s, Afghanistan during the 1980s, and a range of terrorist organizations in the Middle East and Southwest Asia today. Drones, presently the most lethal form of paramilitary operations, may glide softly as a meadowlark through the night air with barely a sound, but there is nothing muffled about the explosions of their Hellfire missiles when they strike targets on the ground. As well, in recent years, the question of whom the CIA should arm in the Syrian civil war has been not so much quiet as, rather, a topic steadily splashed on the front pages of the nation's newspapers, with widespread reporting on the

Agency's shipments of antitank missiles to floundering U.S.-backed rebels, such as Suqour al-Jabal and Division 13.[34]

Myth No. 3: Covert Action Presents an Attractive Alternative to Reliance on America's Diplomats or Marines

Diplomacy can be maddeningly slow and often ineffectual, and sending in the Marines is more cacophonous than a symphony comprising only drums and cymbals. In between lies the so-called third option—yet another euphemism for covert action. It can entail fast and quiet intervention, as when the United States killed Bin Laden in 2011 in a raid into Pakistan that lasted only minutes. Framing foreign-policy options in just these three packages (diplomacy, overt warfare, and covert action) sets up an inertia inside the government, though, that all too often carries the United States toward the use of the third option while slighting other approaches that might merit greater consideration. As a former DNI has noted, "There are many more overt tools of national power available to attack problems in areas of the world than was previously the case where only covert action could be applicable."[35]

Another option is to do nothing—not a bad idea at times for a nation that has been bruised both physically and fiscally by endless interventions abroad, overt and covert, in recent decades. For the most part, other nations or regions must and should determine their own destinies, free of superpower meddling. Another example of a foreign-policy choice outside of the bailiwick of covert action is the "soft power" of setting a good example at home. For the United States to honor the principles of a free press, to eschew torture and extraordinary renditions, and to provide detainees with the basic right of habeas corpus can do more to win admiration and friends abroad than scores of diplomatic negotiations or the "hard power" of armed interventions and covert action. A different sort of hard power—economic statecraft—offers another promising set of options, whether through the establishment of improved trade relations, the use of sanctions, or an extension of development assistance that reaches into poverty-stricken villages from Pakistan to Nigeria with help in the form of health clinics, transportation infrastructure, schools, and clean-water facilities. Soft power can be every bit as useful as hard power and in some instances more so. A judicious foreign policy seeks an intelligent combination of both—what Joseph S. Nye, Jr., has referred to as "smart power."[36]

Myth No. 4: Covert Actions Undergo Rigorous Government Review before They Are Implemented

This myth had limited validity prior to 1975, when covert action approvals often consisted of nothing more than a secure telephone conversation between the

DCI at Langley and the national security adviser in the White House— if that. The Church Committee discovered in 1975 that only about 14 percent of all covert actions from 1961 to 1975 had been authorized by the National Security Council.[37] The committee concluded that these ambiguous arrangements were intentional, designed to protect the president and to blur accountability—the infamous doctrine of plausible deniability, whereby unelected bureaucrats frequently decided when and where covert actions would occur, all in the name of keeping the president's hands clean and the reputation of the United States unsullied. Put another way in bumper-sticker form: No Overseers Allowed!

Since 1974, however, the review of covert action proposals has been far more thorough than during the previous era of benign neglect, although we have seen how the Hughes-Ryan stipulations were completely ignored by the Reagan Administration during the Iran-contra affair. Despite the Hughes-Ryan rules, a consistently rigorous review of proposed covert actions has remained elusive, even beyond the unnerving Iran-contra example. One of the chief obstacles has been the use by the executive branch of "generic" or "worldwide" findings. The word "finding," recall, refers to the president's formal approval of a covert action: the commander-in-chief must "find" that a certain covert action is important and merits White House approval. The expectation on Capitol Hill— insisted upon by Aspin and Mazzoli of the Boland Committee—is that a finding will be accompanied by a specific accounting of the proposed operation, so that lawmakers can understand and evaluate its worthiness.

With generic or worldwide findings, however, specificity is abandoned; the wording of a presidential approval becomes an open-ended opportunity to engage in a covert action, allowing the CIA to fill in the details. The finding, for example, might provide the Agency with authority "to fight global terrorism." This broad language could be interpreted to mean almost anything, with carte blanche to carry out secret operations anywhere, anytime, and against anyone deemed a terrorist. In contrast, a more accountable finding would say something like this: "The CIA has presidential authority to engage in clandestine radio broadcasts from Afghanistan, aimed at the Taliban and transmitted throughout northwestern Pakistan for the next six months at a cost of $2 million." Here are specifics, ideally accompanied by risk assessments that would allow meaningful review by members of SSCI and HPSCI.

The benchmark of rigorous review can disintegrate, too, at the time when Congress is notified about a covert action approval. This notification takes place via separate briefings to both HPSCI and SSCI. Often the intelligence briefers—the DNI (or, earlier in history, the DCI), the CIA director, or their designee (often the DDO)—may try to slip by with thin explanations when appearing before the committees in closed session: the same tactic Admiral Turner attempted unsuccessfully with the Boland Committee. It is up to the lawmakers present at the briefings to flush out the details of a finding by way of thoughtful questioning, all recorded by a stenographer for the committee's archives. Sometimes SSCI and HPSCI members perform this important duty and sometimes they don't.[38]

Timing is important, as well. The Hughes-Ryan law originally provided for *ex post facto* reporting to lawmakers on a finding. "In a timely manner" was the prescription, interpreted by Congress to mean within a day, perhaps two. In 1980, the Intelligence Oversight Act raised the bar to *ante facto* reporting—*before* the covert action went into effect.[39] This rule of *prior notification* to lawmakers of important intelligence activities, not only covert actions, was a powerful form of accountability adopted by Congress, unprecedented in the history of the United States or any other nation. The provision included a temporary escape hatch. As noted in earlier chapters, in emergency situations the CIA chief could limit advanced reporting to only the "Gang of Eight." Nevertheless, even under these special procedures, the Agency was required to follow up within a day by briefing the full membership on both SSCI and HPSCI. Subsequently, with passage of the Intelligence Oversight Act of 1991–1992, this period of permitted delay was extended to a maximum of two days. Yet it is worth recalling from earlier chapters, presidents since 1980 have sometimes chosen to report only to the Gang of Eight and never to the full committees. Or sometimes to only a Gang of Four (an executive branch invention), a Gang of Two (the SSCI and HPSCI chairs), or even to a Gang of Zero, as when the Congress received no reports at all about the Iran-contra operations (the most brazen of all U.S. covert actions).

Myth No. 5: The Approval and Review Process for Covert Action Is Too Cumbersome and Hinders the Nation's Need for a Quick Response to Challenges Overseas

Some intelligence officials long for the halcyon days before the Hughes-Ryan Act and subsequent laws related to covert action made life more complicated at Langley. Better to have a simple telephone call to Dr. Kissinger, or some other national security adviser, than the hurdles posed by findings and concomitant congressional notifications; better still, the vague, generic authority to conduct CAs as the DO saw fit. According to this nostalgic view, the end result of covert action "micromanagement" has been to slow down the Agency in the execution of its important obligation to shield the nation against danger.

In fact, though, the Hughes-Ryan procedures can move with alacrity when necessary, relying on a link-up of secure telephones that allows quick communication among the top intelligence managers, the president, and other key players responsible for greenlighting a covert action. The briefings to Congress can be expedited, as well, through the Gang of Eight provision, which allows for swift action during times of crises. The advantages of the Hughes-Ryan procedures, which were an effort to "democratize" covert action, greatly outweigh the only slightly faster informal (and unaccountable) methods of earlier days. Appropriately, the pernicious doctrine of plausible deniability has been relegated to the landfill and replaced by a clear paper trail of responsibility that leads directly to the Oval Office—at least for covert actions carried out by the CIA. Such accountability is vital to democracy.

The Hughes-Ryan statute brought additional elected representatives of the American people (lawmakers on HPSCI and SSCI, not just the president) into the covert action decision loop. This landmark law introduced at least a modicum of representative democracy into the dark side of foreign policy, providing an opportunity to curb wrong-minded decisions by the executive branch (as epitomized by Iran-contra). Those who place a premium strictly on efficiency may rue the development of a wider circle of accountability for covert actions; however, those wary of power and its potential abuse (that is, anyone who has seriously studied history) will look upon the added precaution of the findings process as a prudent extension of democratic principles into the shadowy corners of America's government—a level of accountability still sorely missing with regard to secret operations conducted by the Pentagon, and even imperfect for the CIA's covert actions despite Hughes-Ryan.

Myth No. 6: Covert Actions Are Closely Monitored by the U.S. Government as They Are Being Implemented

This myth is particularly risible for covert actions carried out under the rubric of a generic finding. When overseers are unclear about the scope and specifics of a covert action in the first place, they are unable to track its path during the implementation phase. Even when a finding is detailed—a rare event and, therefore, the importance of putting flesh on the bones during the Hughes-Ryan briefings before HPSCI and SSCI—the challenges of maintaining accountability in the field are considerable. Clark Clifford, chief author of the National Security Act of 1947 and a former secretary of defense, testified before the Church Committee on this topic:

> I believe on a number of occasions, a plan for covert action has been presented to the NSC and authority is requested for the CIA to proceed from point A to point B. The authority will be given and the action will be launched. When point B is reached, the persons in charge feel it is necessary to go to point C, and they assume that the original authorization gives them such a right. From point C, they go to D and possibly E, and even further.[40]

Clifford's testimony underscores the importance of specific findings that prevent excessive leeway to field operatives. Intelligence managers down the chain of command must strike the right balance between providing flexibility in the field, on the one hand, and ensuring adherence to the intentions of the original finding, on the other hand. A seasoned CIA covert action manager with experience in Afghanistan has written: "[covert action] teams often could respond more quickly and effectively [during the current war in Afghanistan], sometimes before we in HQS [Agency Headquarters at Langley] even knew what action they were taking. This was more than OK—it was what I wanted. The field leaders demonstrated flat, networked intelligence collaboration and covert action at its best."[41] Without a doubt, it is important to avoid the stifling of initiative in the field; nonetheless, if carried too far, this philosophy of management—with its loosey-goosey overtones—can lead some CIA officers to slip from A to what might be a quite inappropriate B, C, D, or even E, in the manner predicted by Clifford. Covert action must be kept within proper boundaries and this necessity calls for specific findings, followed by careful supervision.

Does a devotion to remaining within the white lines of a legal and ethical boundary produce "risk-averse" behavior at the CIA and within the other intelligence agencies, as often claimed?[42] Not in my experience in watching intelligence officers over forty years. Was the thirty-two-year-old Agency officer Johnny "Mike" Spann of Winfield, Alabama, risk-averse when he helped lead the paramilitary operations against the Taliban and Al Qaeda in Afghanistan after the 9/11 attacks, becoming the first American casualty in the ongoing Afghan war? Was the CIA/Navy Seals team that tracked down and killed Bin Laden in 2011 risk-averse? Are the Agency officers fighting against ISIS? Even before 9/11, the CIA and other intelligence agencies have time and again displayed their mettle, as attested to by the 113 gold stars in the Book of Honor in the lobby at Langley. Each star commemorates a man or women who gave their lives overseas to protect the United States, while being anything but risk-averse.[43] Further, as of early 2016, twenty-two NSA officers had died in the line of duty in Afghanistan and Iraq. I once told the *Wall Street Journal* in an interview, "Keep in mind that 95 percent of what the CIA is doing—and has done—is entirely legal and extremely valuable to the country. The record of the CIA and these other agencies is quite outstanding. I hope we don't paint the whole Agency in dark tones just because of some episodes that occurred."[44]

America's intelligence officers are not pansies; they operate, often in dangerous settings, up to the limits of the law. Most of them, though, understand that laws are not suggestions; they are in place for a reason, as the considered judgment of the nation's leaders, subject to change through legitimate procedures if conditions or arguments so convince those in authority. The intelligence officers I've known have not been so much risk-averse as they have been rule-aware.

Most of them get it that officials of the United States are expected to conduct themselves under the law and the Constitution. They honor and respect the white lines. If they disagree with them, they work inside the system to have them clarified, modified, or rescinded. The best of them resign, if necessary, rather than obey an order to violate the law.

It is incontestable, though, that a few intelligence officers have thumbed their noses at the rule of law. Who would have surmised that DCI Casey of the Reagan Administration, with his admirable record as an OSS veteran,[45] or any other DCI, would have involved elements of the Agency in the illegal Iran-contra activities? True, Casey was known as a zealous aficionado of covert action; but that he would go as far as he did with "the Enterprise" is stunning to me at least and to most of my colleagues—though not the more cynical among them, such as one who said to me, "Casey's support for Iran-contra doesn't surprise me at all; his resistance would surprise me."[46] Further, who would have thought the CIA's Office of Security would spy on American citizens during the Cold War (Operation CHAOS)? And probably few people would have predicted that the Agency would recruit Mafia dons to help with its assassination plots against Fidel Castro. Troubling of late is the CIA's hiring of private companies to carry out intelligence operations overseas—so-called outsourcing. Here the chain of command and the lines of accountability are notably vague, and the outside actors are less likely to be socialized into the norms of intelligence-under-the-law, as required by reforms in the post–Church Committee era.[47] To guard against rogue behavior, lawmakers on the Intelligence Committees and their staff have a responsibility to stay on top of covert actions as these operations unfold in the field, not just when they are approved and reported to members of Congress during the findings stage. And sometimes they carry out this responsibility; as I write, a senior SSCI staffer is doing just that in a dangerous region of North Africa.

Myth No. 7: Covert Action Has the Advantage of Allowing the United States to Act Alone in Foreign Affairs, Unencumbered by the Self-interests of Other Nations and Factions

Both diplomacy and the use of military force normally involve a complicated set of relationships among many countries. In the case of global environmental treaties, for instance, well over a hundred nations now gather periodically for negotiations meant to improve the planet's environmental quality; in the recent wars in Iraq, Afghanistan, and against ISIS, although mainly U.S. initiatives, dozens of other nations have operated together in an antiterrorist coalition (many induced to participate by assurances of U.S. foreign aid and weapons sales). These are enterprises of great pitch and moment that require enormous amounts of funding, diplomatic skill, and time investment. In contrast, covert action seems to offer an opportunity for the United States to move unilaterally, with secrecy, dispatch, and no extra weight.

In reality, though, covert actions of any consequence—particularly paramilitary operations—also turn out to be complex ventures. The CIA's covert wars in Laos from 1962 to 1968, as well as against the Soviet military in Afghanistan during the 1980s, for example, swallowed vast amounts of U.S. financial resources and preoccupied the Agency for years. Nor can the United States operate alone in covert ventures of any scope. Indeed, a fundamental tenet of success in this mission is the requirement of having competent and trustworthy allies inside the target nation. In Laos during the 1960s, the partnership was with the Hmong tribesmen (pronounced with a silent "h")—fierce anti-Communist warriors; and in Afghanistan during the 1980s, with the anti-Communist *mujahideen* (who unfortunately grew into the Taliban regime that subsequently provided a safe haven for Bin Laden and the Al Qaeda terrorist organization).[48]

The souring of the war in Indochina, along with presidential candidate Richard Nixon's promise to reduce government spending and to seek détente with the Soviet Union, led to a retreat from open warfare as well as covert actions in Indochina and elsewhere—a downward spiral that would culminate in the lowest frequency of CAs, recorded in that landmark intelligence year of 1975, since the original zero-point when the Agency was created. (See Figure 9.2.[49]) Adding to the lower than expected emphasis on covert action during the Vietnam War was the skepticism of DCI Richard Helms toward the value of CAs. Then, in 1975, came the further distraction of the Church Committee and the other simultaneous inquiries into intelligence operations. The Agency was fighting for its life and had little time for the planning of covert actions (or NIEs—another low point).

Moreover, when the Church Committee's revelations about the attempted coup aimed at Salvador Allende in Chile—along with the assassination plots in other countries—were disclosed, covert action came to a "screeching halt," according to a prominent CIA officer, who said further that it became "nearly impossible to conduct future CA operations."[50] Yet, within a year, President Jimmy Carter—egged on by his hawkish national security adviser Zbigniew Brzezinski—turned to Langley and covert action for solutions to foreign-policy headaches. (These operations remain classified, other than a well-known one in which the Agency worked with Canada to exfiltrate a group of Americans from Tehran during the hostage crisis at the U.S. Embassy in 1979.) It was a 180-degree reversal from Carter's anti–covert action campaign rhetoric and was a much different outcome than direly prophesized by

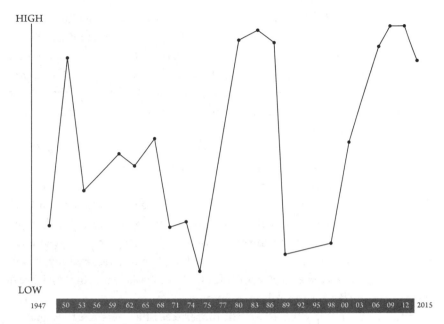

HIGH

LOW

1947 50 53 56 59 62 65 68 71 74 75 77 80 83 86 89 92 95 98 00 03 06 09 12 2015

Figure 9.2 The Ebb and Flow of U.S. Covert Actions, 1947–2015. Source: This trend line is derived from the author's interviews with intelligence professionals over forty-seven years, along with a scouring of the public record. An earlier version of this figure appeared in Loch K. Johnson, *National Security Intelligence: Secret Operations in Defense of the Democracies* (Cambridge, UK: Policy, 2012), p. 90.

Henry Kissinger in January 1977 that "we are unable to do [covert action] anymore."[51]

In fact, the third option sprang to life again under President Carter and, when the Reagan Administration came to power in 1981, this mission entered a Golden Age—a foreign-policy tool turned to even more enthusiastically than its earlier heyday during the Eisenhower years. The Reagan team pursued secret anti-Communism interventions around the world, with El Salvador and Poland prominently in the mix; but above all, in terms of expense and focus, Nicaragua (the Iran-contra affair) and Afghanistan (in support of the *mujahideen*) became the central preoccupations.[52] During the Reagan Administration, the tail of covert action began to wag the dog of American foreign policy as CA funding soared—especially for paramilitary operations—to support what the media labeled the "Reagan Doctrine." This emphasis on covert action surpassed the earlier record set at the time of the Korean War, as President Reagan vowed to take on the Soviet Union and defeat the "Evil Empire." It was also the only time when CAs spiraled upward without being in support of a major U.S. military intervention overseas; this time, the mission was propelled not by battlefield support for the Pentagon but by an administration's anti-Communist zeal. Disclosure of the Iran-contra scandal brought an end to this approach, however, as the president's standing in the polls fell dramatically. The scandal, coupled with the end of the Cold War, sent covert action into cold storage. When George H. W. Bush came to power, he kept covert action below 1 percent of the U.S. intelligence budget—an emphasis far beneath the Reagan years (when Bush had been vice president), as illustrated in Figure 9.2.[53]

Under President Bill Clinton, covert action remained relatively dormant. "Since the public controversies of the eighties over Iran-contra and activities in Central America, we have greatly reduced our capability to engage in covert action," said John Deutch, President Clinton's DCI.[54] As a retired prominent DDO operative opined in 1993 (in an echo of Kissinger's death knell for CA), the third option seemed to have become "largely a thing of the past."[55] Then terrorists struck the United States on 9/11. Like a sputtering engine given a few quarts of fresh oil, the CA engine revved back into action. Before long, covert action would surpass the earlier records for CIA emphasis set during the Korean War and years of the Reagan Administration.

As mentioned in chapter 2, one of the most successful CAs since the Agency's establishment was the routing of the Taliban and Al Qaeda from Afghanistan in the aftermath of the 9/11 attacks; in fact, some senior intelligence officials point to this operation as "the most effective covert-action program in CIA history."[56] A sine qua non for the victory was the internal assistance of the Northern Alliance, a tribe of Afghans who also opposed the Taliban; here was the indispensable "willing partner" for success inside the target country.[57] This paramilitary operation benefited, as well, from support provided by the Joint Special Operations Command in the Pentagon (JSOC) and, overtly, the U.S. Air Force. In more recent covert actions, as in the effort during 2011 to topple the Libyan regime led by Col. Muammar Quaddafi, an added ingredient has been the use of private U.S. (and sometimes foreign) contractors—a reliance on outsourced personnel to beef up America's clandestine presence on the ground. While this augmentation is replete with accountability risks, it has sometimes proved necessary in light of the Agency's limited number of in-house operatives. The sum of these factors: covert actions of any scale do not occur in a vacuum; they have many moving parts and are rarely a quick and easy solution, the beguiling come-on of stealth and quiet notwithstanding.

In the post-9/11 environment, some officials at Langley began to worry, though, that covert action—and especially drone attacks—had grown too dominant in the Agency's global operations, with intelligence analysts becoming more and more focused on the setting of GPS drone-targeting coordinates than on the production of assessments about world affairs. As a foreign-policy specialist has put it, the Obama Administration basically concluded: "'All you need to deal with terrorism is N.S.A. and C.I.A., drones and special ops.' So the C.I.A. gave Obama an angle, if you will, to be simultaneously hawkish and shun using the military."[58] At Langley, though, Director John Brennan, who had served as an analyst throughout his career at the Agency, began to urge the restoration of traditional analysis as the top priority in the CIA's portfolio of responsibilities, with involvement in drone strikes only in limited circumstances.[59] President Obama, heavily influenced by Brennan (who had served earlier as a White House counterterrorist adviser), began in 2013 to taper off the use of Agency drones in the killing fields, reserving them more strictly just for intelligence gathering. In 2014 and after, the CIA reportedly flew no drone missile attacks against ISIS targets in Iraq and Syria, for example, leaving this terrain to the Pentagon. A new debate began in Washington about the Agency's remit: Should it step out of the business of Murder, Inc., altogether, handing over drone warfare exclusively to the Pentagon?[60]

Others opposed the views of the president and the D/CIA on shelving the participation of the CIA in drone attacks. For one thing, argued SSCI's top leaders, Chairman Richard Burr and ranking minority member Dianne Feinstein, sometimes the Pentagon was too slow in sending drones against known terrorist targets in Syria and Iraq, leading to "missed opportunities" once the Agency had spotted ISIS fighters.[61] The CIA's drone operators should be allowed to pull the trigger in those circumstances, they argued (in rare bipartisan unity). Hiding behind this argument were two stronger concerns left unstated by the senators. First, they believed that the CIA was subject to greater congressional accountability than the Pentagon's JSOC (namely, the Hughes-Ryan procedures) and, therefore, should remain in charge of most counterterrorism drone attacks—and certainly those outside the official theaters of war. These official theaters continued to include Afghanistan and, with the spilling of ISIS terrorism from Syria eastward, Iraq as well—and increasingly in Libya. Second, the SSCI leaders (and HPSCI, too) don't want to give up their jurisdiction over drones, because it provides them with a heady closeness to policymaking in the White House and an opportunity to learn what an administration is planning when it comes to foreign intelligence operations.

In a nutshell, during the latest war in Afghanistan and against global terrorism everywhere it cropped up, covert action had gained more attention from U.S. government officials than ever before. Beginning in 2013, however, growing disillusionment with drone warfare at Langley and elsewhere was beginning to draw down such heavy reliance on this segment of the Agency's paramilitary arm.[62]

Myth No. 8: Covert Action Offers a Cheap Fix for Foreign-Policy Dilemmas

Another misconception about covert action is that it is inexpensive. Clearly almost any approach to America's recent woes in Iraq and Afghanistan would have been cheaper than the $2 trillion price tag the U.S. taxpayers have had to pay for these overt military interventions—or more, when all the dust settles. Sometimes costly overt wars are unavoidable, as the brutal actions of the Axis powers properly persuaded the United States in 1941; nevertheless, it would be wrong to assume that covert actions are necessarily a cheap date.

Some small-scale CA operations are reasonably priced. The fee for secretly placing a propaganda article into a foreign newspaper through an Agency media asset is low, although also limited in effect. Large-scale political, economic, and paramilitary operations, in contrast, can run into millions of dollars, even billions, when toting up the costs of covert interventions in such places as Korea and Vietnam (1950–1953 and 1965–1973, respectively, where the CIA operated in harness with America's military intervention); Nicaragua and Afghanistan (the 1980s); and, most recently, Iraq and Afghanistan (as complements to the overt U.S. wars in those nations), as well as in Somalia, Yemen, Pakistan, northern Africa, the Philippines, and elsewhere when groups claiming affiliation with ISIS and Al Qaeda pop up. For example, during the first significant CA intervention abroad in the modern era, in Korea, this mission underwent a sixteen-fold funding increase—a "skyrocketing" of spending, according to the Church Committee—along with a doubling of Agency officers in the field.[63] In recent years, as ISIS, Al Qaeda, Boko Haram, and Al Shabab (the Al Qaeda affiliate in Somalia) metastasized and the United States expanded its struggle against global terrorism with drones leading the way, the cash register for covert action at the CIA and the Pentagon began ringing as never before.

Myth No. 9: Covert Action Is Resorted to Only in Extreme Circumstances That Threaten the United States

The significant expenses of covert action, both in terms of money and America's global reputation, would be more tolerable if this approach were limited to operations designed to protect the United States from immediately perilous circumstances. The record shows, though, that Washington officials have resorted to covert actions in situations far below that standard. Frequently the targets have been small, weak countries. During the Cold War, America's nemesis was the Soviet Union and its satellite states in Eastern Europe (the Warsaw Pact); yet few covert actions were directed against this empire, outside of efforts to infiltrate pro-Western propaganda behind the Iron Curtain. Instead, any developing nation that had the temerity to partner with—or even flirt with—the U.S.S.R. became a target, however remote the chances that these locations presented a genuine threat to the United States. "No country was too small, no foreign leader too trifling, to escape our attention," concluded Senator Church after his committee's sixteen-month investigation into covert action and other intelligence activities.[64] With respect to Nicaragua during the 1980s, the German Nobel laureate in literature, Günter Grass, asked plaintively: "How impoverished must a country be before it is not a threat to the U.S. government?"[65]

Chile is a well-known illustration, with its democratically elected government led by President Allende targeted by the Nixon Administration for a coup during the 1970s. As historian Michael Grow has written with respect to the CIA's various interventions in Latin America, "Cold War presidents and their senior advisers believed that a passive U.S. response to Marxist or otherwise unfriendly regimes in the Western Hemisphere would create a perception of U.S. weakness in the eyes of the international community, with potentially serious long-range consequences for the nation's security."[66] The guiding philosophy became as simple as ABC: Anybody But Communists—a grand strategy embraced with fervor by Secretary of State Henry Kissinger during the Nixon Administration. Yet most of these countries were driven by a deep sense of nationalism, not an attraction to Communism (although some accepted foreign aid from Moscow when turned away by the United States). One can only wonder whether other foreign-policy options would have been more successful in winning over nations in the developing world, such as foreign aid, trade inducements, student and cultural exchanges, and patient diplomacy conducted with a hearing aid rather than a bullhorn.[67]

Myth No. 10: Covert Action Is Driven by the Imperatives of U.S. Security, Rather Than Bureaucratic Politics

Covert action—as with every other policy option—can be strongly influenced by the personal agendas of ambitious bureaucrats and politicians, not just the undeniable security interests of the United States. A classic case involves Richard M. Bissell, Jr., a senior official during the 1960s in the Operations Directorate, home of the stygian Covert Action Staff (CAS) during the Cold War. According to Peter Wyden's exhaustive account of the Bay of Pigs fiasco, Bissell pushed this covert action on President Kennedy in hopes of impressing him by delivering a quick regime change in Cuba and ridding the administration of a persistent irritant: Fidel Castro.[68] The payoff to Bissell—or so he hoped—might be promotion to DCI. Never mind that analysts in the Agency's Intelligence Directorate considered the paramilitary initiative a pipe dream from the start, given the widespread popularity of Castro among the people of Cuba.

The CAS, a unit of the Special Activities Division in the DO, brims with professional intelligence officers with schemes about how their tradecraft can influence the world in a manner beneficial to the United States. That is their job. Further, they are also naturally interested in accelerating their own careers by demonstrating how creative and aggressive they can be. As revealed by the Church Committee, some of the ideas that have percolated up inside CAS have been madcap, from the now well-known exploding cigar for Castro's consumption (it never got to him) to "Operation Elimination by Illumination," also aimed at Cuba.[69] In this plan, U.S. submarines would surface off the island's coast, firing star shells into the midnight darkness. Assets of the CIA in Havana and the Cuban countryside, abetted by leaflets dropped from Agency aircraft, would simultaneously spread the word that "Christ has come! Rise up against the Anti-Christ!" This Second Coming would supposedly lead to the overthrow of Castro, the Anti-Christ, at the hands of the Cuban people. President Kennedy's aides in the White House, no doubt shaking their heads and wondering what people were smoking at Langley, halted this initiative before its launch date.

Myth No. 11: Covert Action Can Be Implemented in a Surgical Manner

Another fantasy about covert action is that it can be used with high precision, as a surgeon would wield a scalpel. *Times* reporter Mazzetti entitled his probe into CIA covert actions against Al Qaeda and the Taliban *The Way of the Knife*.[70] A problem overseas? Send in the CAS or its paramilitary wing, the Special Operations Group (SOG), and the problem will disappear (supposedly) without a trace of evidence implicating the United States. Fed up with the leader of Iran in 1953, Mohammed Mossadeqh, even though he was democratically elected? Send in the CIA, this time working with Britain's MI6, and replace him with a more pliable puppet—the Shah of Iran (Mohammed Reza Shah Pahlavi).[71] This particular operation did proceed with surprising ease, at least over the short run. Long term, though, the Shah proved highly unpopular with his own people, who threw him out of office and replaced him with religious *mullahs* who have remained hateful toward the United States ever since.[72]

Many other operations have been anything but precise or contained, even over the short term. Covert propaganda, for instance, presents the problem of "blowback"—an intelligence term referring to the hazard that propaganda secretly planted overseas by the CIA may be inadvertently reported back to the United States, say, by a *Wall Street Journal* correspondent in a foreign capital who is unaware that a local newspaper article has been placed there by an Agency asset. The *WSJ* reporter may incorporate elements of this article in his or her own dispatch home and, in this manner, the American people become the victims of a U.S. government propaganda operation. Given the ubiquitous nature of social media, blowback is even more likely today.

Using the phrase "blowback" more broadly, some observers have argued that covert actions can have a still wider negative effect on America's standing in the world.[73] The CIA's assassination plots against Castro and the Congo's Patrice Lumumba, for example, stained the reputation of the United States; Washington seemed to be behaving no better than the Soviet KGB, an intelligence organization widely known for its lack of a moral compass. The efforts to over-throw Allende raised further questions about America's apparent willingness to attack even fellow democracies, not just authoritarian and totalitarian regimes. Moreover, as a thoughtful commentator has wondered: "Can a government that deliberately sets out to destroy democratic institutions abroad help but destroy democratic institutions at home?"[74]

Current-day assassination operations against suspected terrorists, carried out by the CIA and the Pentagon using (most frequently) Predators and other types of drones armed with missiles, are viewed by Washington officials as a CA tool that, if not surgically precise, is at least far less likely to injure or kill civilians than an open military invasion. Although a valid consideration, this comparison fails to negate the fact that many civilians have been accidentally killed or maimed by U.S. drone attacks.[75] There is nothing surgically exact about America's drone policy, which elides such fundamental questions as where (on what battlefields or nonbattlefields) the drones may legitimately operate; the criteria for selecting individuals, including American citizens, for inclusion on hit lists; or how proper accountability will be maintained—all the way from target selection through the pulling of the trigger (by distant remote control) to release the drone missiles. The parallel—yet sometimes uncoordinated—drone attacks launched by the CIA and the Pentagon in some countries, with separate kill lists in Yemen (for one illustration), further suggest a lack of surgical planning.[76]

On the matter of drone accountability, President Obama (who increased the number of drone flights to some 400 by 2014, compared to a total of fifty under President Bush), conceded in 2012 that "one of the things we've got to do is put a legal architecture in place—and we need congressional help in order to do that—to make sure that not only am I reined in, but any president is reined in."[77] The president's top counterterrorism adviser at the time, John Brennan, said publicly during his Senate confirmation hearings for the CIA directorship in February 2013 that great care goes into the use of drones. Nonetheless, it remains unclear whether each individual on the "hit list" requires a presidential finding, or if a generic finding permits wide discretion to the Agency, the Pentagon, and the Justice Department in the targeting of suspected terrorists. Even the rules for the assassination by drone strikes of known American citizens abroad are murky, leading many legal authorities to call for the establishment of a special review court to decide on the merits of a presidential request to kill these individuals—judicial accountability brought into the drone CA process, just as it was in 1978 for national security wiretaps against American citizens with the creation of the FISA Court. Senator Angus King (I, Maine) cautions against allowing the White House to serve as "the prosecutor, the judge, the jury, and the executioner all in one," a combination he finds "very contrary to the traditions and the laws of this country."[78]

Disconcerting, too, is a category of drone targets known by the designation "signature." This is a list of individuals who have not been specifically identified as terrorists, but who may be found in a geographic locale—say, northwestern Pakistan—that suggests they could be bad actors. This criterion has the potential to sweep onto the U.S. drone targeting-list virtually every young male not only in Pakistan, but throughout Southwest Asia, as well as in the Middle East and North Africa. Killing people without even knowing who they are, or what they have done or intend to do that may harm the United States and its allies, is a gaping—and unacceptable—departure from the concept of covert action as a scalpel.

Myth No. 12: The Likely Outcomes of Covert Action Can Be Accurately Calibrated

Those who plan covert action are mostly just guessing what the outcomes of their endeavors will be, especially years down the road. In 1953, the Shah may have looked like a good alternative for Iran (or, more accurately, for the United States, the United Kingdom, and their respective oil companies). Glancing back, former DCI William E. Colby offered this evaluation: "The assistance to the Shah . . . was an extremely good move which gave Iran twenty-five years of progress before he was overthrown. Twenty-five years is no small thing."[79] Nor, Colby might have added, is it a small thing that the installation of a pro-Western leader in an oil-rich Middle Eastern country provided a quarter-century of comparative low prices for Americans at their gas pumps. Yet the identification of the United States with the Shah, whose secret police (Savak) tortured dissenters and cast a dictatorial pale over the country, has had a long-term negative effect, beginning with the Revolution of 1979 that overthrew the Shah and installed an anti-American theocracy.

The CIA coup in Guatemala in 1954 may have looked sensible, too, at the time—especially to the United Fruit Company, which feared that the existing regime might expropriate its holdings or charge more at the supply source for the marketing of bananas in the United States. Both DCI Allen Dulles and Secretary of State John Foster Dulles, his brother, had been partners in the prestigious New York City law firm Sullivan and Cromwell, which represented the United Fruit Company.[80] The profit margins of this company aside, journalist Anthony Lewis of the New York Times has reported that the Agency's intervention began "a long national descent into savagery" for Guatemala that lasted for over thirty years.[81] Together, the coups in Iran and Guatemala sent a feeling of euphoria sweeping through the Agency and the White House, producing "an attitude of hubris" in the Eisenhower Administration—but resulting in high costs for the United States in the future, with Iran turning against America in 1979 because of its ties with the Shah, and with people throughout Latin America wary of Washington and its seemingly endless secret interventions in their region of the world.[82] The Bay of Pigs in 1961, described by Barrett as "the most spectacular, publicized and failed covert action in the then-14-year-old history of the Central Intelligence Agency," dampened the notion that the third option was a panacea for America's foreign-policy woes.[83] President Kennedy soon overcame his negative feelings toward the CIA and covert action, however, and ordered it to increase the pressure against Castro and topple his regime.

Not long after, the war in Vietnam again attracted deep involvement by the Agency in paramilitary operations in Indochina that supported U.S. overt military intervention. For example, the CIA-backed fighting in Laos kept the Communists at bay for eight years (1962–1968) and away from killing U.S. troops in Vietnam. All to the good. When the Agency departed Laos in 1968, however, the Hmong found themselves (as Colby summed up in his memoir) "in exile, dead, or living under oppression."[84] When the CIA helped the *mujahideen* drive out the Soviets from Afghanistan in the 1980s (by providing them with Stinger missiles, among other forms of military aid), the resulting retreat of the Soviet Army catapulted this operation onto a high place in the Agency's honor roll of covert actions. Again, at least over the short run. Over the longer run, Afghanistan fell into the hands of Taliban fundamentalists, whom the United States has been fighting inconclusively since 2001.

The CIA's assassination plots during the Cold War also raise the question of the potential value added from controversial covert actions. Would the killing of Fidel Castro have changed much in Cuba? His brother, Raoul, would have replaced him (as he eventually did when Fidel grew too old to govern); at the time of the plots, Raoul Castro was equally truculent toward the United States and friendly toward the Soviet Union. Did the question of whether Patrice Lumumba lived or died matter that much to the course of the Cold War— enough for the United States to plan his murder? Unlikely. And doesn't the use of assassination against foreign leaders invite other nations to retaliate in kind, with our president and other elected officials in the United States (and in other open societies) much more vulnerable than dictators hiding in their armed fortresses? Will unidentified drones bearing missiles soon head for the United States from foreign lands in search of this nation's leaders in the streets of Washington, D.C.? Assassination, by drone or otherwise, is a Pandora's box that must be closed—if that is still possible.[85]

One can wonder, with increased anxiety, about the future of drone warfare advanced by the United States. Over forty nations now have drones. Here is a realm of dimly lit warfare that begs for the establishment of tighter legal restrictions for all nations—rules that define clear boundaries for the use of UAVs. Further, in the not-too-distant future lurks the challenge of nonstate actors who will certainly attempt to acquire this technology, perhaps arming these silent aircraft with weapons of mass destruction—indeed, ISIS is already using primitive drones in Iraq armed with conventional missiles.

Myth No. 13: Covert Action Is Kept within the Boundaries of Moral Acceptability

Each of these myths points to important ethical considerations. Some covert actions have undeniably assisted the cause of freedom around the world. For example, the combined CIA–Navy Seal operation that resulted in the death of Bin Laden brought a form of justice to the chief sponsor of the 9/11 attacks and further signaled to other terrorists that their foul deeds will be avenged. Also, during the Cold War, efforts by the Agency to provide information about the free world to those trapped behind the Iron Curtain brought some hope to the suppressed citizens of the Soviet Bloc and encouraged their resistance to totalitarianism. In another illustration, the CIA's assistance to the Christian Democratic Party in Italy during the 1960s, in its political struggles against the Italian Communist Party, did much to keep that nation free and functioning as an important partner in NATO; and the CIA's paramilitary operations in Laos during the 1960s helped to relieve pressure from the western front on U.S. troops fighting Communist forces next door in Vietnam. Covert action can work, while remaining within the perimeters of ethical acceptability.

At the same time, though, many of America's covert actions have displayed serious moral defects. For one thing, the CIA has often abandoned its covert action partners overseas, leaving them to an uncertain (and often unpleasant) fate against savage opponents—equivalent to starting a fight in a crowded barroom, then ducking out the back door. Among those deserted during the Cold War (from a much longer list) were the Cuban exile invaders at the time of the Bay of Pigs; the Hmong of Laos—the negative side of this intervention (although the Agency did manage to rescue many Hmong and help them resettle in the United States); the Khambas in Tibet; the Nationalist Chinese in Burma; U.S. assets in Saigon at the end of the Vietnam War—all, in the words of critic Ferdinand Mount in the *National Review*, "so many causes and peoples briefly taken up by the CIA and then tossed aside like broken toys."[86]

In addition, CIA assassination plots during the Cold War made the United States appear uncomfortably like its chief nemesis, the Soviet Union. When the Agency established a "Health Alteration Committee" to concoct ways for eliminating disagreeable leaders abroad; when its scientists crafted special weapons for assassinations, such as a poison dart gun and special ballpoint pens that dispensed deadly toxins; when CIA operatives entered into an alliance with mob hitmen, the United States lost sight of its traditional values of honor and fair play.

More recently, the Agency's drone program has precipitated widespread ethical concerns. Reports from Southwest Asia indicate that even pro-Americans in Pakistan (and there are many) question the violation of their nation's airspace by drones, as well as the collateral damage they incur.[87] Moderate, secular Pakistani-Americans, whom I have met at academic conferences and as students in my university classes, have often expressed strong positive feelings toward the United States, but they uniformly question the morality and legality of drone flights and view them as the number one impediment to better relations between the United States and Pakistan. The Obama Administration evidently calculated that the short-term objective of killing Osama bin Laden outweighed the negative response it would draw in some circles in Pakistan, not just among Taliban terrorists in the northwestern region of that country but with a wide cross-section of that country's citizens who object to secret U.S. military operations carried out on their soil. (The other side of that coin, of course, is how the government of Pakistan could have such a prominent fugitive in their country, right next door to a major military base in Abbottabad, without knowing about it—or, more likely, deciding to keep this information from Washington officials.)

During the Cold War, the prominent U.S. diplomat George Ball rejected the use of extreme covert actions.[88] "When we mine harbors in Nicaragua, we fuzz the difference between ourselves and the Soviet Union," he said. "We act out of character, which no great power can do without diminishing itself. . . . When we . . . fight the Russians on their own terms and in their own gutter, we make a major mistake and throw away one of our great assets." Harvard University law professor Roger Fisher expressed similar moral qualms. "When we choose our weapons, let's choose ones we are good at using—like the Marshall Plan—not ones we are bad at—like the Bay of Pigs," Fisher advised, continuing: "To join some adversaries in the grotesque world of poison dart-guns and covert operations is to give up the most powerful weapons we have: idealism, morality, due process of law, and belief in the freedoms of others to disagree, including the right of other countries to disagree with ours."[89] Today, the United States must—and can—fight terrorism without being viewed by people around the world as a perpetrator of unsavory methods.

Myth No. 14: If the Veils of Secrecy Could Be Lifted, the Public
Would Find That Covert Action Has Operated Effectively to
Resolve America's Problems Abroad

Perhaps many of these reservations about covert action—some would say all—could be waved aside if this approach to U.S. foreign policy delivered the goods, that is, if covert action consistently succeeded in protecting and advancing

America's interests in the world. The historical record indicates otherwise, however. The argument that all the really good covert actions remain classified and sealed inside CIA vaults is simply false. Several government investigations have looked into covert action in recent years and the American people know at least the broad outlines regarding most all of them, and certainly almost all of the significant ones. As former secretary of state Dean Rusk has written about America's secret foreign policy, "The argument that 'If you only knew what I knew, you would agree with me' is a phony."[90]

The vast majority of covert actions since the birth of the CIA have been modest in nature, even trivial (as with some of its covert media placements); or, when more ambitious, as at the Bay of Pigs, they have often been unlikely to succeed or remain covert. Furthermore, as illustrated by the cases of the Shah of Iran and support for the Afghan *mujahideen*, the longer-term, unanticipated consequences of covert action can come back to haunt the United States. That America could have gotten by without the small-scale covert actions is plausible; that the nation would have been better off without such failures during the Cold War as the Bay of Pigs or the black mark of assassination plots against Third World figures is self-evident. As former DNI Admiral Dennis Blair has concluded, "Going back to the history of CIA covert operations, I think you can make the argument that if we had done none of them we would probably be better off, and certainly no worse off than we are today."[91]

However valid much of his criticism of covert actions may be, Admiral Blair no doubt overstates the argument against this instrument of foreign policy. After all, the covert action record has had its successes. During the Cold War, a helping hand from the United States to struggling democracies around the world after World War II—along with overt military, economic, and political assistance— allowed nations in Europe, Latin America, Africa, Asia, and the Middle East to resist Communist aggression. More recently in the aftermath of 9/11, the routing of Al Qaeda and Taliban forces in Afghanistan registered a high mark for covert action; here was an outstanding example of the CIA, Pentagon Special Forces, the U.S. Air Force, and local Afghans in the Northern Alliance working together against terrorists.

Moreover, drone strikes and other small-scale paramilitary operations aimed at Al Qaeda, ISIS, and other terrorist organizations have achieved some victories. Indeed, after interviewing hundreds of sources in the United States and overseas, journalist Mazzetti concluded: "Many believe that the drone program is the most effective covert-action program in CIA history."[92] Further, the use of drones may be more acceptable to Americans (and others) than large-scale, overt military invasions. It should be emphasized again, though, that drone covert actions cry out for a warrant process, as well as prior judicial review of proposed targeting against American citizens and timely reporting to SSCI and

HPSCI. Necessary, too, is a closer monitoring by overseers in the executive and legislative branches of how kill lists are coordinated between the Agency and the Pentagon.

Presently, drone assassination initiatives are vetted by lawyers on the NSC working with their counterparts in the IC. The first step is a targeting recommendation drafted by attorneys at the CIA or the Department of Defense; then the NSC Deputies Committee (composed of those second in command at the recommending agency or the DoD) gives the proposal a thorough scrub, before passing it along to the DNI, D/CIA, and the secdef on the Principals Committee for their review and approval. If the potential target is an American citizen, the president must approve, and the congressional oversight committees are informed—although in "extraordinary cases" these steps can be short-circuited, with the president alone making the decision.[93] Beyond these steps, the Obama Administration has redoubled its efforts to avoid casualties among innocent civilians by improving intelligence reconnaissance before a drone attack takes place. Moreover, White House guidelines require that drone assassinations can proceed only if the targeted individual poses a grave threat to the United States; and only if the CIA or DoD feel there is a "near certainty" no civilian casualties will result from the attack. Beyond strengthening these useful Obama Administration rules with increased judicial and congressional involvement in the targeting process, future administrations must seek to establish limits on global drone operations by all nations through the signing of a formal international treaty to that effect.

Among the hundreds of witnesses who appeared before the Church Committee in 1975, two of the most sagacious were Clark Clifford and Cyrus Vance. They had accumulated many years of experience in the government at the cabinet level. When asked their opinions about covert action, they embraced a common theme. "The guiding criterion," said Clifford, "should be the test as to whether or not a certain covert project *truly affects our national security*." Vance, who would soon become secretary of state in the Carter Administration, told the committee similarly that "it should be the policy of the United States to engage in covert actions only when they are *absolutely essential to the national security*."[94] This is the core prescriptive thesis of this chapter as well. The United States needs a covert action capability for some situations, especially related to the struggle against global terrorism. This approach to the conduct of American foreign policy must become much more discriminating than has been the case in the past, however, bearing in mind its many failures. General Stanley McChrystal, one of America's most thoughtful military leaders, emphasizes that "if you go back in history, I can't find a covert fix that solved a problem long term."[95]

In 1995, former DCI William H. Webster shared with the Aspin-Brown Commission his checklist for evaluating the worthiness of a covert action proposal. At Langley, he would always ask top aides who brought him CA proposals:

- Is it legal? (That is, is it in conformity with U.S. laws governing covert action, such as the Hughes-Ryan procedures?)
- Is it consistent with American foreign policy, and, if not, why not?
- Is it consistent with American values?
- If it becomes public, will it make sense to the American people?[96]

The Webster guidelines, coupled with the caveats of Clifford and Vance, should be framed and placed on the office walls of every CA planner, as well as in the Oval Office and the hearing rooms of HPSCI and SSCI.

The Attraction of Covert Action

The trend lines in Figure 9.2 suggest that when the U.S. military is engaged in overt warfare the emphasis on the use of CIA covert actions rises in concert. The prominent illustrations are the Korean War, the Vietnam War, and the current global war against terrorists, coupled with the related conflicts in Iraq and Afghanistan. The Reagan Administration, though, demonstrated that covert action can play a major role in American foreign policy outside the framework of overt warfare. With Ronald Reagan in the White House, CAs took flight Phoenix-like after a post–Vietnam War dormancy—even during a decade of relative peace, with few Americans dying in combat. The missionary anti-Communist zeal of the Reagan Administration fueled this enthusiastic adoption of the third option. Thus, it appears that not only open warfare, but strong ideological convictions as well can turn administrations toward "special activities" (yet another euphemism for covert action, etched in Latin—*Actiones Praecipuae*—at the entrance to the CAS suite of offices at Langley).

The best single predictor of an administration's emphasis on covert action, though, seems to be the amount of spending it devotes to overt military budgets—whether in times of war or peace (see Figure 9.3). Put another way, periods of increased spending on the U.S. military can be as telling as open military intervention, or an administration's ideological zeal against an adversary, when it comes to an increase in the adoption of covert action as an instrument of foreign policy.

Other generalizations about covert action rise from the ups-and-downs of Figure 9.2. Based on America's previous experiences with this approach, one can expect CAs in the future:

- to advance U.S. foreign-policy objectives around the world by way of secret propaganda, political, economic activities, and paramilitary operations;

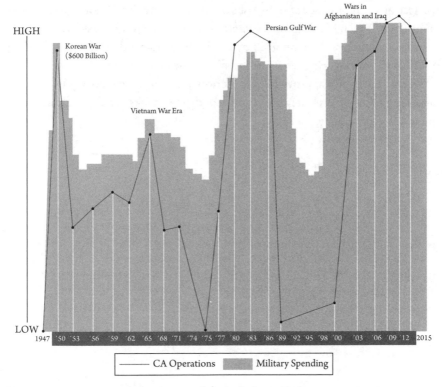

Figure 9.3 Covert Action Emphasis and Overt Military Budgets, 1947–2015. Source:
See note 49 in chapter 9 regarding the covert action estimates presented in this figure; the U.S. defense
spending data are derived from a Department of Defense publication, issued by the Office of the
Under Secretary of Defense (Comptroller): *National Defense Budget Estimates for FY2014* (May 2013),
table 6.2, pp. 97–102, augmented through 2015 with periodic reports in DoD spending found in *New
York Times* articles on this subject.

- to decline in use periodically, as a result of overt military successes (after which covert actions are no longer needed) or failures (no longer wanted); when CAs have been discredited (as with the Bay of Pigs and the Iran-contra scandal); and when pressure to achieve government savings erodes funding support for covert actions (as occurred during the Nixon Administration);
- and to succeed when legitimately approved at home by way of Hughes-Ryan procedures, and when exhibiting well-orchestrated synergism in the field among CIA operatives, U.S. military forces, and a well-disciplined, well-armed indigenous ally within the target nation (the post-9/11 example in Afghanistan).

One conclusion is certain: the third option is here to stay, as presidents and their aides search for ways to promote American interests abroad while avoiding the frustrations of diplomacy and the risks of open warfare. Intelligence overseers—whether on SSCI, HPSCI, or elsewhere—must come to understand when this approach is likely to be embraced by the United States; double down on their questioning during Hughes-Ryan briefings; demand regular reporting on the progress of properly approved covert actions; deal more effectively with drone targeting; and review closely the very use of drone attacks—a disquieting instrument of foreign policy.

10

In the Wilderness

Coping with Counterintelligence

Mirrors, Mirrors Everywhere

Of all the interesting individuals I have met within the IC since 1975—eccentric scientists (including a DS&T expert who waxed on at length about the threat of asteroids striking Earth), a variety of tough paramilitary "snake-eaters," brilliant analysts, steely-eyed security officers, suave legislative liaison staff, and battle-worn DCIs—the most intriguing person is no doubt James J. Angleton, the chief of counterintelligence at the CIA from 1954 to 1974. In his memoirs, DCI Richard Helms referred to him as "the dominant counterintelligence figure in the non-communist world" in his day.[1] One can hardly think of Angleton (he died in 1987) without recalling his oft-repeated reference to counterintelligence as a "wilderness of mirrors"—a poetic description of the bewildering complexities and ambiguities associated with this intelligence mission.[2]

The purpose of this chapter is, first, to provide a feel for the intricacies that accompany the practice—and the oversight—of counterintelligence (CI). I try to impart these intricacies by exploring the mission through the eyes of Angleton, a master practitioner. Second, I examine briefly the evolution of counterintelligence in the United States since the end of the Angleton era. And, third, I suggest some of the key requisites for managing accountability within this mission—a task that is, at times, even more baffling than the difficulties of tracking covert actions.

The Meaning of Counterintelligence

As explored in the previous chapter, the United States collects and analyzes information about threats and opportunities related to the nation's security, from the protection of the homeland and its citizens to the advancement of

America's interests and values worldwide. This information, gathered by the IC, can serve as a shield against danger, as well as a guide to success in diplomatic negotiations, trade talks, covert actions, and warfare. The information comes from open sources, human assets, and sophisticated machines that can look and listen around the planet. The names of the assets and the technical specifications of the machines—"sources and methods"—are among the U.S. government's most carefully kept secrets. The purpose of counterintelligence is to conceal the identity of these assets and their activities from discovery by America's adversaries and to guard the machines against manipulation or destruction by hostile intelligence services or terrorist organizations—including the threat of cyberattacks (cyberterrorism and cybersecurity are important subsets of CI).[3]

Counterintelligence has the further duty, arm-in-arm with law enforcement officials, of helping the United States defend itself more broadly against possible attacks by foreign intelligence services; insider threats like Snowden; subversives within the nation (such as so-called patriot groups—right-wing, extreme antigovernment organizations); "lone wolf" assailants like the San Bernardino killers; and a growing number of international terrorist factions. The modus operandi adopted by these enemies of the United States might include cyberattacks; aerial terrorism; gunfire and bombings at malls and other populated locations; sabotage against nuclear plants, railroads, harbors, and airports; hidden placement of chemical, biological, nuclear, and radioactive materials on freighters bound for U.S. ports; the recruitment of traitors ("moles," such as Ames and Hanssen) inside America's spy agencies; and the infiltration of foreign spies into, say, U.S. weapons laboratories or warplane manufacturing plants. The list of possibilities is lengthy. Formally defined, counterintelligence means "information gathered and activities conducted to identify, deceive, exploit, disrupt or protect against espionage, other intelligence activities, sabotage or assassination conducted for or on behalf of foreign powers, organizations or persons or their agents, or international terrorist organizations or activities."[4] A look back at the Angleton experience with counterintelligence breathes some life into this definition, while underscoring the difficulties of exploring one of the darkest caves in the intelligence community.

Wandering in the Wilderness with James Angleton

My relationship with Angleton began in 1975 when, as an investigator on the Church Committee, I was assigned to report on the CIA's approach to counterintelligence. At the time that meant Angleton's approach.[5] The setting in Washington that year included a resurgent Congress, which had resolved to halt the erosion of its powers at the hands of an imperial presidency, as symbolized most conspicuously by the events referred to in abbreviated form as "Watergate" and "Vietnam." Recall from earlier chapters in this book that, in the decades prior to the domestic spy scandal known as Operation CHAOS, congressional oversight of America's espionage agencies had been less than robust. In response to this feckless congressional authority not only within the intelligence arena but across the broad landscape of public policy, lawmakers took several steps in the mid-1970s toward restoring the status of Congress as an equal branch of government. In the foreign-policy domain, this rehabilitation began formally with passage of the Case-Zablocki Act in 1972, an attempt to gain some control over U.S. diplomacy by requiring improved reporting from the bureaucracy on the use of executive agreements abroad.[6] The next year, lawmakers enacted the War Powers Resolution, a significant—if clumsy and often ignored—attempt to bring Congress back into the game with respect to the nation's war-making powers.[7] In the midst of this institutional uprising came the startling accusations in the *Times* of CIA spying against U.S. citizens.

In 1974, the reporting in the *Times* on Operation CHAOS left an impression of gestapo-like operations occurring inside the United States (see chapter 3). With Watergate and Vietnam as a backdrop, here was a "fatal spark" (as DCI William Colby remembered) that triggered the investigations by the Church Committee and two other panels in the nation's capital.[8] The Year of Intelligence was under way. A rush of additional intelligence reports from Sy Hersh and other journalists followed throughout the winter season. As Colby recollected in his memoir, "Under the steady drumbeat, the Congress was roused to a high state of indignation, and a demand for a wide-ranging investigation of the CIA swept Washington."[9]

Angleton Is Fired

At about this same time in late 1974, Colby dismissed James Angleton, who was known for his secretive management style at the helm of the Agency's Counterintelligence Staff (CIS, a division of the Operations Directorate). According to one account, the DCI axed the CI chief because Angleton had unfairly tagged selected CIA officers as Soviet plants (moles) inside the Agency without adequate evidence to support his claims. His innuendoes against intelligence officers amounted, in Colby's estimation, to a form of McCarthyism at Langley that was ruining the careers of individuals who seemed to have a perfectly honorable record of service. The final straw, according to this account, occurred when Angleton informed the head of French intelligence that the Agency's new chief of station (COS) in Paris was actually a Soviet asset, thereby (to say the least) undermining his effectiveness. The DCI became increasingly convinced that Angleton's overzealous hunt for Soviet plants was harming the

CIA's day-to-day functioning.[10] Colby's son recalls that his father simply "didn't want Angleton in his rice bowl."[11]

At Langley, speculation was rampant that Angleton was overreacting in his search for Soviet infiltrators because he had been so embarrassingly fooled in 1949–1951 by the British MI6 liaison to Washington, Harold A. R. "Kim" Philby. The suave British intelligence officer had developed a friendship with Angleton, who did not suspect at first that the MI6 superstar might actually be a Soviet agent. At the time, Angleton—the vaunted Agency CI chief and an unalloyed Anglophile from his Office of Strategic Services (OSS) days in London—had what turned out to be the KGB's most prized asset right under his nose, as the two frequented Georgetown restaurants and watering holes together during Philby's "service" in Washington. Only belatedly did Angleton begin to have some suspicions about this most brazen and successful of all the Soviet moles aimed at the United States. In 1951, Philby was recalled to London and dismissed from MI6, whose doubts about him had also begun to grow. The well-connected Cambridge University grad was exonerated by the British prime minister, however, and he turned to journalism as a trade, with a domicile in Lebanon. When on the verge of finally being revealed as a Soviet asset by a British agent burrowed deep inside the KGB in Moscow, Philby panicked and boarded a freighter headed for Russia in 1963. When Philby's true allegiance was at last confirmed, Angleton no doubt experienced deep feelings of humiliation and anger, even if he had already started to have his own misgivings about his Georgetown dining companion.[12]

Colby and others at the CIA reached the conclusion in 1974 that Angleton had become harmfully obsessed by the single idea that the KGB had control over all of the Agency's agents and contacts in the U.S.S.R., and, further, that the KGB had managed to riddle Langley with its own spies. Even the so-called Sino-Soviet split of 1962 (a falling apart of political relations between the two large powers, China and Russia) was, according to Angleton's increasingly distorted worldview, dezinformatsiya—a Communist disinformation operation. In reality the split was, he argued, a sham designed to lull the West into complacency. As Colby recalled, "Our concern over possible KGB penetration . . . had so preoccupied us that we were devoting most of our time to protecting ourselves from the KGB and not enough to developing the new sources and operations that we needed to learn secret information about the Soviets and their allies."[13] During Angleton's tenure, Agency attempts to penetrate the Russian intelligence services had ground to a halt. A key question at the CIA became, according to Colby, "whether our operations were totally suspect, as Angleton held, or whether they were being hamstrung by overcautious suspicion."[14] Missing, in the DCI's view, were aggressive activities to recruit Soviet intelligence officers who could serve as moles for the United States inside the Kremlin and its tributaries, an aspiration that Angleton deemed inadvisable because all of the Agency's attempts would likely be discovered and turned against the United States by crafty Soviet intelligence officers who had a team of moles operating within America's intelligence agencies.

Another explanation for Angleton's dismissal is that Colby had become fed up with the fact that the Agency's all-important Israeli account was being handled almost exclusively by the CI chief, who had strong ties to Israel that dated back to friendships he had developed with Jewish resistance leaders during the war against the Nazis.[15] Moreover, Colby wanted to disperse authority for counterintelligence more widely throughout the Agency, rather than have it lodged in the hands of Angleton and his staff within the Operations Directorate. As Colby later recalled, Angleton's "supersecretive style of operation had, at least in recent years, become incompatible with the one I believed essential."[16]

Probably it was a confluence of these concerns that drove the DCI to confront Angleton and send him into forced retirement. For several months, Angleton managed to resist Colby's attempts to remove him. Eventually, though, the DCI concluded that either he or Angleton had to be in charge of the Agency's relations with Israel, so he moved more resolutely against the CI chief. Disgruntled, brooding, his pride injured, Angleton stepped down in December 1974, just as the Agency was about to become engulfed in the "intelligence wars" with the Church, Pike, and Rockefeller panels.

The timing of Angleton's firing made it appear as though he had been selected by Colby as the Agency's scapegoat in response to the *Times* revelations about CHAOS and other improper surveillance activities against Vietnam War protesters in the United States. Many assumed that Angleton's departure was tantamount to an admission of guilt for his involvement in these illegal operations. Privately, though, Angleton blamed the Office of Security (OS) in a different Agency unit—the Directorate of Administration rather than the DO—for the excesses of CHAOS that took place after Colby had transferred the operation from the Counterintelligence Staff to the OS in 1973.[17] At the time of this transfer, Colby took the Agency's counterintelligence liaison relationships with the FBI away from Angleton as well, leaving him with a significantly diminished CI staff.

Preparing for a Wilderness Trek

Early in the Church Committee investigation, Frederick A. O. "Fritz" Schwarz, Jr., the panel's chief counsel, asked me to assist John T. Elliff, a fellow staffer and head of the task force on the FBI, with his examination of the government's counterintelligence activities. Elliff would look at the Bureau; my job was to peer into the Agency's CI practices and prepare for a hearing in which

Angleton would be the star witness. I was given this duty because I was already deeply involved in preparing for hearings on the Huston Plan, which was essentially a blueprint for extreme and often illegal domestic counterintelligence operations approved by President Nixon in 1970. The Angleton assignment led me to a series of lunches and interviews with him throughout the second half of 1975. We would meet at the Army-Navy Club in downtown Washington, his favorite haunt in the District. We also went for occasional drives in his top-of-the-line black Mercedes sedan on a road that bordered the C&O Canal, traveling from Georgetown out into the Maryland countryside and not always within the speed limit.[18]

In preparation for this daunting assignment—the lamb (I was thirty-three) interrogates the lion—I did all the research my time would allow on past counterintelligence cases, as well as on the mysterious leader of the CI staff, a part of the apparatus at Langley that Colby once referred to as the "most secret of Agency crannies."[19] First, I reviewed the history of the "atomic spies." America's construction of atomic bombs under the auspices of the Manhattan Project, in hopes of ending World War II without the horrendous costs of a land invasion of Japan, relied on the highest levels of secrecy. The detonation of a nuclear weapon on Japanese soil would have more persuasive power on the Japanese emperor and his warriors if it came as a surprise weapon. Secrecy means counterintelligence, whose very purpose is to keep America's hush-hush activities secure. Yet as closely guarded as the Manhattan Project's facilities, meetings, and documents were, the United States suffered some of its greatest counterintelligence failures at the site of the bomb construction in Los Alamos, New Mexico.

One of the British scientists allowed to join the Manhattan Project was Klaus Fuchs, who turned out to be the KGB's "single most valuable asset" during the early stages of the Cold War.[20] Only after the end of the war would the United States learn that he had been a Soviet mole working side-by-side with U.S. scientists at Los Alamos. The data he provided the Kremlin likely shaved off several years from the time it would have taken scientists in the U.S.S.R. to build an A-bomb without his kick-start, not to mention saving Moscow millions of rubles in development costs. Fuchs had U.S. confederates in his spy ring, including Julius and Ethel Rosenberg. Others in this Soviet spy ring included David Greenglass and Russell McNutt, who skulked around (respectively) the Manhattan Project facilities in New Mexico and the uranium refinement plant in Oak Ridge, Tennessee, to collect nuclear-weapons information for their Moscow handlers.[21]

Only decades later would the research of Haynes, Klehr, and Vassiliev reveal that some five hundred Americans had been enticed by the KGB or the GRU (Soviet military intelligence) into spying against the United States during the 1930s and 1940s.[22] Many of these individuals were low-level, insignificant assets, clipping newspaper articles about developments in the United States and forwarding them to their KGB handlers; some, though, were truly damaging. Most of the useful assets recruited by the Soviets were working in the private sectors of the American economy, notably engineers with technical information about weaponry and industrial capabilities. A few, however, were also well placed inside government offices in Washington, D.C.

One of the Soviet spies was William Weisband of the NSA, who gave sensitive sigint information to the Kremlin that warned them of the Venona program— the interception by U.S. Army Intelligence of Russian military communications (which had led to the capture of Klaus Fuchs). Weisband's treachery brought a sudden halt to this intelligence fountainhead. A prominent left-leaning American journalist, I. F. Stone, had also been brought into the Communist fold soon after the beginning of the Cold War; so was the personal secretary of the nation's leading newspaper columnist at the time, Walter Lippmann (although the Soviets had been unable to recruit the stellar journalist himself). While not everyone agrees with this conclusion, most CI experts believe further that a senior State Department official and pinstriped member of the Georgetown social elite, Alger Hiss, had been seduced as well by the GRU into joining its stable of penetrations inside the U.S. government.

In my preparations for meeting with Angleton, I learned in addition that the Soviets continued to have significant recruitment successes into the 1960s, including Jack E. Dunlap, an NSA employee, who turned over reams of sigint data to Moscow; and the U.S. Navy Walker family—among the KGB's premier assets—who sold documents to the Kremlin on America's highly classified sigint program for tracing Soviet subs beneath the seas, along with information on the firing codes for U.S. submarine-launched ballistic missiles (SLBMs).[23] Had World War III broken out between the superpowers, this intelligence could have been profoundly damaging to the West.

Angleton: Renaissance Man

Digging into the history of Angleton himself, I learned that—like Frank Church— he was from Boise, Idaho. As a young man, Angleton completed his undergraduate degree at Yale, then headed for Harvard Law School, as would Church a few years later. Church transferred back to Stanford University (where he had completed his undergraduate degree) to finish his legal studies, while Angleton abandoned the study of law altogether after a year and joined the OSS, where he served during World War II in London and later in Italy. Church spent the war years as an Army intelligence officer in China. After the war, Angleton signed on for service in the CIA during its early days and—as a fixture of the Georgetown social scene, aided by his Yale, Harvard, and (especially) OSS connections— he rapidly climbed to the position of the Agency's counterintelligence chief. In this capacity he pursued, in Colby's words, an "unrelenting campaign" to reveal and frustrate Soviet intelligence operations against the United States (perhaps with the haunting specter of Kim Philby leering over his shoulder).[24] Meanwhile, Frank Church had set his eye on the U.S. Senate and, in his first bid for political office, managed to successfully grab this golden ring—in part as a result of his coruscating oratory but also because his Republican opponent (the incumbent) was suffering from rapidly deteriorating health.

The stories about Angleton that floated around the offices of the Church Committee (where he was known as "Mother," one of the many monikers that his Agency colleagues had invented for him privately over the years[25]) painted an impressive portrait. He was a world-class orchid grower; an expert on trout fishing, who tied his own elaborate flies; an outstanding soccer player and golfer in college, as well as being proficient at tennis; and a prominent persona on the Yale campus, as the editor of the avant-garde student literary magazine entitled *Furioso*. During his undergraduate days, he arranged visits to the university by leading poets from around the country (although he was a pedestrian student in most of his classes).[26]

In the OSS, Angleton proved indefatigable as a counterintelligence officer, often sleeping in a bunk by his desk. Moving on to the CIA after the war, he adroitly cultivated the friendship of a succession of prominent DCIs, including Walter Bedell Smith, Allen W. Dulles, and Richard Helms. Much of Angleton's mystique stemmed from his encyclopedic memory of counterintelligence cases through the years. He could cite chapter and verse on the names, postings, objectives, and personal idiosyncrasies of every significant KGB and GRU officer who had ever served around the world since the beginning of the Cold War. Further, he knew the finest details of every CI case that involved foreign penetration operations aimed at the CIA. His Ivy League education, coupled with the impassioned intensity with which he discussed his favorite counterintelligence cases, added to the aura that no one knew better than he how to guard the nation against the machinations of foreign spy services.

Moreover, Angleton was reputed to be a man of highly refined tastes, from his luxury automobile, his elegantly tailored British suits (the CI chief's devotion to all things British had been nurtured by three years as a teen in a British public school, Malvern College), and the wine he drank, to the operatic music he listened to while traveling from his suburban home in Arlington to the Headquarters Building at Langley. The trunk of his car was fitted with an elaborate sound system, designed and installed by NASA engineers he had befriended. As I discovered as we motored along the C&O Canal, the system could flood the interior of the sedan at high volume with his favorite Italian arias. He was fluent in Italian and French. During his boyhood, Angleton spent years in Milan with his family when his father purchased the Italian subsidiary of the National Cash

Register Company. If ever there were a Renaissance Man, the former CIA's chief of counterintelligence seemed to fit the bill.

The Huston Plan

On a darker side, my research indicated that Angleton had also been a key figure in the Huston Plan, the master espionage scheme hatched in 1969–1970 during the Nixon Administration to conduct illegal surveillance against protesters in the anti–Vietnam War movement. Specifically, Angleton had been in charge of the Agency's Project HT Lingual from 1955 to 1973, an element of Operation CHAOS that involved the opening of first-class mail—a criminal offense. HT Lingual existed even before the Huston Plan, with the latter's ironic request for presidential authority to allow CIA mail opening inside the United States that was (unbeknownst to the White House) already under way; the mail opening would continue on even after President Nixon rescinded the authority for the Huston Plan later in the year. Until Colby transferred these assignments to the Agency's Office of Security in 1973, the CI staff had been involved in the broader attempt through Operation CHAOS to address President Nixon's concern (and President Lyndon B. Johnson's before him) about whether the antiwar movement in the United States was being funded and manipulated by the Soviet Union. The answer turned out to be no; the antiwar movement was homegrown, fueled by youthful opposition to America's controversial involvement in a distant civil war roiling in Indochina, and financed by "credit-card revolutionaries" whose travels around the country were financed by generous parents.[27]

Throughout 1968 and 1969, students and other antiwar protesters arrived in Washington by the thousands. The White House resorted to using D.C. Metro buses to circle the White House as a guard against the swelling crowds, as if President Nixon and his aides were pioneers warding off attacks by fierce and resentful Comanche. Historian Theodore H. White recalled the state of affairs in the nation's capital: "Perplexed by a street madness which seemed beyond the control of either his staff, his own efforts, or the FBI, [President Nixon] groped for solutions."[28] Recall from chapter 3 that White House aide John Ehrlichman heard of a young man working with the Republican National Committee (RNC), Tom Charles Huston, who as a student at Indiana University had backed the war in Vietnam and looked upon the shabbily dressed, leftist protesters as a low form of life. Huston had also been a volunteer in the Nixon presidential campaign, as well as a former Army intelligence officer. In 1969, Ehrlichman called him to the Oval Office and, in the name of President Nixon, asked him to write a report for the White House on whether the Soviet Union was funding the antiwar protests. The president appeared briefly at this meeting to give Huston a pep talk and send him on his way, with authority to work with the IC in the preparation of his

study. Pumped up and already imbued with a sense of zeal to carry on his crusade begun at Indiana University against unwashed lefties, Huston immediately
went to FBI Headquarters seeking help in carrying out his presidential orders.

At the Bureau, Huston—carrying the White House baton—got an immediate audience with William C. Sullivan, the number three official at the FBI
and, as the head of the Bureau's domestic intelligence unit, the government's
top counterintelligence officer in charge of thwarting Soviet activities inside
the U.S. homeland. Sullivan prudently asked the youthful presidential emis-
sary to put his request for assistance in writing to FBI Director J. Edgar Hoover.
Huston prepared a letter asking for the Bureau's guidance in determining what
intelligence gaps existed regarding the sources of funding for the protesters. He
sent the letter not only to Hoover, but also to the other top brass in the IC: DCI
Richard Helms, DIA Director Donald Bennett (an Army general), and NSA
Director Noel Gayler (an admiral).

Huston closely followed the counsel of William Sullivan on how to proceed and, in July 1970, a year after being tapped by Ehrlichman, he was ready
to convene the intelligence officials for face-to-face planning about how to
aid the White House against the antiwar throngs continuing to gather on the
Washington Mall. Meeting at the Agency (a popular location for interagency
meetings, because parking was easy on the Langley campus), the four towering
figures in the IC agreed that the legal barriers preventing intelligence collection
against protesters inside the United States would need to be lowered.

In the first week of June, Huston and the nation's spy chiefs took their case
to the president. Sitting at his desk in the Oval, Nixon described the protesters
as misguided youths who were "reaching out for the support—ideological and
otherwise—of foreign powers." They were "radicals" who intended to "destroy
the country." It was up to Hoover and the others to "insure that the fullest possible inter-agency cooperation is being realized and that all our resources are
being utilized to gather the types of information which will enable us to halt the
spread of this terrorism before it gets completely out of hand."[29]

On June 25, 1970—twenty days after their powwow with the president—
Huston and the spy leaders convened in Hoover's downtown office at FBI
Headquarters to sign the top-secret (now declassified), forty-three-page
"Special Report" that became known in the White House as the Huston Plan.
Hoover, Helms, Bennett, and Gayler all signed the document that authorized
illegal counterintelligence operations inside the United States. Huston made
it clear to President Nixon that some of the proposed intelligence operations
involved burglary and were against the law. Among the collection methods given
the go-ahead by the president, nonetheless, included mail coverage and access to
telegrams (abetted by communications companies in the private sector, such as
International Telephone and Telegraph, ITT); break-ins, or what the FBI refers

to as "second-story jobs"; domestic sigint operations; and the development of humint on college campuses.[30] As historian White has written, the Huston Plan allowed the secret agencies to reach "all the way to every mailbox, every college campus, every telephone, every home in America."[31] On July 14, the president officially signed the authorization for the plan to be implemented. Huston's intelligence handiwork in violation of the law was now secret presidential policy.

The plan proved short-lived, however. When Attorney General John Mitchell—no friend of the antiwar movement—caught wind of the Huston Plan, he persuaded Hoover and the president that the risks of public exposure were too high, potentially having a damaging political effect on the White House and the FBI. Hoover withdrew his support and the president quickly followed suit. The attempt to turn America into a counterintelligence state had failed—although no thanks to the IC's leaders or to the Agency's chief of counterintelligence, James Angleton, who knew about the scheme, as well as about the CIA's ongoing CI collection program known as CHAOS. In 1975, the Church Committee would call Huston as its central witness for public hearings into his eponymous plan. Five years after the fact, he expressed remorse for his involvement in the set of spy recommendations recommended to and approved by the president.

The Huston Plan would stay in my mind as I prepared for my meetings with James Angleton, as a reminder that accountability over counterintelligence operations is just as important as it is for any other dimension of intelligence activity. The plan made me doubly wary of my approaching interviews with the former CIA/CI chief.

Tutorials at the Army-Navy Club

Through a CIA liaison officer assigned to the Church Committee, I contacted Angleton in July 1975 and explained that I had been asked by chief counsel Schwarz to explore his views on counterintelligence. A week later, we met for the first time at the Army-Navy Club in the center of Washington on Farragut Square, a few blocks east of the White House. We would have several lunches together at the club in the coming months. Much later I would have a firsthand appreciation for the observation of an Agency historian that Angleton had an air of "I know something you don't know" about him.[32] His physical appearance reminded me of the photographs I had seen of the American poet T. S. Eliot (whom Angleton had befriended in London during World War II). He was tall but stooped, lean, dark-complexioned, grim, and dressed in a somber, Seville-tailored three-piece, dark business suit.[33] Angleton selected a remote table in the club's dining room, situated beneath a ceiling speaker that emitted pop music—including, now and then, themes from a variety of James Bond films. "That awful noise will mask our talk," he said to me in a furtive, whispery voice.

After we ordered lunch at this first meeting, I halfway expected him to pull from his vest pocket a deck of Tarot cards. Instead he began the conversation by explaining the central task of counterintelligence, namely, to construct a "wilderness of mirrors" (I smiled inwardly that he actually used this phrase that I had so often heard associated with him), in which the opponent would be confused and forever lost. This is exactly what he thought the Soviets were achieving against the West. As he ate and drank with refined European manners, Angleton wasted no time launching into the details of some well-known counterintelligence cases from the past, beginning with Yuri Ivanovich Nosenko, the KGB officer who in 1962 offered to spy for the CIA and defected to the United States two years later.[34] Now and then, he would interrupt his tutorial, offer a smile (all the more captivating for its rarity), and ask me something about my interests. For the most part, though, his obsession with the minutiae of cat-and-mouse tales from the world of counterintelligence ruled the day. As he spoke, his voice was low and flat; from his Ivy League diction, one could never have guessed he was from Idaho, except for an occasional "yep" for "yes" in response to some of my questions.

As he delved into past cases, everything revealed seemed to suggest something concealed. The convoluted trail of spies and counterspies spun bewilderingly in my mind after listening to Angleton for a couple of hours. I have some sympathy for Colby's verdict in his memoirs that the CI chief's "explanations were impossible to follow."[35] My conversations with Angleton lacked all semblance of a linear narrative. Counterintelligence is a labyrinthine subject in itself, where the truth is hidden and sometimes impossible to find; but he had a way of making the subject even more obscure and opaque—a cave bathed in an inky gloom within the Agency's blackest catacombs. To draw upon a different metaphor from a book I wrote about the Church Committee, talking with Angleton was like trying to find a new planet through an earthbound telescope: it took constant probing, a sensitivity for nuance, and a willingness to endure vast oceans of silence.[36] He might begin an intriguing and significant account of a CI operation, then it would peter out like a vanishing comet and disappear into a black hole of ambiguity. In a paraphrase of Mark Twain, listening to Angleton for a half hour could make a man dizzy; listening to him for a whole hour would make him drunk.[37] Or as Colby once put it, Angleton's theories about Soviet intelligence operations could be "tortuous."[38]

With or without Angleton's added layers of mystery, the counterintelligence histories we examined could be mind-bending in themselves—a vexing challenge for those engaged in CI accountability. If even counterintelligence experts in the FBI and the CIA periodically fail to agree on a defector's bona fides, how is a lawmaker to evaluate who is correct? Nosenko is a prime example. Leading counterintelligence experts in both the CIA and the FBI spent hundreds of hours interrogating him at the Farm. Sleep deprivation, alternating with loud piped-in music, was used, and this technique can be excruciating after several days—although the interrogators eschewed as ineffective the harsher methods the Agency would embrace after 9/11. Despite these persistent efforts, FBI and CIA counterintelligence specialists could not agree on whether Nosenko was genuine or a false defector sent to the West for the purposes of sowing confusion through disinformation.

In 1959, while a KGB officer, Nosenko had served as Lee Harvey Oswald's case officer when the former U.S. Marine renounced his U.S. citizenship and moved to the Soviet Union. Angleton felt certain that when Nosenko defected to the United States in 1964, he came as a "disinformation officer." His hidden agenda was to bring to the IC the message that Oswald had no connection with the KGB that would implicate the Kremlin in the murder of President John F. Kennedy. Immediately Angleton instinctually drew just the opposite conclusion: Oswald must have still been in Moscow's control on November 22, 1963, when he killed Kennedy. For an insider, let alone an outsider, teasing out the facts in this and other CI investigations can be a brain-wearying exercise—like digging a well with a needle (in the Turkish proverb).

The CI chief remained convinced that Nosenko was a liar. It was true that the defector had failed every polygraph test the Agency gave him; further, the Russian told a number of mistruths during his interrogations, such as claiming he was a KGB lieutenant colonel when he was actually just a captain. Angleton also pointed to the suspicions raised by an earlier KGB defector, Major Anatoli Mikhailovich Golitsyn, who said that his old organization would soon be sending to the United States a false defector who would attempt to discredit him and fool the Agency in many ways through the dissemination of false information. In contrast to Angleton's perspective, FBI interrogators came away from months of questioning Nosenko in full acceptance of his testimony. Eventually, after the CIA kept the Russian in solitary confinement for four years, DCI Colby finally overruled Angleton's misgivings and freed Nosenko, providing him with back pay and hiring him as an Agency consultant on KGB and GRU methods and activities.

Dizzying? Disorienting? Yes, and thus the wilderness of mirrors metaphor. Another illustration is KGB colonel Vitaliy Sergeyevich Yurchenko, who "defected" to the United States in 1995, only to re-defect three months later. Had he been a "dangle," merely sent to America in order to probe the Agency's CI procedures and spread disinformation before fleeing back to Russia? Counterintelligence specialists again disagreed, although most came down on the side of the argument that Yurchenko had been the real thing; but that, soon after his arrival in the United States, he became fearful that the KGB might harm the family he left behind in Moscow. He decided to return home, where by all accounts he remains alive—a condition that supports the "dangle" hypothesis. About half of all the defectors from foreign intelligence services who, with CIA assistance, come to the United States end up being "dangles" or "false defectors." This percentage is sufficiently large to instill some degree of Angleton-like paranoia in even the most well grounded of counterintelligence officers.

Just as Angleton was well practiced at deceiving the Soviets, I was well aware that he could turn his talents toward deceiving others as well. I understood how he might view the Church Committee as just another foreign adversary. Indeed, since the recruitment of agents-in-place was a standard method in the discipline of counterintelligence (recruiting assets, but having them stay within their own foreign intelligence service for on-the-spot spying), he might even try to recruit me. I was on guard. Such an attempt never occurred; but, in our early meetings, Angleton did probe constantly for information about the committee's activities and objectives, all of which I sidestepped. The staff was strictly prohibited from discussing committee matters outside the confines of our suite of offices in the Dirksen Office Building. At the beginning of the investigation, one talented staffer had already been fired from the committee for carelessly violating this important rule—chatting with a friend in a crowded restaurant, where he was overheard by two FBI agents having lunch in an adjacent booth. Angleton finally stopped trying to pump me for information about Frank Church and his colleagues; he settled into a pattern of tutoring his young interviewer on classic CI tradecraft. He perhaps calculated that at least I could be taught the value of this intelligence mission, which was an indispensable set of activities (he would preach), not to be interrupted by the asinine and dangerous distractions of a Senate inquiry.

Although Angleton could often be indecipherable, some of his ideas were quite clear—if dated by stale rhetoric from the early years of the Cold War. Following this first lunch, and all the others that came weekly over the next few months in the summer of 1975, we retired to overstuffed settees in the library of the Army-Navy Club, where old men—an assortment of retired admirals and generals, I assumed, although they were dressed in civilian clothing—either dozed (some rather loudly) or read newspapers. Once comfortably ensconced in a remote corner of the library, Angleton lit up a Merit cigarette (it would be some years to come before smoking was banned inside the club) and continued his tutorial, while with his permission I rapidly took verbatim notes (now part of the Church Committee papers locked up in the National Archives in Washington for fifty years—an absurdly long time after the 1975–1976 inquiry). "Frank Church has never understood counterintelligence," he said one afternoon, needling me about my mentor. "His innocence about the world exceeds that of an unborn child. Doesn't he realize the Soviets seek to destroy American intelligence? Moscow is behind most of the mischief in the world. What will it take to wake him up?" He chain-smoked several more Merits down to their fil-ters, using the dying embers of one cigarette to light the next, which he extracted deftly from a vest pocket in his suit. Brushing aside my attempts at rebuttal, he went on: "Church's objective is transparent: to fashion a statutory straitjacket for the Agency. Whose payroll is he on: KGB? GRU? Or perhaps the Cubans have recruited him. I have a photograph of your senator playing basketball with Fidel in Cuba."

I reminded Angleton that Church had simply been a member of a congres-sional delegation visiting Havana for a few days. All of the lawmakers met with Castro at his villa and shot a few hoops with him.

"I know. They are all as naïve as Church," was his clipped reply.

One afternoon in September, a few weeks before the Church Committee was scheduled to hold its public hearing on counterintelligence, Angleton drank more than his usual two kirs with lunch. As was often the case, he seemed moody, even despondent. In the library, he ordered another kir and soon became agitated. "Moscow's objective is the destruction of the capitalist states," he said, drawing deeply on a cigarette as he peered around the room. The only other person in the library was an elderly man with the features of a well-fed walrus. He slept soundly in a club chair on the other side of the room, his fingers laced across an ample girth, his mustache twitching now and then. I pulled a notepad out of my coat pocket and jotted down Angleton's comments as he continued. "Each day the KGB tries to infiltrate the Western intelligence services," he fumed, "and they have had great success. Soviet agents have been used by the Kremlin to steal secrets from the United States and I have no doubt there is a well-placed mole in the Agency today. And now the KGB has been given even more aggressive instructions: to destroy the CIA by sowing disruption on the inside."

Angleton leaned forward in his chair. His dark eyes stared at me for a while behind wide-rimmed, thick eyeglasses. He finally asked: "And what has been at the center of the Kremlin's strategy against the West?" I knew from experience the question was rhetorical and that his answer would follow. "Deception," he went on, "a strategy that has worked all too well against the gullible liberals in this country, in the media and in Congress." The former CI chief spoke about the Soviet nemesis with such brio that it was hard to resist being caught up in his emotional rants. His eyes glowering, Angleton continued: "The purpose of Soviet deception operations is to destabilize and weaken members of NATO. The techniques used by the KGB are penetrations and 'active measures' [the Soviet term for covert action]. Psychological warfare is a key element of their strategy. In the West, we use deception in military combat; in Russia, it is an integral part of everyday national strategy."

I had heard all of this before during our previous meetings and I was grow-ing weary of the endless diatribes against Senator Church and his committee, as well as Angleton's repetitive theories on Soviet deception operations. At least, though, the counterintelligence theories were more comprehensible than his tireless—and tiresome—harangues about specific CI cases: Nosenko, Golitsyn, and other bugbears of the Red Menace that populated his mind. We would later find out that the CIA chief of counterintelligence might have been better served by focusing more on China, which ended up stealing every single U.S. nuclear-weapon design, allowing the leaders in Beijing to "leapfrog generations of tech-nology development."[39]

"The CIA has been the primary target of Soviet deception," Angleton went on, now on his fourth kir. I had lost count of the many cigarettes he had smoked since lunch. "The KGB feeds disinformation into our channels of intelligence collection, which is passed on to the analysts and then to key policymakers." He blew smoke from the side of his mouth and polished off the drink. "Certain liberals on the Senate Foreign Relations Committee," he resumed, without men-tioning Church and his more progressive colleagues on that panel by name, "have rushed to support SALT, START, and all those other phony arms-control deals, denying all the time that the Russians cheat on every one of them. My staff has uncovered Soviet manipulations of telemetry data on SS-5s, SS-7s, and other Soviet missiles. The Kremlin routinely conceals new weapons systems and encrypts their telemetry. The Soviets continue to construct underground bunkers, subways, tunnels, and caves beneath Moscow and in other locations throughout Russia, all in violation of supposedly solemn treaties with the West." He slouched back into his chair and stared at me in silence for a full minute. "How many senior officials at the CIA are a part of their efforts?" he finally asked. I just stared back at him for a while until he stood up abruptly, put on his black trench coat and black homburg (Angleton was Gothic before it became fash-ionable among some college students), and marched out of the library without a word.

At our next noon repast, Angleton was in a more cheerful mood; but he was drinking kirs with even greater enthusiasm, to the point where his speech began to slur as we sat in the club library. Leaving counterintelligence modus operandi and recent Soviet intelligence ploys behind for the time being, he dredged back into the history of his early days at the CIA. For the first and only time, he asked me to put away my notebook. Over the next hour, he reminisced about the 1950s, claiming that he had helped the Operations Directorate with its propa-ganda operations aimed at Eastern Europe; and that as well he had had a hand in the paramilitary operations of the SOG staff—most significantly, its secret supply of weaponry to pro-democracy rebels in Budapest to encourage their uprising against Communist rule in Hungary. This support helped fuel the 1956 revolt in Budapest, which led to the massacre of mainly young Hungarians—as many as 15,000—in the streets of Budapest, mowed down by Soviet tank fire.

Today in that city one can still see the pock marks in downtown walls made by shells fired by the Red Army. Angleton seemed proud of this support, but I could only wonder about the morality of encouraging youthful revolutionaries to take up arms against nearly hopeless odds, based on pie-crust promises from Angleton and other DO leaders that the United States would come to their rescue once shots were fired.

Angleton spoke, too, about his acquisition of a copy of Nikita Khrushchev's "Secret Speech" in 1956, which the Soviet president delivered to the Twentieth Congress of the Communist Party of the Soviet Union. In its original (provided to Angleton by Israeli intelligence[40]), the speech was already sharply critical of the prior Stalinist regime; Angleton chose, however, to make the language even more damning of the Soviet system. The CI staff's adulterated version of the text was, Angleton told me, circulated throughout Eastern Europe—a claim that has been subsequently discredited by others who say that this intended operation was halted by higher Agency authorities.[41] Further, he hinted at having personally aided the Israeli nuclear-weapon program but remained vague about any details.[42]

At the time, I was unable to verify such allegations. In fact, I couldn't even confirm his take on many of the various counterintelligence cases he told me about. That would have required access to truckloads of classified documents, along with months of research. Even then, I'm not sure what I would have concluded; I knew that several counterintelligence experts in the CIA and the FBI had done just that yet had issued sharply divergent opinions about the trustworthiness of Nosenko, Golitsyn, and others. Here was the true funhouse of multiple mirrors: trying to determine the veracity of Soviet defectors— or, today, verifying who is truly a guilty terrorist among the detainees at Guantánamo, in contrast to who might have been unfairly rounded up by the U.S. military as it swept through the barren landscapes of Afghanistan in the aftermath of the 9/11 attacks.

At any rate, many of Angleton's stories that afternoon went far beyond the parameters of counterintelligence; they amounted, if true, to the venturing of the CIA's Counterintelligence Staff into the realm of covert action, which fell outside of my Church Committee responsibilities—and, one would have thought, outside of Angleton's duties as CI chief. I mentioned some of his more exotic ramblings to colleagues on the committee staff who were working on covert action; however, no one had any evidence related to these matters that might encourage them to take a closer look, including the astonishing claim that his CI staff had contributed significantly to the development of Israel's nuclear-weapon program. Moreover, their plates were full with a host of more immediate covert action inquiries (most related to Chile), as well as with the investigation into CIA assassination plots overseas. I was snowed under, as well, with a plethora of tasks I had on the committee, including the preparation of the Huston Plan and other hearings, writing speeches for the chairman, and keeping him informed about the staff's research findings in a dozen different areas. Time was running out on the life of our investigation, with the final reports due in early 1976; no one was eager to take up fresh lines of research. The validity of Angleton's kirlaced tales would have to await probes by others in the future.[43]

Angleton in the Klieg Lights

A couple of weeks prior to the Church Committee's single public hearing on counterintelligence (not counting the Huston Plan), my assignment was to interrogate Angleton under oath for the record, so that the senators who would be asking him questions on live television would have a sense in advance about what his likely answers would be. This hearing choreography is standard practice on Capitol Hill; lawmakers don't want to be caught blind-sided during a hearing, especially one that is broadcast on national television. On September 12, I sat down with Angleton in a staff office building across the street from the Church Committee quarters in the Dirksen Building. He was accompanied by one of his assistants, as well as counsel from the Agency's Office of Legal Affairs. A couple of aides from the Church Committee joined us, along with a Senate stenographer who recorded the proceedings. Most of my questions had to do with HT Lingual, Operation CHAOS, counterintelligence methodology, and a few ambiguities about some CI cases (especially relating to Nosenko and Golitsyn). After more than two of hours of intense back and forth, both of us were running out of steam and I wound down the session with a final broad question: Was the CIA bound by all of the government's overt orders; or might it be given one set of covert directives while the government's public agencies (say, the Department of State) operated under another overt—and possibly even contradictory—set of directives?

I had in mind the Church Committee's public hearing the previous week that examined the Agency's storehouse of lethal chemicals, part of its assassination capability. This lingering storehouse of substances—shellfish toxin and cobra venom, for example—violated a White House directive from President Nixon to destroy such materials. More broadly, I was also thinking of covert action. I presumed that with these kinds of operations the CIA, on some occasions, might be secretly directed by the White House to undermine a foreign government, while at the same time diplomats in the State Department might be attempting to improve America's ties with the same regime (at least temporarily).

It was a large question and we needed more time to probe its dimensions; I shouldn't have brought it up so late in the deposition. I was expecting Angleton to say something to the effect that this sometimes happens, although only with the clear knowledge and approval of White House officials and intelligence managers; and that such instances would be reported to legislative overseers. Instead, as he was putting his papers together, Angleton replied, "It is inconceivable that a secret intelligence arm of the government has to comply with all the overt orders of the government." I thought I knew what he meant: in unusual circumstances that required some deception, the CIA might be told to carry out Operation X even though the State Department (for instance) might be offering public assurances that the United States would never engage in such an operation. Years later when he looked back at this episode, history professor Robin Winks of Yale University suggested a similar interpretation of Angleton's off-hand remark: "Angleton was saying that there might well be overt orders from 'the government' . . . which would be countermanded by covert ones."[44]

Yet when this pre-hearing deposition was distributed to senators and staff members on the Church Committee the next day, some read these words as an arrogant statement meaning that the CIA was above both the law and supervision by the White House and Congress—as demonstrated in the previous hearing on the Agency's continued sequestering of lethal substances, regardless of a presidential directive to destroy them. Naively no doubt, I had not anticipated this turn of events; or that one of the senators would latch onto this comment as a centerpiece of his questioning during the approaching televised hearing.

As the day of Angleton's appearance before the committee come near, the media quoted him as saying that by cooperating with the congressional and White House investigations "some officials"—a thinly veiled reference to William Colby—had violated the sacrosanct intelligence obligation to protect sources and methods. By telephone, Angleton informed me at the last minute that he might refuse to appear as a witness. I replied that, if this were the case, he would surely be subpoenaed by the committee. Indeed, at the chairman's request, the committee had approved a subpoena two days before the hearing, just in case it might be needed. This measure proved unnecessary. At the eleventh hour, Angleton told me that he would arrive on Capitol Hill at the designated hour for the hearing. The former CI chief would now have a chance to confront the inquisitors whom he so loathed and whom he had criticized Colby for being too friendly toward.

The curtain rose on the CIA counterintelligence hearing at 10:00 on the morning of September 24, 1975, in Room 318 of the Russell Senate Office Building, our regular hearing room where we had recently held our public hearings on the sequestered toxins and also on the Huston Plan. Known by insiders simply as the Caucus Room, formally it was the Richard B. Russell Senate Caucus Room—the site of such major historical events as the hearings on Pearl Harbor in the 1940s, the McCarthy hearings in the 1950s, and the Iran-contra investigation in the 1980s. Suddenly thrust into public prominence after thirty years of a hidden life behind the Agency's high fences, Angleton looked dazed and acutely uncomfortable in front of the bright lights and TV cameras. He sat bent over in his chair, a scowl on his face, his dark-clad body curled into a question mark.

Senator Church gaveled the session to order and observed that the CIA had illegally opened the mail of Hubert H. Humphrey, Richard Nixon (when he was in Congress), Linus Pauling, John Steinbeck, the Ford Foundation, Harvard University, and the Rockefeller Foundation, among many other individuals and groups; and, further, that when President Nixon rescinded the Huston Plan, the CIA had continued its mail-opening program anyway, leaving the president with the false impression that this and related programs of domestic spying had been terminated.[45] Church asked the CIA counter-intelligence chief about this chain of events, leading to an exchange between two men who had little more in common than an Idaho birthplace and a year at Harvard Law School. Angleton placed his right hand behind an ear and bent it forward so he could hear the chairman better in the crowded Caucus Room. Then he replied:

ANGLETON: Mr. Chairman, I don't think anyone would have hesitated to inform the president if he had at any moment asked for a review of intelligence operations.

CHURCH: That is what he did do. That is the very thing he asked Huston to do. That is the very reason that these agencies got together to make recommendations to him, and when they made their recommendations, they misrepresented the facts.

ANGLETON: I was referring, sir, to a much more restricted forum.

CHURCH: I am referring to the mail, and what I have said is solidly based upon the evidence. The president wanted to be informed. He wanted recommendations. He wanted to decide what should be done, and he was misinformed. Not only was he misinformed, but when he reconsidered authorizing the opening of the mail five days later and revoked it, the CIA did not pay the slightest bit of attention to him, did it—the commander-in-chief as you say?

ANGLETON: I have no satisfactory answer for that.

CHURCH: You have no satisfactory answer?

ANGLETON: No, I do not.

CHURCH: I do not think there is a satisfactory answer because, having revoked the authority, the CIA went ahead with the program. So that the commander-in-chief is not the commander-in-chief at all. He is just a problem. You do not want to inform him in the first place, because he might say no. That is the truth of it. And when he did say no, you disregarded it. And then you called him the commander-in-chief.

Church had won the coveted Joffé debating medal as a student at Stanford University and he was a superb public speaker, in league with another great orator from Idahoan, William Borah (1865–1940), whom Church had listened to and mimicked as a boy. Angleton was no match for him in this kind of exchange. Further, the committee chairman was accustomed not just to debate, but to crowds, public hearings, television lights, and cameras; for the reclusive CI chief, however, this was alien territory.

Angleton admitted that the mail opening was illegal, but he tried in a halting manner to defend the program anyway. "From a counterintelligence point of view," he argued, moving his hand from bending his ear to sheltering his eyes against the harsh klieg lights in the room, "it was vitally important to know everything possible about contacts between U.S. citizens and Communist countries." In our Army-Navy Club meetings, Angleton had told me that the CIA opened the mail of only a fraction of letter writers in the United States—some 215,000 instances, he recalled. "That represents about 0.001 percent of the American population," he had said to me with scorn, "and it included people who were involved in criminal fraternization with the enemy." Now, in the public hearing, he merely lamented that "the nature of the threat" posed by the Soviet Union was insufficiently appreciated, and he shot back at Church: "When I look at the map today and see the weakness of power of this country, that is what shocks me."

Senator Robert B. Morgan, a former state attorney general in North Carolina, responded to Angleton that what shocked him was the violation of individual rights represented by the mail-opening program. Another former state attorney general, Senator Walter F. Mondale of Minnesota, joined the fray. He noted how the White House "talking paper" used by President Nixon at the time of the Huston Plan revealed an "enormous, unrestricted paranoid fear about the American people." That paper stated in part that

> hundreds, perhaps thousands, of Americans mostly under 30—are determined to destroy our society. . . . Our people—perhaps as a reaction to the excesses of the McCarthy era—are unwilling to admit the possibility that their children could wish to destroy their country. This is particularly true of the media and the academic community.[46]

Replying to Senator Mondale, Angleton said, "It was not, in my view, paranoia."

Senator Richard S. Schweiker (R, Pennsylvania) zeroed in on the final question that I had posed to Angleton during the pre-hearing deposition. He asked if Angleton had actually said that America's intelligence agencies did not have to comply with all the overt orders of the government.[47]

"Well, if it is accurate," Angleton replied—and it was, as recorded word-by-word by the Senate stenographer, and the senators had a copy of the transcript on the bench before them. "It should not have been said. . . . I would say I had been rather imprudent in making those remarks." When Senator Church entered into this cross-examination, Angleton further replied: "I am sorry, sir, but it does not necessarily represent my views, . . . I withdraw the statement . . . the entire speculation should not have been indulged in."

That was the extent of Angleton's defense and it came across as insufficient, even lame. He could have calmly explained what he had meant, along the lines of Professor Winks's interpretation, but the shock of the public hearings seemed to have dulled Angleton's capacity to engage in effective rebuttal.[48] He had evidently decided that the best strategy was to display some degree of contrition and hope for an early end to this public spectacle.

I felt some personal distress at the time that my questioning had led to Angleton's humiliation. I thought of all the fascinating discussions we had had about counterintelligence and, less formally, about poetry, jazz, and literature; his years in Italy; his family; his hobbies of orchid growing, fly fishing, and photography. Angleton was a remarkable individual in so many ways; however many mistakes he may have made, he had served his country for over thirty years to the best of his ability. During his tenure as counterintelligence chief, no Soviet mole had been able to penetrate the CIA, unlike the rash of traitors that would soon be discovered inside the Agency during the 1980s when Angleton was no longer at Langley and counterintelligence garnered less attention by Agency officers. Now here he was: an object of ridicule. Well deserved, too, his critics would no doubt respond, pointing to the illegal mail opening; his lingering belief in the Sino-Soviet schism as purely a deception operation against the West; the overreach of the "HONETOL" investigations (a joint CIA-FBI operation led by Angleton to expose Soviet spies within the IC) and other overzealous operations; his rigid alliance with Golitsyn against Nosenko and the poor treatment of the latter, in solitary confinement for 1,277 days in a small and Spartan cinder-block building at the Farm; and many additional CI excesses that had ended in tragic outcomes for the parade of individuals Angleton wrongly accused of disloyalty.[49] These mistakes warranted sharp criticism.

Yet lost in the critique against Angleton were the many good things he had done to elevate the profile of counterintelligence at the CIA. He had, after all, won the Distinguished Intelligence Medal, the Agency's highest honor. A former Angleton critic in the IC attempted to catch the nuances of the man by suggesting that the CI chief had gone through several career phases that could be graphed as a bell-shaped curve: "From the mid-1950s to 1963, Angleton and the CI Staff provided a useful voice of caution within the Agency," this observer said, as quoted in a study of Angleton carried out by a number of former Agency officers. "However, from 1963 to 1971, Angleton—distracted by Golitsyn's claims—was involved in a number of counterproductive and destructive efforts."

Then, in his last years, the critique continued, Angleton "was relatively quiet as Chief of the [CI] Staff and had little, if any influence over Agency operations."[50]

Often lost sight of, too, was Angleton's good work in the OSS, as well as the significant value to U.S. intelligence of his contacts in Israel and throughout Europe during the Cold War, including ties with Mafia figures in France and Italy—useful anti-Communist allies for the CIA in the struggle against local Communist fronts in Europe (though the relationship with the mob in the United States was misused during the plots against Castro). Moreover, he enjoyed effective liaison relationships with counterintelligence officials in the FBI—even when for a time in the 1960s Director Hoover and DCI Helms refused to speak to one another because of a disagreement about the bona fides of a Soviet defector. Lost, further, was all recognition of his personal charm and impressive erudition. During the Church Committee's hearing on counterintelligence, the former CI chief could have been legitimately grilled on a host of subjects; but Senator Schweicker's question about the tension between overt-covert government directives was way down the list of important items in my book—and easily defendable by Angleton in less stressful circumstances. Or so I presumed. I was astounded both by Senator Schweicker's elevation of this subject to a status of top billing in the hearing (he was usually one of the committee's best interrogators) and by Angleton's feeble response.

A few days before the hearing, Angleton had complained to me over lunch: "The country is going to hell; there is no interest in national security these days, and your committee is a manifestation of this." I can remember thinking about all the time I had been spending with him, as well as with Tom Charles Huston and Richard Helms, among others. They were not evil individuals by any stretch of the imagination; however, they did have a more pronounced fear of "the enemy" than did most people. For Huston, the enemy had been the young antiwar protesters with their scraggly hair and tattered garb; for Angleton, it was the KGB and other Communist intelligence services for whom the Cold War was a zero-sum game.

"It is the idea of the enemy," former attorney general Ramsey Clark once wrote, "the bad man, the sinister force that we use to deny freedom."[51] Or as Senator Mondale would write in a retrospective (in 2010) on the origins of illegal government surveillance and internment activities at home: "The lesson of American history is that, in threatening times, fear can overtake our better judgment. . . . We have strayed from our values time and again in our history, always in times of fear, and we were almost always ashamed of ourselves when we recovered our senses."[52] The Church Committee found that it was also a matter of intelligence officials failing to consider the deeper, constitutional implications of their acts. In his well-intended efforts to fight Communism, I doubt if Angleton had sufficiently considered the harm he might be inflicting on America's form of democracy.

A few weeks after his ordeal on Capitol Hill, Angleton berated the Church Committee publicly for "a type of McCarthyite hearing in which the denigration of the intelligence community was its goal."[53] I presumed this would be the end of my visits with him, which was a disappointment; I had been learning a lot from Angleton, although I always had my radar switched on for his excesses. I had also developed an affection for him, as one might a favorite worldly uncle. And, as a neophyte to the subject of counterintelligence, I had been grateful for his patience with my endless questions about this arcane field. I would miss my sessions with him.

Early in the new year of 1976, though, he invited me back to the Army-Navy Club, I guess so that he could at least verbally throttle me as a surrogate for Frank Church. After lunch, we adjourned to the library as usual and, although he was drinking less that day, he became agitated nonetheless as he reflected back on the basting he had received at the hands of Senator Church and his colleagues. Angleton compared the investigation to the pillaging of intelligence services in countries that had been overrun and occupied by a foreign power. "Only we have been occupied by Congress," he said angrily, "with our files rifled, our officials humiliated, and our agents exposed." This happened, he said, because of an "impotent executive" that had failed to "carry out its constitutional responsibility to protect the nation's secrets." A reference to Colby again, I assumed. As the afternoon sun began to drop behind D.C.'s modest skyscrapers, I walked with him to his Mercedes. "Let me tell you something," he said, as he slipped behind the wheel, "Washington is a jungle."

When the Church Committee presented its final report in May 1976, Angleton responded with a critique published in a conservative newsletter, deploring the "now shaky and harassed CIA" and "the straitjacket Senator Church and the Committee's staff have brazenly tailored for it." He conceded that the intelligence agencies "did engage in some illegal and ill-advised operations," but he went on to argue that "these were by no means altogether reprehensible, when weighed in light of the national security considerations prevailing at the time."[54]

A month later, Angleton told an Idaho newspaper reporter that the damage wrought by the Church Committee was "very far reaching," and that Senator Church had been "dishonest and demagogic." Recall that during the early days of the Church Committee's inquiry, the senator had become concerned about what seemed to him a pattern of Agency disregard for supervision by the White House or the Congress, as illustrated by the shellfish toxin hearing and the committee's examination of documents on CIA assassination plots. On a Sunday television talk show, Church had referred to the Agency as a "rogue elephant." In the Idaho newspaper interview, Angleton said that "history will show [Church] was the rogue elephant."[55]

I never saw Angleton again, although he would telephone me from time to time over the next several years to fulminate about the state of security in America. I had moved to warm climes in the South in 1979 to take up an attractive academic post at the University of Georgia and, one afternoon in 1987, the former CI chief rang me with a longer-than-usual diatribe against Frank Church, who had been defeated for a fourth term in the 1980 elections (with several former CIA officers traveling to Idaho to join the right-wing campaign launched against him). Following this defeat, the senator contracted pancreatic cancer and had quickly perished three years prior to this call from Angleton. While I held the phone away from my ear, he rambled on loudly for a half-hour about the naiveté of the panels that had investigated intelligence in 1975, and how they had harmed the nation's security. He included the Rockefeller Commission in his diatribe, as if that group—which was just as condemning of improper counterintelligence programs, like Operations CHAOS and HT Lingual, as we were—had been a hotbed of radicals, with such conservatives among its membership as future president Ronald Reagan and former Navy admiral Lyman L. Lemnitzer. Just as my patience was about to run out, he suddenly ended the conversation with the remark: "Remember, it ain't over 'til the fat lady sings. Ciao." I had no idea what Angleton meant by that tired expression, but I supposed it was his uncharacteristically trite way of saying that, eventually, the merits of his unyielding struggle against Soviet penetration operations against the West would be acknowledged.

A few weeks after this telephone call, Angleton died on May 12, 1987, of lung cancer at age sixty nine. He was buried in Morris Hill Cemetery in Boise, Idaho, not far away from the gravesite of Senator Church.

Counterintelligence in the Aftermath of the Angleton Era

When James Angleton departed from the office of CI chief at the Agency in 1974, his laserlike focus on counterintelligence threats disappeared with him. Whether he might have stopped the volcanic spate of spy cases that erupted in the IC subsequent to his departure is unknowable; his supporters, though, believe that much of the treason that occurred within the CIA at least would have been either deterred by his presence or discovered more quickly. Whatever the merits of this argument, no one disputes the mushrooming of counterintelligence setbacks that happened after his departure.

A good way to gain a sense of the range of challenges facing counterintelligence officers, and their overseers, is to examine a few of the prominent failures (from a longer list) in the post-Angleton era, as outlined here. Such lists suggest rampant espionage against the United States, with moles right and left; HPSCI Chair Mike Rogers (2011–2014), among others, frequently remarked that in fact spying against this nation became more prevalent during his time on the Hill than ever before. It should be remembered, however, that those within the IC who have followed the path of treason account for only a minuscule percentage of its workforce. Moreover, the United States has been no more infested with moles than other major powers—indeed probably fewer than our top European allies. Also, during the Cold War the West had its share of penetration successes against the Soviets; it was hardly a one-way street.

The 1970s

After Angleton's dismissal, the first notable counterintelligence stumble in the United States involved Clyde Conrad, an Army noncommissioned officer (NCO). Before he was discovered, Conrad managed—starting in 1975—to engage in a decade-long period of providing Czech and Hungarian intelligence agents (dancing on the puppet strings of their KGB handlers) data on U.S. operational plans if war were to break out with the U.S.S.R. in Europe.[56] Then came the foolish escapades of William P. Kampiles, a first-year CIA officer in 1977, whose evaluation reports were so poor that he was soon eased out of the Agency. He took with him on the way out a manual on U.S. surveillance satellites, which he proceeded to peddle to the Soviets for a measly $3,000 (he probably could have gotten a million). Among other technical specifications, this document revealed to Moscow that America's "Big Bird" satellite had both sigint and geoint capabilities. Kampiles was immediately caught and sentenced to forty years in prison. Further, as usual, the private sector during the 1970s was a favorite KGB target. In 1979, for example, the FBI arrested Dongfan (Greg) Chung, a California engineer employed by a defense contractor in California, for planning to sell data on rocket launching and other technical secrets to the Chinese.

The 1980s

In the 1980s all hell broke loose on the counterintelligence front. In 1983, the KGB enrolled the Agency's Edward Lee Howard on its secret roster of U.S. recruits. He disclosed to his handler several of the Agency's operations in Moscow—including the enormously valuable CIA mole Adolf Tolkachev, a courageous Soviet electronics engineer. Howard escaped to Russia.[57]

Two years later, Aldrich "Rick" Hazen Ames "volunteered" to spy for the Soviets as a well-positioned counterintelligence officer at Langley with a Russian portfolio, causing great damage when he provided the names of the CIA's top agents in Moscow—all nine of whom were immediately murdered. (This response by the KGB displayed surprisingly poor CI tradecraft, because the closely clustered deaths unmistakably signaled to the Agency that Soviet intelligence officials must have a mole inside the CIA's Counterintelligence Staff who had tipped off Moscow about the agents who were quickly executed.) Ames carried on his treachery for almost a full decade before being discovered in 1994. He had essentially ruined the Agency's ability to spy on the Soviet Union during the final years of the Cold War.[58] Even though Ames had shown signs of sudden wealth—a new house in Arlington, an expensive Jaguar sports car, foreign travel, fancy threads—he parried questions from colleagues with the response that his Colombian-born wife (his partner in espionage for the Soviets) had inherited family wealth. Moreover, despite his occasional drunkenness at work, Ames wore a halo: his father had been a much-decorated Agency officer, also in the Operations Directorate. As a result, the younger Ames was given a pass for his besotted behavior. The KGB and its successor after the end of the Cold War, the SVR, were appreciative of his work to the tune of $4.6 million. Unbeknownst to Ames, however, the CIA had developed a mole of its own inside the new SVR who helped to identify him.

The FBI's Robert Hanssen, another well-placed U.S. counterintelligence officer, had taken up treason several years before Ames, and lasted a few years longer than his CIA counterpart before he, too, was identified by the Agency's mole inside the SVR.[59] Hanssen provided documents that supported Ames's series of dead-drop messages to his Russian case officer in Washington, D.C., plus he added some useful findings of his own—such as the location of U.S. listening devices in the newly constructed Soviet Embassy on Wisconsin Avenue in D.C., along with a copy of the emergency plans Washington officials intended to follow if nuclear war broke out between the superpowers. Hanssen's payment came in the form of $1.4 million worth of gems smuggled to him from Russia, but he seemed to be in the "game" chiefly for the intellectual thrill of evading detection by his colleagues at the FBI. Ultimately, though, careless tradecraft combined with clues gleaned by the CIA's penetration into the SVR exposed both Ames and Hanssen and earned them life sentences in federal penitentiaries.

As if this were not enough treason for the decade, Jonathan Jay Pollard was uncovered in 1985 as a Navy intelligence employee who was providing classified documents to Israel. He would remain in prison for the next thirty years.[60] In addition, from his perch within the NSA, Ron Pelton funneled sigint data to Moscow from 1980 to 1985. Inside Moscow itself, a U.S embassy guard by the name of Corporal Clayton J. Lonetree sneaked classified papers to the KGB that he had robbed from the embassy's vaults, in exchange for the company of attractive Russian women. Lonetree, the only Marine ever convicted of espionage against the United States, was lured into treason by a sexual "honey trap"—with its blackmail opportunities— arranged by his Soviet handler.

The 1990s

Treason never takes a holiday. The 1980s were a high point in the frequency of traitorous incidents committed by U.S. intelligence officers; in CI circles, 1985 is remembered as "the year of the spy," and the 1980s "the decade of the spy". The next decade, however, also witnessed several intelligence personnel, along with civilians in sensitive defense industry jobs, defect to the other side. Among them was Harold J. Nicolson, the highest ranking CIA officer ever charged with treason, who began spying for the Soviets at roughly the same time as Ames, Howard, and Hanssen.[61] He betrayed the identities of three graduating classes from the Agency's training school at the Farm. Nicolson was discovered in 1996, thanks in part to post-Ames counterintelligence procedures that required intelligence officers to provide bank account information on their personal finances.

The most wrenching CI failure for the CIA during the 1990s began one January morning in 1993 on Dolly Madison Highway, which runs past the Agency's main entrance at Langley.[62] At 8:00, automobiles driven by Agency employees queued up in the left-turn lane of the highway on their way to work. This access point is heavily guarded by armed officers at a gatehouse, where a shotgun rests on a stand at the ready. Beyond the gatehouse are bollards and Jersey barriers, as well as more armed guards with patrol dogs, backed by a high electrified fence that keeps uninvited guests out of the 213-acre, leafy compound where CIA Headquarters resides. Two hundred meters away from this imposing entrance at Langley, though, Dolly Madison Highway is just a normal and unguarded thoroughfare, with a traffic light at this particular intersection. Inside their cars, Agency employees listened to music or the news on their radios, waiting for a green arrow that would allow them to turn toward the gatehouse and the Agency building beyond. Suddenly a sharp crack rang out. Perhaps a fender-bender? Then the noise became louder with a distinctive popping sound, like firecrackers on the 4th of July.

Jogging slowly along the row of idling cars came a short, dark-haired man with an AK-47 cradled in his arms. His face and his eyes stone cold, he fired at each of the drivers as he passed methodically along the line. Glass shattered, horns blared, trapped drivers and their passengers screamed, several slumping against dashboards and moaning in agony as blood poured from bullet holes in their bodies. After spraying some seventy rounds at close range, the jogger reversed his direction and returned to the first vehicle to pump more bullets into the driver. The victim's wife—unhit by the fusillade—slid out the passenger-side door of the Volkswagen and rolled for cover. Her husband would miraculously recover, but the intelligence officer driving in a car behind him, as well as his passenger, died from their gunshot wounds.

The assassin, Mir Aimal Kansi, sprinted to his getaway car parked nearby, raced back to his apartment not far away, then on to the Dulles International Airport where his expired passport went unnoticed as he boarded a flight to Pakistan, his native land. In the months and—as it turned out—the years to follow, CIA and FBI counterintelligence officials put aside their bureaucratic rivalries and grudges, as they joined forces in the hunt for Kansi.

Four and a half years after the murders on Dolly Madison Highway, a dogged CIA/FBI team finally tracked down Kansi in a small Pakistani village, Dera Ghazi Khan, in the Punjab province near the border of Afghanistan. He was arrested and returned to the United States. In 1997, Kansi was convicted of murder in a Virginia court, and five years later he was executed by lethal injection at that state's Greensville Correctional Center in Jarratt. Before his death, Kansi stated that his motivation had been to retaliate against America's policies toward Muslim countries. Propelled by similar feelings among radical Muslims recruited to Al Qaeda, the counterterrorism (CT) side of counterintelligence was about to move to centerstage in America's national security priorities. Al Qaeda operatives attacked the U.S. embassies in Kenya and Tanzania in 1998, followed by failed efforts to sink the U.S.S. *Cole* off the coast of Yemen in 2000—both unsettling precursors to the most horrific counterintelligence/counterterrorism failure in this nation's history: the tragedy of 9/11.

The FBI had its hands full at home, too, during this period. In 1995—on a day that marked the second anniversary of the Bureau's assault on a compound near Waco, Texas, that killed seventy-two members of the Branch Davidian sect, an event that became a symbol for some "patriot" groups opposed to the federal government—a white supremacist parked his Ryder rental truck on the street near the entrance to the Alfred P. Murrah Federal Building in downtown Oklahoma City. In the truck's storage space was a homemade bomb made up of fifty-five-gallon drums that contained ammonium nitrate and nitromethane. At the press of a remote-control button, the bomb shattered the early morning calm with a powerful blast that crumbled the Federal Building and left 168 people dead inside, including nineteen children killed and another five hundred individuals injured.

The homegrown terrorist, Timothy McVeigh, fled the scene in another vehicle but was pulled over later in the day by a highway patrolman for having an expired license plate. His suspicious behavior led to an arrest and eventually a conviction for the Oklahoma City bombing. McVeigh, who testified that he had shifted from being an "intellectual" in the anti-Washington movement to becoming an "animal" determined to kill in honor of his cause, was put to death for his act of terrorism.[63] Five years later on the eve of the 9/11 attacks, the United States continued to harbor within its borders 602 "hate groups" of the kind McVeigh had joined in Oklahoma; by 2014 that number had risen to 930.[64] With these groups and a rash of ISIS-inspired "lone wolf" attackers, those who prepared intelligence threat assessments in Washington had more to worry about than terrorists based overseas. They would soon learn, though, that the greatest danger to the homeland would come from a terrorist organization in Southwest Asia, known as Al Qaeda (or "the base" in Arabic).

9/11 and After

The attacks against New York City and Washington, D.C., and the airplane brought down by terrorists in the Pennsylvania countryside, will be forevermore seared into the collective memory of the American people. Earlier chapters in this book have presented details on the missed opportunities to intercept the nineteen terrorists (all but four from Saudi Arabia) before the catastrophic events of September 11, 2001. Missing in each instance was hard evidence about the specific intentions of the terrorists—the all-important ingredient of "actionable intelligence." Intelligence officials and policymakers were also distracted by lengthy threat-assessment lists that warned of equally possible terrorist attacks against the D.C. Mall with anthrax sprayed from a crop-duster airplane; poisons dumped in city water supplies around the country; remote-control bombs placed next to nuclear reactors; smallpox-infected terrorists sneaking into the center of Manhattan; and on and on (all outlined in the CIA/CTC terrorism report of 1995, discussed in chapter 6).

The range of threats had a paralyzing effect on decision makers, who ended up doing little of anything to protect against most of these contingencies. Policymakers hoped for the best and kept their fingers crossed, reluctant to spend public money on long-shot speculations about terrorist tactics—the vexing high-cost/low-probability policy conundrum. Just the strengthening of airport security, the sealing of cockpit doors on airliners, and the hiring of sky marshals would send the federal cash registers loudly ringing, offsetting the CTC warning as early as 1995 that aerial terrorism was a distinct possibility— the flying of hijacked commercial aircraft into city skyscrapers.

Just as politicians in Louisiana had pushed to the back burner expensive proposals to strengthen the levees around New Orleans that could withstand a category 5 hurricane—seemingly a remote probability prior to the giant Katrina storm of 2003—so earlier did federal politicians set aside dire threat assessments presented to them by the IC. And these Washington officials were correct most of the time, as with the prediction of an anthrax Mall attack, poisoned reservoirs, sabotage against nuclear reactors, and many other potential disasters. But not about aerial terrorism. The nation paid a horrific toll for the lack of actionable intelligence—or even much intelligence at all—about Al Qaeda and its plotting against the United States; for inadequate CIA-FBI cooperation in tracking the hijackers (which DCI George Tenet later referred to as the event's most serious counterintelligence failure[65]); for the Bureau's feeble responses to warnings from its agents in Minneapolis and Phoenix; and for the lack of serious attention from SSCI, HPSCI, and the White House under both Presidents Clinton and Bush to intelligence counterterrorism reports (however incomplete) in the years that preceded the 9/11 attacks. One of the greatest policy conundrums is how to evaluate the risk of not doing something.

In the wake of 9/11, the United States has been hit by other terrorist assaults against the homeland—fortunately none with the scope and intensity of that September morning. Sometimes intelligence and law enforcement officers have been able to stop the terrorists, as when Faisal Shahzad attempted to set off a bomb in Times Square (2010). At other times, though, America's counterterrorism teams have stumbled, as with Major Nidal Malik Hasan, an Army psychiatrist who murdered thirteen and wounded dozens more at Fort Hood, Texas (2009); Umar Farouk Abdulmutallab, the so-called underwear bomber who attempted to bring down the Detroit-bound airline he was on (2009); the Boston Marathon bombing carried out by the Tsarnaev brothers (2013); and the San Bernardino massacre perpetrated by Syed Rizwan Farook and Tashfeen Malik (2014), along with other lone-wolf attacks in Florida, Minnesota, and New York.

Terrorist threats against the United States are a regular occurrence, whether from ISIS, Al Qaeda, or other Muslim radicals overseas; from *jihadist* recruits within the United States; or white supremacists with a grudge against the U.S. government. The men and women in Washington and the state capitals with responsibility for intelligence accountability, as well as jurists at all levels of government, continue to craft rules flexible enough to permit intelligence and law enforcement to fight effectively against America's enemies, but without providing so much leeway that fundamental American liberties are bent beyond recognition. Counterintelligence and counterterrorist officers, as well as the overseers who supervise them, are on the frontlines of trying to properly manage this ongoing and delicate balancing act.

Treason and Accountability

Treason is a crime driven, above all, by greed—plain old money in the pocket, which has accounted for a majority (53 percent) of traitorous events in the United States in recent decades; followed by ideology (at 24 percent, say, a deluded attraction to *jihadi* "principles" promulgated through social media by ISIS); then by a wide array of lesser incentives, including compromise (as with a blackmail situation) and ego (as with Hanssen's game to "beat the system" for the thrill of it).[66]

Counterintelligence officers sometimes use the mnemonic, MICE, to capture in shorthand this hierarchy of incentives: money, ideology, compromise, or ego. If one stirs into the pot N for "nationality" (spying for the old homeland, as some Chinese-Americans in particular have done in recent years[67]), along with S for "sex" (as in the example of Corporal Lonetree), the mnemonic becomes MINCES. Motivations can change over time, with ideology especially important during the early years of the Cold War, as some Americans were drawn to the tenets of Marxist-Leninism—"the idea of a new kind of society that transcended individualism."[68] Klaus Fuchs, for instance, became convinced that world peace depended on Russia being able to counterbalance America's nuclear capabilities. Pure greed shouldered ideology aside in the 1960s, and today "nationality" has grown in importance—although it lags behind the incentives of cold cash and ideological convictions of one stripe or another.

The art and science of catching traitors lie at the center of counterintelligence. Offensively, the most fruitful method is to penetrate the organization who has deployed or recruited a mole against the United States, whether a foreign intelligence service like the Russian SVR or a terrorist organization like ISIS. Once burrowed inside the enemy camp, America's penetration agent can report back on the espionage operations of the adversary, in the manner that a CIA mole deep within the KGB in the 1990s aided the hunt for the U.S. traitors who turned out to be Ames, Hanssen, and Howard. Sometimes other counterintelligence methods—or timely defections from terrorist camps and hostile intelligence services—can be almost as good as a mole. For instance, in 2016 an ISIS member quit that organization, carrying with him a memory stick stolen from the pocket of that organization's head of internal security, which he provided to German law enforcement authorities and the British broadcast company Sky News. The memory stick appeared to be a bonanza of names and addresses of ISIS recruits and their handlers throughout Europe—if the documents were valid, which some experts questioned.[69]

Tight security at home is vital, too, as a defensive measure against moles or outright terrorist attacks like 9/11. At the Dolly Madison Highway entrance to the CIA, for example, added security measures have been put in place since the Kansi murders. Polygraphs; fences; razor wire; armed guards; bollards and Jersey barriers; identification badges; telephone and social media monitoring (intelligence officers and staff sign away many of their First Amendment rights, in exchange for employment in sensitive jobs); the use of computer encryption, codes, and special firewalls—the list of defensive security measures to protect

America's secrets and its government organizations is extensive (although hardly foolproof, as Snowden as well as Russian and Chinese hacking have demonstrated). When security is lax, the result can be stolen documents or even death, as with the Kansi killings or when seventeen U.S. sailors died during the Al Qaeda attack against the *Cole* in the Aden harbor off the coast of Yemen in 2000. In another example, a Jordanian physician, Humam Khalil Abu-Mulai al-Balawi, was inadequately searched before a meeting in 2009 at Camp Chapman (a CIA base in Khost, Afghanistan) by Agency officers who thought he was a reliable asset. The bomb he wore beneath his clothing killed the Agency's COS in Afghanistan, Jennifer Matthews, along with six other senior Agency officers who were among Langley's most experienced Middle East and Southwest Asian hands.[70]

The problem of cybersecurity looms large, as well, within the disciplines of counterintelligence and counterterrorism. DNI Clapper and others testified on numerous occasions that cyberattacks are the greatest threat facing the United States. Additional CI responsibilities include counterproliferation—always at, or near, the top of the IC's threat assessments; counternarcotics, as the United States remains awash in illegal drugs that infiltrate the homeland from all points of the compass (heroin alone was responsible for the deaths of 129 people a day in the United States during the early weeks of 2016); and, of course, the protection of America's nuclear-weapon stockpile (an Energy Department counterintelligence assignment).[71] Operating closely with the Drug Enforcement Administration and the Pentagon, the CIA devotes considerable resources toward antinarcotics efforts. So far, these activities have been largely unsuccessful; drug dealers are canny and elusive, and this nation's borders are lengthy and relatively porous. As discussed in an earlier chapter, the United States has been able to curb about 20 percent of the illegal drug flows headed toward this country, but that still leaves a deluge of heroin, cocaine, and other narcotics flooding across America's landscape from Maine to California, eddying into big cities and even small, rural townships. In 2016, the governors of New Hampshire and Vermont publicly declared that their states were experiencing a heroin epidemic. This condition afflicts the entire nation, even if other governors have been less public in admitting to the problem.

Over the years, counterintelligence has led to even more public controversies, and sometimes formal investigations, than either covert action or failures of intelligence collection and analysis (see chapter 9). In recent decades, this catalog includes Operation CHAOS and COINTELPRO; the Huston Plan; the Ames and Hanssen cases; 9/11; NSA warrantless and metadata surveillance; and the CIA's renditions and harsh interrogation methods—all in the name of protecting the United States against the KGB, its successor the SVR, and other agents of Communism, as well as, more recently, terrorist factions. In light of this history, one can readily understand the importance of accountability within the counterintelligence domain. Communism and terrorism have been valid dangers that warrant vigorous CI and CT measures; so does the prevention of future insider threats—individuals within the IC who have policy grievances that lead to the unauthorized disclosure of classified information (the Snowden phenomenon). More sensible classification procedures would help; presently far too many documents bear "top secret," "secret," and other inflated designations. So would more reliable whistle-blower protection, as well as a stronger message from SSCI and HPSCI that in their offices whistle-blowers will be protected from retaliation by bosses in the secret agencies. Even with these and other reforms in place, though, the United States will continue to require strong security and other CI defenses, accompanied by the skillful penetrations of adversarial spy and terrorist organizations.[72] As long as the United States has adversaries, so will it need the shields of counterintelligence and counterterrorism.

News in May 2017 jolted the United States again into this realization when it was reported the CIA had learned in 2010 that Beijing officials had executed or imprisoned eighteen to twenty of the Agency's spies in China. A mole hunt, codenamed Honey Badger, had been underway at Langley since then to see if an insider had committed treason by tipping off the Chinese to these humint assets. Or perhaps Chinese intelligence had been able to hack into the Agency's covert computer system used to communicate with its penetration agents. It was a counterintelligence case that rivaled Ames and Hanssen in the scope of losses to the CIA. Signs pointed toward a former Agency officer who had worked on the China account, then resigned to live in Asia at about the same time U.S. assets were being put to death. The CIA's chief of counterintelligence refused to embrace this suspicion, though, until—perhaps remembering the Angleton witchhunts—the evidence became more definitive.[73]

Experience has taught us, though, that the disease of excess zeal can fatally infect well-meaning CI and CT activities, as infamously illustrated by the Huston Plan, CHAOS, COINTELPRO, warrantless wiretapping, the metadata program, and the use of torture. A democracy will not last long if it is unable to establish effective accountability over its counterintelligence and counterterrorism activities. As Tom Charles Huston finally acknowledged, the kid with the picket sign is far different from the kid wearing a suicide vest. Comprehending these differences lies at the heart of the challenge faced by CI/CT officials and their overseers in a democracy.

PART V

THE FUTURE OF INTELLIGENCE ACCOUNTABILITY

Intelligence Accountability and the Nation's Spy Chiefs

Staves of a Barrel, Without a Hoop

Over the years since the creation of the modern intelligence establishment in 1947, America's spy panjandrums have enjoyed few formal authorities to command the espionage agencies that sprawl beneath them.[1] Representative Lee H. Hamilton, a former chairman of HPSCI, observed in 1996, "We don't really have a Director of Central Intelligence. There is no such thing. The DCI at CIA controls only a very small portion of the assets of the Intelligence Community, and there are so many entities you don't have any Director. There is not a Director of Intelligence in the American system, and I think we have to create one."[2]

This absence of meaningful authority at the peak of the intelligence pyramid came about as the result of a fateful last-minute deal cut in 1947 by President Harry S. Truman with the Pentagon brass, in the context of drafting the landmark National Security Act of that year.[3] The president agreed to back away from his desire for a strong, centralized IC with budget and personnel authority lodged firmly in the hands of a DCI, if the military would support the creation of a modern Department of Defense (replacing the War Department) that featured a unified service command under the leadership of a Joint Chiefs of Staff. In this Faustian bargain with its still unspooling consequences, Truman won his unified military command—more or less, although not until 1987 with enactment of the Defense Reorganization Act would the military services truly begin to operate in a cohesive manner.[4] In return, the Pentagon kept its hold over military intelligence without having to worry about a muscular DCI who might try to loosen the grip of admirals and generals over spy assets within the armed services. From the sealing of this agreement until the passage of the Intelligence Reform and Terrorism Protection Act (IRTPA) in 2004, America's spymaster—the DCI—remained more of a cosmetic intelligence chief than a true leader with the reins of all the intelligence agencies firmly in his or (one day) her hands, able to move personnel and budgets as necessary and command the close allegiance of the various "program managers" (directors) who ran each of the operational espionage agencies (sixteen in number today—not counting the administrative Office of the Director of National Intelligence, or ODNI, created by IRTPA).

Thus the modern intelligence "community" was, from the start, a decentralized, fragmented, and stove-piped organization where a dispersion of authority ruled the day. Within this complex, centripetal forces were a rarity and seen for the most part only in times of a national emergency.[5] After the 9/11 terrorist attacks, enactment of IRTPA held out a fleeting opportunity to create a true U.S. national spy leader, more readily able to achieve the goal of maximal intelligence sharing ("all-source fusion," in intelligence jargon). Yet, as had been the case with all the earlier—if less prominent—efforts to unravel Truman's bargain (as when the Aspin-Brown Commission urged the strengthening of the DCI office in 1996), this latest vision of an effective national intelligence leader was thwarted by fierce Pentagon resistance in a counter-IRTPA alliance with its handmaidens on Capitol Hill (most prominently, the Armed Services Committees).[6] As a result of all the heat for reform generated by the 9/11 disaster, accompanied by adroit lobbying by families of the victims and a strong lineup of supporters (including, tepidly, George W. Bush), the significantly diluted IRTPA legislation did manage to abolish the DCI position; however, the new law replaced that office with an even more anemic institution: the Office of the Director of National Intelligence. As noted in chapter 1, the freshly minted ODNI was devoid not only of strong budget and personnel authority to guide the entire IC, but was physically separated as well in a building distant from the wellsprings of a spy chief's most important source of power in Washington: the deep knowledge of world affairs generated by the nation's top strategic analysts located within the Directorate of Analysis at Langley. At least before IRTPA, the DCI benefited from having an office on the seventh floor at Langley, a corridor away from a lineup of seasoned analysts who could brief the director on world affairs at a moment's notice.

Former DCI Stansfield Turner has written that the legislative battle between the Pentagon and intelligence reformers over IRTPA resulted in "the worst of all worlds, that is, a DNI without direct control of the CIA and not enough control of the Intelligence Community to compensate." In his view, "the DNI's hand is weaker than was the DCI's. That, ironically, is the result of legislation that came from the 9/11 Commission's report that recommended empowering the new DNI."[7] Intelligence scholar Amy B. Zegart concurs. "Instead of enhancing coordination and centralization," she writes, "the 2004 legislation has triggered a scramble for turf that has left the secretary of defense with greater power, the director of intelligence with little, and the intelligence community even more disjointed."[8] A commission report published soon after passage of IRTPA described the state of the IC as "fragmented, loosely managed, and poorly coordinated"[9]—just as it had been before enactment of the new law.

The core questions in this chapter are the following: How has this paucity of power at the top of the U.S. intelligence hierarchy affected the practice of intelligence accountability by DCIs; and how did these men (no women have yet served as the nation's spy chief) react, in the aftermath of the Church Committee, to closer supervision over espionage activities by lawmakers and their staffs? The obvious hunch regarding the first question is that a DCI (or now a DNI) who is unable to command his own IC is unlikely to have much success maintaining accountability over the individual spy agencies. Whether this condition has led America's intelligence leaders to turn toward Congress for help with this responsibility is another question addressed in this chapter. This portrait of intelligence accountability as seen from the pinnacle of the IC emerges from my interviews with several DCIs, along with searches through the published archival record on their activities.[10]

I begin with a look at Director Richard Helms's conceptions of intelligence oversight. He came to office in 1966 and, as the last of the "Old Guard" spymasters, he sidestepped relations with "outside" supervisors on Capitol Hill and elsewhere in the government as nimbly as he could. Then his successor, James R. Schlesinger, Jr., assembled the Agency's "Family Jewels"—a classified, in-house list of Agency improprieties (chapter 3). It was the leaking of this document to the media that sent the CIA and its companion agencies spiraling into the maw of the Church Committee investigation in 1975, followed by the establishment of a radically new era of more intensive intelligence oversight in the United States.[11]

The DCI Perspective on Intelligence Accountability

Nineteen men served as DCIs—the high priests of intelligence—from 1947 until 2004, when that position was replaced with the ODNI.[12] (See Figure 11.1.) The first four intelligence directors were Rear Admiral Sidney W. Souers (U.S. Navy Reserve), 1946, a Truman confidant, whose job it was to set up the CIA and establish its ties to the other U.S. spy services; Lt. Gen. Hoyt S. Vandenberg (U.S. Air Force), 1946–1947, a capable man but only briefly in charge of the IC; Rear Admiral Roscoe H. Hillenkoetter (U.S. Navy), 1947–1950, the first director to settle into the office and make a difference; and Gen. Walter Bedell Smith (U.S. Army), 1950–1953, perhaps the most efficient manager and internally popular of all the DCIs. These spy chiefs were not particularly interested in having close ties with Congress; but, as David M. Barrett finds, they did have

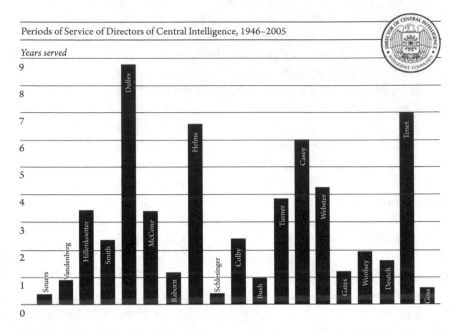

Figure 11.1 Periods of Service, DCIs, 1946–2005. Source: Douglas F. Garthoff, *Directors of Central Intelligence as Leaders of the U.S. Intelligence Community, 1946–2005,* Center for the Study of Intelligence, Central Intelligence Agency, Washington, D.C. (2005), p. 290.

more contact with lawmakers than is usually acknowledged in the scholarly literature. As we have noted in earlier chapters, members of Congress were usually less than eager to share responsibility for the shadowy activities carried out within the crevices of America's national security establishment—and particularly the inevitable failures that would accompany these operations. Now and then, though, lawmakers did speak up and demand corrective action by DCIs, especially when they decided that intelligence budgets had spiraled too high.[13]

Then came the longest-serving and most legendary of the DCIs, Allen W. Dulles (1953–1961), who had been a standout in the OSS during World War II. Subsequently, and buoyed by the fact that he was the brother of Secretary of State John Foster Dulles, the DCI became a lion of Georgetown society and an admired raconteur. He had the misfortune, though, of serving as the nation's intelligence chief at the time of the Bay of Pigs fiasco, a career-ender. As noted earlier in these pages, DCI Dulles once revealed his lack of interest in working closely with lawmakers by remarking that he preferred to share information with the president and no one else—if indeed the president ever bothered to ask.[14]

Next in line to serve as DCI was John McCone (1961–1965), a successful California businessman. Like General Smith, McCone was widely admired inside Langley for his finely honed administrative skills—unlike his successor

William F. Raburn (Vice Admiral, U.S. Navy Ret., 1965–1966), generally considered the least adept of all the DCIs in dealing with spy operations. The years from 1947 to 1966 were for the most part an arid plain in the history of intelligence oversight in the United States, with the DCIs offering little to Congress and lawmakers asking for little. Nor was Richard Helms (1966–1973)—another OSS alumnus, a suave boulevardier, and No. 8 on the chronological list of DCIs—an improvement when it came to working with Congress on matters of intelligence accountability. My conversation with Helms provides a sense of his attitudes toward intelligence supervision by lawmakers, which (according to snippets of information in the public domain—newspaper reports, biographies, histories) were engrained in the minds of the other early Cold War intelligence directors as well.

Richard McGarrah Helms: The "Professional's Professional" (1966–1973)

Helms served as DCI for nearly seven years, surpassed in office longevity only by Dulles and George Tenet (who served under Bill Clinton and George W. Bush).[15] He was the first CIA officer to rise through the ranks, on the operations side, to the Agency's highest perch on the seventh floor at Langley. Though near the top of the CIA's Operations Directorate at the time of the Bay of Pigs, he managed to escape culpability; however, he soon found himself "up to his scuppers" (a favorite phrase of his) in the plots code-named Operation MONGOOSE and aimed at deposing Cuba's president Fidel Castro during the Kennedy years. MONGOOSE turned to all the Agency's dark arts, and then some, in an attempt to end the Castro reign one way or another, including the use of exploding cigars, poison pills, curare-filled ballpoint pens, Mafia hitmen, shellfish toxins, cobra venom, and a newly invented "nondiscernible microbio-inoculator" (dart gun). Helms also signed onto the Huston Plan in 1970, the master spy plan concocted by the Nixon Administration and directed against anti–Vietnam War protesters; and he was deeply implicated in the questionable covert actions directed against President Allende, who had been freely, openly elected by the people of Chile.

None of these activities were reported to Congress during his tenure; indeed, Helms had gone out of his way in public testimony to mislead lawmakers on the Allende operations, to which he entered a plea of nolo contendere in a D.C. court. The judge fined him $2,000, but suspended any jail time.[16] When President Nixon attempted to draw the Agency into the Watergate scandal, Helms—in his finest hour—effectively defended the organization before departing from Langley to accept Nixon's appointment as ambassador to Tehran (where he failed to anticipate the approaching revolution of

1979 that overthrew the Shah).[17] The appointment had all the earmarks of an effort by Nixon to get an uncooperative Helms out of town.

When he returned to Washington after his ambassadorial assignment, Helms started a consulting practice that specialized in the Middle East. He named the firm Safeer, Inc., an Anglicized version of the Arabic and Persian word "safir" or "ambassador" (which he decided to spell with a double "e" to make it simpler for Americans to pronounce). On December 12, 1990, I sat down with him in his K Street office to discuss his thoughts about the spy business.[18] In appearance, he looked about the same as during the days of the Church Committee fifteen years earlier, when I had taken his deposition on the Huston Plan. At seventy-seven, he seemed just as fit and an even more distinguished-looking patrician than I had remembered. He wore a gray suit, with a white pocket handkerchief, a buttoned-down white shirt (de rigueur for Agency officials, current or former), and a subdued tie with a gold clasp. Helms seemed vaguely aware that I had been on the Church Committee staff, which had not been a happy experience for him; but, nonetheless, his demeanor was courtly and welcoming. He was, in fact, a fountain of charm. The Church Committee's chief counsel has commented on this Helms trait, but with a twist. "He was quite charming," recalled Frederick A. O. "Fritz" Schwarz from the time of the investigation in 1975, "but I did not believe him. I think he was not a truth-teller. He was pretty careful in how he failed to tell the truth."[19] This had been my experience with Helms as well, when he adroitly attempted to evade my questions about the Huston Plan.[20]

In my 1990 interview with him, I turned immediately to the question of intelligence accountability.[21]

JOHNSON: What do you think of this experiment in intelligence oversight that we have had, which started in 1975–76?

HELMS: It's definitely here to stay. Whether it started for a good or a bad reason, it now has its own constituency in the Senate and the House; and, as usually happens in those situations, they don't like to give up this constituency. Some of the senators and congressmen feel they have made a genuine contribution to a better understanding of intelligence, better control over covert operations, and so forth.

I would think that the downside of the oversight process is the number of man-hours that it takes out of high officials of the agencies, testifying before various committees, subcommittees, staffers, and Lord knows what. In fact, I was aghast when I heard the number of hours in a year that somebody from the Agency is talking to senators, congressmen, or their staffers. I wonder if, in a rational world, this couldn't be cut down.

JOHNSON: Is this one reason why you have favored a joint intelligence committee?

HELMS: That's one reason why I favor a joint committee. The other reason is that it cuts down on the number of people involved in the secrets of this process. As you well know, the more people who have information, the better chance it has of getting out.

JOHNSON: What do you make of the counter-argument that one committee would be too easy to co-opt; that when you have two oversight committees, you reduce the chances of that happening?

HELMS: That question of co-option has never seemed to me to be very realistic. Let's use an analogy. In the days before the seventies, committee chairmen in both the Senate and the House were very powerful. That all broke down in the sixties and seventies—probably in the seventies. In these earlier days, every senator and every congressman on a committee felt just the opposite: they weren't co-opted. They were too tough. So that [co-optation thesis] doesn't impress me as an argument.

JOHNSON: It's not that easy to co-opt a Richard B. Russell, for example?[22]

HELMS: You could no more co-opt him than you could fly to the moon. He was a man who, in his fairness about these things, nevertheless had opinions, stated them, and was very hard to get off them. So I don't think it's a very good argument.

JOHNSON: Do you believe there was too little congressional interest in intelligence matters before 1975?

HELMS: I didn't ever find there was too little interest. What gave the impression that the Senate wasn't serious about its oversight responsibilities after Senator Russell died [in 1971], and Senator [John] Stennis [D, Mississippi] took over, really went to an entirely different matter, and that was the animosity that existed—the hostility that existed—between Senator Stennis and Senator [Stuart] Symington [D, Missouri]. When Senator Stennis refused to make Senator Symington the chairman of the Preparedness Subcommittee [of the Armed Services Committee], which Stennis had chaired before and which Symington thought he was entitled to, Symington went over to the Foreign Relations Committee and got Senator [and Chairman J. William] Fulbright [D, Arkansas] to give him a comparable subcommittee. So Symington was on both committees [Foreign Relations and Armed Services].

But Stennis did not like having meetings on the Agency when Symington was present—even though Senator [Henry] Jackson [D, Washington] attempted to broker between them. He even suggested to Stennis that he set up a small subcommittee to hear the Agency's problems more frequently, and so forth, in order to avoid this kind of a get-together. Senator Stennis declined and didn't do it. So this was really not the Agency's fault. If the Senate backed up on its responsibilities, it was because of this animosity between two senators.

The House went right along all during this period, without any hiccups at all. They had regular [executive session] hearings; and the budget process in the House Appropriations Subcommittee was very thorough and very good. Mr. [George H.] Mahon [D, Texas, the chairman of the panel] and his predecessors wanted to keep [these meetings] private. They held the meetings in secrecy in the basement of the Capitol Building, where no one knew they were taking place. They had one staffer who did the work and sat in on the meetings; but they had very thorough hearings, and went through the entire budget with the greatest of care.

JOHNSON: And probably no leaks?

HELMS: There were no leaks. The record indicates, as far as the Agency was concerned, that the committees and subcommittees in both the Senate and House for years were absolutely impeccable. They never leaked anything.

JOHNSON: What about today: do you think there is too much access to sensitive intelligence information by the Congress? Have we gone too far?

HELMS: Well, I don't know how to judge that, Dr. Johnson, because I'm not in touch any more. I've been out of the Agency now thirteen years.

JOHNSON: Maybe I can phrase it this way: what do you think of the argument that, because of the delicacy of "sources and methods," Congress shouldn't be given access to sensitive intelligence information from the intelligence community. Is that a good argument?

HELMS: Well, it is a good argument. It is an argument that had great validity before the end of the Cold War. Now the question is whether there isn't more leakage out of the Foreign Relations Committee and the Armed Services Committee than there is out of the Intelligence Committees. In other words, Congress is a sieve.

JOHNSON: What do you make of this concept of *prior* notification on covert actions, to the two Intelligence Committees? Or do you prefer a delayed, forty-eight-hour reporting requirement?

HELMS: Certainly before the end of the Cold War, I would have taken the line that the Agency should have had more than just a forty-eight-hour notification [leeway]. [During the Iranian hostage crisis in 1979] some hostages were in the Canadian Embassy and the Canadians were going to get them out. [The CIA's assistance to the Canadians in helping to exfiltrate the hostages out of Iran] was certainly a covert operation of a sort and should have been notified to the Congress; but the [Carter] administration was scared to death that it might leak. Someone in a cheerful mood might have said, "Great Scott, we're going to get those hostages back!" And the next thing you know it might have been in the papers.

My arguments, I realize, fall on deaf ears with senators, because they think they're just as solid as anybody else: "Don't worry about it; just come up and tell us—the chairman and the deputy chairman. Everything will be all right; you don't need to worry." Well, I was raised in the wrong tradition. My service in intelligence came during World War II, when secrets were really important to keep, and everybody agreed they were important to keep. I've felt that way all the way along. That's the way the Russians do it; the British do it; almost everyone else does it. But we have our own American ways, and I assume that the Senate is going to win out in the end and get some kind of a notification [requirement] like forty-eight hours. You asked my opinion: I'm just opposed to it—even a delayed forty-eight-hour rule, let alone prior notification.

JOHNSON: When would you report, if at all, on these matters?

HELMS: I wouldn't mind prior notice in most cases. I'm not extreme about this; I just think that, once in a while, there are those situations where it shouldn't be required. The devil of these things is that as soon as they write this stuff into law, then somebody—if they break it—is accused of being "above the law." That big argument starts all over again: "What right has this guy got to do that?" This is what's tough about it. This is what that whole Iran-contra argument was about. What was it: the Boland Amendment? Lord, if there's anything that would tear up a man's . . . I was going to say, his soul . . . tear up a man's disposition, it is to deal with a messy thing like that.

JOHNSON: The Boland Amendments went through seven different incarnations.[23]

HELMS: Exactly.

JOHNSON: What do you make of the idea that we need a rewriting of the 1947 National Security Act—a full-blown, detailed legislative "Grand Charter" for intelligence?

HELMS: Don't rewrite anything. Once you start rewriting things in the Congress, you don't know where they are going to go. I would be very much against rewriting anything. Leave it the way it is.

JOHNSON: What about the claim that you didn't always give the martini straight up to the Congress—that you weren't always entirely candid with legislators in hearings?

HELMS: You mean in my testimony?

JOHNSON: Yes.

HELMS. Untrue, totally untrue. The trouble that I got into later was over testimony before the [Senate] Foreign Relations Committee, not before the [Intelligence] Oversight Subcommittee. To the best of my knowledge, I never told an untruth to one of the appropriately appointed oversight committees.

JOHNSON: What about the hearings on Chile before the [Foreign Relations] Subcommittee on Multinational Corporations?

HELMS: That was not my oversight committee. The senators on that Subcommittee [which included Frank Church as the subcommittee chair] had no secrecy inhibitions on them. We had some things going in Chile, where people

[CIA officers and their assets] could have been arrested, or shot, or whatever the case was. I didn't lie, in point of fact; I just didn't tell them everything in that case.

James Rodney Schlesinger: Father of the Family Jewels (1973)

Dr. James R. Schlesinger, a Harvard-trained economist, succeeded Helms in 1973 but proved to be the director who served the shortest period of time. President Nixon initially appointed him DCI, but, after only four months, the president shifted him to the position of secretary of defense. However brief, it was an eventful tenure at Langley, as Schlesinger spent most of his initial time defending the Agency against charges that it had been involved in the Watergate scandal. He also initiated the process of a major downsizing inside the Directorate of Operations (DO), for which the next DCI, Admiral Turner, would take the flak from its officers as he implemented this "rif" (reduction in force). Even more notoriously, Schlesinger issued the internal order for an accumulation of suspected Agency missteps. This list became known as the "Family Jewels" and was leaked by someone in the CIA to journalist Sy Hersh of the *Times* (chapter 3). Schlesinger's few months as DCI were also something of a bridge between the old school of limited congressional accountability and the new school of robust review introduced by the Church Committee.

I met with Schlesinger on June 16, 1994, in another glassy downtown office building in Washington where he held a consultancy position. He offered a cordial greeting as we sat together on a couch. His sturdy frame and square jaw reminded me of my high school football coach. Schlesinger artfully retrieved a worn pipe from a pocket in his suit coat, filled the bowl with tobacco, fumbled around for a match, and lit the brown-leaf concoction. After numerous puffs on the pipe, swirls of smoke enveloped his large and graying head. In the blink of an eye, the former defense secretary seemed transformed from Knute Rockne into Moses—a biblical image reinforced by his deep and authoritative voice. I began by asking what stood out most in his mind from his brief tenure at Langley.

SCHLESINGER: My greatest accomplishment at the Agency was permitting it to survive under circumstances which were difficult, because the Watergate episode had broken in such a way as to hint of some CIA culpability in the affair. After I'd been around for six weeks, I spent much of my time on Capitol Hill testifying about the Watergate activities and the asserted role of the Agency: the real activities, and those of which they had been accused—which were untrue.

The traditional relationship between the Congress and the Agency had been one of general approval, without any detailed knowledge [on the Hill]. Many of the people at the Agency had the attitude that Congress should be denied information. Some of the Old Guard suggested to me that the strategy of plausible denial was the game to be played. To which I responded— this was one morning in a meeting: "The strategy of plausible denial just isn't going to wash. It would be implausible. What we're going to try is the strategy of plausible admission." Many of the Old Guard were shocked; but they didn't really understand, it seemed to me, the constitutional system of the United States, which is that whether agencies of the executive branch like it or not, the Congress has the right to make inquiries into what is going on.[24] To try and stonewall the Congress would have been a constitutional catastrophe, as well as a disaster for the Agency. So when I say "permitting the Agency to survive" was my chief accomplishment, this is what I mean.

Anyhow, the questionable Watergate activities were a very modest involvement [by the CIA] in domestic activities: a profile on Daniel Ellsberg [leaker of the Pentagon Papers and a White House nemesis at the time], providing wigs and whatnot [unknowingly for use by the seven conspirators who broke into the Watergate Hotel in D.C. in search of documents about campaign strategy in the files of the Democratic National Committee, which had offices in this hotel at Foggy Bottom on the banks of the Potomac]. These activities were very much on the periphery; still, they were not entirely proper. Sometime during that period the Agency's security people came to me with a cache of letters from James McCord [a former CIA officer and one of the Watergate burglars]. He had been in correspondence with the [Watergate] people. The letters hinted at this and hinted at that. It was plain there was some kind of undercurrent of communications. Nothing explicit. I said: "I want to know everything related to this [Watergate] affair." This was six or seven weeks or so into my tenure.

One would have thought that something involving one of the Watergate seven would have been brought to my attention, given—what shall I say— the fact that the Agency was not entirely clear of suspicion with regard to the affair. And, yet, these letters had rested downstairs. And there were other things. As someone has said, you turn over these rocks and strange creatures crawl out from beneath them. So that was what led to my instructions to the personnel there [to gather the "Family Jewels"].

JOHNSON: How broad were your instructions?

SCHLESINGER: They were very vague and general. My deputy, Bill Colby, wrote the memorandum and I said, "Keep it vague." I didn't want to say, "You people who know anything about Watergate, McCord, or something, please come and see me." Instead, I said: "Anyone who knows anything untoward." And that led to not only revelations about the Watergate affair, but about a lot of other events in the past, which I had not really wanted to know about and which were now being uncovered.

JOHNSON: Were you shocked?

SCHLESINGER: Shocked may not be the right word. I'd say "surprised." At the time I was there, I did not expect that anything we reported to the Inspector General was going to see the light of day. That was a naive belief.

JOHNSON: Did you spend most of your subsequent time dealing with these Watergate matters that were surfacing?

SCHLESINGER: I spent one helluva lot of time on that. It must have absorbed, after the early weeks, 60 to 70 percent of my time—just going to Capitol Hill and seeing various members of the Congress. At the start of the Nixon Administration, I had done this study for the president when I was at the Bureau of the Budget [BOB, now the Office of Management and Budget, or OMB], driven by the requirement of George Mahon [the chairman of the House Appropriations Committee]. He had told the president that we were going to reduce the spending on intelligence from $5 billion to $3 billion. The president assigned the task to the BOB. So we had underway a squeeze on the entire intelligence community—a very radical reduction.

JOHNSON: Was this unfair of Mahon?

SCHLESINGER: No, it was unfair only in the sense that it was arbitrary. He said, "Look, this is a growing share of the budget and we just can't have it." He left it up to the executive, simply saying: "We're not going to let this part of the defense budget grow as it has in the past." The judgment was correct. As a result of the Vietnam War, many of the intelligence activities had swollen and you know the way bureaucracies are: if you don't take positive steps to shrink the . . . [His voice trailed off, then he continued.] The course of least resistance is to let them be.

JOHNSON: Do we need a secretary of intelligence?

SCHLESINGER: No, I don't think so. I don't think you want to elevate this any more than it is. It may straighten out the boxes in the American government, but it would make foreigners distrust the [intelligence] liaison relationship more than they presently do. If the individual who is DCI has high credibility, I think his recommendations will carry great weight in the final budget process; if he doesn't have credibility, even if he proposes cuts in the service budgets or one thing or another, he is not going to get the Congress to go along. The whole thing, as you know better than I, has shifted since the time I was DCI. The Congress has a helluva lot more detailed information than in the old days.

JOHNSON: Have we gone too far in this direction?

SCHLESINGER: Yeah, I'd be inclined to think so; but it's a reaction against what existed before. I can remember when I was DCI. I went up to the Hill and said, "Mr. Chairman [John Stennis], I want to tell you about some of our programs. . . ." The Senator quickly responded: "No, no, my boy, don't tell me. Just go ahead and do it, but I don't want to know!" You have to make a pass at keeping Congress informed, but if Congress says, "No, I don't want to be informed," you've done your constitutional duty.

William Egan Colby: DCI during the Year of Intelligence (1973–1976)

Although my interviews with DCIs occurred more randomly (according to when I could arrange a meeting with them), they are presented here chronologically according to their terms of tenure as intelligence director. I spoke with the DCI who followed Schlesinger in service—William E. Colby—on January 22, 1991. We met in downtown D.C. again, this time in a fancy suite of law offices (he had earned a J.D. from Columbia University after his OSS days). Colby had struck me during the Church Committee inquiry as a remarkably bright and forthright individual; and, since I was a young man at the time and a fellow Army brat, I had been impressed by his derring-do operations as an OSS paramilitary officer in World War II—a time when he blew up bridges, exchanged gunfire with Germans, and otherwise made his bones in the battle zones of France and snow-swept Norway.[25] He had panache then and, all these years later, he looked to me like someone who could still climb an enemy wall with a dagger between his teeth; indeed, that he would far prefer that assignment—or almost any field action—over sitting in a K Street law office.

Colby had the bad luck of rising to the DCI office during what a CIA historian has referred to as "one of the worst times in Agency history."[26] During the "Year of Intelligence" investigations in 1975, he attempted the difficult task of sailing between a Charybdis and a Scylla: satisfying the Ford White House by refusing to kowtow to the committee's requests for documents and witnesses yet, at the same time, keeping the Church Committee happy by being reasonably cooperative—or else infuriated investigators might have decided to shut down his beloved Agency, which had just been discovered to have spied on American citizens. By no means was Colby always cooperative with the trio of investigations of that year: the Church, Pike, and Rockefeller panels. He resisted Church Committee public hearings on covert action, for instance, and he fought back on many requests for documents, such as a more complete accounting of the Agency's relationships with U.S. journalists. When it came to Operation CHAOS (CIA spying on American citizens), however, Colby was helpful and personally upset that some elements of the Agency had engaged in these wrongful activities.

As Colby courted the Church Committee and promised a "Constitutional Intelligence for America" (his conception of a new kind of "CIA"), Secretary of State Henry Kissinger and former DCI Richard Helms writhed in anger over what they considered an all-too-conciliatory posture struck by the director. "Bill Colby went overboard," Helms said to me during my interview with him, "when he decided that he knew all about the Constitution, and that he was going to send all that material up to those committees." Kissinger and Helms advised President Gerald R. Ford to hunker down until the storm blew over. Eventually the president did fire Colby in the middle of the inquiry but, embarrassingly, had to bring him back to the CIA temporarily until George H. W. Bush could leave his job as U.S. envoy in China and replace the beleaguered DCI. A recent assessment by a retired CIA officer claims that "Colby became a pariah at CIA for collaborating with congressional investigators" in 1975.[27] In my interviews over the years, however, I found that Agency people have been split down the middle on Colby's strategy during the "intelligence wars" (as some embittered CIA officers remember the inquiries of 1975). He was quite popular among those CIA officers—and there are many—who were unhappy about Operation CHAOS and other Agency excesses.

Fortunately for Colby, he was battle-tested from his experiences in the OSS and in Vietnam; risk and adversity were nothing new to him. For example, during and after the war in Indochina, the far left pilloried him for heading up the Agency's Phoenix Program in South Vietnam, an operation designed to "neutralize"—CIA-speak for apprehend or kill—members of the anti-American Viet Cong (VC) infrastructure in league with North Vietnam against the United States and pro-U.S. factions in South Vietnam. The Program led to the death of at least some 20,000 VC and their sympathizers (Colby's estimate), or as many as 60,000 (in the left's claim). No doubt Colby had his enemies within the Agency and among the political left, and those with a conspiratorial mind wondered if his death in 1996 might have had sinister roots. Police accounts, though, concluded that he had suffered a stroke or heart attack while canoeing in bad weather and turbulent waters near his home in Rock Point, Maryland, with no evidence of foul play.

During the Year of Intelligence, I thought he had navigated a sensible, difficult, and courageous route between the White House and the Congress. Although Church Committee chief counsel Schwarz recalls him being "cold" at the time of the investigations, he had always struck me as cordial—if stolid—and I was pleased to see him again for this interview.[28]

JOHNSON: Let me begin by asking you about this "grand experiment" we have been having in intelligence oversight. Do you think it has worked out all right?

COLBY: I think it's worked out very well. Of course, there are glitches here and there, and some arguments. I think Iran-contra was a direct violation of the deal, in both the respects of the refusal to send the finding over [to SSCI and HPSCI] related to the Iranian part, and then coming up with the thesis that the Boland Amendments did not apply to the NSC, which was pure sophistry.[29] I'm surprised that [the Reagan Administration's first DCI, William J.] Casey, didn't pick up on that, because the 1980 Intelligence Oversight Act very clearly says ". . . *any* entity engaged in intelligence activities." So if you're engaged [as was the NSC staff, which planned and led the Iran-contra affair], you're automatically included; it doesn't give you it by name. You will have that kind of thing forever: little things that happen here and there.

JOHNSON: The quality of intelligence oversight often seems uneven.

COLBY: It's the same throughout the government. Sometimes people on the Agriculture Committees worry about what is happening in the Agriculture Department, and sometimes they don't. I think that is typical.

JOHNSON: Do you think that legislators tend to focus in when something goes wrong?

COLBY: Oh, sure. That's the way the Hill works, which is fair enough; but they also look at the annual budget, which is down to a line-item thing. I remember one incident. Some people came to me with the idea of putting a bug out in one of the trust territories in the Pacific. I sent it up to the lawyers [at Langley]. I said, "Look, this is a trust territory. Is it outside the United States, or is it inside the United States?" And a lawyer came back and said, "It's outside." And I said, "Well, I don't think this will be worth a helluva lot; but, okay, let's try it for three months and see what happens." Well, it leaked and Congress complained. I reminded the legislators that the operation had been there all along in the [classified] line-item budget. "It was there for you to ask about," I said. As I say, I never thought it was going to do a helluva lot of good, but I didn't want to put out the word throughout the Agency: "We're going to stop everything because of fear." So I decided, let's do these things. If they work, fine; if they don't, the hell with it.

JOHNSON: How do you develop comity between the branches?

COLBY: I don't think you get comity. It's a deliberate separation of powers. I explained our government to a foreigner one time. I said, "Look, you're familiar with establishing a coalition government in your country. You establish a coalition, you agree on a program, and then everything more or less goes through because you have party discipline. You have to realize that in this country we have to establish a new coalition on each issue. There's no party discipline, so each issue has to have its own coalition." So it's consensus that you need, rather than comity.

There was a case here, I noticed in the paper—though it's a little fuzzy—that apparently before the attack in Panama [an overt military invasion carried out by the George H. W. Bush Administration] somebody came up with the idea of running a coup against that country's president, Manuel Noriega.[30] The possibility was mentioned in the PDB [the President's Daily Brief]. This idea apparently got all the way to one of the congressional oversight committees, as was proper. The Committee's members were being briefed on it, as they should have been, and it got into a discussion. If [President] Noriega is killed in the middle of the coup, is that an assassination? And it went back and forth. They mulled it over, and they finally decided not to do it. Instead [of a covert action], they [the first Bush Administration] sent 24,000 troops and killed several hundred Panamanians. But I suspect that was the right decision, because you'd still be hearing about the assassination of Noriega for the next hundred years; and you will not be hearing about the attack on Panama for the next hundred years.

JOHNSON: Are we likely to have another DCI in the future like Casey who does not appreciate oversight? [Casey's attitude toward intelligence accountability is displayed succinctly in the Casey "interview" below.]

COLBY: Yeah, sure.

JOHNSON: There's no way to get around that?

COLBY: No, you just count on the tension in the constitutional system to work; and if it doesn't work and someone gets caught, then there's a back-up that's supposed to work for a while when someone goes off the reservation. It's like the laws against murder: murders take place even though we have laws, and we punish the guilty party when it happens.

JOHNSON: What about the question of access to information by Congress? Is the "sources and methods" argument a bit phony when it's brought up by the Agency in this context, as a means for avoiding the sharing of information with legislators?

COLBY: I think it's pretty sincere, although they undoubtedly stretch it. Particularly on agent names, we did convince both Church and Pike to leave out the names [in their committee reports]. We pretty well got through that whole thing without names. It was critical. And the return on it was for us to be reasonably responsible. There's your comity. Even when you're antagonists, you can have some degree of comity.

JOHNSON: Unless you're dealing with Otis Pike and some of his people [on the Pike Committee]?

COLBY: Oh, they were impossible!

JOHNSON: A lot of this depends on personality.

COLBY: Yes, of course it does—the character of the people involved.

JOHNSON: What about the timing of Congress's access to information?

COLBY: I think Stan Turner [Admiral Stansfield Turner, DCI during the Carter Administration] put it about as well as anyone. He said at one point, when they were talking about this forty-eight-hour reporting provision, "Look, before Desert One [the attempt to rescue American hostages from the U.S. Embassy in Tehran in 1980], I had sent people over there [to Iran] in little planes to check out the desert to see whether it would hold the weight of a C-15 [a military cargo aircraft]. I am unable to look a young man like that in the eye and tell him that I'm not going to inform ten congressmen [about the mission]; at the same time, I'm not going to lie to him. So I need that kind of flexibility."

I don't think you can write a law to cover it; but I think what you can say is that, after the event, the Congress would then have the right to review whether it was reasonable to withhold the information. In that case, they would have said yes. I imagine there was some kind of briefing: that we are going to run some kind of operation someday, without any particular specifics. I would be surprised if [President Jimmy] Carter hadn't arranged for a few members of the leadership [in Congress] at least to be brought into the fact that we're going to do something to try to get these people out.

JOHNSON: And if Congress doesn't like the rationale?

COLBY: Then it can raise a fuss.

JOHNSON: What do you think about the idea of a "Grand Charter" for intelligence? Has that gone the way of the dinosaurs?

COLBY: That's gone. I was for it. You could diddle with the details, but I've always been interested in getting intelligence a charter—a solid, statutory base—for its functions within the American government.

JOHNSON: How well has the IG [Inspector General] system worked inside the CIA?

COLBY: Well, it's like the IG in the military. They do periodic inspections, and they're a useful investigating team for the director if something is strange. He just tells the IG to look into it. It's a bureaucratic mechanism to get something done; but as a great safety valve, I'm not so sure, any more than the IOB [the Intelligence Oversight Board in the White House]. I mean, it's there . . . but Congress is the real safety check.

JOHNSON: And the press?

COLBY. And the press, certainly; and the feeling that if something is wrong, people will make it known. I have no idea how many sources someone like Seymour Hersh has, but it must be dozens; they must be all over the place. And so if anything serious is wrong, it'll come out.

JOHNSON: Some say the FOIA [Freedom of Information Act] is the most important source of oversight . . .

COLBY: Well, in a way; but now they've exempted the [CIA's] operations files from that—for good reason; it was just a useless exercise. I think it's the press and the Congress; and the traditional feeling that, if something is bad, you should do something about it. The normal, good, loyal American citizen thinks that way.

JOHNSON: Would the CIA have been in big trouble if you hadn't cooperated with the Church and Pike Committees?

COLBY: I thought so. I was walking along by the Library of Congress one time— five, maybe eight, years ago—and this fellow [a former senior staffer on the Church Committee] crossed the street to me, and he said, "I just want to tell you something. I heard that you thought that, if you weren't cooperative with Congress, they would have gone out to destroy the Agency. I just want to tell you, you're absolutely right. We would have." They were out for blood, so I was throwing things at them, trying to be reasonably responsive and trying to protect the Agency at the same time. And I considered really the greatest victory was that Church Committee report is not a bad report; it really is not an unbalanced report. It's a little more sanctimonious than I'd like to have had; but when they came down to that part about covert action, I thought we'd come home free. You know: we shouldn't use it very often, but we shouldn't dismiss it either. I was really a little surprised, because I thought we'd have a little more antagonistic report. The Pike Committee report was useless; but the Church Committee report, if you read it through, hangs together pretty well.[31]

George Herbert Walker Bush: The Spymaster Who Became President (1976–1977)

When George H. W. Bush finally extricated himself from his diplomatic assignment in China, he took Colby's place at Langley, serving a year from January 1976 to January 1977. He began these DCI duties just as the Church Committee was assembling its final report. As Colby graciously recalled in his interview with me, Bush was an instant hit as his successor at the CIA. "Three days after he arrived at the Agency, the new DCI was meeting with staff," Colby recalled. "Somebody said: 'Well, there's a story in the press that says we did this or that.' And Bush replied, 'What are they trying to do to us?' Us! After three days! After that, he had the place in the palm of his hand."

Himself a former member of the U.S. House of Representatives (R, Texas) and his father a well-regarded U.S. senator (Prescott Bush, R, Connecticut) in an earlier generation, Bush was no stranger to the Hill. This legacy helped to calm the waters during the final stages of the Church Committee inquiry, although Senator Church vehemently resisted Bush's appointment as DCI, on the grounds that it was an inappropriate job for a former chairman of the Republican National Committee. I was unable to arrange a sit-down interview with the former president, who had moved to Houston, Texas; but he kindly consented to answer a few questions by mail (which he personally typed and sent to me on January 23, 1994). Here is the brief exchange:

JOHNSON: What do you view as your most important accomplishment as DCI?
BUSH: Restoration of the morale at CIA after the devastating effects and excesses of the Church and Pike investigations.
JOHNSON: How did you divide up your time while serving as DCI?
BUSH: I think about one-third of my time went to Community activities, the rest to CIA.
JOHNSON: Did you find the organization of the Community fragmented?
BUSH: I did not feel there was excessive fragmentation. Certainly there were rivalries; but I felt that, as DCI, I received full cooperation from all the agencies in the Community. When the differences resulted in different interpretations of various data, I was sure the agencies knew they could have a "footnote" [that is, a dissenting opinion in community-wide intelligence reports to policymakers].
JOHNSON: What are your views on intelligence oversight?
BUSH: I think closer oversight was needed, but I think it has gone too far.

Admiral Stansfield Turner: The First DCI under the New Rules (1977–1981)

As DCI, Stansfield Turner made an instant impression: rugged looking (he had played guard on the U.S. Naval Academy football team), sparkling bright (Amherst College and the Naval Academy, where he won a Rhodes Scholarship for graduate study at Oxford University), brimming with self-confidence, and not shy about getting his way. One example: he brought a "Navy mafia" (as it was known at Langley) with him to the Agency to help enforce his directives throughout the intelligence bureaucracy. President Carter, whom he served as DCI and who had been a member of his class at the Naval Academy, had run successfully for the presidency in 1976 in part on a platform that had strong anti-CIA overtones, especially with respect to its use of covert actions in the past. Carter even selected a reform-minded Church Committee member, Walter "Fritz" Mondale, as his running mate.

Turner quickly became one of the least popular DCIs in the Agency's history. His Navy mafia rubbed people the wrong way; and his follow-through on James Schlesinger's plan to fire a large number of DO officers sent waves of resentment throughout the Directorate—even though the officers let go had marginal performance evaluations and were near retirement anyway. As Schlesinger recalled in his interview with me, "I had initiated a reduction in force, across the board. The difference was that I brought in the Agency's deputy directors and said: 'You know who is no longer working very hard, those who may be dead wood, and those who are eligible for retirement. You know who they are, and I don't know; and I'm going to put the responsibility for these reductions on you. You will bring them in and you will tell them why they are leaving.' And I got the Congress to renew the CIA retirement system. The problem Stan had, it seems to me, was that *he* tried to decide; and the numbers [of those fired] were much larger. He also brought in a bunch of fellows from the Navy, who turned out to be his 'heavies,' as it were. It was much more deeply resented. In my case, it was done with some degree of gentleness. No one ever likes to be eased out of an agency; and the CIA, of course, had just accumulated people over the course of the previous thirty years—never let anybody go, never pushed anybody out. So it was a shock to the system."

On May 1, 1991, I met with Admiral Turner at his home in McLean, Virginia, near the CIA. He was dressed in casual attire and seemed ready to spend as much time as I wanted discussing his tenure as director. From our longer conversation, here are the passages that dealt with oversight.[32]

JOHNSON: What's the bottom-line appraisal of how this experiment in intelligence oversight has worked out?

TURNER: Oh, I would grade it a 3.0 out of 4.0, maybe. I don't think the Congress has been tough enough, diligent enough, first. Second, I don't think members of Congress have taken a long-enough view of their responsibilities. Third, I think it has taken quite a while for the [Intelligence] Community to adjust and accept it, although I think that has come along reasonably well in time.

I don't want to appear too critical of the Congress, because I think its members have tried hard and they've done a lot of good. I believe, however, that there is inadequate recognition that oversight of this sort—where there's a sensitive function going on that can embarrass the country, break the laws, or whatever—requires a different congressional procedure than most supervision by the Congress. Most of congressional oversight is done through the budget; and if Congress looks at an agency's budget in detail and checks on it, legislators can check out what the bureaucrats are doing—but you also control it. That's not the same way with intelligence oversight, particularly when some of the money is secret.

JOHNSON: Contingency funds and the like.

TURNER: Right, and while intelligence overseers on the Hill have to control that budget and have to do all that scrutiny, it's important that they take a long-range look, too, and say: "It isn't whether the community buys one satellite or two next year that counts; it's [the question of] what is the weight of reliance we're placing on satellites? Is it right?" Take humint versus satellites, which is always debated. That's something Congress ought to have a hand in; and they really don't, other than worrying about next year's satellite buy. I would only like to encourage the Congress to understand that there are certain areas of activity in the intelligence field that they ought to come at more seriously and ask questions about, for the sake of propriety and legality.

JOHNSON: Without waiting for a crisis?

TURNER: Every so often Congress ought to take a look at covert action writ large—not worrying about the approval of this one that came up yesterday, but worrying about the track record over the last five years. How many have we approved? How many ever accomplished anything? How many are still on the books? Who's telling us what about them? I mean, there are a number of areas like this—some that involve legality and propriety, some that involve effectiveness—where the Congress can provide help.

Let me say, further, that the community needs Congress badly. All professions get myopic, but a secret profession can get more myopic than anybody else. Lawyers at least read in the papers that we all don't like lawyers; doctors read that they charge too much; and so on. But nobody reads an awful lot about what the intelligence people are doing wrong. There's some, of course; but it is much easier, I believe, to become cloistered in the world of secrecy.

JOHNSON: No one is really looking over your shoulder very much.

TURNER: And, therefore, the Congress has got to do that over-the-shoulder work.

JOHNSON: What do you make of the new "within a few days" reporting requirement proposed in the 1991 Intelligence Oversight Act [eventually enacted in 1992] in times of emergency [an *ex post facto* standard in a crisis, rather than the normal prior-notice (*ante facto*) reporting requirement established in the 1980 Intelligence Oversight Act]?

TURNER: That [emergency] formula is acceptable to me, if they make a few changes. First, they should exclude in their definitions Agency support to military operations [SMOs, in Pentagonese], or CIA rescue operations. I had a couple of instances when I—or President Carter—didn't inform the Congress. One was the rescue of the "Canadian Six" by the CIA [during the hostage crisis of 1979 in Iran]—strictly our own operation, but it was a covert action. And another involved several forms of support to the Desert One rescue attempt.

JOHNSON: Like testing the desert soil to see if it could support a landing?

TURNER: Right, and that was dicey for telling anybody about, because lives were very immediately at stake. I think we could redefine covert action in a way to specifically exclude those kinds of operations; but also to point out that a covert action is something that, it is hoped, will remain secret for a long period of time. Those things [military-support missions and rescue operations] only needed to remain secret for a few days, or months; but a covert action is something where you don't want it known that the United States was the acting force. Basically, it's an operational secrecy [versus] a secrecy designed to obscure U.S. participation. I think the definition can be modified; and, then, I think it's desirable to have notification within twenty-four hours, or some reasonable time, because you're now getting to where you might be taking actions covertly that affect U.S. foreign policy.

JOHNSON: Looking at the question of control over the CIA, one former director, Jim Schlesinger, said to me that he thought you had been afraid of the Agency when you went out there—that you didn't relate well to the people [at Langley], that you didn't trust them. How accurate is this?

TURNER: I hope that's not true. I don't think I was afraid of the Agency. Whether I related well is, of course, a matter I can't judge very well. Let me say this: you'd have been a pretty insensitive individual if you stepped in, in 1977, and didn't have some question whether this Agency was running right, whether this Agency was running legally, whether this Agency was running ethically or within the ethical bounds your president wanted it to run in. Lots of people got the wrong impression, though, that "Turner was told to clean house." That was never the case with [President] Carter. He made it clear to all of us that he wanted the government to run legally and ethically; but I never got any orders to go out there and clean up, and that he thought the place was a mess. He wanted secrecy more than I did, often. "Do we tell this to Congress, or we don't?" And he, more often than I, leaned on the side of: "No, we don't. We have to keep this secret."

To get back to your question, I do acknowledge in retrospect that bringing in eight Navy officers with me gave the wrong impression: that I was trying to run it with the Navy. In fact, several of the officers I don't think I saw more than once a year. They did their thing and I never saw them as a group—not once. But it was a poor public relations move.

JOHNSON: What about the DO "purge"?

TURNER: Well, there are several things about that. First of all, not one of the positions removed was overseas. So there was nothing on the cutting edge. Secondly, in the decade since I did that, there has hardly been any American business that hasn't cut 15 or 20 percent out of its headquarters overhead. That's all we were doing. Thirdly, none of the individuals affected were above the bottom 5 percent of their category. So we didn't lose talent; we lost overhead. I think this improved the organization, rather than hurt it.

JOHNSON: Do you think you struck about the right degree of openness with the public when you were DCI?

TURNER: No, I'd like to have been more open. I had a terrible time, for instance, downgrading intelligence Estimates [key research reports prepared by the

IC jointly] to "unclassified." You just can't sit there and do it yourself; and I couldn't get the Agency to be enthusiastic about this. And there is so much information there that could be brought out to the American public, without endangering sources. My gosh, a well-informed public is the whole foundation of the country.

JOHNSON: What is your judgment of the IOB?

TURNER: Reagan emasculated the Board by taking "propriety" out of its mission. It's now only supposed to look into the legality of community activities—but that's the attorney general's job.

JOHNSON: In your time, though, you thought the IOB was a serious organization?

TURNER: Yes. Now I don't say it accomplished a great deal. But I slept better at night because I knew if a disgruntled intelligence guy knew something I should know but wouldn't tell me, because he was afraid he'd lose his job— you can't just walk in on the director: people in the building know you came, and they want to know why you came. So such an individual can go to the Oversight Board. It was a safety valve for me, and I think it was a great mistake to change its charter. The people on that Board were very helpful; they were detached enough, but knowledgeable enough.

The PFIAB [President's Foreign Intelligence Advisory Board], which we [the Carter Administration] did away with, was so politicized at the time as to be ineffective. If asked if I'd still have a PFIAB today, I could be talked into it; but the combination of it having such an ultra-right wing membership at that time, along with my need already to report to the new intelligence oversight committees in Congress, pushed me against the panel. My feeling was: let's absorb the congressional oversight and not have me reporting to yet another group over here [in the executive branch]. I mean, how many hours a day can I spend telling people what we're doing! Now that that's all settled, as I say, I could be talked into it—with a chance to select a broad cross-section of members.

JOHNSON: Do you think the CIA has a good idea of what standards society wants it to adhere to?

TURNER: On the one hand, yes, we certainly heard through the Church Committee reports—and the reactions of the public to those reports—the things they didn't want the Agency to do; but, on the other hand, it isn't just negative guidance that you need. What bothers me is that the public and the Congress were not more enraged at the CIA's role in Iran-contra. The public and the Congress did not send the right message to the Agency after that. There is no question that the Agency broke the law; there's no question that a couple of people up there [high in the Reagan Administration] ought to have gone on trial; there's no question they destroyed messages that they shouldn't have; and so on. And the fact that that's been pushed under the rug is a bad signal to the Agency, because legality is not something you tamper with. It's not gray; it's black and white. Ethics or propriety are, of course, more subjective; but unless you insist that the organization adheres to the law, it's pretty hard to set some ethical standards for it!

JOHNSON: What was your greatest achievement as DCI?

TURNER: I look on the successful launching of oversight with Congress as probably my most important accomplishment. I had the confidence of the two Intelligence Committees.

William Joseph Casey, Rogue DCI (1981–1987)

Another OSS veteran and a former member of PFIAB, Casey had made good money as a financial guru in New York. A member of the strongly conservative wing of the Republican Party, he had the connections and the wherewithal to head up Ronald Reagan's successful presidential campaign in 1980. He had reportedly hoped for the position of secretary of state in the new administration; but, when that post went to George P. Shultz, he settled for DCI, serving from 1981 until his death from a brain tumor in 1987 (just before the beginning of the Iran-contra investigative hearings). Never had a national presidential campaign manager headed the Agency, and it was little surprise that politics and intelligence often became intertwined during his tenure. Although his personality could be spiky, Casey brought an admirable energy to some intelligence activities that had begun to sag, such as the writing of National Intelligence Estimates (NIEs). The tragedy of his service as DCI, though, was the Iran-contra scandal, for which he will be mainly remembered. He was also the least cooperative director among the set examined here when it came to dealing with Congress, although Richard Helms was not far behind.

Educated to some degree by his own fiery run-ins with lawmakers, Helms beneficently attempted in retirement to nudge Casey toward greater civility when it came to relations on Capitol Hill. He took Casey to lunch and suggested: "You can tell the people on the [oversight] committees just about anything and they cooperate—but only if you're above board. . . . You will find the only thing you can't tell them are operations you should not be in in the first place, like the Bay of Pigs."[33]

My only opportunity to question Casey occurred at a small dinner party held on June 11, 1984, in the DCI's dining room on the Agency's top floor. The guests were a group of visiting scholars attending a scholarly conference at Langley. Here is the brief exchange, grumbled by the DCI in his inimitable gravelly voice—and offered at the very time he was in negotiations with SSCI to improve the Agency's oversight cooperation:

JOHNSON: What is the role of Congress in intelligence?
CASEY: The business of Congress is to stay the f— out of my business.

Only when Senator Barry Goldwater (who had served on the Church Committee) confronted Casey angrily about his poor briefing to SSCI on the mining of harbors in Nicaragua did Casey, with mumbled apologies, scramble back from the rim of a black hole in the CIA's relations with the congressional oversight committees. Even then, for most members of SSCI and HPSCI, the DCI had become all gall and wormwood. Few could even understand his briefings on Nicaragua—a combination of Casey's poor enunciation and his unwillingness to speak candidly with lawmakers. During closed sessions, he would constantly mispronounce "Nicaragua" as "Nicawawa," giving every indication that he believed he was saying the name properly. After one session, a cabal of senators on SSCI drafted a resolution, tongue-in-cheek, that declared "henceforth, no monies shall be spent from the federal treasury for any intelligence operations or related activities in any country that the Director of Central Intelligence cannot pronounce correctly."[34]

The most serious event occurred, though, when an SSCI member asked Casey whether the CIA was mining harbors in Nicaragua, as discussed in chapter 8. The DCI said no—in his barely coherent fashion. Only later was it clear that Casey had relied on a misleading technical point: the Agency was not mining harbors; it was mining *piers* within the harbors. The DCI's attempt to toy with the SSCI angered the committee's leader, Goldwater, leaving the high-profile senator with a deep bruise of humiliation. Until this episode, Goldwater had been an alter ego for Casey; now the institutional instincts of the SSCI chair flared and, temporarily at least, trumped his core blind allegiance to the office of the president and the CIA on anything to do with security.

William Hedgcock Webster, Mr. Integrity (1987–1991)

In the aftermath of the Iran-contra debacle, the Reagan Administration and the CIA were in desperate need for a reset of the intelligence accountability button and, to switch metaphors, a cleansing of the putrid air of scandal that had engulfed the White House. As a replacement for Casey, President Reagan wisely selected William H. Webster, a man known throughout the nation's capital for his moral rectitude—just the person to take over the Agency's reins in the midst of the Iran-contra scandal. Judge Webster (as he was often called) had served as a U.S. District Court judge in eastern Missouri, as well as on the Court of Appeals for the Eighth Circuit; and, subsequently, he led the FBI for almost a decade (1978–1987). A former Amherst College student with a law degree from Washington University, the judge held impeccable academic and public service credentials, as well as social grace and a handsome visage. The sole criticism that stuck to him was a sense that he often enjoyed playing long afternoon tennis matches, to the detriment of providing the vigorous leadership needed by the Agency to restore its image after the effects of Cyclone Casey. Still, at the time, high integrity seemed a rare trait in government circles and this gift to the administration from the judge was alone worth a good deal, both to Langley and the White House. Webster was still DCI at the time we met, in the director's office at Langley on May 2, 1991, three months before he retired.

JOHNSON: How would you evaluate the experiment in intelligence oversight?

WEBSTER: I arrived on the scene here [in Washington] in 1978, so I began—on the FBI side—to catch the impact of the oversight process. On balance, I think the oversight process has been clearly useful and helpful. In many ways, oversight makes it possible for us to do our business in critical times—"critical" in the sense where people are critical of intelligence—when we might not be able to perform well, because of the rush toward legislative restrictions. The intelligence oversight committees function properly as surrogates, representing to their colleagues and the public that we are doing our business as we should be doing it.[35]

JOHNSON: Has appearing before Congress made too great a surcharge on your time as DCI?

WEBSTER: No, it hasn't. It comes in bunches, usually in the spring during the budgetary process. And then, of course, when some activity has come under question—perhaps a covert action program or something of that kind. If legislators call for an inquiry into what is going on, and, if it's serious enough and various questions are raised, I think I should be there [on Capitol Hill]. Truth be known, I always find that preparing for something like that increases the likelihood that I will know everything I need to know about a particular subject. Where we have had some level of burden that I doubt was fully anticipated is in responding to Agency staffing requirements [brought about by burgeoning requests for information posed by lawmakers and their staffs]. Last year we provided over 1,000 briefings, and over 5,000 reports, to Congress. That has two risks: one, it statistically increases the possibility of some of that getting out into the public domain, where it may not belong; and, two, it draws a lot of our expert time in responding to more detailed, technical questions.

JOHNSON: Do you sometimes feel that matters are so sensitive that you prefer only to talk to the Committee chairman?

WEBSTER: Yes, and we have worked out a good working relationship on that. Not all chairmen have been willing to accept that burden—they call it a "burden."

We've had half-awkward periods of uncertainty on how to proceed when a chairman hasn't been willing to do it. If you have a chairman and a ranking minority member who are both willing to accept that responsibility, it works fine because both parties are covered. I have never felt that I would condition my telling them on their commitment not to tell the others. My approach has been to say: "This is so sensitive we would prefer to tell you and ask that, if at any time you consider it necessary to go beyond that, you let us know so we can protect our sources in whatever way is appropriate."

JOHNSON: Do you feel that the Congress has gotten too involved in the details of the CIA—"micromanagement"?

WEBSTER: Sometimes I do; and the White House thinks there is far too much micromanagement. None of us is too wise to listen to suggestions on how we might do something better; but sometimes we have to stand up to the Congress. An example would be legislators wanting to tell us which candidates to support during a covert action designed to shape a foreign election. That is directly related to administration policy, which the CIA is supposed to carry out. We don't make policy judgments. It's maddening if at that point Congress says, "If you don't do it our way, then there'll be no money," or even: "We'll wipe out the program if you proceed in this way." We live in that wonderful world of the separation and balancing of powers that our founding fathers created for us, and we all have to exercise some restraint. Micromanagement comes when someone wants to work their will on us as we do something, rather than to review what we have done and to say, "You should have been more attentive to this issue or to that issue, or this process or that process." This is really, from an executive branch point-of-view, what oversight is supposed to do. I sometimes say "oversight" is "after it's over"— but nobody agrees with me! It's not a realistic position, I concede, because there will be some involvement of legislators who sometimes want to save us from ourselves.

JOHNSON: When the history of the Webster years at the CIA is written, what do you most want to be remembered for?

WEBSTER: I have tried to demonstrate that the intelligence community is trustworthy; that it has no political ax to grind; that it will report intelligence competently, objectively, and in a timely way. I tried to do that in a number of ways, including how we testify—the rules for giving testimony to Congress. I insist that our testimony must be complete, candid, and correct.

JOHNSON: That was desperately needed.

WEBSTER: This was needed. There was some dancing and disingenuousness— at least Congress thought we were maybe being disingenuous. Part of the problem was that CIA witnesses were blindsided by unexpected questions. The simplest thing to do—as we put out in our guidelines—was to say: "I'm not authorized to answer that question. I'll report the question back to Headquarters and we'll work the problem up." [This approach was necessary] so I could protect our sources and methods responsibility and, at the same time, give the committee what it needed to know. I think restrictive legislation generally comes when members of Congress don't trust you to work with them and tell them the truth—let them know what's happening.

I found that our people over here [at Langley] are not hostile to the concept of accountability under the law. What we needed was support in showing how legal guidance could be something helpful to the Agency. I see myself portrayed as "Mild Bill," instead of "Wild Bill" [a reference to William J. Casey], every time someone writes an article, while my whole history in Washington shows that I'm willing to take risks and to do things—as long as I know they are lawful. That is very, very important. You lose that, then you lose trust; and then you have another Church-Pike series and things don't happen. You don't get the money you need; instead, you get restrictions. I brought the CIA's lawyers onto the campus [at Langley]; they had been off in some other location [in North Arlington], where they weren't likely to be consulted as regularly. I want our people to be aggressive; but if you're going to be really aggressive, you need to know where the lines are.

When we have covert action reviews, I ask a couple of questions: Is it legal? Is it consistent with our overt foreign policy? Is it consistent with American values? If it becomes public, will it make sense to the American people?

Robert M. Gates, Analyst as DCI (1991–1993)

Bob Gates earned a Ph.D. in Russian studies from Georgetown University and was the only analyst to rise to the office of DCI. (When the office of the DCI became the office of the Director/CIA in 2005, another analyst rose to the top of the Agency hierarchy: John O. Brennan.) Gates later served as deputy national security adviser in the first Bush Administration, and as secretary of defense for both Presidents George W. Bush and Barack Obama. At the CIA, he dramatically increased the production of NIEs and otherwise moved the collection-and-analysis mission to center stage.[36] Here are his perspectives on oversight from an interview I had with him on March 28, 1994, in his downtown D.C. consulting office.[37]

JOHNSON: What are your views on intelligence oversight?
GATES: I closely identify with Colby. When the congressional investigations began [in 1975], he decided that the only way to save the Agency was to cooperate in the investigation—give them substantially all they wanted. Kissinger and [National Security Adviser Brent] Scowcroft to this day believe

he went too far, and obviously so did Helms. My view is that Colby had no choice; that he made the right decision. A few months after pardoning Nixon, President Ford simply was not in a position to precipitate a constitutional crisis by exerting executive privilege over papers involved in a congressional investigation. They had just been through that a year before, and it just wasn't going to happen. So the Agency would have lost anyway; however, by being up front about it, I think Colby not only earned some credit on the Hill, but he bought enough time so that by the end of 1975 the kind of "feeding frenzy" that goes on here in Washington had abated. As I wrote in *Foreign Affairs*, the Agency was moved in effect to an equidistant position between the Congress and the executive; and, if anything, it has probably moved more toward the Congress.[38]

The notion, then, is that Congress has to become a constituency; and I think it has worked. The Agency hates covert action; and policymakers basically don't care about NIEs. Where intelligence and CIA gain their support is what I call "the river of information"—the flow of useful intelligence from around the world to policymakers. Over the past twenty years, the Agency has built a constituency on the Hill of people who have served on the Intelligence Committees. With a couple of eccentric exceptions, like [Daniel Patrick] Moynihan [D, New York], there is basically a broad consensus on the Hill crossing partisan and philosophical lines that, yeah, this is something we need to preserve. The oversight process has built that. In addition to being healthy for the country, oversight has also been healthy for the intelligence community.

JOHNSON: Is Congress a sieve with respect to intelligence?

GATES: I have had far worse problems with leaks out of the executive branch over the past eight years than I ever had with the Congress. The only real leaks that came out of the Congress had to do with controversial covert actions during the early 1980s—primarily in Central America, but also in Afghanistan. It was a period of confrontation, with Casey and everything; so I think it was a unique period. One of the tragedies of the history of that period is that the Congress really only got its act together to do real oversight in a systematic way with the Oversight Act of 1980; and it is a tragedy that the first DCI they had to deal with after that—Casey—was guilty of contempt of Congress from the day he showed up for the job. So there was no reservoir of trust or credit there to draw on; and I think that since the beginning of 1987, we've been able to build that trust.

JOHNSON: Do you think the United States has gone too far in the direction of intelligence oversight?

GATES: No, I don't; but there are four basic problems on the Hill. The first is an inclination to micromanage. I remember Malcolm Wallop [R, Wyoming] in the early 1980s trying to tell me exactly how many analysts to assign to each country and things like that. The director's flexibility to run the Agency has eroded enormously. I don't think that's unique to the CIA, however; it's the same throughout the executive branch—overseas pay and what level should it be relative to the Foreign Service, and stuff like that.

The second problem is the split between the authorizing and appropriating committees. It used to be that the appropriators would essentially take what the authorizers did and put that into the appropriations bill; now what is worse than their disagreements is that sometimes the appropriators will write something into the law that they want CIA to do, but it won't be authorized. The Agency can't spend the money that's appropriated, because it hasn't been authorized. I remember I had a terrible set-to with Ted Stevens [R, Alaska], who said: "You're breaking the law. We appropriated money and you're not spending it."

And I said: "Senator, have you read the law? The law says I can't spend this unless it's been authorized."

And he said, "Who wrote that law!"

It was funny; he didn't even realize that. And the reverse is happening: we'll be authorized to do things, but the appropriators won't appropriate the money for it. And we're looking at hundreds of millions of dollars that can't be spent. It's a netherworld that's either not authorized or not appropriated, so it can't be touched. So we lose hundreds of millions of dollars in the budget each year.

I tried to get everybody in the government to agree, including the Hill, when I first became director. Everybody agreed we needed to strengthen our efforts on non-proliferation [of WMDs], counterterrorism, and counternarcotics; and I asked for, I think, $63 million of the non-appropriated funds. It had been authorized, but not appropriated. I had to get the agreement of eight committees [of Congress] to use the $63 million; and it took me from January to July—even though nobody disagreed with a single thing I intended to do. Guys would engage in the usual kind of Hill blackmail: "Well, I want you to spend this amount on my project," or "I want to add this to it for that project." And then someone else would say, "Well, if you do that for him, I won't vote for it because that's a waste of money." It was a matter of trying to mediate among the different committees on the Hill to get the damn thing done. It was incredibly frustrating. For example, Dave McCurdy [the SSCI chair, D-Oklahoma] and John Murtha [the Defense Appropriations Subcommittee chair, D-Pennsylvania] hated each other.

The third problem is the rotation of members off of SSCI and HPSCI. About the time they begin to become effective on the committees, they're gone. The result is that you're always starting over with people who don't know anything about the business, and you waste a lot of time bringing them up to speed.[39]

Finally, there has been no particular effort by the members [of SSCI and HPSCI] to carve out extra chunks of their time to learn about intelligence. It seems to me that if they are going to be on those committees, the leadership ought to extract a commitment from them that they will devote the time to it to become effective. So here I am, a professional intelligence officer asking for more congressional oversight! But what I'm talking about is oversight by members, not staff.

R. James Woolsey, Techint Champion (1993–1995)

Yale Law, Rhodes Scholar, military service—the Woolsey résumé had "success" written all over it, yet it didn't extend to his relations as DCI with either President Bill Clinton (despite a common Yale and Rhodes experience) or with the SSCI chairman. When a small airplane crash-landed by pilot error on the White House grounds early in Woolsey's tenure, the joke around Washington was that this accident was the DCI's desperate attempt to get an appointment with the president, who rarely asked to see him. Moreover, Woolsey had a running feud with the SSCI chair, Dennis DeConcini (D, Arizona). In frustration, Woolsey left Langley after a couple of years, but he did make something of a mark helping to develop technical collection platforms and integrate them more effectively throughout the IC—his main interest. On September 29, 1993, I sat down with Woolsey in the director's seventh-floor spacious suite, with a view of the forest at Langley and, in the distance, the Potomac River sparkling in the sunlight. We mostly discussed technical intelligence collection activities, but I posed to him a few questions related to accountability.

JOHNSON: How do you handle the Hill side of your job?

WOOLSEY: I handle it by spending an awful lot of time up there. I used to be, for three years, general counsel of the Senate Armed Services Committee in the early seventies. Although a lot of the players have changed, some are still around. I like the Hill. I spend a lot of time not just in hearings but going up there, one-on-one, to explain to senators and congressmen the nature of the intelligence budget. You can't just deal with the Intelligence Committees. They can look into wrongdoing, and we basically have no secrets from them; but we also try to keep other members of Congress informed. We treat alike anyone who has an election certificate. There's no difference between the way we deal with those things between Intelligence Committee members and non-committee members.

JOHNSON: How do you handle the covert action "finding" briefings?

WOOLSEY: There hasn't been a finding since I became DCI—although some operations have continued on from earlier administrations. Covert actions are way down, under 1 percent of what the intelligence community does these days.

JOHNSON: Are PFIAB and IOB any good?

WOOLSEY: The IOB is probably going to get merged into PFIAB, as a subcommittee. PFIAB itself is only just getting off the ground [having been temporarily disbanded during the Carter Administration]; but we will soon ask them to do such things as provide an objective look at how good or bad the estimates have been in a certain area over the course of the last decade or so. Four or five of the members know the [intelligence] community inside out; and then there's the larger group of extremely bright people who are just getting into the business. I'm looking forward to working with them.

JOHNSON: How does one guard against another scandal like the Iran-contra affair?

WOOLSEY: What we have done so far—and Tony [Anthony Lake, the national security adviser at the time] has done it at NSC—is to make it absolutely clear that nobody will come within a country mile of anything that could be regarded as covert action without having a finding. There isn't going to be any halfway covert action, or partial covert action, or "Well, gee, this is very close to a covert action, but maybe we could say it's not."

JOHNSON: What do you hope will be your legacy as DCI?

WOOLSEY: I hope adequate funding, programs, and structure for the consolidations that are now necessary within the intelligence community. We need the different parts working together more effectively. Especially important is the construction of an architecture for the dissemination of imagery in the field [chiefly photography from sophisticated, high-resolution cameras on satellites and reconnaissance aircraft].[40]

John Deutch, Scientist as DCI (1995–1997)

Like Woolsey, John Deutch was a "techie"—although, as a senior chemistry professor at MIT and a long-time "hardware" whiz at the Pentagon (surveillance satellites, reconnaissance aircraft) when on leave from the university, he qualified as a true, in-the-weeds, bona fide technology expert. He brought this interest in "techint" with him when he moved from the number two position at the Defense Department to the DCI slot. I visited him in Cambridge, Massachusetts, on October 29, 1998, a couple of years after his retirement from government. In his large, cluttered hideaway office near one of the long corridors of MIT's imposing main building, he almost immediately said that during his time at Langley he had found the CIA "a troubled and confused agency." Two years had been enough for him, he told me, before he bailed out as director (nudged along by President Bill Clinton, which Deutch didn't tell me[41]). His emphasis on intelligence collection platforms, as well as on more detailed guidance for the DO in foreign agent recruitment, along with his skepticism about most covert actions and a gruff personality, made him as unpopular as Admiral Turner had been at Langley—if not more so. He has the dubious distinction of being the only DCI ever booed in the Agency's auditorium ("the Bubble" in front of the Langley complex of buildings) as he addressed senior Agency staff one afternoon. The opprobrium came chiefly from the DO section of the auditorium; its officers disliked his occasional interference with, but largely his lack of interest in, their covert action and humint activities.

Most of my time with Deutch that afternoon was spent on a discussion of his favorite subject: intelligence hardware—techint; but I slipped in a few questions about accountability. He had been DCI during the time of the Aspin-Brown inquiry into the state of U.S. intelligence in 1995, so I started there.[42]

JOHNSON: Did the Aspin-Brown Commission have any effect?

DEUTCH: [Laughter.] There were three people who liked the Aspin-Brown Commission: the president [Clinton], Tony Lake, and myself. I thought it was a step forward. Everybody else hated it. The secretary of defense [William J. Perry] hated it; the secretary of state [Warren M. Christopher] hated it; the attorney general [Janet Reno] hated it.

JOHNSON: Why?

DEUTCH: Because, when the smoke cleared, it gave the director [DCI] more authority. So [as a result of this high-powered opposition to its recommendations, especially the strengthening of the DCI position] it vanished virtually without a trace.[43]

JOHNSON: The effort to acquire more authority for the DCI never went anywhere?

DEUTCH: Never. In fact, Tony [Lake] said to me, "John, you ought to push this." But I did not want to fight with Chris [Secretary Christopher] and Bill [Secretary Perry].

JOHNSON: Would you comment, please, on the question of intelligence accountability and oversight?

DEUTCH: Well, one of the top challenges is to keep the Congress fully and currently informed on the intelligence operations. You do that by just giving them everything. This is always a big dispute, because it permits Congress to make more aggressive efforts in foreign policy. Today the real dispute is over intelligence-sharing with Congress. Legislators can totally redo the budget, based on new information from the intelligence community. DCIs keep telling legislators, "Plan the budget ahead for five years." Instead, the budget goes up and down, with changes in chairmanships. I don't have any trouble keeping Congress informed with respect to covert operations or intelligence collection; I just don't think they are very influential. The real mischief from Democrats and Republicans, however, enters in with the budget, because they change the budget too often.

JOHNSON: Is the prior-notice debate important?

DEUTCH: It's not of consequence.

JOHNSON: Is covert action really that useful?

DEUTCH: I think it's very useful, although we are very bad at it. Historically, it has been used to get rid of governments you didn't like, in the fifties and sixties. Here the record is mixed, and not too pertinent. However, covert action having to do with [WMD] proliferation and with terrorism is highly useful, to disrupt or kill—end—them. Preempt the operations. This is terribly important. If you find out that Osama bin Laden has a chemical plant, you may want to go there and destroy that plant. If you use the U.S. Marine Corps, you've got a military battle on your hands. So I think it is very important, but not for the classical reasons.

JOHNSON: What do you consider your most important success as director?

DEUTCH: The change in relationships between the FBI and the CIA. We established one counterintelligence effort, not two. That's very important. Another success was much better customer relations. And I think I stopped the downward trend of negative congressional attitudes toward the CIA.

George Tenet, From Hill Staffer to Intelligence Chief (1997–2004)

Perhaps the most affable of the DCIs interviewed in this chapter is George Tenet (before he had reached that pinnacle). He had enjoyed unique opportunities to see the world of intelligence accountability from three key vantage points: as SSCI staff director; as the top NSC staffer for intelligence (one of the only people in that position to be selected from outside the ranks of the CIA); and by way of leadership positions at the Agency (first as deputy DCI, then DCI). He accrued the second longest period of service as director, behind only Allen Dulles.[44] Convivial, with a ready smile and handshake, Tenet thrived on the interactions that accompanied these leadership positions.

Alas, though, as DCI he was at the helm when terrorists attacked the U.S. embassies in Kenya and Tanzania (1998) and attempted to sink the U.S.S. *Cole* in the Gulf of Aden (2000). Even more significantly, this was also a time when America suffered in 2001 its worst homeland attack since the War of 1812, when British Redcoats torched the White House and sent President James Madison galloping away on horseback into the Virginia countryside. It was a time, too, in 2002, when the CIA mistakenly reported the likely presence of WMDs in Iraq, leading the United States into a war against that nation the next year based on a false premise (2003). No DCI can be charged with a comparably dismal record. Moreover, even though he was one of the nation's leading mavens on the subject of intelligence accountability, he fought furiously with SSCI and HPSCI members—as well as with members of the Robb-Silverman Commission—over their requests for documents and witnesses during inquiries into the 9/11 attacks and, in the case of Robb-Silverman, into the Iraqi WMD misjudgments.

I intercepted him for an interview on June 17, 1994, at a midpoint in his career between service on the Hill and at Langley. Tenet's job at that time was the NSC point man for intelligence during the Clinton presidency. We met in an ornate office in the Old Executive Office Building (now named the Eisenhower Building), adjacent to the West Wing of the White House. I asked him first about the relatively obscure job he was holding.

JOHNSON: How does this office [the NSC Senior Director for Intelligence] fit in?
TENET: Its primary mission is to ensure that the policy priorities of the administration are reflected in the operations that U.S. intelligence undertakes in support of the president and his national security decision-makers. I have a liaison function with all the other senior program directors on the NSC staff. It's also a real management and oversight function, with regard to the Community, on behalf of the national security adviser [Lake]. Tony is my boss, and any actions I take are at his request, and on his behalf and his authority. I keep an eye on particularly sensitive collection and operational issues, to ensure they are being properly vetted and that the risk and policy considerations are being fully considered. The DCI [Woolsey at the time], who also has an office in this building, has a weekly meeting—every Wednesday, or sometimes on Friday—with the national security adviser for purposes of reviewing the intelligence agenda. It's an informational meeting, and sometimes it is for purposes of getting decisions made. It's a two-way street between Jim [Woolsey] and Tony. Tony may reflect on a piece of analysis he saw, or a piece of raw intelligence: "Can we get more information on X, Y, or Z?" he might say. Also, the annual review of covert action activities is done by this office.

On a given day, I'm working on Haiti; on North Korea; on the executive order regarding declassification. I'm working on a new NPD [National Presidential Directive] on security structure. There is a lot going on; but, for the most part, anything that affects the community—in terms of policy issues, performance, and priorities that Tony's dealing with—this office deals with. Providing intelligence support to military operations is a huge part of what we do.
JOHNSON: What is your appraisal of Hill oversight for intelligence activities?

TENET: I think it's quite extensive. I don't believe there is micromanagement. I think that what Congress does is healthy. For the most part, it has been a productive, cooperative relationship that has benefitted the intelligence community. There are always dust-ups; there are always disagreements that I think could be handled better. Sometimes I questioned some of the things when I was on the Hill; then you come to the executive branch and evaluate the needs of your new client. You have a different perspective. But, for the most part, the system of oversight is extremely beneficial to the executive branch. The three of us in this office [Tenet and two aides] can't be looking at all the things the Congress is looking at; thus, a healthy bipartisan relationship with the White House, the intelligence community, and the oversight committees is a big insurance policy for the president. The process is very, very healthy. There are disagreements about priorities, no doubt; but the interesting thing about the Hill is the continuity up there on the staffs—terrific, and very helpful.

JOHNSON: Have SSCI and HPSCI been co-opted by the intelligence community?

TENET: No, I don't see any co-optation. For the most part, those staffs are extremely professional, well-run, and quite understanding of the problems—and also committed to intelligence, but not in a way that blinds them to the need to make changes.

JOHNSON: Do some of the members of SSCI and HPSCI fail to take oversight seriously?

TENET: It depends on the issue. The Senate Intelligence Committee had pretty good participation; but there was a great deal of trust placed on the chairman and vice-chairman. They spend an inordinate amount of time on these issues. I'm not sure that the time devoted by the rest of the committee members is any different than on any other committee. When things really matter, all the members are there. The chairman and vice-chairman have to carry the load on a lot of mundane, arcane matters; however, when it matters, the rest show up.

Intelligence Accountability as Viewed from the DCI's Seventh Floor Aerie

From these interviews, along with oversight episodes chronicled in the academic literature and newspaper reports (see the bibliography), one can derive some conclusions about how the leaders of the IC have felt about the new intelligence accountability put in place following the Church, Pike, and Rockefeller inquiries. The overarching finding is that most of America's spymasters, however reluctantly in some cases, have accepted the idea of more rigorous review (and, often, preview) of their activities. The exception is William J. Casey—always the exception of Casey, who looked upon Congress about the same way as Senator Moynihan (an SSCI member) came to look upon the CIA: as an organization to be dismantled or, at any rate, ignored in the name of better government and the improved security of the American people.[45] Although Casey was the most extreme, each of the DCIs interviewed in this chapter advanced some reservations in their embrace of a fully rigorous form of intelligence oversight after the Year of Intelligence.

Helms came across as unenthusiastic about congressional oversight for intelligence, as befitting his deep-seated resistance to accountability from the Hill while serving at Langley. Although he seemed resigned to the reality of the new oversight rules, he thought that DCIs had to spend too much time coddling lawmakers and their staffs; that too many people in Congress were involved in intelligence oversight; and that the Hill was leaky—not so much SSCI and HPSCI as the other committees dealing with security matters (Foreign Relations, Armed Services, and Appropriations). I had the sense that it wouldn't ruin his day if Capitol Hill were suddenly squashed by a giant meteor from outer space.

Schlesinger, too, felt that maybe the United States had gotten a little too carried away with bringing democracy into the inner sanctums of the intelligence agencies. He was prepared, however, to face the new circumstances—if not with glee then at least with a willingness to cooperate, if lawmakers really proved to be interested enough to listen to briefings (unlike his experience with Senator Stennis).

Colby, as with Helms an up-through-the-ranks DO professional, may well have been inclined to share Helms's perspective on congressional accountability, were it not for the Church Committee and Colby's conviction that intransigence might well have led to the Agency's demise at the hands of legislative reformers. He bit the bullet and adopted some degree of belief in a constitutional balance that included a serious role for Congress in the intelligence domain. His legal training may have made him sensitive, as well, to constitutional matters—although legal training (St. Johns School of Law) seemed to have had no such effect on William Casey. Colby refused to go full bore on the accountability front, however, and fought back when lawmakers went too far (in his opinion), as with their requests for public hearings on covert action.

George H. W. Bush reminded me of the stances taken by Helms and Schlesinger: reluctantly willing to accept the new intelligence accountability, but wishing it would keep a lower profile—and not pleased at all about the idea of prior notice for all significant intelligence activities (as required by the Intelligence Oversight Act of 1980). Over the years, Bush has also been an acid-tongued critic of the Church Committee. Recall his public reference to the staff of the Church and Pike panels as "untutored little jerks."[46]

With Admiral Turner, the DCI office took a sharper turn toward a position of pro-accountability. He even argued that lawmakers had not been serious and tough enough during the Carter years when it came to their questioning of intelligence activities. As a practicing DCI, the admiral tried to get away with whispering some briefings into the ears of only the SSCI and HPSCI chairs; but when Boland rejected this approach, Turner gamely briefed the full committee membership. At one point early in his tenure as DCI, recall (chapter 3) how Turner attempted to press his case for limited briefings with no transcription allowed—no recording of his briefings to HPSCI and SSCI, or any of the Q and A that followed. He retreated, however, when Les Aspin, Roman Mazzoli (D, Kentucky), and some other HSPCI members insisted—over the angry objections of Chairman Boland—on having a verbatim transcript of the briefings on presidential findings.[47]

Casey summed up his views on oversight with admirable, if salty, brevity at the DCI's dinner party: congressional review was unnecessary (to put the case more gently than he did). He was also one of the chief architects of the Iran-contra affair, and he spurned many an NIE that failed to resonate with his political views and those of the Reagan White House.

When Judge Webster followed Casey into the director's office, it was a return to the attitude that Turner had displayed toward accountability: a sense that congressional review could actually add to the legitimacy of intelligence operations. Webster established laudable, pro-transparency rules for giving testimony to Congress, and he set clear standards for judging the merits of covert action proposals. Like the other earlier directors (if more explicit), Webster would have preferred to discuss intelligence activities only with the "Gang of Four," that is, the chairs and vice chairs on SSCI and HPSCI, or—even better—with just the two chairmen; but, like Turner, he was prepared to back away from this exclusivity if the leaders of these committees balked. Also, in the vein of all the DCIs, Webster would like to have seen accountability reserved to an *ex post facto* review of programs, rather than giving Congress an *ante facto* opportunity to object before a program was under way (the key provision of the 1980 Intelligence Oversight Act). This *ante facto* approach clearly complicates matters for DCIs and presidents; however, it is the only truly meaningful form of oversight, unless one believes that trying to corral the intelligence horse after it has already bolted from the barn is the proper approach to congressional oversight and a constitutional balance between the branches of government.

Bob Gates conceded to being a Colby clone on oversight—basically on board for the new era of closer supervision from Capitol Hill. Still he, too, blanched at the instances of micromanagement he had confronted as DCI, especially the absurdly detailed attempts at cue-giving offered by Senator Malcolm Wallop. Gates also lamented the confusion about budgeting, most notably the lack of close coordination between the intelligence oversight committees and the appropriations committees. With a dollop of Turner in his critique, he further wished that SSCI and HPSCI members would take their duties more seriously and spend the amount of time it takes to become experts on intelligence issues. On balance, though, he devoted more time working with lawmakers on accountability questions than any other DCI—and, for the most part, he seemed to enjoy it.

Agreeing with Gates about the maddening unpredictability of budgeting on Capitol Hill, John Deutch longed for better long-range planning by members of Congress. Essentially, though, he had bought into the notion of a full partnership role between the IC and Congress in the intelligence affairs of the nation; however, he had a fairly low regard for the influence and effectiveness of lawmakers in the policy process.

While engaged as the top NSC staff official for intelligence, George Tenet—who by training and early experience as an SSCI staff director could have been voted the most likely to endorse oversight—certainly gave lip service to the new intelligence accountability. His later approach to the Hill as DCI, however, suggests that a shadow can fall between pro-oversight rhetoric and its actual practice in the case of some intelligence directors. While at the helm of the IC, Tenet's theoretical embrace of a genuine congressional oversight role vanished when pressed by SSCI and HPSCI to cooperate with investigative probes into the major mishaps that occurred during his tenure. When it mattered during the 9/11 and WMD inquiries, Tenet was right: the SSCI and HPSCI membership did show up for investigative hearings; however, Tenet and his staff often did not.

Nor would Tenet's successor, Porter Goss, the last DCI (2004–2005), bother much with tending garden on Capitol Hill. While a member of the Aspin-Brown Commission, he had been a vigorous advocate of intelligence oversight (though ideally practiced by only a Joint Committee in Congress; see chapter 4). Then, when he became director, he, too, like Tenet, took on the coloration of the Agency's seventh floor, which seemed to encourage a jaded view of lawmakers among most residents of the DCI's office.

A rough estimate of my best judgment on where these DCIs stood with respect to intelligence oversight is presented in Table 11.1.[48] When it came to cooperating with Congress in oversight activities, the DCIs fell into three categories: weak, moderate, and strong. One-third of the total—four directors—could be found in each category. As the continuum suggests, considerable variation has existed among the oversight perspectives of the intelligence chiefs interviewed for this book. While the individual personalities of the directors played a part in shaping their responses to Congress (Casey being the best example, but Woolsey

Table 11.1 **An Estimated Continuum of Support by DCIs for Rigorous Intelligence Oversight by the Congress, 1966–2005**

DCI Support for Rigorous Intelligence Oversight by the Congress										
Weak				Moderate						Strong
WJC	RH	GB	JW	GT PG	JS	JD	WC WW		ST RG	
<										>

Key:
Weak: William J. Casey (WJC); Richard Helms (RH); George Bush (GB, as in George H. W. Bush); James Woolsey (JW)
  Moderate: George Tenet (GT); Porter Goss (PG); James Schlesinger (JS); John Deutch (JD)
  Strong: William E. Colby (WC); William Webster (WW); Stansfield Turner (ST); Robert Gates (RG)

illustrative, too), much of the explanation for their perspectives resided in the circumstances they faced. For example, Operation CHAOS forced Colby into cooperating with lawmakers—or perhaps witness them tear his beloved Agency apart; Turner was required by the recent passage of the Hughes-Ryan Act to work with members of SSCI and HPSCI on covert actions; Webster and Gates came into office after the Iran-contra scandal and were expected by their administrations to mend fences on Capitol Hill; Tenet, like the Bush Administration he served, became so obsessed after 9/11 by the possibility of more terrorist attacks against the United States that he reacted in a belligerent manner toward lawmakers who seemed to question his counterterrorism operations.[49]

In culling through these interviews and the records of DCI public statements on intelligence accountability since the Year of Intelligence, the observations of Colby, Webster, Turner, and Gates strike the most resonant cords with those who reject a return to the "good old days" when spy chiefs were able to run America's secret agencies without much concern for the views of Congress. For example, in the wake of the Church Committee experience, Colby observed that the congressional investigations and the new oversight rules had actually strengthened the CIA and clarified the boundaries "within which it should, and should not operate."[50] From the shores of retirement, and while appearing on *Larry King Live*, he even proffered useful insider advice on how to handle an age-old accountability conundrum posed by the CNN host:

KING: How can Congress be sure that the Agency will tell them what's happening?

COLBY: They just have to ask and wait and see if anything comes out that violates what the Agency tells them, and then hang the director if he hasn't told them about something.[51]

Judge Webster's enlightened rules for reporting to Congress, and his discerning eye for raising questions about covert action, stand out. Further, in his early weeks at Langley, Admiral Turner sent a message to all of the CIA's field offices around the world in which he underscored the importance of intelligence accountability. "Oversight can be a bureaucratic impediment and a risk to security," he acknowledged, but went on to say: "It can also be a tremendous strength and benefit to us. It shares our responsibilities. It ensures against our becoming separated from the legal and ethical standards of our society. It prevents disharmony between our foreign policy and intelligence efforts. It helps us build a solid foundation for the future of our intelligence operations."[52] Turner's memoir is the only one among those written by DCIs interviewed here that has an entry in the index for "accountability" or "oversight."

The last word from the DCIs in this chapter, though, goes to Bob Gates, for no leader in the U.S. intelligence community has so well captured the value of intelligence accountability as he did in his memoir:

> Some awfully crazy schemes might well have been approved had everyone present not known and expected hard questions, debate, and criticism from the Hill. And when, on a few occasions, Congress was kept in the dark, and such schemes did proceed, it was nearly always to the lasting regret of the Presidents involved. Working with Congress was never easy for Presidents but, under the Constitution, it wasn't supposed to be. I saw too many in the White House forget that.[53]

Amen.

12

The Ongoing Quest for
Security and Liberty

Have the intelligence reforms introduced in the mid-1970s worked? This is the central question I have sought to address in this book. My sense is that the new oversight procedures adopted in 1975, and strengthened over the next twenty years, have indeed improved the balance between liberty and security in the United States; today this nation's spy agencies are held to a much higher standard of accountability than before the Year of Intelligence. Moreover, the sheer fact that scores of SSCI and HPSCI staffers now labor, gimlet-eyed and prick-eared, every day on the review—and, in some instances, the preview—of intelligence activities, as well as keeping a microscopic watch on budgets, means that a much closer scrutiny of intelligence activities is occurring in contemporary America than was remotely the case in the "good old days" from 1947 to 1974.

Further, before 1975 the major newspapers in the United States rarely carried a story about intelligence. Since then, as I started clipping articles from the *New York Times* and other sources on this subject, I find myself filling up scrapbooks at a rapid rate—several pieces each week and sometimes several in a single day. Conscious of this new public awareness of what were once opaque underground caverns within the government, lawmakers on SSCI and HSPCI (and elsewhere in Congress) have had to pay closer attention to intelligence operations—doubly so now that the experiences of the 9/11 attacks, as well as an unpopular war in Iraq, have demonstrated, painfully, the importance of getting intelligence right. A further incentive for the public and its elected representatives to take intelligence seriously is, on the security side, the growing threat of global terrorism (notably ISIS, Al Qaeda, and Boko Haram), along with the ever-present worry of North Korea and its bizarre behavior—not to mention the need to strengthen cyber and food security, and to confront environmental threats like climate change. On the liberty side stand the perils to freedom inherent in the rise of mass surveillance capabilities, the government's embrace of medieval torture techniques, and the enduring moral and legal ambiguities surrounding the use of drones for assassination operations against suspected terrorists—including American citizens and, in some parts of the Middle East and Southwest Asia, practically any young male picked up in the sights of UAV cameras.

Yet, having concluded in one breath that the post-1975 oversight reforms have taken root (despite periodic setbacks like the Iran-contra scandal), I would hasten to add in a second breath that the quality and consistency of intelligence accountability falls far short of the aspirations advanced by reformers at the time of the Church Committee inquiry. While the period preceding the reform movement was one of oversight darkness, the light that accompanied the reforms has been patchy and at times barely more than a hazy dawn. One thinks again of Iran-contra, as well as the secret slide of the second Bush White House toward overzealous NSA wiretap and metadata programs, and the CIA's descent—with dubious authorization—into the tar pit of torture. For intelligence overseers, the headwinds have been consistently strong. In this chapter, I further explore why the advocates of an improved state of accountability for America's spy agencies have come up short in their objectives, and what might be done to advance a more reliable and acceptable union of liberty and security.

The argument in the preceding chapters of this book has followed this train of thought:

- The United States and other democracies must have both security and liberty—the ability to survive and prosper in an uncertain, often hostile world, but in a society that honors freedom, privacy, and individuality (introduction).
- The intelligence agencies in the United States mushroomed into an enormous bureaucratic apparatus (the world's largest), accompanied by relatively modest efforts to keep track of these organizations and their activities (chapter 1).
- Historically, in the United States, intelligence operations were accorded a special status, an exceptionalism, which encouraged independence and self-initiative among the secret agencies, but that—left unbridled—ran contrary to the concept of Madisonian checks and balances that applies to the rest of the government (chapter 2).
- The idea of intelligence exceptionalism crashed and burned when the CIA and other agencies violated their trust and spied on American citizens participating in lawful antiwar and civil rights protests, which led to major investigations into the activities of the nation's agencies and an insistence that they become part of America's constitutional system of checks and balances (chapter 3).

- As this experiment in robust intelligence accountability—the first in history—began to unfold, it was punctuated by remarkably bold initiatives at improved supervision over America's spies, as with the Intelligence Oversight Act of 1980, but by some backsliding as well—most alarmingly, the Iran-contra affair (chapter 4).
- The attacks against the United States on 9/11 dramatically challenged the nation's devotion to vigorous intelligence accountability as, in a climate of fear, the second Bush Administration cast aside several of the most important new safeguards against mass surveillance and other espionage excesses (chapter 5).
- Over the years since 1975, the pattern of intelligence accountability in the United States began to reveal itself as a reactive process, in which overseers entered into the serious monitoring of the secret agencies chiefly when major scandals or intelligence failures resulted in a degree of public shock that forced lawmakers to become more attentive to their oversight duties (chapter 6).
- Strong accountability has seldom occurred since 1975 unless accompanied by major media coverage that ratcheted up the pressure on overseers to investigate controversial intelligence scandals or failures (chapter 7).
- On a day-to-day basis since 1975, lawmakers have displayed various levels of commitment to intelligence accountability, extending from a complete lack of interest all the way through to a useful blend of criticism and support for the spy agencies—although mostly members of Congress have exhibited a propensity to "cheerlead" on behalf of the espionage services (chapter 8).
- The missions of collection and analysis, along with covert action, have presented overseers with multiple challenges, and several setbacks, in an intelligence world that remains highly secretive, recondite, and fast-moving (chapter 9).
- Similarly, the mission of counterintelligence has posed arcane—and sometimes baffling—puzzles for even the most dedicated overseers (chapter 10).
- Almost all of the nation's spymasters since the Year of Intelligence have accepted the new rules of accountability, with various degrees of enthusiasm; but periodically they have chosen to resist serious outside supervision through misleading or belated briefings and other methods of evasion (chapter 11).

These findings leave us at a crossroads. Intelligence accountability has now traveled far enough and gained sufficient experience to display from time to time an impressive capacity to perform well, just as reformers had hoped in 1975. For example, in a reliable and bipartisan report, SSCI recently completed a study on the intelligence failures (and other circumstances) that led to the death in 2012 of America's ambassador in Libya, J. Christopher Stevens, and three other

Americans. Also impressive were the committee's reports on terrorist attacks against U.S. airlines, including the incident of the "Underwear Bomber" in 2009.[1] Further, in 2014, when ISIS seized Mosul in Iraq, SSCI immediately began reviewing data from the previous six months to determine what the various U.S. intelligence agencies had known about the possibility of a major offensive by the Syrian-based terrorist organization. Lawmakers and their staffs would never have been able, or even been interested in trying, to prepare reports like these in the years prior to 1975.

The new system of accountability has also operated well, most of the time, during SSCI's confirmation proceedings and in the periodic trips abroad taken by SSCI and HPSCI members and staff to inspect intelligence operations overseas, where COSs are appropriately queried about their in-country activities—an experience bound to keep intelligence officers on their toes. The intelligence oversight committees have also been effective in day-to-day secure telephone calls to the intelligence agencies, along with agency visits, secure email exchanges, and all the other informal contacts that ensure the nation's spies understand that properly designated overseers are steadily watching their activities. The SSCI Torture Report, though flawed by the lack of Republican participation, is also a remarkable feat of research and reporting: an in-depth oversight inquiry into questionable interrogation methods in hopes of improving intelligence practices—a five-year act of self-appraisal that no other government in the world would be willing and equipped to undertake. Even the now-and-then sluggish nature of accountability by Congress in recent years remains a striking improvement over the dark ages that preceded the Year of Intelligence.

Yet, at the same time (as traced in earlier chapters), intelligence accountability in the United States has revealed recurring instances of lethargy and even collapse. Few observers of the new intelligence accountability are happy with the arrogance shown by some ranking CIA officers during the SSCI's torture study; the ongoing ambiguities of drone targeting; the often poor quality of intelligence briefings to SSCI and HPSCI—including the highly misleading testimony of the General Hayden "tummy slapping" variety; the lackluster commitment of many lawmakers to their oversight responsibilities; or the lack of appreciation from the American public when their representatives pursue the slow boring of hard boards that a dedicated close review of intelligence activities entails. The list goes on, including the unacceptable restrictions that intelligence agencies often put on members during briefings. "All of the 'can'ts' get in the way of oversight," bemoans a senior SSCI staffer, shaking his head: "Can't take notes, can't take docs; must have a 'minder,' must use the SCIF" (a sensitive compartmented information facility).[2]

This uneven record of intelligence accountability has bred a sense of pessimism among close observers of the national security apparatus in the

United States. "The Edward Snowden revelations provided only the latest reminder that protecting civil rights and liberty at home requires congressional oversight of the national-security state that is well resourced, expert, and unhindered by partisan opportunism," writes Steve Coll, who concludes: "On the present evidence, it is hard to imagine Congress meeting that burden."[3] In this concluding chapter, I explore the most important reasons why intelligence accountability has often stalled out, sometimes leading to crash landings and, almost always, to a sinking feeling that things are less well supervised in the world of spies than democratic principles would admonish.

The Ingredients for Successful Intelligence Accountability

As we have noted throughout this book, the two most fundamental ingredients for the success of spy accountability are, first, cooperation from the executive branch in the sharing of intelligence information and, second, a reasonably high level of oversight motivation on Capitol Hill. Unfortunately, both ingredients are frequently in short supply.

Cooperation from the Executive Branch

The first requirement for effective intelligence accountability is the good-faith embrace of the concept by the executive branch and its intelligence apparatus—an acknowledgment that the constitutional principles extolled by the nation's founders apply to the veiled agencies of government, too, not just to the more open departments like Agriculture and Commerce. As emphasized in almost every earlier chapter, lawmakers only know about intelligence activities to the extent that the president and the attorney general, plus the DNI, the D/CIA, and other intelligence agency managers, keep them informed.[4] One study of accountability in the shuttered house of spies puts the case this way: intelligence oversight will succeed "only if there is honesty and completeness in what the members of the intelligence community tell their congressional overseers."[5]

Nevertheless, even this basic requirement is often absent. A vivid illustration occurred during the Church Committee inquiry. A Defense Department two-and-a-half-ton truck delivered reams of documents to the panel's guarded doorstep at the Senate Dirksen Office Building—enough to keep the staff busy for weeks. The problem was, as DoD well knew and the committee soon found out, the mountain of papers was merely a gimcrack, devoid of a single useful paper. For the Defense Department, fortified by the triple steel of practiced evasiveness, stonewalling was the name of the game as it pertinaciously hindered and obstructed the committee at every turn.[6]

Similarly, in 2002, recall how the Joint Committee investigating the 9/11 attacks ran into extensive delaying tactics adopted by the second Bush Administration. When asked questions by lawmakers about why the CIA was taken by surprise, DCI George Tenet resorted to a mini-filibuster in the Agency's defense. Recall how the committee co-chair Bob Graham (D, Florida) politely requested that the director keep his opening remarks brief, but instead Tenet went on for almost an hour and in a "somewhat defiant tone."[7] The DCI also rejected the committee's request to declassify and publish information in its final report about Saudi Arabia's role in the 9/11 attacks—even though, in the opinion of these responsible lawmakers, the public had the right to know the truth and disclosure would not have harmed America's foreign-policy interests.[8] Nor would it have harmed the kingdom of Saudi Arabia, assuming it was not involved in the 9/11 attacks. Adding kindling to the fire, Tenet refused as well to allow certain Agency witnesses to testify, yanking them from an appearance before the panel just as a hearing was scheduled to begin. "Witnesses are requested, refused, requested again, granted, and then—at the last minute—refused again," groused a member of the Joint Committee.[9]

During the hearings, a staff member cautioned the Joint Committee members that certain CIA witnesses might present less than candid testimony. Tenet learned about this warning and lambasted the committee in public for supposedly prejudging the veracity of Agency officers. Yet it could hardly be denied that intelligence officers in the past had stiff-armed the Congress. Several CIA officers misled Iran-contra investigators; and, in another example (from 1995–1996), a senior SSCI staffer accused Agency officials of "flat lying" to the Senate Intelligence Committee when it attempted to investigate the CIA's ties to a controversial military officer and asset in Guatemala who had been accused of complicity in the murder of an American citizen (the Alpirez case, discussed in chapter 4).[10] More recently, a long-time SSCI staffer, Edward Levine, accused DCI Tenet of having misled the Senate committee about the weakness of the evidence regarding possible WMDs in Iraq in the lead-up to the 2003 invasion of that country.[11]

According to a staff aide, as the Joint Committee continued its investigation into 9/11, Senator Bob Graham "toughened his stance toward the intelligence agencies when the Administration began to stonewall."[12] Rather than relenting, Tenet further blocked the flow of requested documents to staff investigators and, rubbing salt in the wound, at the last minute he canceled his own appearance before a closed session of the committee. Reaching a boiling point, Graham accused the Agency of "obstructionism" and "unacceptable" behavior.[13] In the judgment of a seasoned Hill staffer, the DCI had "stuck its fingers in the eye of the oversight committee, which under Graham was waking up very late to the fact that it is being rolled."[14]

Open lines of communication between intelligence overseers and the nation's spy leaders—especially, the DNI, D/CIA, D/FBI, and D/NSA—are of utmost importance for effective accountability. In the manner of several of his DCI predecessors, Tenet tended to ignore the rank-and-file membership on SSCI and HPSCI, preferring to discuss issues one-on-one with the chairs and ranking minority members on these committees—the Gang of Four, a board fabricated by the executive branch to limit the number of witting lawmakers. Sometimes in the past this approach was used as a ploy by DCIs to honor "oversight" more in the breach than in the observance. They would whisper into the ear of a committee chair, then count on him or her to support the IC if an operation cratered and junior members—the Aspins and Mazzolis in the lower ranks—demanded to know why they had never been informed.

At least the rank-and-file members of SSCI and HPSCI have access to liaison officers from the spy agencies. Often these individuals are personable, knowledgeable, and respectful of Congress's constitutional right to information from the executive branch; these liaison officers can build bridges of trust between the intelligence community and Capitol Hill. Yet, with the exceptions of NSA, DIA, and Army Intelligence, the turnover rate of these officers from across the IC has been high. This has resulted in a significant decline in rapport between the Congress and the secret agencies. Further, a few liaison officers—especially those recruited from the Agency's Directorate of Operations—have seemed to view the legislative branch as another foreign target to be assessed, charmed, and controlled. Conspiratorial observers might even wonder if the CIA's purpose has been less to inform the oversight committees than to woo, penetrate, and manipulate them—an argument buttressed by the fact that a disproportionate percentage of the Agency's liaison officers assigned to the Hill have had DO backgrounds.

As shown throughout this book, executive branch secrecy has been yet another substantial barrier for those who take intelligence accountability seriously.[15] Representative Lee Hamilton, a model intelligence overseer, has observed that "the great task is to strike a balance between the need to ensure accountability and the Intelligence Community's need to gather and protect information. It's the balance between oversight and secrecy."[16] Some forms of secrecy are obviously justified—even vital—such as protecting the identities of CIA officers and their assets overseas, or the blueprints of DoD weapons systems on the drawing boards. Nonetheless, at the core of democratic theory is the requirement of an informed citizenry, which in turn depends on openness in government—not stamping everything in sight SECRET, TOP SECRET, or above.

The second Bush Administration displayed a marked preference for secrecy over openness. For example, in 2001 the number of classified documents rose by 44 percent over the previous year. In another illustration of keeping information bottled up within the executive branch, the Justice Department systematically ignored queries from the Senate Judiciary Committee throughout 2002 about operations related to the FISA Court.[17] Even John Warner (R, Virginia), the chairman of the Senate Armed Services Committee, as well as a senior SSCI member and a staunch supporter of the Bush Administration and the CIA, complained about being left "out of the loop" on significant national security decisions. "I will not tolerate a continuation of what's been going on the last two years," he declared in 2003.[18] That same year, a long-toothed newspaper reporter noted that "exhibiting a penchant for secrecy that has been striking," the administration's attorney general, John Ashcroft, issued a directive permitting government agencies to reject requests for documents under the Freedom of Information Act.[19]

One canard about the protection of secrets can be dismissed right away: the notion that Congress cannot keep its collective mouth shut, that it is a "sieve"— in a favorite characterization of those who like to attack the idea of congressional accountability for intelligence (including DCI Helms in the interview presented in chapter 11). Every study, and every DCI (even Casey), has been laudatory on the capacity of HPSCI and SSCI to keep the nation's secrets. The only significant exception occurred in 1995, when HPSCI lawmaker Robert G. Torricelli (D, New Jersey) disclosed information related to CIA activities in Guatemala that should never have been released by a member of Congress (the Alpirez case).[20] He was reprimanded by HPSCI, but Torricelli soon left the House anyway in a bid for a Senate seat representing New Jersey. Recall that he managed to win that election even after his embarrassing record in the House; however, the rookie senator was convicted of campaign fraud and sentenced to prison. Torricelli was not the Hill's finest overseer.

The Torricelli example aside, the praiseworthy forty-two-year record of Congress for handling classified materials responsibly since the establishment of SSCI and HPSCI is widely acknowledged. So is the well-demonstrated fact that almost all leaks involving classified information have come from the executive branch, with Snowden the most well-known recent example. Digging deeper still, the most damaging "leaks" to the United States have come from traitors inside the IC, such as the CIA's Aldrich Ames and the FBI's Robert Hanssen. Moreover, virtually every study on secrecy (such as the one carried out by the Moynihan Commission in 1996–1997) has concluded that far too much information—some 85 percent—is unnecessarily classified by intelligence and military bureaucrats in the first place.[21]

Another aspect of secrecy bears emphasis: the significance and danger of leaks have been exaggerated. Here is how Secretary of State Dean Rusk saw it: "At any given time there are only a few truly critical secrets: in the nuclear field, espionage activity, military research, negotiating positions, and maybe a few others. But in truth—and consider that this comes from someone who has held a number of classifications above top secret—I don't know of many subjects on which a private citizen could not make a reasonable judgment by reading information readily available on that subject."[22]

Related to secrecy is the question of how much overseers can tell the public about intelligence activities. While executive classification of documents spiraled upward during the second Bush Administration, open hearings on intelligence on Capitol Hill declined. Both SSCI and HPSCI have proven to be poor purveyors of information and insight about intelligence to the American public. Adding insult to injury, the new SSCI chair, Richard Burr, declared upon assuming this office in 2015 that the committee would scale back sharply on open hearings, including the DNI's usual annual "threat assessment" presentation in public. On June 16, 2016, though, he did try his hand at an open hearing—with CIA Director Brennan on current threats—and it went well, with no classified information revealed and the public coming away with a better sense of why we must have spy services. Public hearings on some intelligence topics are possible, helpful, and certainly in the spirit of democracy.

The Obama Administration was practically as secretive as the second Bush Administration, and in fact (as noted earlier in this book) has prosecuted three times the number of "leak" cases as every other administration before it combined. A former HPSCI staff director, Timothy R. Sample, praised this upward trend in secrecy that began in earnest with the second Bush presidency. "Too many people in the world today know how we go about our business," he argued, illustrating how even some congressional overseers have sought to limit public access to information about IC activities.[23] The executive branch has resisted making intelligence available to the public, and the Congress has weakly complied, even though—as the Church Committee demonstrated with its NSA open hearings—intelligence information can be shared with the public about the IC without jeopardizing sources and methods.[24]

America relies not so much on a dogmatic interpretation of divided power among the branches of government—a prescription for deadlock—but rather on the sharing of power among these institutions. Nonetheless, the executive branch has frequently chosen to dismiss this spirit of power sharing, refusing to keep lawmakers in the loop on important intelligence activities. As noted in previous chapters of this book, the ploys adopted to keep Congress deaf and dumb have ranged from complete silence to verbal legerdemain. An example of silence is the NSA's warrantless sigint collection programs initiated soon after the 9/11 attacks. The Bush Administration chose to bypass the Foreign Intelligence Surveillance Act of 1978 by simply ordering the director of the NSA at the time,

General Hayden, to proceed with wiretaps based solely on presidential authority. The appropriate approach would have been to go to Congress with a request to amend or repeal the 1978 surveillance law, not simply pretend it never existed. As related in chapter 5, the administration did tell a few specially anointed lawmakers about the extralegal NSA wiretaps; but even these chosen few subsequently claimed, when the illegal operations surfaced in the *Times* in 2005, that they had been denied details and prohibited from discussing the program with their professional staff—or even with fellow colleagues on the intelligence oversight committees. This selective and circumscribed reporting is a far cry from the intent of the Intelligence Oversight Act of 1980 and its companion legislation.

The same thing happened again with the NSA's metadata collection activities, disclosed by Snowden in 2013. The Bush and Obama Administrations informed a few lawmakers; but, again, they were barred from taking notes, discussing the legal ramifications with professional staff, or debating the merits of this approach to espionage—even within the secret confines of SSCI and HPSCI. Further, both administrations turned their backs on meaningful *ante facto* reporting. Even when the NSA decided at least to inform the FISA Court about some of its domestic collection activities, in three significant instances—according to a 2013 statement from John D. Bates, a judge on the court—the reports misrepresented the operations and contained "repeated inaccurate statements."[25]

The administration of George W. Bush was hardly the first to stiff the Congress. In 1975, for instance, the Ford White House attempted to hide from the Church Committee information about CIA assassination plots; but President Ford was forced to retreat when it became clear that Republicans and Democrats alike on the committee insisted on examining this macabre side of American foreign policy—and were willing to go to court if necessary to obtain the relevant documents. Recall how, a decade later in the lead-up to the Iran-contra scandal, CIA officers and staff members of the NSC (including national security advisers McFarlane and Poindexter) attempted to elude congressional investigators by flatly denying knowledge of the unauthorized covert actions in Iran and Nicaragua. Remember, too, in 1995, how the CIA kept concealed the presence of a Guatemalan murderer on its payroll (Alpirez), even though—as Acting DCI Studeman acknowledged—the Intelligence Oversight Act of 1980 requires reports to Congress on any suspected improprieties.

In the aftermath of the 9/11 attacks, when Congress attempted to learn why the intelligence agencies had failed to warn the nation, lawmakers once more ran into a wall of obduracy and obfuscation. Slow-rolling and stonewalling replaced the Constitution's prescription for power sharing. Similarly, both Presidents George W. Bush and Barack Obama have tried to turn the Gang of Eight rule—meant to apply only in emergencies—into the normal reporting requirement, informing only eight lawmakers (if that many) instead of the required full memberships of SSCI and HPSCI. In addition, the Obama Administration continued the Bush Administration's practice of sometimes limiting intelligence briefings even further, to the Gang of Four, with warnings to them not to mention what they have been told to anyone else. No doubt most attractive of all to many in the executive branch is the Gang of Zero, informing no one at all on Capitol Hill about its secret activities—the approach often adopted by the second Bush Administration.

Motivation on Capitol Hill

The second vital ingredient for successful intelligence accountability is the will of individual members of Congress to engage in a meaningful examination of spy programs. As an experienced Hill staffer has emphasized, "Determination is the key. Members [of Congress] have to be willing to break arms and legs. Not too many are willing."[26] A former special assistant to DCI Casey urged the Kean 9/11 Commission to pursue its investigative responsibilities with a "helicopter-raids-at-dawn, break-down-the-doors, kick-their-rear-ends sort of operation"—although this was not exactly the approach to oversight favored by his Congress-bashing boss during the 1980s.[27] An individual involved in government accountability for decades has summed up the most important requirement for success: "the need for lawmakers to take oversight seriously."[28]

Feel-good exhortations on behalf of robust accountability aside, the truth is that most lawmakers on SSCI and HPSCI rarely even make it to executive-session hearings, let alone conduct helicopter raids on the CIA or the NSA. High percentages of lawmakers on these congressional panels appear at "firefighting" hearings that deal with scandals and failures; but their participation in routine, "police-patrolling" hearings (sans TV cameras) is usually spotty at best. Only approximately one-third of the total SSCI and HPSCI membership participated, on average, in executive session hearings during recent years, according to my interviews with staff on these committees. Citing Woodrow Wilson's adage that "Congress in committee-rooms is Congress at work," I concluded in an earlier study on SSCI and HPSCI that "a good many legislators failed to show up for work."[29] A recent HPSCI staff director has claimed, however, that in more recent years upward of 70 percent of the lawmakers on that panel have been attending hearings, perhaps stirred by the failures of 9/11 and the misguided Iraq WMD hypothesis.[30]

Among those members who did appear at public hearings on intelligence during the years from 1975 to 1990, I found in earlier research that the quality of the questions posed to CIA witnesses by lawmakers varied widely, ranging from easy "softball" to more serious "hardball" questions. SSCI's Senator Goldwater, a classic "ostrich" during much of his tenure on that committee, managed to turn a hearing on how to improve intelligence into a harangue about the imperfections of Congress. The Arizonan decried—amusingly but without the benefit of evidence—that "this place has more leaks than the men's room at Anheuser-Busch."[31] I discovered in my research that some members did engage in a thorough cross-examination of witnesses, and at times even a harsh criticism of CIA operations; yet, for the most part, the questioning by lawmakers leaned more toward the advocacy side of the ledger—cheerleading on behalf of the spy services. The exception is when scandals and major intelligence failures rocked the nation and become the focus of attention on Capitol Hill; then, with the television cameras whirring in the hearing room, a majority of members elevate the degree of their involvement to a higher level of newsworthy, hardball queries into controversial programs.

Former HPSCI member Timothy J. Roemer (D, Indiana) has expressed his concern about the lack of commitment by members of Congress to the earnest practice of accountability. "We've gotten away from the Church Committee emphasis on oversight," he said. "There aren't even oversight subcommittees on HPSCI or SSCI anymore."[32] Adopting one useful measure to give HPSCI more energy and focus, House Democrats decided in 1992 to bring several young lawmakers onto the committee, since older members seemed to have had too many other committee assignments that distracted them from participation in the panel's oversight activities.

As we have seen in earlier chapters, even DCIs have criticized the flaccid nature of oversight. "Congress is informed to the degree that Congress wants to be informed," testified former DCI Colby, observing that several members of SSCI and HPSCI had expressed little interest in briefings on current operations by the CIA.[33] In the same vein, in DCI Turner's recollection, "the committees of Congress could have been more rigorous with me [during the Carter Administration].... It would be more helpful if you are probing and rigorous."[34] Were he still alive, no doubt DCI Casey would disagree—quite likely with scatological emphasis; and, in line with Casey, most lawmakers have displayed a clear preference for the role of intelligence advocate over adversary: the "cheerleading" role examined in chapter 8. For them, the president and the intelligence leaders know best in this sensitive policy domain; it is better to follow these experts in the executive branch than to second-guess—and perhaps harm—America's intelligence efforts against terrorism and other threats. Deference to the president, along with a blinkered embrace of security and efficiency as the most important values in our cultural narrative, is a safer bet than trying to exercise greater accountability while wringing one's hands over the loss of liberty.

In the early decades of the Cold War, this attitude of deference tended to be persuasive to most lawmakers when it came to foreign policy generally—until the war in Vietnam demonstrated how wrong-minded a "Daddy knows best" philosophy can be. That ill-fated war, as well as Watergate, underscored for law-makers that Congress was designed by the Constitution's founders to be an equal branch of government, not merely a cockboat drifting along in the wake of the U.S.S. *White House*. Yet, even after these important lessons, lawmakers in the 1990s resorted back to their attitude of deference toward the executive branch on all matters dealing with foreign and security policy. As a Senate major-ity leader, Robert Byrd (D, West Virginia), lamented, the legislative branch had lost its "will to lead."[35]

The Strengthening of Intelligence Accountability

A core objective of intelligence reformers has been to ensure greater access for overseers to information within the executive branch regarding the conduct of intelligence activities. Stated simply, conscientious lawmakers have wanted to know what is going on. To know would be to place them in a position of being able to advise, and perhaps to help avoid such disasters as another Bay of Pigs, Operations CHAOS and COINTELPRO, the poor counterterrorism coordi-nation of the CIA and the FBI prior to the 9/11 attacks, and the blithe accep-tance of false hypotheses like the one regarding the existence of WMDs in Iraq in 2002. What follows are some key questions that more specifically go to the heart of ongoing efforts aimed at improving intelligence accountability. Answers to these questions reveal the current state of America's responses to the funda-mental issue of oversight: *Which overseers should have access to what information from whom, and when?*

Who Should Be Informed?

In the pre-1975 era of intelligence oversight, the answer to this question was quite often: *no one* on Capitol Hill should be informed—as happened, to give some examples, with CHAOS, COINTELPRO, SHAMROCK, MINARET, the assassination plots, and the covert actions against Allende. Sometimes the number of people in the "witting circle" (as CIA officials refer to those in the know) might be expanded to include a single "outside" person or maybe even two—say, Senator Richard Russell and Representative Carl Vinson (both Georgia Democrats with intelligence review responsibilities, such as they were at the time). Passage of the Hughes-Ryan Act in 1974 shot that number up to some sixty-three lawmakers and a few staff aides, when it came to the mandatory covert action briefings in both the Senate and the House. Three years later, that number was reduced—with the creation of SSCI and HPSCI—to a more rea-sonable thirty-seven members of Congress and a couple of staffers. Enactment of the Intelligence Oversight Act of 1980 ensured that the number of thirty-seven or so in the witting circle—the total number has fluctuated slightly over the years, according to how many lawmakers are on these panels and how many staffers are admitted into the top-secret Hughes-Ryan briefings (always very few)—was extended to hearings on all important intelligence activities, not just covert action.

Is thirty-seven a number too large and imprudent as a list of those in Congress with access to the nation's highest secrets? Or is this number acceptable, for a democracy of 321 million citizens, to guarantee some vestige of democracy in the monitoring by SSCI and HPSCI of the nation's spy programs? People can disagree on this question, with Allen Dulles perhaps preferring the number one or none, while Snowden would opt for the whole world to know America's secrets. This number of SSCI and HPSCI members and staff with access to covert action and other briefings strikes me as a reasonable compromise; and, it bears repeating, SSCI and HPSCI have consistently demonstrated their abilities to keep the nation's secret intact.

What Information Should Be Reported?

As stipulated in the 1980 Oversight Act and reinforced by its 1991 sequel, lawmakers now have access—in theory at least—to *all* information provided to the executive branch by the intelligence community, with the exception of the *President's Daily Brief* (and even in the case of the *PDB*, most of its information comes to SSCI and HPSCI in other current-intelligence reports). In reality, however, we have seen earlier in this book how Congress has often had to throw a hissy fit before the IC officials become responsive—although, to put accountability into historical perspective, the level of access afforded SSCI and HPSCI far exceeds what congressional overseers ever received prior to 1975. As a means for guaranteeing a more systematic flow of information to the Hill, members of Congress have established formal reporting requirements. The strongest are in statutory form; others have come by way of either written or (weaker) oral agreements between SSCI and HPSCI leaders and the DCI (now the DNI and the D/CIA).

Members of Congress and intelligence officers cleave into two camps on this topic. Many lawmakers believe that reporting requirements, such as the prior-notice stipulation for covert actions (except in times of emergency) laid out first in the 1980 Oversight Act, are an indispensable means of leverage for keeping SSCI and HPSCI informed. Intelligence officers, though, often balk at what they see as excessive legislative involvement in the delicate workings of intelligence—the "micromanagement" argument much relished by those who oppose accountability. They complain, as did Helms in the interview comments presented in chapter 11, of the unwarranted surcharge on the time of intelligence officials who could otherwise be dealing with terrorism and other threats to the nation, rather than wasting their time writing reports for HPSCI and SSCI, or driving up to the Hill through snarled D.C. traffic for briefings. "Needless red tape," as a British Public Safety minister has called efforts in the United Kingdom to strengthen intelligence reporting; a good many U.S. spy managers would raise a pint to that sentiment.[36]

Proponents of robust accountability stress, however, that without regular reporting to SSCI and HPSCI, intelligence managers might brief lawmakers merely when the D/CIA or DNI felt so inclined, or when forced to by a scandal or a conspicuous failure of intelligence analysis or warning. Better to have important operations automatically brought to the attention of overseers, who might otherwise never know about them. Obviously reporting requirements should not be excessive in number, and they should focus on significant activities. "Oversight has become too complicated," complained future DNI Clapper to me earlier in his career when he was head of the National Geospatial-Intelligence Agency (NGA). "There are too many jurisdictions, too much paperwork."[37] He pointed to the eighty-seven reports that were due from the intelligence community on the approaching first day of May in 2002, as requested by HPSCI.

I agreed: that number did seem excessive. Even an SSCI staffer shook his head in dismay when complaining to me during an interview about "too many notification deadlines" that had been imposed by his committee. He spoke of an example that required the NRO to report to SSCI and HPSCI anytime a spy satellite had suffered a broken part.[38] Yet one person's "over-reporting" can be another person's vital oversight information. Recently, under Dianne Feinstein's initiative, SSCI requested regular reporting from the DNI on cases where outside contractors might be engaged in activities that could be conducted just with governmental employees. Is this request unreasonable? I don't think it is unreasonable; and this initiative has expanded usefully into periodic DNI inventories on the number and purpose of external contracts—something the oversight committees in Congress (and the ODNI) must be on top of in this age of widespread intelligence outsourcing.

While some of the criticism of excessive reporting requirements may be legitimate, there is another side to that coin. The 92 percent delinquency rate in providing reports on time to SSCI and HPSCI in 2002 reflected poorly on the attitude of the IC toward accountability, as well as on the efforts of the spy agencies to communicate well with members of Congress and their staffs.[39] Moreover, lawmakers have learned from experience that the oversight committees need to be provided with prior notice of any secret executive codicils or new interpretations of surveillance laws (one of the lessons from the metadata controversy), along with other waivers of established law and procedure, such as the rules guiding intelligence agency relations with accredited American journalists. Recall how in 1995 DCI Deutch argued in hearings that, in emergency circumstances, he had the right to waive established prohibitions against CIA connections with accredited U.S. journalists. This in turn led DCI Turner to admit, when prodded by journalists and lawmakers, that he had made such waivers three times during his tenure. All this was news to SSCI and HPSCI, and these panels passed legislation to ensure that, in the future, they would be informed of any such waivers.

The purpose of oversight is not to suffocate the vital work of the spy agencies, but rather to maintain their effectiveness while at the same time preserving civil liberties and budgetary discipline—along with, as former SSCI member William S. Cohen has put it, the important objective of bringing to fruition "the combined wisdom of both branches."[40] If one is dead set against a role for Congress in intelligence matters, however, one is more likely to end up in the place preferred by Admiral Poindexter, the national security adviser of Iran-contra infamy, who looked upon Congress and its reporting requirements as nothing more than an "outside interference" (chapter 4). That road leads to a return of the unfettered imperial presidency, often blamed for Watergate and the war in Vietnam. Or, more accurately, since it was Poindexter who failed to keep even the president well informed (preferring the old, discredited approach of plausible deniability), that road leads to an unfettered imperial national-security bureaucracy.[41]

Who Is Responsible for Reporting to Intelligence Overseers?

Here the pre-1975 answer was the CIA (infrequently, in practice), because that is where the DCI was housed. The DCI might have been called upon to answer a few budget questions, or to respond to flaps like the one that arose when the Agency was unable to anticipate the outbreak of war on the Korean Peninsula in 1950. With the advent of Hughes-Ryan, however, the president was required both to formally endorse covert action proposals and to ensure they were reported to Congress. Thus, the answer evolved to mean that the president and the CIA are responsible for reporting to the Hill on covert actions, and the president, the CIA, and other intelligence agencies on spy initiatives (depending on which "int" or mission is involved).

When Should the Intelligence Agencies Report to Congress?

The "when" of anything is important—as in, for example, "When are you going to pay me back that $1,000 you owe me?" Before 1975, reporting to Congress took place mainly at the discretion of the DCI and his aides at Langley. Then Hughes-Ryan introduced the notion of reporting, at least on covert action approvals, "in a timely manner"—defined in floor debate in Congress as within twenty-four hours. While this formula was still *ex post facto* in character, it wove a fairly short leash nonetheless. With the 1980 Oversight Act, the revolutionary requirement for prior notice (*ante facto* reporting) became the official standard, and—in an example of breathtaking assertiveness by proponents of accountability—it would be not just for covert actions but for *all* important intelligence activities. This legal requirement is essential for genuine accountability; however, it has often been ignored by officials in the executive branch who at the same time, speaking from the other side of their mouths, profess allegiance to the rule of law.

Here was true accountability: reporting to thirty-seven (or so) members of Congress and senior staff, on *every* important intelligence activity, by *every* agency in the intelligence community, and *in advance*. No nation in the world has rules this demanding for intelligence oversight—a set of prescriptions that is the envy of intelligence reformers in all of the parliamentary democracies. Even the Gang of Eight provision—the escape hatch in times of dire emergencies—made sense, especially since according to the 1980 and 1991 Intelligence Oversight Acts the full complements of SSCI and HPSCI would be briefed in these circumstances within a couple of days (supposedly). Alas, though, as chronicled in earlier chapters, game playing entered the picture, as from time to time officials in the executive branch have ignored these stipulations; have modified them to treat the Gang of Eight as though this group alone were the full memberships of SSCI and HPSCI; or have gone so far as to rely instead on a Gang of Four, a Gang of Two, a Gang of One, and sometimes a Gang of None. Other evasive tactics adopted by the secret agencies have included lying to overseers, or otherwise misleading them (DCI Casey's "piers" instead of "harbors" in Nicaragua is a classic illustration), or briefing select members to one degree of thoroughness or another, but with orders to the lawmakers not to inform staff—the very people who have the time and expertise to check on the validity of the briefing information.

All of which is to say that the law is one thing, and it is important; but forcing officials to adhere to its black-letter intent can be yet another matter, especially when dealing with individuals like Dick Cheney who believe that only the executive branch should make foreign and national security policy. In the face of such challenges, SSCI and HPSCI must grasp the nettle of institutional retaliation, reminding the executive branch that Congress is its constitutional equal in governing authority. Significant sanctions are at hand for lawmakers, starting with the power of the purse. Few democracies have provided their lawmakers with the kinds of oversight powers enjoyed by SSCI and HPSCI (the subpoena power high among them); the question is whether Congress has the intestinal fortitude to use these tools when necessary. During the embattled torture investigation, SSCI never used its powers of subpoena, budget control, contempt of Congress citations, or the release of classified information (with proper adherence to the procedures of the Senate)—all so many glittering swords of accountability allowed to rust.

If the executive branch insists on flaunting rules of accountability, Congress can—and has—shut off funds for intelligence activities. The most well-known example is the increasingly restrictive set of Boland Amendments to curb covert actions in Nicaragua during the Reagan Administration. Further, lawmakers can call for committee hearings to place questionable programs under closer scrutiny; and, if held in public, such hearings can cause great embarrassment to officials accused of malfeasance or ineptitude (as demonstrated by the Church Committee, the Iran-contra inquiry, and the probes into 9/11 and the Iraqi WMD forecasts). Naming and shaming can be a powerful deterrent—though naming in the case of intelligence officers and assets on active duty in the field is never appropriate, because as a result their lives may be endangered.

The large cudgel of the subpoena power is particularly menacing as a means of forcing reluctant witnesses to testify—or pay heavy fines and even face a stiff jail sentence. Without subpoena powers, oversight committees have little leverage over the agencies they supervise; yet few parliaments abroad have provided their intelligence oversight committees (if indeed they have any) with subpoena authority. Recall, too, that SSCI and HPSCI can seek the publication of classified documents, so the American people can understand the issues and weigh in. The best instrument of oversight, though, is the questioning in hearings that lawmakers, with their thick archive of experience, can provide as a means for improving intelligence programs—or halting improper ones. The top question overseers can pose to intelligence managers: What could go wrong with the program you propose?

Congress: The One-Armed Intelligence Overseer
Reelection Obsessions

The politics of Congress is central to any discussion of intelligence oversight. The incentive structure on Capitol Hill favors the passage of bills, with one's name on the title as a sponsor, particularly new laws that channel federal funds back to the home district—what Professor David Mayhew has referred to as a "credit-claiming" opportunity, vital for a lawmaker's career longevity.[42] Everything lawmakers do is patched to reelection considerations, leaving intelligence oversight (for many) as little more than a faint penumbra outside this central obsession. Despite the optimism expressed on behalf of intelligence accountability by reformers, members of Congress often doubt that devotion to this aspect of their legislative activities will be understood and appreciated by their constituents. The drudgery of posing questions to intelligence witnesses in hearings (which are normally closed because of the sensitive topics examined), or combing through intelligence budgets line by line, produce few or usually no headlines—unless SSCI and HPSCI have been startled into investigative mode as a result of a spy scandal in Washington or a significant intelligence failure that harms the nation's security. An eight-year member of SSCI, former senator Sam Nunn (D, Georgia), has recalled that "there was little payoff back home from being on the Intelligence Committee."[43]

Despite the stinging experiences of CHAOS and COINTELPRO, the Iran-contra scandal, the 9/11 failures, and the Iraqi WMD mistakes, the prevailing "know-nothing" philosophy on Capitol Hill that characterized the pre-1975 era of spy accountability continues to be attractive for some lawmakers who seek to shield themselves from intelligence flaps. Ironically, the waiting list to become a member of SSCI and HPSCI is long, because many members of Congress enjoy the James Bond aura that accompanies service on these panels—bound to impress the Kiwanis Club. Once selected, however, many soon lose interest in the day-to-day grind of oversight work and are more attracted to district-oriented, reelection opportunities, from fundraisers to pork-barrel legislation. "Intelligence oversight is a tough business—harder than with any other of the executive branch agencies," emphasizes a senior congressional staffer. She points to "the secrecy, the chilling effect that comes with dealing with classified information, and the intimidation that intelligence officers are good at."[44]

Some members of Congress have resigned from SSCI and HPSCI early into their tenure, once the aura of intrigue and glamor fades. An illustration, though less from intimidation than from a sense of disappointment and ennui, is Senator Slade Gordon (R, Washington). He recalled to me that SSCI meetings soon struck him as a snooze-fest, in which he "never heard anything that he hadn't already read in the newspapers."[45] From his perspective, the SSCI may just as well have been the now-defunct Senate Committee on Weights and Measures—as if, in the grand scheme of things, intelligence accountability were hardly more pressing than a game of Hunt the Slipper. Such lack of appreciation for the day-by-day value of intelligence oversight contributes mightily to the discouraging entropy that, short of firefighting episodes, often infuses SSCI and HPSCI.

For these reasons and others examined throughout this book, Congress as an intelligence overseer typically acts with one arm tied behind its back or, more accurately, with at least one arm—and sometimes two—busily engaged in other institutional and reelection obligations. These arms are unavailable for the heavy lifting that comes with tracking the spy agencies. On the Hill, the demands for fund-raising are nearly nonstop, at times with every hour of the work day (meals included) devoted to romancing donors. "Considering how pressed we are for time, locking in a whole lunch [for fund-raising] is a lot," but necessary, recently sighed Sheldon Whitehouse, a Democratic senator from Rhode Island.[46] In the keen eye of journalist Nicholas Kristof, "Elected officials are hamsters on a wheel, always desperately raising money for the next election."[47] A *60 Minutes* investigation found that members of Congress need to raise about $18,000 a day if they hope to be reelected. They do this by becoming Capitol Hill telemarketers, many of them calling fund-raisers at least four hours a day—compared to an estimated two hours a day spent by lawmakers on committee work.[48]

Such pressures led intelligence scholar Amy Zegart to the conclusion that intelligence accountability on the Hill soon becomes viewed by SSCI and HPSCI members as too much like hard labor, along with being "a political loser" when it comes to appealing to voters back home or attracting campaign financing for the next election cycle.[49] Add to these daily reelection concerns the polarization that has gripped Capitol Hill, along with the antigovernment attitude of many Tea Party members of Congress and the Trump Administration, whose chief goal frequently seems to be bringing the federal government to its knees (the Pentagon, with its many military bases in their home districts excepted), and the result is a toxic environment for the serious practice of intelligence accountability—or any other kind of oversight.

The Trap of Co-optation

When it comes to accountability practices, a further danger always exists for lawmakers: going "native." Like ambassadors abroad accused of taking on the political hue of the country where they are stationed ("localitis") rather than the country they represent, HPSCI and SSCI members and staff can end up identifying more with the intelligence agencies they supervise than with their roles as detached and objective guardians of the public weal. "They are very nice to [SSCI and HPSCI members]," former HPSCI chair Hamilton recalls, "inviting them to Langley, treating them to dinner, wining and dining them."[50] Further, congressional members and staff who had earlier careers in one of the spy agencies might be especially prone toward favoring their old stomping grounds. Two-thirds of the staff members on the Intelligence Committees have had previous lives in one of the espionage agencies or with the military—although lawmakers who have served as intelligence officers (as did HPSCI chairs Porter Goss and Mike Rogers) are rare.

Despite this potential for misplaced loyalties, though, experienced Congress watchers have found that former intelligence officers often provide the most energetic oversight as Hill staffers. They know where the bodies are buried back in their respective former agencies; moreover, they are professionals who do the best they can for whoever may be their current employee.[51] As one senior aide (himself once an FBI agent) has put it, "Former IC staffers tend to be the most aggressive at oversight; they are the ones who take the deep dives."[52] Occasionally, a staffer may exhibit an inability to criticize his or her former spy agency (I observed this only once in a while when I was on the HPSCI staff); more often, though, SSCI and HPSCI have benefited from having staff aides who can tell whether their former IC colleagues are playing it straight with Congress or engaged in spinning. A much larger problem is the pervasive philosophy among lawmakers that the legislative branch should pay unwavering deference to the executive branch when it comes to matters of foreign policy and national security—the Dick Cheney School of Public Affairs.

The employment relationship between the community and Congress is a two-way street. A sizable number of SSCI and HPSCI staffers take up, or resume, positions in the IC after a tour of duty on one of the oversight committees. The most well-known illustration is DCI Tenet, the one-time SSCI staff director. Others include former Church Committee staffers L. Britt Snider, the former SSCI chief counsel who served as IG at the Agency as well as in Pentagon counterintelligence; and John Elliff, the head of the Church Committee's FBI Task Force, who later in his career went to work for the Bureau. Like most of the intelligence officers who moved to the Hill, each of these individuals traveling in the opposite direction displayed loyalty—though not blind loyalty—to the branch where they were newly employed (the proper ethical stance), not where they were once employed.[53]

In Search of Liberty and Security

The intelligence agencies are indispensable to the security of the United States, and intelligence officers are among the brightest and most dedicated of the nation's public servants. Over the years, the overwhelming majority of these men and women have been patriotic, competent, and law-abiding. Former Church Committee staff John Elliff has remarked on their response to the findings of the intelligence investigations derived during the Year of Intelligence in 1975:

> People who spent their careers in the Intelligence Community since the Church Committee have worked hard to earn the trust of the oversight committees and the American people that they will follow the rules. In that sense, they are very upset with all of the post-Snowden concern. "We can't trust them! We can't trust them! They will go back to spying on Martin Luther King!" No, we aren't going to do that, is their attitude.

We know better, we've got lawyers everywhere. We've got checks and balances built into the system. And all of that is the product of the Church Committee.[54]

I have witnessed this devotion to law and accountability, as well, while on the job as intelligence overseer in Washington and during most of my interviews with intelligence officers. Nevertheless, one can hardly dismiss the memory of Operation CHAOS, COINTELPRO, and Iran-contra; lapses in counterintelligence (Ames, for one; tracking the 9/11 terrorists, for another); faulty analysis from time to time (Iraqi WMDs); and the gaming of Congress as if it were a hostile nation to be manipulated rather than a valued partner in the defense of the United States.

My study of the Church Committee published in 1986 ended with an expression of concern that intelligence accountability might be too demanding for lawmakers.[55] The soon-breaking Iran-contra scandal confirmed the fragility of the oversight system put in place by the Church Committee. This setback reminds me of a remark made by the celebrated historian Fritz Stern. "The fragility of freedom is the simplest and deepest lesson of my life and work," he said.[56] As with all statutes (against armed robbery, for instance), the legal scaffolding for intelligence accountability remains vulnerable to individuals and institutions who are willing to violate the law. As William Colby suggested in chapter 11, the remedy in such instances is to catch the perpetrators and apply the appropriate legal penalties.

Lost Oversight Opportunities

The purpose of intelligence accountability is to help ensure that America's secret agencies obey the law, spend the taxpayers' money prudently, and operate as effectively as possible to warn of dangers to the United States and its allies. When accountability is lax, the pursuit of these important goals suffers. One can imagine how SSCI and HPSCI members, as dedicated police patrollers, might have prevented the conditions that eventually led to the traumatizing intelligence "fire alarms" discussed in this book. Consider again the "what ifs" raised earlier in this book.

With Iran-contra, for instance, what if lawmakers had followed through—more energetically and with a stronger dose of skepticism—on the rumors in Washington that the Boland Amendments were being secretly sidestepped by the Reagan Administration? Recall that members of SSCI and HPSCI did question McFarlane and Poindexter, along with the Iran-contra point man Lt. Col. Oliver L. North of the NSC staff, about the rumors; but the lawmakers too easily accepted the false denials of the White House officials, without ever taking their testimony formally and under oath.[57]

Or what if extensive hearings had been held by SSCI and HPSCI (behind closed doors on this delicate subject) into counterintelligence before the Ames disaster? Perhaps such sessions would have caused the Agency to question more seriously the possibility of "moles" inside its walls, checking the bank accounts of Ames and other top Agency officers (now a standard practice in the aftermath of this scandal).

What if the oversight committees had examined CIA-FBI liaison relations before the 9/11 attacks, a fairly obvious subject of interest for those interested in an effective, coordinated response to global terrorist threats? The committees would have discovered a fractured relationship, which had tragic consequences in September 2001. Earlier in that year, the Agency and the Bureau failed to communicate effectively about the entry of the 9/11 terrorists into the United States (recall how at least two were tracked by the CIA as they entered California).[58] What if the committees had held hearings and looked more deeply into the Agency's Counterterrorism Center report of 1995 that predicted aerial terrorism inside the United States?[59] Might that have led to a recommendation for tighter airport security, perhaps along with an improved protection of cockpit doors in commercial airliners, the arming of pilots, and more sky marshals onboard each plane?

What if the committees had probed into the quality of the data for the Iraqi WMD premise in 2002? Surely an inquiry would have raised questions about the obvious softness of the evidence, especially in light of reservations churning inside the Bureau of Intelligence and Research (INR) in the State Department, along with doubts raised in the intelligence units of the Energy Department and the U.S. Air Force.[60] What if lawmakers or their staff had asked why Saddam Hussein, the leader of Iraq, might have wanted to claim possession of WMDs even if this assertion seemed unlikely? That line of thought may have led them to consider how highly threatened Iraq felt by Iran, and how Saddam Hussein (a Sunni) might be trying to keep this Shia enemy at bay by bluffing Tehran's leaders into believing he possessed a nuclear, biological, and chemical deterrent. As it was, Congress—not to mention the Bush Administration—failed to demand even the writing of a National Intelligence Estimate on Iraq until the very eve of America's invasion into that country. Recall that when lawmakers finally insisted on the preparation of an Estimate, the spy agencies threw the assessment together hastily, with the cautionary reservations about the WMD hypothesis held by INR, Energy, and the Air Force buried deep in the report and never mentioned in the Executive Summary. Particularly disheartening is the realization that most of the NIE was never read by most members of Congress.[61]

What if in executive session SSCI and HPSCI had conducted routine police-patrolling hearings into the activities of the FISA Court in the aftermath of the 9/11 attacks? They may have discovered, long before word came out in the *Times* in 2005, that the White House and the NSA were violating the Court's rules that require wiretap warrants in national security cases.[62]

Such questions underscore how vital intelligence accountability can be. Dedicated police patrollers on SSCI and HPSCI are in a position to save the nation from much grief—even tragedy, as the casualties from the 9/11 attacks and the extended war in Iraq remind us, along with the costs, turmoil, and embarrassment of major *ex post facto* inquiries. Intelligence reformers in favor of greater accountability are, as playwright Tennessee Williams might put it, disappointed but not discouraged. Their core hopes remain unreached, but they are still alive and feasible, namely, that the United States will find an effective equilibrium between the goals of security and liberty; and that SSCI and HPSCI will evolve into panels of dedicated police patrollers acting as guardians—not just firefighters—willing to steadfastly monitor the world of American intelligence activities on a daily basis. To achieve this challenging but reachable objective, the congressional oversight committees will have to clear several hurdles.

Ongoing Obstacles to Meaningful Intelligence Accountability
Separate Institutions That Share Power

Everything ultimately reduces down to the twin missing links in intelligence accountability: the will of executive branch officials to provide SSCI and HPSCI with full information about significant intelligence activities, and the will of lawmakers to study and weigh the merits of these initiatives, helping to correct missteps when necessary.

As several of the DCIs in chapter 11 noted, strong incentives exist for achieving these goals. When intelligence is provided to members of Congress, the executive branch has a partner with whom to share the blame if things go wrong.[63] Moreover, experienced lawmakers are in a position to provide valuable insights into security matters; some members of Congress have served for decades on the Hill—five decades in the case of Georgia's influential Carl Vinson in earlier times—and are excellent corporate memories of what kinds of policies have worked in the past and what kinds have not. In addition, it is worth emphasizing, who among the Congress wishes to be AWOL in his or her responsibility for bolstering America's intelligence shield—the nation's first line of defense against future 9/11 attacks or worse? A working relationship between intelligence officers and Hill supervisors is a win-win for both branches of government. The legislature, though, would benefit from a number of structural improvements for their intelligence oversight committees. The 9/11 Commission described their performance as "dysfunctional." What might be done to improve the effectiveness of SSCI and HPSCI?

Organizational Improvements on Capitol Hill

Addressing the Jurisdictional Morass

For starters, the jurisdictional tangle on Capitol Hill related to intelligence accountability cries out for reform. The clear and proper solution is to fold almost all intelligence matters (including budget authorizations) into the SSCI and HPSCI baskets. While this proposal tends to give members of the Armed Services Committees indigestion, it really shouldn't when its members consider three important facts. First, their plates are already overflowing with the task of conducting accountability over everything else the Pentagon does—a nearly impossible task in itself.[64] Second, by rule, recall that SSCI and HPSCI always have some Armed Services members on their roster (usually two); these lawmakers can keep the Armed Services panels informed of any new developments related to tactical military intelligence that arise, which the Armed Services Committees would then be in a position to protest and block if necessary. Third, members of SSCI and HPSCI view with great seriousness the importance of providing the best tactical intelligence the nation can acquire for the protection and advancement of U.S. troops under fire or in potentially dangerous settings; on this point, the Intelligence Committees and the Armed Services Committees are of one mind. Thus, the transfer of tactical intelligence fully into SSCI's ambit—the evolutionary pathway already being pursued by HPSCI—could occur without much dislocation and few, if any, policy changes in support to military operations.

Further on the jurisdictional question, the Judiciary Committees like to have authority over the FISA Court and that does make some sense, given the large number of attorneys among the committee's membership; but, again, the House and Senate Judiciary Committees already have a packed agenda without addressing FISA questions. Moreover, SSCI and HPSCI have overlapping memberships with the judicial panels as well; so full responsibility for FISA Court oversight could be lodged in SSCI and HPSCI with greater jurisdictional clarity, no change in policy, and complete, ongoing awareness of FISA matters among judiciary members as a result of the overlapping memberships. The outcome of these changes would be clearer lines on the Hill for intelligence accountability, making life easier and more rational for everyone—certainly not least the intelligence managers in the executive branch.

Repairing the Authorization and Appropriations Bridge

Pressing, too, is the necessity of honoring the constitutional and traditional meanings of "authorization" and "appropriation." The Intelligence Committee must, by compromise and agreement among their members, authorize intelligence benchmarks every year for policy substance and budget recommendations;

and the Appropriations Committees must then match final appropriations figures with the authorizing stipulations provided by SSCI and HPSCI. Capitol
Hill has sometimes drifted away from this basic constitutional sequence—just
as its members have allowed a constitutional majority-vote rule to transform
into a sixty-vote rule on too many bills that come before the Senate, which has
often had the devastating effect of paralyzing the legislative process. (At least, in
2013, the Democrats forced through a Senate procedural change that permitted approval of most presidential nominees by a simple majority vote.) Strong
leadership at the top in both parties will have to insist on adherence to sensible
authorization and appropriations procedures, as well as an end to the unconstitutional and unrealistic sixty-vote rule in the Senate—that is, if they wish
Congress to be a respected, well-functioning representative institution. The
argument that this sixty-vote procedure protects the filibuster is a canard; on
truly extraordinary policy debates, which happen rarely, the filibuster option will
remain alive and well.

Focusing and Redoubling Oversight Activities

Further, as an experienced oversight practitioner has suggested, it would be valuable for both SSCI and HPSCI to have dedicated Oversight Subcommittees.[65]
The House committee had this focus when it started; I was the inaugural staff
director of the panel's Subcommittee on Oversight from 1977 to 1980. The committee eventually eliminated this subunit, however, then brought it back again
after 9/11, only to dispense with it once more in recent years. The committees
could also develop better membership recruitment procedures, screening out
those—like Slade Gordon—who have only a superficial interest in intelligence.
Probably nothing would improve congressional oversight more than if SSCI and
HPSCI members doubled the time they spent on this responsibility, from an
estimated five hours to ten hours a week.[66] As an encouragement to invest more
time on accountability, SSCI and HPSCI members could be allowed a one-
committee assignment reduction—say, three instead of the normal four in the
Senate. (Some members, though, might view this as a punishment, preferring
to be on four or even five committees if that will bring them more publicity and
visibility to voters back home.)

    As mentioned earlier in this book, particularly dedicated overseers could
also be recognized with special perks on the Hill bestowed by congressional leaders: better parking and office space (a larger room with a view of the
Capitol is something that matters for members of Congress), for instance, and
increased staff allotments. The Congress, as well as outside groups, could also
present "Intelligence Overseer of the Year" awards to the Aspins, Mazzolis, and
Robinsons who labor indefatigably on SSCI and HPSCI, which would add to the

lawmaker's luster back home. Media and academic groups (such as the American Political Science Association and the International Studies Association) could also present high-profile prizes to individuals in Congress and elsewhere in the government who have contributed to effective and fair accountability in the intelligence domain.

Improving Resources for Oversight

Important, as well, would be an increase in resources for the two Intelligence Committees. The staffs on both panels have declined in number in recent years; and the Government Accountability Office (GAO), which could help SSCI and HPSCI on some intelligence topics (such as drone budgets), has experienced a two-thirds staff reduction since 1979. "We should double the number of staff on SSCI," urges one of the committee's top staff investigators, echoing a suggestion I have heard many times over the years from a variety of individuals inside and outside the government.[67] Currently, for example, SSCI and HPSCI have only two staffers each assigned to review CIA programs—even though the other intelligence agencies attract less attention from committee members. (These other agencies often escape attention chiefly because their activities are too technically arcane to grasp easily, such as the intricacies of surveillance satellite management. For most lawmakers, the details of sigint tradecraft falls somewhere in interest between proofs of Euclidian geometry and the conjugation of German irregular verbs.) This understaffing is all the more peculiar in light of the fact that CIA covert action draws the most interest among SSCI and HPSCI members, especially Hughes-Ryan briefings.[68]

The Legislative Agenda

The Grand Charter experiment—the drafting of legislation to provide more detailed guidance to the entire IC—failed in the aftermath of the Church Committee investigations. The effort proved too grandiose, and it managed to mobilize all the agencies of the IC and their allies to lobby against its omnibus provisions. The idea of strengthened charters for each of the spy agencies continues to make sense, though; a worthy project for SSCI and HPSCI, over a several-year period, would be to enact charters for each of the agencies, then knit them together into one whole. Congress still needs to establish clearer "red lines" for each of the espionage services, so that their managers and officers understand more exactly what society expects of them.

Further, a larger number of public hearings—patches of sunlight between the shadows—could be presented by SSCI and HPSCI. Remember how the Church Committee demonstrated with its open session on Operation SHAMROCK that even sensitive material can be reviewed before the public in a responsible way, coordinated together by the IC and the oversight agencies as a means for providing information to citizens about intelligence objectives without harming sources and methods. In 2014, HPSCI held a useful set of open hearings on the NSA metadata program that allowed both those members in favor of this approach, as well as those against, to explain their views to the public while, at the same time, avoiding tradecraft details. These sessions helped to inform a national debate on the subject—exactly what should happen in a democracy. A senior SSCI staffer quickly scotched the idea of more public hearings, however, when I tried it out on him. "The material is too sensitive," he said, "and, moreover, the members would just use the occasion for posturing."[69] I continue to think, however, that truly sensitive material can be avoided while still keeping the public better informed, and that lawmakers will act responsibly when the nation is tuned into televised hearings—or be quickly reined in by their leaders, colleagues, and critics back home.

Congress and the Declassification of Executive Branch Documents

On top of these measures, the Congress must address more clearly the question of when it can declassify intelligence documents on its own—an especially delicate subjects on those (frequent) occasions when the executive branch opposes declassification. Constitutional authority Louis Fisher has written: "The President does not have plenary or exclusive authority over national security information," adding: "The scope of the President's power over national defense and foreign affairs depends very much on what Congress does in asserting its own substantial authorities in these areas."[70]

Among these authorities is Section 8 of Senate Resolution 400 (Senate Rule 9.7), the same measure used to create SSCI in 1976. This resolution provides the Senate with authority to release classified information unilaterally (that is, the Senate acting alone); however, so far SSCI has never asked the full chamber to vote on the release of a classified document. It is an elaborate procedure, which requires prior notification to the president and the starting of a five-day clock. If the president objects (in writing) to a Senate committee's intention to release classified material within this period, a majority of the SSCI membership (or the Senate majority and minority leaders jointly) may refer the matter to the full Senate. Within four to nine days, senators must take a public vote on the question, with the option of deciding to release only part of the document under consideration. Most likely, the executive and legislative branches would work out their differences informally before the disagreement came to a vote— the case so far (as with the Church Committee reports, as well as the Executive Summary of the SSCI Torture Report). Nevertheless, as Fritz Schwarz has noted, "A believable threat to use this power [to unilaterally declassify] should deter administration stalling of the sort there has been with the torture report."[71]

The ongoing debate in Washington over the release (at long last) of a bottled-up portion of the Joint 9/11 Committee (the Graham-Porter panel), dealing with the relationship between the terrorist attackers and the government of Saudi Arabia, revealed again the ambiguities that continue to surround legislative declassification of documents. As a *Times* reporter asked, "Would it take a vote by the House and the Senate? Would it be left up to the House and Senate Intelligence Committees, which first produced the report?" The HPSCI and SSCI chairs expressed reluctance for their panels to make this decision.[72] My interpretation of Senate Rule 9.7 is that neither SSCI nor HPSCI has the authority to release on their own volition classified information provided to them by the executive branch, without first going to their parent chamber for a vote. If the documents in question have been written and stamped classified by one of the committees themselves, though, then either SSCI or HPSCI should be able to release the material if the chairman and vice chairmen of the panel consent—or, in the case of a joint report, with the consent of the chairs and vice chairs of both oversight committees, or by majority vote within both committees.

The question remains whether the current rules are too restrictive. Perhaps SSCI and HPSCI, acting together or separately, ought to have authority to declassify documents from the intelligence agencies (not just their own documents). After all, the members of these panels are going to be much more interested in the question of disclosure than the average lawmaker asked to consider the question during a debate on the floor, as well as quite knowledgeable about the implications of a declassification decision. Shouldn't their opinions trump other members of Congress on this matter, since the latter would be coming in cold to a Senate or House floor debate?

In the instance of the Church Committee's interim report on *Alleged Assassination Plots* (November 1975), the committee duly took the report to the Senate floor, where a majority of the panel's members argued that this was an informational session and, therefore, a vote was not required; the committee could release its own report. Some lawmakers objected to this reasoning, because much of the report was based on documents and testimony acquired from the executive branch. They insisted on a vote. During the presentation of the report, however, many senators drifted out of the chamber and there were never enough members present for the necessary quorum to take a vote. The Church Committee thus released its own report on assassination plots by default, leaving a bitter taste in the mouths of those senators (lobbied intensely by the Ford Administration to block the release of the report) who claimed that the panel had exceeded its authority.[73]

My own approach would be to support authority for SSCI and HPSCI to release intelligence documents themselves when a two-thirds approval of those present and voting in the committee deemed this action useful to the public interest—even when the document had come from the executive branch. I doubt if such a vote would take place often, if ever; more likely, the two branches would negotiate a workable settlement beforehand. It could be useful, though, to have this option available when the executive branch is merely trying to cover up its intelligence mistakes or scandals by blocking congressional declassification of telling documents.

Development of Intelligence Oversight Algorithms

The intelligence oversight committees might benefit from bringing in RAND or McKinsey consultants to help them develop a sophisticated set of intelligence oversight algorithms for each of the primary intelligence missions: collection and analysis, covert action, and counterintelligence. A good illustration of this approach can be seen in the restaurant safety industry.[74] Some considerations of accountability are prominent in this domain: Are employees washing their hands? Is the fish iced down? Is hot food served at a temperature of at least 140 degrees? Is cold food refrigerated at 40 degrees and below? Are dirty dishes washed in hot water close to boiling? Are records maintained for all shellfish?

One of the problems in this industry is that large cities have many restaurants, but few public health inspectors—reminiscent of how the IC has many agencies and subsidiary units, but relatively few congressional overseers. In the restaurant safety business, the Public Health Department in Chicago has come up with a computer program that crunches a dozen variables based on publicly available (and regularly updated) information. Among these variables are

- a restaurant's previous sanitation violations;
- the length of time since the last inspection;
- how long the restaurant has been operating;
- whether the place is licensed to sell tobacco (smoking is prohibited in restaurants); and
- the three-day average high in temperature in Chicago (a time when maintaining food temperature becomes more challenging).

An algorithm takes data like these and weights them in terms of their significance for predicting whether a critical violation is likely to occur at a specific restaurant. The higher the coefficient, the more likely it is that there will be a serious violation. The Public Health team in Chicago found that by using an algorithm it was able to increase its discovery of violations by a factor of 25 percent and seven days earlier than with its previous off-the-cuff inspections. The computer program allowed the restaurant overseers to place in priority the establishments they needed to focus on the most. Violations earned fines. Moreover, the results were published online, which causes restaurant owners to take them seriously in an age when consumers thrive on easily accessible online dining-out reviews. In addition, in Chicago food safety teams respond to consumer complaints that come in by Twitter or other social media—an analog of intelligence whistle-blowing. Tweets lead to further inspections, although inspectors in Chicago have found the algorithm approach more reliable than tweets.

Using the covert action (CA) mission as an illustration, overseers might especially concentrate on such variables as the following:

- Does the covert action have a paramilitary (PM) component?
- Does that PM component involve a coup d'état or an assassination?
- Will the operation cost more than $1 million?
- Is it focused on a particularly dangerous target, say, North Korea or ISIS?
- Is it a joint operation with another nation's secret service (and, therefore, far more complicated)?
- Have planners connected with a local faction inside the target nation with similar objectives (usually vital for success)?
- What has been the previous experience with the use of CA against the target?

The actual writing of intelligence oversight algorithms is beyond the parameters of this book, but the approach holds promise for channeling limited accountability resources into key areas of intelligence that carry the greatest risk for error and embarrassment to the United States.

The Judicial Side of Intelligence Accountability

On the judicial side of oversight, the FISA Court must have a less partisan membership selection process.[75] Continuing to allow the Chief Justice of the Supreme Court (presently, John G. Roberts, Jr., a Republican from New York) to pick members will continue to result in the unfair packing of the Court, as with GOP judges in the case of Justice Roberts. To bring about a more balanced representation of party leanings, new appointments should alternate between selections made by the most senior justice on the Supreme Court nominated by a Republican president (Roberts was chosen by President George W. Bush) and the most senior Supreme Court justice chosen by a Democratic president (most recently Ruth Bader Ginsburg, selected by President Bill Clinton). Sensible, too, would be the establishment of a separate Terrorist Targeting Court (or TTC) along the lines of the FISA Court, but dedicated to a review of presidential requests for the targeted killing by a drone (or other method) of specific Americans abroad suspected of engaging in terrorist activities against the United States.

Moreover, the judicial branch will have to improve its FISA Court procedures for the review of warrant requests for intelligence collection operations, with less of an inclination to defer automatically to executive branch attorneys. Judge James Robertson, a former member of the FISA Court, has observed that the judges on the court have no body of opinions or precedents to help them interpret warrant requests; they are simply expected to approve a warrant application or not—yes or no, up or down. Further, recall how Judge Bates admonished the NSA in public for misleading him and his colleagues about the scope of that agency's metadata collection program. In at least one of these cases, NSA analysts were using a telephone log database in a manner that went beyond what the judges thought they had approved. The court should encourage the presence of non-IC attorneys in the room when warrants are reviewed, as now allowed by the USA FREEDOM Act of 2015.

Oversight Help from the Media and the Academy

Along with the fundamental requirement of oversight cooperation between Congress and the executive branch, the injection of some degree of democracy into the hidden side of government will depend on ongoing, diligent media probes into spy activities. Indeed, recall how the vast majority of intelligence scandals and failures in the United States have been brought to light by investigative journalists, not members of Congress. Recent events, though, have raised the barriers against investigative journalism, as the Obama Administration escalated Justice Department efforts to extinguish the right of the media to talk with government officials about security policies. The public outing of the NSA's metadata program by Snowden, and concomitant government counterintelligence probes into ties between the media and spies, has revealed an increased capacity of the intelligence agencies to trace telephone calls and other means of communications between journalists and government sources. Should these interactions dry up, the chances for citizens to know at least some things about their intelligence community will diminish even further. The American media have displayed a high level of responsibility in dealing with secrets that come their way, almost always contacting the government first for a dialogue about the implications of publishing, then stopping the presses if the government's argument is reasonable and not merely a cover-up.[76] With respect to national security topics, the First Amendment will become something of a quaint historical relic if the government moves further toward the overzealous prosecution of journalists for their reporting on national security issues.

Academia can provide valuable insights into intelligence activities, too. The International Studies Association now boasts some twenty-four panels at its annual conventions dedicated strictly to intelligence topics; the American Political Science Association has an "Organized Group" on intelligence studies. The field also has three prominent scholarly journals—*Intelligence and National Security*; *International Journal of Intelligence and Counterintelligence*; and *Studies in Intelligence* (a publication of the CIA's Center for the Study of Intelligence)—as well as several less widely distributed (but high-quality) periodicals that focus on intelligence specialties like sigint and cryptography. Moreover, professors across the United States and in other democracies now write scores of books and offer well over two hundred college courses on intelligence—most of them not "how-to" courses, but studies devoted to the theory of intelligence, along with practical, evidence-based examinations on how intelligence informs policymaking, as well as when the secret agencies succeed in their missions and when they fail (see this book's bibliography). As with journalists, college and high school teachers can also play a vital role in educating the public about this esoteric but important component of national security and foreign policy—and the necessity for accountability over intelligence activities.

Improvements in Whistle-blowing and Warrant Procedures

Among the most pressing reforms is to make legitimate whistle-blowing more feasible and acceptable. If leakers with moral or legal objections to government activities could more easily approach the intelligence oversight committees on Capitol Hill, for example, or some other responsible venue of accountability in the government (such as the IOB), perhaps they would stay home and work within the system rather than bolting recklessly to China or Russia with their objections. I think Snowden would have found a receptive ear among some members of SSCI and HPSCI, but he never tried—apparently because he believed such an effort would be futile. In fact, he would have been heard. That doesn't mean, of course, that he could have persuaded a majority of the lawmakers to oppose the metadata program. After all, some SSCI members who had been briefed on the program opposed it (such as Senators Wyden and Udall), but were unable to convince a majority of their colleagues to join them in opposition or to make the program public. Snowden might have been persuasive, though, given his firsthand knowledge of the program, and that is the point: to make sure whistle-blowers have a chance to make their case in a responsible manner, without having to go to jail or abandon their country. The establishment in the IC of a "dissent channel," as exists in the Department of State, whereby whistle-blowers can send messages anonymously to an IG or some other investigator (including SSCI and HPSCI), would be a useful step as well.[77]

A Citizens Intelligence Advisory Board

In 1937, the Brownlow Committee on Administrative Management completed a report for President Franklin D. Roosevelt on the staffing requirements and reorganization of the executive branch to meet modern demands. Its conclusion was straightforward: "The president needs help."[78] The examination of intelligence accountability in the United States in this book leads to a similar conclusion with respect to Congress: lawmakers need help. This is not to say that Congress has failed to move forward with intelligence oversight since the days of the Church Committee; as we have seen, lawmakers have laudably crafted several important laws and guidelines to help monitor secret operations. It is to say, however, that for all the reasons discussed here and in earlier chapters, members of Congress are unable to handle the duties of intelligence accountability by themselves. SSCI and HPSCI have had a valuable, if uneven, record of accomplishment; nevertheless, the IC is too vast, and its activities too complex and dispersed, for these committees to address the activities of the secret agencies unaided. The intelligence oversight panels need a helping hand from a newly created, permanent, and independent intelligence commission.

The idea of providing extra help for lawmakers assigned to intelligence accountability has gained currency throughout the democracies. The United Kingdom, whose intelligence accountability committee in Parliament (the Intelligence and Security Committee) is far weaker than SSCI and HPSCI, has an auxiliary Investigatory Powers Tribunal that serves as a supplementary watchdog. Australia has an Inspector-General of Intelligence and Security who reviews the activities of the Australian IC. The Netherlands has established a nonparliamentary, independent committee for intelligence oversight, abbreviated in Dutch as the CTIVD. Canada has a Security Intelligence Review Committee composed of five former politicians and members of the Privy Council Office, supported by a staff of eighteen experts; and some of Canada's intelligence reformers have called for a new external watchdog agency to assist further with intelligence accountability. Hansjörg Geirger, the former president of the BND (the German foreign intelligence service), advocates the creation in his country of a "commissioner for the intelligence services"—a person appointed by Berlin lawmakers who could monitor, with staff support, the activities of Germany's espionage agencies and provide outside backup to the existing—but still weak—intelligence oversight panel in the *Bundestag* (the German parliament).

In addition, the United Nations Human Rights Council has created a "rapporteur" who will monitor, investigate, and report on privacy issues; advise governments about compliance; and even investigate alleged violations. In the United States, Paul Pillar (a thoughtful former National Intelligence officer and Middle East expert) has advocated the idea of an outside group of intelligence experts to assist SSCI and HPSCI with their oversight duties. This is a position I have also come to, independently.[79]

Each of these proposals is based on the widespread observation that lawmakers in every democracy simply lack the time and expertise to manage intelligence accountability by themselves, under the current conditions that place such a premium on fund-raising for reelection. Pillar envisions the creation of a "congressional intelligence office," which he defines as "a permanent, nonpartisan watchdog modeled after the Government Accountability Office and the Congressional Budget Office." Its job would be to augment SSCI and HPSCI by providing "scrutiny and vigilance regarding the substantive use and misuses of intelligence, including politicization."[80]

I believe that SSCI and HPSCI can already handle many of the duties outlined by Pillar, but other responsibilities will require assistance. SSCI has divided its mandate into four categories: responding to daily events; preparing for confirmation hearings; drafting legislation; and engaging in major reviews and investigations. As they presently stand, the members and staff of both SSCI and HPSCI can—and are well tailored to—manage the first three categories of responsibility, even though lawmakers are torn by their other legislative duties as well as fund-raising sirens. Where the committees need help the most is with the fourth category: major reviews and investigations. This job can be highly time-consuming, as illustrated by special inquiries like the Joint Committee probe into 9/11, or the deep-dive research effort into the CIA torture program and the NSA metadata activities.

In my own version of an outside oversight helper, the United States would establish by statute a broadly focused Citizens Intelligence Advisory Board (CIAB). It could comprise nine members, aided by a staff of a dozen specialists. The members would be chosen in this fashion (or something similar): two by SSCI (one by the majority party, one by the minority party, each of whom would also continue to serve on SSCI); two from HPSCI (under comparable arrangements); two private citizens selected by the Supreme Court (one chosen by the Chief Justice and one by the senior judge appointed by the opposite party as the president who appointed the Chief Justice); two selected by the incumbent president; and a chairperson selected by a majority vote of the deans at the top five ranked schools of international and public affairs in the United States (with the balloting monitored by the IOB in the White House).

The term of service for each CIAB member would be five years, with the possibility of an additional five-year term. The CIAB membership positions would be full-time, except for the four lawmakers who would serve part-time as they fulfilled concurrently their work on SSCI or HPSCI. Four of the CIAB staffers would be designees assigned to, and chosen by, these four lawmakers. The congressional members would have to be a special breed—an Aspin, Hamilton, Mazzoli, or Robinson—with a strong interest in intelligence to sustain this double duty. They would also have to have a reasonably safe reelection constituency. It is vital to have congressional participation in CIAB activities, as a means of providing a connection to the organization that funds the IC: the U.S. Congress. Nothing so attracts the attention of intelligence bureaucrats as the power of the purse.

The CIAB, SSCI, and HPSCI, along with the GAO (for special assignments), would work together as an intelligence accountability coalition, coordinated by a management team composed of the four SSCI and HPSCI members and the CIAB chairperson (who would be overall leader of the team). The purpose of the CIAB would be to supplement the work of the intelligence oversight committees, not duplicate or interfere with their agendas. When SSCI and HPSCI are, at certain times in their history, captured by ostriches and cheerleaders, the less political and more independent CIAB could take up the slack in congressional guardianship. The CIAB would issue annual public reports, as well as classified reports to SSCI, HPSCI, the congressional leadership, and the White House. It would also hold hearings, with at least a few each year in open session; conduct formal inquiries when necessary, with full subpoena powers and the leverage of contempt citations that accompany them; take on special research projects that SSCI and HPSCI did not have time to pursue (say, an examination of intelligence reporting requirements to Congress to see if they are either excessive or too limited, which the committees themselves may be too close to evaluate fairly); and disclose to the public any spy activities that violate the laws of the United States or the nation's established societal norms.

Should operations like CHAOS, COINTELPRO, SHAMROCK, and MINARET, as well as torture and unbridled metadata programs, be stopped in their tracks before they begin? Should the likes of the Bay of Pigs and other questionable covert actions have been subjected to closer scrutiny? The poor intelligence performance associated with the 9/11 attacks and the question of WMDs in Iraq? In each case, clearly the answer in a democracy must be yes; and this will simply not happen—thoroughly, steadily—with SSCI and HPSCI acting alone, however well intended and hardworking its members and staff may be. The proposed CIAB would not be an overly complex new system that overburdens the IC, but rather a separation out from SSCI and HPSCI of the extraordinarily demanding tasks of special reviews and investigations—responsibilities that busy lawmakers are ill-equipped to handle. The CIAB would be a godsend to SSCI and HPSCI, in the sense of serving as a helpful hand to those committees, as well as a clear focal point for the IC during intelligence flaps.

Citizen Responsibilities

Professor Wesley Wark has emphasized, with reference to the reform of intelligence oversight procedures in Canada, that "while we pursue new forms of reassurance about intelligence operations, we will still want these agencies to spy, and spy well."[81] Exactly so for the United States as well. Again, the challenge is to find the proper equilibrium between security and liberty. Operations CHAOS and COINTELPRO (among others) should impress upon each of us that the government has in the past—and could in the future—use its secret powers to counter lawful protest, even ruin the lives of people because some bureaucrat (J. Edgar Hoover in the case of COINTELPRO) doesn't like the way they look, what they say or write, or the content of their political beliefs. It is incumbent upon all Americans to take a more active role in demanding the protection of this nation's fundamental constitutional freedoms, electing only those presidents, senators, and representatives who vow to take intelligence accountability seriously. The citizens of this great nation must either fight for their right of privacy or lose it. The security side of the equation is well represented by the intelligence bureaucracy and its allies in the private sector (such as drone and satellite manufacturers); the counterbalance of a well-organized and well-funded coalition of privacy groups has yet to form coherently in the United States. The CIAB could help adjust that imbalance and help educate the American people about the importance of maintaining an equilibrium between security and liberty.

Above all, the intelligence community must always remember that its most important possession is its honor and reputation. If the American people believe that their spy agencies have become more of a danger to democracy and the honor of the United States than a protection against foreign and domestic threats, the secret agencies will have lost what they need the most: the full support of the public for the indispensable security objectives they have been created to perform.

These are all significant challenges. They are no more daunting, though, than the obstacles Americans have already overcome on the road toward a more perfect union. A classified CIA review of a paper presented on intelligence accountability by Professor Harry Howe Ransom at the American Political Science Association annual meeting in 1962—finally declassified fifty-one years later—ended with a sarcastic observation that Ransom had expressed a desire at the meeting "to know what was going on in a 'gigantic' organization which admittedly had to operate in secret but which needed some control, the nature of which the political scientist was unable to determine."[82]

Since then, the Church Committee, political scientists, law professors, think tanks, journalists, and others have determined what kinds of improved controls over intelligence activities are necessary, including better incentives on Capitol Hill for guardians to engage in steady police patrolling—lawmakers who will insist on full and timely (normally, *ante facto*) reporting to Congress. The next step is the adoption of the further reforms examined in this chapter, along with the selection of men and women for high office who are prepared to bring meaningful accountability into this intelligence shadowland. The way is long and hard, but not beyond the capacity of those who believe in the full flowering of democratic principles in the United States, even in—or perhaps most of all in—its spy agencies.

Epilogue

Intelligence in the Early Trump Administration

Politicians as Spymasters

Intelligence controversies moved center stage in the lead-up to the Trump Administration and, as this book was going into production, throughout its early weeks in office.[1] The first appointment proposed by President-elect Donald J. Trump was a politician, Representative Mike Pompeo (R, Kansas), to head the CIA. He was clearly brainy enough for the job, graduating first in his class at West Point and earning a law degree from Harvard University. Critics wondered, however, whether Pompeo—a Tea Party devotee—could maintain the nonpartisan neutrality expected in this sensitive post. His appointment of Gina Haspel, who had been a top CIA officer involved in the Agency's controversial torture activities after 9/11, along with the destruction of evidence about this program, as his deputy did little to reassure observers that Pompeo would provide level-headed intelligence leadership —although Haspel had just served with merit as the CIA's chief of station in the important London posting.[2]

Of its previous twenty-three directors since President Harry S. Truman founded the Agency in 1947, only five have been individuals with a markedly political background. Three were Republicans and two were Democrats. The first was career politician George H. W. Bush, who assumed the CIA directorship in January 1976. Recall that he had been a former head of the Republican National Committee (RNC), as well as a member of the House of Representatives from Texas. Bush took over the Agency's reins in the middle of the Church Committee inquiry. Though unsuccessful, Senator Church vehemently resisted Bush's appointment as the nation's spy chief, on the grounds that it was an inappropriate job for a former head of the RNC.

Bush served for only a year at the CIA (from January 1976 to January 1977), devoting the first six months of his tenure to the launching of a charm offense on Capitol Hill designed to wind down the Church panel's investigation.

Throughout this turbulent period of inquiry, it was survival time for Agency and other intelligence officers as they wondered if their jobs would still exist after the Senate probe. While Director Bush and the CIA concentrated on weathering the investigation, covert actions overseas ground almost to a complete halt; and the production of National Intelligence Estimates (NIEs), the nation's most detailed intelligence reports, reached a historic low point.

Bush reached out to Democrats and Republicans alike in Congress, seeking to tone down criticism aimed at the Agency. His service in the House, along with the fact that his father, Prescott Bush, had been a popular senator, meant that he was no stranger to Capitol Hill. This legacy, as well as Bush's diplomatic skills and his willingness to interact with lawmakers on both sides of the aisle, eased the tensions between Congress and the CIA during the Year of Intelligence. When the dust settled in May 1976, the Church Committee garnered near-unanimous support for its final report, presented to the public that month. In this instance, having a moderate politician as the nation's intelligence director may have been helpful during a period of tense executive-legislative relations. Moreover, even if he had wanted to, Bush was too preoccupied with the inquiry to bring politics into the CIA's day-to-day intelligence reports and operations.

In the 1980s William J. Casey, who had been President Ronald Reagan's presidential campaign manager, projected a rather different profile as CIA director. Casey was unapologetically political inside the Agency, even tearing up NIEs on occasion and writing his own intelligence reports that were more in tune with the Reagan Administration's anti-Communist global objectives. During his rocky tenure (1981–1987), Casey slipped the moorings of neutrality altogether and led the nation secretly into the quagmire of the Iran-contra affair. He treated intelligence oversight laws enacted by a Democratic Congress as if they were written in invisible ink: unseen and readily ignored.

The third *homo politicus* to assume the role of America's spymaster was a former Democratic staff director of the Senate Intelligence Committee, George J. Tenet (1997–2004). In the tradition of most CIA leaders over the years, he played it straight politically for much of his lengthy tenure. After the 9/11 attacks, however, Tenet—who had developed chummy relations with the Bush White House—was drawn into the pro-war politics of the administration. In 2002–2003, he failed to assess with a sufficiently critical eye the obstinate belief held by the Bush team that an invasion of Iraq was necessary to rid that nation of weapons of mass destruction (WMDs). Vice President Dick Cheney and the neoconservatives in the administration managed to erode the CIA director's willingness to search more deeply for facts about the validity of the hypothesis that Iraq possessed WMD. A high-cost invasion would prove the hypothesis false. The neocons had their own agenda: topple Saddam Hussein as a dangerous enemy of Israel, establish on Iraqi soil a beachhead for democracy in the

Middle East, and pay for the whole venture with Iraqi oil sales. Tenet, the former Democrat, had bought into the war aims of the GOP administration all too readily, departing from his obligation as spy chief to insist that President Bush weigh more carefully the dissenting views in the intelligence community that questioned the existence of Iraqi WMDs.

Like Pompeo, the fourth political figure, Representative Porter Goss (R, Florida), had served on the House Intelligence Committee before his appointment as CIA director by George W. Bush. While still in Congress, Goss had publicly displayed a visceral disdain for the Clinton Administration. He carried this pronounced partisanship with him to Agency Headquarters at Langley during his brief, eight-month stint as intelligence director. Similarly, Pompeo has revealed a deep-seated animosity toward the Clintons, going after former secretary of state Hillary Clinton during House hearings on Benghazi with a vengeance that startled even his Tea Party colleagues.

In 2009–2011 during the Obama Administration, Leon E. Panetta served as the nation's fifth politician-turned-spymaster. He had previously been a Democratic member of the House of Representatives, as well as White House chief-of-staff for President Clinton. At Langley, Panetta kept his political views in check for the most part; but, periodically, he relied on close party ties with President Obama to help him fend off attempts by intelligence bureaucrats to challenge the CIA's leadership over the wider IC. In one instance, for example, tight political bonds with the president allowed Panetta to have his way against those—including one of the early DNIs (Admiral Blair)—who sought White House permission to open up the chief-of-station slots overseas to officers in other spy agencies, not just reserve them for the CIA.

One of the most well known of the Agency directors, Richard Helms (1966–1973), stressed in an interview that I conducted with him in 1990 that the high councils in Washington are saturated with partisan policy wonks. What was needed when a president gathered his national security experts together was someone in the room "who was not trying to formulate a policy, carry out a policy, or defend a policy, someone who could say: 'Now listen, this isn't my understanding of the facts.'" Is that the role Pompeo is prepared to play? The cardinal sin of intelligence is politicization, the twisting of intelligence reports to buttress the policy goals of those in the Oval Office and other high government aeries. As the example of William Casey underscores, individuals previously involved in politics may be notably susceptible to these siren calls.

The National Security Act of 1947, which created the CIA, stipulated that the chairman of the Joint Chiefs of Staff (C/JCS) and the Agency's director would serve as advisers to the National Security Council (though not members, of which there are only four: the president, vice president, secretary of state, and secretary of defense), as a way to ensure that neutral parties would be present to safeguard the facts related to any issue before the Council. One of President Trump's early moves was to announce that, henceforth, neither the C/JSC, the CIA director, nor the director of national intelligence (DNI) would be invited on a regular basis to NSC sessions—a shocking disregard for evidentiary-based foreign-policy and national security affairs. The administration soon relented on this rule for the CIA director, and then weeks later decided that the C/JSC and the DNI should be present as well for NSC meetings. How firm these commitments were to having intelligence experts on hand for NSC gatherings remained uncertain; and the fact that the president's choice for DNI—Dan Coats (R, Indiana)—was not confirmed by the Senate until mid-March of 2017 added to the perception that intelligence was a low priority for the administration.

Double Jeopardy

Compounding the concern about mixing politics and intelligence raised by the Pompeo nomination was the new president's choice for DNI. Coats was another career politician and former member of the House Intelligence Committee (HPSCI), as well as a senator (for several nonconsecutive terms) who served on that chamber's intelligence committee oversight panel (SSCI).

Thus the Trump Administration will have a former politician running the overall IC as DNI (Coats), and another politician running the community's highest profile spy organization, the CIA (Pompeo)—a double whammy to the tradition of sheltering America's intelligence activities from political influence. Perhaps they will manage to remain neutral in their new positions, dedicating themselves strictly to fact-finding and unbiased analysis, even if banished from NSC meetings. The historical record of politicians in these roles is hardly reassuring, though—especially the Casey example.

Honest Broker or Broken Honesty?

An additional controversy resulted at the beginning of the Trump years from another intelligence-related appointment: the national security adviser. The paramount obligation of this office is to serve as an honest broker, ensuring that the views of key agencies in the national security domain are presented to the president in a fair and timely manner, and that the findings of the intelligence agencies are kept free of political spin. For this position (which does not require Senate confirmation, unlike the top posts at the CIA and the Office of the DNI), President Trump turned to Lt. Gen. Michael J. Flynn. He was a former director of the Defense Intelligence Agency (DIA), one of the eight agencies within the

DoD framework. General Flynn brought with him mixed reviews for this vital post. While serving in Iraq and Afghanistan, Flynn earned high marks for delivering useful battlefield intelligence, earning him three stars on his epaulettes. He became the longest service flag officer in the Iraq and Afghan war zones. Yet when he returned to Washington to run the DIA, widespread complaints soon arose over his disorganized management practices and blustering style.

More troubling still, he developed a reputation for politicizing intelligence within the DIA, reportedly insisting (for instance) that its analysts support his conclusion that Iran is an implacable enemy of the United States. Flynn lasted only twenty-four days as national security advisor, brought down by media leaks about his questionable contacts with Russian officials during the presidential campaign while serving then as an aide to Trump. What angered the administration most was the fact that, after the election, Flynn lied to the vice president and others about these contacts. As this book went to press, he had just been subpoenaed by HSPCI to testify on the Trump Administration's possible collusion with Russia in America's presidential election. He vowed to evoke the Fifth Amendment rather than testify.

The administration turned next to another lieutenant general, Herbert Raymond "H. R." McMaster, considered an Army intellectual by virtue of his Ph.D. from the University of North Carolina, his widely read book critical of military passivity in dealings with President Lyndon B. Johnson and his approach to the war in Vietnam (*Dereliction of Duty*), and his predilection to cite political philosophers in discussions of warfare strategy. A former tank commander with battlefield experience in Iraq and Afghanistan, the more organized and less strident McMaster seemed a reasonable choice for national security adviser. His selection gave yet a further military coloration to the Trump team, though, with former military leaders already in place as secretary of defense and as the director of the Department of Homeland Security (along with Pompeo's service as an Army tank commander before he turned to a political career).

The Blind Leading the Blind

Compounding his questionable appointments to the CIA and ODNI, Trump set a record for refusing intelligence briefings during the presidential campaign, dismissing their value out-of-hand. In office, he showed little interest at first in the *President's Daily Brief*—the early morning roundup of world affairs presented by the CIA and valued by many previous presidents. Despite the fact that the United States was spending over $70 billion annually to collect and understand the intelligence that goes into the *PDB* and other intelligence reports, the president seemed to prefer tweeting and watching TV. Initially, General Flynn had presented to the president the NSC staff's version of a daily brief, a document that was unlikely to match in depth and objectivity the traditional *PDB* brought to the White House for the past fifty years by the CIA on behalf of the entire IC. McMaster and Pompeo faced a difficult challenge, it appeared, in convincing the president that the *PDB*—and intelligence in general—was worth his attention. By June, however, they were having some success in convincing the president to sit still for a while in the morning for an intelligence briefing—although it was clear from media reports quoting insiders that he was not a detail man during these sessions.[3]

During these early weeks in office, Trump liked to point to past errors made by the spy agencies, as with their failure to anticipate the 9/11 attacks or, prior to the U.S. invasion of Iraq in 2003, the conclusion reached by a majority of agencies in the IC that the leaders in Baghdad harbored WMDs that might be used against the United States. It should be remembered, though, that academic researchers around the nation came to the same conclusion that Iraq probably possessed unconventional weaponry. The fact that it didn't, as it turned out, came as a surprise to experts across the United States. That fact doesn't absolve George Tenet from his failure to insist on more digging into the WMD hypothesis before an invasion of Iraq, but it does place the analytical errors into context. A more balanced appraisal of the IC would acknowledge that, as organizations run by humans, its seventeen agencies will make mistakes but that they typically provide accurate—and sometimes invaluable—information. Examples include the Agency's important fact-finding during the Cuban missile crisis, or more recently, on the details of Russian machinations in Eastern Europe. For a president to ignore intelligence would be equivalent to crossing Fifth Avenue wearing a blindfold.

President Trump also clung to his campaign position that CIA torture was a useful approach to intelligence gathering and that he would go beyond even waterboarding—regardless of the fact that Pompeo and the president's new secretary of defense, James N. Mattis, both rejected the Agency's thoroughly discredited counterterrorism interrogation methods. The president insisted that unnamed Agency sources swore by its results, even though the report from the Senate Intelligence Committee had reached just the opposite conclusion, relying on CIA testimony and other research.

Cyber Concerns

Controversial, too, was the finding by three key agencies in the IC (the CIA, the FBI, and the NSA) that Russia had hacked into the computers of the Democratic National Committee during the 2016 presidential election, perhaps even tilting—to some unknown degree—the outcome toward a Trump victory over Russian president Vladimir Putin's nemesis, Hillary Clinton. It is far-fetched, however, to presume that Russian computer mischief produced the massive anti-establishment protest vote in favor of Donald Trump. This outcome was a complex result of the Democratic Party taking white, blue-collar voters for granted, coupled with the unpopularity of candidate Clinton, plus the loss of jobs in the nation stemming from workplace automation and the effects of globalization. Nonetheless, it is disturbing that Moscow would recklessly attempt to shape the outcome of an American presidential election.

Politicians of all stripes made it clear that cyberattacks against the United States will not be tolerated from any source. Both HPSCI and SSCI started up inquiries into the allegations, as did the Department of Justice and the FBI. If proven true, lawmakers will sternly warn Russia against further engagement in these forms of intelligence harassment—or else face serious cyber and other countermeasures. Most likely, both nations will seek an agreement to curb cyberattacks aimed at one another, realizing that neither the Russians nor the Americans benefit from such behavior, and understanding that the danger is great that electronic warfare could spin out of control and escalate into a military response.

During this controversy, President Trump alleged in March—shockingly and without precedent—that former president Obama had ordered wiretaps against him during the election, a charge denied by DNI James R. Clapper, Jr., and FBI Director James B. Comey. (Clapper retired at the end of the Obama Administration, and President Trump soon fired Comey.) The president asked members of Congress to investigate the possibility of intelligence surveillance aimed at him by the Obama Administration at Trump Tower in New York City during the election and perhaps since then. Further, the new president asked lawmakers to add to their list of subjects for investigation the question of whether he and his aides had been influenced by Russia during the presidential election—although he soon made a point of ridiculing the need for any kind of inquiry at all into his alleged ties with Russia. Madness seemed to have descended on Washington, D.C.

There is at least a whiff of hypocrisy in the revulsion expressed in Washington about Moscow's "active measures" (the Russian name for covert action) against the United States and its presidential election. As widely reported by the media and scholars over the decades, the CIA has been aggressively engaged worldwide in the use of covert actions, including electoral and other political meddling—even against fellow democracies. (The prime example is the Allende regime in Chile during the 1970s.) There is arguably a place for covert action in world affairs, notably against ISIS and other terrorist organizations; however, as related in chapter 9, this approach is often resorted to indiscriminately and with unfortunate consequences. The Church Committee concluded that covert actions should be adopted only as a last resort, not as normal practice. Leaders in Moscow and Washington would do well to weigh more carefully the possible results of secret interventions into one another's elections and governmental affairs.

The Ongoing Challenge of Intelligence Reform

Yet another intelligence dustup loomed as the new administration moved toward a possible deep-tissue restructuring of America's intelligence organizations and activities. While president-elect, Donald Trump vividly expressed his contempt for the nation's IC. He even accused anonymous U.S. intelligence officers of having leaked a Russian dossier regarding alleged sexual improprieties engaged in by Trump when he presided over a Miss Universe contest held in Moscow in 2013. Trump denied these charges (as did President Putin) and compared the leak, which he remained convinced came from U.S. intelligence agencies, to approaches used by Hitler during the Third Reich to defame adversaries. Needless to say, this comparison did not sit well at Langley or in the Office of the DNI—although the incumbent DNI at the time, Clapper, said after a meeting with the president-elect during this flare-up that the discussions had been mutually cordial and respectful.

Regardless of the momentary mending of relations, the new president and his national security aides seemed intent on addressing the shortcomings they perceived in America's spy apparatus. If Trump moves in the direction of reform, one of his first challenges will be to resolve the tensions that have evolved between CIA directors and DNIs.

In the aftermath of 9/11 and the subsequent investigation by the Kean Commission into intelligence and policy failures associated with the terrorist attack, reformers sought to strengthen America's intelligence capabilities. As discussed earlier in this book, they conceived of a DNI Office as a means for bringing about closer coordination among the spy agencies—a missing element that contributed to the failures that led to that tragic morning in 2001. Recall, for instance, how the CIA and the FBI had fumbled their liaison efforts to track the whereabouts of two suspected terrorists living in San Diego who subsequently became part of the 9/11 airline hijacking operation.

Yet by selecting the CIA director (Pompeo) early on, the Trump team cast a cloud over the future of American's top intelligence figure: the DNI. As related in chapter 5, Congress created the DNI office—under pressure from the Kean Commission and the reform-minded families of the 9/11 victims—as a means for bringing greater cohesion to the IC. The families were persuasive lobbyists as they descended on Washington, D.C., in search of ways to prevent more tragedies like the one that had claimed the lives of their loved ones. Fueled by the Kean Commission's findings, the families had become convinced—rightly so—that a lack of effective coordination among America's intelligence organizations had contributed significantly to the nation's lack of preparedness to defend against "aerial terrorism" in 2001 and potential attacks in the future. Today, the nation's cyber defenses have displayed a further lack of institutional integration, as Russian hacking illustrated anew (not to mention widespread Chinese theft of electronic data and other cyberattacks against the United States).

Under the pressure of public opinion and with sympathy toward the 9/11 families, Congress established the Office of the DNI in 2004 as part of the Intelligence Reform and Terrorism Prevention Act (IRTPA). As this book has related, during the legislative maneuvering that accompanied passage of this law, however, a majority in Congress retreated from the original concept of providing the new DNI position with meaningful budget and appointment powers over all the spy agencies. Without these authorities, organizational integration of the IC would remain elusive. Thanks to effective lobbying by the Defense Department against the creation of a robust DNI office, the United States ended up with a cosmetic spymaster for the IC, rather than a true leader with full spending and personnel powers. The DoD, led by the redoubtable bureaucratic in-fighter Secretary Donald Rumsfeld at the time, feared that a muscular DNI might lead to excessive civilian control over military intelligence and a diminution of what intelligence professionals refer to as SMO (support to military operations).

The weaknesses of the DNI position led the first three DNI incumbents to throw up their hands in exasperation over the feebleness of their office and resign after short terms. The fourth, General Clapper, became the only director so far to stay more than two years. He began as DNI in 2010 and retired on the final day of the Obama Administration in 2017. Clapper's prior fifty-year career as an intelligence officer allowed him to develop close professional ties at the various spy agencies well before he accepted the DNI job. These community-wide contacts made it possible for him to cajole the agency directors—several of whom he had mentored and all of whom he knew personally—toward a stronger sense of team play. Clapper's retirement leaves his Trump-selected replacement, Dan Coats, in the unenviable position of trying to coordinate the vast IC without Clapper's extensive—indeed, unparalleled—ties to the nation's intelligence professionals.

In the language of America's spies, the gold standard of intelligence is "all-source fusion," that is, an integrated, holistic presentation to the president and his aides of reports about current events and conditions around the world in which all of the secret agencies combine their best information under the DNI's guidance. By naming its choice for Agency director several weeks before addressing who would serve as DNI, the incoming Trump Administration sent a signal that the status of the DNI Office and the integration of the spy agencies is of secondary importance—and perhaps of no importance at all. The end result is likely to be a backslide toward bureaucratic fragmentation or "stovepiping" within the IC, along with the sowing of confusion regarding the relationship between the CIA and the DNI.

DCI versus DNI

President Obama's outgoing CIA director, John Brennan, instituted some useful reforms within the Agency during his tenure. For example, in 2015, he established a new Directorate of Digital Innovation (DDI), a response to the importance of computers in today's world, along with a continuing concern about hackers and even the possibility of a massive cyberattack against the United States—an electronic Pearl Harbor that would wreak havoc across this densely wired nation. In most need of reform measures, however, is the broader IC. If the Trump Administration becomes serious about addressing intelligence shortcomings at this level, it will have to consider two prominent organizational models.

The first model would amend the IRTPA law by providing the DNI belatedly with authorities over money, along with the hiring and firing of the sixteen agency managers (in consultation with departmental secretaries). This would allow the establishment of a meaningful national spy director who could more readily bring about the goal of all-source fusion. The Rumsfeld worry that a strong DNI would diminish SMO has always been a false argument. No Director of Intelligence is going to jeopardize the safety of America's fighting men and women on foreign battlefields by eroding intelligence support to them; President Trump, or any other chief executive, would immediately fire any spymaster who allowed this to happen. A stronger DNI, though, would allow for the improved integration of intelligence reporting not only for military matters but across the broad subjects the White House needs to know about, including questions of global politics, economics, health (the danger of pandemics), environmental degradation, cultural upheavals, and other nonmilitary subjects.

A second model for achieving the objective of closer cooperation among the spy agencies would be to abolish the DNI office altogether by repealing that portion of IRTPA. Then the DCI position could be reinstated and provided, at long last, with the means to accomplish community-wide integration: the budget and personnel authorities consistently stripped from the DCI position throughout the years. The attractiveness of this second approach is that the DCI would be located at CIA Headquarters (as before), where a majority of the nation's top strategic intelligence analysts reside—the core knowledge base of the IC. Only now, however, the DCI would have long-sought-after authority to actually lead both the Agency and the entire IC. This is the scheme envisioned by the Truman Administration and several commissions of inquiry since then (including the Aspin-Brown Commission in 1996). After all, the CIA was meant to be the *Central* Intelligence Agency, designed originally to be the hub of the national intelligence wheel with its many spokes.

Under this plan, the CIA director would serve not only as the Agency's leader (D/CIA), but also as the head of all the spy agencies (DCI), equipped finally with authority necessary to properly integrate the broad IC. The DCI would delegate day-to-day guidance of the CIA to a deputy (DD/CIA), allowing the DCI to focus on community-wide intelligence integration. Here is the pre-DNI approach to strengthening intelligence organization in the United States, but with the vital reform of providing the Director of Central Intelligence with the budget and appointment authorities this office never enjoyed from 1947 to 2004, when replaced by the weak DNI office.

The Third Option

A third option is available to the Trump Administration: a further disparagement of the spy agencies as displayed periodically by the president, who often seemed in the first months of his tenure to prefer playing the game of Blind Man's Bluff on the world stage. Based on Trump's remarks during the lead-up to his inauguration, one could conclude that this third option is a real possibility. Yet, as president his first stop on the day after the inauguration ceremonies was to CIA Headquarters. "I'm so behind you," he told an admiring audience gathered in the Agency's foyer. (Afterward, CBS News reported that the new president had taken his own studio audience with him to Langley.) He referred to Pompeo as "perhaps my most important appointment" and added "there's nobody I respect more" than America's intelligence officers. "We're going to win again," he continued, "and you'll be leading the charge." These remarks—were they just rhetoric or did they reflect reality?—could lead one to just the opposite conclusion, namely, that the new president was deeply aware of the importance of intelligence for U.S. security and ready to rely on the work of the secret agencies.

Perhaps President Trump will pay some attention to the findings of the CIA and its companion agencies, especially in times of international crisis, but without ever addressing the underlying organizational weaknesses of the IC—the regrettable "stovepiping" that has prevented its agencies from sharing their fully integrated findings to the White House with as many pieces of the global jigsaw puzzle put together as possible.

If President Trump abandons attempts to integrate the spy agencies more effectively, citizens will have to rely on Congress, investigative journalists, and scholarly studies for guidance on how America's vital intelligence shield can be strengthened to prevent future 9/11s. Fundamental reform in the IC, in conjunction with the oversight reforms discussed throughout this book, will put the United States back on the right track for having the best—and most accountable— intelligence services in world history.

ACKNOWLEDGMENTS

I have had the opportunity to serve in the legislative and executive branches of the federal government, with responsibilities for monitoring America's secret intelligence agencies. Along the way, I benefited greatly from an association with several outstanding national leaders, mentors, and colleagues who helped me understand the hidden side of Washington, D.C. I take this opportunity to offer my deepest appreciation to President George H. W. Bush and Vice President Walter F. Mondale; Senator Frank Church of Idaho, as well as Senators Wyche Fowler of Georgia, Gary Hart of Colorado, Sam Nunn of Georgia, and Carl Levin of Michigan; Secretary of State Dean Rusk and U.S. Ambassadors Martin Hillenbrand, Karl F. Inderfurth, and Don Johnson, as well as Ambassador Dieter Kastrup of Germany; and representative, as well as subsequently secretary of defense, Les Aspin of Wisconsin.

I have also benefited significantly from conversations with many intelligence officers, including CIA Chief of Counterintelligence James Angleton; Director of Central Intelligence (DCI) William J. Casey; Director of National Intelligence James R. Clapper, Jr.; DCI William E. Colby; Jack Davis; DCI John Deutch; Nicholas Dujmović; DCI Robert M. Gates (who also served as secretary of defense); DCI Richard Helms; Frederick P. Hitz; Arthur S. Hulnick; Mark M. Lowenthal; Fred F. Manget; Hayden B. Peake; Paul R. Pillar; Paul J. Redmond; David Robarge; DCI James R. Schlesinger, Jr. (another intelligence director who went on to serve as secretary of defense); J. Warren Stembridge; DCI George Tenet; DCI Stansfield Turner; DCI William H. Webster; Joe Wippl; and DCI R. James Woolsey. I benefited significantly as well from discussions with Capitol Hill staff colleagues, including in the Senate, Barry Carter, John Elliff, Peter Fenn, James Johnston, Elliott Maxwell, Frederick A. O. Schwarz, Jr., L. Britt Snider, and Gregory F. Treverton; and in the House, Dick Giza, Thomas K. Latimer, and Diane LaVoy. Since I left the government, I have met other congressional staff aides who have been helpful in their discussions about intelligence with me, including Michael Allen, Clete Johnson, Daniel J. Jones, and Paul Matulic, plus Library of Congress experts on intelligence: Richard A. Best, Jr., Al Cummings, and Fred Kaiser.

I also owe a debt to several colleagues in the academic and think-tank worlds, especially Joel Aberbach, Steven Aftergood, Matthew M. Aid, Christopher Andrew, David M. Barrett, Richard K. Betts, Arthur C. Campbell, Francis M. Carney, Laura K. Donohue, Stuart Farson, Michael German, Peter Gill, Michael J. Glennon, Michael Handel, Glenn Hastedt, Michael Herman, Peter Jackson, Robert Jervis, David Kahn, Jennifer Kibbe, William W. Keller, Wolfgang Krieger, Sébastien Laurent, Geneieve Lester, William Nolte, Joseph S. Nye, Jr., Mark Phythian, Vernon Puryear, Jeffrey Richelson, Martin Rudner, Harry Howe Ransom, Jennifer Sims, Frank J. Smist, Jr., John D. Stempel, Stan A. Taylor, Patrick F. Walsh, Wesley K. Wark, Michael Warner, Bradford Westerfield, James J. Wirtz, and Amy B. Zegart. Influential, too, on my thinking has been the reporting of journalists Seymour M. Hersh, Ian Masters, Mark Mazzetti, Dana Priest, James Risen, Charles Savage, Scott Shane, Jeff Stein, David Wise, and Bob Woodward; and, in the judicial world, Judges Morris S. "Buzz" Arnold and James E. Baker. The bibliography, as well as the notes, offer further testimony of my indebtedness to a wider range of scholars. Of course, none of these good people bear any blame for the interpretations that I settle on in these pages, or for any error of fact.

Over the past forty years, I have written about intelligence accountability from time to time in various scholarly journals. In this book I sometimes draw from the scattered fragments of this earlier work: a few anecdotes about, and quotes by, intelligence officials, which helped to provide historical perspective on the subject. I want to acknowledge my appreciation to the editors of these journals for allowing me to repurpose some of this earlier research (see the bibliography) in the preparation of this book.

Further, I would like to express my appreciation to President Jere W. Morehead, the president of the University of Georgia, for his friendship and steady support for my research, teaching, and public service endeavors; to Provost Pamela S. Whitten for her warm encouragement along the way; to David C. Lee, the vice president for research at the university; and Markus M. L. Crepaz, the Head of the Department of International Affairs in the School of Public and International Affairs, for their support for this project. I also thank my colleagues Louis Fisher (Scholar in Residence with the Constitutional Project in Washington, D.C.) and David M. Barrett (Villanova University) for taking the time to read the full manuscript and suggest valuable ideas for revision; my Ph.D. students at the University of Georgia, particularly Lt. Col. James Borders (U.S. Air Force) and Lt. Col. Joshua N. K. Massey (U.S. Marine Corps), for assistance with fact-checking and their broader insights into intelligence topics; and my Honors students for their preparation of several briefing books on aspects of intelligence accountability as class projects, as well as another undergraduate, Zach Hawkins, for his assistance on specific research questions.

I also extend special, heartfelt thank yous to my extraordinary wife, Leena S. Johnson, for her unfailing support and sure-footed editorial suggestions, while keeping the Johnson family happy and close; to our daughter, Kristin E. Swati, and her husband, Jamil Swati, for stimulating conversations and insights about world affairs; to Claire Sibley and Helen Nicholson of Oxford University Press in America for their clear and cheerful guidance; to Chris Dahlin for her outstanding copyediting; and, last but not least, to the immensely talented president of Oxford University Press in America, Niko Pfund, as well as my thoughtful senior editor, David McBride, for their steady encouragement and wise counsel.

Appendix A

THE ORGANIZATION OF THE U.S. INTELLIGENCE COMMUNITY, 2017

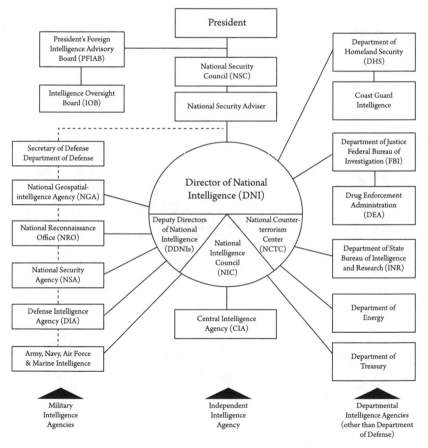

* From 1947 to 2004, a Director of Central Intelligence (DCI) led the Intelligence Community, rather than a Director of National Intelligence. The Department of Homeland Security and the Coast Guard did not become part of the IC until 2003, and the Drug Enforcement Administration, in 2006.

Appendix B

U.S. INTELLIGENCE LEADERSHIP, 1946–2017

Director, National Intelligence (DNI)

2005–2007	Amb. (ret.) John D. Negroponte
2007–2009	Gen. (ret.) J. M. "Mike" McConnell
2009–2010	Adm. (ret.) Dennis C. Blair
2010–2017	Gen. (ret.) James R. Clapper, Jr.
2017– Sen.	Dan Coates

Director, Central Intelligence (DCI)

1946	Adm. Sidney William Souers
1946–1947	Lt. Gen. Hoyt Sanford Vandenberg
1947–1950	Rear Adm. Roscoe H. Hillenkoetter
1950–1953	Gen. Walter Bedell Smith
1953–1961	Allen W. Dulles
1961–1965	John A. McCone
1965–1966	Vice Adm. William F. Raborn, Jr.
1966–1973	Richard Helms
1973	James R. Schlesinger
1973–1976	William E. Colby
1976–1977	George H. W. Bush
1977–1981	Adm. Stansfield Turner
1981–1987	William J. Casey
1987–1991	William H. Webster
1991–1993	Robert M. Gates
1993–1995	R. James Woolsey
1995–1997	John M. Deutch

1997–2004   George J. Tenet
2004–2005   Porter J. Goss

Chair, Senate Select Committee on Intelligence (SSCI)

1976–1977   Daniel K. Inouye, Democrat, Hawaii
1977–1981   Birch Bayh, Democrat, Indiana
1981–1985   Barry Goldwater, Republican, Arizona
1985–1987   David Durenberger, Republican, Minnesota
1987–1993   David L. Boren, Democrat, Oklahoma
1993–1995   Dennis DeConcini, Democrat, Arizona
1995–1997   Arlen Specter, Republican, Pennsylvania
1997–2001   Richard C. Shelby, Republican, Alabama
2001–2003   Bob Graham, Democrat, Florida
2003–2006   Pat Roberts, Republican, Kansas
2007–2008   John D. Rockefeller IV, Democrat, West Virginia
2009–2014   Dianne Feinstein, Democrat, California
2015–   Richard M. Burr, Republican, North Carolina

Chair, House Permanent Select Committee on Intelligence (HPSCI)

1977–1985   Edward P. Boland, Democrat, Massachusetts
1985–1987   Lee H. Hamilton, Democrat, Indiana
1987–1989   Louis Stokes, Democrat, Ohio
1989–1991   Anthony C. Beilenson, Democrat, California
1991–1993   Dave McCurdy, Democrat, Oklahoma
1993–1995   Dan Glickman, Democrat, Kansas
1995–1997   Larry Combest, Republican, Texas
1997–2004   Porter J. Goss, Republican, Florida
2004–2006   Peter Hoekstra, Republican, Michigan
2006–2011   Silvestre Reyes, Democrat, Texas
2011–2014   Mike Rogers, Republican, Michigan
2015–   Devin Nunes, Republican, California

Appendix C

THE INTELLIGENCE OVERSIGHT ACT OF 1980

Title V of the National Security Act of 1947, 50 USC 413

Accountability for Intelligence Activities

Congressional Oversight*

Sec. 501. (a) To the extent consistent with all applicable authorities and duties, including those conferred by the Constitution upon the executive and legislative branches of the Government, and to the extent consistent with due regard for the protection from unauthorized disclosure of classified information and information relating to intelligence sources and methods, the Director of Central Intelligence and the heads of all departments, agencies, and other entities of the United States involved in intelligence activities shall—

    (1) keep the Select Committee on Intelligence of the Senate and the Permanent Select Committee on Intelligence of the House of Representatives (hereinafter in this section referred to as the "intelligence committees") fully and currently informed of all intelligence activities which are the responsibility of, are engaged in by, or are carried out for or on behalf of, any department, agency, or entity of the United States, including any significant anticipated intelligence activity, except that (A) the foregoing provision shall not require approval of the intelligence committees as a condition precedent to the initiation of any such anticipated intelligence activity, and (B) if the President determines it is essential to limit prior notice to meet extraordinary circumstances affecting vital interests of the United States, such notice shall be limited to the chairmen and ranking

minority members of the intelligence committees, the Speaker and minority leader of the House of Representatives, and the majority and minority leaders of the Senate;

(2) furnish any information or material concerning intelligence activities which is in the possession, custody, or control of any department, agency, or entity of the United States and which is requested by either of the intelligence committees in order to carry out its authorized responsibilities; and

(3) report in a timely fashion to the intelligence committees any illegal intelligence activity or significant intelligence failure and any corrective action that has been taken or is planned to be taken in connection with such illegal activity or failure.

(b) The President shall fully inform the intelligence committees in a timely fashion of intelligence operations in foreign countries, other than activities intended solely for obtaining necessary intelligence, for which prior notice was not given under subsection (a) and shall provide a statement of the reasons for not giving prior notice.

(c) The President and the intelligence committees shall each establish such procedures as may be necessary to carry out the provisions of subsections (a) and (b).

(d) the House of Representatives and the Senate, in consultation with the Director of Central Intelligence, shall each establish, by rule or resolution of such House, procedures to protect from unauthorized disclosure all classified information and all information relating to intelligence sources and the methods furnished to the intelligence committees or to Members of the Congress under this section. In accordance with such procedures, each of the intelligence committees shall promptly call to the attention of its respective House, or to any appropriate committee or committees of its respective House, any matter relating to intelligence activities requiring the attention of such House or such committee or committees.

(e) Nothing in this Act shall be construed as authority to withhold information from the intelligence committees on the grounds that providing the information to the intelligence committees would constitute the unauthorized disclosure of classified information or information relating to intelligence sources and methods.

*This act is less formally known by government officials as the 1980 Intelligence Oversight Act.

NOTES

Introduction

1. George Orwell, *1984* (London: Secker & Warburg, 1949).
2. For my account of the Church Committee investigation, see Loch K. Johnson, *A Season of Inquiry: The Senate Intelligence Investigation* (Lexington: University Press of Kentucky, 1985), republished with a new introduction and postscript as *A Season of Inquiry Revisited: The Church Committee Confronts America's Spy Agencies* (Lawrence: University Press of Kansas, 2015).
3. For the Richard Harris quote, see his "Reflections: Secrets," *New Yorker* (April 10, 1978), p. 84. Le Carré has put the core question of intelligence accountability this way: "how far can we go in the rightful defense of our Western values without abandoning them along the way?" "Fifty Years Later," a foreword to a new edition of John le Carré, *The Spy Who Came in from the Cold* (New York: Penguin, 2013), p. xiv.
4. See David Cole and James X. Dempsey, *Terrorism and the Constitution* (New York: New Press, 2006); Louis Fisher, *Defending Congress and the Constitution* (Lawrence: University Press of Kansas, 2001); and Richard A. Posner, *Not a Suicide Pact: The Constitution in a Time of National Emergency* (New York: Oxford University Press, 2006).
5. Fred F. Manget, essay, in Mark Phythian, ed., "An INS Special Forum: The US Senate Select Committee Report on the CIA's Detention and Interrogation Program," *Intelligence and National Security* 31/1 (January 2016), p. 20.
6. Quoted in Richard D. Lyons, "Schorr Relieved of Duties by CBS," *New York Times* (February 24, 1976), p. A1.
7. Dean Rusk, as told to Richard Rusk and edited by Daniel S. Papp, *As I Saw It* (New York: Norton, 1990), p. 557.
8. *Knauff v. Schaughnessy*, 338 U.S. 537, 551 (1950). I am grateful to constitutional scholar Louis Fisher for bringing this case to my attention.
9. Martin Petersen, "Questions about the War on the Terrorists," *Washington Times* (February 22, 2015), A18.
10. Eric Lichtblau and Katie Benner, "As Apple Resists, Encryption Fray Erupts in Battle," *New York Times* (February 18, 2016), p. A1.
11. Michael D. Shear, "Obama Calls for Law Enforcement Access in Encryption Fight," *New York Times* (March 12, 2016), p. A1.
12. Matt Apuzzo, "Messaging App Is Latest Front in Tech Debated," *New York Times* (March 13, 2016), p. A1.
13. William J. Bratton, the City's police commissioner, and John J. Miller, the deputy commissioner for counterterrorism and intelligence, "Why Apple Should Unlock an iPhone," *New York Times* (February 23, 2016), p. A27.
14. Mike McPhate, "Gates Says Government Must Find a Balance on Privacy," *New York Times* (February 24, 2016), p. B4.

15. Ibid.
16. Nicole Perlroth, "Digital Security Experts Find Unlikely Allies, in Ex-Officials," *New York Times* (March 5, 2016), p. B1.
17. Michael D. Shear and David E. Sanger, "Apple Battle Bares Fissure in U.S. Policy," *New York Times* (March 6, 2016), p. A1.
18. Eric Lichtblau and Joseph Goldstein, "Justice Dept. Wants Apple to Unlock More Phones," *New York Times* (February 24, 2016), p. B1.
19. The quotes from Bankston and Schiff are reported by Michael D. Shear, "Torn, but Obama Nods to Security," *New York Times* (February 20, 2016), p. B5.
20. Quoted in Cecilia Kang and Eric Lichtblau, "F.B.I. Error Prompted Lockdown of iPhone," *New York Times* (March 2, 2015), p. B1.
21. Quoted by Michael D. Shear, David E. Sanger, and Katie Benner, "iPhone Battle Strikes Nerve," *New York Times* (March 14, 2016), p. A1.
22. Ron L. Meyers, New York, "Letters," *New York Times* (March 20, 2016), p. SR10.
23. Quoted by Cecilia Kang, "A Tug of War over Data Security Intensifies in the Nation's Capital," *New York Times* (May 9, 2016), p. B6.
24. Eric Lichtblau, "Security Czars on Apple's Side in Privacy War," *New York Times* (April 23, 2016), p. A1 (quote at p. B2). The cost for this outside help exceeded $1 million ("NewsHour," *PBS Television* [April 23, 2016]).
25. Scott Shane, Matthew Rosenberg, and Andrew W. Lehren, "Documents Said to Reveal Hacking Secrets of C.I.A.," *New York Times* (March 8, 2017), p. A1. *Times* reporters concluded that, according to the WikiLeaks documents, the CIA had already "found security flaws [in smartphones and other communications equipment], kept them secret and then used them for surveillance and intelligence gathering" (Steve Lohr and Katie Benner, "How Worried Should You Be about Your Phone, Computer or TV?" *New York Times* [March 8, 2017]), p. A10).
26. Wesley Wark, "C-51 and the Canadian Security and Intelligence Community: Finding the Balance for Security and Rights Protections," in Edward Iacobucci and Stephen Toope, eds., *After the Paris Attacks: Responses in Canada, Europe and around the Globe* (Toronto: University of Toronto Press, 2015).
27. Binyamin Appelbaum, "A Nobel Winner on Net Neutrality, Amazon and More," *New York Times* (October 15, 2014), p. B3. In just one of many examples of what can happen when regulations and accountability operate poorly, two critics of the U.S. automobile industry report that there were more than fifty million vehicles recalled in 2014. They note that "when regulators sleep and auto companies place profits over safety, safety defects pile up" (Clarence Ditlow and Ralph Nader, "Weak Oversight, Deadly Cars," *New York Times* [October 29, 2014], p. A23). A noble example of the value to society that a persistent quest for accountability can yield is the work of government overseer Dr. Frances Oldham Kelsey. Formerly a family doctor and teacher in South Dakota, she stood up fearlessly to powerful corporate interests as she gathered evidence for the Food and Drug Administration in the 1960s. Her focus was on a drug best known by its generic name, thalidomide, which was causing thousands of babies in Europe, North America, and the Middle East to be born with flipperlike arms and legs, as well as other defects. "Her exceptional judgment in evaluating a new drug for safety for human use has prevented a major tragedy of birth deformities in the United States," said President John F. Kennedy at a White House ceremony honoring her achievement (see Robert D. McFadden, "An F.D.A. Stickler Who Saved U.S. Babies from Thalidomide," *New York Times* [August 8, 2015], p. A1).
28. Quoted by Attorney General Robert Kennedy, speech, Law Day, University of Georgia School of Law, Athens, Georgia (May 6, 1961).
29. See, for instance, *Report of the Commission on Protecting and Reducing Government Secrecy* (Moynihan Report, chaired by Senator Daniel Patrick Moynihan, D, New York), Senate Document 105-2, 103rd Congress (Washington, DC: U.S. Government Printing Office, 1997). See also, Frederic A. O. Schwarz, Jr., *Democracy in the Dark: The Seduction of Government Secrecy* (New York: New Press, 2015).
30. Jack Anderson, "How the CIA Snooped inside Russia," *Washington Post* (December 10, 1973), p. B17.

31. Ben Bradlee, *A Good Life: Newspapering and Other Adventures* (New York: Simon & Schuster, 1995), pp. 323, 433, 453–486.
32. *New York Times Co. v. United States*, 403 US 713, 751 (1971).
33. James B. Stockdale, *In Love and War* (New York: Bantam, 1985), p. 17. See also John Prados, "Essay: 40th Anniversary of the Gulf of Tonkin Incident," National Security Archive, Washington, D.C. (August 4, 2004); and Robert J. Hanyok, "Skunks, Bogies, Silent Hounds, and the Flying Fish: The Gulf of Tonkin Mystery, 2–4 August 1964," *Cryptologic Quarterly* (declassified by the NSA on November 3, 2005).
34. Lincoln Caplan, "Leaks and Consequences," *American Scholar* (August 2013), pp. 20–31, quote at p. 31.
35. Richard A. Clarke, quoted by Sean Deuby, "Richard Clarke at RSA Conference," *Windows IT Pr.com* (February 26, 2014). An expert on the Constitution has noted plainly that "when you don't feel safe, democracy is hard" (Akhil Reed Amar, Sterling Professor of Law and Political Science, Yale University, "The Constitution at a Crossroads," lecture, University of Georgia, Athens, Georgia [September 16, 2016]).
36. Quoted in Karen Korematsu, "When Lies Overruled Rights," *New York Times* (February 18, 2017), p. A21.
37. The widely admired secretary of state at the time, former general Colin Powell, told the United Nations that, based on the "solid intelligence" he was receiving, he could report that Iraq was engaged in a robust WMD program. Several years later he wrote in a memoir that the errors in his speech to the UN were "a blot, a failure, that will always be attached to me" (Colin Powell, with Tony Koltz, *It Worked for Me: In Life and Leadership* [New York: Harper, 2012], p. 223).
38. On the Church Committee, see (in addition to *A Season of Inquiry Revisited*, op. cit.) my "Congressional Supervision of America's Secret Agencies: The Experience and Legacy of the Church Committee," *Public Administration Review* 64 (January 2004), pp. 3–14; and Frederick A. O. Schwarz, Jr., and Aziz Z. Huq, *Unchecked and Unbalanced: Presidential Power in a Time of Terror* (New York: Free Press, 2007). For the other two intelligence investigations of 1975 (examined in chapter 3), see the study on the Pike Committee: J. Leiper Freeman, "Investigating the Executive Intelligence: The Fate of the Pike Committee," *Capitol Studies* 5 (Fall 1977), pp. 103–117; for commentary of the Rockefeller Commission, see Daniel Schorr, *Clearing the Air* (New York: Houghton Mifflin, 1977); and, generally for this era, Frank J. Smist, Jr., *Congress Oversees the United States Intelligence Community, 1947–1989* (Knoxville: University of Tennessee Press, 1990).
39. See Dr. Ray Cline, a former deputy director for Intelligence, "Should the CIA Fight Secret Wars?" *Harpers* (September 1984) (a roundtable discussion with national security experts), p. 39.
40. Author's notes of remarks made by Dr. Ray Cline, "Controlling Intelligence," a panel at the annual meeting of the American Political Science Association, Chicago, Illinois (September 6, 1987), original emphasis. A well-regarded former British intelligence officer similarly recalls that ministerial approvals and legal considerations often gave him and his colleagues—even though they understood the need for regulations—a sense that the "procedures [were] designed to turn our sprint into a hurdle race" (Michael Herman, an inaugural interview by Mark Phythian for the "Profiles in Intelligence" series, *Intelligence and National Security* 7 [December 2016], p. 4).
41. James Q. Wilson, "Reducing Discord over Foreign Policy," *New York Times* (December 24, 1986), p. A25.
42. Vice Admiral John M. Poindexter, testimony, U.S. Senate Select Committee on Secret Military Assistance to Iran and the Nicaraguan Opposition and U.S. House of Representatives Select Committee to Investigate Covert Arms Transactions with Iran (the Inouye-Hamilton Committees), *Hearings*, vol. 8, 100th Cong., 1st Sess., Washington, D.C. (1987), p. 159. On the National Security Council, see Karl F. Inderfurth and Loch K. Johnson, eds., *Fateful Decisions: Inside the National Security Council* (New York: Oxford University Press, 2004).
43. 9/11 Commission, *Final Report of the National Commission on Terrorist Attacks upon the United States* (New York: Norton, 2004), p. 420.
44. Jose A. Rodriguez, "Don't We Want to Stop Terrorism?" *Washington Post* (December 12, 2014), p. B1.

45. Executive Summary, *Committee Study of the Central Intelligence Agency's Detention and Interrogation Program*, Senate Select Committee on Intelligence, U.S. Senate, Washington, D.C. (December 14, 2014).

46. Loch K. Johnson, "Supervising America's Secret Foreign Policy: A Shock Theory of Congressional Oversight for Intelligence," in David P. Forsythe, Patrice C. McMahon, and Andrew Wedeman, eds., *American Foreign Policy in a Globalized World* (New York: Routledge, 2006), pp. 173–192.

47. See Bruce D. Berkowitz and Jeffrey T. Richelson, "The CIA Vindicated," *National Interest* 41 (Fall 1995), pp. 36–47; "An Evaluation of the CIA's Analysis of Soviet Economic Performance, 1970–1990," Report, Permanent Select Committee on Intelligence, U.S. House of Representatives, 102nd Cong., 1st Sess., Washington, D.C. (November 18, 1991); Loch K. Johnson, *Secret Agencies: U.S. Intelligence in a Hostile World* (New Haven, CT: Yale University Press, 1996), pp. 187–193; David M. Kennedy, "Sunshine and Shadow: The CIA and the Soviet Economy," Kennedy School of Government, Harvard University, Case Program No. C16-91-1096.0, Cambridge, MA (1991); and Kirsten Lundberg, "CIA and the Fall of the Soviet Empire: The Politics of 'Getting It Right,'" Kennedy School of Government, Harvard University, Case Program No. C16-94-125.1, Cambridge, MA (1994).

48. Letter to me from Representative Wyche Fowler, Jr. (D, Georgia), Washington, D.C. (February 18, 1985).

49. Reported by Steven Aftergood, *Secrecy News*, FAS [Federation of American Scientists; hereafter FAS] Project on Government Secrecy 2004/90 (October 14, 2004).

50. Mark Mazzetti and Matt Apuzzo, "Saudis, the C.I.A. and the Arming of Syrian Rebels," *New York Times* (January 24, 2016), p. A1.

51. This is a phrase Churchill used during a speech before the House of Commons that criticized governmental sleight-of-hand in the United Kingdom (*Hansard*, February 22, 1906, p. 555).

52. Outside of the specialized scholarly periodicals on intelligence (see the bibliography), the literature published on this subject by leading political science journals is, given the significance of intelligence in the making of foreign-policy decisions, oddly thin. The *American Political Science Review*, for instance, has published only one article on intelligence (about analysis) since the journal's founding in 1906. Nor has the *APSR* published a single article on climate change or global warming, which says more about the state of the discipline of political science than about the importance of these topics. See Amanda Goodall and Andrew Oswald, "Do the Social Sciences Need a Shake-Up?" *Times Higher Education,* United Kingdom (October 9, 2014); and Amy B. Zegart, "Cloaks, Daggers, and Ivory Towers: Why Political Science Professors Don't Study U.S. Intelligence," in Loch K. Johnson, ed., *Essential of Intelligence* (Santa Barbara, CA: Praeger Security International, 2015), pp. 31–48.

Chapter 1

1. Lee H. Hamilton and Jordan Tama, *A Creative Tension: The Foreign Policy Roles of the President and Congress* (Washington, DC: Woodrow Wilson Center Press, 2002), p. 56. Hamilton has also observed that "oversight is designed to look into every nook and cranny of governmental affairs, expose misconduct, and shine the light of publicity on it. Oversight can protect the country from the imperial presidency and from bureaucratic arrogance" (Lee H. Hamilton, "Oversight vs. Glitzy Investigation," *Christian Science Monitor* [July 15, 1999], p. 11).

2. Remark to the author, cited in Loch K. Johnson, *The Threat on the Horizon: An Inside Account of America's Search for Security after the Cold War* (New York: Oxford University Press, 2011), p. 201. Columnist Maureen Dowd, discussing the problem of the former NBC News anchor Brian Williams (fired from NBC and now with CNN) and his occasional tendency to inflate his own biography, quotes an NBC News reporter about the scandal: "There was no one around to pull his chain when he got too over-the-top" ("Anchors Aweigh," *New York Times* [February 8, 2015], p. Wk. 11). That is an accountability responsibility of government overseers as well: pulling the chain on overzealous or lax bureaucrats when necessary.

3. Writing about intelligence oversight in Germany, a legal scholar in that nation remarks that "the lawfulness of intelligence operations is the main criterion of oversight," adding that an additional important objective of overseers is to ensure "the usefulness of intelligence

activities" (Jan-Hendrik Dietrich, "Of Toothless Windbags, Blind Guardians and Blunt Swords: The Ongoing Controversy about the Reform of Intelligence Services Oversight in Germany," *Intelligence and National Security* 31/3 [April 2016], pp. 397–415, quotes at pp. 399, 400). These are universal standards for the conduct of intelligence accountability in the democracies.

4. This Court is known also, especially in some law journals, as the FIS Court or simply FISC.
5. David S. Cohen, speech, "Governing Intelligence" Conference, Center on Law and Security, NYU School of Law (April 21, 2016), Washington, D.C.
6. Joel D. Aberbach, *Keeping a Watchful Eye: The Politics of Congressional Oversight* (Washington, DC: Brookings Institution, 1990), p. 2.
7. On the Snowden leaks in 2013, see Loch K. Johnson, ed., "An *INS* Special Forum: Implications of the Snowden Leaks," *Intelligence and National Security* 29 (December 2014), pp. 793–810; and on other recent leakers: Matt Apuzzo, "Letter Calls Plea Deal for Retired General Petraeus a 'Profound Double Standard,'" *New York Times* (March 16, 2015), p. A14.
8. Steven Aftergood, "A New IC Award for 'Reporting Wrongdoing,'" *Secrecy News*, FAS (September 26, 2016), p. 1.
9. Jane Mayer, "Torture and the Truth," *New Yorker* (December 22 and 29, 2014), p. 43.
10. Remarks, Dick Cheney, Fox Television *Evening News* (December 10, 2014).
11. Amy Zegart and Julie Quinn, "Congressional Intelligence Oversight: The Electoral Disconnection," *National Security and Intelligence* 25/6 (December 2010), pp. 744–766.
12. The former FBI Task Force leader on the Church Committee staff, John T. Elliff, has put it this way: "Before the Church Committee [in 1975], Congress was blind" (in Katherine Scott, ed., *Oral History Interviews, Church Committee*, U.S. Senate Historical Office, Washington, D.C. [February 21, 2014], p. 110). Intelligence scholar Anne Daugherty Miles has observed, "Quiet, behind the scenes oversight happens constantly. Most is at the staff level" ("Congressional Oversight of the U.S. Intelligence Community [IC]: Who Does What?" paper, International Studies Association, annual meeting, New Orleans [March 2014], p. 43). One example: in 2016, SSCI staffers began to review each CIA drone strike overseas (Ken Dilanian, "Secret Dispute over Whether CIA Drones Should Be Killing ISIS Targets," *NBC News Investigations* [March 24, 2016]). While some forms of "quiet oversight" took place before 1975 (see David M. Barrett, *The Congress and the CIA* [Lawrence: University Press of Kansas, 2005]), since that year it has occurred more continually and with a much larger number of congressional staffers involved.
13. I based these observations on a matching up of a chair's state with a description from the *New York Times* of which states lean more conservative or more moderate (presented in that newspaper by Nate Cohn and Josh Keller [February 3, 2016], p. A1); my thanks to my undergraduate assistant, Zachery Hawkins, for the data about regional representation on the committees over the years.
14. M. D. McCubbins and T. Schwartz, "Congressional Oversight Overlooked: Police Patrols and Fire Alarms," *American Journal of Political Science* 28 (1984), pp. 165–179, quote at 166.
15. Morris S. Ogul and Bert A. Rockman, "Overseeing Oversight: New Departures and Old Problems, *Legislative Studies Quarterly* 15 (2003), p. 14.
16. Aberbach, op. cit., p. 98.
17. Ibid.
18. The GAO has had a long history of competence in the investigation of cost overruns and other questionable activities in the executive branch, and it has occasionally assisted the Congress with intelligence inquiries; for the most part, though, SSCI and HPSCI have resisted its "intrusion" into "their" territory—an unfortunate posture of turf protection on Capitol Hill that undermines the use of an important asset that could help the intelligence oversight committees with their staggering review responsibilities. In a helpful new direction, the Office of the Director of National Intelligence issued Intelligence Community Directive 114 in 2014. This document grants the GAO authorized access to intelligence in certain domains, such as gathering data on the IC's contractor workforce (a project assigned to the GAO by the Senate's Homeland Security and Governmental Affairs Committee). The principal deputy director of the ODNI, Stephanie O'Sullivan, constructively observed that she welcomed these "outside eyes" to help her office "find problems" (quoted in *Secrecy News*, FAS 2016/26 [March 22, 2016], p. 3).

19. Morris S. Ogul, *Congress Oversees the Bureaucracy: Studies in Legislative Supervision* (Pittsburgh: University of Pittsburgh Press, 1976), p. 159.

20. Frank Smist, Jr., *Congress Oversees the United States Intelligence Community*, 2nd ed. (Knoxville: University of Tennessee Press, 1994).

21. Author's interview with C. Mellon, a SSCI staffer, Washington, D.C. (February 5, 2003).

22. Aberbach, op. cit., p. 123.

23. Johnson, *Threat on the Horizon*, op. cit.

24. For an optimistic viewpoint, see R. L. Calvert, M. D. McCubbins, and B. R. Weingast, "A Theory of Political Control and Agency Discretion," *American Journal of Political Science* 33 (1989), pp. 588–611; and, on the more pessimist side, D. B. Spence, "Agency Policy Making and Political Control: Modeling Away the Delegation Problem," *Journal of Public Administration Research and Theory* 2 (1997), pp. 199–219.

25. John F. Bibby, "Congress; Neglected Function," in Melvin R. Laird, ed., *The Republican Papers* (New York: Anchor, 1968), p. 477.

26. "Committee Reform Amendments of 1974," Committee on Committees [the Bolling Committee], U.S. House of Representatives, *H. Rept. 93-916*, 93rd Cong., 2nd Sess. (1974), p. 62.

27. Ogul, op. cit., pp. 183–186.

28. Aberbach, op. cit., p. 118.

29. Loch K. Johnson, "Playing Ball with the CIA: Congress Supervises Strategic Intelligence," in Paul E. Peterson, ed., *Congress, the Executive, and the Making of American Foreign Policy* (Norman: University of Oklahoma Press, 1994), pp. 49–73.

30. Quoted in F. Davis, "GOP-Controlled Senate Expected to Give Less Scrutiny to War on Terror," *Miami Herald* (November 7, 2002), p. A1.

31. Quoted in Renee Schoof, "Richard Burr, Incoming Head of Senate Intelligence, Plans Scrutiny of CIA," *McClatchy* (December 13, 2014).

32. Aberbach, op. cit., p. 213.

33. Christopher J. Deering, "Alarms and Patrols: Legislative Oversight in Foreign and Defense Policy," in C. C. Campbell, N. C. Rae, and J. F. Stack, Jr., eds., *Congress and the Politics of Foreign Policy* (Upper Saddle River, NJ: Prentice Hall, 2003), pp. 112–138, quote at 135.

34. Anthony Madonna and Ian Ostrander, "If Congress Keeps Cutting Its Staff, Who Is Writing Your Laws? You Won't Like the Answer," *Monkey Cage Newsletter, Washington Post Blog* (August 20, 2015). A recent study from the Brookings Institution traces the steady decline in staff numbers on Capitol Hill from 1975 to 2015 (see Curtlyn Kramer, "Vital Stats: Congress Has a Staffing Problem, Too," *Brookings Blog* [May 24, 2017]).

35. Dean Rusk, as told to Richard Rusk and edited by Daniel S. Papp, *As I Saw It* (New York: Norton, 1990), pp. 554–555.

36. See Karl F. Inderfurth and Loch K. Johnson, *Fateful Decisions: Inside the National Security Council* (New York: Oxford University Press, 2004).

37. See Malcolm Byrne, *Iran-Contra: Reagan's Scandal and the Unchecked Abuse of Presidential Power* (Lawrence: University Press of Kansas, 2014).

38. "Inquiry Shows Secret Aid to Many Foreign Leaders," *New York Times* (January 26, 1976), p. A1, citing findings from the House Select Committee on Intelligence (the Pike Committee).

39. Michael J. Glennon, *National Security and Double Government* (New York: Oxford University Press, 2015), p. 7.

40. See Kenneth Michael Absher, Michael C. Desch, and Roman Popadiuk, *Privileged and Confidential: The Secret History of the President's Intelligence Advisory Board* (Lexington: University Press of Kentucky, 2012).

41. My interview with a senior SSCI staffer, Washington, D.C. (June 5, 2015). See Nadia Hilliard, *The Accountability State: US Federal Inspectors General and the Pursuit of Democratic Integrity* (Lawrence: University Press of Kansas, 2017).

42. My interview, Washington, D.C. (June 6, 2015).

43. Steven Aftergood, "Intelligence Whistleblower Law Has Been Used Infrequently," *Secrecy News*, FAS, 2014/25 (March 27, 2014), pp. 1–2.

44. Steven Aftergood, "IC Inspector General Oversees the Intelligence Community," *Secrecy News*, FAS 2014/81 (December 3, 2014), pp. 2, 3.

45. John Goldsmith, *The Terror Presidency: Law and Judgment inside the Bush Administration* (New York: Norton, 2007), p. 33.

46. David E. Sanger and Mark Landler, "Obama's Latest View on Secrecy Overlooks Past Prosecution of Leaks," *New York Times* (April 12, 2016), p. A14.

47. "Punishing Leaks through Administrative Channels," *Secrecy News*, FAS 2016/39 (May 3, 2016), pp. 1–2.

48. PCLOB, *Report on the Telephone Records Program Conducted under Section 215 of the USA PATRIOT Act and on the Operations of the Foreign Intelligence Surveillance Court* (January 23, 2014), p. 184.

49. Quoted by Charlie Savage, "Limits on Privacy Board Face Challenge in Senate," *New York Times* (July 15, 2016), p. A13.

50. Senator Ron Wyden (D, Oregon), quoted in *Secrecy News*, FAS (June 20, 2016), p. 2.

51. Steven Aftergood and Rep. Rush Holt (D, New Jersey), "The House Committee on Intelligence Needs Oversight of Its Own," *MSNBC Television* op-ed (May 30, 2014). For an inventory of several oversight entities within the NSA with the sole mission of scrutinizing the propriety of the agency's activities, see Margo Schlanger, "Intelligence Legalism and the National Security Agency's Civil Liberties Gap," *Harvard National Security Journal* 6 (January 2015), pp. 112–205. While having robust internal oversight is important, sometimes— indeed, some of the most important times—a questionable operation is so tightly held that only the top tier in an organization knows about it and all the oversight entities in the building become irrelevant. Examples: DCI William J. Casey's running of the Iran-contra affair from Langley's seventh floor; and General Michael V. Hayden and his general counsel running STELLARWIND, an illegal sigint surveillance program, from their NSA offices (see, respectively, Malcolm Byrne, *Iran-Contra: Reagan's Scandal and the Unchecked Abuse of Presidential Power* [Lawrence: University Press of Kansas, 2014]; and Michael V. Hayden, *Playing to the Edge: American Intelligence in the Age of Terror* [New York: Penguin, 2016], p. 77).

52. "ISOO Director Fitzpatrick Moves to NSC," *Secrecy News*, FAS 2016/4 (January 11, 2016).

53. Steven Aftergood, "Fixing Pre-Publication Review: What Should Be Done?" *Just Security Blog* (January 15, 2016).

54. See, for example, Jack Goldsmith and Oona A. Hathaway, "The Government's Prepublication Review Process Is Broken," *Washington Post Blog* (December 25, 2015), who conclude that the system is "too expansive, slow and susceptible to abuse" and "an intolerable cost to our democracy." They acknowledge that the "government must be able to keep its secrets, but First Amendment values also matter"—another balancing act for democracies in the domain of national security. Also Richard H. Immerman, *The Hidden Hand: A Brief History of the CIA* (New York: John Wiley, 2014), pp. xii–xv; and Johnson, *Threat on the Horizon*, op. cit., pp. xx–xxi.

55. *New York Times Co. v. United States* (403 U.S. 713). On contemporary Justice Department national security prosecutions, see Matt Apuzzo, "New Rules for National Security Prosecutions after Missteps," *New York Times* (April 27, 2016), p. A14, which notes that "all cases affecting national security, even tangentially, now require coordination and oversight in Washington."

56. See, respectively, Frank Snepp, *Irreparable Harm* (New York: Random House, 1999); and Allan A. Ryan, *The 9/11 Terror Cases: Constitutional Challenges in the War against Al Qaeda* (Lawrence: University Press of Kansas, 2015).

57. Dietrich, op. cit., p. 404.

58. "There is nothing surprising about the fact that the Foreign Intelligence Surveillance Court has overwhelmingly approved the surveillances that have come to them," says a former Church Committee staff attorney. "The agencies know enough not to be testing the limit. They don't want a record of being turned down and being accused of being 'rogue elephants' " (Frederick D. Barron, in Scott, ed., *Oral History Interviews*, op. cit. [May 28, 2015], p. 34).

59. Glennon, op. cit., p. 104. Ohio State University law professor Peter M. Shane has referred to the FISA Court as "typically deferential to the Justice Department's statutory and constitutional arguments" ("The NSA and the Legal Regime for Foreign Intelligence Surveillance," *I/S: A Journal of Law and Policy for the Information Society*, [2014], p. 285). Another study concludes that the court "currently operates more closely to an executive adjunct," not an

objective, independent judiciary body—a "rubber stamp on behalf of government programs [rather] than a neutral check against executive overreach" (Walter F. Mondale, Robert A. Stein, and Caitlinrose Fisher, "No Longer a Neutral Magistrate: The Foreign Intelligence Surveillance Court in the Wake of the War on Terror," *Minnesota Law Review* 100/6 [June 2016], pp. 2291, 2294).

60. My interview with Judge Morris S. "Buzz" Arnold, Little Rock, Arkansas (November 26, 2014), who served on the FISA Appeals Court from 2008 to 2013. My thanks to Al Gates for arranging this interview.

61. James Risen and Eric Lichtblau, "Bush Lets U.S. Spy on Callers without Courts," *New York Times* (December 16, 2005), p. A1.

62. Elizabeth Goitein and Faiza Patel, "What Went Wrong with the FISA Court," Brennan Center for Justice, New York University School of Law, www.brennancenter.org/ (2015).

63. Charlie Savage and Jonathan Weisman, "N.S.A. Collection of Bulk Call Data Is Ruled Illegal," *New York Times* (May 8, 2015), p. A1.

64. See Louis Fisher, "Rethinking the State Secrets Privilege," in Loch K. Johnson, ed., *The Oxford Handbook of National Security Intelligence* (New York: Oxford University Press, 2010), pp. 657–672. Fisher was the research director of the House Iran-Contra Committee in 1986–1987.

65. Quoted in Matt Apuzzo and Al Baker, "Sued over Spying, New York Police Get Oversight," *New York Times* (January 8, 2016), p. A1.

66. Claudia Hillebrand, "Intelligence Oversight and Accountability," in Robert Dover, Michael S. Goodman, and Claudia Hillebrand, eds., *Routledge Companion to Intelligence Studies* (London: Routledge, 2014), pp. 305–312. See also Glenn Hastedt, "Washington Politics, Homeland Security, and the Struggle against Global Terrorism," in Loch K. Johnson, ed., *Essentials of Strategic Intelligence* (Santa Barbara, CA: Praeger Security International, 2015), pp. 387–416.

67. See Katherine A. Scott, *Reining in the State: Civil Society and Congress in the Vietnam and Watergate Eras* (Lawrence: University Press of Kansas, 2013).

68. The Poitras phrase is from Sarah Lyall, "The Art of Surveillance," *New York Times* (January 31, 2016), p. AR3. See also Mike Lofgren, *The Deep State: The Fall of the Constitution and the Rise of a Shadow Government* (New York: Viking, 2016), whose definition of a "deep state" is wider than just the intelligence community, but whose perspective is close to Poitras's: the government is driven by national security concerns and tilted strongly toward executive power. On the matter of how many entities should be involved in intelligence accountability, Australia intelligence scholar Patrick Walsh (among others) believes the U.S. approach involves too many institutions, with the result of a fragmented effort that clouds who exactly is in charge. He prefers the Australian model, where such authority is lodged with the Inspector General for Intelligence and Security (IGIS), who has sweeping powers to investigate wrongdoing, including the right to issue subpoenas for witnesses and documents (email communication from Professor Walsh to me [August 8, 2014]). Just the opposite argument might be applied to IGIS, however: that it is too small an institution to properly monitor Australia's sizable intelligence community—although it certainly does have the virtue of pinpointing ultimate responsibility for intelligence supervision, as Walsh emphasizes. In between the examples of the United States (which has the most intelligence oversight entities of any nation by far—a separate question from how successfully they perform) and Australia is a range of approaches, with Canada, the United Kingdom, and Germany among those who take the matter seriously and have established credible oversight review panels. France has yet to provide its parliament with such duties, and a report on Dutch intelligence oversight indicates a relatively passive approach (Constant Hijzen, "More Than a Ritual Dance: The Dutch Practice of Parliamentary Oversight and Control of the Intelligence Community," *Security and Human Rights* [2013], pp. 227–238). For comparative perspectives on intelligence supervision, see James Burch, "A Domestic Intelligence Agency for the United States? A Comparative Analysis of Domestic Intelligence Agencies and Their Implications for Homeland Security," *Homeland Security Affairs* 3 (June 2007), pp. 1–16; and Hans Born, Ian Leigh, and Loch K. Johnson, *Who's Watching the Spies? Establishing Intelligence Service Accountability* (Washington, DC: Potomac Books, 2005). For an argument that the CIA "is the most open secret organization in the world . . . scrutinized by more organs of accountability than any other intelligence

service," see David Robarge (a CIA historian), "CIA in the Spotlight: The Central Intelligence Agency and Public Accountability," *Journal of Intelligence History* 9/1–2 (2009), pp. 105–112, quote at 105. Like Professor Walsh, Robarge also sees the U.S. system of intelligence accountability as "uniquely fragmented and fractious" (p. 126).

69. See, for example, Loch K. Johnson, *National Security Intelligence: Secret Operations in Defense of the Democracies* (Cambridge: Polity, 2012) and *America's Secret Power: The CIA in a Democratic Society* (New York: Oxford University Press, 1989).

70. Amy Zegart, "September 11 and the Adaptation Failure of U.S. Intelligence Agencies," *International Security* 29/4 (Spring 2005), pp. 78–111.

71. Siobhan Gorman, "NSA Has Higher Profile, New Problems," *Baltimore Sun* (September 8, 2006), p. A1

72. On these intelligence budget figures, see Walter Pincus, "Intelligence Spending at Record $80.1 Billion in First Disclosure of Overall Figure," *Washington Post* (October 28, 2010), p. A1; and a Congressional Research Service report, *Intelligence Spending and Appropriations: Issues for Congress* (September 5, 2013), Library of Congress, Washington, D.C. In the United States, the base annual defense budget—not counting supplements for the wars in Iraq and Afghanistan—increased (in adjusted dollars) from $378 billion in 1998 to $600 billion in 2010 (unsigned editorial, "A Better, Not Fatter, Defense Budget," *New York Times* [May 9, 2016], p. A18]). See also Steven Aftergood, "Intelligence Spending Increased in 2016," *Secrecy News*, FAS (October 31, 2016), p. 3. On party differences regarding support for intelligence activities, see Johnson, "Playing Ball with the CIA," op. cit., pp. 49–73.

73. Philip Johnston, "GCHQ and the License to Eavesdrop," *Daily Telegraph*, London (August 27, 2010), p. A1.

74. Admiral Dennis C. Blair, Director of National Intelligence, media roundtable, Washington, D.C. (September 15, 2009). The documents leaked to the *Washington Post* by Edward Snowden present a much lower personnel number of 107,035 employees in the IC; however, this appears to include only full-time-equivalent (FTE) civilian employees, while Admiral Blair's figure must include military intelligence personnel and perhaps personnel outside the government who are short-term contract employees. See Wilson Andrews and Todd Lindeman, "The Black Budget: An Interactive Graphic," *Washington Post* (August 29, 2013), p. 6.

75. Barton Gellman and Greg Miller, "'Black Budget' Summary Details U.S. Spy Network's Successes, Failures and Objectives," *Washington Post* (August 29, 2013), p. A1.

76. On the "ints," see Mark M. Lowenthal and Robert M. Clark, eds., *The Five Disciplines of Intelligence Collection* (Washington, DC: CQ Press, 2016).

77. David Brooks, "Warren Can Win," *New York Times* (December 16, 2014), p. A25.

78. "Cleaning House," *New York Times Book Review* (March 6, 2016), p. 14.

79. John Sipher, quoted by Ken Dilnian, "Former Spooks Criticize CIA Director John Brennan for Spying Comments," *NBCNews.com* (March 2, 2016). This "stealing" phrase is not appreciated at the CIA, which notes that "it does not do justice to the real work our officers do" (Cohen, "Governing Intelligence," op. cit.).

80. Both 85 percent figures, which have remained steady over the years, are from *Preparing for the 21st Century: An Appraisal of U.S. Intelligence*, Report of the Commission on the Roles and Capabilities of the United States Intelligence Community [the Aspin-Brown Commission] (Washington, DC: U.S. Government Printing Office, March 1, 1996), p. 49.

81. See, for example, James R. Clapper, "Foreword," in *The National Intelligence Strategy of the United States, 2014*, Office of the Director of National Intelligence (Washington, DC, 2014), p. 17. In this document, the DNI noted that it was an important matter of professional ethics to "report wrongdoing through appropriate channels ... [to] remain accountable to ourselves, our oversight institutions, and through those institutions, ultimately to the American people ... [and to be] respectful of privacy and civil liberties" (pp. 3, 13).

82. See Michael Allen, *Blinking Red: Crisis and Compromise in American Intelligence after 9/11* (Washington, DC: Potomac Books, 2013).

83. Steven Aftergood, "DNI Establishes Intelligence Transparency Council," *Secrecy News*, FAS 2016/33 (April 11, 2016), pp. 3–4. Clapper has also led an effort inside the community to bring about secrecy reform, requesting in March 2016 a "fundamental classification guidance

review" designed to hasten the declassification of documents considered sensitive only for a short time; see Steven Aftergood, "DNI Clapper Embraces Review of Secrecy System," *Secrecy News*, FAS 2016/31 (April 6, 2016), pp. 1–2, as well as Sanger and Landler, "Obama's Latest View on Secrecy," op. cit. See also Michael D. Shear, "Clinton Had No Ill Intent on Emails, Obama Says," *New York Times* (April 10, 2016), p. A10.

84. My interview with R. James Woolsey, CIA Headquarters, Langley, Virginia (September 29, 1993).

85. My interview with Adm. Stansfield Turner, at the former DCI's home, McLean, Virginia (May 1, 1991). For vivid descriptions of the admiral's difficulties in trying to manage the CIA, let alone the larger IC, see his *Secrecy and Democracy: The CIA in Transition* (Boston: Houghton Mifflin, 1985). Intelligence scholars Zegart and Quinn have observed that "when senior officials within an intelligence agency have a hard time learning what others in their organization are doing, legislators outside the agency are unlikely to stand a better chance of monitoring activities" ("Congressional Intelligence Oversight: The Electoral Disconnection," *Intelligence and National Security* 26/6 [December 2010], p. 751).

86. David F. Sanger, "Top-Secret Code Released by Hackers Points to Breach at N.S.A.," *New York Times* (August 17, 2016), p. A1.

87. My most recent visit with the OCA staff at Langley occurred on April 28, 2016, and I have interviewed staff in that office on several other occasions since 1975; see, for example, Loch K. Johnson, *Bombs, Bugs, Drugs, and Thugs: Intelligence and America's Quest for Security* (New York: New York University Press, 2000), as well as *Secret Agencies: U.S. Intelligence in a Hostile World* (New Haven, CT: Yale University Press, 1996).

88. This is substantially less engagement with Congress than what the OCA reported to me in 1993, when the figure was 1,512 contacts (Johnson, *Secret Agencies*, op cit., p. 54, based on my interview with the head of that office on April 1, 1994).

89. These data are drawn from Cohen, "Governing Intelligence," op. cit.

90. 462 U.S. 919, 957–59, 967–68, 1002 (1983).

91. Email communication to me (May 9, 2016).

92. Cohen, "Governing Intelligence," op. cit.

93. Edward S. Corwin, *The President: Office and Powers, 1987–1957*, rev. ed. (New York: New York University Press, 1957), p. 171.

94. See Johnson, *Bombs, Bugs, Drugs, and Thugs*, op. cit., ch. 3.

95. Quoted in Ken Dilanian, "CIA's Brennan to Overhaul Spy Agency's Management Structure," *Associated Press* (March 6, 2015).

96. "Information Sharing: U.S. GAO Review of DHS Assessment of Fusion Center Capabilities," Government Accountability Office, GAO-15-155 (November 4, 2014).

97. Dana Priest and William M. Arkin, "A Hidden World, Growing beyond Control," *Washington Post* (July 19, 2010), p. A1, and their "National Security Inc.," *Washington Post* (July 20, 2010), p. A1.

98. *Domestic Security: Confronting a Changing Threat to Ensure Public Safety and Civil Liberties*, Business Executives for National Security (BENS) Task Force, Washington, D.C. (January 2015), with a more expansive list of IC candidates on p. 21.

99. James Risen and Matt Apuzzo, "C.I.A., on Path to Torture, Chose Haste over Analysis," *New York Times* (December 12, 2014), p. A1.

Chapter 2

1. *Hansard* (November 11, 1947), House of Commons, London, England, p. 207.

2. See Edward J. Larson, *The Return of George Washington, 1783–1789* (New York: Morrow/HarperCollins, 2014); and David Robertson, *The Original Compromise: What the Constitution's Framers Were Really Thinking* (New York: Oxford University Press, 2013).

3. Max Farrand, ed., *The Records of the Federal Convention of 1787*, vol. 1 of 4 vols. (New Haven, CT: Yale University Press, 1937), p. 475, cited by Robertson, *The Original Compromise*, op cit., p. 7.

4. See Loch K. Johnson, *American Foreign Policy and the Challenges of World Leadership: Power, Principle, and the Constitution* (New York: Oxford University Press, 2015), ch. 11.

5. Edward J. Larson, remarks to the Folio Book Club, Athens, Georgia (October 30, 2014).

6. James Madison, speech before the Virginia State Constitutional Convention (December 1, 1829), in Kermit L. Hall and Kevin T. McGuire, eds., *The Judicial Branch* (New York: Oxford University Press, 2005), p. 68.

7. Thomas Jefferson, "Draft of the Kentucky Resolutions" (October 1798), in Merrill D. Peterson, ed., *Thomas Jefferson: Writings* (New York: Library of America, 1984), p. 455.

8. John Emerich Edward Dalberg-Acton (Lord Acton), letter to Bishop Mandell Creighton (April 5, 1887), in John Bartlett, *Familiar Quotations*, ed. Emily Morison Beck, 14th ed. (Boston, Little, Brown, 1968), p. 750.

9. James Madison, *Federalist Paper No. 51* (February 8, 1788), reprinted in *The Federalist* (New York: Modern Library, 1937), p. 337.

10. 272 U.S. 52.293 (1926), emphasis added.

11. David Brooks, "President Obama Was Right," *New York Times* (June 6, 2014), p. A23.

12. For a well-written and thoughtful argument that is more pessimistic about how well the Madisonian system of government has worked, see Michael J. Glennon, *National Security and Double Government* (New York: Oxford University Press, 2015).

13. See a classic statement in favor of the Madisonian over the parliamentary system, see Kenneth Waltz, *Foreign Policy and Democratic Politics: The American and British Experience* (New York: Little, Brown, 1967).

14. As described by Jacob S. Hacker and Paul Pierson, "Why Trump Can't Break the G.O.P.," *New York Times* (April 3, 2016), p. SR3.

15. Quoted in Loch K. Johnson, *America's Secret Power: The CIA in a Democratic Society* (New York: Oxford University Press, 1989), p. 10, drawing on the *Final Report*, Select Committee to Study Governmental Operations with Respect to Intelligence Activities (the Church Committee), Sen. Rept. No. 94-755, vol. 1, U.S. Senate, 94th Cong., 2nd Sess. (Washington, DC: U.S. Government Printing Office, 1976), p. 9, citing the *Doolittle Commission Report* (1954).

16. Church Committee, *Final Report*, op. cit., vol. 1, p. 9.

17. In his only public speech as DCI, Richard Helms said, "The nation must to a degree take it on faith that we, too, are honorable men devoted to her service" (quoted in *Profiles in Leadership: Directors of the Central Intelligence Agency and Its Predecessors*, Office of Public Affairs, Central Intelligence Agency [September 2013], p. 48). Another intelligence chief during the Cold War era, William E. Colby, entitled his memoir *Honorable Men: My Life in the CIA* (New York: Simon & Schuster, 1978, with Peter Forbath). James Madison would have blanched at the notion of accepting anything about the activities of powerholders "on faith." Key studies of the Bay of Pigs adventure have chronicled the red flags that accompanied the planning of the invasion, including the muted enthusiasm from the Pentagon, the skepticism of the CIA's Cuban analysts (as opposed to its operations staff in the DO), and the triumph of ambition for promotion over a sober assessment of the chances for success by the top CIA individual leading the effort, Richard B. Bissell, a sailing and social pal of the president's. Despite the widespread reservations outside the CIA's Directorate of Operations, the top appointed national security aides in the Kennedy Administration went along with the proposal—until the covert action disintegrated on the island's beaches in the face of fierce Cuban resistance, just as anticipated by the Agency's ignored Latin American analysts (see Irving L. Janis, *Groupthink*, 2nd ed. [Boston: Houghton Mifflin, 1982]; and Peter Wyden, *Bay of Pigs: The Untold Story* [New York: Simon & Schuster, 1979]).

18. In recent years, the aggregate intelligence budget figure has become a matter of official public record. For the $80.1 billion figure in 2010, see *Secrecy News*, FAS 112 (October 31, 2012), p. 1; and, for the more current figure, Siobhan Gorman, "U.S. Intelligence Spending Rises for First Time since 2011," *Wall Street Journal* (October 31, 2014), p. A1. On the general question of intelligence spending, see Loch K. Johnson and Kevin J. Scheid, "Spending for Spies: Intelligence Budgeting in the Aftermath of the Cold War," *Public Budgeting & Finance* 17 (Winter 1997), pp. 7–27.

19. See Paul R. Erlich, et al., "The Long-Term Biological Consequences of Nuclear War," *Science* 222 (December 23, 1983), pp. 145–149.

20. Public remarks, University of Georgia (April 6, 1992).

21. President Dwight D. Eisenhower, press conference (November 14, 1956), Washington, D.C.

22. Albert D. Wheelon, "CORONA: A Triumph of American Technology," in Dwayne A. Day, John M. Logsdon, and Brian Latell, eds., *Eye in the Sky: The Story of the Corona Spy Satellites* (Washington, DC: Smithsonian Institution Press, 1998), p. 38. I thank intelligence scholar Richard A. Best, Jr., for drawing my attention to this quote.

23. Dean Rusk, as told to Richard Rusk, with editing by Daniel S. Pape, *As I Saw It* (New York: Norton, 1990), p. 237. Unfortunately, this comment leaked to the media, which annoyed Rusk greatly; at this delicate moment in the crisis, he did not want the Soviet leader, Nikita Khrushchev, to feel humiliated by the Americans.

24. The CIA's performance during this period of crisis warrants high praise, although it was hardly perfect. Indeed, the harsh reality of intelligence is that no agency or individual is able to claim that the world has become fully transparent to them or that they are able to flawlessly predict the future ("crystal-gaze," as British intelligence officers put it). In the case of the Cuban missile crisis, CIA analysts initially predicted that the Soviet Union would never be so provocative and foolish as to place nuclear-armed missiles just ninety miles off America's eastern seaboard; further, none of the intelligence agencies were aware (until Soviet archives opened after the Cold War) that the Kremlin had placed over two hundred tactical nuclear warheads on the island before the crisis unfolded and also had Ilyusian bombers sitting on Cuban runways armed with atomic bombs in their cargo hatches. Had the United States invaded the island—the initial plan—these weapons would probably have been used against the American troops, resulting in an upward spiral toward a full-scale nuclear war between the superpowers. While obviously it would have been extremely helpful to know about this other weaponry, the U2 photographs of the bases—along with the gift of knowledge that a fortnight remained before the strategic missiles would be a threat to the United States—was so critical in itself as to be viewed as one of the great accomplishments in the history of the CIA. The bottom line: intelligence consists not just of careful planning and extensive collection activities, but considerable guesswork and luck as well. It can be improved substantially, though, with sufficient financial investment, hard work, ingenuity, and accountability.

25. See Loch K. Johnson, *Bombs, Bugs, Drugs, and Thugs: Intelligence and America's Quest for Security* (New York: New York University Press, 2000).

26. The specifics of this case remain classified, but the broad outline of events was related to me by a senior DO officer, Washington, D.C. (February 20, 1996).

27. My conversation with the former ambassador and U.S. senator, Athens, Georgia (March 20, 2015).

28. Steven Aftergood, "Intel Agencies Have a 'Duty to Warn' Endangered Persons," *Secrecy News*, FAS 2015/54 (August 24, 2015), p. 2.

29. Charlie Savage, "Internal Newsletter Items Detail N.S.A. Employee Life," *New York Times* (May 17, 2016), p. A11.

30. See Hugh Wilford, *The Mighty Wurlitzer: How the CIA Played America* (Cambridge, MA: Harvard University Press, 2008).

31. *Preparing for the 21st Century: An Appraisal of U.S. Intelligence*, Report of the Commission on the Roles and Capabilities of the United States Intelligence Community (Washington, DC: U.S. Government Printing Office, March 1, 1996), p. 13.

32. Richard A. Best, Jr., "Intelligence and U.S. National Security Policy," draft paper (November 2014).

33. Remark to me, Athens, Georgia (May 21, 1983).

34. Robert M. Gates, *From the Shadows* (New York: Simon & Schuster, 1996), p. 560. So reportedly was every agent the CIA ran against North Vietnam during the war in Vietnam (Jeff Stein, "New Vietnam Spy Tale Sheds Light on How the U.S. Lost the War," *Newsweek Online* [April 30, 2015]).

35. On these counterintelligence cases, see Ben Macintyre, *A Spy among Friends: Kim Philby and the Great Betrayal* (New York: Crown, 2014); plus David Wise, *Nightmover* (New York: Random House, 1992), and his *Spy: The Inside Story of How the FBI's Robert Hanssen Betrayed America* (New York: Random House, 2002).

36. See the *9/11 Commission Report* (New York: Norton, 2004). After the 9/11 attacks, the Minnesota-based terrorist (Moussaoui) was arrested, convicted, and is now serving a life sentence in a U.S. prison.

37. See Paul R. Pillar, *Intelligence and U.S. Foreign Policy: Iraq, 9/11, and Misguided Reform* (New York: Columbia University Press, 2011).

38. Janis, *Groupthink*, op. cit., p. 29.

39. See Johnson, *America's Secret Power*, op. cit.

40. See Malcolm Byrne, *Iran-Contra: Reagan's Scandal and the Unchecked Abuse of Presidential Power* (Lawrence: University Press of Kansas, 2014).

41. A remark by Representative Don Edwards (D, California), to the *San Jose Mercury News*, quoted in Adam Clymer, "Don Edwards, Rights Champion in House, Dies at 100," *New York Times* (October 3, 2015), p. A19.

42. Harry Howe Ransom, "Secret Intelligence Agencies and Congress," *Society* 123 (1975), pp. 33–38, quote at p. 36.

43. Loch K. Johnson, "Congress and the CIA: Monitoring the Dark Side of Government," *Legislative Studies Quarterly* 5 (1980), pp. 477–499.

44. William H. Jackson, Jr., book review, *Intelligence and National Security* 5 (1990), pp. 253–254.

45. The USA PATRIOT Act bore the jaw-twisting formal title of "United and Strengthening America by Providing Appropriate Tools Required to Intercept and Obstruct Terrorism"; §214(b), 115 Stat. 287 (amending 50 U.S.C. §§1843[a],[b]); Pub. L. No. 107–56 (2001).

46. Jonathan Weisman and Jennifer Steinhauer, "PATRIOT Act Faces Curbs Supported by Both Parties," *New York Times* (May 1, 2015), p. A1.

47. Alissa J. Rubin, "France Moves to Vastly Widen Domestic Spying," *New York Times* (May 6, 2015), p. A8.

48. Steven Erlanger and Kimiko de Freytas-Tamura, "A Rattled Europe Tilts toward Bolder Security, Starting a Rights Debate," *New York Times* (November 20, 2015), p. A14.

49. Alissa J. Rubin, "French Muslims Say Emergency Powers Come at Too High a Cost," *New York Times* (February 18, 2016), p. A8.

50. Anthony Glees, "Privacy Must Yield to the Needs of Security," *New York Times* (online) (November 11, 2015).

51. Interview conducted by Patrick Steck (one of my graduate students in the Department of International Affairs), University of Georgia, Atlanta (April 22, 2015).

52. Fareed Zakaria, "Why They Hate Us," *CNN Television* (August 21, 2016).

53. Quoted in Scott Shane, "Debates on Limits over Surveillance Burst Open Again," *New York Times* (November 17, 2015), p. A12.

54. Al Baker and Marc Santora, "California Attackers Discussed Jihad Privately, F.B.I. Says," *New York Times* (December 17, 2015), p. A22.

55. Presidential speech (June 14, 2016), quoted in an unsigned editorial, "The Threat to Gay Americans," *New York Times* (June 15, 2016), p. A24.

56. Bill Moyers, *The Secret Government: The Constitution in Crisis*, PBS Documentary (1987).

57. See William L. Shirer, *The Rise and Fall of the Third Reich: A History of Nazi Germany* (New York: Simon & Schuster, 1959).

58. Edward Gibbon, *The Decline and Fall of the Roman Empire* (New York: Viking, 1952), p. 85.

Chapter 3

1. "An Overview of American Intelligence until World War II," *Factbook on Intelligence*, Central Intelligence Agency (Langley, VA: Central Intelligence Agency, n.d., but published in the 1980s).

2. See William R. Corson, *The Armies of Ignorance: The Rise of the American Intelligence Empire* (New York: Dial, 1977).

3. James S. Van Wagenen, "A Review of Congressional Oversight," paper, Central Intelligence Agency, 1997.

4. See Select Committee to Study Governmental Operations with Respect to Intelligence Activities (the Church Committee), *Final Report, Book I* (Rept. 94–755), U.S. Senate, 94th Cong., 2nd Sess. (Washington, DC: U.S. Government Printing Office, May 1976).

5. David M. Barrett, *The CIA and Congress: The Untold Story from Truman to Kennedy* (Lawrence: University Press of Kansas, 2005); L. Britt Snider, *The Agency and the Hill: CIA's Relationship with Congress, 1946–2004*, Center for the Study of Intelligence (Washington, DC: Central

Intelligence Agency, 2008), which extensively mines an unpublished and undated internal CIA draft manuscript on the subject of intelligence accountability (which on p. 4, note 4, Snider cites as a "Draft CIA Study").

6. David M. Barrett, "Congressional Oversight of the CIA in the Early Cold War, 1947–63," in Loch K. Johnson, ed., *Strategic Intelligence: Intelligence and Accountability*, vol. 5 (Westport, CT: Praeger Security International, 2007), p. 13.

7. See, for example, Harry Howe Ransom, *The Intelligence Establishment* (Cambridge, MA: Harvard University Press, 1970); and Jerrold L. Walden, "The C.I.A.: A Study in the Arrogation of Administrative Powers," *George Washington Law Review* 39 (October 1970), pp. 66–101. Barrett finds that although congressional accountability over intelligence was hardly robust in the late 1940s and throughout the 1950s, it was not "simply passive or static" (*CIA and Congress,* op. cit., p. 458).

8. Barrett, *CIA and Congress,* op. cit., p. 230; Snider, *The Agency and the Hill,* op. cit., p. 9.

9. My interview, Tufts University, Boston (February 26, 1988).

10. Snider, *The Agency and the Hill,* op. cit., pp. 8, 32. Senator Saltonstall recalled meeting "at least twice a year" with CIA representatives when he led the Armed Services Subcommittee on intelligence oversight; and "at least once a year," he remembered, the Agency would meet with the Appropriations Subcommittee on intelligence matters (*Congressional Record* [April 9, 1956], p. 5924).

11. Walter Norblad (R, Oregon), remarks, *Congressional Record* (August 15, 1963), p. 15086.

12. David Robarge, "CIA in the Spotlight: The Central Intelligence Agency and Public Accountability," *Journal of Intelligence History* 9/1–2 (2009), p. 114 (original emphasis). Frank J. Smist, Jr., notes that when lawmakers on a CIA subcommittee in Congress found out—after the fact—about the Agency's plan to overthrow Prime Minister Mossadegh of Iran, their reaction was merely to express surprise by "how very cheaply" the operation had been carried out (see his *Congress Oversees the United States Intelligence Community* [Knoxville: University of Tennessee Press, 1990], p. 6).

13. *Congressional Record* (April 9, 1956), p. 5924.

14. Respectively, Senate Committee on Government Operations, *Hearing on Oversight of U.S. Government Operations,* U.S. Senate, 94th Cong., 2nd Sess. (February 3, 1976), p. 362; and remarks, *Today Show,* NBC Television (June 10, 1975).

15. Snider, *The Agency and the Hill,* op. cit., pp. 9–10.

16. Harry Howe Ransom (who had interviewed Dulles), "Congress, Legitimacy and the Intelligence Community," paper, annual convention, Western Political Science Association, San Francisco, California (April 6, 1976).

17. Oral History No. 86, taped by Hughes Cates (February 22, 1977), Richard B. Russell Library, University of Georgia, Athens, Georgia.

18. Quoted by Tom Braden (a former senior CIA officer), "What's Wrong with the CIA?" *Saturday Review* 2 (April 5, 1975), p. 14.

19. Snider, *The Agency and the Hill,* op. cit., p. 13.

20. Harry Howe Ransom, "Congress and the Intelligence Agencies," in Harvey C. Mansfield, ed., *Congress against the President* (New York: Praeger, 1975), p. 162.

21. Quoted in a letter to Theodore Green, dated January 16, 1956, Dr. Frank J. Smist, Jr., Collection, University of Oklahoma, cited in Smist, *Congress Oversees,* op. cit., p. 6.

22. Quoted by Bob Wiedrich, "Can Congress Keep a Secret?" *Chicago Tribune* (February 3, 1976), p. A16.

23. Barrett, *CIA and Congress,* op. cit., pp. 231–232.

24. My interview with Walter L. Pforzheimer, Watergate Hotel (where he lived in one luxurious apartment for himself, with an adjoining apartment for his extensive library, later given to Yale University, where he had been a student), Washington, D.C. (May 30, 1983).

25. Rhodri Jeffrey-Jones, *The CIA and American Democracy* (New Haven, CT: Yale University Press, 1989); and Loch K. Johnson, *America's Secret Power: The CIA in a Democratic Society* (New York: Oxford University Press, 1989).

26. Snider, *The Agency and the Hill,* op. cit., p. 25.

27. Ibid., p. 27.

28. Tom Wicker et al., "C.I.A.: Maker of Policy, or Tool?" *New York Times* (April 25, 1966), p. A1.

29. See Samuel Dash, *Chief Counsel: Inside the Ervin Committee—The Untold Story of Watergate* (New York: Random House, 1976).

30. Snider, *The Agency and the Hill*, op. cit., p. 30.

31. See Dash, *Chief Counsel*, op. cit., p. 214. According to a reliable staff member on the Ervin Committee, one of its members—Howard Baker (R, Tennessee)—attempted to shield President Nixon by claiming inside the confines of the panel that the CIA had been involved in the DNC break-in by (as the staffer has written) "initially assisting then undermining the Watergate burglars in order to damage the president" (Scott Armstrong, "What to Remember About Watergate," *New York Times* [May 21, 2017], p. SR7). For lack of evidence to back up his preposterous charges, Baker's attempts at exonerating the president collapsed.

32. See Katherine A. Scott, *Reining in the States: Civil Society and Congress in the Vietnam and Watergate Eras* (Lawrence: University Press of Kansas, 2013).

33. See John Prados, *The Family Jewels* (Austin: University of Texas Press, 2014). In 1973, before the leak, DCI James R. Schlesinger had sent a memo around the Agency that said: "Let me know of anything we've done that we shouldn't have done" (journalist David Wise, comment, "Moles, Defectors, and Deceptions: James Angleton and His Influence on U.S. Counterintelligence," conference, Woodrow Wilson International Center for Scholars and the Georgetown University Center for Security Studies, Washington, D.C. [March 29, 2012]); see also chapter 11 of this book. The results of this request from Dr. Schlesinger are what eventually made their way to the *Times*. A seasoned bureaucrat, Schlesinger was ensuring that he would not be blamed for anything improper that might have occurred at the Agency before he arrived at Langley that year.

34. Snider, *The Agency and the Hill*, op. cit., p. 34.

35. National security adviser (and later secretary of state) Henry Kissinger of the Nixon Administration said, during an NSC meeting on covert action planning against presidential candidate Salvador Allende, "I don't see why the United States should stand by and watch Chile go communist merely due to the stupidity of the Chilean people" (cited by Gregory F. Treverton, "Covert Action: Forward to the Past?" in Loch K. Johnson, ed., *Essentials of Strategic Intelligence* [Santa Barbara, CA: Praeger, 2015], pp. 179–180).

36. See Johnson, *America's Secret Power*, op. cit., pp. 108–117.

37. Amendment to the Foreign Assistance Act (Pub. L. No. 93-559, §32, 88 Stat. 1804).

38. See the *Congressional Record* (January 21, 1975, pp. H524–S529; and January 27, 1975, pp. S967–S984).

39. *New York Times* (December 22, 1974), p. A1. Hersh has commented on why, in his view, he has been the recipient of government leaks over the years: "You know why sources speak? Why they risk their careers, their reputations, their very lives to talk to me? They talk because the weight becomes simply too great to bear. And so they dump it on me. They go home to their wives and say, 'I did something good today.' And that weight is released" (remark, interview with Hersh by journalists Aaron and Jordan Kandell, New York City [May 5, 2016], shared by email with me).

40. On the political and philosophical orientations of Frank Church, see my "Operational Codes and the Prediction of Leadership Behavior," in Margaret G. Herman, ed., *A Psychological Examination of Political Man* (New York: Free Press, 1977), pp. 80–119; and Church's own statement regarding his Madisonian-like suspicion of the executive branch powers in "Of Presidents and Caesars," *Congressional Record* 116 (April 30, 1970), pp. 13563–13566.

41. On the Church Committee, see my studies *A Season of Inquiry Revisited: The Church Committee Confronts America's Spy Agencies* (Lawrence: University Press of Kansas, 2015); "The Church Committee Investigation of 1975 and the Evolution of Modern Intelligence Accountability," *Intelligence and National Security* 23/2 (2008); "Accountability and America's Secret Foreign Policy: Keeping a Legislative Eye on the CIA," *Foreign Policy Analysis* 1 (Spring 2005), pp. 99–120; and "Congressional Supervision of America's Secret Agencies: The Experience and Legacy of the Church Committee," *Public Administration Review* 64 (January 2004), pp. 3–14. See, as well, Walter F. Mondale, with David Hage, *The Good Fight: A Life in Liberal Politics* (New York: Scribner, 2010); several works by the committee's chief counsel, Frederick A. O. Schwarz, Jr.: "The Church Committee and a New Era of Intelligence Oversight," *Intelligence and National Security* 22 (April 2007), pp. 270–297; "Intelligence Oversight: The Church

Committee," in Johnson, *Strategic Intelligence*, op. cit., pp. 19–46, plus chapters in the following books: *Democracy in the Dark: The Seduction of Government Secrecy* (New York: Free Press, 2015); and with coauthor Aziz Z. Huq, *Unchecked and Unbalanced: Presidential Power in a Time of Terror* (New York: New Press, 2007). Smist, too, has important insights into the Church Committee, Smist, *Intelligence Community*, op. cit. The Church Committee files will remain sealed in Senate vaults until 2025—fifty years after the investigation, at least twenty-five years longer than would seem necessary.

42. Robert L. Grenier, *88 Days to Kandahar: A CIA Diary* (New York: Simon & Schuster, 2015), p. 20.

43. Paul C. Light, *Government by Investigation: Congress, Presidents, and the Search for Answers, 1945–2012* (Washington, DC: Brookings Institution Press, 2014), p. 193. Government investigations can have a dark side, too. The most infamous example in the modern era was the set of hearings held in the 1950s by Senator Joseph McCarthy (R, Wisconsin) into alleged Communists in the U.S. Army—a probe that revealed the unfairness of the senator's charges, which were composed chiefly of innuendoes. The Army's outside counsel, Joseph Walsh of Boston, skillfully exposed and ridiculed the senator's antics before millions of television viewers—the first TV coverage of a congressional inquiry (see Richard H. Rovere, *Senator Joe McCarthy* [Berkeley: University of California Press, 1959]). More recent illustrations of dubious legislative inquiries include the politically tinged probe by the Select Committee on Benghazi, House of Representatives, into Secretary of State Hillary Clinton's responsibility for the attacks against U.S. diplomatic and intelligence personnel in Benghazi, Libya; and the House Select Investigative Panel on Infant Lives that in 2016 looked into fetal tissue research, a probe described by medical school officials as a "witch hunt" that could halt scientific inquiry into a broad range of illnesses (the Benghazi inquiry has been reported on widely in the media during 2015 and 2016; on the fetal tissue investigation, see Gardiner Harris, "House Fetal Tissue Inquiry Worries Abortion Rights Advocates," *New York Times* [March 25, 2016], p. A1).

44. When Church went to visit Senator John Stennis in January 1975 to solicit his vote to become chair of the investigative committee, the former Rhodes scholar patrician from Mississippi and a long-time unwavering CIA defender, said, "I will not vote to investigate the CIA. However, if my views do not prevail, I shall vote for you for chairman"—as he did (Betty K. Koed, Senate Historian, "Choosing a Chairman," *Senate Historical Minutes*, Office of the Historian, U.S. Senate [March 9, 2016]). On the Church Committee, see also Katherine (Kate) A. Scott, ed., *Church Committee Members and Staff, 1975–1976, Oral History Interviews* (July 24, 2013–March 10, 2015), U.S. Senate Historical Office, Washington, D.C. (2016).

45. "The CIA Report the President Doesn't Want You to Read: The Pike Papers," *Village Voice* (February 16 and 23, 1976). Despite an intensive investigation, the FBI never determined who leaked the Pike Committee report. The CIA pointed a finger at the committee; some committee members pointed back, speculating that the Agency had tried to further disparage the panel by leaking the document and blaming the committee.

46. See Johnson, *Season of Inquiry Revisited*, op. cit., p. 206.

47. See Commission on CIA Activities within the United States, *Report to the President* (Washington, DC: U.S. Government Printing Office, 1975).

48. Frederick "Fritz" A. O. Schwarz, Jr., in Scott, *Oral Histories*, op. cit. (October 28, 2014), pp. 450–451.

49. Quoted by James Hohmann, Tom Hamburger, and Elise Viebeck, "The Daily 202: Walter Mondale Frustrated with Obama's Handling of CIA Torture Report," *Washington Post* (October 19, 2014).

50. Schwarz, in Scott, *Oral History Interviews*, op. cit., p. 465.

51. For Schwarz's comment, see Scott, *Oral History Interviews*, op. cit., p. 463; on the Welch media spectacle, see Johnson, *Season of Inquiry Revisited*, op. cit., pp. 162–163.

52. These recollections come from my presence in the room for all Church Committee deliberations and hearings, during which time I took careful notes on the proceedings (now stored in the National Archives, along with the rest of the committee's papers). The Church Committee reviewed these notes and the book manuscript, eventually published in 1986 as *A Season of Inquiry: The Senate Intelligence Investigation* (Lexington: University Press of Kentucky), as did

the CIA's Publications Review Board, to ensure no classified information was inadvertently included. The PRB insisted that I delete the phrase "satellite surveillance" in the manuscript and use in its place "National Technical Means"—even though the former phrase had been used by President Lyndon B. Johnson in an open press conference.

53. He might have noted that the NSA list mostly included the names of innocent American citizens, like similar watch lists discovered by the Church Committee at the CIA and the Internal Revenue Service (IRS). The Agency's mail-opening list, for example, included Senator Hubert Humphrey, Richard Nixon (when he was in Congress), the scientist and double Nobel Laureate Linus Pauling, John Steinbeck, the Ford Foundation, Harvard University, and the Rockefeller Foundation, among many others. In his usual style of selective recollection, former NSA director Michael V. Hayden attempted in his memoir to belittle the Church panel's inquiry into the NSA by suggesting that the agency had only been spying on antiwar dissenters—"the likes of Jane Fonda, Joan Baez, and Benjamin Spock," as if their peaceful protests deserved the espionage carried out against them along with the thousands of others opposed to the war in Vietnam whose only "crime" was to engage in the First Amendment right to peacefully protest government policies (see Michael V. Hayden, *Playing to the Edge: American Intelligence in the Age of Terror* [New York: Penguin, 2016], p. 3).

54. See *Final Report, Book I: Foreign and Military Intelligence, Final Report, Book I*, Sen. Rept. No. 94-465, 94th Cong., 2nd Sess., as well as *Book II: Intelligence Activities and the Rights of Americans; Book III: Supplementary Detailed Staff Reports on Intelligence Activities and the Rights of Americans* (Washington, DC: U.S. Government Printing Office, 1976); and *Interim Report: Alleged Assassination Plots Involving Foreign Leaders* (Washington, DC: U.S. Government Printing Office, 1975). The Church Committee also published seven volumes of hearings testimony related to the assassination plots. One of the most dramatic moments in the committee's history was when Senator Church held up a CIA weapon before the television cameras during public hearings in the Russell Caucus Room—a "nondiscernible microbioinnoculator" in spy-speak (dart gun, for short) the size of a .45-caliber pistol that fired a small dart filled with poison. The pistol could fire silently and with remarkable accuracy for 100 meters. Although never used, it was a vivid symbol of the Agency's covert action arsenal. A photograph of the weapon held aloft by the chairman appeared in newspapers across the country. Some, on and off the committee, criticized Church for staining the reputation of the Agency by evoking an image of the organization as an international Godfather, knocking off enemies of the United States around the world. The chairman's view was that the committee had to have some drama in its public hearings as a means for attracting public attention to intelligence excesses and the need to reform the spy agencies, although he was unwilling to go so far as to examine in public hearings the specifics of CIA assassination plots. President Ford fired DCI Colby for cooperating too much with the Church Committee by providing the dart gun and, in the president's view, too many documents to the panel's staff investigators (William E. Colby and Peter Forbath, *Honorable Men: My Life in the CIA* [New York: Simon & Schuster, 1978], pp. 440–441).

55. Church Committee, *Final Report, Book II*, op. cit., p. 6.

56. Ibid., p. 218.

57. My interview with former vice president Mondale, Minneapolis, Minnesota (February 17, 2000). See also Mondale, *Good Fight*, op. cit.

58. "The Day the Sixties Died," PBS documentary (April 27, 2015). The president and practically everyone else in the United States properly condemned the burning of ROTC buildings on campuses, as occurred at Kent State University (for example) days before the governor of Ohio called out the state's National Guard in early May 1970. Such acts are significant crimes and had to be dealt with seriously—although certainly not with the heavy-handed approach chosen by the governor. He allowed the National Guard to enter a chaotic campus scene with live ammunition. Some of these troops opened fire on peaceful protesters, killing four students (only one of whom had been involved—only moderately—in campus protests). Days later, state patrolmen killed several more students at Mississippi State University who were also peacefully protesting the expansion of the war by President Nixon in Vietnam into neighboring Cambodia, as well as advocating expanded civil rights for African-Americans. These tragedies were two of the most shameful episodes in U.S. history. Little did the public know

at the time that President Nixon was also secretly about to grant unprecedented authority for the nation's major intelligence agencies to spy on students and other protesters—the Huston Plan (discussed later in this chapter).

59. Church Committee, *Final Report, Book II*, op. cit., pp. 10–12, 65–94, 211–223.

60. Published by the University of Michigan Press (Ann Arbor, 1960).

61. Church Committee, *Final Report, Book II*, op. cit., pp. 216–219.

62. Church Committee, *Final Report, Book II*, op. cit., pp. 11, 220–221; *Book III*, pp. 158–161.

63. As described by journalist Colman McCarthy, "Philip Hart: The Gentle Way Is the Effective Way," *Washington Post* (February 2, 1976), p. A16.

64. Questioning by Senator Mondale and responding testimony by the Church Committee chief counsel, Fredrick A. O. Schwarz, Jr., *Hearings: Vol. 6: Federal Bureau of Investigation*, Church Committee, 94th Cong., 2nd Sess. (November 18, 1975), p. 42.

65. My interview with Frederick A. O. Schwarz, Jr., New York City (April 27, 2000); see also Schwarz and Huq, *Unchecked and Unbalanced*, op. cit. Michael German of the Brennan Center in New York noted in 2016 that "the FBI shouldn't have authority to use unfettered powers to chase down vague intelligence unconnected to a crime" (quoted by Cora Currier, "Amid Clinton Controversy, FBI Documents Show Why Americans Should Worry about Intelligence Gathering," *Intercept* [November 7, 2016]).

66. Church Committee, *Book II*, op. cit., p. 4.

67. Testimony of NSA Deputy Director Benson Buffham, *Hearings, Vol. 5: The National Security Agency and Fourth Amendment Rights*, Church Committee (1975), 94th Cong., 2nd Sess., p. 45. During a deposition, the NSA's chief counsel told the Church Committee's chief counsel that "the Constitution does not apply to the NSA" (Schwarz, in Scott, ed., *Oral History Interviews*, op. cit., p. 460). The NSA's leadership did not appreciate the public grilling by the Church Committee and soon after the investigation they awarded the agency's top leaders with a special lapel pin: an Idaho potato with a pike stuck through it—considered a badge of honor at Ft. Meade.

68. Church Committee, *Book II*, op. cit., p. 141.

69. See Hannah Arendt, *The Origins of Totalitarianism* (New York: Harcourt, 1973).

70. Church Committee, *Book II*, op. cit., p. 141.

71. Peter M. Shane, "The NSA and the Legal Regime for Foreign Intelligence Surveillance," *IS: A Journal of Law and Policy for the Information Society*" (2014), p. 299.

72. Henry Steele Commager, "Intelligence: The Constitutional Betrayed," *New York Review of Books* (September 30, 1976), p. 32.

73. Remarks, *Congressional Record* (May 17, 1976), p. S7340. In contrast, Mark Bowden, author of *Black Hawk Down*, remembers the Church and Pike Committees as "a venerable posse" that "damn near lynched the entire intelligence community" (foreword to William J. Daugherty, *Executive Secrets: Covert Action and the Presidency* [Lexington: University Press of Kentucky, 2004], p. xi).

74. Jonathan Weisman and Jennifer Steinhauer, "Patriot Act Faces Curbs Supported by Both Parties," *New York Times* (May 1, 2015), p. A17.

75. Dean Rusk, as told to Richard Rusk and edited by Daniel S. Papp, *As I Saw It* (New York: Norton, 1990), p. 397. When I told a colleague about this Rusk observation, he responded with a fair critique, "Yes, but remember, too, that Iran did not use a covert operation to remove a U.S. president and replace him with someone loyal to Iran" (July 2016).

76. As polling data from the Pew Global Attitudes Report and other sources on worldwide opinions toward the United States have indicated, however, this high standing was tarnished by the second Bush Administration's invasion of Iraq in 2003; see Loch K. Johnson, *Seven Sins of American Foreign Policy* (New York: Longman, 2007), ch. 2.

77. Quoted by Charles B. Seib and Alan L. Otten, "Fulbright: Arkansas Paradox," *Harper's* (June 1954), p. 61.

78. For a comparative analysis of oversight in the United States and other nations, see Hans Born, Ian Leigh, and Loch K. Johnson, eds., *Who's Watching the Spies? Establishing Intelligence Service Accountability* (Washington, DC: Potomac Books, 2005).

79. The Senate and House established these committees by way, respectively, of Senate Resolution 400 (enacted on May 19, 1976) and House Resolution 658 (enacted on July 14, 1977).

80. See Richard F. Grimmett, "9/11 Commission Recommendations: Implementation Status," *Congressional Research Report*, RL33742, Congressional Research Service, Library of Congress, Washington, D.C. (December 4, 2006).
81. Discussed by Amy Zegart, prepared statement, *Hearings on Congressional Oversight of Intelligence Activities*, Select Committee on Intelligence, U.S. Senate, 119th Cong., 1st Sess., Rept. 110–794 (November 13, 2007), p. 47.
82. Author's telephone interview with John T. Elliff, staff leader for the FBI Task Force, Church Committee (April 14, 2000).
83. See, for example, note 73 above and 84 below.
84. Scott, ed., *Oral History Interviews*, op. cit. (March 10, 2015), p. 425. The work of the Church Committee had its distractors beyond the macho novelists Bowden and Tom Clancy, including such prominent people as former president George H. W. Bush, former secretary of state James Baker (also in the first Bush Administration), and—of all people—former national security adviser Robert C. McFarlane, one of the Iran-contra conspirators. Baker has said, for example, that the committee "unilaterally disarm[ed] . . . our intelligence capabilities." The *Wall Street Journal* joined in the chorus, observing in an editorial soon after the 9/11 attacks in 2001 that the IC had been "reeling" ever since the investigation in 1975. One could only wonder, as Fritz Schwarz has put it, how the intelligence agencies could "still be 'reeling' after twenty-five years and six administrations"; or, if true, why Bush and Baker had "failed to know" or "lacked the power to rehabilitate supposedly neutered agencies." For these quotes, see Schwarz, *Democracy in the Dark*, op. cit., pp. 173–174.
85. William E. Colby, with Peter Forbath, *Honorable Men: My Life in the CIA* (New York: Simon & Schuster, 1978), p. 442.
86. Cited in Snider, *The Agency and the Hill*, op. cit., p. 36.
87. *Congressional Record* (November 11, 1975).
88. On the Huston Plan, see Johnson, *America's Secret Power*, op. cit., ch. 7; and Loch K. Johnson, "National Security, Civil Liberties, and the Collection of Intelligence: A Report on the Huston Plan," in *Supplementary Detailed Staff Reports on Intelligence and the Rights of Americans*, Select Committee to Study Governmental Operations with Respect to Intelligence Activities (the Church Committee), Book III, U.S. Senate (April 23, 1976), pp. 921–986.
89. These subjects are discussed in depth in the Church Committee's *Final Report*, op. cit.
90. For these various episodes, see *Alleged Assassination Plots Involving Foreign Leaders, An Interim Report*, Select Committee to Study Governmental Operations with Respect to Intelligence Activities (the Church Committee's formal name), U.S. Senate (1975), also published commercially under the same title (New York: Norton, 1976), pp. 84, 86, 128–133; William Harvey testimony, Church Committee (June 25, 1975), pp. 72–73; and John Roselli testimony, Church Committee (June 24, 1976), p. 43. Further, Bundy had to step in to halt plans concocted by military intelligence that would have introduced the parasite Bunga into Cuba for purposes of destroying the island's sugar-cane industry, along with a proposed operation to spread hoof-and-mouth disease among Cuba's draft animals (Loch K. Johnson, *National Security Intelligence: Secret Operations in Defense of the Democracies*, 2nd ed. [Cambridge, UK: Polity, 2017], pp. 87–88, based on unclassified documents from the Johnson Presidential Library at the University of Texas in Austin, Texas). Moreover, the *Times* noted in 1962 that, in a "harum-scarum project that illustrated problems of controls," the Agency had contaminated sugar bound from Cuba to a Russian port on a British freighter, the *S.S. Stretham Hill* (under Soviet lease), using a harmless but unpalatable substance. The White House heard about this operation, which the Agency claimed had been within "approved instructions," and quickly stopped it before it began ("C.I.A. Operations: A Plot Scuttled," *New York Times* [April 28, 1966, p. A1]). In 1977, investigative journalists accused the Agency of providing "at least tacit backing" for another dubious operation in which "operatives linked to anti-Castro terrorists introduced African swine fever virus into Cuba in 1971," which led to the forced slaughter of half-a-million pigs to prevent a nationwide animal epidemic (Drew Fetherson and John Commings, "CIA Linked to 1971 Swine Virus in Cuba," *Washington Post* [January 9, 1977], p. A1).
91. *Alleged Assassination Plots*, op. cit., pp. 44–48.
92. Frederick D. Baron, in Scott, *Oral History Interviews*, op. cit. (May 28, 2015), p. 15.

93. David Ignatius, "The Senate's CIA Report Is a Necessary Public Accounting," *Washington Post* (December 11, 2014), p. A18. A CIA historian similarly blasts the entire Church Committee for its chairman's premature remark (Robarge, "CIA in the Spotlight," op. cit., p. 110).

94. To mention just one example here, the evidence continues to mount that the CIA chief of station in the Congo in 1961, during the Agency's assassination plot against Congo's leader, Patrice Lumumba, shaped policy on his own to bring about Lumumba's demise at the hands of African rivals. The station chief failed to inform his superiors at Langley about his actions at a crucial moment when officials in Washington were still pondering what to do about Lumumba during the waning days of the Eisenhower Administration (see Stephen R. Weissman, "An Extraordinary Rendition," *Intelligence and National Security* 25/2 [April 2010], pp. 198–222, and his book review in *Studies in Intelligence* 5/4 [December 2015], pp. 53–54). Other nations, including the United Kingdom, have experienced rogue intelligence behavior. For example, Jack Straw, the British foreign secretary (responsible for MI6), told the public in December 2005 that "there is simply no truth in the claims that the United Kingdom has been involved in [CIA rendition operations], full stop." When MI6's participation in CIA renditions in Libya came to public light, however, Straw retreated to the feeble admission that "no foreign secretary can know all the details of what its intelligence agencies are doing at any one time" (Nick Hopkins and Richard Norton-Taylor, "Blair Government's Rendition Policy Led to Rift Between UK Spy Agencies," *Guardian* [May 31, 2016]).

95. Johnson, *Season of Inquiry Revisited,* op. cit., p. 283.

96. Robert M. Gates, *From the Shadows* (New York: Simon & Schuster, 1996), p. 61.

Chapter 4

1. This phrase, widely used by intelligence chiefs and lawmakers prior to the Church Committee, should say "women" as well, since they have played a significant role over the years in the intelligence activities of the United States (including service as COSs overseas).

2. Loch K. Johnson, *Secret Agencies: U.S. Intelligence in a Hostile World* (New Haven, CT: Yale University Press, 1996), pp. 89–94.

3. The author was present at this meeting, as the senior HPSCI staff member with responsibilities for covert action reviews (along with the committee's staff director, Thomas K. Latimer).

4. R. W. Apple, Jr., "The Lives They Lived: Les Aspin, Vietnam's Student," *New York Times Magazine* (December 31, 1995), p. 9.

5. Often members of Congress can be even more enthusiastic for a covert action proposal than executive branch briefers, as when lawmakers pushed for the overthrow of President Jacobo Arbenz in Nicaragua in 1954, or for support to the anti-Soviet *mujahideen* in Afghanistan during the Reagan presidency. See, respectively, David M. Barrett, *The CIA and Congress: The Untold Story from Truman to Kennedy* (Lawrence: University Press of Kansas, 2005); and George Crile, *Charlie Wilson's War* (New York: Grove, 2003). Charlie Wilson was an influential senior member of HPSCI at the time.

6. Allen E. Goodman, quoted by Time Weiner, "Call in the C.I.A. and Cross Your Fingers," *New York Times* (September 15, 1996), p. E3.

7. Wesley Wark, "C-51 and the Canadian Security and Intelligence Community: Finding the Balance for Security and Rights Protections," in Edward Iacobucci and Stephen Toope, eds., *After the Paris Attacks: Responses in Canada, Europe and around the Globe* (Toronto: University of Toronto Press, 2015), p. 179.

8. 50 U.S.C. §§1801-1911 (Supp. V 1981). As Charles Savage notes, though, the NSA's collection capabilities have expanded greatly since 1978: "FISA covers a narrow band of surveillance: the collection of domestic or international communications from a wire on American soil, leaving most of what the N.S.A. does uncovered" ("U.S. Set to Expand Sharing of Intercepted Calls and Email," *New York Times* [February 26, 2016], p. A18). After 9/11, the second Bush Administration should have brought FISA up-to-date with congressional amendments, rather than simply ignoring the concept of a FISA warrant and setting loose the NSA to bypass judicial approvals altogether for much of their collection (as probed in the next chapter).

9. One of the leading staffers on the Church Committee, David Aaron, had moved on to the Carter Administration, where he participated in the Intelligence Charter negotiations as

deputy director for national security. Aaron thought the charter failed because of SSCI's instance on being informed of covert actions in advance, even in times of emergency. Another Church Committee staffer, Anne Karalekas, pointed to the excessive detail of the proposal as one of the main defects that doomed the initiative. See David Aaron, testimony, *Hearings on Congressional Oversight of Covert Activities*, Permanent Select Committee on Intelligence, U.S. House (September 22, 1983), p. 98; and Anne Karalekas, "Intelligence Oversight: Has Anything Changed?" *Washington Quarterly* 6 (Summer 1983), pp. 22–30.

10. S.2525, the National Intelligence Reorganization and Reform Act of 1978, Congressional Record, 95th Cong., 2nd Sess, (1978), pp. 3110–3141; for President Carter's Executive Order No. 12036, see §§3–4, 43 Fed. Reg. (1978), p. 3678.

11. 94 Stat. 1981, title 4, sec. 501, 50 U.S.C. 413.

12. Loch K. Johnson, "Legislative Reform of Intelligence Policy," *Polity* 17 (1985), pp. 549–753.

13. Loch K. Johnson, *American Foreign Policy and the Challenges of World Leadership* (New York: Oxford University Press, 2015), chs. 10 and 11.

14. *To Authorize Appropriations for Fiscal Year 2003*, Select Committee on Intelligence, U.S. Senate, 107th Cong., 2nd Sess., S. Rpt. 107–149 (May 13, 2002), p. 7, cited by Jennifer Kibbe, "Congressional Oversight of Intelligence: Is the Solution Part of the Problem?" *Intelligence and National Security* 25/1 (February 2010), p. 35.

15. See Loch K. Johnson, *The Making of International Agreements: Congress Confronts the Executive* (New York: New York University Press, 1984).

16. Steven Aftergood, "SSCI Bill Adopts Fundamental Classification Review," *Secrecy News*, FAS (June 10, 2016), p. 2.

17. Gregory F. Treverton, "Intelligence: Welcome to the American Government," in Thomas E. Mann, ed., *A Question of Balance: The President, Congress and Foreign Policy* (Washington, DC: Brookings Institution, 1990), pp. 70–108.

18. 18 U.S.C. app. III §§1–16.

19. Graymail may be formally defined as "a tactic employed by a defendant who threatens to disclose classified information with the hopes that the prosecution will choose not to prosecute in order to keep the information protected" (Stephen Dycus, Arthur L. Berney, William C. Banks, and Peter Raven-Hansen, *National Security Law*, 3rd ed. [New York: Aspen, 2002], p. 883, n. 5).

20. Public Law 97-200.

21. Philip Agee, *Inside the Company: CIA Diary* (Harmondsworth, UK: Penguin, 1975).

22. 50 U.S.C. §4310432 (1994 & Supp. V 1999).

23. L. Britt Snider, *The Agency and the Hill: CIA's Relationship with Congress, 1946–2004*, Center for the Study of Intelligence (Washington, DC: CIA, 2008), p. 146. For the language of the Act, see 50 U.S.C. § 431-432 (1994 & Supp. V 1999).

24. Quoted by George Lardner, Jr., *Washington Post* (July 22, 1981), p. A1.

25. The letter, dated April 9, 1984, appeared in the *Post* on April 11 (p. A17).

26. Quoted in the *New York Times* (April 16, 1984), p. A6. Moynihan resigned from the committee, returning only after Casey made his amends (Senator Daniel Patrick Moynihan, "Secrecy as Government Regulation," Marver H. Bernstein Lecture, Georgetown University [March 3, 1997]).

27. Quoted in *Newsweek* (October 10, 1983), p. 38. Another irate lawmaker lamented that Casey had been consistently less than forthcoming: "He wouldn't tell you if your coat was on fire if you didn't ask him" (quoted by Frank Smist, Jr., *Congress Oversees the United States Intelligence Community*, 2nd ed. [Knoxville: University of Tennessee Press, 1994], p. 214).

28. Stansfield Turner, *Secrecy and Democracy: The CIA in Transition* (Boston: Houghton Mifflin, 1985), pp. 167–168.

29. Snider, *The Agency and the Hill*, op. cit., p. 62. Intelligence scholar Jennifer Kibbe notes that "members have complied for so long [with the Gang of Eight provision as a substitute for full reporting to SSCI and HPSCI] that it is now entrenched practice and hard to reverse" "Congressional Oversight of Intelligence," (op. cit., p. 35).

30. See Alfred Cumming, *"Gang of Four" Congressional Intelligence Notifications*, Congressional Research Service Report, Library of Congress, Washington, D.C. (January 29, 2010), pp. 1–14.

31. Leon Panetta, Statement for the Record, *Confirmation Hearings*, Select Committee on Intelligence, U.S. Senate (February 5, 2009), p. 4. On the Gang of Four as a fabrication, see

Marshall Curtis Erwin, "Gang of Four Congressional Intelligence Notifications," *Congress Research Service*, Library of Congress, Washington, D.C. (2013).

32. On the Iran-contra affair, see Malcolm Byrne, *Iran-Contra: Reagan's Scandal and the Unchecked Abuse of Presidential Power* (Lawrence: University Press of Kansas, 2014), as well as the official congressional *Report on the Iran-Contra Affair*, Senate Select Committee on Secret Military Assistance to Iran and the Nicaraguan Opposition and House Select Committee to Investigate Covert Arms Transactions with Iran (the Inouye-Hamilton Committee, after co-chairs Senator Daniel K. Inouye, D, Hawaii, and Representative Lee H. Hamilton, D, Indiana), Sen. Rept. 100-216 and H. Rept. 100-433 (Washington, DC: U.S. Government Printing Office, November 1987). Valuable, too, is an account by two members of the committee: William S. Cohen and George Mitchell, *Men of Zeal: A Candid Inside Story of the Iran-Contra Hearings* (New York: Viking, 1988); President's Special Review Board, *The Tower Commission Report* (Washington, DC: U.S. Government Printing Office, 1987), which criticized President Reagan for his passive management style during the affair—a rare criticism from John Tower (vice chair of the Church Committee) of a GOP president; and a scathing indictment by the special prosecutor assigned to investigate the scandal, Lawrence E. Walsh, *Firewall: The Iran-Contra Conspiracy and Cover-Up* (New York: Norton, 1997).

33. Department of Defense Appropriations Act 1985, Pub. L. No. 98–473, §8066, 98 Stat. 1935 (1984). Knowing that a Democratically controlled Congress had enough votes to override a presidential veto, President Reagan signed the Boland Amendments. Seldom has ink on parchment meant so little.

34. Byrne, *Iran-Contra*, op. cit., p. 376, n. 37.

35. Testimony, Inouye-Hamilton Committee, op. cit., *Joint Hearings*, vol. 100-5 (June 9, 1987), p. 552.

36. Byrne, *Iran-Contra*, op. cit., p. 82. "You don't lie," McFarlane explained to investigators. "You put your own interpretation on what the truth is" (testimony, *Final Report*, vol. 1, Office of Independent Council, Trial of Oliver North, Washington, D.C. [1989], p. 87).

37. Byrne, *Iran-Contra*, op. cit., p. 78.

38. Laurence H. Tribe, "Reagan Ignites a Constitutional Crisis," *New York Times* (May 20, 1987), p. A31.

39. For these examples and quotes, see Byrne, *Iran-Contra*, op. cit., pp. 18, 22, 43, 253–255.

40. According to the notes of several staffers at a White House meeting on November 10, 1986: Byrne, *Iran-Contra*, op. cit., p. 258.

41. Inouye-Hamilton Committee, *Report on the Iran-Contra Affair*, op. cit., p. 437. Successive Republican administrations had no compunction about hiring leading figures involved in the scandal. For example, Poindexter served in the Pentagon during the second Bush Administration, until his leadership behind a proposal for a massive domestic intelligence collection operation came to light and he had to leave office. In this same administration, Elliot Abrams served on the National Security Council, despite his conviction in 1991 on two misdemeanor counts of unlawfully withholding information from lawmakers at the time of their inquiry into the Iran-contra affair. During the start-up weeks of the Trump Administration, the new secretary of state, Rex W. Tillerson, selected Abrams as his deputy. The president first accepted this key appointment, then vetoed the choice when his aides discovered that Abrams had written a sharply critical article about Trump during the presidential campaign, thereby flunking the White House loyalty test.

42. Lawrence E. Walsh, *Nightline*, ABC News (December 24, 1992). For a persuasive litany of evidence that Vice President Bush was well aware of the affair, see Byrne, *Iran-Contra*, op. cit.

43. Byrne, *Iran-Contra*, op. cit., p. 76.

44. See Joseph J. Ellis, *The Quartet Orchestrating the Second American Revolution, 178–1789* (New York: Knopf, 2015). An important book on Cheney's approach to security and foreign policy is Charles Savage, *Takeover: The Return of the Imperial Presidency and the Subversion of American Democracy* (New York: Little, Brown, 2007), see especially pp. 54–62.

45. Arthur L. Liman, quoted in Cohen and Mitchell, *Men of Zeal*, op. cit., pp. 318–20.

46. The quote is a conclusion drawn by Byrne, *Iran-Contra*, op. cit., p. 334. For John W. Dean's confession about his participation in the Watergate cover-up as a result of his own career aspirations and an overzealous devotion to President Nixon, see *Blind Ambition: The White House Years* (New York: Simon & Schuster, 1976).

47. Loch K. Johnson, "Playing Ball with the CIA: Congress Supervises Strategic Intelligence," in Paul E. Peterson, ed., *Congress, the Executive, and the Making of American Foreign Policy* (Norman: University of Oklahoma Press, 1994), pp. 49–73.

48. CIA Inspector General Act of 1989 (§20 CIA Act of 1949, as amended).

49. Snider, *The Agency and the Hill*, op. cit., p. 69.

50. Pub. L. No. 102-88, 105 Stat. 441.

51. Public Law No. 102-88, 105 Stat. 441, Sec. 602. ("Oversight of Intelligence Activities"). See David L. Boren, "The Winds of Change at the CIA," *Yale Law Journal* 100 (1992), pp. 853–857. At the time, Robert M. Gates was President Bush's DCI nominee. Gates publicly stated that a delay in notifying SSCI and HPSCI should last no longer than a few days and that he would contemplate resignation as the intelligence director if it extended beyond that time period (*Congressional Quarterly Almanac* 47 [1991], p. 482). Even Secretary of State Henry Kissinger, no champion of intelligence accountability, told the Church Committee that covert actions should be briefed to the congressional oversight panels before being implemented (remarks, November 21, 1975).

52. Marvin C. Ott, "Partisanship and the Decline of Intelligence Oversight," *International Journal of Intelligence and Counterintelligence* 16 (2003), pp. 69–94, quote at p. 81.

53. Joel D. Aberbach, "What's Happened to the Watchful Eye?" *Congress & the Presidency* 29 (2002), pp. 3–23, quote at p. 20.

54. Quoted by Peter Baker, "A Steady Drip of Lost Pride," *New York Times* (October 22, 2014), p. A3.

55. Stephen F. Knott, "The Great Republican Transformation on Oversight," *International Journal of Intelligence and Counterintelligence* 13 (2000), pp. 49–63, quote at p. 57.

56. Ott, "Partisanship and the Decline of Intelligence Oversight," op. cit., pp. 82–83.

57. Ibid., p. 87; John Prados, *Safe for Democracy* (Chicago: Ivan R. Dee, 2006), p. 619.

58. Senator Bob Graham, "The Lehrer News Hour," *PBS Television* (October 17, 2002).

59. Carroll J. Doherty, "On Hill, Latest CIA Uproar Revives Issue of Trust," *Congressional Quarterly Weekly Report* 53 (April 15, 1995), p. 1073.

60. Tim Weiner, "C.I.A. Severs Ties to 100 Foreign Agents," *New York Times* (March 3, 1997), p. A12. Deutch was an unpopular figure among DO officers to begin with, because of his cutbacks in that Directorate; in retaliation, they attempt to portray his new "rule" as diminishing the Agency's humint programs across the board, including in the counterterrorism (CT) domain. On the contrary, the Deutch rule did not apply to CT asset recruitment. With its counterattack, the DO attempted to suggest that the new DCI was weak on U.S. security (see Loch K. Johnson, *The Threat on the Horizon: An Inside Account of America's Search for Security after the Cold War* [New York: Oxford University Press, 2011]). The Deutch rule has been substantially relaxed in recent years; but, as a deputy director of the CIA has said, when the Agency does continue its relationships with foreign governments or groups that pose human rights concerns, "we have done so because of the critical intelligence" involved. In these instances, the CIA emphasizes that "our partners must respect human rights" and, "where appropriate, we develop guidance and training to improve their conduct, and we may also adjust the nature or depth of our cooperation." The DD/CIA went on to say, "In all of these cases—no matter the result—we keep Congress informed. We describe the basis of the concerns that arise, whether confirmed or not, and how we've chosen to address the situation" (David S. Cohen, speech, "Governing Intelligence" Conference, Center on Law and Security, NYU School of Law, Washington, D.C. [April 21, 2016]).

61. Unsigned editorial, "Robert Torricelli for the Senate," *New York Times* (October 28, 1996), p. A12.

62. These quotes from Cohen, Shelby, and Studeman are from the transcript, "Guatemala and the Reported Murders of Michael Devine and Efrain Bamaca," *Hearings*, Select Committee on Intelligence, U.S. Senate, 104 Cong., 1st Sess. (April 4, 1995), pp. 42, 50–53.

63. *Hearings on the Huston Plan*, U.S. Senate Select Committee on Intelligence, 94th Cong., 1st Sess. (September 23, 1975); Loch K. Johnson, *A Season of Inquiry Revisited: The Church Committee Confronts America's Spy Agencies* (Lawrence: University Press of Kansas, 2015). Often witnesses known for their brilliance and steel-trap minds will suddenly suffer from amnesia when questioned about past intelligence excesses, a condition known in the Pentagon

as CRS, or "Can't Remember Shit"—a most convenient malady (see Seymour M. Hersh, "The General's Report," *New Yorker* [June 25, 2007], p. 60).

64. On the Huston Plan, see Loch K. Johnson, *America's Secret Power: The CIA in a Democratic Society* (New York: Oxford University Press, 1986), ch. 7.

65. Frederick D. Baron, in Katherine Scott, ed., *Oral History Interviews, Church Committee*, U.S. Senate Historical Office, Washington, D.C. (May 28, 2015), p. 11.

66. These instances of dubious amnesia can be found in Richard Helms's testimony, Rockefeller Commission (April 23 and 24, 1975), pp. 160–163 and 389–391, respectively; and his testimony to the Church Committee, U.S. Senate (June 13, 1975)—see Johnson, *Season of Inquiry Revisited*, op. cit.

67. William E. Colby, testimony, *Hearings on Congressional Oversight of Covert Activities*, HPSCI, op. cit., p. 29.

68. Inouye-Hamilton Committee, *Report on the Iran-Contra Affair*, op. cit., p. 142.

69. These reflections on the Aspin-Brown Commission were published initially in book-length form: Johnson, *Threat on the Horizon*, op. cit. They are repurposed here to focus on questions of intelligence accountability.

70. Steven Komarow, "In Turnabout, the CIA Finds Itself under a Microscope," *USA Today* (July 15, 1994), p. 5A.

71. Ibid.

72. Unsigned editorial, "Mr. Aspin: Pick Up the Pace," *New York Times* (January 16, 1995), p. A16.

73. Commission Fowler often said to me, in contrast, that he liked the rotational rule, which brought a larger number of lawmakers onto the Intelligence Committees, limiting the chances for co-option and educating the Congress as a whole on matters of intelligence.

74. Snider, *The Agency and the Hill*, op. cit., p. 76.

75. Quoted in Robert Pear, "A Shake-Up at Spy Agency as Secret Fund Is Disclosed," *New York Times* (September 25, 1995), p. A12.

76. Tim Weiner, "A Secret Agency's Secret Budgets Yield Lost Billions, Officials Say," *New York Times* (January 30, 1996), p. A1.

77. Tony Capaccio, "CIA Ends Reagan-Era Pact That Kept Pentagon from NRO Books," *Defense Week* (October 2, 1995), p. 1. An intelligence official who came into the NRO after the scandal recalls that the agency had a largely negative view toward SSCI and HPSCI in its early days. " 'We're not going to tell you anything, and you can't make us,' was the attitude," he said (remarks, my notes, "National Intelligence and Technology Symposium," CIA Conference, Langley, Virginia [November 6, 1998]).

78. Commission on the Roles and Capabilities of the United States Intelligence Community, *Preparing for the 21st Century: An Appraisal of U.S. Intelligence* (Washington, DC: U.S. Government Printing Office, 1996).

79. Hart-Rudman Commission, *Road Map for National Security: Imperative for Change* (Washington, DC: U.S. Government Printing Office, 2001); see William M. Nolte, "The Hart-Rudman Commission: Starting Point for Rethinking American National Security," *Intelligence and National Security* 31/1 (January 2016), p. 93.

80. Remark, former senator Gary Hart, "Strengthening Intelligence Oversight," Symposium, Brennan Center for Justice, New York University School of Law in Washington, D.C. (May 28, 2015).

81. Gregory F. Treverton, *Intelligence for an Age of Terror* (Cambridge: Cambridge University Press, 2009), p. 232.

Chapter 5

1. This is not to say that partisanship waned in the new environment. The failure of SSCI to pass an authorization bill in each of the years from 2006 to 2009 is a telling illustration of how party politics undermined one of the committee's most basic oversight responsibilities (see Jennifer Kibbe, "Congressional Oversight of Intelligence: Is the Solution Part of the Problem?" *Intelligence and National Security* 25 [February 2010], pp. 24–49). At times, though, SSCI (and HPSCI) could be fully united, when topics were more amenable to cross-aisle agreement. Examples include SSCI's unanimous vote in favor of its critical six-hundred-page report

on intelligence failures related to WMDs in Iraq (*Report on the U.S. Intelligence Community's Prewar Intelligence Assessments on Iraq*, S. Rpt. 108-301, Select Committee on Intelligence, U.S. Senate [July 9, 2004]), and its balanced report on Benghazi (*Review of the Terrorist Attacks on U.S. Facilities in Benghazi, Libya, September 11–12, 2012*, S. Rpt. 113-134, Select Committee on Intelligence, U.S. Senate [January 15, 2014]).

2. L. Britt Snider, *The Agency and the Hill: CIA's Relationship with Congress, 1946–2004*, Center for the Study of Intelligence, Central Intelligence Agency (2008), p. 187.

3. Loch K. Johnson, "Glimpses into the Gems of American Intelligence: The *President's Daily Brief* and the National Intelligence Estimate," *Intelligence and National Security* 23 (June 2008), pp. 333–370.

4. Commission on Terrorist Attacks Upon the United States (Kean Commission), *9/11 Report* (Washington, DC: U.S. Government Printing Office, 2004); also published commercially as *The 9/11 Commission Report* (New York: Norton, 2004).

5. It is worth noting that, based on IC information, the Navy Seals were able to raid the Pakistani secret compound of the Al Qaeda leader, Osama bin Laden, and kill him ten years after the 9/11 attacks. So sometimes the military can leave a small footprint, but Schlesinger's warning remains valid most of the time.

6. See Richard A. Clarke, *Against All Enemies: Inside America's War on Terror* (New York: Free Press, 2004).

7. *9/11 Commission Report*, op. cit., p. 275.

8. See Loch K. Johnson, *The Threat on the Horizon: An Inside Account of America's Search for Security after the Cold War* (New York: Oxford University Press, 2011), p. 123.

9. For excerpts from this *PDB*, see the *9/11 Commission Report*, op. cit., pp. 261–62.

10. Michael Allen, *Blinking Red: Crisis and Compromise in American Intelligence after 9/11* (Washington, DC: Potomac Books, 2014). The formal cite for IRTPA is 118 Stat. 3638; Pub. L. 108-458.

11. See Loch K. Johnson, "A Centralized Intelligence System: Truman's Dream Deferred," *American Intelligence Journal* (Autumn/Winter 2005), pp. 6–15.

12. Journalist Maureen Dowd wrote in 2004: "Because of 9/11, they [those in the Bush White House] think they can suspend the Constitution, blow off investigators, attack nations pre-emptively, and keep Americans afraid by waging a war against terrorism that can never be won" ("Sorry, Right Number," *New York Times* [February 29, 2004], p. Wk. 13).

13. Dana Priest, "Congressional Oversight of Intelligence Criticized," *Washington Post* (April 27, 2004), p. A1.

14. *9/11 Report*, op. cit.

15. Bill Gertz, *Breakdown* (Washington, DC: Regnery, 2002), p. 113.

16. Karen J. Greenberg, *Rogue Justice: The Making of the Security State* (New York: Crown, 2016). The FISA Court ruled that the PATRIOT Act permitted bulk collection, holding further in a 2013 decision that (according to an authoritative study) "*all* Americans' phone records were relevant to authorized international terrorism investigations because they may be used in some unforeseen, future search" (see Walter F. Mondale, Robert A. Stein, and Caitlinrose Fisher, "No Longer a Neutral Magistrate: The Foreign Intelligence Surveillance Court in the Wake of the War on Terror," *Minnesota Law Review* 100/6 [June 2016], p. 2265, original emphasis). Section 215 of this law ordered Verizon Communications to provide the NSA with all of its telephone metadata collected every single day (House of Representatives, *Report No. 114-109*, pt. 1, p. 2 [2015]).

17. Laura K. Donohue, "NSA Surveillance May Be Legal—But It's Unconstitutional," *Washington Post* (June 21, 2013).

18. Greenberg, *Rogue Justice*, op. cit., p. 233.

19. See, for instance, an Associated Press poll that found more than 60 percent of the respondents in the United States said they valued privacy over the NSA's antiterror protections (poll conducted by Eileen Sullivan and Jennifer Agiesta, [January 27, 2014]).

20. Suzanne E. Spaulding (former general counsel for SSCI and HPSCI), "Power Play: Did Bush Roll Past the Legal Stop Signs?" *Washington Post* (December 25, 2005), p. B1.

21. David S. Kris, "On the Bulk Collection of Tangible Things," *Journal of National Security Law & Policy* 7 (2014), p. 212.

22. My interview with Judge Morris S. "Buzz" Arnold, United States Court of Appeals for the Eighth Circuit, Little Rock, Arkansas (November 26, 2014).
23. Eric Lichtblau, "Security Czars on Apple's Side in Privacy War," *New York Times* (April 23, 2016), p. A1. STELLARWIND and PRISM are just two among myriad NSA collection programs whose codenames seem to have sprung from an overheated imagination: MYSTIC, BULLRUN, TUMULT, MONSTERMIND, TURMOIL, among scores of others that have no intrinsic meaning (see Greenberg, *Rogue Justice*, op. cit., p. 233), but that make keeping track of the agency's collection activities a game of sigint Whac-a-Mole.
24. Jane Mayer, "United States of Secrets (Part One): The Program," transcript, *Nightline*, PBS Television (2015), p. 24. For Hayden's unapologetic recollections of this era, see his *Playing to the Edge: American Intelligence in the Age of Terror* (New York: Penguin, 2016).
25. James Risen, *State of War: The Secret History of the CIA and the Bush Administration* (New York: Free Press, 2006), p. 43.
26. Quoted in Scott Shane, "At Security Agency, News of Surveillance Program Gives Reassurances a Hollow Ring," *New York Times* (December 22, 2005), p. A14.
27. Peter M. Shane, "The NSA and the Legal Regime for Foreign Intelligence Surveillance," *I/S: A Journal of Law and Policy for the Information Society* (2014), p. 272. Or, as Mike Lofgren puts it with respect to the FISA Amendments Act of 2008, "This legislation retroactively legalized the Bush administration's illegal and unconstitutional surveillance first revealed by the *New York Times* in 2005 and indemnified the telecommunications companies for their cooperation in these acts. The bill passed easily: All that was required was the invocation of the word 'terrorism' and most members of Congress responded like iron filings obeying a magnet" (Mike Lofgren, "Essay: Anatomy of the Deep State," *Moyers & Company*, BillMoyers.com [February 21, 2014], p. 6).
28. Pub. L. No. 110-261, 122 Stat. 2436, amending 50 U.S.C. §1801 (2008).
29. Press release, Office of Senator Wyden (June 30, 2014).
30. Mondale, Stein, and Fisher, "No Longer a Neutral Magistrate," op. cit., p. 2268; Mondale served on the Church Committee as an activist against improper surveillance methods.
31. See, for example, John C. Yoo, *The Powers of War and Peace: The Constitution and Foreign Affairs after 9/11* (Chicago: University of Chicago Press, 2005). Just a few days after the 9/11 attacks, Yoo wrote in an OLC memo that, in the face of devastating terrorist attacks, "the government may be justified in taking measures which in less troubled conditions could be seen as infringements of individual liberties" (cited in Hayden, *Playing to the Edge*, op. cit., p. 58). The phrasing echoed what former president Nixon had claimed in response to questions posed to him by the Church Committee: "there have been—and will be in the future—circumstances in which presidents may lawfully authorize actions in the interests of the security of this country, which if undertaken by other persons, or even by the president under different circumstances, would be illegal" (Richard M. Nixon, "Supplementary Detailed Staff Reports on Foreign and Military Intelligence," *Final Report*, Book IV Appendix, Select Committee to Study Governmental Operations with Respect to Intelligence Activities, Rept. No. 94-755, U.S. Senate [April 23, 1976], pp. 157–158). These perspectives boil down to a belief that a president can do whatever he or she wants in a time of genuine or perceived crisis—not a good democratic principle short of a circumstance when, as faced by Abraham Lincoln, the survival of the Republic is at stake, in which case a president would have to act boldly and face the consequences afterward. General Hayden refers to Vice President Cheney's top aide, attorney David Addington, as the "alleged architect of the 'unitary executive' theory" (Hayden, *Playing to the Edge*, op. cit., p. 73). Perhaps Yoo and Addington can share this title. Harvard-trained Addington and the Yale-trained Yoo (like Hayden's deputy counsel cited in this chapter) could at least agree on one thing, despite their old-school rivalries: in foreign affairs, only Article II of the Constitution counted.
32. Michael V. Hayden, interview, "United States of Secrets," op. cit., p. 8.
33. Hayden, *Playing to the Edge*, op. cit., p. 68.
34. Vito Potenza, interview, "United States of Secrets," op. cit., p. 9.
35. Ibid., p. 19. While Hayden relied on the FISA Court to provide the authority he sought, he would later make clear his views on the relationship between judges and intelligence activities. Judges, he wrote, "know nothing about the subject and cannot be held to account for

adverse outcomes" (Michael V. Hayden and Michael B. Mukasey, "NSA Reform That Only ISIS Could Love," *Wall Street Journal* [November 17, 2014]). Hayden also wrote in his memoir: "We informed the third branch of government, the judiciary, in early 2002, *not because anyone thought that the president doing this under his Article 2 authorities needed the court's permission*, but rather because Justice was understandably concerned that the STELLARWIND-derived data could work its way into applications for routine FISA warrants" (*Playing to the Edge*, op. cit., p. 81, emphasis added). The FISA Court of Appeals apparently shares this view, stating in its very first (of few) rulings: "We take for granted that the president does have . . . inherent authority to conduct warrantless searches to obtain foreign intelligence information" (cited by Hayden, *Playing to the Edge*, p. 82)—a legal opinion many attorneys and others would find objectionable. In his memoir, Hayden also recalls how he was asked by Addington if he would join the White House in support of STELLARWIND even if the acting AG—the chief law enforcement officer of the United States—questioned its legality. "Yes, I would" was Hayden's response (p. 87).

36. Interview with General Hayden (April 7, 2010), conducted by Genevieve Lester, *When Should State Secrets Stay Secret? Accountability, Democratic Governance, and Intelligence* (New York: Cambridge University Press, 2015), p. 43. Hayden's boundary lines seemed wide enough to accommodate an entire rugby scrum.

37. The letter was dated January 4, 2006, and cited in Michael German, ed., *Strengthening Intelligence Oversight*, Brennan Center for Justice, New York University School of Law (2015), p. 11. Representative Harman complained further that use of a Gang of Four for reporting under the Intelligence Oversight Act of 1980 was, in fact, a violation of that law, which allows only a Gang of Eight—and, even in that case, for only a couple of days before SSCI and HPSCI must be fully informed.

38. In contrast, Hayden has opined (*Playing to the Edge*, op. cit.), in the context of NSA's briefings to Congress on STELLARWIND, TSP, and PRISM, that the "executive has discretion, though, in limiting how many members actually get briefed" (p. 77). Hayden acknowledged, however, that "politically it was a mistake [to limit the briefings to only a few members of Congress] and strategically it led to a loss of political and, more important, popular support for what we were doing" (p. 80). The general noted further: "A better course would have been to brief the entire House and Senate Intelligence Committees along with a limited number of staff on the whole program, effectively daring them to take action to stop *any* of it" (p. 80, original emphasis). Not until 2006—five years after its inception—was the full membership of SSCI and HPSCI briefed on STELLARWIND.

39. On the Snowden leaks, see Glenn Greenwald, *No Place to Hide: Edward Snowden, the NSA, and the U.S. Surveillance State* (New York: Metropolitan Books, 2014). Greenwald notes at the beginning of this book that he derived its title from a passage in a speech given by Frank Church in 1975, in which the senator spoke of the government's growing "capability to monitor everything—telephone conversations, telegrams, it doesn't matter. There would be no place to hide."

40. Quoted by Ken Dilanian, "NSA Weighed Ending Phone Program before Leak," *Associated Press* (March 30, 2015).

41. Quoted in Darren Samuelsohn, "Hill Draws Criticism over NSA Oversight," *Politico* (March 2, 2014), p. 2.

42. Paul J. Quirk and William Bendix, "Secrecy and Negligence: How Congress Lost Control of Domestic Surveillance," *Issues in Governance Studies*, Brookings Institution, Washington, D.C. (March 2, 2015), pp. 9, 13.

43. My interview (June 16, 2015), Washington, D.C., original emphasis. For a scholarly argument in favor of using "fishing expeditions" to find terrorists and their affiliates, see Richard K. Betts, *Enemies of Intelligence* (New York: Columbia University Press, 2007), p. 173.

44. Diane Roark, interview, "United States of Secrets," op. cit., p. 2.

45. My interview with SSCI staffer (June 16, 2015), Washington, D.C.

46. Samuelsohn, "Hill Draws Criticism over NSA Oversight," op. cit., p. 1.

47. Civil liberties activists maintain that only one domestic terrorism defendant, an individual convicted of raising $15,000 for a Somali terrorist organization, was uncovered (in part) by the metadata program (Dilanian, "NSA Weighed Ending Phone Program," op. cit.).

48. Samuelsohn, "Hill Draws Criticism over NSA Oversight," op. cit., p. 3.
49. Quoted by Matthias Schwartz, "Who Can Control N.S.A. Surveillance?" *New Yorker* (January 23, 2015).
50. See "United States of Secrets," op. cit., p. 25; and Ken Dilanian, "Before Snowden, a Debate inside NSA," *Associated Press* (November 19, 2014).
51. Dilanian, "NSA Weighed Ending Phone Program," op. cit.
52. The formal name of the panel is the President's Review Group on Intelligence and Communications Technologies, which urged that privacy must be protected as a "central aspect of liberty" (*Liberty and Security in a Changing World*, U.S. Government Printing Office, Washington, D.C. [December 12, 2013], p. 47).
53. Samuelsohn, "Hill Draws Criticism over NSA Oversight," op. cit., p. 4.
54. Senator Dianne Feinstein, remark, "This Week with George Stephanopoulos," *ABC News* (June 9, 2013).
55. Jack Goldsmith, interview, "United States of Secrets," op. cit., p. 16. On the legal front, the White House counsel, Alberto Gonzales, has said (channeling Watergate's John Dean) that he signed the Addington document "because [he] wanted to protect the president" ("United States of Secrets," p. 18).
56. Michael J. Morell, quoted in David E. Sanger, "In Book, Ex-C.I.A. Official Rebuts Republican Claims on Benghazi Attack," *New York Times* (May 4, 2015), p. A8.
57. Jennifer Steinhauer, "Senate Is Sharply Split over Extension of N.S.A. Phone Data Collection," *New York Times* (May 22, 2015), p. A15.
58. Dilanian, "NSA Weighed Ending Phone Program," op. cit., p. 3.
59. See Steinhauer, "Senate Is Sharply Split," op. cit.; and David E. Sanger, "Sky Isn't Falling after Snowden, N.S.A. Chief Says," *New York Times* (June 30, 2014), p. A1.
60. Unsigned editorial, "Edward Snowden, Whistle-Blower," *New York Times* (January 2, 2014), p. A18. In contrast, Hayden wrote in a memoir that he wanted to put Snowden on a "different list" than the short list for the European Parliament's Sakharov Prize for Freedom of Thought, for which Snowden had been nominated (eventually won by teenager Malala Yousafzai of Pakistan). Hayden's critics jumped on this comment as a veiled allusion to a "kill list" for terrorists and other enemies of the United States—an accusation that Hayden later in his memoir called "ludicrous," although he never specified what kind of list he had in mind (Hayden, *Playing to the Edge*, op. cit., p. 421).
61. Charlie Savage, "House Intelligence Committee Urges Obama Not to Grant Snowden Pardon," *New York Times* (September 16, 2016), p. A16. The *Washington Post* editorial board opposed a pardon, too, bowing to the HPSCI position that Snowden possibly caused "tremendous damage" to U.S. national security with his release of some classified documents unrelated to the NSA, even if he should be thanked for revealing that agency's "excesses." One example of damage: disclosure of U.S. cooperation with Scandinavian services against Russia. The *Post* recommended that Snowden return home and "hash out all of this before a jury of his peers" (see Editorial Board, "No Pardon for Edward Snowden," *Washington Post* [September 17, 2016]). For an overview of the Snowden affair, see Loch K. Johnson, ed., "An INS Special Forum: Implications of the Snowden Leaks," *Intelligence and National Security* 29/6 (December 2014), pp. 793–810. For cogent arguments against a pardon, see Jack Goldsmith, "Why President Obama Won't, and Shouldn't, Pardon Snowden," *Lawfare* (September 16, 2016); and, in favor, Kenneth Roth and Salil Shetty, "Pardon Snowden," *New York Times* (September 15, 2016), p. A25.
62. Quoted in Steven Aftergood, "Sorting through the Snowden Aftermath," *Secrecy News*, FAS (September 19, 2016), p. 3. Aftergood properly observed that "the fact [that] U.S. intelligence surveillance policies had to be modified in response to the public controversy over Snowden's disclosures was a tacit admission that intelligence oversight behind closed doors had failed to fulfill its role up to that point" (p. 2). On November 28, 2016, fifteen former senior members of the Church Committee staff (including Chief Counsel Schwarz and Staff Director Miller) sent a letter to President Obama urging him "to extend leniency to Edward Snowden in negotiating a fair and just settlement of the criminal charges against him, based on the public benefits that resulted from his disclosures." I and a few other senior staffers who had served on the Committee did not sign the letter, on grounds that Snowden's leaks had gone

far beyond revealing the metadata program—to include classified documents whose release proved harmful to the United States. The president took no action on Snowden before leaving office in January 2017.

63. Hayden and Mukasey, "NSA Reform That Only ISIS Could Love," op. cit.

64. *Congressional Record* 160 (November 18, 2014), p. S6077.

65. See, for example, Wyden press release (June 30, 2014), Washington, D.C.

66. See, respectively, Steinhauer, "Senate Is Sharply Split," op. cit.; and unsigned editorial, "Rand Paul's Timely Takedown on the Patriot Act," *New York Times* (May 22, 2015), p. A24.

67. Jennifer Steinhauer, "Senate to Try Again Next Week after Bill on Phone Records Is Blocked," *New York Times* (May 24, 2015), p. A14.

68. Charlie Savage, "Surveillance Court Rules That N.S.A. Can Resume Bulk Data Collection," *New York Times* (July 1, 2015), p. A14.

69. Lawrence Wright, "The Al Qaeda Switchboard," Comment, *New Yorker* (January 13, 2014), p. 3; see also Philip Shenon, "An Explosive New 9/11 Charge," *Daily Beast* (June 21, 2014), which accuses DCI George Tenet of blocking the information sharing with the FBI. A senior SSCI staffer said to me, "The CIA wanted to be the hero in stopping the 9/11 terrorists; therefore, it never informed the FBI about the Qaeda members in San Diego" (June 18, 2015).

70. For a chronology of the torture program, see Wilson Andrews and Alicia Parlapiano, "A History of the C.I.A.'s Secret Interrogation Program," *New York Times* (December 9, 2014).

71. For the pro-interrogation views of one Agency attorney, see Fred F. Manget, retired Deputy General Counsel of CIA, in Mark Phythian, ed., "An *INS* Special Forum: The US Senate Select Committee Report on the CIA's Detention and Interrogation Program," *Intelligence and National Security* 31/1 (January 2016), p. 19. On the U.S. torture programs, see as well Jane Mayer, *The Dark Side* (New York: Doubleday, 2008).

72. Jane Mayer, "Torture and the Truth," *New Yorker* (December 22, 2014).

73. Steven Aftergood, "CIA Torture Report: Oversight, but No Remedies Yet," *Secrecy News*, FAS 2014/83 (December 10, 2014), p. 2.

74. In a failed effort to stop Goldsmith, Vice President Cheney's lawyer—Addington—resorted to fear tactics. "If you rule that way," he told Goldsmith, "the blood of the 100,000 people who die in the next attack will be on your hands" (interview with Goldsmith, *Frontline*, PBS Television transcript [October 16, 2007]).

75. An HPSCI member recalls urging the CIA, in a letter to the Agency's General Counsel (Scott Muller) in 2003, not to destroy the interrogation videotapes; see Jane Harman (D, California), "America's Spy Agencies Need an Upgrade," *Foreign Affairs* (March/April 2015), p. 103.

76. Colonel North referred to this destruction of "Enterprise" aircraft by the CIA as "the ultimate cover-up" (Oliver L. North with William Novak, *Under Fire: An American Story* [New York: HarperCollins, 1991], p. 272). See also Malcolm Byrne, *Iran-Contra: Reagan's Scandal and the Unchecked Abuse of Presidential Power* (Lawrence: University Press of Kansas, 2014), p. 253. In 1973 during the Watergate controversy, Senator Mike Mansfield (D, Montana) sent a letter to federal agencies asking them to preserve all their files related to the incident for review by the pending Senate investigation. At the time, DCI Richard Helms had his secretary destroy all the tapes of conversations in his office over his seven-year tenure as the nation's intelligence chief (see Commission on CIA Activities within the United States [the Rockefeller Commission], *Report to the President* [June 1975], p. 204).

77. Senator Dianne Feinstein, "Dianne Feinstein: The CIA 'Cannot Shove the Laws Aside,'" *Nightline*, PBS Television transcript (May 19, 2015), p. 2.

78. My interview, Washington, D.C. (June 17, 2014).

79. Feinstein, "Dianne Feinstein: The CIA 'Cannot Shove the Laws Aside,'" op. cit., p. 1.

80. Dianne Feinstein, remarks concerning the Committee Report on CIA Detention, Interrogation Program, U.S. Senate floor (December 9, 2014).

81. *Committee Study of the Central Intelligence Agency's Detention and Interrogation Program*, Senate Select Committee on Intelligence, U.S. Senate, 113th Cong., 2nd Sess. (December 3, 2014), p. 38, hereafter the Senate Torture Report. For a series of thoughtful essays on the report, see "*INS* Special Forum," op. cit., pp. 8–27. In his memoir, Hayden persists in arguing (without evidence) that the information obtained by waterboarding detainees was "incredibly valuable" (Hayden, *Playing to the Edge*, op. cit., pp. 189, 224).

82. In Bill Harlow, ed., *Rebuttal: The CIA Responds to the Senate Intelligence Committee's Study of Its Detention and Interrogation Program* (Annapolis, MD: Naval Institute Press, 2015), pp. 8–9.
83. Every now and then, though, Russell would surprise the CIA and block what he considered was too steep a spending request for its annual budget (see, for example, Snider, *The Agency and the Hill*, op. cit., p. 175); Chambliss's support for intelligence was far less alloyed.
84. My interview (June 17, 2015), Washington, D.C.
85. Remark, Washington, D.C. (April 27, 2016).
86. See Loch K. Johnson, "Educing Information: Interrogation, Science and Art," *Studies in Intelligence* 51 (December 2007), pp. 43–46. George Packer notes that professional jargon in government (and elsewhere) "can be a fence raised to keep out the uninitiated and permit those within it to persist in the belief that what they do is too hard, too complex, to be questioned" ("Can You Keep a Secret?" *New Yorker* [March 7, 2016], p. 67).
87. Senate Torture Report, op. cit., Findings and Conclusions Section, p. 3. See also Scott Shane, "Waterboarded, He Now Makes Case to Go Free," *New York Times* (August 24, 2016), p. A1, which reports that "American intelligence officials wrongly concluded that [Zubaydah] was a top-ranking leader of Qaeda who might have knowledge of forthcoming plots."
88. See Adam Goldman, "Military Prosecutor: Senate Report on CIA Interrogation Program Is Accurate," *Washington Post* (February 10, 2016), p. A1.
89. Remark to Eric Bradner, "John Brennan Defends CIA," *CNN Politics* (December 12, 2014).
90. An important insider, Representative James Sensenbrenner (R, Wisconsin), the chief sponsor of the PATRIOT Act in 2001, told correspondent Mattathias Schwartz that "the intelligence community has never made a compelling case that bulk collection stops terrorism." As Schwartz further reports, several outside critiques of the metadata and torture programs concluded, in harmony with the findings of the SSCI investigators, that the results were meager ("Who Can Control N.S.A. Surveillance?" op. cit). For similar conclusions, see also Michael German, "No NSA Poster Child: The Real Story of 9/11 Hijacker Khalid al-Mihdhar," *Defense One* (October 16, 2013); John Mueller and Mark G. Stewart, "Secret without Reason and Costly without Accomplishment: Questioning the National Security Agency's Metadata Program," *I/S: A Journal of Law and Policy for the Information Society* (2014), pp. 407–429; and Senators Ron Wyden, Mark Udall, and Martin Heinrich (D, New Mexico), Amicus Curiae, *First Unitarian Church v. NSA* (No. 13-3287, November 2013).
91. John Brennan, public remarks, Brookings Institution, Washington, D.C. (July 13, 2016). The Republican presidential nominee in 2016, Donald Trump, had a rather different view. "I would bring back waterboarding," he said on the campaign trail (February 2, 2016), adding, "and I'd bring back a hell of a lot worse than waterboarding."
92. President Barack Obama, statement, White House (December 9, 2014).
93. Mark Hosenball, "CIA Deceived White House, Public over 'Brutal' Interrogations," *Reuters* (December 9, 2014).
94. Based on my interviews with James Angleton periodically throughout the summer and fall of 1975, Washington, D.C.; see also chapter 10 in this book. Angleton would have nodded his head knowingly at a recent report on the use of torture by South Korean intelligence against suspected home-grown spies for North Korea. "They made me naked and beat me randomly, threatening to burn my genitals with cigarettes," remembered one victim, later exonerated. "They threatened to rape my fiancée and even her mother. In the end, I told them I would confess to whatever they wanted me to" (Lee Cheol, in a documentary film by investigative journalist Choi Seungho, "Spy Nation" [2016], quoted in Choe Sang-Hun, "Film Shines Light on South Korean Spy Agency's Fabrication of Enemies," *New York Times* [September 18, 2016], p. A9).
95. On rapport interrogation and its successes, see the comments of FBI special agent Ali H. Soufan, "What Torture Never Told Us," *New York Times* (September 6, 2009), p. A9, who concluded that the CIA's interrogation methods were "ineffective, unreliable, unnecessary and destructive." According to a CIA report issued five years before the 9/11 attacks, "Quite apart from moral and legal considerations, physical torture or extreme mental torture is not an expedient device" ("The Interrogation of Suspects under Arrest," Center for the Study of Intelligence, Central Intelligence Agency, Langley, Virginia [July 2, 1996]). On the

Israeli experience, see Joseph Lelyveld, "Interrogating Ourselves," *New York Times Sunday Magazine* (June 12, 2005), pp. 36ff.

96. Rumsfeld is quoted by John C. Yoo, "From Guantanamo to Abbottabad," *Wall Street Journal* (May 4, 2011); and Karl Rove was interviewed by Chris Matthews, *Hardball with Chris Matthews*, MSNBC Television (June 22, 2005).
97. My personal experience, Oslo (September 19, 2003).
98. My personal experience at Yale University, New Haven, Conn. (Fall Semester, 2005).
99. This message appeared in December 2014.
100. Eric Severeid, interview with William O. Douglas, *CBS Evening News* (January 19, 1980).
101. J. William Fulbright, remarks, *Congressional Record* (May 17, 1966), p. 10808, cited by Randall Bennett Woods, *Fulbright: A Biography* (New York: Cambridge University Press, 1955), p. 420.
102. My interview, Washington, D.C. (June 16, 2015).
103. Dick Cheney, *In My Time: A Personal and Political Memoir* (New York: Threshold, 2012), pp. 522–523.
104. John Rizzo, *Company Man: Thirty Years of Controversy and Crisis in the CIA* (New York: Scribner, 2014).
105. Fred F. Manget, remarks, Symposium on William E. Colby, University of Georgia, Athens, Georgia, quoted in Lee Shearer, "Panelists Discuss Controversial Ex-CIA Chief," *Athens Banner-Herald* (November 16, 2012), p. A4. CIA attorney John Rizzo notes that the Office of Legal Counsel in the Department of Justice issued ten major opinions to the CIA confirming the legality of the interrogation program between 2002 and 2007 (Rizzo, *Company Man*, op cit., pp. 188–189, 212–216). Former DCI and HPSCI chair Porter Goss, who condoned waterboarding when he was at Langley, also dismissed the notion that the Agency had engaged in torture. The interrogations were not brutal, he argued in testimony to SSCI in 2006. "It's more of an art," he said, "or a science" (my interview with an SSCI staffer present at the Goss presentation [June 17, 2015], Washington, D.C.). Another CIA officer, though, objected strenuously to the adoption of harsh interrogation methods and he viewed the Torture Report as really "important." He went on: "In the future, if the CIA faces a situation where it comes to the edge, hopefully it will know to go back—and understand that it cannot do *anything*" (quoted by Connie Bruck, "The Inside War," *New Yorker* [June 22, 2015], p. 54, original emphasis). See also John W. Schiemann, *Does Torture Work?* (New York: Oxford University Press, 2016), an analysis using game theory that leads to the answer "no"; and Douglas A. Johnson, Alberto Mora, and Averell Schmidt, "The Strategic Costs of Torture: How 'Enhanced Interrogation' Hurt America," *Foreign Affairs* 95/5 (September/October 2016), pp. 121–132.
106. My interview with a senior SSCI staffer, Washington, D.C. (June 18, 2015).
107. Former vice president Dick Cheney, remarks, *Fox Television Evening News* (December 10, 2014); for Cheney's at-length defense of the interrogation program, see interview by Chuck Todd, "Meet the Press," *NBC Television* (December 14, 2014).
108. Jose A. Rodriguez, "Don't We Want to Stop Terrorism?" *Washington Post* (December 12, 2014), p. B1. In early 2017, incoming CIA Director Mike Pompeo selected Rodriguez's former deputy in the torture program, Gina Haspel, as his top deputy at Langley. Her name had appeared on the CIA cable that ordered the destruction of the torture videotapes (see Matthew Rosenberg, "C.I.A.'s New Deputy Had Leading Role in Torture of Detainees," *New York Times* [February 3, 2017], p. A10).
109. Hayden, *Playing to the Edge*, op. cit. In a thirty-eight-page document, Senator Feinstein has chronicled a long list of "factual errors and other problems" in Hayden's memoirs (https://www.feinstein.gov/public/). For essays (with Hayden, Rodriguez, McLaughlin, and Porter Goss among the authors) that dismiss SSCI's report on the grounds of Democratic staff bias, see Harlow, *Rebuttal*, op. cit. A top intelligence expert and journalist, James Bamford has written that Hayden "shifted from playing far from the edge to leaping over it"—especially when he agreed to STELLARWIND simply because the White House wanted it, even though the acting attorney general at the time and later FBI Director James Comey had declared the program unlawful (*Nation*, June 1, 2016).

110. Senator Dianne Feinstein, press conference remarks on Torture Report, Washington, D.C. (December 9, 2014).

111. Connie Bruck, "The Inside War," *New Yorker* (June 22, 2015), p. 43.

112. John McLaughlin, "John McLaughlin: CIA Interrogations Were Legal, Moral and Effective," *Nightline*, PBS Television transcript (May 19, 2015), p. 9.

113. Feinstein, *Nightline*, op. cit., p. 4; also Senator Mark Udall, interviewed by Scott Raab, "Mark Udall Promises America Will 'Be Disgusted' by CIA Torture Report," *Esquire* (January 2015).

114. Bruck, "Inside War," op. cit., p. 45.

115. Quoted anonymously by Jeremy Herb in *The Hill* (March 6, 2014), p. 11.

116. Bruck, "Inside War," op. cit., p. 46.

117. See the Senate Torture Report (Executive Summary), pp. 401–408. Shortly after the release of this Executive Summary, former CIA directors Tenet, Goss, and Hayden joined forces with McLaughlin and others in an op-ed noting that SSCI had ignored the frightening nature of the times in the weeks immediately after 9/11. They concluded: "The Al Qaeda leadership has not managed another attack on the homeland in the 13 years since [9/11], despite a strong desire to do so. The CIA's aggressive counterterrorism policies and programs are responsible for that success" (George J. Tenet, et al., "Ex-CIA Directors: Interrogations Saved Lives," *Wall Street Journal* [December 10, 2014]). For an example of how the CIA is not above conducting espionage operations against American journalists whom they view as misguided, see David M. Barrett, "JFK, FBI, CIA, and PFIAB: Playing Hardball over an Intelligence Leak to the *New York Times*, 1962," *Intelligence and National Security* 32 (January 2017), pp. 37–53.

118. On Abu Ghraib, see Eric Fair, *Consequence* (New York: Henry Holt, 2016); Philip Gourevitch and Errol Morris, *Standard Operating Procedure* (New York: Penguin, 2008); and Karen J. Greenberg and Joshua L. Dratel, eds., *The Torture Papers: The Road to Abu Ghraib* (New York: Oxford University Press, 2005).

119. McLaughlin, *Nightline*, op. cit., p. 5. For an example of another retired Agency officer (an attorney) who relies on this reasoning, see "*INS* Special Forum," op. cit., p. 20.

120. See Lelyveld, "Interrogating Ourselves," op. cit., p. 48. An experienced former FBI agent, Michael German of the Brennan Center at the New York University School of Law, has noted that "when you're the good guy and you're on the side of truth and democracy and the American way, anything that is an impediment to you is naturally bad, and needs to be overcome, even if it's the law" (quoted by Ken Dilanian, "A Legacy Shaped by Big Data," *Los Angeles Times* [April 1, 2014], p. A1).

121. Lelyveld, "Interrogating Ourselves," op. cit., p. 44.

122. Oslo, Norway (December 10, 2009). On the question of ideals and ethics, even if one prefers to skirt such topics when it comes to intelligence, there are practical reasons for avoiding the anger of other countries whose leaders may take such matters seriously. As a State Department Assistant Secretary for European and Eurasian Affairs during the second Bush Administration has put it, discounting the effects of questionable intelligence programs (his specific examples were the absence of habeas corpus and the use of torture at Guantánamo) "hurt everything we tried to do. . . . It cost us political capital" (Daniel Fried, quoted in Connie Bruck, "Why Obama Has Failed to Close Guantánamo," *New Yorker* (August 1, 2016), p. 38).

   A major CIA intelligence collection operation in the 1970s, Project Jennifer, underscores how different people—all well meaning—can judge the merits of specific espionage activities in different ways. The objective of Project Jennifer was to raise a sunken Soviet submarine from the bottom of the Pacific Ocean, using a deep-sea mining vessel, the *Glomar Explorer*, contracted by the Agency from millionaire Howard Hughes. When the story leaked to the media, Senator Frank Church said that "if we are prepared to pay Howard Hughes $350 million for an obsolete Russian submarine, it's little wonder we are broke." His colleague, Barry Goldwater, offered a contrasting point of view. "Frankly," he said, "if they hadn't gone out and raised that sub, I'd be mad" (see Loch K. Johnson, *A Season of Inquiry Revisited: The Church Committee Confronts America's Spy Agencies* [Lawrence: University Press of Kansas, 2015], pp. 28, 32). One of the CIA officers involved in the project wrote a book about the experience that professed its high value: David H. Sharp, *The CIA's Greatest Covert Operation* (Lawrence: University Press of Kansas, 2012).

123. Lelyveld, "Interrogating Ourselves," op. cit., p. 4.
124. Feinstein, *Nightline*, op. cit., p. 3. See, also Ken Dilanian, "Two Psychologists Who Helped Run CIA Interrogations Had Never before Conducted One," *Associated Press* (December 10, 2014).
125. Connie Bruck, "Inside War," *New Yorker* (June 22, 2015), p. 48.
126. See Mark Mazzetti and Matt Apuzzo, "C.I.A. Officers Are Cleared in Senate Computer Search," *New York Times* (January 15, 2015), p. A8.
127. Cristian Farias, "American Public Is Not Entitled to See Full Senate Torture Report, Court Rules," *Huffington Post* (March 13, 2016).
128. Remarks to the Senate (December 9, 2014).
129. Tenet, et al., "Ex-CIA Directors," op. cit.
130. David Ignatius, "The Torture Report's One Glaring Weakness," *Washington Post* (December 11, 2014). A senior CIA official has argued that when it came to keeping lawmakers informed about the interrogation program, their claim to have been misled is "farcical, not true. . . . I can tell you, I had difficulty getting on the calendars of senators I wanted to brief. Their ardor for the truth is greater now than it was then, in some cases" (interview with Robert Grenier, former CIA/CTC Director, 2004–2006, *News Hour*, PBS Television ([December 9, 2014]).
131. Mike Glennon, Fletcher School of Law and Diplomacy, remarks, Levin Center Conference on Intelligence Accountability, U.S. Senate (October 20, 2015).
132. See Amy Zegart, "*INS* Special Forum," op. cit., p. 25. The denials of normative bias in the report were expressed by several participants in the Levin Center Conference, op. cit., both on the SSCI staff and outsiders.
133. Dianne Feinstein, "NSA's Watchfulness Protects America," *Wall Street Journal* (October 13, 2013). In a Senate hearing, Feinstein—in support of the NSA sigint programs that had become controversial—rued "how little information" the United States had about Al Qaeda before the 9/11 attacks. "They will come after us, and I think we need to prevent an attack wherever we can" (Schwartz, "Who Can Control N.S.A. Surveillance?" op. cit.).
134. Professor Pfiffner, "*INS* Special Forum," op. cit., p. 23.
135. Feinstein, *Nightline*, op. cit., p. 6.
136. Statement, U.S. Senate floor (December 9, 2014), cited by Professor Pfiffner in "*INS* Special Forum," op. cit., p. 23. McCain said elsewhere that he "totally agree[d] with the report" (Matt Sledge and Michael McAuliff, "CIA Torture Report Approved by Senate Intelligence Committee," *Huffington Post* [October 13, 2012]).
137. Pfiffner, "*INS* Special Forum," op. cit., p. 24; see also Emma Harries, "The Incoherence of the Only Serious Argument for Torture," *Intelligence and National Security* 32/2 (March 2017), pp. 463–483.
138. Public Law 109-148, div. A, tit. X, §§ 1001–1006, 119 Stat. 2680, 2739-44 (2005).

Chapter 6

1. The Kean Commission, *The 9/11 Commission Report: Final Report of the National Commission on Terrorist Attacks Upon the United States* (New York: Norton, 2004), p. 420.
2. See Louis Fisher, *Defending Congress and the Constitution* (Lawrence: University Press of Kansas, 2011), pp. 326–327, and his "The State Secrets Privilege: From Bush II to Obama," *Presidential Studies Quarterly* 46/1 (March 2016), pp. 173–193.
3. Remarks, "Meet the Press," *NBC Television* (November 21, 2004).
4. James Risen and Eric Lichtblau, "Bush Lets U.S. Spy on Callers without Courts," *New York Times* (December 16, 2005), p. A1.
5. Representative Nancy Pelosi, "The Gap in Intelligence Oversight," *Washington Post* (January 15, 2006), p. B7.
6. Matthew D. McCubbins and Thomas Schwartz, "Congressional Oversight Overlooked: Police Patrols and Fire Alarms," *American Journal of Political Science* 26 (1984), pp. 165–179.
7. Harry H. Ransom, "Secret Intelligence Agencies and Congress," *Society* 123 (1975), pp. 33–38.
8. See David Mayhew, *The Electoral Connection* (New Haven, CT: Yale University Press, 1974).
9. Richard A. Clarke, *Against All Enemies: Inside America's War on Terror* (New York: Free Press, 2004), pp. 238–239.

10. I first presented an exploration of these patterns of accountability in "Supervising America's Secret Foreign Policy: A Shock Theory of Congressional Oversight for Intelligence," in David P. Forsythe, Patrice C. McMahon, and Andrew Wederman, eds., *American Foreign Policy in a Globalized World* (New York: Routledge, 2006), pp. 173–192.

11. Hijzen arrived at this observation after a January 23, 2012, interview with Joris Voorhoeve, a member of the Dutch parliamentary oversight committee; see Constant Hijzen, "More Than a Ritual Dance: The Dutch Practice of Parliamentary Oversight and Control of the Intelligence Community," *Security and Human Rights* 24 (2013), p. 232.

12. I am grateful to my research assistant, Rachael Lee Stewart, for helping me gather these data (and the data in chapter 7) from the *New York Times* archives, stored in the University of Georgia Main Library, Athens, Georgia.

13. Harry H. Ransom, email communication to me (February 7, 2006). The Trump statement comes from a tweet sent out by the new president on February 17, 2017, and widely quoted (see, for example, Amanda Erickson, "Trump Called the Media an 'Enemy of the American People,'" *Washington Post* [February 18, 2017], p. A1). Historian Michael Beschloss reminds us of a comment from President Richard M. Nixon to his secretary of state Henry Kissinger: "The press is the enemy, the establishment is the enemy, the professors are the enemy" (December 1972 tape, quoted by Maureen Dowd, "Trapped in Trump's Brain," *New York Times* [February 19, 2017], p. SR11). Trump's attacks, though, became even more persistent, shrill, and public in his media-bashing.

    In contrast, the long-time CBS correspondent, Dan Rather, has described "journalism as the red beating heart of democracy" (quoted by Tad Friend, "The Pictures," *New Yorker* [November 2, 2015]). Less floridly, Martin Baron, a *Washington Post* editor (and earlier a heroic figure of investigative journalism at the *Boston Globe*, as depicted in the 2016 film *Spotlight*, the only movie about journalists ever to win the Academy Award for Best Picture), has said, "Somebody needs to hold powerful institutions and individuals accountable, and we're the ones [the media] who have that particular role in our society" (interview, "NewsHour," *PBS Television* [February 29, 2016]). Perhaps the most famous investigative reporter of all in the United States, the *Washington Post*'s Bob Woodward has commented that his first thought when he wakes up each morning is "what are the bastards hiding"—a mantra for everyone involved in the business of government accountability (quoted in *Amherst*, a magazine published by Amherst College in Massachusetts [Fall 2014], p. 5, drawing on remarks he made at the college in an open forum during the fall semester of 2014).

    Intelligence scholar Jennifer Kibbe believes that, because of the classified nature of espionage work, "in all but a few exceptional cases, the media is effectively precluded" from playing a supporting role with Congress in monitoring the secret agencies (Jennifer Kibbe, "Congressional Oversight of Intelligence: Is the Solution Part of the Problem?" *Intelligence and National Security* 25/1 [February 2010], p. 25). While secrecy does make the media's reporting on spies difficult, I think that journalists have done a remarkably good job in reporting on intelligence mishaps and setting an oversight agenda for SSCI and HPSCI (see chapter 7); unfortunately, though, newspapers across the nation have been forced, in an age of a dire economic turndown for print media, to cut their staffs and investigative units as cost-saving measures—especially within the foreign-policy and national security realms.

14. Hans Born, Loch K. Johnson, and Ian Leigh, eds., *Who's Watching the Spies? Establishing Intelligence Service Accountability* (Washington, DC: Potomac Books, 2005).

15. Edward Wong, "Chinese Leader's News Flash: Journalists Must Serve Party," *New York Times* (February 23, 2016), p. A1.

16. Loch K. Johnson, John C. Kuzenski, and Erna Gellner, "The Study of Congressional Investigations," *Congress & the Presidency* 19 (Autumn 1992), pp. 138–156.

17. See, for instance, Scott Shane, "Senate Panel's Partisanship Troubles Former Members," *New York Times* (March 12, 2006), p. A18.

18. For a recollection of these years, see my "Congressional Supervision of America's Secret Agencies: The Experience and Legacy of the Church Committee," *Public Administration Review* 64 (January 2004), pp. 3–14.

19. For the Church Committee reports, see Select Committee to Study Governmental Operations with Respect to Intelligence Activities, *Final Report*, 94th Cong., 2nd Sess., Sen. Rept. No.

94-755, 6 vols. (Washington, DC: U.S. Government Printing Office, March 1976). The Pike Committee report was leaked and published as "The CIA Report the President Doesn't Want You to Read: The Pike Papers," *Village Voice* (February 16 and 23, 1976). For an overview of these episodes, see Loch K. Johnson, *A Season of Inquiry Revisited: The Church Committee Confronts America's Spy Agencies* (Lawrence: University Press of Kansas, 2015).

20. U.S. Congress, *Report on the Iran-Contra Affair*, Senate Select Committee on Secret Military Assistance to Iran and the Nicaraguan Opposition (the Inouye Committee) and House Select Committee to Investigate Cover Arms Transactions with Iran (the Hamilton Committee), with the committees operating jointly, Sen. Rept. 100-216 and H. Rept. 100-433 (November 1987). For overviews, see Malcolm Byrne, *Iran-Contra: Reagan's Scandal and the Unchecked Abuse of Presidential Power* (Lawrence: University Press of Kansas, 2014); and William S. Cohen and George J. Mitchell, *Men of Zeal: A Candid Inside Story of the Iran-Contra Hearings* (New York: Viking, 1988).

21. On the deaths in Somalia, see Mark Bowden, *Black Hawk Down: A Story of Modern War* (Berkeley, CA: Atlantic Monthly Press, 1999); and Robert Patman, *Strategic Shortfall: The Somalia Syndrome and the March to 9/11* (Westport, CT: Praeger Security International, 2010). On the specifics of the Ames case, see David Wise, *Nightmover* (New York: HarperCollins, 1995); and "An Assessment of the Aldrich H. Ames Espionage Case and Its Implications for U.S. Intelligence," *Staff Report*, Senate Rpt. 103-90, Select Committee on Intelligence, U.S. Senate, 103rd Cong., 2nd Sess. (November 1994). For the Aspin-Brown Commission report, see *Preparing for the 21st Century: An Appraisal of U.S. Intelligence*, Report of the Commission on the Rules and Capabilities of the United States Intelligence Community (Washington, DC: U.S. Government Printing Office, March 1, 1996); and for a detailed case study of this inquiry, see Loch K. Johnson, *The Threat on the Horizon: An Inside Account of America's Search for Security after the Cold War* (New York: Oxford University Press, 2011).

22. Joint Inquiry into Intelligence Community Activities before and after the Terrorist Attacks of September 11, 2001, *Final Report*, U.S. Senate Select Committee on Intelligence and U.S. House Permanent Select Committee on Intelligence (Washington, DC: U.S. Government Printing Office, December 2002); and Kean Commission, *The 9/11 Commission Report*, op. cit.

23. "Intelligence Authorization Act for Fiscal Year 2005," *Report*, H. Rept. 108–558, Permanent Select Committee on Intelligence, U.S. House of Representatives, 108th Cong., 2nd Sess. (June 21, 2004), pp. 23–27. On the subject of humint, see Frederick P. Hitz, *The Great Game: The Myth and Reality of Espionage* (New York: Knopf, 2004).

24. Robert Jervis, *Why Intelligence Fails: Lessons from the Iranian Revolution and the Iraq War* (Ithaca, NY: Cornell University Press, 2010); Loch K. Johnson, "The Failures of U.S. Intelligence and What Can Be Done about Them," *Yale Journal of International Affairs* 2 (February 2006), pp. 116–131, as well as *Threat on the Horizon*, op. cit.

25. For his recollections, see Colin Powell, with Tony Koltz, *It Worked for Me: In Life and Leadership* (New York: HarperCollins, 2012), pp. 217–224.

26. Bob Woodward, *Plan of Attack* (New York: Simon & Schuster, 2004), p. 249. Tenet subsequently maintained in his memoirs that he used the "slam dunk" phrase simply to underscore for the president his belief that the IC could come up with a strong case for the public that Iraq probably had WMDs (George Tenet with Bill Harlow, *At the Center of the Storm: My Years at the CIA* [New York: HarperCollins, 2007], p. 362)—a distinction without a difference.

27. See, for example, the memoirs of former SSCI chairman Bob Graham, with Jeff Nussbaum, *Intelligence Matters* (New York: Random House, 2004).

28. Tenet, *At the Center of the Storm*, op. cit., p. 449.

29. *Report to the President*, the Commission on the Intelligence Capabilities of the United States Regarding Weapons of Mass Destruction, led by former senator Charles S. Robb (D, Virginia) and Judge Laurence H. Silberman (Washington, DC: U.S. Government Printing Office, March 13, 2005).

30. *Report on the U.S. Intelligence Community's Prewar Intelligence Assessments on Iraq* (the Roberts Report), Senate Select Committee on Intelligence (the Roberts Committee), U.S. Senate, 108th Cong., 2nd Sess. (July 7, 2004), which (like the Robb-Silberman Report) chastised the IC for its poor coverage of WMD developments in Iraq prior to the U.S. invasion in 2003,

and also offered a sensible catalog of recommendations to improve the core intelligence mission of collection and analysis.

31. See Loch K. Johnson, "The CIA and the Media," *Intelligence and National Security* 1 (May 1986), pp. 143–169; on the *Washington Post* article published in 1996, see Alicia Upano, "Will a History of Government Using Journalists Repeat Itself under the Department of Homeland Security?" *News Media & the Law* (Winter 2003), p. 10.

32. Johnson, *Threat on the Horizon*, op. cit., p. 340.

33. See Tim Weiner, "Chief Defends Secrecy, in Spending and Spying, to Senate," *New York Times* (February 23, 1996), p. A1; and Walter Pincus and R. Jeffrey Smith, "CIA Defends Rule on Use of Reporters," *Washington Post* (February 23, 1996), p. A1.

34. Public Law 104-293.

35. Title VII, Intelligence Authorization Act for FY 1999. When the Whistleblowers Protection Act passed, it inadequately covered IC employees. On October 10, 2012, President Obama issued Presidential Policy Direction 19 to provide more comprehensive protections for potential whistle-blowers; see Joe Davidson, "Obama Issues Whistleblower Directive to Security Agencies," *Washington Post* (October 11, 2012), Federal Eye Blog; Thomas F. Gimble, testimony, "National Security Whistleblower Protection," Hearings, House Committee on Government Reform (February 14, 2006), especially p. 6; and *Secrecy News*, FAS (October 11, 2012). An executive order is no substitute for enduring statutory language, however, and reformers continued to urge Congress to make the provisions of the order permanent.

36. For a legislative history of this landmark statute, see Loch K. Johnson, "Legislative Reform of Intelligence Policy," *Polity* 17 (Spring 1985), pp. 549–573.

37. Powell, *It Worked for Me*, op. cit., p. 222.

38. See Rhodri Jeffreys-Jones, "Why Was the CIA Established in 1947?" in Rhodri Jeffreys-Jones and Christopher Andrews, eds., *Eternal Vigilance? 50 Years of the CIA* (London: Cass, 1997), pp. 20–41; and Loch K. Johnson, "A Central Intelligence System: Truman's Dream Deferred," *American Journal of Intelligence* 21 (February 2006), pp. 16–36.

39. These events are chronicled in various volumes; see, for example: Rhodri Jeffreys-Jones, *The CIA & American Democracy* (New Haven, CT: Yale University Press, 1989); Loch K. Johnson, *America's Secret Power: The CIA in a Democratic Society* (New York: Oxford University Press, 1989), as well as *Secret Agencies: U.S. Intelligence in a Hostile World* (New Haven, CT: Yale University Press, 1996); and John Ranelagh, *The Agency: The Rise and Decline of the CIA* (New York: Simon & Schuster, 1987).

40. See the often-overlooked but insightful memoir by one of the White House conspirators, Egil "Bud" Krogh, written with the assistance of Matthew Krogh and entitled *Integrity: Good People, Bad Choices, and Life Lessons from the White House* (New York: Public Affairs, 2007), quote at p. 74. On Watergate (which has spawned a rich literature, both in the form of books and government reports), see also Samuel Dash, *Chief Counsel: Inside the Ervin Committee—the Untold Story of Watergate* (New York: Random House, 1976); and Bob Woodward and Karl Bernstein, *All the President's Men* (New York: Simon & Schuster, 1994).

41. This analysis does not attempt to include every intelligence scandal or failure; that list is much longer. See, for instance, the discussion of miscues in tracking Soviet military activities during the Cold War, in Johnson, *Threat on the Horizon*, op. cit., ch. 7; or the litany in Uri Friedman, "The Ten Biggest American Intelligence Failures," *Foreign Policy* (January 3, 2012), which includes Pearl Harbor (1941), the Bay of Pigs (1962), the Tet offensive in Vietnam (1968), the outbreak of the Yom Kippur War (1973), the Iranian Revolution (1979), the Soviet invasion of Afghanistan (1979), the collapse of the Soviet Union (1990), the Indian nuclear test (1998), the 9/11 attack (2001), and the Iraqi WMD mistake (2002). I include only the last two of the events on Friedman's list—the ones I think are the most significant in terms of a major public and investigative response since the time of the CIA's creation in 1947 (after Pearl Harbor, which was also the subject of a major inquiry); plus, I include the CHAOS, Iran-contra, and Somalia/Ames failures. Not everyone will agree with my choices. For instance, some (like Friedman, as well as Senator Daniel Moynihan) believe that the CIA's failure to predict the fall of the Soviet Union is one of the most important analytic errors in the Agency's history (see, for example, Daniel P. Moynihan, "Do We Still Need the C.I.A.? The State Department Can Do the Job," *New York Times* [May 19, 1991], p. E17). This sets the

bar too high, in my view, for no one could or did—not even the top academic Soviet specialists in the United States—predict that epic event with any precision. The Agency's group of Soviet analysts (SOVA) performed remarkably well, however, in its week-to-week monitoring of the Soviet economy's decline during the 1980s; SOVA suggested this sharply downward trend could lead to a profound political upheaval in Russia and its satellite states in Eastern Europe (see Johnson, *Threat on the Horizon,* op. cit.). The excellence of this tracking by SOVA is why the surprise about the precise timing of the Soviet fall is not included here as a major failure. Another significant intelligence failure not examined here is the CIA's conclusion during the Vietnam War that arms funneled by the North Vietnam enemy to its troops and allies (the Viet Cong or VC) in South Vietnam were arriving chiefly by way of the Ho Chi Minh Trail corridor, when in fact the port of Sihanoukville in Cambodia was the primary channel (see Kenneth Conboy, *The Cambodian Wars: Clashing Armies and CIA Covert Operations* [Lawrence: University Press of Kansas, 2013], p. 33). This was a costly error, but, as a tactical aspect of the war in Vietnam, it lies outside the scope of the major fire alarms explored in this chapter.

42. David Grondin, University of Ottawa, book review, *Perspectives on Politics* 13/3 (September 2015), p. 924, original emphasis.

43. Timothy J. Burger, "A New White House Memo Excludes CIA Director," *Time* (June 5, 2005), p. 21; and my several interviews with DNI James R. Clapper, Jr., from 2013 to 2016 (DNI Headquarters, Liberty Crossing, Virginia, and elsewhere).

44. David M. Barrett noted, however, in his *The CIA and Congress: The Untold Story from Truman to Kennedy* (Lawrence: University Press of Kansas, 2005), that lawmakers did not ignore their oversight duties completely; sometimes they even behaved as aggressive patrollers, including the strongly pro-CIA Senator Richard B. Russell of Georgia, as in the example given earlier in this book about his objection to what he considered a bloated Agency budget in one fiscal year. For the most part, though, Barrett found that the state of intelligence accountability prior to 1974 paled in comparison to the degree of supervision that occurred after Congress established SSCI and HPSCI as permanent and well-staffed panels on the Hill. This is the same conclusion reached by another thorough study: L. Britt Snider, *Congress and the Agency: CIA's Relationship with Congress, 1946–2004* (Washington, DC: Center for the Study of Intelligence, Central Intelligence Agency, 2008).

45. See Richard K. Betts, "Analysis, War and Decision: Why Intelligence Failures Are Inevitable," *World Politics* 31 (October 1978), pp. 61–89, and his *Enemies of Intelligence: Knowledge & Power in American National Security* (New York: Columbia University Press, 2007).

46. Remarks, *CNN* (October 14, 2002); see also Kevin Whitelaw and David E. Kaplan, "Don't Ask, Don't Tell," *U.S. News & World Report* (September 13, 2004), p. 36.

47. The Graham quote is from his appearance on "The Lehrer News Hour," *PBS Television* (October 17, 2002); see, as well, Senator Bob Graham with Jeff Nussbaum, *Intelligence Matters: The CIA, the FBI, Saudi Arabia, and the Failure of America's War on Terror* (New York: Random House, 2004). The comparison of the number of CIA case officers abroad and FBI agents in New York City comes from my interviews with various intelligence personnel and Hill staffers in recent years.

48. See Joel D. Aberbach, *Keeping a Watchful Eye: The Politics of Congressional Oversight* (Washington, DC: Brookings Institution, 1990); and *Workshop on Congressional Oversight and Investigations,* U.S. House of Representatives, 96th Cong., 1st Sess. (October 22, 1979).

49. Colin Powell (having been a highly decorated combat general) told former president Bill Clinton several years later that he never would have approved of a Black Hawk operation like the one in Somalia, unless it were conducted at night when U.S. forces have an advantage because of specialized equipment—such as nighttime goggles; see Bill Clinton, *My Life* (New York: Knopf, 2004), p. 553. Important details like this operational flaw are precisely what can be flushed out by lawmakers during executive session oversight hearings—ideally in advance of an operation. On this unhappy warfare on the Horn of Africa, see also Kenneth Allard, *Somalia Operations: Lessons Learned* (Ft. McNair, Washington, DC: National Defense University Press, January 1995); Walter Clarke and Jeffrey Herbst, eds., *Learning from Somalia: The Lessons of Armed Humanitarian Intervention* (Boulder, CO: Westview, 1997); Robert Oakley, *Somalia and Operation Restore Hope* (Washington, DC: U.S. Institute for

Peace Press, 1995); and Karen Von Hippel, *Democracy by Force: U.S. Military Intervention in the Post–Cold War World* (New York: Cambridge University Press, 2000).

50. John F. Elliff and Loch K. Johnson, "Counterintelligence," in Church Committee, *Foreign and Military Intelligence, Final Report,* op. cit.

51. See Richard A. Clark, *Against All Enemies* (New York: Free Press, 2004); and Johnson, *Threat on the Horizon,* op. cit.

52. See the Kean Commission Report, *The 9/11 Commission Report,* op. cit.; and Loch K. Johnson, "Framework for Strengthening U.S. Intelligence," op. cit.

53. Louis Freeh (the former FBI director), "Why Did the 9/11 Commission Ignore 'Able Danger'?" *Wall Street Journal* (November 17, 2005), p. A16.

54. David Barstow, William J. Broad, and Jeff Gerth, "How the White House Used Disputed Arms Intelligence," *New York Times* (October 3, 2004), p. A18.

55. See Loch K. Johnson, "Congress and the CIA: Monitoring the Dark Side of Government," *Legislative Studies Quarterly* 5 (November 1980), pp. 477–499.

56. See Loch K. Johnson, "Accountability and America's Secret Foreign Policy: Keeping a Legislative Eye on the CIA," *Foreign Policy Analysis* 1 (Spring 2005), pp. 99–120; and L. Britt Snider, "Congressional Oversight of Intelligence after September 22," in Jennifer E. Sims and Burton Gerber, eds., *Transforming U.S. Intelligence* (Washington, DC: Georgetown University Press, 2006), pp. 239–258.

57. This phrase is often attributed to Thomas Jefferson, but John Philpot Curran, the Lord Mayor of Dublin, also said in a speech in 1790 that "the condition upon which God hath given liberty to man is eternal vigilance" (John Bartlett, *Familiar Quotations,* 14th ed. [Boston: Little, Brown, 1968], p. 479).

58. Quoted in Bob Drogin, "Spy Agencies Fear Some Applicants Are Terrorists," *Los Angeles Times* (March 8, 2005), p. A1.

59. Ken Mehlman, remarks, "This Week with George Stephanopoulos," *ABC News* (February 5, 2006).

60. The Poindexter quote is from the final report of the Inouye-Hamilton Committee (discussed in chapter 4 of this book), vol. 8, p. 159; on the resistance of the Bush Administration to keeping SSCI and HPSCI fully informed on NSA wiretapping, see Scott Shane and Eric Lichtblau, "Full Committee Gets Briefing on Eavesdropping," *New York Times* (February 9, 2006), p. A20.

61. Arthur Conan Doyle, "The Blue Carbuncle," in *The Adventures of Sherlock Holmes* (New York: Oxford University Press, 1993), p. 164.

62. Remarks, *Frontline,* op. cit.

63. Interview with Suzanne E. Spaulding (April 6, 2011), conducted by Genevieve Lester, *When Should State Secrets Stay Secret? Accountability, Democratic Governance, and Intelligence* (New York: Cambridge University Press, 2015), pp. 119–120.

64. See, respectively, http://www.gwu.edu/nsarchiv and http://fas.org/irp/news/2005.

65. Remarks to me from OCA staff, CIA Headquarters (April 28, 2016).

66. Quoted in Peter Wallsten, "Lawmakers Say Obstacles Limited Oversight of NSA's Telephone Surveillance Program," *Washington Post* (August 10, 2013), p. A1. General Hayden has claimed that Rockefeller was happy to have the Al Qaeda terrorist Khalid Shaikh Mohammed tortured in 2003 and, in his memoirs, the general quotes the SSCI chair as saying on CNN at the time: "I wouldn't take anything off the table"—yet only to go on to denounce the CIA for its interrogation methods a decade later in the committee's Torture Report (see Michael V. Hayden, *Playing to the Edge: American Intelligence in the Age of Terrorism* [New York: Penguin, 2016]). Yet given the elliptical briefings from Hayden, the senator had at best only limited knowledge of the methods being used by the Agency in 2003; moreover, "wouldn't take anything off the table" is a standard Washington response on talk shows related to potential foreign-policy responses of the United States, as a way of signaling to America's enemies that they should tread carefully. For a thoughtful essay on SSCI's Torture Report, see Robert Jervis, "The Torture Blame Game: The Blotched Senate Report on the CIA's Misdeeds," *Foreign Affairs* (May/June 2015), who argues that "torture contributed to the belief that the U.S. was hypocritical in its proclaimed defense of liberty and human rights and prone to treat Muslims as less than fully human.... Perhaps torture was effective in gaining information but not in furthering the American national interests."

67. Interviewed by Stephen R. Weissman (June 8, 1994) and quoted in his *A Culture of Deference: Congress's Failure of Leadership in Foreign Policy* (New York: Basic Books, 1995), p. 112.

68. Remarks, *Hearings on Congressional Oversight of Intelligence Activities*, Select Committee on Intelligence, U.S. Senate, 119th Cong., 1st Sess., Rept. 110-794 (November 13, 2007), p. 35.

69. Gregory F. Treverton, "Covert Action: Forward to the Past?" in Loch K. Johnson, ed., *Essentials of Strategic Intelligence* (Santa Barbara, CA: Praeger, 2015), p. 200.

70. On the Keating letter, see Michael S. Schmidt, "F.B.I. Said to Find It Could Not Have Averted Boston Attack," *New York Times* (August 3, 2013), p. A13; on the quest for information about the drone program, see Mark Mazzetti and Mark Landler, "Drone War Rages On, Even as Administration Talks about Ending It," *New York Times* (August 3, 2013), p. A4; as well as Scott Shane, "U.S. Drone Strikes Are Said to Target Rescuers at Sites," *New York Times* (February 2, 2012), p. A4; Declan Walsh, Eric Schmitt, and Ihsanullah Tipu Mehsud, "Drones at Issue as U.S. Rebuilds Ties to Pakistan," *New York Times* (March 19, 2012), p. A1; and Scott Shane, "Election Spurred a Move to Codify U.S. Drone Policy," *New York Times* (November 25, 2012), p. A1. Shane has also written a first-rate book on the CIA's use of a drone attack against an American citizen in Yemen, entitled *Objective Troy: A Terrorist, a President, and the Rise of the Drone* (New York: Tim Duggan, 2015).

71. Kibbe, "Congressional Oversight of Intelligence," op. cit., p. 37. SSCI Chair John D. "Jay" Rockefeller IV has also testified that he found many of his briefings from intelligence officials "superficial" and "inconsequential" (remarks, *Hearings on Congressional Oversight of Intelligence Activities*, op. cit., p. 26).

72. As noted in the previous chapter, when further queried about his misleading answers to lawmakers on the Iran-contra investigative panel, a high-ranking CIA officer replied that he had been "technically correct, [if] specifically evasive" (*Hearings*, Inouye-Hamilton Committees, op. cit., p. 142). An important, if reluctant, witness to the scandal was Secretary of State George Shultz of the Reagan Administration. He admonished the vice president at the time, George H. W. Bush (who was aware of the expanding Iran-contra operations), that he ought to exercise greater caution in dealing with the plotters on the NSC staff. Bush said he would be careful in what he said publicly about their activities, leading Shultz to emphasize to him (according to notes taken by the secretary's aide), "You can't be tech[nically] right, you have to be right" (Malcolm Byrne, *Iran-Contra: Reagan's Scandal and the Unchecked Abuse of Presidential Power* [Lawrence: University Press of Kansas, 2015], p. 257). The CIA would have benefited from adopting the Shultz approach at the time. During a later period of controversy over the NSA warrantless collection programs, its director, General Hayden, displayed another tendency toward game-playing with language: "there was *no* DOJ opinion that [STELLARWIND] was unlawful, just a refusal to currently commit to its lawfulness" (Hayden, *Playing to the Edge*, op. cit., p. 88, original emphasis). When the acting AG and the FBI director threatened to resign unless STELLARWIND were placed on firmer legal footing, the White House moved at long last to seek congressional support.

73. My interview with a senior SSCI investigator who worked on the committee's Torture Report (June 18, 2015), Washington, D.C.

74. Dexter Perkins, *The Evolution of American Foreign Policy* (New York: Oxford University Press, 1948), p. 168.

Chapter 7

1. On the relationships among intelligence, the media, and oversight activities, see Vian Bakir, "Political-Intelligence Elites, Strategic Political Communication, and the Press: The Need for, and Utility of, a Benchmark of Public Accountability Demands," *Intelligence and National Security* 7 (December), pp. 1–22; Claudia Hillebrand, "The Role of News Media in Intelligence Oversight," *Intelligence and National Security* 27 (October 2012), pp. 689–706; Robert Dover and Michael S. Goodman, eds., *Spinning Intelligence: Why Intelligence Needs the Media, Why the Media Needs Intelligence* (New York: Columbia University Press, 2009); David P. Hadley, "A Constructive Quality: The Press, the CIA, and Covert Intervention in the 1950s," *Intelligence and National Security* 31/2 (March 2016), pp. 246–265; Loch K. Johnson, "The CIA and the Media," *Intelligence and National Security* 1 (May 1986), pp. 143–169; Shlomo Shpiro,

Intelligence and the Media (London: Cass, 2002); and Amy B. Zegart, "The Domestic Politics of Irrational Intelligence Oversight," *Political Science Quarterly* 126 (Spring 2011), pp. 1–27.

2. See, for example, Christopher J. Deering, "Alarms and Patrols: Legislative Oversight in Foreign and Defense Policy," in C. C. Campbell, N. C. Rae, and J. F. Stack, Jr., *Congress and the Politics of Foreign Policy* (Upper Saddle River, NJ: Prentice Hall, 2003), pp. 112–138.

3. Matthew D. McCubbins and Thomas Schwartz, "Congressional Oversight Overlooked: Police Patrols and Fire Alarms," *American Journal of Political Science* 28 (1984), pp. 165–179.

4. Quoted by Philip Shenon, "As New 'Cop on the Beat,' Congressman Starts Patrol," *New York Times* (February 6, 2007), p. A18.

5. These ten shock cases strike the author as the most important since the creation of the CIA. Nonetheless, one can think of other high-profile intelligence failures that could qualify as contenders, such as the mistaken Agency estimate about the timing of a first Soviet nuclear test in 1949; or, more recently, the scandal related to the CIA's use of harsh interrogation methods in the struggle against global terrorists. In neither of these cases, though, were there major follow-up government inquiries. The weakest entry on the list of shocks presented here is the CIA-Watergate case, because it didn't prove to be much of a scandal; it is included, however, because it was widely perceived at the time as a potential major shock, had the CIA truly been involved in the burglary or the cover-up. While the list could vary somewhat, certainly the ten cases examined here are widely viewed as significant scandals or intelligence failures. (See also note 41 in chapter 6.)

6. S. Timmermans and A. Mauck, "The Promises and Pitfalls of Evidence-Based Medicine," *Health Affairs* 24 (2005), pp. 18–28.

7. For appraisals of the intelligence studies field, see Loch K. Johnson, "The Development of Intelligence Studies," in Robert Dover, Michael S. Goodman, and Claudia Hillebrand, eds., *The Routledge Companion to Intelligence Studies* (London: Routledge, 2013), ch. 1; Peter Gill and Mark Phythian, "What Is Intelligence Studies?" *International Journal of Intelligence, Security and Public Affairs* 18/1 (2016), pp. 5–19; Loch K. Johnson and Allison M. Shelton, "Thoughts on the State of Intelligence Studies: A Survey Report," *Intelligence and National Security* 28 (February 2013), pp. 109–120; Stephen Marrin, "Improving Intelligence Studies as an Academic Discipline," *Intelligence and National Security* 31/2 (March 2016), pp. 266–279; and Damien Van Puyvelde and Sean Curtis, " 'Standing on the Shoulders of Giants': Diversity and Scholarship in Intelligence Studies," *Intelligence and National Security* 32/1 (February 2017).

8. Mike McConnell, "Remarks on Lessons from the World of Journalism," Woodrow Wilson International Center, Washington, D.C. (November 13, 2007), cited by David Omand, "Intelligence Secrets and Media Spotlights: Balancing Illumination and Dark Corners," in Dover, Goodman, and Hillebrand, *The Routledge Companion to Intelligence Studies*, op. cit., p. 55, emphasis added. Heated congressional attention to the use of drones by the CIA for killing suspected terrorists abroad—including American citizens—seems to have been prodded by the extensive news coverage of these paramilitary operations. One media analyst concluded, for example, "The news coverage has finally goosed Congress off the sidelines" (David Carr, "Debating Drones, in the Open," *New York Times* [February 11, 2013], p. B8). Yet no major government inquiry has been conducted into the use of drones for intelligence purposes, such as examining the merits of how targets for death are selected by the White House.

9. This examination of the Korean case draws on David M. Barrett, *The CIA and the Congress* (Lawrence: University Press of Kansas, 2005), pp. 82–89, quotes from pp. 83, 86.

10. On the Bay of Pigs operation, see Peter Wyden, *The Bay of Pigs: The Untold Story* (New York: Simon & Schuster, 1979). Hillebrand refers to several roles the media plays with respect to intelligence oversight, highlighting (as does this chapter) "the media as an information transmitter and stimulator for formal scrutinizers" ("The Role of News Media," op. cit., p. 692).

11. Barrett, *The CIA and the Congress*, op. cit., p. 453.

12. Cited in Victor Marchetti and John D. Marks, *The CIA and the Cult of Intelligence* (New York: Knopf, 1974), p. 52.

13. Barrett, *The CIA and the Congress*, op. cit., p. 455.

14. See Sol Stern, "A Short Account of International Student Politics & the Cold War, with Particular Reference to the NSA, CIA, etc.," *Ramparts* (March 1967), pp. 87–97; and William Grimes, "Warren Hinckle, Editor of *Ramparts* and Voice for Radical Left, Dies at 77," *New*

York Times (August 26, 2016), p. B14. On the CIA's ties to domestic organizations in the United States, see Loch K. Johnson, *America's Secret Power: The CIA in a Democratic Society* (New York: Oxford University Press, 1989).

15. Bob Woodward and Carl Bernstein, *The Final Days* (New York: Simon & Schuster, 1976).

16. Samuel Dash, *Chief Counsel: Inside the Ervin Committee—the Untold Story of Watergate* (New York: Random House, 1976), p. 214.

17. Carl Bernstein and Bob Woodward, *All the President's Men* (New York: Simon & Schuster, 1974).

18. Remark, Bill Keller, managing editor of the *New York Times*, interviewed by Terry Gross, "Fresh Air," National Public Radio (February 1, 2011).

19. James Risen and Eric Lichtblau, "Bush Lets U.S. Spy on Callers without Courts," *New York Times* (December 16, 2005), p. A1.

20. James Risen, *State of War: The Secret History of the CIA and the Bush Administration* (New York: Free Press, 2006), p. 57.

21. For example, the American Civil Liberties Union, as well as the Brennan Center for Justice; on the former, see Kathleen Hennessey and Michael A. Memoli, "CIA Torture Report Not Likely to Result in Reforms or Prosecutions," *Los Angeles Times* (December 14, 2014), p. A1; on the latter, see Michael German, ed., *Strengthening Intelligence Oversight* (Brennan Center for Justice, New York University, 2015), with several participants from the Church Committee, including Senators Walter Mondale and Gary Hart, as well as the panel's chief counsel, Frederick A. O. "Fritz" Schwarz, Jr.

    Paul C. Light of New York University reports on Pew polls that have gauged "News Interest" in various events from the 9/11 attacks forward. According to this data, the 9/11 attacks and the Iraq WMD fiasco recorded the highest percentages of interest (along with the Abu Ghraib prison scandal). No major inquiry—a special commission or a congressional investigation—came about regarding Abu Ghraib, supporting the notion that in a climate of global terrorism the U.S. government has been reluctant to take on a major probe into the IC that might hinder its counterterrorism activities. The exception of the WMD case is understandable, because the White House had claimed that Iraq was developing nuclear weapons that could lead to "mushroom clouds" in Americans' backyards (as both President George W. Bush and national security adviser Condoleezza Rice put it); that this prognosis was so wrong on such a significant topic meant that a serious inquiry was all but inevitable. (The NSA sigint controversies do not appear in Light's study.) See Paul C. Light, "Vision + Action = Faithful Execution: Why Government Daydreams and How to Stop the Cascade of Breakdowns That Now Hunts It," *PS: Political Science and Policy* 49/1 (January 2016), pp. 5–20.

22. Cited by Risen, *State of War*, op. cit., p. 56.

23. Cited in ibid.

24. See John Yoo, *The Powers of War and Peace: The Constitution and Foreign Affairs after 9/11* (Chicago: University of Chicago Press, 2010). For Nixon's views on presidential preeminence, see his remarks during a Church Committee deposition: "Supplementary Detailed Staff Reports on Foreign and Military Intelligence," Appendix, Book IV, *Final Report*, Select Committee to Study Governmental Operations with Respect to Intelligence Activities (the formal name of the Church panel), Report No. 94–755, U.S. Senate (April 23, 1976), pp. 157–158.

25. On the PATRIOT Act, see David Cole and James X. Dempsey, *Terrorism and the Constitution* (New York: New Press, 2006).

26. A. Glees and P. H. J. Davies, *Spinning the Spies* (London: Social Affairs Unit, 2004), p. 35.

27. See Lars Willnat and Jason Martin, "Foreign Correspondents: An Endangered Species," in David H. Weaver and Lars Willnat, eds., *The Global Journalist in the 21st Century* (New York: Routledge, 2012), pp. 495–510.

28. See James Poniewozik, "In Battle of Candidates, Lauer Is the Loser," *New York Times* (September 9, 2016), p. A16.

Chapter 8

1. For these numbers, I am grateful to my undergraduate assistant Zachery Hawkins for his search through *Congressional Quarterly* committee membership lists since 1976.

2. Joel D. Aberbach, *Keeping a Watchful Eye: The Politics of Congressional Oversight* (Washington, DC: Brookings Institution, 1990), p. 123.

3. Americans for Democratic Action, *Voting Records* (1976–2016), http://www.adaaction.org/.

4. This point is based on my personal observations while staff director of the HPSCI Subcommittee on Oversight during its start-up phase (1977–1980).

5. "The CIA and the Media," *Hearings*, Subcommittee on Oversight, Permanent Select Committee on Intelligence, U.S. House of Representatives (Washington, DC: U.S. Government Printing Office, 1979).

6. Drawn from Loch K. Johnson, "It's Never a Quick Fix at the CIA," *Washington Post* (August 30, 2009), Outlook Section, p. A1, although this story has appeared in one variation or another in many places over the years.

7. On this philosophy, see L. Britt Snider, *Sharing Secrets with Lawmakers: Congress as a User of Intelligence: An Intelligence Monography*, CSI 97-10001, Center for the Study of Intelligence, Central Intelligence Agency (Langley, VA: February 1997), p. 52.

8. An intelligence scholar in the Netherlands relates how a former member of the Dutch security service "once stated that when his minister had to go to a session of the parliamentary committee he always carried two pieces of paper, implying that one of those was a 'light version' and the other a more thorough account of the latest operations and activities. The second piece of paper always remained in the minister's briefcase" (Constant Hijzen, "More Than a Ritual Dance: The Dutch Practice of Parliamentary Oversight and Control of the Intelligence Community," *Security and Human Rights* 24 [2013], p. 232).

9. The question was posed to HPSCI Chairman Reyes by *Newsweek*'s Jeff Stein, as referred to in Stein's piece, "Cleaning House," *New York Times Book Review* (March 6, 2016), p. 14.

10. At least in the early days of HPSCI for which data are available, Aspin held the record for visiting the committee's premises to participate in individual briefings from staff and during formal committee meetings. The committee began its life in September 1977; from that starting point until the end of December that year, Aspin came to the panel's secluded suite of offices in the Capitol Building thirty-seven times for individual informal briefings with staff, followed by sixty-two such visits in 1978. As for more formal committee briefings and hearings, Aspin attended seven of these full committee meetings and briefings in 1977, as well as twenty-nine additional committee briefings on more narrow intelligence topics. In 1978, HPSCI's first full year in operation, Aspin attended seventeen full committee meetings, briefings, markups, and conference committee sessions; and twenty-five less formal committee briefings on special topics.

    The total number of times that Aspin came to the committee, then, was 73 visits in 1977 (over a four-month period) and 104 visits in 1978 (over a full year). These numbers strike me as robust, as one might hope from a "guardian" (and the first four months of setting up the committee were particularly demanding on members, before HPSCI entered into its more routine gatherings). In 1995, Aspin also broke all attendance records for the Aspin-Brown Commission on Intelligence, before he passed away in the middle of the panel's year of inquiry into the intelligence agencies (see Loch K. Johnson, *The Threat on the Horizon: An Inside Account of America's Search for Security after the Cold War* [New York: Oxford University Press, 2011]).

11. See Richard F. Fenno, *Congressmen in Committee* (Boston: Little, Brown, 1973), who emphasizes the importance of a lawmaker's fundamental interests in a topic for understanding how much time he or she devotes to oversight and other committee work, an observation that certainly holds up in my forty years of observing intelligence overseers (see the Aspin and Mazzoli examples on HPSCI in chapter 4). As Fenno writes, some lawmakers (in his examples, on the committees of Education and Labor, as well as Foreign Affairs, both in the House) "emphasize a strong personal interest in and a concern for the content of public policy in their committee's subject matter; in short, they want *to help make good public policy*" (p. 9, original emphasis). Lawmakers attend intelligence oversight hearings, for example, to the extent they are drawn to the topic, with action-oriented covert action hearings usually the most popular attraction.

    Even for some well-meaning members, though, attendance at HPSCI and SSCI hearings can wane after a year or two. As a former SSCI staff director, Charles Battaglia, has commented, the details of operations become "too arcane and technical," and accountability turns out to be "not as sexy as they thought it would be" (interview by Jennifer Kibbe, in "Congressional Oversight of Intelligence: Is the Solution Part of the Problem?" *Intelligence and National Security* 25/1 [February 2010], p. 49). I found this diminishing interest especially true with respect to complicated NSA and NGA techint collection activities (see my *Threat on the Horizon*, op. cit.).

12. See, for example, Amy Zegart, *Spying Blind: The CIA, the FBI, and the Origins of 9/11* (Princeton, NJ: Princeton University Press, 2007).

13. For a sample of Lasswell's views, see Harold D. Lasswell, *Power and Personality* (New York: Norton, 1948); Singer's quote is from his remarks, "Sarajevo and Arms Control," *In Brief*, the newsletter of the United States Institute of Peace 5 (March 1989), pp. 2–3.

14. Stanley Hoffman, "Heroic Leadership: The Case of Modern France," in Lewis J. Edinger, ed., *Political Leadership in Industrialized Societies: Studies in Comparative Analysis* (New York: Wiley, 1967), p. 109.

15. Harold D. Lasswell, "Political Systems, Styles and Personalities," in Edinger, *Political Leadership in Industrialized Societies*, op. cit., p. 320. See also Alexander L. George and Juliette L. George, *Woodrow Wilson and Colonel House: A Personality Study* (New York: Dover, 1964), for a compelling Lasswellian analysis of the relationship between President Wilson and Senator Lodge.

16. Elsewhere, I have tried to grapple with this question of engagement by looking at the quality of questions asked by members of the Intelligence Committees; but the analysis was sharply limited in that only the few public hearings held by these panels could be examined. In the difficult field of intelligence studies, you take what shards of public evidence you can find. See Loch K. Johnson, "Playing Ball with the CIA: Congress Supervises Strategic Intelligence," in Paul E. Peterson, ed., *Congress, the Executive, and the Making of American Foreign Policy* (Norman: University of Oklahoma Press, 1994), pp. 49–73.

17. Frederick A. O. Schwarz, Jr., in Katherine Scott, ed., *Oral History Interviews, Church Committee*, U.S. Senate Historical Office, Washington, D.C. (October 29, 2014), p. 476.

18. See David M. Barrett, "Congressional Oversight of the CIA in the Early Cold War, 1947–1963," in Loch K. Johnson, ed., *Intelligence and Accountability: Safeguards against the Abuse of Secret Power*, vol. 5, *Strategic Intelligence* (Westport, CT: Praeger, 2007), pp. 1–18; Loch K. Johnson, *America's Secret Power: The CIA in a Democratic Society* (New York: Oxford University Press, 1987); and Harry Howe Ransom, *The Intelligence Establishment* (Cambridge, MA: Harvard University Press, 1970).

19. Tim Weiner, *Legacy of Ashes: The History of the CIA* (New York: Doubleday, 2007), p. 337.

20. L. Britt Snider, *The Agency and the Hill: CIA's Relationship with Congress, 1946–2004* (Washington, DC: Center for the Study of Intelligence, Central Intelligence Agency, 2008), p. 42.

21. Connie Bruck, "The Inside War," *New Yorker* (June 22, 2015), p. 55.

22. My interview, Washington, D.C. (June 18, 2014). For empirical evidence in line with this remark, see Johnson, "Playing Ball with the CIA," op. cit.

23. From James Bamford, "Five Myths about the National Security Agency," *Washington Post* (June 21, 2013), quoted in Michael J. Glennon, *National Security and Double Government* (New York: Oxford University Press, 2014), p. 57.

24. NSC memo, Clarke to Rice, "Observations at the Principals Meeting on Al Qida" (September 4, 2001), reprinted in *The 9/11 Commission Report* (New York: Norton, 2004), p. 212. The text italicized here is underlined in the original memo; "Al Qida" is an alternative spelling of Al Qaeda.

25. On the frequency and seriousness with which CIA officers have been questioned by lawmakers in several public hearings, see Johnson, "Playing Ball with the CIA," op. cit.

26. For histories of these failures, Weiner, *Legacy of Ashes*, op. cit.; and Zegart, *Spying Blind*, op. cit.

27. Daniel Patrick Moynihan, "Do We Still Need the C.I.A.? The State Dept. Can Do the Job," *New York Times* (May 19, 1991), p. E17.

28. For an account of the Torricelli case, see Mark M. Lowenthal, *Intelligence: From Secrets to Policy*, 3rd ed. (Washington, DC: CQ Press, 2006), pp. 271–272.

29. Edward Gibbon, *The Decline and Fall of the Roman Empire* (New York: Viking, 1952), p. 85. Church had a resolute distrust of executive branch power, seared into him by the Vietnam and

Watergate experiences and (before that) his government classes at Stanford University (see Frank Church, "Of Presidents and Caesars: The Decline of Constitutional Government in the Conduct of American Foreign Policy," *Idaho Law Review* 6/1 [Fall 1969], pp. 1–15, which favorably quotes Gibbon's criticism of the Roman Caesars); for an essay that traces Church's perspective on the misuse of government power by the presidency, see Loch K. Johnson. "Operational Codes and the Prediction of Leadership Behavior," in Margaret G. Herman, ed., *A Psychological Examination of Political Man* (New York: Free Press, 1977), pp. 80–119.

30. Quoted by F. Davies, "GOP-Controlled Senate Expected to Give Less Scrutiny to War on Terror," *Miami Herald* (November 7, 2002), p. A1.

31. Interviewed by Cynthia Nolan, Washington, D.C. (October 15, 2003), author of "More Perfect Oversight: Intelligence Oversight and Reform," in Johnson, *Strategic Intelligence,* op. cit., pp. 115–140, quote at 126–127.

32. For such allegations against the Agency regarding drugs during the tenure of DCI John Deutch in the mid-1990s (neither substantiated nor likely), see Johnson, *Threat on the Horizon,* op. cit., p. 365; on CIA proprieties, see Johnson, *America's Secret Power,* op. cit.

33. Remarks, *Congressional Oversight of Intelligence Activities,* Select Committee on Intelligence, U.S. Senate, 110th Cong., 1st Sess., Sen. Rept. 110-794 (November 13, 2007), p. 28.

34. See U.S. Senate Select Committee on Secret Military Assistance to Iran and the Nicaraguan Opposition and U.S. House of Representatives Select Committee to Investigate Covert Arms Transactions with Iran, *Report of the Congressional Committees Investigating the Iran-Contra Affair,* Sen. Rept. No. 100-216 and H. Rept. No. 100-433, 100th Cong., 1st Sess. (Washington, DC: U.S. Government Printing Office, November 1987).

35. William Shakespeare, *As You Like It,* Act II, Scene vii, line 139.

36. B. Drogin, "Senator Says Spy Agencies Are 'in Denial,'" *Los Angeles Times* (May 4, 2004), p. A1.

37. Select Committee on Intelligence (the Roberts Committee), *Report on the U.S. Intelligence Community's Prewar Intelligence Assessments on Iraq,* U.S. Senate, 108th Cong., 1st Sess. (2004). The Roberts Committee remained riven by partisanship, despite the chairman's efforts (short-lived) to rally the panel behind a thorough inquiry. Democrats on the committee insisted on probing into why the Bush Administration had promoted the false Iraqi WMD hypothesis, while Roberts sought to avoid this line of inquiry. The Senate Majority Leader Bill Frist (R, Tennessee) finally had to step in and calm down the wrangling, separating the WMD inquiry into two parts: the intelligence failures and, only after the presidential election, both the Clinton and Bush Administration failures (see L. Britt Snider, "Congressional Oversight of Intelligence after September 11," in Jennifer E. Sims and Burton Gerber, eds., *Transforming U.S. Intelligence* [Washington, DC: Georgetown University Press, 2008], pp. 239–258).

38. See Richard A. Clarke, *Against All Enemies: Inside America's War against Terror* (New York: Free Press, 2004); and Bob Woodward, *A Plan of Attack* (New York: Simon & Schuster, 2004).

39. Philip Shenon, "G.O.P. Senator Proposes a Plan to Split Up C.I.A.," *New York Times* (August 23, 2004), p. A1.

40. Remarks, "Intelligence Reform and Oversight: The View from Congress," Council on Foreign Relations (June 26, 2008), cited in Kibbe, "Congressional Oversight," op. cit., p. 26.

41. Email response to me (March 8, 2016).

42. Interview conducted by Kibbe, "Congressional Oversight," op. cit., p. 33.

43. Quoted by Helen Fessenden, "Sept. 11 Commission's Proposals Spur Urgency, Caution in Congress," *CQ Weekly Report* (July 24, 2004), p. 1815.

44. Interview with L. Britt Snider, conducted by Kibbe, "Congressional Oversight," op. cit., p. 27.

45. Russell Baker, "Chill on the Hill," *Nation* (October 2002), p. 13.

46. Porter J. Goss, remarks, transcript, "United States of Secrets (Part One): The Program," *Frontline* (May 20, 2014).

47. Joseph Lelyveld, "Interrogating Ourselves," *New York Times Sunday Magazine* (June 12, 2005), p. 37.

48. Representative Porter Goss, "Crossfire," *CNN Television* (May 16, 2001).

49. See, for instance, Stein, "Clearing House," op. cit.

50. Johnson, *Threat on the Horizon,* op. cit. As Kibbe notes, "The joint committee proposal has been widely criticized because it is hard to see how oversight will be strengthened with fewer eyes devoted to the problem" ("Congressional Oversight," op. cit., p. 42).

51. Johnson, *Threat on the Horizon*, op. cit.
52. A former CIA officer and keen critic of intelligence accountability has said, "To do the job of rigorous oversight a member of Congress needs to be a junkyard dog" (my notes, remarks, Mel Goodman, Symposium on Intelligence, University of Tulsa, Tulsa, Oklahoma, October 21, 2008).
53. Senior CIA officer, email response to me (October 8, 2014).
54. See Loch K. Johnson, *A Season of Inquiry Revisited: The Church Committee Confronts America's Spy Agencies* (Lawrence: University Press of Kansas, 2015).
55. William Shakespeare, *King Richard II*, edited by Peter Ure (London: Methuen, 1956), Act v, Scene v, p. 174.
56. My interview with an SSCI staff aide, Washington, D.C. (December 10, 2004).
57. My interview with an SSCI staff aide, Washington, D.C. (June 16, 2014).
58. See *Congressional Record*, 119 (1973), p. 24532; and Pat Holt, *The War Powers Resolution: The Role of Congress in U.S. Armed Intervention* (Washington, DC: American Enterprise for Public Policy Research, 1978).
59. Quoted in "U.S. Aid to Nicaraguan Rebels—Lawmakers Speak Out," *U.S. News & World Report* (May 2, 1983), p. 29.
60. Ibid.
61. Executive Order No. 12333 on United States Intelligence Activities (December 4, 1981), which replaced President Carter's Executive Order No. 12036 (issued on January 24, 1977).
62. John T. Elliff, in Scott, *Oral History*, op. cit. (February 21, 2014), p. 112.
63. The letter was dated April 9, 1984 (see Letters to the Editor, *Washington Post* [April 11, 1984], p. A17).
64. Email communication to me from Dr. Elliff (April 24, 2016).
65. Historian Ernest R. May attributed Woolsey's problems on Capitol Hill primarily to his siding with the Armed Services Committees in favor of spending on surveillance satellites, rather than supporting an emphasis on human-agent intelligence preferred by the SSCI leadership. See Ernest R. May, "The Twenty-first Century Challenge for U.S. Intelligence," in Sims and Gerber, *Transforming U.S. Intelligence*, op. cit., pp. 3–13, with reference to Woolsey at pp. 6–7.
66. James Risen, *State of War: The Secret History of the CIA and the Bush Administration* (New York: Free Press, 2006), p. 9.
67. Richard C. Shelby, "September 11 and the Imperative of Reform in the U.S. Intelligence Community," Additional Views of Senator Richard C. Shelby, Vice Chairman, Senate Select Committee on Intelligence, *Joint Inquiry Report* (Washington, DC: U.S. Government Printing Office, December 10, 2002), p. 135.
68. Philip Sherwell, "US Shutdown: 1995 Flashback When Newt Gingrich Was "Snubbed" on Air Force One," *Telegraph* (October 1, 2013).
69. For Graham's memoir, see Bob Graham with Jeff Nussbaum, *Intelligence Matters: The CIA, the FBI, Saudi Arabia, and the Failure of America's War on Terror* (New York: Random House, 2004).
70. K. Guggenheim, "Tenet Defends CIA's Pre-9/11 Efforts," *Washington Post* (October 17, 2002), p. A1.
71. Neil A. Lewis, "Senator Insists C.I.A. Is Harboring Iraq Reports," *New York Times* (October 4, 2002), p. A12. Tenet had become a master at Fabian delay in his relations with Congress, in the style of the ancient Roman leader Quintuz Fabius Maximus Verrucosus Cunctator—this last name translated as the "delayer" (Mary Beard, *SPQR: A History of Ancient Rome* [New York: Liveright, 2015], p. 181).
72. See Graham, *Intelligence Matters*, op. cit. The director of the CIA, John Brennan, had this to say about these charges on *Meet the Press* (*NBC News*, May 1, 2016): "The 9/11 Commission took that joint inquiry [by the Graham-Goss Committee] and those 28 pages or so, and followed through on the investigation. And they came out with a very clear judgment that there was no evidence that indicated that the Saudi government as an institution, or Saudi officials individually, had provided financial support to Al Qaeda." Left unstated was the possibility that wealthy Saudis outside the government, with strong ties to the royal family, had provided financial support to the 9/11 terrorists. In July 2016, the Obama Administration approved the release by Congress of the twenty-eight pages. Nonetheless, Graham pressed his case further by declaring

that "questions about whether the Saudi government assisted the terrorists remain unanswered." He called for the release of additional documents generated by the Kean Commission and still kept classified (see Bob Graham, "The Questions of 9/11, Still Unanswered," *New York Times* [September 10, 2016], p. A19).

73. Bruck, "The Inside War," op. cit., p. 54.

74. For example, while Feinstein opposed waterboarding detainees, a former senior CIA officer recalls, "As far as Saxbe is concerned, we didn't waterboard enough of them often enough. He's a jingoist" (email to me, September 8, 2015).

75. Quoted by Ed O'Keefe, "Proposal to Restrict NSA Phone-tracking Program Defeated," *Washington Post* (July 25, 2013), cited by Glennon, *National Security*, op. cit., p. 72 (emphasis added by Glennon and retained here).

76. Cited in Michael Doyle, "Terror Attack Greets Intelligence Panel Chief in First Days on the Job," *McClatchy* (January 10, 2015), based on data collected by American University, Washington, D.C.

77. Senator Richard Burr, remarks to David Welna, "The Challenge of Keeping Tabs on the NSA's Secretive Work," *Morning Edition*, NPR (July 23, 2014).

78. Quoted by Ali Watkins, "GOP Plans to Give Explosive Document Back to CIA," *Huffington Post* (January 20, 2015).

79. Quoted in Renee Schoof, "Sen. Burr Deflects Questions about Calling for Drone Killing," *News Observer*, Charlotte, N.C. (April 29, 2015). One of the senator's constituents, who spent a career on Capitol Hill as a foreign-policy specialist, has commented that "the Agency and the Senate Intelligence Committee—under his leadership—have become a mutual admiration society" (William E. Jackson, Jr., "Senate Intelligence Committee Chair Richard Burr: The Stealth Senator?" *News Observer* [November 12, 2015]).

80. William E. Jackson, Jr., "Richard Burr, Our Protector of the National Security State," *Raleigh News & Observer* (March 13, 2016).

81. Quoted in Steven T. Dennis, "Virginia Lawmaker Questions Burr about Quashing Stories on Russia Interference with Election," *Bloomberg* (February 25, 2017).

82. Senator Mark Udall, remarks on the Senate floor, quoted in George Zornick, "Senator Udall Discloses CIA Findings on Torture and Blasts Obama's Inaction," *Nation* (December 10, 2014).

83. Bruck, "The Inside War," op. cit., p. 54.

84. Welna, NPR, op. cit.

85. See my interview with DNI Clapper: Loch K. Johnson, "A Conversation with James R. Clapper Jr., the Director of National Intelligence in the United States," *Intelligence and National Security* 30 (February 2015), pp. 1–25. In the wake of this flap, Senator Feinstein observed that "there is no more direct and honest person [than Jim Clapper]," "This Week with George Stephanopoulos," *ABC News* (June 9, 2013).

86. Doyle, "Terror Attack Greets Intelligence Panel Chief," op. cit.

87. Karoun Demirjian, "House Intelligence Chairman Denies Evidence of Trump Team's Ties to Russia," *Washington Post* (February 27, 2017), p. A1.

88. Michael S. Schmidt, "Leaders of House Panel Sharply Split on Russia Inquiry," *New York Times* (February 28, 2017), p. A13. Like the White House, Burr and Nunes expressed concern chiefly about government leaks, not Russian influence over the Trump Administration.

89. Craig Whitlock, "Admiral Pleads Guilty in Scandal," *Wall Street Journal* (June 10, 2016), p. A11.

90. Representative Rush Holt and Steven Aftergood "The House Committee on Intelligence Needs Oversight of Its Own," op-ed, *MSNBC* (May 30, 2014). Holt retired from the House in 2014 after serving eight terms.

Chapter 9

1. On the collection-and-analysis mission, see Richard K. Betts, "Analysis, War and Decision: Why Intelligence Failures Are Inevitable," *World Politics* 31 (October 1978), pp. 61–89 (reprinted in Loch K. Johnson and James J. Wirtz, eds., *Intelligence: The Secret World of Spies*, 4th ed. [New York: Oxford University Press, 2015], pp. 141–157); Robert M. Clark, *Intelligence Analysis: A Target-Centric Approach*, 3rd ed. (Washington, DC: CQ Press, 2010); Harold P. Ford,

Estimative Intelligence: The Purposes and Problems of National Intelligence Estimating (New York: University Press of America, 1993); Jeffrey A. Friedman and Richard Zeckhauser, "Why Assessing Estimative Accuracy Is Feasible and Desirable," *Intelligence and National Security* 31/2 (March 2016), pp. 178–200; Robert Jervis, *Why Intelligence Fails: Lessons from the Iranian Revolution and the Iraqi War* (Ithaca, NY: Cornell University Press, 2010); Loch K. Johnson, "Glimpses into the Gems of American Intelligence: The *President's Daily Brief* and the National Intelligence Estimate," *Intelligence and National Security* 23 (June 2008), pp. 333–370; Stephen Marrin, ed., "Special Issue on Intelligence Analysis," *Intelligence and National Security* 32 (August 2017); David Omand, "The Cycles of Intelligence," in Robert Dover, Michael S. Goodman, and Claudia Hillebrand, eds., *Routledge Companion to Intelligence Studies* (New York: Routledge, 2014), pp. 59–70; Paul R. Pillar, "Adapting Intelligence to Changing Issues," in Loch K. Johnson, ed., *Handbook of Intelligence Studies* (New York: Routledge, 2007), pp. 148–162; Richard L. Russell, *Sharpening Strategic Intelligence* (New York: Cambridge University Press, 2007); Jennifer E. Sims, "Decision Advantage and the Nature of Intelligence Analysis," in Loch K. Johnson, ed., *The Oxford Handbook of National Security Intelligence* (New York: Oxford University Press, 2010), pp. 375–388; L. Britt Snider, *The Agency and the Hill: CIA's Relationship with Congress, 1946–2004* (Washington, DC: Center for the Study of Intelligence, Central Intelligence Agency, 2008), pp. 193–257, which looks at oversight for both collection and analysis; Gregory F. Treverton, "Intelligence Analysis: Between 'Politicization' and Irrelevance," in Roger Z. George and James B. Bruce, eds., *Analyzing Intelligence: Origins, Obstacles, and Innovations* (Washington, DC: Georgetown University Press, 2008); and Timothy Walton, *Challenges in Intelligence Analysis* (New York: Cambridge University Press, 2010).

2. Richard Helms, with William Hood, *A Look over My Shoulder: A Life in the Central Intelligence Agency* (New York: Random House, 2003), p. 234.

3. For a more detailed examination of the intelligence cycle and its complications, see Arthur S. Hulnick, "What's Wrong with the Intelligence Cycle?" in Loch K. Johnson, ed., *Strategic Intelligence, Vol. 2: The Intelligence Cycle* (Westport, CT: Praeger, 2007), pp. 1–22; and Mark Phythian, ed., *Understanding the Intelligence Cycle* (Abington, UK: Routledge, 2013).

4. See Loch K. Johnson, *Bombs, Bugs, Drugs, and Thugs: Intelligence and America's Quest for Security* (New York: New York University Press, 2000), ch. 3.

5. My interviews with cyber intelligence officers in attendance at the International Studies Association annual meeting, Atlanta, Georgia (March 16–18, 2016). In a joint statement, the SSCI ranking minority member Dianne Feinstein and her HPSCI counterpart, Adam Schiff, said that "the Russian intelligence agencies are making a serious and concerted effort to influence the U.S. election" (quoted by Michael Isikoff, *Yahoo News* [September 23, 2016]). Further, during that month, Iran's Islamic Revolutionary Guards Corps launched cyberattacks against dozens of U.S. banks and even attempted to take control of a small dam in a New York suburb (David Sanger, "U.S. Indicts 7 Tied to Iranian Unit in Cyberattacks," *New York Times* [March 25, 2016], p. A3). On the hacking of the DNC, see David E. Sanger, "Questions Loom over a Response to Cyberattacks," *New York Times* (July 31, 2016), p. A1.

6. Loch K. Johnson, "Evaluating 'Humint': The Role of Foreign Agents in U.S. Security," *Comparative Strategy* 29 (September–October 2010), pp. 308–333; Jeffrey T. Richelson, "The Technical Collection of Intelligence," in Loch K. Johnson, ed., *Handbook of Intelligence Studies* (New York: Routledge, 2007), pp. 105–117.

7. Richard K. Betts, *Enemies of Intelligence: Knowledge and Power in American National Security* (New York: Columbia University Press, 2007); Mark M. Lowenthal and Robert M. Clark, *The 5 Disciplines of Intelligence Collection* (Los Angeles: Sage, 2016).

8. Willmoore Kendall, "The Function of Intelligence," *World Politics* 1 (1948–1949), pp. 542–552; Sherman Kent, *Intelligence for American World Policy* (Princeton, NJ: Princeton University Press, 1949), as well as "Estimates and Influence," *Foreign Service Journal* (April 1969); and William M. Nolte, "Intelligence Analysis in an Uncertain Environment," in Loch K. Johnson, ed., *Oxford Handbook of Intelligence Studies*, op. cit., pp. 404–421.

9. Stephanie Carvin, "Where Is the Review of Intelligence Analysis in CSIS?" *Globe and Mail*, Canada (November 4, 2016).

10. Michael S. Goodman, *The Official History of the Joint Intelligence Committee, Vol. 1: From the Approach of the Second World War to the Suez Crisis* (London: Routledge, 2014), p. 7.

11. See Jack Davis, "A Policymaker's Perspective on Intelligence Analysis," *Studies in Intelligence* 38 (1995), pp. 7–15; and Mark M. Lowenthal, "Tribal Tongues: Intelligence Consumers, Intelligence Producers," *Washington Quarterly* 15 (Winter 1992), pp. 157–168.

12. See Loch K. Johnson, *The Threat on the Horizon: An Insider's Account of America's Search for Security in the Aftermath of the Cold War* (New York: Oxford University Press, 2011), p. 347; and George Tenet with Bill Harlow, *At the Center of the Storm: My Years at the CIA* (New York: HarperCollins, 2007), p. 449.

13. Helene Cooper, "Military Officials Distorted Intelligence on ISIS, Report Says," *New York Times* (August 12, 2016), p. A6. For the ten-page report, see *Initial Findings of the U.S. House of Representatives Joint Task Force on U.S. Central Command Intelligence Analysis*, prepared by GOP members of HPSCI, the Armed Services Committee, and the Defense Appropriations Subcommittee (August 10, 2016).

14. Ibid.

15. Drawn from Loch K. Johnson, *National Security Intelligence: Secret Operations in Defense of the Democracies*, 2nd ed. (Cambridge, UK: Polity, 2017), pp. 67–69.

16. John Lauder, Director, DCI Nonproliferation Center, comment, Oxford University seminar, Oxford, England (September 26, 1999), my notes, in Johnson, *Bombs, Bugs, Drugs, and Thugs*, op. cit., p. 24. For a prominent disbelieving journalist, see Daniel Schorr, "Washington Notebook," *New Leader* (May 17–31, 1999), p. 5. The factory owner had no success in court suing the United States.

17. See Loch K. Johnson, "Analysis for a New Age," *Intelligence and National Security* 11/5 (October 1996), pp. 657–671.

18. Aki Peritz, "Think U.S. Intel Is in Decline?" *Washington Post* (February 19, 2016).

19. *Hamlet*, Act II, Scene 2, lines 90–91.

20. President Richard M. Nixon, *Memorandum for Bob Haldeman, Copy for Fred Malek, from the President*, White House, Washington, D.C. (May 18, 1971, reproduced from the open files of the Nixon Presidential Materials Staff, White House Historical Office [declassified document, Church Committee files, U.S. Senate, Washington, D.C., 1975]).

21. David S. Cohen (DD/CIA), speech, "Governing Intelligence" Conference, Center on Law and Security, NYU School of Law (April 21, 2016), Washington, D.C.

22. The exploration of covert action myths here grew out of an essay by the author in *Atlantic.com* (January 2013); followed by a paper prepared for a conference on covert action at Georgetown University (February 7, 2013); then a longer piece, entitled "Myths of Covert Action," *Virginia Policy Review* 7 (Winter 2014), pp. 52–64; and finally a paper on covert action presented at the 2015 annual meeting of the International Studies Association in New Orleans. The present iteration elaborates on these earlier themes and incorporates the best of the recent journalistic reporting on this subject. On covert action in the academic and policy literature, see James A. Barry, "Covert Action Can Be Just," *Orbis* 37 (Summer 1993), pp. 375–390; Frank Church, "Covert Action: Swampland of American Foreign Policy," *Bulletin of the Atomic Scientists* 32 (February 1976), pp. 7–11; William J. Daugherty, "Approval and Review of Covert Action Programs since Reagan," *International Journal of Intelligence and Counterintelligence* 17 (Spring 2004), pp. 62–80, and *Executive Secrets: Covert Action and the Presidency* (Lexington: University Press of Kentucky, 2004); Roy Godson, *Dirty Tricks or Trump Cards: U.S. Covert Action and Counterintelligence* (New Brunswick, NJ: Transaction, 2000); Loch K. Johnson, "On Drawing a Bright Line for Covert Operations," *American Journal of International Law* 86 (April 1992), pp. 284–309, as well as *National Security Intelligence*, op. cit., ch. 3, and a book I edited, entitled *Strategic Intelligence, Vol. 3*, op. cit., which has nine essays on the subject by various experts; Stephen F. Knott, *Secret and Sanctioned: Covert Operations and the American Presidency* (New York: Oxford University Press, 1996); Todd Stiefler, "CIA's Leadership and Major Covert Operations: Rogue Elephants or Risk-Averse Bureaucrats?" *Intelligence and National Security* 19 (Winter 2004), pp. 632–654; and Gregory F. Treverton, *Covert Action: The Limits of Intervention in the Postwar World* (New York: Basic Books, 1987).

23. Pub. L. No. 102-88, 105 Stat. 441 (August 14, 1991). DCI Deutch of the Clinton Administration defined covert action simply as "those activities CIA undertakes to influence events overseas that are intended not to be attributable to this country" (my notes on his speech at the National Press Club, Washington, D.C. [September 12, 1995]).

24. An illustration: during the 1970s, the CIA distributed political lapel buttons (some 50,000 of them) to pro-Western guerrillas in an African nation, proclaiming "I am a member of [the faction's acronym]." Cost: $2,500. The DO considered forwarding bumper stickers to the war zone, too; however, a quick count indicated the lack of enough automobiles in the jungle setting to justify the effort (my interview with a former DO officer, Washington, D.C. [October 23, 1980]). An experienced retired DO officer said to me during an interview on September 3, 2014, in Boston, "Most covert action has nothing to do with lethality but is aimed at influencing foreign audiences."

25. Isabel Kershner, "Meir Dagan, Israeli Who Disrupted Iranian Nuclear Program, Dies at 81," *New York Times* (March 18, 2016), p. B15; see also David E. Sanger, *Confront and Conceal: Obama's Secret Wars and Surprising Use of American Power* (New York: Crown, 2012). The "turning point" assessment here is from David E. Sanger, "Unlikely Spy Who Fed Secrets to the U.S. Is Executed in Iran," *New York Times* (August 8, 2016), p. A3. Insightful, too, is James Bamford, "Michael Hayden Played Right Up to the Edge of Legality—and Then Took a Big Leap Off," *Nation* (June 1, 2016).

26. See William S. Cohen and George J. Mitchell, *Men of Zeal* (New York: Penguin, 1988); Stephen Dycus, Arthur L. Berney, William C. Banks, and Peter Raven-Hansen, *National Security Law*, 3rd ed. (New York: Aspen Law & Business, 2002), pp. 473–542; and *Hearings*, Select Committee on Secret Military Assistance to Iran and the Nicaraguan Operation (the Inouye-Hamilton Joint Committee, U.S. Congress [July/August 1987], plus the panel's final report, entitled *Iran-Contra Affair*, Sen. Rept. No. 100-216 and H. Rept. No. 100-433 [November 1987]).

27. See Jennifer D. Kibbe, "Covert Action and the Pentagon," in Loch K. Johnson, ed., *Strategic Intelligence, Vol. 3*, op. cit., pp. 131–144; and Mark Mazzetti, *The Way of the Knife: The CIA, a Secret Army, and a War at the Ends of the Earth* (New York: Penguin, 2013), p. 76. Data regarding SOCOM (the U.S. Special Operations Command) are rare, but its commander, Adm. Eric T. Olson, disclosed in 2011 that the organization's budget had risen from about $2 billion in 2001 to a projected $10.5 billion in 2012. "On an average day, in excess of 12,000 Special Operations Forces (SOF) and SOF support personnel are deployed in more than 75 countries across the globe," he wrote in "Special Operations," *Joint Publication* 3-05, Department of Defense (April 18, 2011), as reported by Steven Aftergood, "Special Operations Forces on the Rise," *Secrecy News*, FAS 2011/40 (May 2, 2011), p. 1. On the broad question of covertly supplying arms to friends abroad, President Obama has noted: "I actually asked the CIA to analyze examples of America financing and supplying arms to an insurgency in a country that actually worked out well. And they couldn't come up with much" (quoted in David Remnick, "Annals of the Presidency: Going the Distance," *New Yorker* [January 27, 2014], p. 57).

28. An amendment to the Foreign Assistance Act, Pub. L. No. 93-559, 32, 88 Stat. 1804.

29. Mazzetti, *Way of the Knife*, op. cit., p. 132.

30. Ibid., p. 311. The acronym JSOC stands for Joint Special Operations Command, which is the entity in charge of the Pentagon's Special Operations Forces.

31. Loch K. Johnson, *America's Secret Power: The CIA in a Democratic Society* (New York: Oxford University Press, 1986), based on my interviews in the 1980s with several DO personnel.

32. Louis Menand, "Table Talk: How the Cold War Made Georgetown Hot," *New Yorker* (November 10, 2014), p. 77.

33. Hugh Wilford, *The Mighty Wurlitzer: How the CIA Played America* (Cambridge, MA: Harvard University Press, 2008).

34. See, for example, Mark Mazzetti, Anne Barnard, and Eric Schmitt, "Military Success in Syria Is Giving Putin Leverage," *New York Times* (August 7, 2016), p. A1.

35. Admiral Dennis Blair, DNI from 2009 to 2010, quoted in Mazzetti, *Way of the Knife*, op. cit., p. 235.

36. Joseph S. Nye, Jr., "Public Diplomacy and Soft Power," *Annals of the American Academy of Political and Social Science* 616 (2008), pp. 94–109.

37. *Final Report*, Select Committee to Study Governmental Operations with Respect to Intelligence Activities (the Church Committee), 94th Cong., 2nd Sess., Sen. Rept. No. 94-755 (1976), pp. 56–57.

38. For illustrations, see Loch K. Johnson, *Secret Agencies: U.S. Intelligence in a Hostile World* (New Haven, CT: Yale University Press, 1996), pp. 92–93. On a few occasions, criticism of a covert

action by members of SSCI or HPSCI has been so strong at the time of a Hughes-Ryan briefing that the executive branch has backed away from the proposal altogether.

39. Pub. L. No. 96-450, 407(b), 94 Stat. 1981 (1980).
40. Quoted in Johnson, *A Season of Inquiry Revisited: The Church Committee Confronts America's Spy Agencies* (Lawrence: University Press of Kansas, 2015), p. 148. In 2005, MI6 in the United Kingdom kept from foreign secretary Jack Straw the fact that it had been involved in a rendition operation involving Libya. When this deception became public knowledge, Straw shrugged his shoulders and said that he couldn't be expected to know all the details of intelligence activities—the A-B-C-D-E problem. Prime Minister Tony Blair added that he did not have "any recollection at all" of the rendition. These suggestions that MI6 may have been operating beyond Cabinet orders incensed the agency's Sir Richard Dearlove, who responded that rendition was "a political decision [based on] serious calculation about where the overall balance of our national interests stood" (see Nick Hopkins and Richard Norton-Taylor, "Blair Government's Rendition Policy Led to Rift between UK Spy Agencies," *Guardian* [May 31, 2016]).
41. Henry A. Crumpton, *The Art of Intelligence* (New York: Penguin, 2012), p. 206.
42. The *9/11 Commission Report* stated that the CIA is "institutionally averse to risk" (New York: Norton, 2004, p. 93); and a leading legal authority in the United States has declared that "a paralyzing culture of risk-averse legalism" infected the military and the CIA before the 9/11 attacks (Jack Goldsmith, *The Terror Presidency: Law and Judgment inside the Bush Administration* [New York: Norton, 2007], p. 94).
43. See Ted Gup, *The Book of Honor: Covert Lives and Classified Deaths at the CIA* (New York: Doubleday, 2000).
44. Peter Nicholas, "Intelligence Agencies Face a Credibility Test," *Wall Street Journal* (December 9, 2014).
45. See Douglas Waller, *Disciples* (New York: Simon & Schuster, 2015).
46. Remark, email to me (July 29, 2016).
47. See Morten Hansen, "Intelligence Contracting: On the Motivations, Interests, and Capabilities of Core Personnel Contractors in the US Intelligence Community," *Intelligence and National Security* 29 (February 2014), pp. 58–81; and Tim Shorrock, *Spies for Hire: The Secret World of Intelligence Outsourcing* (New York: Simon & Schuster, 2008).
48. On the CIA's operations in Laos, see William E. Colby and Peter Forbath, *Honorable Men: My Life in the CIA* (New York: Simon & Schuster, 1978), pp. 191–202; Kenneth Conboy, *The Cambodian Wars: Clashing Armies and CIA Covert Operations* (Lawrence: University Press of Kansas, 2013); Joshua Kurlantzick, *A Great Place to Have a War: America in Laos and the Birth of a Military CIA* (New York: Simon & Schuster, 2016); and John Prados, *William Colby and the CIA: The Secret Wars of a Controversial Spymaster* (Lawrence: University Press of Kansas, 2007), as well as his *President's Secret Wars: CIA and Pentagon Covert Operations since World War II* (New York: William Morrow, 1986). On the Agency's covert action in Afghanistan during the Reagan Administration, see Steve Coll, *Ghost Wars: The Secret History of the CIA, Afghanistan, and Bin Laden, from the Soviet Invasion to September 10, 2011* (New York: Penguin, 2004); George Crile, *Charlie Wilson's War* (New York: Grove, 2003); and Doug Stanton, *Horse Soldiers: The Extraordinary Story of a Band of U.S. Soldiers Who Rode to Victory in Afghanistan* (New York: Scribner, 2009).
49. While covert action is among the most closely held secrets within the U.S. national security establishment, a sufficient number of unclassified government documents have surfaced since 1975 to provide some insights into the nature of America's shadowy foreign policy. In this chapter, these sources have been complemented by studies from insiders at (or retired from) the CIA and lawmakers responsible for intelligence accountability; as well as reports from journalists and biographers; scholarly studies from academe and the nation's think tanks; and intelligence memoirs (see the bibliography).

Fitting together these unclassified pieces of the covert action jigsaw puzzle, I have been able to derive what I believe is a reasonably accurate portrait of when the United States has emphasized this instrument of foreign policy, and when this approach has been relatively dormant. A more precise tracking would require access to specific budget figures for covert action, year by year, since 1947. That information is highly classified and unlikely to appear in the public domain any time soon. In lieu of this hard data, I have supplemented the archival record by interviewing scores of active-duty and retired intelligence officials since 1980, as well as academic experts, about my estimated trend line for covert action, with the objective of making the portrait as accurate as possible. This is an art form akin, I suppose, to the method used by forensic sketch artists employed by police crime labs, whose drawings help witnesses and officers on the beat identify suspected perpetrators. With this analogy I don't intend to equate covert actions with criminal acts. They can be, as with the Iran-contra affair in the 1980s; or they may be entirely legitimate, at least with respect to U.S. law: say, the secret supplying of arms to counterterrorist groups allied with the United States overseas, with proper congressional authorizations and appropriations.

50. These quotes are, respectively, from my interview in Washington, D.C. (October 10, 1980); see, as well, my *Threat on the Horizon*, op. cit., p. 179.

51. Henry Kissinger, in a top-secret briefing to the NSC (now declassified), Document 83, *Foreign Relations of the United States (FRUS), 1969–1976*, vol. 38/2, U.S. Department of State (December 2014).

52. A former CIA covert action specialist suggests, though, that "perhaps the most successful political action program ever was a broad-based effort to undermine the legitimacy of the Polish military government that came to power in 1980 while concurrently supporting the independence movement headed by Polish labor union Solidarity" (William J. Daugherty, "Political Action as a Tool of Presidential Statecraft," in Loch K. Johnson, ed., *Essentials of Strategic Intelligence* [Santa Barbara, CA: Praeger, 2015], pp. 203–216).

53. Letter to me from former president George H. W. Bush (dated January 23, 1994).

54. Deutch, speech, op. cit.

55. Charles G. Cogan, "Partners in Time: The CIA and Afghanistan," *World Policy Journal* 10 (Summer 1993), pp. 73–82.

56. Cited by Mazzetti, *Way of the Knife*, op. cit., p. 318.

57. Milt Bearden, the senior CIA officer in charge of CA in Pakistan and Afghanistan from 1986 to 1989, "Lessons from Afghanistan," *New York Times* (March 2, 1998), p. A19.

58. Mark Landler, "H Is for Hawk," *New York Times Sunday Magazine* (April 24, 2016), p. 31.

59. Mark Mazzetti, "C.I.A. to Focus More on Spying, a Difficult Shift," *New York Times* (May 24, 2013), p. A1.

60. See Mazzetti, *Way of the Knife*, op. cit.; and Scott Shane, *Objective Troy: A Terrorist, a President, and the Rise of the Drone* (New York: Tim Duggan Books/Penguin Random House, 2015).

61. Ken Kilanian, "Secret Dispute over Whether CIA Drones Should Be Killing ISIS Targets," *NBS News Investigations* (March 24, 2016).

62. On the turndown in drone attacks in the second term of the Obama Administration, see Steve Coll, "The Unblinking Stare," *New Yorker* (November 24, 2014), p. 108.

63. John Ranelagh, *The Agency: The Rise and Decline of the CIA* (New York: Simon & Schuster, 1987), p. 220; and Church Committee, *Final Report*, Sen. Rept. No. 94-755 (1976), op. cit., p. 31. See also Church Committee, "Covert Action," *Hearings*, U.S. Senate, 94th Cong., 2nd Sess. (October 23, 1975), as well as its "Alleged Assassination Plots Involving Foreign Leaders," *Interim Report*, Sen. Rept. No. 94-465 (November 20, 1975), reprinted by Norton (New York, 1976); and Anne Karalekas, "History of the Central Intelligence Agency," *Supplementary Detailed Staff Reports on Foreign and Military Intelligence, Final Report*, Sen. Rept. No. 94-755 (April 23, 1976) (all from the U.S. Government Printing Office, Washington, D.C.). The trend line in figure 9.2 does not mean to indicate that roughly equal sums of money were spent on covert action during the Korean War, the 1980s, and the post-9/11 era. In fact, much more funding went into the latter two periods, especially during the drone-led counterterrorism CAs of the second Bush and the Obama Administrations. Rather, the line is meant to suggest the relative degrees of the CIA preoccupation with covert action over the years: the time, energy, and attention devoted to this mission—its overall profile in American foreign policy—as estimated by archival research into the inventory of published scholarly articles on covert action, augmented by my interviews with insiders over the years.

64. Church, "Covert Action," op. cit., quote at p. 11.

65. Günter Grass, "Solidarity with the Sandinistas," *Nation* 236 (March 12, 1983), p. 301.

66. Michael Grow, *U.S. Presidents and Latin American Interventions* (Lawrence: University Press of Kansas, 2008), p. 187. See also *Alleged Assassination Plots*, op. cit.; Hal Brands, *Latin America's Cold War* (Cambridge, MA: Harvard University Press, 2010); and Treverton, *Covert Action*, op. cit.

67. For an elaboration of this argument, see Loch K. Johnson, *American Foreign Policy and the Challenges of World Leadership: Power, Principle, and the Constitution* (New York: Oxford University Press, 2015).

68. Peter Wyden, *Bay of Pigs: The Untold Story* (New York: Simon & Schuster, 1979).

69. *Alleged Assassination Plots*, op. cit. See also Johnson, *National Security Intelligence*, op. cit., pp. 144–176.

70. Mazzetti, *Way of the Knife*, op. cit.

71. See Kermit Roosevelt, *Countercoup: The Struggle for the Control of Iran* (New York: McGraw-Hill, 1979).

72. Secretary of State Madeleine Albright of the Clinton Administration has noted that the U.S.- and U.K.-sponsored coup was "clearly a setback for Iran's political development. And it is easy to see now why many Iranians continue to resent this intervention by America in their internal affairs" (quoted in Stephen Kinzer, *All the Shah's Men: An American Coup and the Roots of Middle East Terror* [New York: Wiley, 2003], p. 212). Photographs in this book show the revolutionaries of 1979 carrying portraits of Mossadegh through the streets of Tehran—a symbol of their determination to avenge the 1953 coup.

73. See, for example, Chalmers Johnson, *The Sorrows of Empire: Militarism, Secrecy, and the End of the Republic* (New York: Henry Holt, 2004).

74. Richard Harris, "Reflections: Secrets," *New Yorker* (April 10, 1978), p. 86.

75. See, for example, Mark Mazzetti, Charlie Savage, and Scott Shane, "A U.S. Citizen, in America's Cross Hairs," *New York Times* (March 10, 2013), p. A1; Charlie Savage, "U.S. Releases Drone Strike 'Playbook' for Targeting Terrorism Suspects," *New York Times* (August 7, 2016), p. A10; and the outstanding book on the subject of drone warfare: Shane, *Objective Troy*, op. cit. In recent years, the CIA may have turned primarily to drones as instruments for assassinating terrorists, but evidently some old fashion approaches remain in play. For example, in 2008, the Agency reportedly joined forces with Israeli intelligence in a paramilitary operation that relied on a car bomb to kill Imad Mugnlyah, the international operations chief for Hezbollah (Matthew Rosenberg and Adam Goldman, "In C.I.A. Iran Chief, Sign of Trump's Hard Line," *New York Times* [June 3, 2017], p. A1).

76. Mazzetti, *Way of the Knife*, op. cit., p. 311.

77. Remarks by the president to Jon Stewart, "The Daily Show," *Comedy Network* (October 18, 2012). The number of drone flights comes from Richard Engel, "Meet the Press," *NBC News* (December 14, 2014).

78. Quoted by Karen Greenberg, "Rethinking How We Try Terrorists," *American Scholar* (Summer 2016), p. 15; see also Scott Shane, "An Al Qaeda Martyr's Enduring Pitch," *New York Times* (September 18, 2016), p. SR 5.

79. Interviewed on "Larry King Live," *CNN Television* (February 2, 1987).

80. Peter Grose, *Gentleman Spy: The Life of Allen Dulles* (Boston: Houghton Mifflin, 1994), p. 317.

81. Anthony Lewis, "Costs of the C.I.A.," *New York Times* (April 25, 1997), p. A19. On the coup in 1954, see Richard H. Immerman, *The CIA in Guatemala: The Foreign Policy of Intervention* (Austin: University of Texas Press, 1982); and David Atlee Phillips, *The Night Watch* (New York: Atheneum, 1977).

82. William J. Daugherty, *Executive Secrets: Covert Action and the Presidency* (Lexington: University Press of Kentucky, 2004), p. 140. A leading British scholar on intelligence, Christopher Andrew of Cambridge University, looks back on CIA covert actions in the 1950s with some admiration. "They were a great adventure," he has said, "and killed far fewer people than [overt] warfare" (my notes on his comments made at the conference on "James Angleton and His Influence on U.S. Counterintelligence," Woodrow Wilson International Center and Georgetown University Center for Security Studies, Washington, D.C. [March 29, 2013]).

83. David M. Barrett, "If an Off-the-Record Briefing about Covert Action Remains Secret, Did It Ever Happen? JFK, Bay of Pigs, and a Secret Press Briefing," paper, annual meeting, International Studies Association, Atlanta, Georgia (April 16, 2016), p. 1.

84. Colby and Forbath, *Honorable Men*, op. cit., p. 198. See also Kurlantzick, *A Great Place to Have a War*, op. cit.
85. See James E. Baker and W. Michael Reisman, *Regulating Covert Action: Practices, Contexts and Policies of Covert Coercion Abroad in International and American Law* (New Haven, CT: Yale University Press, 1992). Experts have noted that drones are the perfect vehicle for delivering biological and chemical agents (see, for example, Micah Zenko and Sarah Kreps, *Limiting Armed Drone Proliferation* [New York: Council on Foreign Relations Press, 2014]).
86. Ferdinand Mount, "Spook's Disease," *National Review* 32 (March 7, 1980), p. 300.
87. See, for example, Declan Walsh, "U.S. Disavows 2 Drone Strikes over Pakistan," *New York Times* (March 15, 2013), p. A1.
88. "Should the CIA Fight Secret Wars?," a roundtable discussion in *Harpers* (September 1984), pp. 37–44.
89. Roger Fisher, "The Fatal Flaw in Our Spy System," *Boston Globe* (February 1, 1976), p. A21.
90. Dean Rusk, as told to Richard Rusk and edited by Daniel S. Papp, *As I Saw It* (New York: Norton, 1990), p. 562.
91. Cited in Mazzetti, *Way of the Knife*, op. cit., p. 80, based on his interview with Blair.
92. Ibid., p. 318.
93. On these provisions, see Charlie Savage, "U.S. Releases Drone Strike 'Playbook' for Targeting Terrorism Suspects," *New York Times* (August 7, 2016), p. A10.
94. Church Committee, "Covert Action," *Hearings*, U.S. Senate (October 23, 1975), emphases added to both quotes.
95. General Stanley McChrystal, "Generation Kill: A Conversation with Stanley McChrystal," *Foreign Affairs* (March/April 2013).
96. Remarks, Aspin-Brown Commission staff interview, Washington, D.C. (1996), quoted in Johnson, *Threat on the Horizon*, op. cit., p. 281. The fourth guideline is often referred to as "the *New York Times* test." The review group looking into the NSA metadata program in 2013 similarly advocated a "front-page rule," requiring the spy agencies to ask themselves whether the American people would find a proposed intelligence initiative necessary and proper if it appeared on the front page of the newspaper (President's Review Group on Intelligence and Communications Technologies, *Liberty and Security in a Changing World*, U.S. Government Printing Office, Washington, D.C. [December 12, 2013], p. 170). See also the views of Representative Les Aspin, "Covert Action: Questions to Answer," *First Principles* 6 (May 1981), pp. 9–11. Aspin had considerable experience with covert action as an overseer (on the Pike Committee and later on HPSCI, as well as when he chaired the House Armed Services Committee, and then when serving as secretary of defense under President Bill Clinton and as chair of the Aspin-Brown Commission). In his *First Principles* essay, he warned against turning to the CIA for major war-fighting—an assignment best reserved for the Department of Defense, in his view. In contrast, recall my conversation with James R. Schlesinger (chapter 4) when the former DCI and SecDef cautioned against allowing the Pentagon into the paramilitary field. As a rule, the CIA is better equipped than the Pentagon for conducting covert action for four reasons: it can move faster; it is smaller (the "subtlety" factor); it is less leaky ("more operationally secure," in spy talk); and it is more "non-attributable"—Agency paramilitary officers don't wear uniforms. On the normative side of this question, Senator Church maintained that "covert actions have a cumulative effect, giving this country such a bad reputation that we are really doing ourselves in. Our capacity to exert moral leadership is evaporating" (remarks to me, Washington, D.C. [September 4, 1975]). For more on prescriptive guidelines for covert action, see Johnson, "On Drawing a Bright Line," op. cit.; Gregory F. Treverton, "Covert Action: Forward to the Past?" in Johnson, *Strategic Intelligence*, op. cit., pp. 1–21; and James M. Scott and Jerel A. Rosati, "'Such Other Functions and Duties': Covert Action and American Intelligence Policy," in Johnson, *Strategic Intelligence*, op. cit., pp. 83–105.

Chapter 10

1. Richard Helms, with William Hood, *A Look over My Shoulder: A Life in the Central Intelligence Agency* (New York: Random House, 2003), p. 275.
2. Angleton was an aficionado of poetry during his undergraduate student days at Yale University; this phrase comes from T. S. Eliot's poem "Gerontion."

3. The literature on counterintelligence is voluminous. Here are some samples: Raymond J. Batvinis, *The Origins of FBI Counterintelligence* (Lawrence: University Press of Kansas, 2007); Cleveland C. Cram, "Of Moles and Molehunters: A Review of Counterintelligence Literature," Center for the Study of Intelligence, CIA, Report No. CSI 93-002 (October 1993); Richard C. Clarke, *Against All Enemies: Inside America's War on Terror* (New York: Free Press, 2004); J. Ehrman, "Toward a Theory of CI: What Are We Talking about When We Talk about Counterintelligence," *Studies in Intelligence* 53/2 (2009); Edward Jay Epstein, "The Spy War," *New York Times Sunday Magazine*, sec. 6 (September 28, 1980); John Earl Haynes, Harvey Klehr, and Alexander Vassliev, with translations by Philip Redko and Steven Shabad, *Spies: The Rise and Fall of the KGB in America* (New Haven, CT: Yale University Press, 2009); Robert Jervis, "Intelligence, Counterintelligence, Perception, and Deception," in Jennifer E. Sims and Burton Gerber, eds., *Vaults, Mirrors, and Masks: Rediscovering U.S. Counterintelligence* (Washington, DC: Georgetown University Press, 2009), pp. 69–79; Loch K. Johnson, *National Security Intelligence: Secret Operations in Defense of the Democracies*, 2nd ed. (Cambridge, UK: Polity, 2017), ch. 4, and "Stock and (James) Bonds: Spies in the Global Marketplace," in Loch K. Johnson, *Bombs, Bugs, Drugs, and Thugs: Intelligence and America's Quest for Security* (New York: New York University Press, 2000), pp. 32–50; William R. Johnson, *Thwarting Enemies at Home and Abroad: How to Be a Counterintelligence Officer* (Washington, DC: Georgetown University Press, 1987); David Martin, *The Wilderness of Mirrors* (New York: Harper & Row, 1980); J. M. Olson, "A Never Ending Necessity: The Ten Commandments of CI," *Studies in Intelligence* (Fall–Winter 2001), pp. 81–87; Paul J. Redmond, "The Challenges of Counterintelligence," in Loch K. Johnson, ed., *The Oxford Handbook of National Security Intelligence* (New York: Oxford University Press, 2010), pp. 537–554; Stan A. Taylor and Daniel Snow, "Cold War Spies: Why They Spied and How They Got Caught," *Intelligence and National Security* 12 (April 1997), pp. 101–125; Athan Theoharis, *Chasing Spies* (Chicago: Ivan R. Dee, 2002); Michelle K. Van Cleave, *Counterintelligence and National Strategy* (Washington, DC: National Defense University Press, 2007); and Frederick L. Wettering, "Counterintelligence: The Broken Triad," *International Journal of Intelligence and Counterintelligence* 13 (Fall 2000), pp. 265–299.
4. Executive Order 12333, Sec. 3.5, of the Reagan Administration, as amended on July 31, 2008. German intelligence officers refer to the successful recruitment of one of their own by a foreign power as "a hole in the bucket."
5. These recollections about Angleton and his views on counterintelligence are drawn from my "James Angleton and the Church Committee," *Journal of Cold War Studies* 15 (Fall 2013), pp. 128–147. My observations on Angleton and counterintelligence have been enriched by personal experiences—what political scientists refer to as "participant observation," whereby the scholar hovers near the subject of his or her research to see firsthand how governmental activities are carried out. On this valuable, but insufficiently used, methodology—one that informs this book throughout—see Richard F. Fenno, Jr., *Watching Politicians: Essays on Participant Observation* (Berkeley: Institute of Governmental Studies, University of California at Berkeley, 1990). On Angleton, see Seymour M. Hersh, "The Angleton Story," *New York Times Magazine* (June 25, 1978), pp. 13ff., and *The Samson Option: Israel's Nuclear Arsenal and American Foreign Policy* (New York: Random House, 1991), ch. 17; Michael Holzman, *James Jesus Angleton, the CIA, and the Craft of Counterintelligence* (Amherst: University of Massachusetts Press, 2008); William Hood, James Nolan, and Samuel Halpern, "Myths Surrounding James Angleton: Lessons for American Counterintelligence," Working Group on Intelligence Reform, Consortium for the Study of Intelligence (Washington, D.C, 1994); Tom Mangold, *Cold Warrior: James Jesus Angleton, the CIA's Master Spy Hunter* (New York: Simon & Schuster, 1991); and Robin W. Winks, "The Theorist," in his *Cloak and Gown: Scholars in the Secret War, 1939–1961* (New York: William Morrow, 1987), pp. 322–372, reprinted in Loch K. Johnson, *Intelligence, Vol. III, Counterintelligence: Shield for National Security Intelligence* (New York: Routledge, 2011), pp. 115–161.
6. See Loch K. Johnson, *The Making of International Agreements: Congress Confronts the Executive* (New York: New York University Press, 1984).
7. Louis Fisher, *Congressional Abdication on War and Spending* (College Station: Texas A&M University Press, 2000).

8. William Colby and Peter Forbath, *Honorable Men: My Life in the CIA* (New York: Simon & Schuster), p. 391.
9. Ibid., p. 397.
10. See Martin, *Wilderness of Mirrors*, op. cit., pp. 199, 213.
11. My notes on Carl Colby's remarks, "James Angleton and His Influence on U.S. Counterintelligence," Woodrow Wilson International Center and Georgetown University Center for Security Studies, Washington, D.C. (March 29, 2013). William Colby had served in Vietnam and periodically used this old military expression.
12. See John Ranelagh, *The Agency: The Rise and Decline of the CIA* (New York: Simon & Schuster, 1987), p. 151.
13. Colby and Forbath, *Honorable Men*, op. cit., pp. 244–245.
14. Ibid., p. 297. Paranoia is a condition that comes with the territory in the counterintelligence business—a "murky world," in the words of a British journalist who has waded into the subject, a world "full of risks, dangers, personal jealousies and never-ceasing suspicions that the man in the office next to yours may be a Soviet agent. It is a situation that creates paranoia, corroding men's character" (Henry Brandon, "The Spy Who Came and Then Told," *Washington Post*, National Weekly Edition [August 24, 1987], p. A36). Just how much paranoia is enough is a question that has "no easy answer," writes political scientist Jervis, "Intelligence, Counterintelligence," op. cit., p. 75. Angleton clearly went too far on several occasions late in his career, even calling DCI and later secretary of defense James R. Schlesinger, Jr., of "Family Jewels" fame a Soviet mole (see Robert M. Gates, *From the Shadows* [New York: Simon & Schuster, 1996], p. 34).
15. The Center of Special Studies in Israel offers scholarly recognition for distinguished study in the field of intelligence with a prize named the "Jim Angleton Award."
16. Colby and Forbath, *Honorable Men*, op. cit., p. 334.
17. My interview with Angleton, Army-Navy Club, Washington, D.C. (August 12, 1975); see also Colby and Forbath, ibid., p. 396.
18. Angleton told me that he drove the seemingly block-long Mercedes instead of a preferred Rolls-Royce because he didn't think the Agency's Chief of CI should be "conspicuous." Perhaps the brand name had added appeal; his mother's middle name was Mercedes.
19. Colby and Forbath, *Honorable Men*, op. cit., 314.
20. Nicholas Lemann, "Spy Wars: The Real Legacy of Soviet Spying in America," *New Yorker* (July 27, 2009), pp. 70–75, quote at p. 74.
21. Haynes, Klehr, and Vassiliev, *Spies*, op. cit.; Timothy Gibbs, "Catching an Atom Spy: MI5 and the Investigation of Klaus Fuchs," in Johnson, *Oxford Handbook*, op. cit., pp. 555–568.
22. Haynes, Klehr, and Vassiliev, *Spies*, op. cit. See also Lemann, "Spy Wars," op. cit.
23. See Martin, *Wilderness of Mirrors*, op. cit., and Ranelagh, op. cit.
24. Colby and Forbath, *Honorable Men*, op. cit., p. 243.
25. Once I got to know Angleton, he would telephone me periodically at my townhouse in Southwest Washington. One evening, my wife answered the telephone and, putting her hand over the receiver, called to me with a grin: "It's Mother." I thought she meant my own mother and I answered the phone enthusiastically with a "Hi, Mom!" Silence. Then: "This is Jim Angleton." With a red face on my end of the line, we talked about plans for our next lunch and interview.
26. See Winks, "The Theorist," op. cit.
27. This phrase is from an FBI counterintelligence officer, testimony, *Huston Plan Hearings*, Select Committee on Intelligence Activities (the Church Committee), U.S. Senate, 94th Cong., 1st Sess. (September 25, 1975), p. 137.
28. Theodore H. White, *Breach of Faith: The Fall of Richard Nixon* (New York: Atheneum, 1975), p. 133.
29. Presidential Talking Paper, prepared by Tom Charles Huston and used by President Richard Nixon, Oval Office (June 5, 1970), Church Committee files (declassified on February 28, 1975), "Security/FBI," Container Number 12-1.
30. For a more complete account, see Loch K. Johnson, *America's Secret Power: The CIA in a Democratic Society* (New York: Oxford University Press, 1987), ch. 7.
31. White, *Breach of Faith*, op. cit., p 133.
32. My notes of CIA historian David Robarge's comment, "Moles, Defectors, and Deceptions," op. cit.

33. David Robarge has inventoried a wide range of Angleton depictions from fictional and nonfictional accounts of the man, all painted in dark hues (" 'Cunning Passages, Contrived Corridors': Wandering in the Angletonian Wilderness," *Studies in Intelligence* 53 [2009], pp. 43–55).

34. For background on Nosenko and other key counterintelligence cases, see Martin, *Wilderness*, op. cit.; Mangold, *Cold Warrior*, op. cit.; and David Wise, *Molehunt* (New York: Random House, 1992).

35. Colby and Forbath, *Honorable Men*, op. cit., p. 364.

36. This metaphor is from my *A Season of Inquiry: The Senate Intelligence Investigation* (Lexington: University Press of Kentucky, 1985), p. 82, republished as *A Season of Inquiry Revisited: The Church Committee Confronts America's Spy Agencies* (Lawrence: University Press of Kansas, 2015).

37. Mark Twain, "Dinner Speech: General Grant's Grammar," *Collected Tales, Sketches, Speeches, & Essays: 1852–1890* (New York: Library of America, 1967), p. 907. Twain's reference was to Matthew Arnold, the British poet and cultural critic. Former DCI and Secretary of Defense James R. Schlesinger has said that "listening to Jim [Angleton] was like looking at an Impressionist painting" (quoted by Tom Mangold, *Cold Warrior: James Jesus Angleton, the CIA's Master Spy Hunter* [New York: Simon & Schuster, 1991], p. 153). I would say that Cubism or, even better, Surrealism would be closer to the mark. Angleton was the Giorgio de Chirico of counterintelligence.

38. Colby and Forbath, *Honorable Men*, op. cit., p. 364.

39. Michelle Van Cleave, "Foreign Spies Are Serious. Are We?" *Washington Post* (February 8, 2009), p. B9. Van Cleave served as the head of U.S. counterintelligence from July 2003 through March 2006.

40. See Dan Raviv and Jossi Melman, *Every Spy a Prince* (Boston: Houghton Mifflin, 1990), p. 89.

41. Hersh, "Angleton Story," op. cit.; Colby and Forbath, *Honorable Men*, op. cit., p. 133; John M. Crewdson, "The C.I.A.'s 3-Decade Effort to Mold the World's Views," *New York Times* (December 25, 1977), p. A1; and Jerry D. Ennis, "Anatoli Golitsyn: Long-time CIA Agent?" *Intelligence and National Security* 21 (February 2006), p. 41.

42. Following Angleton's death, an American journalist could only conclude (without details or a specific source) that "Angleton reportedly aided Israel in obtaining technical nuclear data" (Glenn Frankel, "The Secret Ceremony," *Washington Post* [December 5, 1987], Style Section, p. B1). Others once close to Angleton have said to me since the Church Committee inquiry that he and his staff siphoned off minute amounts of fissionable material from U.S. stockpiles—so small in quantity at any given time as to be unnoticed by nuclear security personnel—and passed it along to Israeli contacts. I have no way of evaluating the truthfulness of that stunning allegation, and I am inclined to doubt its validity on the grounds alone of the risk posed to Angleton by such a venture and the unlikely technical prowess this would require on behalf of his staff. On the topic of Angleton and the Israeli atomic bomb program, see Samuel Katz, *Soldier Spies: Israeli Military Intelligence* (Novato, CA: Presidio Press, 1992).

43. For some evidence in support of Angleton's involvement in the Hungarian Revolt, see Hersh, "Angleton Story," op. cit.

44. Winks, "The Theorist," op. cit., p. 119.

45. "Huston Plan," *Hearings on Intelligence Activities*, vol. 2, Senate Select Committee to Study Governmental Operations with Respect to Intelligence Activities, the Church Committee (Washington, DC: U.S. Government Printing Office, 1976), pp. 52–93.

46. Huston, "Presidential Talking Paper," op. cit.

47. For accounts of this exchange, see Johnson, *Season of Inquiry*, op. cit., pp. 86–88; Mangold, *Cold Warrior*, op. cit., p. 351; and Winks, "The Theorist," op. cit., pp. 118–120.

48. During a 2012 conference on the topic of James Angleton, CBS newsman David Martin (who covered the Church Committee proceedings in 1975) said during a panel discussion that Angleton told him after the hearing that he had been on medication that day to help ensure he would not have to leave for the bathroom in the middle of the proceedings, and that the medication had affected his ability to respond well to questioning ("Moles, Defectors, and Deceptions," op. cit.).

49. See Martin, *Wilderness*, op. cit.; and Mangold, *Cold Warrior*, op. cit.

50. Hood, Nolan, and Halpern, "Myths Surrounding James Angleton," op. cit., p. 32, paraphrasing an anonymous source.

51. Ramsey Clark, foreword to Allan Reitman, ed., *The Pulse of Freedom* (New York: Norton, 1975), p. 18.
52. Walter F. Mondale, with David Hage, *The Good Fight: A Life in Liberal Politics* (New York: Scribner, 2010), p. 136.
53. From an interview Angleton gave to an Idaho newspaper while visiting there in 1976 (Jay Shelledy, "Former Top Spymaster Has Bitter Words for Harshest Critic of the Cloak and Dagger," *Lewiston Morning Tribune* [June 6, 1976], p. A5). The former CI chief had been expressing similar sentiments around Washington, D.C., ever since the Church Committee's counterintelligence hearing.
54. James Angleton and Charles J. V. Murphy, "On the Separation of Church and State," *American Cause, Special Report* (June 1976), p. 2. Most of the sections on counterintelligence in the Church Committee final papers remain classified and are stored in a special section of the National Archives. The few paragraphs in the public *Final Report* devoted to CIA counterintelligence, which I wrote, simply warned of the risks involved in what appeared to be less of an emphasis placed on this mission in the aftermath of the Angleton excesses. Angleton's successor, George T. Kalaris, a bright, tough-minded individual, had little previous experience in counterintelligence, but he did possess a warmer personality than Angleton and he proved to be an outstanding leader in many ways. Kalaris cleaned up Angleton's chaotic filing system, so important to the CI tradecraft, and he brought a fresh sense of responsibility and openness to the Agency's Counterintelligence Staff. The CI mission, though, had a diminished profile at Langley overall, which lasted until 1994 when the discovery of Aldrich Ames renewed attention to this vital topic. As an Agency historian has put it, "Counterintelligence became degraded after Angleton, and a security laxity set in" (Robarge, "Moles, Defectors, and Deceptions," op. cit.).

When I wrote the passages on CIA counterintelligence in the Church Committee's final report, the classification levels were so high that all that remained in the public version was some brief language about the organizational debates raging inside the Agency. They chiefly dealt with the subject of whether CI should be centralized, in the Angleton model, or decentralized as Colby and Kalaris preferred. Given the power changes at the Agency (Angleton's firing), the Colby/Kalaris approach won out. More recently, the former CIA senior official John McLaughlin has sung the praises of decentralization: "Counterintelligence should be a part of the mental toolbox of everyone," he told a conference on Angleton in 2012 ("Moles, Defectors, and Deceptions," op. cit.). Centralization did make some sense, though; by having all of the counterintelligence files in one place, they could be cross-referenced easily in the search for connections between suspected moles inside the Agency and, more common in the daily work of CI officers, for the careful tracing of what SVR officer had served where, what Russian "diplomat" had been PNGed from which country for "extracurricular" (spying) activities, and myriad other subtle pieces of a mosaic that might add up to identifying foreign spies—the warp and wool of the counterintelligence profession. Moreover, by widely dispersing the CI mission, no one had overall responsibility, which makes accountability all the more difficult and, further, has a way of degrading the everyday importance of this critical barrier against foreign intelligence agencies and terrorists. In light of the 9/11 attacks, the counterterrorism compartment of CI did slowly embrace more centralization, culminating with the passage of the Intelligence Reform and Terrorism Prevention Act in 2004 and its creation of a National Counterterrorism Center (NCTC), located in the Office of the DNI but with direct reporting lines to the president as well.

The managerial vexation of intelligence centralization versus decentralization took another turn as a result of the 9/11 attacks. With the clumsy CIA-FBI counterintelligence coordination in the buildup to the attacks in mind, the Kean Commission's key recommendation was that the U.S. intelligence agencies should adopt better methods for sharing information across agencies' boundaries. Yet "sharing" is a concept anathema to CI specialists. They prefer to keep intelligence in separate "compartments," so that a future Ames or Hanssen will be able to inflict only limited damage, rather than have access to a broad range of secrets cutting across the entire IC. This managerial dispute remains a lively topic of debates inside the secret agencies, with sharing surging ahead so far. On this bureaucratic dilemma between centralization and decentralization as it has affected the Department of State, see

Bert A. Rockman, "America's *Departments* of State: Irregular and Regular Syndromes of Policy Making," *American Political Science Review* 75 (December 1981), pp. 911–927, original title emphasis.

55. Shelledy, "Former Top Spymaster," op. cit., p. A4.
56. On Conrad, see Redmond, "The Challenges of Counterintelligence," op. cit., and for a longer list of counterintelligence cases, see Johnson, *National Security Intelligence,* op. cit., ch. 4; as well as Norman Polmar and Thomas B. Allen, eds., *The Encyclopedia of Espionage* (New York: Gramercy Books, 1997).
57. On Lee, see David Wise, *The Spy Who Got Away: The Inside Story of Edward Lee Howard* (New York: Random House, 1988); and on Tolkachev, David E. Hoffman, *The Billion Dollar Spy: A True Story of Cold War Espionage and Betrayal* (New York: Doubleday, 2015).
58. See Redmond, "The Challenges of Counterintelligence," op. cit. (who played a major role in uncovering Ames), along with *An Assessment of the Aldrich H. Ames Espionage Case and Its Implications for U.S. Intelligence,* Staff Report, Select Committee on Intelligence, U.S. Senate, Sen. Rpt. 103-90, 103rd Cong., 2nd Sess. (Washington, DC: U.S. Government Printing Office, November 1, 1994); and David Wise, *Nightmover: How Aldrich Ames Sold the CIA to the KGB for $4.6 Million* (New York: HarperCollins, 1993). In tracking down moles like Ames, U.S. counterintelligence sleuths use a methodology informally called "walking back the cat"—tracing back in time the whereabouts and activities of various suspects to see if clues can be found that lead to the mole.
59. David Wise, *Spy: The Inside Story of How the FBI's Robert Hanssen Betrayed America* (New York: Random House, 2003).
60. See Seymour M. Hersh, "The Traitor," *New Yorker* (January 18, 1999), pp. 26–33.
61. David Johnston and Tim Weiner, "On the Trail of a C.I.A. Official from Asia Travel to Bank Files," *New York Times* (November 21, 1996), p. A1; Walter Pincus and Roberto Suro, "Rooting Out the 'Sour Apples' inside the CIA," *Washington Post,* National Weekly Edition (November 25–December 1, 1996), p. A30; and Wesley Wark, "For Love of Money," *Ottawa Citizen* (February 7, 2009).
62. See Mary Anne Weaver, "The Stranger," *New Yorker* (November 13, 1995), pp. 59–72.
63. Jo Thomas, "Letter by McVeigh Told of Mind-Set," *New York Times* (May 9, 1977), p. A1. For a fascinating broader account, see Stuart A. Wright, *Patriots, Politics, and the Oklahoma City Bombing* (New York: Cambridge University Press, 2007).
64. Reported by "NewsHour," *PBS Television* (March 25, 2016).
65. George Tenet, public testimony, *Hearings,* National Commission on Terrorist Attacks upon the United States (the 9/11 Commission, April 14, 2014), p. 5, cited by Amy B. Zegart, *Spying Blind: The CIA, the FBI, and the Origins of 9/11* (Princeton, NJ: Princeton University Press, 2007).
66. Taylor and Snow, "Cold War Spies," op. cit.
67. See Scott Shane, "A Spy's Motivation: For Love of Another Country," *New York Times* (April 20, 2008), p. Wk 3, who draws on a study by Katherine L. Herbig (a DoD contractor) about the rise of Chinese-American espionage in the United States.
68. Lemann, "Spy Wars," op. cit., p. 74.
69. Mark Piggott, "Isis: British Daesh Militant Details in 22,000 Documents: A Major Victory for Counter-Terrorism," *International Business Times,* U.K. (March 10, 2016); on the skepticism, see Melissa Eddy, "Germany Obtains Files Said to List ISIS Recruits," *New York Times* (March 11, 2016), p. A11.
70. Mark Mazzetti, "Officer Failed to Warn C.I.A. before Attack," *New York Times* (October 20, 2010), p. A1.
71. The heroin statistic is from "Evening News," *ABC Television* (March 10, 2016); on the vulnerabilities of U.S. nuclear weapons, see Eric Schlosser, "Break-In at Y-12," *New Yorker* (March 9, 2015), pp. 46ff.
72. John A. McCone, DCI during the Kennedy Administration, once observed that "experience has shown penetration to be the most effective response to Soviet and Bloc [intelligence] services" (declassified Agency memorandum, 1962, Church Committee files, p. 167). In 2009, DNI Admiral Dennis C. Blair said, similarly, that "the primary way" the IC determines which terrorist groups pose a direct and immediate threat to the American homeland is "to penetrate them and learn whether they're talking about making attacks against the United

States" (quoted by Karen DeYoung and Walter Pincus, "Success against al-Qaeda Cited," *Washington Post* [September 30, 2009], p. A1).
73. See Mark Mazzetti, Adam Goldman, Michael S. Schmidt, and Matt Apuzzo, "Killing C.I.A. Informants, China Stifled U.S. Spying," *New York Times* (May 21, 2017), p. A1.

Chapter 11

1. Loch K. Johnson, *America's Secret Power: The CIA in a Democratic Society* (New York: Oxford University Press, 1989).
2. Quoted in John H. Hedley, "The Intelligence Community: Is It Broken? How to Fix It," *Studies in Intelligence* 39 (1996), p. 17.
3. Loch K. Johnson, "A Centralized Intelligence System: Truman's Dream Deferred," *American Intelligence Journal* 23 (Autumn/Winter 2005), pp. 6–15.
4. See James R. Locher III, *Victory on the Potomac: The Goldwater-Nichols Act Unifies the Pentagon* (College Station: Texas A&M University Press, 2002).
5. President Truman had perhaps learned a lesson in creating the CIA, namely, that government by statute (as the Constitution extols) can be a difficult, unpredictable procedure, during which the White House must compromise with several stakeholders—most dauntingly, the Department of Defense. With the next intelligence agency he created, the NSA, the president took an easier route: the issuance of a presidential directive, in this case entitled simply "Communications Intelligence" (NSC Intelligence Directive No. 9, signed on October 24, 1952). See Matthew M. Aid, *The Secret Sentry: The Untold History of the National Security Agency* (New York: Bloomsbury, 2009), pp. 43–44. Truman's shortcut move seems to have drawn little criticism, probably because sigint is an arcane topic and lawmakers knew little about this form of intelligence—and, even if they did, the oversight capacity on the Hill to do anything about the presidential order remained in its infancy. The sprouting up of intelligence agencies by executive order over the years has contributed to the institutional fragmentation in the IC and makes the argument in favor of an Intelligence Charter attractive, as a means for bringing all the parts of the IC together into a more cohesion and rational framework.
6. See Michael Allen, *Blinking Red: Crisis and Compromise in American Intelligence after 9/11* (Washington, DC: Potomac Books, 2013).
7. Admiral Stansfield Turner, *Burn before Reading: Presidents, CIA Directors, and Secret Intelligence* (New York: Hyperion, 2005), pp. 254, 262.
8. Amy Zegart, *Spying Blind: The CIA, the FBI, and the Origins of 9/11* (Princeton, NJ: Princeton University Press, 2007), p. 183.
9. *Report of the Commission on the Intelligence Capabilities of the United States Regarding Weapons of Mass Destruction* [the Silberman-Robb Commission on the intelligence errors related to hypothesized Iraqi WMDs], p. 17.
10. I conducted these interviews with DCIs between the years 1986 and 1998 in Washington, as well as at Langley and in Boston. They covered a wide gamut of intelligence topics and, in this chapter, I draw on the sections that dealt with intelligence accountability. The CIA has published an in-house history of the DCIs, which is helpful in portraying the decisions they made over the years; but neither "accountability" nor "oversight" is listed in the index and little attention is paid to this subject in the volume (see Douglas F. Garthoff, *Directors of Central Intelligence as Leaders of the U.S. Intelligence Community, 1946–2005*, Center for the Study of Intelligence, Central Intelligence Agency, Washington, D.C. [2005]).
11. In an exchange of emails with a senior CIA officer, now retired, I once referred to the so-called Family Jewels as a "Pandora's box of horrors." He accused me of being overdramatic about the abuses revealed in the Jewels list, most of which were alleged and never addressed by the *New York Times*. "There is no nuance in outside comments on the 'family jewels,'" he said, "no search for what the CIA was trying to do [that is, make an internal accounting of any improprieties its officers may have committed, in order to correct these abuses] and the restraints it actually worked under" (correspondence with me, dated September 5, 2014). He had a point, but, nonetheless, I thought he was too readily dismissive of Operation CHAOS, as well as the Agency's covert actions in Chile.
12. For article-length biographies, see Garthoff, *Directors of Central Intelligence*, op. cit.

13. See David M. Barrett, *The CIA and Congress: The Untold Story from Truman to Kennedy* (Lawrence: University Press of Kansas, 2005). Barrett points out that, while more intelligence oversight took place in Congress than is often assumed, on the whole most lawmakers were happy to avoid responsibility for the nation's secret operations, which sometimes resulted in controversy (as with the Bay of Pigs in 1961). On the uneven—and usually weak—efforts of elected representatives to review intelligence activities, see Harry Howe Ransom, *The Intelligence Establishment* (Cambridge, MA: Harvard University Press, 1970).

14. Harry Howe Ransom (a political scientist who had interviewed Dulles), "Congress, Legitimacy and the Intelligence Community," paper presented at the Western Political Science Association annual convention, San Francisco, CA (April 6, 1976).

15. The phrase "the professional's professional" comes from Roy Jonkers, "In Memoriam," *Electronic Newsletter*, Association of Foreign Intelligence Officers (October 26, 2002—the year Helms died from multiple myeloma at the age of eighty-nine).

16. See the case study by Mark Lilla, entitled *The Two Oaths of Richard Helms*, Kennedy School of Government, Harvard University (Cambridge, MA, 1983); and Richard Harris, "Reflections: Secrets," *New Yorker* (April 10, 1978), pp. 44–86.

17. For his memoir, see Richard Helms with William Hood, *A Look over My Shoulder: A Life in the Central Intelligence Agency* (New York: Random House, 2003). See also Thomas Powers, *The Man Who Kept the Secrets: Richard Helms and the CIA* (New York: Simon & Schuster, 1979).

18. The session, which I recorded with his permission, lasted an hour, as was the case with the other interviews presented in this chapter, except for the remarks by President Bush (the result of a letter exchange) and the brief comment by DCI Casey (during a dinner conversation).

19. Frederick "Fritz" A. O. Schwarz, Jr., in Katherine Scott, ed., *Oral History Interviews, Church Committee*, U.S. Senate Historical Office, Washington, D.C. (October 28, 2014), p. 458.

20. See my *A Season of Inquiry Revisited: The Church Committee Confronts America's Spy Agencies* (Lawrence: University Press of Kansas, 2015).

21. What follows are excerpts from the interview that relate to intelligence accountability; for the full interview—one of two (along with a session with William E. Colby) that I have published previously from among those found in this chapter—see Loch K. Johnson, "Spymaster Richard Helms, an Interview with the Former US Director of Central Intelligence," *Intelligence and National Security* 18/3 (Autumn 2003), pp. 24–44; and note 28 below.

22. Russell was a long-time member of the Senate Armed Services Committee and the Appropriations Committee, with responsibilities for intelligence oversight.

23. The purpose of the Boland Amendments, sponsored by HPSCI Chair Edward P. Boland (D, Massachusetts) during the early 1980s, was to restrict various aggressive forms of CIA covert action directed against the Sandinista regime in Nicaragua—especially paramilitary operations. See Malcolm Byrne, *Iran-Contra: Reagan's Scandal and the Unchecked Abuse of Presidential Power* (Lawrence: University Press of Kansas, 2014).

24. Schlesinger's remarks reminded me at the time of a comment Dean Rusk had once made to me: "There are many, many instances where Congress has played a major role, usually behind the scenes, in the conduct of our diplomacy. Sometimes this influence can be positive and sometimes negative—but in our complicated constitutional system, I see no way to avoid such involvement or to strike a balance sheet" (letter from Dean Rusk, School of Law, University of Georgia, Athens, Georgia [May 31, 1982]).

25. For an account, see Douglas Waller, *Disciples* (New York: Simon & Schuster, 2015).

26. David S. Robarge, "Intelligence in Recent Public Literature," *Studies in Intelligence* 47 (2003). For Colby's memoirs, see William E. Colby with Peter Forbath, *Honorable Men: My Life in the CIA* (New York: Simon & Schuster, 1978); also John Prados, *Lost Crusader: The Secret Wars of CIA Director William Colby* (New York: Oxford University Press, 2003).

27. Nicholas Reynolds (CIA, Ret.), book review, *Studies in Intelligence* 60/1 (March 2016), p. 65.

28. Schwarz, *Oral History Interviews*, op. cit., p. 459. For the full interview, see Loch K. Johnson, "A Conversation with Former DCI William E. Colby: Spymaster during the 'Year of the Intelligence Wars,'" *Intelligence and National Security* 22/2 (April 2007), pp. 250–269.

29. The word "finding," recall, refers to the bold requirement in the Hughes-Ryan Act of 1974 that the CIA take all important covert action proposals to the White House, so the president could find (or not find) them suitable for approval—the end of plausible deniability, replaced by a direct paper trail to the Oval Office.

30. During the George H. W. Bush Administration, the United States invaded Panama between mid-December 1989 and late January 1990 in "Operation Just Cause," designed to oust its corrupt president (which it did).

31. For these reports, see Select Committee to Study Governmental Operations with Respect to Intelligence Activities, *Final Report*, 94th Cong., 2nd Sess, Sen. Rept. No. 94-755, 6 vols. (Washington, DC: U.S. Government Printing Office, November 20, 1975); and, on the Pike Committee report (leaked to the media), "The CIA Report the President Doesn't Want You to Read: The Pike Papers," *The Village Voice* (February 16 and 23, 1976).

32. For Turner's memoir, see Admiral Stansfield Turner, *Secrecy and Democracy: The CIA in Transition* (Boston: Houghton Mifflin, 1985). An accomplished author who didn't need the help of a ghost writer, Turner published several other works on intelligence, including (with co-author George Thibault), "Intelligence: The Right Rules," *Foreign Policy* 48 (Fall 1982), pp. 122–138, as well as (on his own) "Purge the C.I.A. of K.G.B. Types," *New York Times* (October 2, 1985), p. A24; "Has Reagan Killed CIA Oversight?" *Christian Science Monitor* (September 26, 1985), p. A14; *Terrorism and Democracy* (Boston: Houghton Mifflin, 1991); and *Burn before Reading*, op. cit.

33. Quoted by Joseph Persico, *Casey* (New York: Penguin, 1990), p. 334. I am grateful to Professor Glenn Hastedt, an intelligence studies colleague, for drawing my attention to this quote.

34. Told to me by former senator Sam Nunn (D, Georgia) during his visit to the University of Georgia on April 26, 2016.

35. A German scholar of intelligence has concluded that "the better the control of [intelligence] services, the larger the legitimacy of their actions" (Jan-Hendrik Dietrich, "Of Toothless Windbags, Blind Guardians and Blunt Swords: The Ongoing Controversy about the Reform of Intelligence Services Oversight in Germany," *Intelligence and National Security* 31/3 [April 2016], pp. 397–415, quote at p. 415).

36. See Loch K. Johnson, "Glimpses into the Gems of American Intelligence: The President's Daily Brief and the National Intelligence Estimate," *Intelligence and National Security* 23 (June 2008), pp. 333–370.

37. See also his remarks on this subject in my *The Threat on the Horizon: An Inside Account of America's Search for Security after the Cold War* (New York: Oxford University Press, 2011).

38. Robert M. Gates, "The CIA and American Foreign Policy," *Foreign Affairs* 66 (Winter 1987/88), pp. 215–230. See, as well, Gates's "Strengthening Congressional Oversight of Intelligence," *National Security Law Report*, American Bar Association (February 1993); and his memoir, entitled *From the Shadows* (New York: Simon & Schuster, 1996).

39. Since this interview, the Intelligence Committees have removed the rotational requirement. Both before and after this rule change, though, the turnover rates have been high among SSCI and HPSCI chairs: three years for both committees, on average, with Representative Boland (1977–1985) serving the longest on HPSCI at eight years, and SSCI's David L. Boren (D, Oklahoma, 1987–1993) and Diane Feinstein (D, California, 2009–2014) tied at six years each on SSCI. Three years seems to be a magical span of time for government service in many positions related to national security. For instance, the nineteen DCIs served on average about three years each, as have the nation's secretaries of state and defense (Garthoff, *Directors of Central Intelligence*, op. cit., p. 276). America has a government in continual flux.

40. Above all else, the goal is to provide U.S. warfighters with reliable pictures of battlefield conditions ("situational awareness," in Pentagon lingo)—a huge advantage for those in combat.

41. See Johnson, *Threat on the Horizon*, op. cit., pp. 365–366.

42. I served as special assistant to Les Aspin (D, Wisconsin) and a staff investigator during this period.

43. For a more sanguine appraisal of the Commission, see my *Threat on the Horizon*, op. cit.

44. For his memoir, see George Tenet with Bill Harlow, *At the Center of the Storm: My Years at the CIA* (New York: HarperCollins, 2007).

45. For Moynihan's views, see Daniel Patrick Moynihan, "Do We Still Need the C.I.A.? The State Dept. Can Do the Job," *New York Times* (May 19, 1991), p. E17.

46. Quoted in Bob Drogin, "Spy Agencies Fear Some Applicants Are Terrorists," *Los Angeles Times* (March 8, 2005), p. A1.

47. I served as the staff director for HPSCI's Oversight Subcommittee in 1977–1980 and witnessed these confrontations, which are related in chapter 3 of this book.

48. I derive this manner of depicting an attitudinal continuum from my research on "operational codes," a useful methodology for analyzing the perspectives of public figures on various policy issues; see my "Operational Codes and the Prediction of Leadership Behavior," in Margaret G. Herman, ed., *A Psychological Examination of Political Man* (New York: Free Press, 1977), pp. 80–119. One can conceive of the spy chiefs being arrayed along three other dimensions as well, according to their support for the core triad of major intelligence missions (collection and analysis, covert action, and counterintelligence) with, for example, DCI Casey easily the most gung-ho on the use of covert action.

49. On the importance of the collision between circumstances and personalities for understanding behavior in government office, see Loch K. Johnson, *American Foreign Policy and the Challenges of World Leadership: Power, Principle, and the Constitution* (New York: Oxford University Press, 2015), chap. 1; and Stephen Skowronek, *Presidential Leadership in Political Time: Reprise and Reprisal*, 2nd ed. (Lawrence: University Press of Kansas, 2011).

50. William E. Colby, "After Investigating U.S. Intelligence," *New York Times* (February 26, 1976), p. A11.

51. William E. Colby, remarks, *Larry King Live, CNN* (February 2, 1987).

52. Message from DCI Turner to all CIA stations, 1978 (declassified), as quoted in my *America's Secret Power: The CIA in a Democratic Society* (New York: Oxford University Press, 1989), p. 231. See also Turner and Thibault, "Intelligence," op. cit.

53. Gates, *From the Shadows*, op. cit., p. 559. "If we can't convince our oversight committees that our activities are worth the cost and risk," observed the CIA's deputy director in 2016, "then maybe we need to reconsider what we're doing, or how we are assessing risk, cost and gain." The DD/CIA added: "For CIA officers, rigorous oversight may feel onerous from time to time; it may make our jobs more complicated and the days a bit longer. But we know that for the sake and security of our democratic society, we must be accountable for our actions. And we understand that such oversight is both right and wise" (David S. Cohen, speech, "Governing Intelligence" conference, Center on Law and Security, NYU School of Law [April 21, 2016], Washington, D.C.).

Chapter 12

1. *Review of the Terrorist Attacks on U.S. Facilities in Benghazi, Libya, September 11–12, 2012*, Sen. Rpt. 113-134, Senate Select Committee on Intelligence, U.S. Senate (January 15, 2014). This SSCI report is not to be confused with the work of the Select Committee on Benghazi, created by House Republicans in 2014 (see David M. Herszenhorn, "A Panel's Pace on Benghazi Fuels Doubts," *New York Times* [May 19, 2016], p. A1; and his "Benghazi Panel Finds No Misdeeds by Clinton," *New York Times* [June 29, 2016], p. A1). This latter panel, led by Representative Trey Gowdy (R, South Carolina), was reportedly motivated by a desire to smear the reputation of former secretary of state Hillary Clinton in the midst of her 2016 presidential candidacy. The Gowdy Committee, which lasted longer than the Watergate or Iran-contra investigations, spent almost $7 million on its probe into Secretary Clinton's decisions related to the terrorist attack on U.S. government facilities in Benghazi, in eastern Libya in September 2012. The committee found no misdeeds by Clinton, but managed to smear her reputation over a period of two years. As for the so-called Underwear Bomber, this terrorist was a Nigerian by the name of Umar Farouk Abdulmutallab, who hid plastic explosives in his undergarments on a flight from Amsterdam to Detroit on December 25, 2009; fortunately, the explosives malfunctioned as the aircraft approached Detroit.

2. My interview, Washington, D.C. (June 5, 2015). A "minder" is someone from one of the intelligence agencies, often an in-house attorney, who is sent by intelligence managers to sit in whenever overseers interview or depose an intelligence officer. From the point of view of accountability, the presence of a minder has a chilling effect on the candor of answers from the officer being interviewed. The Church Committee sometimes succeeded in its efforts to banish minders during interviews and depositions, but not always; it was a constant fight. A SCIF is essentially a sealed room—say, within a U.S. embassy overseas—invulnerable to outside electronic eavesdropping. A retired senior CIA officer conceded to me that "Congress is often manipulated and deceived" by the Agency; but he also believed that—despite her

denials—House Speaker Nancy Pelosi had been briefed on the CIA's interrogation methods, but that her staff aide had probably not been with her. Lawmakers suffer from "information overload," he noted further. "The staffer has to concentrate his or her member's thoughts" (email communication to me [September 8, 2015]).

3. Steve Coll, "Comment: Dangerous Gamesmanship," *New Yorker* (April 27, 2015), p. 20.

4. See William H. Jackson, Jr., "Congressional Oversight of Intelligence: Search for a Framework," *Intelligence and National Security* 5 (1990), p. 115; and L. Britt Snider, *Sharing Secrets with Lawmakers: Congress as a User of Intelligence* (Washington, DC: Center for the Study of Intelligence, Central Intelligence Agency, 1997).

5. James Currie, "Iran-Contra and Congressional Oversight of the CIA," *International Journal of Intelligence and Counterintelligence* 11 (1988), pp. 185–210. An HPSCI chairman, Peter Hoekstra (R, Michigan), complained in a letter to President George W. Bush that the legislative branch "simply should not have to play Twenty Questions to get the information that it deserves under our Constitution" (reported by Eric Lichtblau and Scott Shane, "All Told Bush Project Secrecy Might Be Illegal," *New York Times* [July 9, 2006], p. A1).

6. For this and many other examples, see Loch K. Johnson, *A Season of Inquiry Revisited: The Church Committee Confronts America's Spy Agencies* (Lawrence: University Press of Kansas, 2015).

7. K. Guggenheim, "Tenet Defends CIA's Pre-9/11 Efforts," *Washington Post* (October 17, 2002), p. A1.

8. See Senator Bob Graham, with Jeff Nussbaum, *Intelligence Matters: The CIA, the FBI, Saudi Arabia, and the Failure of America's War on Terror* (Lawrence: University Press of Kansas, 2008). The twenty-eight pages were at last released on July 15, 2016, by HPSCI after being declassified by the Obama Administration with only a few redactions. The document revealed some contacts between the 9/11 hijackers and Saudi officials—"a catalog of meetings and suspicious coincidences," concluded the *New York Times* report on the release, including evidence of checks from Saudi royals to cutouts in contact with the terrorists. In the words of the *Times* account, however, the evidence was "by no means a Rosetta Stone" that clearly implicated the Saudi government in the 9/11 attacks (Mark Mazzetti, "In 9/11 Document, View of Saudi Effort to Thwart U.S. Action on Al Qaeda," *New York Times* [July 16, 2016], p. A13). The twenty-eight pages could be read differently by different people, though, and Senator Graham remained a skeptic about the conclusion that the Saudi government was not involved in the attacks. "This [document] makes a very compelling case that the Saudis were the source of assistance to the 9/11 hijackers," he commented (*Bloomberg Business News* [July 15, 2016]). An expert on the subject, Simon Henderson at the Washington Institute for Near East Policy, suggests that the evidence will not support the proposition that the royal family directly financed the 9/11 terrorists; however, "official Saudi money ended up in the pockets of the attackers, without a doubt" (see his "What We Know about Saudi Arabia's Role in 9/11," *Foreign Policy* [July 18, 2016]).

9. Senator Richard C. Shelby (R, Alabama), *Congressional Record* 148 (2002), p. 59085.

10. My interview with a senior HPSCI staffer, Washington, D.C. (February 6, 2003).

11. Remarks, Levin Center Conference on the Church Committee, Kennedy Caucus Room, Russell Building, U.S. Senate, Washington, D.C. (October 20, 2015).

12. Author's interview with a senior staff aide, Washington, D.C. (February 6, 2003).

13. N. A. Lewis, "Senator Insists C.I.A. Is Harboring Iraq Reports," *New York Times* (October 4, 2002), p. A12.

14. Email communication to me (October 4, 2002).

15. See Daniel Patrick Moynihan, *Secrecy: The American Experience* (New Haven, CT: Yale University Press, 1998); Frederick A. O. Schwarz, Jr., *Democracy in the Dark: The Seduction of Government Secrecy* (New York: New Press, 2015); and Trent Lott and Ron Wyden, "Hiding the Truth in a Cloud of Black Ink," *New York Times* (August 26, 2004), p. A18.

16. Lee H. Hamilton, "Opening Statement," *Hearings*, Committee on Government Reform, U.S. House of Representatives (July 18, 2001), p. 3.

17. See, respectively, *Annual Report*, Information Security Oversight Office, National Archives (2002); and D. Eggan, "Ashcroft Assailed," *Washington Post* (August 21, 2002), p. A1.

18. Robert Novak, "GOP Senators on the Warpath," *Chicago Sun-Times* (January 13, 2003), p. A1.

19. Adam Clymer, "Government Openness at Issue as Bush Holds on to Records," *New York Times* (January 3, 2002), p. A1.
20. Mark M. Lowenthal, *Intelligence: From Secrets to Policy*, 6th ed. (Los Angeles: Sage/CQ, 2015), pp. 419–420.
21. Commission on Protecting and Reducing Government Secrecy (the Moynihan Commission), *Secrecy* (Washington, DC: U.S. Government Printing Office, 1997); See also Schwarz, *Democracy in the Dark*, op. cit; and Rhodri Jeffrey-Jones, *The CIA & American Democracy* (New Haven, CT: Yale University Press, 1989).
22. Dean Rusk, as told to Richard Rusk and edited by Daniel S. Papp, *As I Saw It* (New York: Norton, 1990), pp. 561–562.
23. My interview with HPSCI staff director Tim Sample, Washington, D.C. (January 29, 2003).
24. Michael Hayden, a former NSA and CIA director, has noted that when controversial NSA collection programs were subject to public hearings in 2008, "the debate was indeed extraordinarily long, but the inner workings of the program were *not* exposed" (Michael V. Hayden, *Playing to the Edge: American Intelligence in the Age of Terror* [New York: Penguin, 2016], p. 87, original emphasis).
25. See Charlie Savage and Scott Shane, "Top-Secret Court Castigated N.S.A. on Surveillance," *New York Times* (August 23, 2013), p. A1; and *Report on the Surveillance Program Operated Pursuant to Section 702 of the Foreign Intelligence Surveillance Act*, Privacy and Civil Liberties Oversight Board (July 2, 2014), Washington, D.C.
26. My interview with senior SSCI staff, Washington, D.C. (February 4, 2003).
27. Herbert E. Meyer, "A Memo to the 9/11 Commission," *National Review Online* (January 6, 2003).
28. Eleanor Hill (who skillfully directed the staff of the Graham-Goss Joint Committee inquiry into the 9/11 intelligence failures), remark, Levin Center Conference, op. cit.
29. Loch K. Johnson, "Playing Ball with the CIA: Congress Supervises Strategic Intelligence," in Paul E. Peterson, ed., *Congress, the Executive, and the Making of American Foreign Policy* (Norman: University of Oklahoma Press, 1994), pp. 49–73, quote at p. 56. The Wilson quote is from his *Congressional Government: A Study in American Politics* (New York: Meridian, 1885), p. 69.
30. My interview with Sample, op. cit.
31. Johnson, "Playing Ball with the CIA," op. cit., p. 100. In contrast, another former Church Committee member, Gary Hart (D, Colorado), has noted that the first SSCI membership (often known as the Inouye Committee, after the panel's inaugural SSCI chair, Daniel K. Inouye, D, Hawaii) kept secrets well—a "huge historic achievement" that set the tone for subsequent SSCI members and signaled to the IC (and others) that Congress could be trusted with the nation's deepest secrets (remark, Conference on the Church Committee, New York University's Brennan Center in Washington, D.C. [June 5, 2015]). The inaugural Boland Committee displayed good discipline on the House side, too.
32. My interview with Timothy J. Roemer, Washington, D.C. (February 5, 2003).
33. William E. Colby, testimony, "Congressional Oversight of Covert Activities," *Hearings*, Permanent Select Committee on Intelligence, U.S. House of Representatives, 98th Cong, 2nd Sess. (September 20, 1983), p. 29.
34. Stansfield Turner, testimony, "H.R. 1013, H.R. 1317, and Other Proposals Which Address the Issue of Affording Prior Notice of Covert Actions in the Congress," *Hearings*, Permanent Select Committee on Intelligence, U.S. House of Representatives, 100th Cong., 2nd Sess. (April–June 1987), p. 66.
35. Quoted by Stephen R. Weissman, *A Culture of Deference: Congress's Failure of Leadership in Foreign Policy* (New York: Basic Books, 1995), p. 194.
36. Minister Steven Blaney, quoted in Alex Boutilier, "Review Body for Canada's Electronic Spy Agency Warns It Can't Keep Up," *Toronto Star* (April 1, 2015).
37. My interview with Lt. Gen. (ret.) James R. Clapper, Jr., NGA, Bethesda, Maryland (February 6, 2003).
38. My interview with SSCI staffer Jon Rosenwasser, Washington, D.C. (June 16, 2014).
39. This statistic is from Walter Pincus, "Overdue Intelligence Reports," *Washington Post* (December 1, 2002), p. A12.

40. William S. Cohen, "Congressional Oversight of Covert Actions," *International Journal of Intelligence and Counterintelligence* 2 (1988), pp. 155–162.

41. See Michael J. Glennon, *National Security and Double Government* (New York: Oxford University Press, 2015).

42. David Mayhew, *The Electoral Connection* (New Haven, CT: Yale University Press, 1974).

43. Remark to me during one of his visits to the University of Georgia, Athens, Georgia (April 26, 2016).

44. Remark, Levin Center Conference, op. cit.

45. Remark to me at the Conference on Freedom and Security, Boise State University, Idaho (October 2, 2003).

46. Quoted in Ashley Parker, "On Senate Menu, Bean Soup and a Soupçon of Partisanship," *New York Times* (August 20, 2014), p. A1.

47. Nicholas Kristof, "America the Unfair?" *New York Times* (January 21, 2016), p. A23. "Every hour a member of Congress spends on call time [to donors] is an hour less spent on critical issues," observed dismayed Representative Steve Israel (D, New York), in announcing his retirement from Congress (quoted in an unsigned editorial, "Beggars Banquet in Congress," *New York Times* [January 7, 2016], p. A22).

48. *CBS News* (April 24, 2016).

49. Amy Zegart, *Eyes on the Spies: Congress and the United States Intelligence Community* (Stanford, CA: Hoover Institution Press, 2011), pp. 115–116.

50. Lee Hamilton, remark to me during his visit to the University of Georgia, Athens (April 9, 2008).

51. Remarks by various senior staffers from SSCI and from the Graham-Goss Joint Committee, Levin Center Conference, op. cit.

52. Daniel Jones, SSCI staffer, Levin Center Conference, op. cit.

53. A former CIA senior officer recalls that "only two staffers in the history of HPSCI have been former case officers, that is, people who were practicing operations officers. The Directorate [DDO] hated these two guys and spread rumors about them as being disaffected. The real reason for the hatred is that they knew what questions to ask" (email to me, September 8, 2015).

54. Katherine Scott, ed., *Oral History Interviews, Church Committee*, U.S. Senate Historical Office, Washington, D.C. (March 28, 2014), p. 111.

55. Johnson, *Season of Inquiry Revisited*, op. cit., p. 276.

56. From his book *Five Germanys I Have Known* (New York: Farrar, Straus, and Giroux, 2006), quoted by William Grimes, "Fritz Stern, 90, Noted Historian on Germany, Dies," *New York Times* (May 19, 2016), p. A18.

57. See Malcolm Byrne, *Iran-Contra: Reagan's Scandal and the Unchecked Abuse of Presidential Power* (Lawrence: University Press of Kansas, 2014). Lee Hamilton, HPSCI chair at the time of the Iran-contra affair, recalls, "They [McFarlane and North] lied to me. So did Elliott Abrams" (an assistant secretary in the State Department also caught up in the Iran-contra scheme). Remarks to me during Representative Hamilton's visit to the University of Georgia, Athens (April 9, 2008).

58. See *The 9/11 Commission Report* (New York: Norton, 2004).

59. See Loch K. Johnson, *Threat on the Horizon: An Inside Account of America's Search for Security after the Cold War* (New York: Oxford University Press, 2011), pp. 123–124.

60. Robert Jervis, *Why Intelligence Fails: Lessons from the Iranian Revolution and the Iraq War* (Ithaca, NY: Cornell University Press, 2010); Loch K. Johnson, "A Framework for Strengthening U.S. Intelligence," *Yale Journal of International Affairs* 2 (February 2006), pp. 116–131.

61. Paul R. Pillar, *Intelligence and U.S. Foreign Policy: Iraq, 9/11, and Misguided Reform* (New York: Columbia University Press, 2009).

62. James Risen and Eric Lichtblau, "Bush Lets U.S. Spy on Callers without Courts," *New York Times* (December 16, 2005), p. A1.

63. On this general theme, see Gordon Silverstein, *Imbalance of Powers: Constitutional Interpretation and the Making of American Foreign Policy* (New York: Oxford University Press, 1997). A former Church Committee attorney observes that the protection afforded them by a

system of judicial warrants is "a good thing for the intelligence and law enforcement agencies" (Frederick D. Barron, in Scott, *Oral History Interviews*, op. cit. [May 28, 2015], p. 27).

64. A prominent member of the Armed Services Committee, John McCain (R, Arizona), told the 9/11 Commission in 2004 that if his panel had spent about ten minutes considering the intelligence budget it would have been a good year (Jonathan Weisman, "Democrats Reject Key 9/11 Panel Suggestion; Neither Party Has an Appetite for Overhauling Congressional Oversight of Intelligence," *Washington Post* [November 30, 2006], p. A1).

65. Eleanor Hill, remark, Levin Center Conference, op. cit.

66. This estimate comes from my interviews with SSCI and HPSCI staff members in 2014 and 2015, Washington, D.C., and is consistent with my own observations of HPSCI activities in the late 1970s—although in those early days a few lawmakers, like Les Aspin (D, Wisconsin) and Keith Robertson (R, Virginia), normally put in some fifteen hours a week on intelligence reviews, and more when special hearings were under way (including on weekends).

67. Daniel Jones, SSCI staffer, Levin Center Conference, op. cit.

68. My interviews with SSCI and HPSCI staff aides, Washington, D.C. (June 16, 2014).

69. My interview, Washington, D.C. (June 18, 2014).

70. Louis Fisher, "Congressional Access to National Security Information: Precedents from the Washington Administration," *Report No. 2009-002846*, Law Library of Congress (May 22, 2009), p. 7.

71. Schwarz, *Democracy in the Dark*, op. cit., p. 195.

72. Carl Hulse, "Fearing a Last-Minute Obstacle in a Push to Release 9/11 Findings," *New York Times* (May 24, 2016), p. A15.

73. Johnson, *Season of Inquiry Revisited*, op. cit.

74. See "Up to Code," *PBS Newshour* (February 12, 2016).

75. See *Justice in the Surveillance State*, Alliance for Justice, Washington, D.C. (2013).

76. There is a vast literature on this subject, but a good starting place is the reflections of former *Washington Post* executive editor Ben Bradlee, *A Good Life: Newspapering and Other Adventures* (New York: Simon & Schuster, 1996).

77. See Ellen Barry, "To the U.S. in the '70s, A Dissenting Diplomat," *New York Times* (June 28, 2016), p. A6.

78. *Administrative Management in the Government of the United States*, President's Committee on Administrative Management (Washington, DC: U.S. Government Printing Office, 1937); see also Barry D. Karl, *Executive Reorganization and Reform in the New Deal* (Cambridge, MA: Harvard University Press, 1963).

79. On these proposals, see (on the U.K.) James Ball, "GCHQ Views Data without a Warrant, Government Admits," *Guardian* (October 29, 2014); and Mark Phythian, "The British Experience with Intelligence Accountability," in Loch K. Johnson, ed., *Essentials of Strategic Intelligence* (Santa Barbara, CA: Praeger Security International, 2015), pp. 447–470; (on Australia) Patrick F. Walsh, *Intelligence and Intelligence Analysis* (New York: Routledge, 2011), and John Coyne, "The Intel on Intelligence Gathering in Times of Terror," *Huffington Post*, Australian (March 29, 2016); (on the Netherlands) Constant Hijzen, "More Than a Ritual Dance: The Dutch Practice of Parliamentary Oversight and Control of the Intelligence Community," *Security and Human Rights* 24 (2003), pp. 227–238; (on Canada) Colin Kenny, "What Real Intelligence Oversight Would Look Like," *National Post* (March 2, 2015), Ian MacLeon, "Spy Agency Watchdog 'in a Difficult Position' with Huge Budget Cuts Looming," *National Post* (March 24, 2016), and Wesley Wark, "Canada's Spy Watchdogs: Good, but not Good Enough," *Globe and Mail* (February 1, 2016); (on Germany) Jan-Hendrik Dietrich, "Of Toothless Windbags, Blind Guardians and Blunt Swords: The Ongoing Controversy about the Reform of Intelligence Services Oversight in Germany," *Intelligence and National Security* 31/3 (April 2016), pp. 397–416; (on the UN) Ewen MacAskillo, "UN Establishes Role of Privacy Chief in Wake of Snowden Leaks," *Guardian* (March 28, 2015); and (on the U.S.) Pillar, *Intelligence and U.S. Foreign Policy*, op. cit.; and Loch K. Johnson, *National Security Intelligence: Secret Operations in Defense of the Democracies* 2nd ed. (Cambridge, UK: Polity, 2017), pp. 210–213. For a comparative overview of intelligence oversight in the democracies, see Hans Born, Loch K. Johnson, and Ian Leigh, eds., *Who's Watching the Spies: Establishing Intelligence Service Accountability* (Washington, DC: Potomac Books, 2005); and Peter Gill,

Intelligence Governance and Democratisation: A Comparative Analysis of the Limits of Reform (London: Routledge, 2016).
80. Pillar, *Intelligence and U.S. Foreign Policy*, op. cit., p. 316.
81. Wark, "Canada's Spy Watchdogs," op. cit.
82. Walter Pforzheimer, Memorandum for the Record, prepared for DCI Allen Dulles, Central Intelligence Agency (September 7, 1962), sanitized for release on September 5, 2013; Professor David M. Barrett discovered this document in the National Archives and I thank him for sharing it with me.

Epilogue

1. This epilogue draws upon my, 'Kiss of Death? The Politicization of U.S. Intelligence Under Trump," *World Politics Review* 11 (March 21, 2017), pp. 1–8.
2. My interviews with two senior intelligence officials, Washington, D.C. (May 25, 2017). Pompeo, the former tank commander turned spy chief, seemed to bring with him to Langley a militaristic view of the Agency's roles in the struggle against global terrorism. "The tradition we came out of [is] the OSS and Wild Bill Donovan," he told a reporter in June of 2017. "The warriors are here," he continued. "Release the bridle and allow this agency to do the things that will serve and protect America in ways that frankly the last administration just didn't let them do. We're going to do it. We're going to get out there. You can't win if you don't take risk. The President has directed the CIA to win, and we're going to do it" (Hugh Hewitt, "Interview with CIA Director Mike Pompeo," *MSNBC Television* [June 24, 2017]).
3. See Philip Rucker and Ashley Parker, "How President Trump Consumes—or Does Not Consume—Top-Secret Intelligence," *Washington Post* (May 29, 2017), p. A1. In June 2017, CIA Director Pompeo said that he was spending some 35 to 40 minutes with the president "nearly every day," and that he found Trump "an avid consumer of the products we provide." (Hewitt, ibid.). The extent to which the president paid attention to intelligence, aside, clearly the new administration sought to increase funding for the spy agencies, in step with Pentagon budget increases. The National Intelligence Program (NIP—see chapter 1) rose from a requested $54.9 billion in FY 2017 to $57.7 billion in 2018; and the Military Intelligence Program (MIP) from $18.5 billion in FY 2017 to $20.7 billion in FY 2018 (Steven Aftergood, "Intelligence Budget Requests for FY 2018 Published," *Secrecy News*, FAS 2017/47 [June 19, 2017], p. 4).

ABBREVIATIONS AND CODENAMES

Too many abbreviations in a book can be a source of annoyance for the reader, so I have tried to keep the number down; at the same time, they are inevitable within the realm of national security writing. For instance, no reader wants to see "Senate Select Committee on Intelligence" over and over again; therefore, the acronym SSCI makes sense, for purposes of parsimony. Below are the abbreviations I have found useful—and certainly in wide currency among Washington officials involved in intelligence work.

ACLU	American Civil Liberties Union
AFIO	Association of Former Intelligence Officers
AG	attorney general
Agency, the	Central Intelligence Agency
APSA	*American Political Science Review*
AUMF	Authorization of the Use of Military Force
AWOL	absent without leave
BENS	Business Executives for National Security
Big Bird	U.S. satellites having both sigint and geoint capabilities
BND	Bundesnachtrichtendienst (German intelligence agency)
Bureau, the	Federal Bureau of Investigation
BW	biological weapons
C-15	military cargo plane
CA	covert action
CAS	Covert Action Staff (CIA)
CB	chemical-biological
CBW	chemical-biological warfare
CE	counterespionage
CENTCOM	U.S. Central Command
CHAOS	codename for illegal CIA domestic spying operation, revealed in 1974
CI	counterintelligence
CIA	Central Intelligence Agency (known by insiders as the Agency)
CIAB	Citizens Intelligence Advisory Board (proposed)
CIA/IG	Central Intelligence Agency Inspector General
CIC	Counterintelligence Center (CIA)
CIPA	Classified Information Procedures Act
CIS	Counterintelligence Staff (CIA)
CMS	Community Management Staff
CN	Congressional Notification (from CIA to Congress)
CNSS	Center for National Security Studies

COINTELPRO	FBI Counterintelligence Program
COS	chief of station, the top intelligence officer in a country overseas
CRS	Congressional Research Service (Library of Congress); also, "Can't remember shit" (a Pentagon slang expression for false amnesia)
CSG	Counterterrorism Security Group
CSIS	Canadian Security and Intelligence Service
CTC	Counterterrorism Center (CIA)
CTIVD	Dutch intelligence oversight committee
CW	chemical weapons
D	Democrat
DA	Directorate of Administration (now Directorate of Support, CIA); also, Directorate of Analysis (CIA)
DCI	Director of Central Intelligence
D/CIA or DCIA	Director of the Central Intelligence Agency
DDA	Deputy Director for Analysis (CIA)
DDCI	Deputy Director of Central Intelligence
DD/CIA or DDCIA	Deputy Director, Central Intelligence Agency
DDDI	Deputy Director of Digital Innovation (CIA)
DDI	Deputy Director for Intelligence (now DDA); also, Directorate of Digital Innovation (CIA)
DDNI	Deputy Director for National Intelligence (ODNI)
DDO	Deputy Director for Operations (CIA)
DDS	Deputy Director for Support (CIA)
DDS&T	Deputy Director for Science and Technology (CIA)
DEA	Drug Enforcement Administration
D/FBI	Director of the Federal Bureau of Investigation
DHS	Department of Homeland Security; also, Defense Humint Service (DoD)
DI	Directorate of Intelligence (CIA)
DIA	Defense Intelligence Agency
DIRNSA	Director of the National Security Agency (also, D/NSA)
DNI	Director of National Intelligence
DNC	Democratic National Committee
D/NSA	Director of the National Security Agency
DO	Directorate of Operations (CIA)
DoD	Department of Defense
DoE	Department of Energy
DoJ	Department of Justice
DoS	Department of State
DoT	Department of Transportation
DS&T	Directorate for Science and Technology (CIA)
EAB	External Advisory Board (CIA)
EBIS	evidence-based intelligence studies
EBM	evidence-based medicine
EITs	enhanced interrogation techniques (CIA)
EKG	electrocardiogram
EO (or eo)	executive order
EOP	Executive Office of the President
FAA	FISA Amendments Act (2008)
FAS	Federation of American Scientists
FBI	Federal Bureau of Investigation (also referred to as the Bureau)
FISA	Foreign Intelligence Surveillance Act
FISC	Foreign Intelligence Surveillance Court
FOIA	Freedom of Information Act
FSB	Federal Security Service (Russia)
FTE	full-time equivalent (personnel measure)
GAO	Government Accountability Office (Congress)

GCHQ	Government Communications Headquarters (UK)
geoint	geospatial intelligence
GOP	Grand Old Party (Republican Party)
GPS	Global Positioning System
GRU	Soviet military intelligence
HONETOL	a joint CIA-FBI operation to expose Soviet spies
Honey Badger	codename, CIA/CI hunt for Chinese mole in recent years
HPSCI	House Permanent Select Committee on Intelligence
HRP	Historical Review Board (CIA)
HT Lingual	codename for an improper mail-opening operation in the 1960s (CIA)
humint	human intelligence (espionage assets)
I	Independent
IC	intelligence community
ICTC	Intelligence Community Transparency Council (ODNI)
IC21	Intelligence Community 21 (title of a HPSCI report in 1996)
IG	Inspector General
IGIS	Inspector General for Intelligence and Security (Australia)
imint	imagery intelligence (photography; geoint)
INC	Iraqi National Congress
INR	Bureau of Intelligence and Research (Department of State)
Int-Q-Tel	a CIA venture capital fund located in Silicon Valley
ints	intelligence collection methods (for example: "sigint")
IOB	Intelligence Oversight Board (White House)
IRS	Internal Revenue Service
IRTPA	Intelligence Reform and Terrorism Prevention Act
ISIS	Islamic State in Syria (also known as Islamic State, ISIL, or, in Arabic, *Dawlat* [The State], or another Arabic term viewed by ISIS members as insulting: *Daesh*)
ISOO	Information Security Oversight Office
IT	information technology
ITC	Intelligence Transparency Council
I&W	indicators and warning
JCS	Joint Chiefs of Staff (U.S.)
JIC	Joint Intelligence Committee (U.K.)
JROC	Joint Reconnaissance Operations Center
JSOC	Joint Special Operations Command
KGB	Soviet Secret Police and Foreign Intelligence
KSM	Khalid Shaikh Mohammed
masint	measurement and signatures intelligence
MI	military intelligence
MICE	money, ideology, compromise, and ego (a CI phrase)
MI5	British Security Service
MINCES	money, ideology, nationality, compromise, ego, and sex (a CI phrase)
MINERAT	codename for NSA domestic telephone eavesdropping, revealed in 1975
MIP	Military Intelligence Program
MI6	Secret Intelligence Service (SIS-UK)
MK-ULTRA	a drug experimentation program (CIA)
MON	Memorandum of Notification
MONGOOSE	a CIA program to overthrow the Fidel Castro regime in Cuba
Mossad	Israeli intelligence agency
MOU	Memorandum of Understanding
NATO	North Atlantic Treaty Organization
NBC	nuclear, biological, and chemical (weaponry)
NCA	National Command Authority
NCO	noncommissioned officer
NCPC	National Counterproliferation Center (ODNI)

NCS	National Clandestine Service (now DO, CIA)
NCTC	National Counterterrorism Center (ODNI and the White House)
NFIP	National Foreign Intelligence Program (now NIP)
NGA	National Geospatial-Intelligence Agency
NGO	nongovernmental organization
NIC	National Intelligence Council
NIE	National Intelligence Estimate
NIO	National Intelligence Officer
NIP	National Intelligence Program
NIPF	National Intelligence Priorities Framework
NOC	nonofficial cover
NPC	Nonproliferation Center (CIA)
NPD	National Presidential Directive
NPIC	National Photographic Interpretation Center (NGA, and formerly CIA)
NRO	National Reconnaissance Office
NSA	National Security Agency (or National Student Association)
NSC	National Security Council (White House)
NSDD	National Security Decision Directive
NTM	National Technical Means
OBE	overtaken by events (a periodic criticism of analysis)
OC	official cover
OCA	Office of Congressional Affairs (CIA)
ODNI	Office of the Director of National Intelligence
OLC/DoJ	Office of Legal Counsel (Department of Justice)
OLC/CIA	Office of Legal Counsel (Central Intelligence Agency)
OMB	Office of Management and Budget
ONI	Office of Naval Intelligence
OPEC	Organization of Petroleum Exporting Countries
op-ed	editorial opinion piece
osint	open-source intelligence
OSS	Office of Strategic Services
PCLOB	Privacy and Civil Liberties Oversight Board
PDB	*President's Daily Brief*
PDD	Presidential Decision Directive
PFIAB	President's Foreign Intelligence Advisory Board (as of 2008, PIAB)
PGMs	Precision Guided Munitions
phoint	photographic intelligence (also, photoint; imint; geoint)
PIAB	President's Intelligence Advisory Board (White House)
PIDB	Public Interest Declassification Board (Congress and the White House)
PM ops	paramilitary operations (CIA)
PNG	persona non grata
PR	public relations
PRB	Publication Review Board (CIA)
PRC	People's Republic of China
PRISM	codename for the NSA's communications metadata program aimed at foreigners
R	Republican
RAND	Research and Development (Washington and California think tank)
RDI	post-9/11 rendition, detention, and interrogation program (CIA)
rif	reduction in force
RNC	Republican National Committee
SA	special activities (covert action)
SALT	Strategic Arms Limitation Treaty
Savak	secret service in Iran during the reign of the Shah
SCIF	sensitive compartmented information facility

SCRC	Security Classification Reform Committee (White House)
SDO	support to diplomatic operations
Secedef	secretary of defense
Seq	sequestration (budget)
SF	Special Forces (Green Berets—U.S. Army)
SHAMROCK	codename for NSA domestic cable-reading operations revealed in 1975
sigint	signals intelligence
SIOP	Select Intelligence Oversight Panel (Congress)
SIS	Secret Intelligence Services (British, also known as MI6)
SIU	Special Investigations Unit (the Nixon White House)
SLBM	submarine-launched ballistic missile
SMO	support to military operations
SNIE	Special National Intelligence Estimate
socmint	social media intelligence
SOCOM	Special Operations Command (Pentagon)
SOE	Special Operations Executive (British)
SOF	Special Operations Forces (U.S.)
SOG	Special Operations Group (PM/CAS/CIA)
SOVA	Office of Soviet Analysis (DI/CIA—now DA/CIA)
SR-21	U.S. spy plane (see U-2)
SSCI	Senate Select Committee on Intelligence
SS-5, SS-7	Soviet missilery
START	Strategic Arms Reduction Treaty
STELLARWIND	codename for a post-9/11 warrantless wiretap program (NSA)
SVR	Foreign Intelligence Service (Russia, successor of the KGB)
techint	technical intelligence
TIARA	tactical intelligence and related activities
TOR	terms of reference (for NIE and *PDB* drafting)
TSP	Terrorist Surveillance Program (NSA)
TTC	Terrorist Targeting Court (proposed)
215	code number for NSA metadata communications program targeting American citizens
UAV	unmanned aerial vehicle (drone)
UK	United Kingdom
UN	United Nations
USAF	U.S. Air Force
USC	U.S. Code (a statutory identification system)
USN	U.S. Navy
USSR	Union of Soviet Socialist Republics
U2	CIA spy plane (known by the U.S. Air Force as SR-71)
VC	Viet Cong (South Vietnam)
VENONA	codename for U.S. sigint intercepts against Soviets (1943–1980)
VX	a lethal nerve agent and chemical weapon
WI-ROGUE	codename for a specific, reckless CIA operative in the 1960s
WMD	weapon of mass destruction
YAF	Young Americans for Freedom (pro–Vietnam War student group)

BIBLIOGRAPHY

Aberbach, Joel D. 1977. "Changes in Congressional Oversight," *American Behavioral Scientist* 22 (May 7): 493–515.

———. 1987. "The Congressional Committee Intelligence System: Information, Oversight and Change," *Congress and the Presidency* 14: 51–76.

———. 1990. *Keeping a Watchful Eye: The Politics of Congressional Oversight.* Washington, DC: Brookings Institution.

———. 2002. "What's Happened to the Watchful Eye?" *Congress & the President* 29: 3–23.

Absher, Kenneth Michael, Michael C. Desch, and Roman Popadiuk. 2012. *Privileged and Confidential: The Secret History of the President's Intelligence Advisory Board.* Lexington: University Press of Kentucky.

———. 2012. "The President's Foreign Intelligence Advisory Board." In Loch K. Johnson, ed., *The Oxford Handbook of National Security Intelligence.* New York: Oxford University Press. 172–188.

Adelsberg, Samuel S. 2012. "Bouncing the Executive's Blank Check: Judicial Review and the Targeting of Citizens," *Harvard Law & Policy Review* 6: 437–457.

Adler, Emanuel. 1979. "Executive Control and the CIA," *Orbis* 23: 671–696.

Aid, Matthew M. 2009. *The Secret Sentry: The Untold History of the National Security Agency.* New York: Bloomsbury.

———. 2015. "Prometheus Embattled: A Post-9/11 Report Card on the National Security Agency." In Loch K. Johnson, ed., *Essentials of Strategic Intelligence.* Santa Barbara, CA: Praeger Security International. 417–446.

Aldrich, Richard. 2005. "Whitehall and the Iraq War: The UK's Four Intelligence Enquiries." *Irish Studies in International Affairs* 16 (November): 73–88.

———. 2009. "US-European Intelligence Cooperation on Counter-Terrorism: Low Politics and Compulsion." *British Journal of Politics and International Relations* 11(1): 122–139.

Allen, Michael. 2013. *Blinking Red: Crisis and Compromise in American Intelligence after 9/11.* Washington, DC: Potomac Books.

Ambinder, M. 2009. "The Real Intelligence Wars: Oversight and Access." *Atlantic* (November 18).

Andrew, Christopher. 1995. *For the President's Eyes Only: Secret Intelligence and the American Presidency from Washington to Bush.* New York: HarperCollins.

Andregg, Michael. 2010. "Ethics and Professional Intelligence." In Loch K. Johnson, ed., *The Oxford Handbook of National Security Intelligence.* New York: Oxford University Press. 735–756.

Angleton, James, and Charles J. V. Murphy. 1976. "On the Separation of Church and State." *American Cause: Special Report,* American Security Council. Washington, D.C. (June).

Anonymous. 1996. "Making the C.I.A. Accountable," *New York Times* (unsigned editorial) (August 18): E14.

Arnold, Jason Ross. 2014. *Secrecy in the Sunshine Era: The Promise and Failures of U.S. Open Government Laws.* Lawrence: University Press of Kansas.

Arsenault, Elizabeth Grimm. 2016. *The Gloves Came Off: Lawyers, Policymakers, and Norms in the Debate on Torture.* New York: Columbia University Press.

Ashby, LeRoy, and Rod Gramer. 1994. *Fighting the Odds: The Life of Senator Frank Church.* Pullman: Washington State University Press.

Aspin, Les. 1980. "Covert Acts Need Even More Oversight." *Washington Post* (February 24): B7.

———. 1981. "Misreading Intelligence." *Foreign Policy* 43: 166–172.

Aspin-Brown Commission (led by former secretaries of defense Les Aspin and Harold Brown). 1996. *Preparing for the 21st Century: An Appraisal of U.S. Intelligence: Report of the Commission on the Roles and Capabilities of the United States Intelligence Community* (March 1), Washington, D.C.

Auerswald, David P., and Colton C. Campbell, eds. 2012. *Congress and the Politics of National Security.* New York: Cambridge University Press.

Baker, James A. 2008. "Intelligence Oversight." *Harvard Journal on Legislation* 45/1 (Winter): 199–208.

Baker, James E. 2007. *In the Common Defense: National Security Law for Perilous Times.* Cambridge, UK: Cambridge University Press.

———. 2015. "From Cold War to Long War to Gray War: Covert Action in U.S. Legal Context." In Loch K. Johnson, ed., *Essential of Strategic Intelligence.* Santa Barbara, CA: Praeger Security International. 217–236.

Bakir, Vian. 2015. "News, Agenda Building, and Intelligence Agencies: A Systematic Review of the Field from the Discipline of Journalism, Media, and Communications." *International Journal of Press/Politics* 20: 131–144.

———. 2016. "Political Intelligence Elites, Strategic Political Communication, and the Press: The Need for, and Utility of, a Benchmark of Public Accountability Demands." *Intelligence and National Security* 7 (December): 1–22.

Baldino, Daniel, ed. 2010. *Democratic Oversight of Intelligence Services.* Annandale, Australia: Federation Press.

Balla, Steven J., and Christopher Deering. 2013. "Police Patrols and Fire Alarms: An Empirical Examination of the Legislative Preference for Oversight." *Congress & the Presidency* 40/1: 27–40.

Bamford, James. 2004. *A Pretext for War: 9/11, Iraq, and the Abuse of America's Intelligence Agencies.* New York: Doubleday.

———. 2016. "Michael Hayden Played Right Up to the Edge of Legality—and Then Took a Big Leap Off." *Nation* (June 1, 2016).

Banks, William C. 2007. "The Death of FISA." *Minnesota Law Review* 91: 1209–1301.

Barnds, William J. 1969. "Intelligence and Foreign Policy: Dilemmas of a Democracy," *Foreign Affairs* 47 (January): 281–295.

Barrett, David M. 1998. "Glimpses of a Hidden History: Sen. Richard Russell, Congress, and Early Oversight of the CIA." *International Journal of Intelligence and Counterintelligence* 11: 271–299.

———. 2004. "An Early 'Year of Intelligence': CIA and Congress, 1958." *International Journal of Intelligence and Counterintelligence* 17: 468–501.

———. 2005. *The CIA and Congress: The Untold Story from Truman to Kennedy.* Lawrence: University Press of Kansas.

———. 2007. "Congressional Oversight of the CIA in the Early Cold War, 1947–63." In Loch K. Johnson, ed., *Strategic Intelligence: Intelligence and Accountability, Safeguards against the Abuse of Secret Power,* vol. 5. Westport, CT: Praeger Security International. 1–18.

———. 2016. "Explaining the First Contested Confirmation of a Director of Central Intelligence: John McCone, The Kennedy White House, the CIA and the Senate, 1962." *Intelligence and National Security* 31: 74–87.

Bawn, Kathleen. 1995. "Political Control versus Expertise: Congressional Choices about Administrative Procedures." *American Political Science Review* 89/1: 62–73.

————. 1997. "Choosing Strategies to Control the Bureaucracy: Statutory Constraints, Oversight and the Committee System." *Journal of Law, Economics and Organization* 13: 101–126.

Bedan, Matt. 2007. "Echelon's Effect: The Obsolescence of the U.S. Foreign Intelligence Legal Regime." *Federal Communications Law Journal* 59: 426–444.

Bell, Griffin B., with Ronald J. Astrow. 1982. *Taking Care of the Law*. New York: Morrow.

Bendix, William, and Paul J. Quirk. 2015. "Secrecy and Negligence: How Congress Lost Control of Domestic Surveillance." *Issues in Governance Studies* 68 (March): 1–19.

Benton, M., and M. Russell. 2013. "Assessing the Impact of Parliamentary Oversight Committees: The Select Committees in the British House of Commons." *Parliamentary Affairs* 66: 772–797.

Beres, Louis Rene. 1991. "The Permissibility of State-Sponsored Assassination during Peace and War." *Temple International & Comparative Law Journal* 5 (Fall): 231–249.

Berger, Raoul. 1974. *Executive Privilege: A Constitutional Myth*. Cambridge, MA: Harvard University Press.

Berkowitz, Bruce. 2002. "Is Assassination an Option?" *Hoover Digest* 1: 1–5.

Berkowitz, Bruce, and Allen Goodman. 2000. *Best Truth: Intelligence in the Information Age*. New Haven, CT: Yale University Press.

Berman, Emily. 2014. "Regulating Domestic Intelligence Collection." *Washington and Lee Law Review* 71: 3–91.

Berry, James A. 1992. "Managing Covert Political Action: Guideposts from Just War Theory." *Studies in Intelligence* 36: 19–31.

————. 1993. "Covert Action Can Be Just." *Orbis* 37 (Summer): 375–390.

Best, Richard A., Jr. 2006. *Intelligence Estimates: How Useful to Congress?* Congressional Research Service (November 21).

————. 2010. *Intelligence Reform after Five Years: The Role of the Director of National Intelligence (DNI)*. Congressional Research Service (June 22).

Betts, Richard K. 2004. "The New Politics of Intelligence: Will Reforms Work This Time?" *Foreign Affairs* 83: 2–8.

————. 2007. *The Enemies of Intelligence: Knowledge and Power in American National Security*. New York: Columbia University Press.

Bibby, John F. 1968. "Congress' Neglected Function." In Melvin R. Laird, ed., *The Republican Papers*. New York: Arbor. 477–488.

Bickel, Alexander M. 1975. *Morality of Consent*. New Haven, CT: Yale University Press.

Bissell, Richard M., Jr., with Jonathan E. Lewis and Frances T. Pudlo. 1996. *Reflections of a Cold Warrior*. New Haven, CT: Yale University Press.

Blanton, T. 2003. "National Security and Open Government in the United States: Beyond the Balancing Test." In *National Security and Open Government: Striking the Right Balance*. Syracuse, NY: Campbell Public Affairs Institute, Syracuse University.

Bloom, Robert M., and William J. Dunn. 2006. "The Constitutional Infirmity of Warrantless NSA Surveillance: The Abuse of Presidential Power and the Injury to the Fourth Amendment." *William and Mary Bill of Rights Journal* 15: 147–202.

Bochel, Hugh, Andrew Defty, and Andrew Dunn. 2010. "Scrutinising the Secret State: Parliamentary Oversight of the Intelligence and Security Agencies." *Policy & Politics* 38: 483–487.

Bochel, Hugh, Andrew Defty, and Jane Kirkpatrick. 2015a. "'New Mechanisms of Independent Accountability': Select Committee and Parliamentary Scrutiny of the Intelligence Services." *Parliamentary Affairs* 68: 314–337.

————. 2015b. *Watching the Watchers: Parliament and the Intelligence Services*. New York: Palgrave/Macmillan.

Boren, David L. 1992. "The Winds of Change at the CIA." *Yale Law Journal* 101: 853–865.

Boren, David L., and William S. Cohen. 1987. "Keep Two Intelligence Committees." *New York Times* (August 17): A19.

Born, Hans, Ian Leigh, and Loch K. Johnson. 2005. *Who's Watching the Spies? Establishing Intelligence Service Accountability*. Washington, DC: Potomac Books.

Born, Hans, and Ian Leigh. 2005. *Making Intelligence Accountable: Legal Standards and Best Practice for Oversight*. Oslo: Publishing House of the Parliament of Norway.

———. 2007. "Intelligence Accountability: A Comparative Perspective." In Loch K. Johnson, ed., *Strategic Intelligence: Intelligence and Accountability, Safeguards against the Abuse of Secret Power*, vol. 5. Westport, CT: Praeger Security International. 47–66.

Born, Hans, Ian Leigh, and Marina Caparini, eds. 2007. *Democratic Control of Intelligence Services: Containing Rogue Elephants*. Aldershot, UK: Ashgate.

Born, Hans, Ian Leigh, and Aidan Wills. 2015. *Making International Intelligence Cooperation Accountable*. Geneva Centre for the Democratic Control of Armed Forces Books.

Born, Hans, and Thorsten Wetzling. 2007. "Intelligence Accountability: Challenges for Parliaments and Intelligence Services." In Loch K. Johnson, ed., *Handbook of Intelligence Studies*. New York: Routledge. 315–329.

Bovens, Mark. 2007. "Analysing and Assessing Accountability: A Conceptual Framework." *European Law Journal* 13/4 (2007): 447–468.

Braat, Eleni. 2016. "Recurring Tensions between Secrecy and Democracy: Arguments about the Security Service in the Dutch Parliament, 1975–1995." *Intelligence and National Security* 31/4 (June): 532–555.

Braden, Tom. 1975. "What's Wrong with the CIA?" *Saturday Review* (April 5): 8–14.

Bradley, Alison A. 2002–2003. "Extremism in the Defense of Liberty? The Foreign Intelligence Surveillance Act and the Significance of the USA PATRIOT Act." *Tulane Law Review* 77: 465–493.

Bradlee, Benjamin C. 1986. "The Press Is Not Reckless about National Security." *Washington Post, National Weekly Edition* (June 23): 24–25.

Breglio, Nola K. 2003. "Leaving FISA Behind: The Need to Return to Warrantless Foreign Intelligence Surveillance." *Yale Law Journal* 113: 179–217.

Brown, Harold, with Joyce Winslow. 2012. *Star Spangled Security: Applying Lessons Learned over Six Decades Safeguarding America*. Washington, DC: Brookings Institution Press.

Bruck, Connie. 2015. "The Inside War." *New Yorker* (June 22): 43–55.

Bruneau, Thomas C., and S. C. Boraz, eds. 2007. *Reforming Intelligence: Obstacles to Democratic Control and Effectiveness*. Austin: University of Texas Press.

Burch, James. 2007. "A Domestic Intelligence Agency for the United States? A Comparative Analysis of Domestic Intelligence Agencies and Their Implications for Homeland Security." *Homeland Security Affairs* 3 (June): 1–16.

Business Executives for National Security (BENS). 2015. *Domestic Security: Confronting a Changing Threat to Ensure Public Safety and Civil Liberties*. Washington, D.C. February.

———. 2016. *Domestic Security Revisited: Concluding Status Report*. February.

Byrne, Malcolm. 2014. *Iran-Contra: Reagan's Scandal and the Unchecked Abuse of Presidential Power*. Lawrence: University Press of Kansas.

Cain, Bruce E., Patrick Egan, and Sergio Fabbrini. 2003. "Toward More Open Democracies: The Expansion of Freedom of Information Laws." In Bruce E. Cain, Russell J. Dalton, and Susan E. Scarrow, eds., *Democracy Transformed? Expanding Political Opportunities in Advanced Industrial Democracies*. New York: Oxford University Press. 115–139.

Calvert, R. L., M. D. McCubbins, and B. R. Weingast. 1989. "A Theory of Political Control and Agency Discretion." *American Journal of Political Science* 33: 588–611.

Caplan, Lincoln. 2013. "Leaks and Consequences." *American Scholar* (Autumn): 20–31.

Carter, Ralph G., and James M. Scott. 2009. *Choosing to Lead: Understanding Congressional Foreign Policy Entrepreneurs*. Durham, NC: Duke University Press.

Central Intelligence Agency, Inspector General. 2007. *OIG Report on CIA Accountability with Respect to the 9/11 Attacks: Executive Summary* (June).

Champion, J. Christopher. 2005. "The Revamped FISA: Striking a Better Balance between the Government's Need to Protect Itself and the 4th Amendment." *Vanderbilt Law Review* 58: 1671–1703.

Chan, Janet. 1999. "Governing Police Practice: Limits of New Accountability." *British Journal of Sociology* 50/2: 249–268.

Charles, Douglas M. 2007. *J. Edgar Hoover and the Anti-Interventionists: FBI Political Surveillance and the Rise of the Domestic Security State, 1939 1945*. Columbus: Ohio State University Press.

Cheney, Dick. 1990. "Congressional Overreach in Foreign Policy." In Robert A. Goldwin and Robert A. Licht, eds., *Foreign Policy and the Constitution*. Washington, DC: American Enterprise Institute. 101–121.

Chesterman, Simon. 2011. *One Nation under Surveillance: A New Social Contract to Defend Freedom without Sacrificing Liberty*. New York: Oxford University Press.

Chu, V. S., A. Nolan, and R. M. Thompson. 2014. *Reform of the Foreign Intelligence Surveillance Court (FISC): Selection of Judges*. Congressional Research Service (March).

Church, Frank. 1969. "Of Presidents and Caesars: The Decline of Constitutional Government in the Conduct of American Foreign Policy." *Idaho Law Review* 6/1 (Fall): 1–15.

———. 1976. "Covert Action: Swampland of American Foreign Policy." *Bulletin of the Atomic Scientist* 32 (February): 7–11.

———. 1983. "Do We Still Plot Murders?" *Los Angeles Times* (June 14): A5.

CIA. 2007. "Oral History Archives: Reflections of DCI Colby and Helms on the CIA's 'Time of Troubles.'" *Studies in Intelligence* 51/3: 11–28.

Cinquegrana, Americo R. 1988–1989. "Dancing in the Dark: Accepting the Invitation to Struggle in the Context of 'Covert Action,' the Iran-Contra Affair and the Intelligence Oversight Process." *Houston Journal of International Law* 11: 77–209.

Clapper, James R., Jr. 2010. "The Role of Defense in Shaping U.S. Intelligence Reform." In Loch K. Johnson, ed., *The Oxford Handbook of National Security Intelligence*. New York: Oxford University Press. 629–639.

Clark, Kathleen. 2010. "The Architecture of Accountability: A Case Study of the Warrantless Surveillance Program." *Brigham Young University Law Review* 2: 357–420.

———. 2010. "'A New Era of Openness?' Disclosing Intelligence to Congress under Obama." *Constitutional Commentary* 26: 313–337.

———. 2011. "Congress's Right to Counsel in Intelligence Oversight." *University of Illinois Law Review* 3.

Clarke, Conor. 2014. "Is the Foreign Intelligence Surveillance Court Really a Rubber Stamp? *Ex Parte* Proceedings and the FISC Win Rate." *Stanford Law Review Online* 66: 125–133.

Clarke, Duncan L., and Edward L. Neveloff. 1984. "Secrecy, Foreign Intelligence, and Civil Liberties: Has the Pendulum Swung Too Far." *Political Science Quarterly* (Fall): 493–513.

Clarridge, Duane R., with Digby Diehl. 1997. *A Spy for All Seasons: My Life in the CIA*. New York: Scribner's.

Clift, A. Denis. 2007. "The Coin of Intelligence Accountability." In Loch K. Johnson, ed., *Strategic Intelligence: Intelligence and Accountability, Safeguards against the Abuse of Secret Power*, vol. 5. Westport, CT: Praeger Security International. 165–182.

Clinton, Joshua, David Lewis, and Jennifer Selin. 2014. "Influencing Bureaucracy: The Irony of Congressional Oversight." *American Journal of Political Science* 38: 387–340.

Cogan, Charles G. 1993. "Covert Action and Congressional Oversight: A Deontology." *Studies in Conflict and Terrorism* 16: 32–38.

Cohen, David S. 2016. Speech, "Governing Intelligence" Conference, Center on Law and Security, NYU School of Law, Washington, D.C.

Cohen, William S. 1988. "Congressional Oversight of Covert Actions." *International Journal of Intelligence and Counterintelligence* 2: 155–162.

———. 1989. "Congressional Oversight of Covert Actions: The Public's Stake in the Forty-Eight Hour Rule." *Harvard Journal of Law & Public Policy* 12/2: 285–301.

Cohen, William S., and George Mitchell. 1988. *Men of Zeal: A Candid Inside Story of the Iran-Contra Hearings*. New York: Viking.

Colaresi, Michael P. 2012. "A Boom with Review: How Retrospective Oversight Increases the Foreign Policy Ability of Democracies." *American Journal of Political Science* 56: 671–689.

———. 2014. *Democracy Declassified: The Secrecy Dilemma in National Security*. New York: Oxford University Press.

Colby, William E. 1976a. "After Investigating U.S. Intelligence." *New York Times* (February 26): A11.

———. 1976b. "Intelligence Secrecy and Security in a Free Society." *International Security* 1/2: 121–128.

———. 1978. "Gesprach mit William E. Colby." *Der Spiegel* (January 23) 56: 112–114.

Colby, William E., and Richard Helms. 2007. "Oral History: Reflections of DCI Colby and Helms on the CIA's 'Time of Troubles.'" *Studies in Intelligence* 51: 11–28.

Cole, David, and Martin S. Lederman. 2006. "The National Security Agency's Domestic Spying Program: Framing the Debate." *Indiana Law Journal* 81: 1355–1425.

Cole, David, and James X. Dempsey. 2006. *Terrorism and the Constitution: Sacrificing Civil Liberties in the Name of National Security.* New York: New Press, 2006.

Colton, David Everett. 1988. "Speaking Truth to Power: Intelligence Oversight in an Imperfect World." *University of Pennsylvania Law Review* 571: 571–613.

Commager, Henry Steele. 1976. "Intelligence: The Constitution Betrayed." *New York Review of Books* (September 30): 32–37.

Commission on Protecting and Reducing Government Secrecy (the Moynihan Commission). 1997. *Secrecy.* Washington, DC: U.S. Government Printing Office.

Commission on the Roles and Capabilities of the United States Intelligence Community (the Aspin-Brown Commission). 1996. *Preparing for the 21st Century: An Appraisal of United States Intelligence.* Washington, DC: U.S. Government Printing Office.

Connor, William E. 1991–1992. "Reforming Oversight of Covert Actions after the Iran-Contra Affair: A Legislative History of the Intelligence Authorization Act for FY 1991." *Virginia Journal of International Law* 32: 871–928.

———. 1993a. "Congressional Reform of Covert Action Oversight Following the Iran-Contra Affair." *Defense Intelligence Journal* 2: 37–42.

———. 1993b. *Intelligence Oversight: The Controversy behind the FY 1991 Intelligence Authorization Act.* Intelligence Profession Series, No. 11. McLean, VA: Association of Foreign Intelligence Officers.

Corson, William R. 1967. *The Armies of Ignorance: The Rise of the American Intelligence Empire.* New York: Dial.

Council on Foreign Relations. 1996. "Making Intelligence Smarter: The Future of U.S. Intelligence." Report of an Independent Task Force. New York.

Cox, Douglas, and Ramzi Kassem. 2014. "Off the Record: The National Security Council, Drone Killings, and Historical Accountability." *Yale Journal on Regulation* 31: 363–400.

Crabb, Cecil V., Jr., and Pat M. Holt. 1984. *Invitation to Struggle: Congress, the President and Foreign Policy*, 2nd ed. Washington, DC: CQ Press.

Crile, George. 2003. *Charlie Wilson's War.* New York: Grove.

Cummings, Alfred. 2010a. *"Gang of Four" Congressional Intelligence Notifications.* Congressional Research Service Report, Library of Congress, Washington, D.C. (January 29): 1–14.

———. 2010b. *Sensitive Covert Action Notifications: Oversight Options for Congress.* Congressional Research Service Report, Library of Congress, Washington, D.C. (January 29): 1–14.

Currie, J. 1998. "Iran-Contra and Congressional Oversight of the CIA." *International Journal of Intelligence and Counterintelligence* 11: 185–210.

Darling, Arthur B. 1990. *The Central Intelligence Agency: An Instrument of Government, to 1950.* University Park: Pennsylvania State University Press.

Dash, Samuel. 1976. *Chief Counsel: Inside the Ervin Committee—The Untold Story of Watergate.* New York: Random House.

Daugherty, William J. 2004. *Executive Secrets: Covert Action and the Presidency.* Lexington: University Press of Kentucky.

Davidson, Roger H. 1977. "The Political Dimensions of Congressional Investigations." *Capitol Studies* 5 (Fall): 41–63.

Davies, Philip H. J. 2012. *Intelligence and Government in Britain and the United States.* Vols. 1 and 2. Santa Barbara, CA: Praeger/ABC-Clio.

Deering, Christopher J. 2003. "Alarms and Patrols: Legislative Oversight in Foreign and Defense Policy." In C. C. Campbell, N. C. Rae, and J. F. Stack, Jr., eds., *Congress and the Politics of Foreign Policy*. Upper Saddle River, NJ: Prentice Hall. 112–138.

Defty, Andrew. 2008. "Educating Parliamentarians about Intelligence: The Role of the British Intelligence and Security Committee." *Parliamentary Affairs* 61: 621–641.

DeRosa, Mary. 2003. "Privacy in the Age of Terror." *Washington Quarterly* 26: 27–41.

Dershowitz, Alan, et al. 2006. "Warrantless Wiretaps." Opening Argument. *Yale University School of Law* 1 (February): 1–8.

Dickinson, Laura A. 2012. "Outsourcing Covert Activities." *Journal of National Security Law & Policy* 5: 521–537.

Dietrich, Jan-Hendrik. 2016. "Of Toothless Windbags, Blind Guardians and Blunt Swords: The Ongoing Controversy about the Reform of Intelligence Services Oversight in Germany." *Intelligence and National Security* 31/3 (April): 397–415.

Donaldson, Patrick J. 2010. "Infiltrating American Intelligence: Difficulties Inherent in the Congressional Oversight of Intelligence and the Joint Committee Model." *American Intelligence Journal* 28/1: 13–28.

Donner, Frank J. 1981. *The Age of Surveillance: The Aims and Methods of America's Political Intelligence Surveillance*. New York: Vintage.

Donohue, Laura K. 2006. "Criminal Law: Anglo-American Privacy and Surveillance." *Journal of Criminal Law and Criminology* 96: 234–258.

———. 2013. "NSA Surveillance May Be Legal—But It's Unconstitutional." *Washington Post* (June 21).

———. 2014. "FISA Reform." *I/S: A Journal of Law and Policy for the Information Society* 16: 599–639.

Dover, R., and Michael S. Goodman, eds. 2009. *Spinning Intelligence: Why Intelligence Needs the Media, Why the Media Needs Intelligence*. London: Hurst.

Dycus, Stephen, Arthur L. Berney, William C. Banks, and Peter Raven-Hansen. 2002. *National Security Law*, 3rd ed. New York: Aspen.

Easton, Eric B., and Martin E. Halstuk. 2006. "Of Secrets and Spies: Strengthening the Public's Right to Know about the CIA." *Stanford Law and Policy Review* 17: 353–389.

Edwards, George C., III, and B. Dan Wood. 1999. "Who Influences Whom? The President, Congress and the Media." *American Political Science Review* 93/2: 327–344.

Eiran, Ehud. 2016. "The Three Tensions of Investigating Intelligence Failures." *Intelligence and National Security* 31/4 (June): 598–618.

Elliff, John T. 1977. "Congress and the Intelligence Community." In Lawrence C. Dodd and Bruce I. Oppenheimer, eds., *Congress Reconsidered*. New York: Praeger. 193–206.

———. 1979. *The Reform of FBI Intelligence Operations*. Princeton, NJ: Princeton University Press.

Erwin, Marshall Curtis. 2013a. *House Intelligence Committee Calls on DOD to Inform Committee of Intelligence Activities*. Congressional Research Service Report.

———. 2013b. *Enduring Oversight Issues*. Congressional Research Service (April 23): 4–7.

———. 2013c. *Sensitive Covert Action Notifications: Oversight Options for Congress*. Congressional Research Service (April 10).

———. 2014. *"Gang of Four" Congressional Intelligence Notifications*. Congressional Research Service (March 14).

Farley, B. R. 2011. "Targeting Anwar Al-Aulaqi: A Case Study in U.S. Drone Strikes and Targeted Killing." *National Security Law Brief*, 2: 57–87.

Farson, Stuart A. 1996. "In Crisis in Flux? Politics, Parliament and Canada's Intelligence Policy." *Journal of Conflict Studies* 16: 1–21.

———. 2000. "Parliament and Its Servants: Their Role in Scrutinizing Canadian Intelligence." *Intelligence and National Security* 15/2 (March): 235–249.

Farson, Stuart A., and Mark Phythian, eds. 2011. *Commissions of Inquiry and National Security: Comparative Approaches*. Santa Barbara, CA: Praeger Security International.

Farson, Stuart A., and Reg Whitaker. 2010. "Accounting for the Future or the Past? Developing Accountability and Oversight Systems to Meet Future Intelligence Needs." In Loch K.

Johnson, ed., *The Oxford Handbook of National Security Intelligence*. New York: Oxford University Press. 673–698.

Fenno, Richard F., Jr. 1973. *Congressmen in Committees*. Boston: Little, Brown.

Fessenden, H. 2005. "The Limits of Intelligence Reform." *Foreign Affairs* 84: 106–120.

Fisher, Louis. 1972. *President and Congress: Power and Policy*. New York: Free Press.

———. 1989. "How Tightly Can Congress Draw the Purse Strings?" *American Journal of International Law* 83: 758–766.

———. 2003. "Congressional Investigations: Subpoenas and Contempt Power." *Congress Research Service*, Report RL 31836 (April 2).

———. 2007. "The State Secrets Privilege: Relying on Reynolds." *Political Science Quarterly* 122 (Fall): 385–408.

———. 2008. *9/11 and the Constitution*. Lawrence: University Press of Kansas.

———. 2010. "Rethinking the State Secrets Privilege." In Loch K. Johnson, ed., *The Oxford Handbook of National Security Intelligence*. New York: Oxford University Press. 657–672.

———. 2011. *Defending Congress and the Constitution*. Lawrence: University Press of Kansas.

———. 2016. "The State Secrets Privilege: From Bush II to Obama." *Presidential Studies Quarterly* 46/1 (March): 173–193.

Fisher, Roger. 1976. "The Flaw in Our Spy System." *Boston Globe* (February 1): A18.

Ford, Christopher. 2007. "Intelligence Demands in a Democratic State: Congressional Intelligence Oversight." *Tulane Law Review* 81: 721–776.

Forsythe, David P. 1992. "Democracy, War and Covert Action." *Journal of Peace Research* 29: 385–395.

Fowler, Linda L. 2015. *Watchdogs on the Hill: The Decline of Congressional Oversight of U.S. Foreign Relations*. Princeton, NJ: Princeton University Press.

Fowler, Wyche, Jr. 1984. "Legislative Control of Covert Operations." *First Principles* 9 (March/April): 1, 4–7.

Franck, Thomas M., and Edward Weisband. 1974. *Secrecy and Foreign Policy*. New York: Oxford University Press.

———. 1979. *Foreign Policy by Congress*. New York: Oxford University Press.

Franks, C. E. S. 1989. "Accountability for Security Intelligence Agencies." In P. Hanks and J. McCamus, eds., *National Security: Surveillance and Accountability in a Democratic Society*. Cowansville, Quebec: Yvon Blais.

Freeman, J. Leiper. 1977. "Investigating the Executive Intelligence: The Fate of the Pike Committee." *Capitol Studies* 5 (Fall): 103–117.

Fritz, Antje. 2004. "Watching the Watchdogs: The Role of the Media in Intelligence Oversight in Germany." Paper, Geneva Centre for the Democratic Control of Armed Forces 138 (April): 1–64.

Fuchs, Meredith, and G. Gregg Webb. 2006. "Judging Secrets: The Role of the Courts in Preventing Unnecessary Secrecy." *Administrative Law Review* 58/1: 210–222.

Fuller, Christopher J. 2017. See It, Shoot It: The Secret History of the CIA's Lethal Drone Program. New Haven, CT: Yale University Press.

Fyffe, Greg. 2011. "The Canadian Intelligence Community after 9/11." *Journal of Military & Strategic Studies* 13: 1–17.

Garrett, Hatch. 2012. *Privacy and Civil Liberties Oversight Board: New Independent Agency Status*. Congressional Research Service, RL34385 (August 27).

Garthoff, Douglas F. 2005. *Directors of Central Intelligence as Leaders of the U.S. Intelligence Community, 1946–2005*. Center for the Study of Intelligence. Washington, DC: Central Intelligence Agency, 2005.

Gates, Robert M. 1987–1988. "The CIA and American Foreign Policy." *Foreign Affairs* 66 (Winter): 215–230.

———. 1993. "Strengthening Congressional Oversight of Intelligence." *National Security Law Report*, American Bar Association (February).

———. 1996. *From the Shadows*. New York: Simon & Schuster.

Gelb, Leslie H. 1986. "Overseeing of C.I.A. by Congress." *New York Times* (July 7): A11.

Gellman, Barton. 2016. *Dark Mirror: Edward Snowden and the American Surveillance State*. New York: Penguin.

German, Michael, ed. 2015. *Strengthening Intelligence Oversight*. Brennan Center for Justice, School of Law, New York University.

Gertz, B. 2002. *Breakdown*. Washington, DC: Regnery.

Gibbon, Edward. 1952. *The Decline and Fall of the Roman Empire*. New York: Viking.

Gill, Peter. 1991. "The Evolution of the Security Intelligence Debate in Canada since 1976." In A. Stuart Farson, David Stafford, and Wesley Wark, eds., *Security and Intelligence in a Changing World*. London: Frank Cass. 75–94.

———. 1996. "Reasserting Control: Recent Changes in the Oversight of the UK Intelligence Community." *Intelligence and National Security* 11: 313–331.

———. 2007. "Evaluating Intelligence Oversight Committees: The UK Intelligence and Security Committee and the War on Terror." *Intelligence and National Security* 22: 14–37.

———. 2012. "Intelligence, Threat, Risk and the Challenge of Oversight." *Intelligence and National Security* 27: 206–222.

———. 2016. *Intelligence Governance and Democratisation: A Comparative Analysis of the Limits of Reform*. Routledge: London.

Gill, Peter, and Mark Phythian. 2012. *Intelligence in an Insecure World*, 2nd ed. Cambridge, UK: Polity Press.

Glees, Anthony, and Philip H. J. Davies. 2004. *Spinning the Spies: Intelligence, Open Government, and the Hutton Enquiry*. London: Social Affairs Unit.

———. 2006. "Intelligence, Iraq, and the Limits of Legislative Oversight during Political Crisis." *Intelligence and National Security* 21/5: 848–883.

Glees, Anthony, Philip H. J. Davies, and J. N. L. Morrison. 2006. *The Open Side of Secrecy: Britain's Intelligence and Security Committee*. London: Social Affairs Unit.

Glennon, Michael J. 1981. "Investigating Intelligence Activities: The Process of Getting Information for Congress." In Thomas E. Franck, ed., *The Tethered Presidency*. New York: New York University Press.

———. 1987. "The Boland Amendment and the Power of the Purse." *Christian Science Monitor* (June 15) 79: A12.

———. 2015. *National Security and Double Government*. New York: Oxford University Press.

Goitein, Elizabeth, and Faiza Patel. 2015. "What Went Wrong with the FISA Court." Paper, Brennan Center for Justice, New York University School of Law.

Goldman, Jan, ed. 2006. *Ethics of Spying*. Lanham, MD: Scarecrow Press.

Goldsmith, Jack. 2007. *The Terror Presidency: Law and Judgment inside the Bush Administration*. New York: Norton.

———. 2012. *Power and Constraint*. New York: Norton.

Goldwater, Barry. 1983. "Congress and Intelligence Oversight." *Washington Quarterly* 6 (Summer): 16–21.

Goodale, James C. 2013. *Fighting for the Press: The Inside Story of the Pentagon Papers and Other Battles*. New York: CUNY Journalism Press.

Goodman, Melvin. 2008. *Failure of Intelligence: The Rise and Fall of the C.I.A.* New York: Rowman and Littlefield.

Graham, Senator Bob. 2002. "Remarks." *Lehrer News Hour*, PBS Television (October 17).

Graham, Senator Bob, with Jeff Nussbaum. 2004. *Intelligence Matters: The CIA, the FBI, Saudi Arabia, and the Failure of America's War on Terrorism*. New York: Random House.

Graham-Goss Committees (led by Senator Bob Graham, D, Florida, and Representative Porter J. Goss, R, Florida). 2002. "Joint Inquiry into Intelligence Community Activities before and after the Terrorist Attacks of September 11, 2001." Final Report, U.S. Senate Select Committee on Intelligence and U.S. House Permanent Select Committee on Intelligence. Washington, D.C.

Greenberg, Harold. 2005. "The Doolittle Commission of 1954." *Intelligence and National Security* 20: 687–694.

Greenberg, Karen J. 2016. *Rogue Justice: The Making of the Security State*. New York: Crown.

Greenberg, Karen J., and J. L. Dratel. 2005. *The Torture Papers: The Road to Abu Ghraib*. Cambridge, UK: Cambridge University Press.

Greenwald, Glenn. 2014. *No Place to Hide: Edward Snowden, the NSA, and the U.S. Surveillance State*. New York: Henry Holt.

Grier, Peter. 2014. "NSA Chief: Snooping Helped Thwart 50 Terrorist Attack in 20 Countries." *Christian Science Monitor* (June 18) 106: A1.

Grossman, Serge, and Michael Simon. 2008. "And Congress Shall Know the Truth: The Pressing Need for Restructuring Congressional Oversight of Intelligence." *Harvard Law & Policy Review* 2 (July): 435–447.

Gumina, Paul. 1992. "Title VI of the Intelligence Authorization Act: Fiscal Year 1991: Effective Covert Action Reform or 'Business as Usual'?" *Hastings Constitutional Law Quarterly* (Fall) 31: 149–205.

Gup, Ted. 2004. "Covering the CIA in Times of Crisis: Obstacles and Strategies." *Harvard International Journal of Press/Politics* 9: 28–39.

———. 2007. *Nation of Secrets: The Threat to Democracy and the American Way of Life*. New York: Doubleday.

Haass, Richard N. 1996. "Don't Hobble Intelligence Gathering." *Washington Post* (February 15): A27.

Haines, Gerald K. 1998–1999. "The Pike Committee Investigation and the CIA: Looking for a Rogue Elephant." *Studies in Intelligence* (Winter).

Halchin, Elaine L., and Frederick M. Kaiser. 2012. *House and Senate Select Committees on Intelligence*. Congressional Research Service.

———. 2014. *Congressional Oversight of Intelligence*. Congressional Research Service.

Hall, Richard, and Alan Deardorff. 2006. "Lobbying as Legislative Subsidy." *American Political Science Review* 100: 69–84.

Halperin, Morton H., Jerry J. Berman, Robert L. Borosage, and Christine M. Marvick. 1976. *The Lawless State: The Crimes of the U.S. Intelligence Agencies*. New York: Penguin.

Hamilton, Alexander, John Jay, and James Madison. 1788. *The Federalist*. New York: Modern Library.

Hamilton, Lee H. 1987. "View from the Hill." Extracts from Studies in Intelligence. Langley, VA: Central Intelligence Agency (September): 65–76.

———. 1999. "Oversight vs. Glitzy Investigation." *Christian Science Monitor* (July 15) 91: A11.

Hamilton, Lee H., and Jordan Tama. 2002. *A Creative Tension: The Foreign Policy Roles of the President and the Congress*. Washington, DC: Woodrow Wilson Center Press.

Hardy, Timothy S. 1994. *Intelligence Reform in the Mid-1970s*. Central Intelligence Agency.

Harknett, Richard J., and James A. Stever. 2011. "The Struggle to Reform Intelligence after 9/11." *Public Administration Review* 51 (September–October): 700–706.

Harlow, Bill, ed. 2015. *Rebuttal: The CIA Responds to the Senate Intelligence Committee's Study of Its Detention and Interrogation Program*. Annapolis, MD: Naval Institute Press.

Hart, Gary. 2006. *The Shield and the Cloak: The Security of the Commons*. New York: Oxford University Press.

Hastedt, Glenn P. 1986a. "The Constitutional Control of Intelligence." *Intelligence and National Security* 1 (May 1986): 255–271.

———. 1986b. "Controlling Intelligence: The Role of the DCI." *International Journal of Intelligence and Counterintelligence* 1 (1986): 25–40.

———. 1991a. *Controlling Intelligence*. London: Frank Cass.

———. 1991b. "Controlling Intelligence: Defining the Problem." In Glenn P. Hastedt, ed., *Controlling Intelligence*. London: Frank Cass. 6–8.

———. 2007. "Foreign Policy by Commission: Reforming the Intelligence Community." *Intelligence and National Security* 22 (November): 443–472.

———. 2010. "The Politics of Intelligence Accountability." In Loch K. Johnson, ed., *The Oxford Handbook of National Security Intelligence*. New York: Oxford University Press. 719–734.

———. 2015a. "How Intelligence Organizations View Congressional Oversight." Paper, annual meeting, American Political Science Association (September 5), San Francisco.

———. 2015b. "Washington Politics, Homeland Security, and the Struggle against Global Terrorism." In Loch K. Johnson, ed., *Essentials of Strategic Intelligence*. Santa Barbara, CA: Praeger Security International. 387–416.

———. 2016. "Exploring New Perspectives on the Congressional Oversight of Intelligence." Paper, annual meeting, American Political Science Association (September 2), Philadelphia.

Hatch, Garrett. 2012. *Privacy and Civil Liberties Oversight Boards: New Independent Agency Status*. Congressional Research Service.

Hayden, Michael V. 2016. *Playing to the Edge: American Intelligence in an Age of Terror*. New York: Penguin.

Hayez, Phillippe. 2011. "National Oversight." In Aidan Willis, Ian Leigh, and Hans Born, eds., *International Intelligence Cooperation and Accountability*. New York: Routledge. 142–160.

Hedley, John Hollister. 1994. "The CIA's New Openness." *International Journal of Intelligence and Counterintelligence* 7 (Summer): 129–142.

———. 1998. "Secrets, Free Speech, and Fig Leaves." *Studies in Intelligence* 41/5.

Helms, Richard, with William Hood. 2003. *A Look over My Shoulder*. New York: Random House.

Henkin, Louis. 1971. "The Right to Know and the Duty of Withhold." *University of Pennsylvania Law Review* 120/2.

Herman, Michael. 1996. *Intelligence Power in Peace and War*. Cambridge, UK: University of Cambridge Press.

———. 2004. "Ethics and Intelligence after September 2001." *Intelligence and National Security* 19 (Summer): 180–194.

Hersh, Seymour M. 1974a. "Congress Is Accused of Laxity on C.I.A.'s Covert Activity." *New York Times* (December 31): A1.

———. 1974b. "Huge C.I.A. Operation Reported in U.S. against Antiwar Force, Other Dissidents in Nixon Years." *New York Times* (December 22): A1.

———. 1978. "The Angleton Story." *New York Times Magazine* (June 25): 13ff.

Hess, Sigurd. 2009. "German Intelligence Organizations and the Media." *Journal of Intelligence History* 9/1: 75–87.

Hijzen, Constant. 2013. "More Than a Ritual Dance: The Dutch Practice of Parliamentary Oversight and Control of the Intelligence Community." *Security and Human Rights* 24: 227–238.

Hillebrand, Claudia. 2011. "Guarding EU-wide Counter-terrorism Policing: The Struggle for Sound Parliamentary Scrutiny of Europol." *Journal of Contemporary European Research* 7: 500–519.

———. 2012. "The Role of News Media in Intelligence Oversight." *Intelligence and National Security* 27/5: 689–706.

———. 2014. "Intelligence Oversight and Accountability." In Robert Dover, Michael S. Goodman, and Claudia Hillebrand, eds., *Routledge Companion to Intelligence Studies*. New York: Routledge. 305–312.

Hilliard, Nadia. 2017. *The Accountability State: US Federal Inspectors General and the Pursuit of Democratic Integrity*. Lawrence: University Press of Kansas.

Hinckley, Barbara. 1994. *Less Than Meets the Eye: Foreign Policy Making and the Myth of the Assertive Congress*. Chicago: University of Chicago Press.

Hinrichs, Christine E. 2009. "Flying under the Radar or an Unnecessary Intelligence Watchdog: A Review of the President's Foreign Intelligence Advisory Board." *William Mitchell Law Review* 35 (January 3): 5109–5117.

Hirschman, Albert O. 1970. *Exit, Voice, and Loyalty: Response to Decline in Firms, Organizations, and States*. Cambridge, MA: Harvard University Press.

Hitz, Frederick P. 2002. "Unleashing the Rogue Elephant: September 11 and Letting the CIA Be the CIA." *Harvard Journal of Law and Public Policy* 25: 390–396.

Hoekstra, Pete. 2005. *Secrets and Leaks: The Costs and Consequences for National Security*. Washington, DC: Heritage Foundation (September 6).

Holt, Pat M. 1995. *Secret Intelligence and Public Policy*. Washington, DC: CQ Press.
———. 2000. "Who's Watching the Store? Executive-Branch and Congressional Surveillance."
     In C. Eisendrath, ed., *National Insecurity: US Intelligence after the Cold War*. Philadelphia:
     Temple University Press.
Huber, John D., and Charles R. Shipan. 2000. "The Costs of Control: Legislators, Agencies, and
     Transaction Costs." *Legislative Studies Quarterly* 25/1: 25–52.
Hughes, Thomas L. 1976. *The Fate of Facts in a World of Men: Foreign Policy and Intelligence-Making*.
     Headline Series No. 233. Washington, DC: Foreign Policy Association.
Hulnick, Arthur S. 1999. *Fixing the Spy Machine: Preparing American Intelligence for the Twenty-
     First Century*. Westport, CT: Praeger.
———. 1999–2000. "Openness: Being Public about Secret Intelligence." *International Journal of
     Intelligence and Counterintelligence* 12 (Winter): 463–483.
Ignatius, David. 2014. "The Torture Report's One Glaring Weakness." *Washington Post* blog
     (December 11).
Immerman, Richard H. 2014. *The Hidden Hand: A Brief History of the CIA*. New York: John Wiley.
Isikoff, Michael. 2005. "Sen. Bond Pulls GOP Staff Off Torture Investigation." *Newsweek*
     (September 25).
Jackson, William H., Jr. 1990. "Congressional Oversight of Intelligence: Search for a Framework."
     Intelligence and National Security 8 (July): 113–147.
Jeffreys-Jones, Rhodri. 1989. *The CIA and American Democracy*. New Haven, CT: Yale University
     Press.
———. 2013. *In Spies We Trust: The Story of Western Intelligence*. New York: Oxford University Press.
Jeffreys-Jones, Rhodri, and Christopher Andrew, eds. 1997. *Eternal Vigilance? 50 Years of the CIA*.
     London: Frank Cass.
Jervis, Robert. 2006. "Reports, Politics, and Intelligence Failures: The Case of Iraq." *Journal of
     Strategic Studies* 29: 3–52.
———. 2007. "Intelligence, Civil-Intelligence Relations, and Democracy." In Thomas C. Bruneau
     and Steven C. Boraz, eds., *Reforming Intelligence: Obstacles to Democratic Control and
     Effectiveness*. Austin: University of Texas Press. vii–xx.
———. 2009. "Intelligence, Counterintelligence, Perception, and Deception." In Jennifer E. Sims
     and Burton Gerber, eds., *Vaults, Mirrors, and Masks: Rediscovering U.S. Counterintelligence*.
     Washington, DC: Georgetown University Press. 69–80.
———. 2010. *Why Intelligence Fails: Lessons from the Iranian Revolution and the Iraq War*. Ithaca,
     NY: Cornell University Press.
———. 2015. "The Torture Blame Game: The Blotched Senate Report on the CIA's Misdeeds."
     Foreign Affairs (May/June).
Johnson, Chalmers. 2004. *The Sorrows of Empire: Militarism, Secrecy, and the End of the Republic*.
     New York: Henry Holt.
Johnson, Douglas A., Alberto Mora, and Averell Schmidt. 2016. "The Strategic Costs of Torture:
     How 'Enhanced Interrogation' Hurt America." *Foreign Affairs* 95/5 (September/October):
     121–132.
Johnson, Loch K. 1976. "National Security, Civil Liberties, and the Collection of Intelligence:
     A Report on the Huston Plan." In *Supplementary Detailed Staff Reports on Intelligence and
     the Rights of Americans*, Final Report, Select Committee to Study Governmental Operations
     with Respect to Intelligence Activities, Book III, U.S. Senate (April 23): 921–986.
———. 1979. "Legislative Oversight and the Central Intelligence Agency." *Workshop on
     Congressional Oversight and Investigations*, U.S. House of Representatives, House Document
     No. 96-217 (October 22): 15–17.
———. 1980a. "The CIA: Controlling the Quiet Option." *Foreign Policy* 39 (Summer): 143–152.
———. 1980b. "Congress and the CIA: Monitoring the Dark Side of Government." *Legislative
     Studies Quarterly* 5 (November): 477–499.
———. 1984. "Legislative Control of Paramilitary Operations." *First Principles* (March/April):
     1–4.

————. 1985a. "Legislative Reform of Intelligence Policy." *Polity* 17 (Spring): 549–573.

————. 1985b. *A Season of Inquiry: The Senate Intelligence Investigation.* Lexington: University Press of Kentucky. Reprinted in 2015 (Lawrence: University Press of Kansas).

————. 1989a. *America's Secret Power: The CIA in a Democratic Society.* New York: Oxford University Press.

————. 1989b. "Controlling the CIA: A Critique of Current Safeguards." *Harvard Journal of Law and Public Policy* 12 (Spring): 371–396.

————. 1989c. "Covert Action and Accountability: Decision-Making for America's Secret Foreign Policy." *International Studies Quarterly* (March) 13: 81–110.

————. 1989d. "Foreign Policy and the Rule of Law." In *Official Accountability Act*, Subcommittee on Criminal Justice, Committee on the Judiciary, U.S. House of Representatives, House Document No. 98-455: 22–35.

————. 1992. "On Drawing a Bright Line for Covert Operations." *American Journal of International Law* 86 (April): 284–309.

————. 1992–1993. "Smart Intelligence." *Foreign Policy* 89: 67–69.

————. 1994. "Playing Ball with the CIA: Congress Supervises Strategic Intelligence." In Paul E. Paterson, ed., *Congress, the Executive, and the Making of American Foreign Policy.* Norman: University of Oklahoma Press. 49–73.

————. 1996. *Secret Agencies: U.S. Intelligence in a Hostile World.* New Haven, CT: Yale University Press.

————. 1997a. "Balancing Security and Liberty." *Freedom Review* 28 (Summer): 37–44.

————. 1997b. "The CIA and the Question of Accountability." *Intelligence and National Security* 12/1.

————. 1998. "Intelligence and the Challenge of Collaborative Government." *Intelligence and National Security* 13/2.

————. 2000. *Bombs, Bugs, Drugs, and Thugs: Intelligence and America's Quest for Security.* New York: New York University Press.

————. 2002. "Congress's Experiment Overseeing Spies." *New York Times* (June 9): WK15.

————. 2003. "Governing in the Absence of Angels: On the Practice of Intelligence Accountability in the U.S. Congress." *Congress Project*, Woodrow Wilson Center, Washington, D.C., May.

————. 2004a. "Congressional Supervision of America's Secret Agencies: The Experience and Legacy of the Church Committee." *Public Administration Review* 64: 3–14.

————. 2004b. "Presidents, Lawmakers, and Spies: Intelligence Accountability in the United States." *Presidential Studies Quarterly* 34 (December): 828–837.

————. 2005. "Accountability and America's Secret Foreign Policy: Keeping a Legislative Eye on the CIA." *Foreign Policy Analysis* 1 (Spring): 99–120.

————. 2006a. "The Failures of U.S. Intelligence and What Can Be Done about Them." *Yale Journal of International Affairs* 2 (February): 116–131.

————. 2006b. "Supervising the Secret Foreign Policy: A Shock Theory of Congressional Oversight for Intelligence." In David P. Forsythe, Patrice C. McMahon, and Andrew Wedeman, eds., *American Foreign Policy in a Globalized World.* New York: Routledge. 259–277.

————. 2007a. "A Conversation with Former DCI William E. Colby, Spymaster during the 'Year of the Intelligence Wars.'" In Loch K. Johnson, ed., *Strategic Intelligence: Intelligence and Accountability, Safeguards against the Abuse of Secret Power,* vol. 5. Westport, CT: Praeger Security International. 47–66.

————. 2007b. "A Shock Theory of Congressional Accountability for Intelligence." In Loch K. Johnson, ed., *Handbook of Intelligence Studies.* New York: Routledge. 343–360.

————, ed. 2007c. *Strategic Intelligence, Vol. 5: Intelligence and Accountability.* Westport, CT: Praeger Security International.

————. 2008a. "The Church Committee Investigation of 1975 and the Evolution of Modern Intelligence Accountability." *Intelligence and National Security* (June) 23/2: 333–370.

————. 2008b. "Congress, the Iraq War, and the Failures of Intelligence Oversight." In James P. Pfiffner and Mark Pythian, eds., *Intelligence and National Security Policymaking on Iraq: British and American Perspectives*. College Station: Texas A&M University Press.

————. 2008c. "Ostriches, Cheerleaders, Skeptics, and Guardians: Role Selection by Congressional Intelligence Overseers." *SAIS Review* 28: 93–108.

————. 2009. "It's Never a Quick Fix at the CIA." *Washington Post* (August 30): B1.

————, ed. 2010. "Intelligence Accountability." In *The Oxford Handbook of National Security Intelligence* (Part IX). New York: Oxford University Press. 629–756.

————, ed. 2011a. *Intelligence: Critical Concepts in Military, Strategic and Security Studies, Vol. IV: Holding National Security Intelligence Accountable*. New York: Routledge.

————. 2011b. *The Threat on the Horizon: An Inside Account of America's Search for Security after the Cold War*. New York: Oxford University Press.

————. 2013a. "James Angleton and the Church Committee." *Journal of Cold War Studies* 15 (Fall): 128–147.

————. 2013b. "The Myths of America's Shadow Wars." *Atlantic Monthly Online* (January 31).

————. 2014a. "Intelligence Shocks, Media Coverage, and Congressional Accountability, 1947–2012." *Journal of Intelligence History* (January) 13: 1–21.

————, ed. 2014b. "*INS* Special Forum: Implications of the Snowden Leaks." *Intelligence and National Security* 29/6 (December): 1–18.

————. 2014c. "The Myths of Covert Action." *Virginia Policy Review* 7 (Winter): 52–64.

————. 2015. "Security, Privacy, and the German-American Relationship." *Bulletin of the German Historical Institute* 6 (Fall): 47–74.

————. 2016. "Congress and the American Experiment in Holding Intelligence Agencies Accountable." *Journal of Policy History* 28/8: 494–514.

————. 2017. *National Security Intelligence: Secret Operations in Defense of the Democracies*, 2nd ed. Cambridge, UK: Polity.

————. 2017. "Kiss of Death? The Politicization of U.S. Intelligence Under Trump." *World Politics Review* (March): 1–8.

Johnson, Loch K., and John T. Elliff. 1976. "Counterintelligence." In *Foreign and Military Intelligence*, Final Report, Select Committee to Study Governmental Operations with Respect to Intelligence Activities, Book I, U.S. Senate (April 26): 63–78.

Johnson, Loch K., John C. Kuzenski, and Dana Gellner. 1992. "The Study of Congressional Investigations: Research Strategies." *Congress & the Presidency* 19 (Autumn): 138–156.

Johnson, Loch K., and James J. Wirtz, eds. 2018. "Accountability and Civil Liberties." In *Intelligence: The Secret World of Spies*, 5th ed., Part VII. New York: Oxford University Press. 349–424.

Johnson, Robert David. 2006. *Congress and the Cold War*. Cambridge, UK: Cambridge University Press.

Johnson, Roberta A. 2003. *Whistleblowing: When It Works—and Why*. Boulder, CO: Lynne Rienner.

Jos, Philip, Mark E. Tompkins, and Steven W. Hays. 1989. "In Praise of Difficult People: A Portrait of the Committed Whistleblower." *Public Administration Review* 49/6.

Kaiser, Frederick M. 1988. "Congressional Rules and Conflict Resolution: Access to Information in the House Select Committee on Intelligence." *Congress and the Presidency* 15 (Spring): 49–73.

————. 1989. "The Watchers' Watchdog: The CIA Inspector General." *International Journal of Intelligence and Counterintelligence* 3 (1989): 5–75.

————. 1992. "Congress and the Intelligence Community: Taking the Road Less Traveled." In Roger H. Davidson, ed., *The Post-reform Congress*. New York: St. Martin's Press. 279–300.

————. 1994. "Impact and Implications of the Iran-Contra Affair on Congressional Oversight of Covert Action." *International Journal of Intelligence and Counterintelligence* 7: 205–234.

————. 2008. *Congressional Oversight of Intelligence: Current Structure and Alternatives*. Congressional Research Service Report, Library of Congress, Washington, D.C. (September 16).

————. 2012. *Congressional Oversight of Intelligence: Current Structure and Alternatives*. Congressional Research Service Report, Library of Congress, Washington, D.C. (April 1).

Kaplan, Fred. 2016. *Dark Territory: The Secret History of Cyber War*. New York: Simon & Schuster.

Karalekas, Anne. 1983. "Intelligence Oversight: Has Anything Changed?" *Washington Quarterly* 6: 22–30.

Kaunert, Christian, Sarah Léonard, and Alex MacKenzie. 2015. "The European Parliament in the External Dimension of EU Counter-terrorism: More Actorness, Accountability and Oversight 10 Years On?" *Intelligence and National Security* 30: 357–376.

Kean Commission (led by Thomas H. Kean, former governor of New Jersey). 2004. *The 9/11 Commission Report: The National Commission on Terrorist Attacks upon the United States*. New York: Norton.

Kean, Thomas H., and Lee H. Hamilton. 2006. *Without Precedent: The Inside Story of the 9/11 Commission*. New York: Knopf.

Keller, William W. 1989. *The Liberals and J. Edgar Hoover*. Princeton, NJ: Princeton University Press.

Kenny, Colin. 2015. "What Real Intelligence Oversight Would Look Like." *National Post* (Canada), March 2.

Kibbe, Jennifer. 2010a. "Congressional Oversight of Intelligence: Is the Solution Part of the Problem?" *Intelligence and National Security* (February) 25: 24–49.

———. 2010b. "Covert Action, Pentagon Style." In Loch K. Johnson, ed., *The Oxford Handbook of National Security Intelligence*. New York: Oxford University Press. 569–586.

Kissinger, Henry. 1987. "A Matter of Balance." *Los Angeles Times* (July 26): B1.

Kitrosser, Heidi. 2015. *Reclaiming Accountability: Transparency, Executive Power, and the U.S. Constitution*. Chicago: University of Chicago Press.

Kitts, Kenneth. 1996. "Commission Politics and National Security: Gerald Ford's Response to the CIA Controversy of 1975." *Presidential Studies Quarterly* 26: 1081–1098.

Knott, Stephen F. 1996. *Secret and Sanctioned: Covert Operations and the American Presidency*. New York: Oxford University Press.

———. 1998. "Executive Power and the Control of American Intelligence." *Intelligence and National Security* 13/2.

———. 2002. "The Great Republican Transformation on Oversight." *International Journal of Intelligence and Counterintelligence* 13: 49–63.

Koh, Harold Hongju. 1988. "Why the President (Almost) Always Wins in Foreign Affairs: Lessons of the Iran-Contra Affair." *Yale Law Journal* 97 (June): 1255–1342.

———. 1990. *The National Security Constitution: Sharing Power after the Iran-Contra Affair*. New Haven, CT: Yale University Press.

Kornbluh, Peter. 1987–1988. "The Iran-Contra Scandal: A Postmortem." *World Policy Journal* (Winter) 37: 129–150.

Kornbluh, Peter, and Malcolm Byrne, eds. 1993. *The Iran-Contra Scandal: The Declassified History*. New York: New Press.

Kramer, Jay. 2011. "The Director of National Intelligence and Congressional Oversight of the Intelligence Community: Much Needed Statutory Clarification and Necessary Institutional Reforms." *Kansas Journal of Law & Public Policy* 20 (September): 452–476.

Krieger, Wolfgang. 2009. "Oversight of Intelligence: A Comparative Approach." In Gregory F. Treverton and Wilhelm Agrell, eds., *National Intelligence Systems: Current Research and Future Prospects*. Cambridge: Cambridge University Press. 210–234.

Kriner, Douglas L. 2009. "Can Enhanced Oversight Repair 'the Broken Branch'?" *Boston University Law Review* 89/2: 765–793.

Kris, David S. 2014. "On the Bulk Collection of Tangible Things." *Journal of National Security Law & Policy* 22: 284–312.

Kwoka, M. 2013. "Deferring to Secrecy." *Boston College Law Review* 54: 185–242.

Lamanna, Lawrence J. 2007. "Documentary Evidence for Differences between American and British Approaches to Intelligence." In Loch K. Johnson, ed., *Strategic Intelligence: Intelligence and Accountability, Safeguards against the Abuse of Secret Power*, vol. 5. Westport, CT: Praeger Security International. 89–114.

Lander, S. 2001. "The Oversight of Security and Intelligence." *RUSI Journal* 146: 30–34.

Latimer, Thomas K. 1979. "U.S. Intelligence and the Congress." *Strategic Review* (Summer): 47–56.

———. 1981. "United States Intelligence Activities: The Role of Congress." In Robert L. Pfaltzgraff, Jr., Uri Ra'anan, and Warren Milberg, eds., *Intelligence Policy and National Security.* Hamden, CT: Archon Books.

Lee, Laurie Thomas. 2003. "The USA PATRIOT Act and Telecommunications: Privacy under Attack." *Rutgers Computer & Technology Law Journal* 29: 371–403.

Lee, Timothy B. 2013. "Obama Says the NSA Has Had Plenty of Oversight. Here's Why He's Wrong." *Washington Post* (June 7): A12.

Lefebvre, Stéphane. 2010. "Canada's Legal Framework for Intelligence." *International Journal of Intelligence and Counterintelligence,* 23/2: 247–295.

———. 2012. "Croatia and the Development of a Democratic Intelligence System (1990–2010)." *Democracy and Security* 8 (April): 115–163.

Leigh, Ian. 2005. "More Closely Watching the Spies: Three Decades of Experience." In Hans Born, Loch K. Johnson, and Ian Leigh, eds., *Who's Watching the Spies? Establishing Intelligence Service Accountability.* Washington, DC: Potomac Books. 3–11.

———. 2009. "The Accountability of Security and Intelligence Agencies." In Loch K. Johnson, ed., *Handbook of Intelligence Studies.* New York: Routledge. 67–81.

———. 2010. "Intelligence and the Law in the United Kingdom." In Loch K. Johnson, ed., *The Oxford Handbook of National Security Intelligence.* New York: Oxford University Press. 640–656.

Lelyveld, Joseph. 2005. "Interrogating Ourselves." *New York Times Sunday Magazine* (June 12): 36ff.

Lester, Genevieve. 2015. *When Should State Secrets Stay Secret? Accountability, Democratic Governance, and Intelligence.* New York: Cambridge University Press.

Lichtblau, Eric. 2008. *Bush's Law: The Remaking of American Justice.* New York: Pantheon.

Light, Paul C. 2014. *Government by Investigation: Congress, Presidents, and the Search for Answers, 1945–2012.* Washington, DC: Brookings Institution.

Lindsay, James M. 2012. "The Senate and Foreign Policy." In Burdett A. Loomis, ed., *The U.S. Senate: From Deliberation to Dysfunction.* Washington, DC: Sage/CQ Press.

Liu, Edward C., Andrew Nolan, and Richard M. Thompson II. 2014. *Overview of Constitutional Challenges to NSA Collection Activities and Recent Developments.* Congressional Research Service.

Lizza, Ryan. 2013. "State of Deception." *New Yorker* (December 16).

Lofgren, Mike. 2014. "Essay: Anatomy of the Deep State." *Moyers & Company,* BillMoyers.com (February 21).

———. 2016. *The Deep State: The Fall of the Constitution and the Rise of a Shadow Government.* New York: Viking.

Lotz, George B, II. 2007. "The United States Department of Defense Intelligence Oversight Programme: Balancing National Security and Constitutional Rights." In Hans Born and Marina Caparini, ed., *Democratic Control of Intelligence Services: Containing Rogue Elephants.* Aldershot, UK: Ashgate.

Lowenthal, Mark M. 2015. *Intelligence: From Secrets to Policy,* 6th ed. Washington, DC: Sage/CQ Press.

Lundberg, Kirsten. 2001. *Congressional Oversight and Presidential Prerogative.* Harvard Case Study, C14-01-1605.0.

Lupia, Arthur, and Matthew D. McCubbins. 1998. *The Democratic Dilemma: Can Citizens Learn What They Need to Know?* Cambridge, UK: Cambridge University Press.

Lustgarten, Lawrence, and Ian Leigh. 1994. *In from the Cold: National Security and Parliamentary Democracy.* Oxford: Clarendon Press.

Lyon, David. 2015. *Surveillance after Snowden.* Cambridge, UK: Polity.

Manget, Fred F. 1996. "Another System of Oversight: Intelligence and the Rise of Judicial Intervention." *Studies in Intelligence* 39: 43–50.

―――. 2007. "Intelligence and the Rise of Judicial Intervention." In Loch K. Johnson, ed., *Handbook of Intelligence Studies*. New York: Routledge. 329–342.

Manjikian, Mary. 2016. "Two Types of Intelligence Community Accountability: Turf Wars and Identity Narratives." *Intelligence and National Security* 31/5: 686–698.

Mann, Thomas E., and Norman J. Ornstein. 2006. *The Broken Branch: How Congress Is Failing America and How to Get It Back on Track*. New York: Oxford University Press.

―――. 2012. *It's Even Worse Than It Looks: How the American Constitutional System Collided with the New Politics of Extremism*. New York: Basic Books.

Marchetti, Victor, and John D. Marks. 1974. *The CIA and the Cult of Intelligence*. New York: Dell.

Marrin, Stephen. 2014. "Systems of Intelligence: The United States." In Robert Dover, Michael S. Goodman, and Claudia Hillebrand, eds., *Routledge Companion to Intelligence Studies*. New York: Routledge. 305–312.

Martin, David C. 1980. *Wilderness of Mirrors*. New York: Harper & Row.

Martin, Kate. 2004. "Domestic Intelligence and Civil Liberties." *SAIS Review* 24: 7–21.

Marty, Dick. 2007. *Alleged Secret Detentions and Unlawful Inter-state Transfers of Detainees Involving Council of Europe Member States*. Parliamentary Assembly, Council of Europe.

Matei, Florina Cristiana. 2014. "The Media's Role in Intelligence Democratization." *International Journal of Intelligence and Counterintelligence* 27/1: 73–108.

Matei, Florina Cristiana, and Thomas Bruneau. 2011. "Policymakers and Intelligence Reform in the New Democracies." *International Journal of Intelligence and Counterintelligence* 24 (2011): 656–691.

Maury, John M., Jr. 1974. "CIA and the Congress." *Studies in Intelligence*, Central Intelligence Agency.

Mayer, Jane. 2008. *The Dark Side*. New York: Doubleday.

Mayhew, David. 1974. *Congress: The Electoral Connection*. New Haven, CT: Yale University Press.

Mazzetti, Mark, and Scott Shane. 2007. "Watchdog of C.I.A. Is Subject of C.I.A. Inquiry." *New York Times* (October 11): A1.

McCarthy, G. C. 2002. "Oversight of Intelligence in the Clinton Era." *International Journal of Intelligence and Counterintelligence* 15: 26–51.

McCubbins, Matthew D., and Thomas Schwartz. 1984. "Congressional Oversight Overlooked: Police Patrols and Fire Alarms." *American Journal of Political Science* 26: 165–179.

McDonough, Denis, Mara Rudman, and Peter Rundlet. 2006. "No Mere Oversight: Congressional Oversight of Intelligence Is Broken." Report, Center for American Progress (June).

McNeal, Greg S. 2014. "Targeted Killing and Accountability." *Georgetown Law Journal* 102 (2014): 681–794.

Miles, Anne Daugherty. 2013. "'Taking a Footnote': Budgetary Oversight of the Intelligence Community and the Role of OMB." Paper, annual meeting, International Studies Association, Toronto (April).

―――. 2014. "Congressional Oversight of the U.S. Intelligence Community (IC): Who Does What?" Paper, annual meeting, International Studies Association, New Orleans (March).

―――. 2016. *Intelligence Community Spending: Trends and Issues*. Congressional Research Service. November 8.

Miller, Greg, and Dana Priest. 2014. "CIA Unlikely to Lose Power in Wake of Interrogation Report." *Washington Post* (December 9): A1.

Miller, Russell, ed. 2008. *U.S. National Security, Intelligence and Democracy: From the Church Committee to the War on Terror*. New York: Routledge.

Moe, Terry. 1987. "An Assessment of the Positive Theory of 'Congressional Dominance.'" *Legislative Studies Quarterly* 12: 56–68.

Mondale, Walter F., with David Hage. 2010. *The Good Fight: A Life in Liberal Politics*. New York: Scribner.

Mondale, Walter F., Robert A. Stein, and Caitlinrose Fisher. 2016. "No Longer a Neutral Magistrate: The Foreign Intelligence Surveillance Court in the Wake of the War on Terror." *Minnesota Law Review* 100/8 (June): 2251–2312.

Morgan, Richard E. 1980. *Domestic Intelligence: Monitoring Dissent in America*. Austin: University of Texas Press.

Moyers, Bill. 1988. *The Secret Government: The Constitution in Crisis*. Washington, DC: Seven Locks Press.

Moynihan, Daniel Patrick. 1991. "Do We Still Need the C.I.A.? The State Department Can Do the Job." *New York Times* (May 19): E17.

———. 1998. *Secrecy: The American Experience*. New Haven, CT: Yale University Press.

Mueller, John, and Mark G. Stewart. 2014. "Secret without Reason and Costly without Accomplishment: Questioning the National Security Agency's Metadata Program." *I/S: A Journal of Law and Policy for the Information Society* 16: 407–432.

Mulgan, Richard. 2003. *Holding Power to Account: Accountability in Modern Democracies*. New York: Palgrave.

Müller-Wille, Björn. 2006a. "Improving the Democratic Accountability of EU Intelligence." *Intelligence and National Security* 21 (February): 100–128.

———. 2006b. "Intelligence and Democratic Accountability: A Blessing, Not a Curse." *European Security* 15: 491–506.

Newbery, Samantha. 2016. *Interrogation, Intelligence and Security: The Origins and Effects of Controversial British Techniques, 1969–2003*. Manchester, UK: Manchester University Press.

9/11 Commission. 2004. *Final Report of the National Commission on Terrorist Attacks upon the United States*. New York: Norton.

Nolan, Cynthia M. 1999. "Seymour Hersh's Impact on the CIA." *International Journal of Intelligence and Counterintelligence* 12: 1–34.

———. 2007. "More Perfect Oversight: Intelligence Oversight and Reform." In Loch K. Johnson, ed., *Strategic Intelligence: Intelligence and Accountability, Safeguards against the Abuse of Secret Power*, vol. 5. Westport, CT: Praeger Security International. 115–140.

———. 2010. "The PFIAB Personality: Presidents and Their Foreign Intelligence Boards." *International Journal of Intelligence and Counterintelligence* 23 (Spring): 27–60.

North, Oliver L., with William Novak. 1991. *Under Fire: An American Story*. New York: HarperCollins.

Oakley, David. 2009. "Taming the Rogue Elephant?" *American Intelligence Journal* (Winter) 27: 61–67.

O'Connell, Anne Joseph. 2006. "The Architecture of Smart Intelligence: Structuring and Overseeing Agencies in the Post-9/11 World." *California Law Review* 94 (December): 1655–1744.

Odum, Lt. Gen. William E. 2002. *Fixing Intelligence*. New Haven, CT: Yale University Press.

Ogul, M. S. 1976. *Congress Oversees the Bureaucracy: Studies in Legislative Supervision*. Pittsburgh: University of Pittsburgh Press.

Ogul, M. S., and Bert A. Rockman. 1990. "Overseeing Oversight: New Departures and Old Problems." *Legislative Studies Quarterly* 15: 5–24.

Olmsted, Katherine. 1996. *Challenging the Secret Government: The Post-Watergate Investigations of the CIA and FBI*. Chapel Hill: University of North Carolina Press.

———. 2006. "Lapdog or Rogue Elephant? CIA Controversies from 1947 to 2004." In Athan Theoharis, Richard Immerman, Loch K. Johnson, Kathrine Olmsted, and John Prados, eds., *The Central Intelligence Agency: Security under the Scrutiny*. Westport, CT: Greenwood Press.

Ombres, Devon. 2015. "NSA Domestic Surveillance from the PATRIOT Act to the FREEDOM Act: The Underlying History, Constitutional Basis, and the Efforts at Reform." *Seton Hall Legislative Journal* 39: 27–58.

Opderbeck, David. 2014. "Drone Courts." *Rutgers Law Journal* 44 (Spring): 460.

Oseth, John M. 1985. *Regulating United States Intelligence Operations: A Study in Definition of the National Interest*. Lexington: University Press of Kentucky.

Ott, Marvin C. 2003. "Partisanship and the Decline of Intelligence Oversight." *International Journal of Intelligence and Counterintelligence* 16: 69–94.

Papandrea, Mary-Rose. 2014. "Leaker Traitor Whistleblower Spy: National Security Leaks and the First Amendment." *Boston University Law Review* 94: 449–544.

Parry, Robert, and Peter Kornbluh. 1988. "Iran-Contra's Untold Story." *Foreign Policy* 7 (Fall): 3–30.

Pelosi, Rep. Nancy. 2006. "The Gap in Intelligence Oversight." *Washington Post* (January 15): B7.

Peterzell, Jay. 1983. "Can Congress Really Check the CIA?" *Washington Post* (April 21): A25.

Pfiffner, James P. 2009. *Power Play: The Bush Presidency and the Constitution.* Washington, DC: Brookings Institution.

———. 2010. *Torture as Public Policy.* Boulder, CO: Paradigm.

Pfiffner, James P., and Mark Phythian, eds. 2008. *Intelligence and National Security Policymaking on Iraq: British and American Perspectives.* Manchester, UK: Manchester University Press.

Phythian, Mark. 2005. "Hutton and Scott: A Tale of Two Inquiries." *Parliamentary Affairs* 58: 124–137.

———. 2005–2006. "Still a Matter of Trust: Post-9/11 British Intelligence and Political Culture." *International Journal of Intelligence and Counterintelligence* 18: 653–681.

———. 2007a. "The British Experience with Intelligence Accountability." *Intelligence and National Security* 22: 75–98.

———. 2007b. "Intelligence Oversight in the UK: The Case of Iraq." In Loch K. Johnson, ed., *Handbook of Intelligence Studies.* New York: Routledge. 301–314.

———. 2010. "'A Very British Institution': The Intelligence and Security Committee and Intelligence Accountability in the United Kingdom." In Loch K. Johnson, ed., *The Oxford Handbook of National Security Intelligence.* New York: Oxford University Press. 699–718.

———. 2013a. "Between Covert and Overt Action: The Obama Administration's Use of Armed Drones as a Tool of Counterterrorism Policy." *Contemporary Issues in Law* 12/4: 283–310.

———, ed. 2013b. *Understanding the Intelligence Cycle.* Abingdon, UK: Routledge.

———, ed. 2016. "INS Special Forum: The US Senate Select Committee Report on the CIA's Detention and Interrogation Program." *Intelligence and National Security* 31/1 (January): 8–27.

Phythian, Mark, and Peter Gill. 2012. *Intelligence in an Insecure World,* 2nd ed. Cambridge: Polity Press.

Phythian, Mark, Peter Gill, and Stephen Marrin, eds. 2008. *Intelligence Theory: Key Questions and Debates.* London: Routledge.

Phythian, Mark, and James P. Pfiffner, eds. 2008. *Intelligence and National Security Policymaking on Iraq: British and American Perspectives.* Manchester, UK: Manchester University Press; College Station: Texas A&M University Press.

Pickett, George. 1985. "Congress, the Budget, and Intelligence." In Alfred C. Maurer, James M. Keagle, and Marion D. Tunstall, eds., *Intelligence: Policy and Process.* Boulder, CO: Westview Press.

Pike Committee (led by Representative Otis Pike, D, New York). 1976. "The CIA Report the President Doesn't Want You to Read: The Pike Papers." Leaked to the *Village Voice* (February 16 and 23): full issues. Also published as *CIA: The Pike Report* (Nottingham, UK: Spokesman Books, 1977).

Pillar, Paul R. 2009. *Intelligence and U.S. Foreign Policy: Iraq, 9/11, and Misguided Reform.* New York: Columbia University Press.

Pincus, Walter. 2002. "Overdue Intelligence Reports." *Washington Post* (December 1): A1.

Pines, Daniel L. 2009. "The Central Intelligence Agency's 'Family Jewels': Legal Then? Legal Now?" *Indiana Law Journal* 84: 637–688.

Posner, Richard A. 2004. "Torture, Terrorism, and Interrogation." In Sanford Levinson, ed., *Torture: A Collection.* New York: Oxford University Press, 2004. 291–298.

———. 2005. *Preventing Surprise Attacks: Intelligence Reform in the Wake of 9/11.* Stanford, CA: Hoover Institution Press.

———. 2006a. *Not a Suicide Pact: The Constitution in a Time of National Emergency.* New York: Oxford University Press.

————. 2006b. *Uncertain Shield: The U.S. Intelligence System in the Throes of Reform*. Lanham, MD: Rowman & Littlefield.

Powe, Scot. 1986. "Espionage, Leaks, and the First Amendment." *Bulletin of the Atomic Scientists* (June–July) 41: 8–10.

Powers, Richard Gid. 1987. *Secrecy and Power: The Life of J. Edgar Hoover*. New York: Free Press.

Powers, Thomas. 1979. *The Man Who Kept the Secrets: Richard Helms and the CIA*. New York: Simon & Schuster.

Pozen, David E. 2010. "Deep Secrecy." *Stanford Law Review* 62/2.

————. 2013. "The Leak Leviathan: Why the Government Condemns and Condones Unlawful Disclosures of Information." *Harvard Law Review* 127: 513–635.

————. 2015. "The Mosaic Theory, National Security, and the Freedom of Information Act." *Yale Law Journal* 115: 628–679.

Prados, John. 2003. *Lost Crusader: The Secret Wars of CIA Director William Colby*. New York: Oxford University Press.

————. 2006. *Safe for Democracy*. Chicago: Ivan R. Dee.

————. 2013. *The Family Jewels: The CIA, Secrecy, and Presidential Power*. Austin: University of Texas Press.

President's Review Group. 2013. *Liberty and Security in a Changing World*. Report and Recommendations to the President's Review Group on Intelligence and Communications Technology (December 12).

Priest, Dana. 2004. "Congressional Oversight of Intelligence Criticized." *Washington Post* (April 27): A1.

Priest, Dana, and William M. Arkin. 2011. *Top Secret America: The Rise of the New American Security State*. New York: Little, Brown.

Privacy and Civil Liberties Oversight Board. 2014. "Report on the Telephony Records Program Conducted under Section 215 of the USA PATRIOT Act on the Operations of the Foreign Intelligence Surveillance Court." Washington, DC: U.S. Department of Justice.

Pyle, Christopher. 1970. "CONUS Intelligence: The Army Watches Civilian Politics." *Washington Monthly* (January).

Quirk, Paul, and William Bendix. 2015. "Secrecy and Negligence: How Congress Lost Control of Domestic Surveillance." *Issues in Governance Studies* 88 (Washington, DC: Brookings Institute).

Quirk, Paul, and Sarah Binder, eds. 2005. *The Legislative Branch and American Democracy: Institutions and Performance*. New York: Oxford University Press.

Radsan, Afsheen John, and Ryan M. Check. 2010. "One Lantern in the Darkest Night: The CIA's Inspector General." *Journal of National Security Law & Policy* 4: 247–294.

Ranelagh, John. 1986. *The Agency: The Rise and Decline of the CIA*. New York: Simon & Schuster.

Ransom, Harry Howe. 1961. "Secret Mission in an Open Society." *New York Times Magazine* (May 21): 20, 77–79.

————. 1970a. *The Intelligence Establishment*. Cambridge, MA: Harvard University Press.

————. 1970b. "Much Policy, Little Intelligence." *New York Times* (December 26): A23.

————. 1975a. "Congress and the Intelligence Agencies." In Harvey C. Mansfield, ed., *Congress against the President*. New York: Praeger. 153–166.

————. 1975b. "Secret Intelligence Agencies and Congress." *Society* 123: 33–38.

————. 1975c. "The Uses and Abuses of Secret Power." *Worldview* 18 (May): 11–15.

————. 1976. "Congress, Legitimacy, and the Intelligence Community." Paper, annual meeting, Western Political Science Association (April): 1–14.

————. 1977. "Congress and Reform of the C.I.A." *Policy Studies Journal* 5 (Summer): 476–480.

————. 1980. "Being Intelligent about Intelligence." *American Political Science Review* 74 (March): 141–148.

————. 1981. "Don't Make the C.I.A. a K.G.B." *New York Times* (December 24): A23.

————. 1983. "Strategic Intelligence and Intermestic Politics." In Charles W. Kegley, Jr., and Eugene R. Wittkopf, eds., *Perspectives on American Foreign Policy*. New York: St. Martin's Press. 299–319.

———. 1984. "CIA Accountability: Congress as Temperamental Watchdog." Paper, annual meeting, American Political Science Association (September 1): 1–24.

———. 1987. "The Politicization of Intelligence." In Stephen J. Cimbala, ed., *Intelligence and Intelligence Policy in a Democratic Society*. Dobbs Ferry, NJ: Transnational Press.

———. 2007. "A Half Century of Spy Watching." In Loch K. Johnson, ed., *Strategic Intelligence: Intelligence and Accountability, Safeguards against the Abuse of Secret Power*, vol. 5. Westport, CT: Praeger Security International. 183–194.

Reisman, W. Michael, and James E. Baker. 1992. *Regulating Covert Action: Practices, Contexts, and Policies of Covert Coercion Abroad in International and American Law*. New Haven, CT: Yale University Press.

Rempel, R. 2004. "Canada's Parliamentary Oversight of Security and Intelligence." *International Journal of Intelligence and Counterintelligence* 17: 634–654.

Richelson, Jeffrey T. 2015. *The US Intelligence Community*. Boulder, CO: Westview.

Ringqist, Evan J., Jeff Worsham, and Marc Allen Eisner. 2003. "Salience, Complexity, and the Legislative Direction of Regulatory Bureaucracies." *Journal of Public Administration Research and Theory* 13/2: 141–164.

Risen, James. 2006. *State of War: The Secret History of the CIA and the Bush Administration*. New York: Free Press.

Risen, James, and Eric Lichtblau. 2005. "Bush Lets U.S. Spy on Callers without Courts." *New York Times* (December 16): A1.

Rizzo, John. 2012. "The CIA-Congress War." *Defining Ideas*, the Hoover Institution (March 30).

———. 2014. *Company Man: Thirty Years of Controversy and Crisis in the CIA*. New York: Scribner.

Robarge, David. 2009. "CIA in the Spotlight: The Central Intelligence Agency and Public Accountability." *Journal of Intelligence History* 9 (June): 105–126.

Roberts, Patrick S., and Matthew Dull. 2013. "Guarding the Guardians: Oversight Appointees and the Search for Accountability in U.S. Federal Agencies." *Journal of Policy History* 25: 87–239.

Robertson, K. G. 1988. "Accountable Intelligence: The British Experience." *Conflict Quarterly* 8: 3–28.

Rockefeller Commission (led by Vice President Nelson A. Rockefeller). 1975. Report to the President on the Commission on CIA Activities within the United States. June, Washington, D.C.

Rockman, Bert A. 1984. "Executive-Legislative Relations and Legislative Oversight." *Legislative Studies Quarterly* 9 (August): 387–440.

Rodriguez, Jose A., and Bill Harlow. 2012. *Hard Measures: How Aggressive CIA Actions after 9/11 Saved American Lives*. New York: Threshold Editions.

———. 2014. "Don't We Want to Stop Terrorists?" *Washington Post* (December 12): B1.

Rollins, John, and Rebecca S. Lange. 2012. "'Gang of Four' Congressional Intelligence Notifications." Report No. R40698, Congressional Research Service, Washington, D.C. (November 19).

Rosen, Bernard. 1998. *Holding Government Bureaucracies Accountable*, 3rd ed. Westport, CT: Praeger.

Rosenbach, Eric B., and Aki Peritz. 2009. *Confrontation or Collaboration? Congress and the Intelligence Community*. Cambridge, MA: Belfer Center for Science and International Affairs, Kennedy School of Government, Harvard University (July).

Rouke, Francis E. 1960. "Administrative Secrecy: A Congressional Dilemma." *American Political Science Review* 65 (September): 684–694.

Rovner, Joshua. 2011. *Fixing the Facts: National Security and the Politics of Intelligence*. Ithaca, NY: Cornell University Press.

Rovner, Joshua, and Austin Long. 2006. "How Intelligent Is Intelligence Reform?" *International Security*, Correspondence to the Editors, 30/4 (Spring): 196–203.

Rudner, Martin. 2007. "Canada's Communications Security Establishment, Signals Intelligence, and Counter-Terrorism." *Intelligence and National Security* 22 (August): 473–490.

Rusk, Dean. 1977. *Oral History*, Richard B. Russell Library, University of Georgia (February 22): No. 86.

Rusk, Dean, as told to Richard Rusk, with editing by Daniel S. Papp. 1990. *As I Saw It*. New York: Norton.

Russett, Bruce M. 1990. *Controlling the Sword: The Democratic Governance of National Security*. Cambridge, MA: Harvard University Press.

Sagar, Rahul. 2013. *Secrets and Leaks: The Dilemma of State Secrecy*. Princeton, NJ: Princeton University Press.

Sample, Timothy R. 2009. In Jennifer E. Sims and Burton Gerber, eds., *Vaults, Mirrors, and Masks: Rediscovering U.S. Counterintelligence*. Washington, DC: Georgetown University Press. 241–260.

Sanger, David E. 2012. *Confront and Conceal: Obama's Secret Wars and Surprising Use of American Power*. New York: Crown.

Savage, Charlie. 2007. *Takeover: The Return of the Imperial Presidency and the Subversion of American Democracy*. New York: Little, Brown.

———. 2008. "President Weakens Espionage Oversight: Board Created by Ford Loses Most of Its Power." *Boston Globe* (March 14): A1.

Scher, Seymour. 1963. "Conditions for Legislative Control." *Journal of Politics* 25 (August): 526–551.

Schiemann, John W. 2016. *Does Torture Work?* New York: Oxford University Press.

Schlanger, Margo. 2015. "Intelligence Legalism and the National Security Agency's Civil Liberties Gap." *Harvard National Security Journal* 6: 112–205.

Schlesinger, Arthur M., Jr. 1976. "Reform of the CIA?" *Wall Street Journal* (February 25): A10.

———. 2004. *The Imperial Presidency*, reprint edition. Boston: Mariner Books.

Schmitt, Gary J. 1985. "Congressional Oversight of Intelligence." *Studies in Intelligence* (Spring) 39: 17–43.

Schneier, Bruce. 2015. *Data and Goliath: The Hidden Battles to Capture Your Data and Control Your World*. New York: Norton.

Schoenfeld, Gabriel. 2010. *Necessary Secrets: National Security, the Media and the Rule of Law*. New York: Norton.

Schorr, Daniel. 1977. *Clearing the Air*. New York: Houghton Mifflin.

Schwartz, Paul M. 2009. "Warrantless Wiretapping, FISA Reform, and the Lessons of Public Liberty: A Comment on Holmes' Jorde Lecture." *California Law Review* 97: 407–432.

Schwarz, Frederick A. O., Jr. 1976. "Intelligence Activities and the Rights of Americans." New York Bar Association meeting, New York City (November 16), reprinted in the *Congressional Record* (January 28, 1977): 51,627–51,629.

———. 1987. "Recalling Major Lessons of the Church Committee." *New York Times* (July): A25.

———. 2007a. "The Church Committee and a New Era of Intelligence Oversight." *Intelligence and National Security* 22 (April): 270–297.

———. 2007b. "Intelligence Oversight: The Church Committee." In Loch K. Johnson, ed., *Strategic Intelligence: Intelligence and Accountability, Safeguards against the Abuse of Secret Power*, vol. 5. Westport, CT: Praeger Security International. 19–46.

———. 2015. *Democracy in the Dark: The Seduction of Government Secrecy*. New York: Free Press, 2015.

Schwarz, Frederick A. O., Jr., and Aziz Z. Huq. 2007. *Unchecked and Unbalanced: Presidential Power in a Time of Terror*. New York: New Press.

Sciaroni, Bretton G. 1989. "The Theory and Practice of Executive Branch Oversight." *Harvard Journal of Law and Public Policy* 12: 397–432.

Scott, James M., and Ralph G. Carter. 2002. "Acting on the Hill: Congressional Assertiveness in U.S. Foreign Policy." *Congress & the Presidency* 29/2: 151–169.

Scott, Katherine (Kate) A. 2013. *Reining in the State: Civil Society and Congress in the Vietnam and Watergate Eras*. Lawrence: University Press of Kansas.

———, ed. 2016. *Church Committee Members and Staff, 1975–1976*. Oral history interviews (July 24, 2013–March 10, 2015), U.S. Senate Historical Office, Washington, D.C.

Scott, Len V., and Peter D. Jackson, eds. 2004. *Understanding Intelligence in the Twenty-First Century: Journeys into Shadows*. London: Routledge.

Shane, Peter M. 2009. *Madison's Nightmare: Executive Power and the Threat to American Democracy.* Chicago: University of Chicago Press.

———. 2014. "The NSA and the Legal Regime for Foreign Intelligence Surveillance." *I/S: A Journal of Law and Policy for the Information Society* 16: 259–300.

Shane, Scott. 2006. "Senate Panel's Partisanship Troubles Former Members." *New York Times* (March 12, 2006): A18.

Shapiro, S., and R. Steinzor. 2006. "The People's Agent: Executive Branch Secrecy and Accountability in an Age of Terrorism." *Duke Law Journal* 69: 100–129.

Sharp, David H. 2012. *The CIA's Greatest Covert Operation.* Lawrence: University Press of Kansas.

Shipan, Charles R. 2004. "Regulatory Regimes, Agency Actions, and the Conditional Nature of Congressional Influence." *American Political Science Review* 98 (August): 467–480.

Shorrock, Tim. 2008. *Spies for Hire: The Secret World of Intelligence Outsourcing.* New York: Simon & Schuster.

Shpiro, Shlomo. 2002. *Intelligence and the Media.* London: Cass.

Silberman-Robb Commission (led by Judge Laurence H. Silberman and former senator Charles S. Robb). 2004. *Final Report: Commission on the Intelligence Capabilities of the United States Regarding Weapons of Mass Destruction.* Washington, D.C.

Silverstein, Gordon. 1997. *Imbalance of Powers: Constitutional Interpretation and the Making of American Foreign Policy.* New York: Oxford University Press.

Sims, Jennifer E., and Burton Gerber. 2005. *Transforming U.S. Intelligence.* Washington, DC: Georgetown University Press.

Sinnar, Shirin. 2013. "Protecting Rights from Within? Inspectors General and National Security Oversight." *Stanford Law Review* 65: 1027–1086.

Slick, Stephen B. 2014. "Modernizing the IC 'Charter.'" *Studies in Intelligence* 58/2 (June).

Slick, Stephen B., and William C. Inboden, project directors. 2016. *Intelligence and National Security in American Society.* Policy Research Project Report Number 189, Policy Research Project on Intelligence in American Society, Lyndon B. Johnson School of Public Affairs, Austin, Texas (May).

Smist, Frank, Jr. 1994. *Congress Oversees the United States Intelligence Community,* 2nd ed. Knoxville: University of Tennessee Press.

Snider, L. Britt. 1997. *Sharing Secrets with Lawmakers.* Center for the Study of Intelligence, Central Intelligence Agency (February).

———. 1999–2000. "Unlucky Shamrock: Recollections from the Church Committee Investigation of NSA." *Studies in Intelligence,* Central Intelligence Agency (Winter).

———. 2001. "Creating a Statutory Inspector General at the CIA." *Studies in Intelligence* 44: 15–21.

———. 2007. "A Unique Vantage Point: Creating a Statutory Inspector General at the CIA." *Studies in Intelligence,* Central Intelligence Agency (September).

———. 2008a. *The Agency and the Hill: CIA's Relationship with Congress, 1946–2004.* Washington, DC: Center for the Study of Intelligence, Central Intelligence Agency.

———. 2008b. "Congressional Oversight of Intelligence after September 11." In Jennifer E. Sims and Burton Gerber, eds., *Transforming U.S. Intelligence.* Washington, DC: Georgetown University Press. 239–258.

Solove, Daniel J. 2011. *Nothing to Hide: The False Tradeoff between Privacy and Security.* New Haven, CT: Yale University Press.

Soufan, Ali H. 2009. "What Torture Never Told Us." *New York Times.* September 6: Wk9.

Spaulding, Suzanne E. 2008. "Building Checks and Balances for National Security Policy: The Role of Congress." *Advance: The Journal of the American Constitution Society* (February) 10: 16–26.

Spence, D. B. 1997. "Agency Policy Making and Political Control: Modeling Away the Delegation Problem." *Journal of Public Administration Research and Theory* 2: 199–219.

Stennis, John C., and J. William Fulbright. 1971. *The Role of Congress in Foreign Policy.* Washington, DC: American Enterprise Institute.

Stone, Geoffrey R. 2009. "Free Speech and National Security." *Indiana Law Journal* 84: 939–962.

Strong, J. Thompson. 1986. "Covert Activities and Intelligence Operations: Congressional and Executive Roles Redefined." *International Journal of Intelligence and Counterintelligence* 1: 63–72.

Sturtevant, M. 1992. "Congressional Oversight of Intelligence: One Perspective." *American Intelligence Journal* (Summer) 10: 17–20.

Swire, Peter. 2004. "The System of Foreign Intelligence Surveillance Law." *George Washington Law Review* 72: 1306–1329.

Tama, Jordan. 2011. *Terrorism and National Security Reform.* Cambridge, UK: Cambridge University Press.

Tenet, George, with Bill Harlow. 2007. *At the Center of the Storm: My Years at the CIA.* New York: HarperCollins.

Tetlock, Philip E. 1995. "Accountability in Social Systems: A Psychological Perspective." In Philip C. Stenning, ed., *Accountability for Criminal Justice: Selected Essays.* Toronto: University of Toronto Press.

Tetlock, Philip E., and Barbara A. Mellers. 2011. "Intelligence Management of Intelligence Agencies: Beyond Accountability Ping-Pong." *American Psychologist* 66 (September): 542–554.

Theoharis, Athan G. 1978. *Spying on Americans: Political Surveillance from Hoover to the Huston Plan.* Philadelphia: Temple University Press.

———, ed. 1998. *A Culture of Secrecy: The Government versus the People's Right to Know.* Lawrence: University Press of Kansas.

———. 2002. *Chasing Spies.* Chicago: Dee.

———, ed. 2006. *The Central Intelligence Agency: Security under Scrutiny.* Westport, CT: Greenwood Press.

Toh, Amos, Faiza Patel, and Elizabeth (Liza) Goitein. 2016. *Overseas Surveillance in an Interconnected World.* New York: Brennan Center, New York University.

Tower Commission (led by Senator John Tower, R, Texas). 1987. *Report of the President's Special Review Board* [on the Iran-contra affair]. Washington, D.C. (February 26).

Treverton, Gregory F. 1987. "Covert Action and Open Society." *Foreign Affairs* 65 (Summer): 995–1014.

———. 1987a. *Covert Action: The Limits of Intervention in the Postwar World.* New York: Basic Books.

———. 1987b. "From 'Covert' to 'Overt.'" *Daedalus* 116/2: 120.

———. 1990. "Intelligence: Welcome to the American Government." In Thomas E. Mann, ed., *A Question of Balance: The President, the Congress, and Foreign Policy.* Washington, DC: Brookings Institute. 70–108.

———. 2011. *Intelligence for an Age of Terror.* Cambridge: Cambridge University Press.

Trouteaud, Alex R. 2004. "Civil Liberties." In John G. Geer, ed., *Public Opinion and Polling around the World: A Historical Encyclopedia.* Santa Barbara, CA: ABC-CLIO, 2004.

Tsang, Steve, ed. 2007. *Intelligence and Human Rights in the Era of Global Terrorism.* Westport, CT: Praeger Security International.

Turner, Admiral Stansfield. 1985a. "Has Reagan Killed CIA Oversight?" *Christian Science Monitor* (September 26) 77: A14.

———. 1985b. "Purge the C.I.A. of K.G.B. Types." *New York Times* (October 2): A24.

———. 1985c. *Secrecy and Democracy: The CIA in Transition.* Boston: Houghton Mifflin.

———. 2005. *Burn before Reading: Presidents, CIA Directors, and Secret Intelligence.* New York: Hyperion.

Turner, Admiral Stansfield, and George Thibault. 1982. "Intelligence: The Right Rules." *Foreign Policy* 48 (Fall): 122–138.

Turner, Michael A. 2004. *Why Secret Intelligence Fails.* Washington, DC: Potomac.

Tye, John Napier. 2014. "Meet Executive Order 12333: The Reagan Rule That Lets the NSA Spy on Americans." *Washington Post* (July 18).

U.S. House of Representatives. 1976. *Recommendations of the Final Report.* No. 94-883, Select Committee on Intelligence (the Pike Committee), House, 94th Cong., 2nd. Sess. Washington, DC: U.S. Government Printing Office.

———. 1994. *Legislative Oversight of Intelligence Activities: The US Experience: Report of the Select Committee on Intelligence.* No. 103-88, Senate, 103d Cong., 2nd Sess. Washington, DC: U.S. Government Printing Office.

———. 1996. *IC21: The Intelligence Community in the 21st Century: Staff Study.* Permanent Select Committee on Intelligence, House, 104th Cong., 1st Sess. Washington, DC: U.S. Government Printing Office: ch. XV (on oversight).

U.S. Senate. 1975. *Alleged Assassination Plots Involving Foreign Leaders.* Interim Report, Select Committee to Study Governmental Operations with Respect to Intelligence Activities (the Church Committee), 94th Cong., 1st Sess. (November).

———. 1976. *Final Report.* No. 94-755, Select Committee to Study Governmental Operations with Respect to Intelligence Activities (the Church Committee), Senate, 94th Cong., 2nd Sess. (May).

———. 1994. *Legislative Oversight of Intelligence Activities: The U.S. Experience.* Select Committee on Intelligence, 103rd Cong., 2nd Sess.

———. 2007. "Congressional Oversight of Intelligence Activities." Hearings, Select Committee on Intelligence, 110th Cong., 1st Sess. (November 13).

———. 2015. *Report 114-8.* Select Committee on Intelligence, 114th Cong., 1st Sess. (March 31).

Van Buuren, Jelle. 2013. "From Oversight to Undersight: The Internationalization of Intelligence." *Security & Human Rights* 24 (September): 239–252.

Van Puyvelde, Damien. 2006. "Intelligence, Democratic Accountability, and the Media in France." *Democracy and Security* 10 (July): 287–305.

———. 2013. "Intelligence Accountability and the Role of Public Interest Groups in the United States." *Intelligence and National Security* 28 (April): 139–158.

———. 2016. *The US Intelligence Community and the Private Sector.* Ithaca, NY: Cornell University Press.

Van Wagenen, James S. 1997. "A Review of Congressional Oversight." *Studies in Intelligence* 40/5: 97–102.

Walden, J. L. 1970. "The C.I.A.: A Study in the Arrogation of Administrative Power." *George Washington Law Review* 39: 66–101.

Waldron, Jeremy. 2003. "Security and Liberty: The Image of Balance." *Journal of Political Philosophy* 11: 191–210.

Walker, Matthew B. 2007. "Reforming Congressional Oversight of U.S. Intelligence." *International Journal of Intelligence and Counterintelligence* 19/4: 702–720.

Walsh, Lawrence E. 1990. "Secrecy and the Rule of Law." *Oklahoma Law Review* 43: 568–592.

———. 1993. *Final Report of the Independent Counsel for Iran/Contra Matters.* U.S. Court of Appeals for the District of Columbia Circuit (August 4).

———. 1997. *Firewall: The Iran-Contra Conspiracy and Cover-Up.* New York: Norton.

Walsh, Patrick F. 2011. *Intelligence and Intelligence Analysis.* New York: Routledge.

Wark, Wesley K. 2001. "The Access to Information Act and the Security and Intelligence Community in Canada." Report No. 20, Access to Information Review Task Force (August). Ottawa.

———. 2015. "C-51 and the Canadian Security and Intelligence Community: Finding the Balance for Security and Rights Protection." In Edward Iacobucci and Stephen Toope, eds., *After the Paris Attacks: Responses in Canada, Europe and around the Globe.* University of Toronto. 38–47.

Warner, Michael, and J. Kenneth McDonald. 2005. *US Intelligence Community Reform Studies since 1947.* Washington, DC: CIA Center for the Study of Intelligence.

Watts, L. 2004. "Conflicting Paradigms, Dissimilar Contexts: Intelligence Reform in Europe's Emerging Democracies." *Studies in Intelligence* 48: 11–25.

Weber, Ralph E., ed. *Spymasters: Ten CIA Officers in Their Own Words.* Wilmington, DE: SR Books.

Weiner, Tim. 2007. *Legacy of Ashes: The History of the CIA.* New York: Doubleday.

Weingast, Barry R., and Mark J. Moran. 1983. "Bureaucratic Discretion or Congressional Control? Regulatory Policymaking by the Federal Trade Commission." *Journal of Political Economy* 91: 475–520.

Weissman, Stephen R. 1995. *A Culture of Deference: Congress's Failure of Leadership in Foreign Policy.* New York: Basic Books.

Weller, Geoffrey. 2000. "Political Scrutiny and Control of Scandinavia's Security and Intelligence Services." *International Journal of Intelligence and Counterintelligence* 13: 171–192.

White, Laura. 2003. "The Need for Governmental Secrecy: Why the U.S. Government Must Be Able to Withhold Information in the Interest of National Security." *Virginia Journal of International Law* 43/4.

Whittaker, Reginald. 1999a. "Designing a Balance between Freedom and Security." In J. Fletcher, ed., *Ideas in Action: Essays on Politics and Law in Honour of Peter Russell.* Toronto: University of Toronto Press. 126–149.

———. 1999b. *The End of Privacy: How Total Surveillance Is Becoming a Reality.* New York: New Press.

Willis, Aidan, Mathias Vermeulen, Hans Born, Miartin Scheinin, and Micha Thornton. 2001. *Parliamentary Oversight of Security and Intelligence Agencies in the European Union.* European Parliament.

Wise, David. 1976. *The American Police State: The Government against the People.* New York: Random House, 1976.

———. 1978. "Is Anybody Watching the CIA?" *Inquiry* (November 27): 17–21.

———. 1997. *The Politics of Lying: Government Deception, Secrecy, and Power.* New York: Random House.

Witcombe, A. 2000. "Shaken, Not Stirred: Parliamentary Oversight of the Intelligence and Security Agencies." *Public Sector* 23: 10–14.

Wolff, Hugh W. 1978. *Intelligence Community: Congressional Oversight.* Congressional Research Service (January 3).

Wong, Katherine. 2006. "The NSA Terrorist Surveillance Program." *Harvard Journal on Legislation* 43: 517–534.

Wood, B. Dan. 2011. "Congress and the Executive Branch: Delegation and Presidential Dominance." In Eric Schickler and Frances E. Lee, eds., *The Oxford Handbook of the American Congress.* New York: Oxford University Press. 789–811.

Woods, Chris. 2015. *Sudden Justice: America's Secret Drone Wars.* New York: Oxford University Press.

Woods, Randall Bennett. 1995. *Fulbright: A Biography.* Cambridge, UK: Cambridge University Press.

Woodward, Bob. 1987. *Veil: The CIA Secret Wars, 1981–87.* New York: Simon & Schuster.

———. 2004. *Plan of Attack.* New York: Simon & Schuster.

Xiu, Jie. 2004. "The Roles of the Judiciary in Examining and Supervising the Changing Laws of Electronic Surveillance." *Seton Hall Legislative Journal* 28: 229–258.

Yale University. 2006. "Symposium on Warrantless Wiretaps." *Opening Arguments,* School of Law (February): 1–8.

Yamamoto, Erik K. 2005. "White (House) Lies: Why the Public Must Compel the Courts to Hold Presidents Accountable for National Security Abuses." *Law and Contemporary Problems* 68: 285–340.

Yoo, John. 2005. *The Powers of War and Peace: The Constitution and Foreign Affairs after 9/11.* Chicago: University of Chicago Press.

———. 2006. "Courts at War." *Cornell Law Review* 91/2: 573–601.

———. 2007. "The Terrorist Surveillance Program and the Constitution." *George Mason Law Review* 14: 565–604.

Zaller, John, and Dennis Chiu. 1996. "Government's Little Helper: U.S. Press Coverage of Foreign Policy Crises, 1945–1991." *Political Communications* 13/4: 385–405.

Zegart, Amy B. 2005. "September 11 and the Adaptation Failure of U.S. Intelligence Agencies." *International Security* 29/4 (Spring): 78–111.

———. 2006a. "An Empirical Analysis of Failed Intelligence Reforms before September 11." *Political Science Quarterly* 121: 33–60.

———. 2006b. "How Intelligent Is Intelligence Review?" *International Security*, Response to Correspondence to the Editors 30/4 (Spring): 203–208.

———. 2007a. Prepared Statement, *Hearings on Congressional Oversight of Intelligence Activities*, Select Committee on Intelligence, U.S. Senate, 119th Cong., 1st Sess. Rept. 110–794 (November 13).

———. 2007b. *Spying Blind: The CIA, the FBI, and the Origins of 9/11*. Princeton, NJ: Princeton University Press.

———. 2011a. "The Domestic Politics of Irrational Intelligence Oversight." *Political Science Quarterly* 126/1: 1–25.

———. 2011b. *Eyes on Spies: Congress and the United States Intelligence Community*. Palo Alto, CA: Hoover Institute, Stanford University.

———. 2011c. *The Roots of Weak Congressional Oversight*. Palo Alto, CA: Hoover Institute, Stanford University.

Zegart, Amy B., and Julie Quinn. 2010. "Congressional Intelligence Oversight: The Electoral Disconnection." *Intelligence and National Security* 24 (December): 744–766.

ABOUT THE AUTHOR

Loch Kingsford Johnson is the Regents Professor of Public and International Affairs at the University of Georgia, as well as a Meigs Distinguished Teaching Professor. He is the author of more than two hundred articles and essays, and the author or editor of more than thirty books on U.S. national security, including most recently, *National Security Intelligence*, 2nd ed. (Polity, 2017); *American Foreign Policy and the Challenges of World Leadership* (Oxford, 2015); *The Essentials of Intelligence* (ABC-Clio/Praeger, 2015); *A Season of Inquiry Revisited: The Church Committee Confronts America's Spy Agencies* (Kansas, 2015); *The Threat on the Horizon* (Oxford, 2011); and *The Oxford Handbook of National Security Intelligence* (Oxford, 2010). He has published editorials in the *New York Times*, the *Washington Post*, the *Chicago Tribune*, the *Philadelphia Inquirer*, the *Atlanta Journal-Constitution*, the *Baltimore Sun*, and elsewhere.

Professor Johnson served as a special assistant to Chairman Frank Church on the Senate Select Committee on Intelligence (1975–1976); as a staff aide on the U.S. Senate Foreign Relations Committee (1976–1977); as the first staff director of the Subcommittee on Intelligence Oversight, U.S. House Permanent Select Committee on Intelligence (1977–1979); as a senior staff member on the Subcommittee on Trade and International Economic Policy, Committee on Foreign Affairs, U.S. House of Representatives (1980); and as a special assistant to Chairman Les Aspin on the Aspin-Brown Commission on the Roles and Missions of Intelligence (1995–1996). He was the Issues Director for Senator Church during Church's presidential campaign (1976); served as a foreign policy adviser to President Jimmy Carter during his 1980 reelection campaign (and coauthored the Presidential Briefing Book on Foreign Policy used during the presidential debates); and is currently a consultant to several government and civic organizations.

Professor Johnson has won the "Certificate of Distinction" from the National Intelligence Study Center in Washington, D.C.; the "Studies in Intelligence Award" from the Center for the Study of Intelligence in Washington, D.C.; the "Best Article Award" from the Century Foundation's Understanding Government Project; and the V. O. Key "Best Book" Prize (with Charles S. Bullock III) from the Southern Political Science Association. He has served as secretary of the American Political Science Association and as chair of its Intelligence Studies Organized Group; and he has been president of the International Studies Association, South. Professor Johnson is the senior editor of the international journal *Intelligence and National Security*, and he has served on the editorial advisory board for several other journals, including *Foreign Policy Analysis* and the *Journal of Intelligence History*. In 2008–2009, Professor Johnson was named a Phi Beta Kappa Visiting Scholar, and he is now on the Phi Beta Kappa National Board for the Visiting Scholar Program. He has been a Distinguished Visiting Scholar at Yale University and at Oxford University. In 2012, he was selected as the inaugural "Professor of the Year" by the consortium of fourteen universities in the Southeast Conference. At the 2014 annual meeting of the International Studies Association, he was awarded the "Distinguished Professor" prize, a recognition bestowed occasionally by the Intelligence Studies Section; and, in 2015, he was presented with a Lifetime Achievement Award from the International Association for Intelligence Education. In 2017, he was the recipient of the Faculty Service Award from the Alumni Association at the University of Georgia.

Born in Auckland, New Zealand, Professor Johnson received his Ph.D. in political science from the University of California, Riverside. In postdoctoral activities, he was awarded an American Political Science Association Congressional Fellowship. He has also studied nuclear weapons policy at Harvard University and MIT, and he has conducted research on Congress as a Carl Albert Visiting Fellow at the University of Oklahoma. Professor Johnson has lectured at more than 140 universities and think tanks worldwide. At the University of Georgia he led the founding of the School of Public and International Affairs, established in 2001.

INDEX

Note: Page references followed by a "*t*" indicate table; "*f*" indicate figure.

Index